THE VENONA SECRETS

THE VENONA SECRETS

Exposing Soviet Espionage and America's Traitors

Herbert Romerstein and Eric Breindel

Since 1947
REGNERY PUBLISHING, INC.
An Eagle Publishing Company • Washington, DC

Library of Congress Cataloging-in-Publication Data

Romerstein, Herbert.
    The Venona secrets : exposing Soviet espionage and America's traitors /
    Herbert Romerstein and Eric Breindel.
        p.   cm.
    Includes bibliographical references and index.
    ISBN 0-89526-275-4
    1. Espionage, Soviet—United States—History. 2. Soviet Union. Komitet gosudarstvennoæ bezopasnosti—History. 3. Soviet Union. Glavnoe razvedyvatel§'oe upravlenie—History. 4. United States. Signal Security Agency—History. 5. Cryptography—United States—History—20th century. 6. World War, 1939-1945—Cryptography. 7. Soviet Union—Foreign relations—United States—History. 8. United States—Foreign relations—Soviet Union—History. I. Breindel, Eric, 1955-1998. II. Title.

DK266.3 .R66 2000
940.54'8647—dc21

Published in the United States by
Regnery Publishing, Inc.
An Eagle Publishing Company
One Massachusetts Avenue, NW
Washington, DC 20001

Visit us at <www.regnery.com>.

Distributed to the trade by
National Book Network
4720-A Boston Way
Lanham, MD 20706

Printed on acid-free paper
Manufactured in the United States of America

10 9 8 7 6 5 4 3 2 1

Books are available in quantity for promotional or premium use. Write to Director of Special Sales, Regnery Publishing, Inc., One Massachusetts Avenue, NW, Washington, DC 20001, for information on discounts and terms or call (202) 216-0600.

CONTENTS

PREFACE

ERIC BREINDEL AND I HAD BEEN FRIENDS for about fifteen years at the time the National Security Agency (NSA) began releasing the *Venona* documents in 1995. *Venona* was the U.S. code word given secret Soviet spy communications, equivalent to the word *Ultra* used for the Nazi secret messages. Eric and I had met when I was a professional staff member of the House Permanent Select Committee on Intelligence, and Eric was my counterpart on the Senate Intelligence Committee. We realized shortly after we met that we were kindred souls—we both had an interest in history, in particular the history of espionage and of Communism. Eric's death in 1998 was a loss to me in many ways—as a coauthor, of course, but also as a valued friend with whom I would discuss these matters long into the night.

When *Venona* appeared in 1995 our late-night telephone sessions increased both in frequency and in length. Each time one of us would discover something new, he would call the other, causing my wife to complain about being awakened in the middle of the night to hear about an exciting finding that Eric and I had made.

Eric's interest in these matters, as Norman Podhoretz explained at Eric's memorial service, stemmed from the fact that, as the son of Holocaust survivors, he understood the nature of Nazi and Communist totalitarianism. My own interest stemmed from a teenage infatuation with Communist slogans, which I lost as soon

Preface

as I learned more about that ideology. An earlier generation referred to the awakening of people to the Communist menace as their Kronstadt—taken from the 1921 Communist massacre of sailors who demanded democracy at the Kronstadt fortress. My Kronstadt was the North Korean invasion of South Korea in June 1950, when theory was transformed into practice. I served there with the U.S. Army in 1953, during which time I saw Korean civilians risk their lives crossing the enemy lines in the midst of fighting to escape from a Communist regime. That was an important lesson to me.

After returning from Korea, I worked for the state of New York investigating Communist summer camps for children and charity rackets in which innocent people contributed money to supposedly good causes—money that went instead to pay for Communist propaganda. In 1965 I became an investigator for the House Committee on Un-American Activities, and from 1971 to 1975 I was the minority chief investigator for its successor, the House Committee on Internal Security.

In 1978 I became a professional staff member for the House Intelligence Committee, where I assisted Congressman John Ashbrook (R-Ohio) and C. W. "Bill" Young (R-Florida) to oversee the Central Intelligence Agency (CIA) and the Federal Bureau of Investigation (FBI) and worked on the committee's study of KGB activities, including the extensive Soviet disinformation campaign.

I left the committee in 1983 to become head of the Office to Counter Soviet Disinformation at the United States Information Agency. I retired in 1989 but continued to study, lecture, and write on the subject. In 1992 and 1993 my wife and I had the opportunity to work in the archives of the former Soviet Union and later in Czechoslovakia and Germany.

While we were working in Russia, we learned that unreconstructed Communists were unhappy that we and other American

Preface

researchers were given access to Soviet archives. An article in a hard-line Russian newspaper in April 1993 said: "What right do the Americans have to conduct research into secret materials in our archives? Which traitor to Russia's interests opened the door to them?"[1] But before the hard-liners succeeded in convincing Boris Yeltsin to restrict some of the more interesting sections, we had obtained thousands of pages of documents from the archives of the Communist International. Other researchers shared thousands more with us, and we in turn shared the material with Eric Breindel.

Eric was only forty-two when he died in March 1998. A magna cum laude graduate of Harvard in 1977, where he was editorial chairman of the *Harvard Crimson*, Eric confronted leftist mythology while he was still in college. In 1982 he received his law degree from Harvard Law School and joined the staff of the Senate Intelligence Committee, where he worked for Senator Daniel Patrick Moynihan (D-New York). There he learned details of Soviet intelligence operations against the United States as well as what our government was doing about it. Eric then served as editorial page editor of the *New York Post* from 1986 to January 1997, when he became senior vice president of the *Post*'s parent company, News Corporation. An outstanding spokesman for conservative views, he was moderator of a weekly news show on public affairs on the Fox News channel. But despite his busy schedule, Eric continued to study Soviet intelligence operations. The release of *Venona* gave him the chance to put his knowledge to work.

When Eric and I compared the *Venona* material with the documents we had obtained from the Soviet archives and with material the FBI had released about its investigations, we realized that the whole story had not yet been told. Working together, we drew a number of important conclusions. It was obvious that the earlier view of the United States government—that American Communists,

Preface

because of their loyalty to the Soviet Union, might spy on their own government—was true, but it did not go far enough. *Venona*, together with our other sources, made it clear that American Communists with access to sensitive information were expected by the Party to turn it over to the Soviets. More importantly, the American Communist Party leadership sought out such members and turned them over to work for the Soviets. To guarantee their ideological loyalty, the Party checked them through its own secret files, and Soviet intelligence double-checked them through the files of the Communist International. Earl Browder, head of the American Communist Party, was deeply involved in recruiting Party members and vetting them for espionage.

Of particular interest to both Eric and me was the Soviet attitude toward Jews as revealed in *Venona*. We were not surprised that the NKVD, the Soviet foreign intelligence service, showed disdain for and made cynical use of those Jews willing to work for them. What surprised us was the *Venona* code name for Jews—"Rats." An NKVD program was set up to spy on and disrupt Jewish organizations that were helping Jewish victims in Europe, people who would have significant contacts in the postwar period. Why? Because the Soviets saw European Jews who supported democracy as an impediment to Soviet control in Eastern and Central Europe. Both as Americans and as Jews, we concluded that the Soviet Union and its intelligence operations were the enemies of our freedom.

Study of the documents raised a number of questions. Do intelligence and espionage operations matter? Was Soviet espionage a significant factor in the projection of Soviet power? Was the demise of the Soviet Empire hastened, delayed, or, perhaps, unaffected by America's response?

The answers: Espionage by American Communists provided the Soviet Union with an atom bomb years before its scientists

Preface

could have produced one, and subsequently the threat of atomic warfare enabled the Soviet Union to project its power and to influence Western thinking. Soviet-controlled agents of influence in the U.S. government during World War II helped the USSR achieve its goals in Central Europe and Asia. The existence of Soviet-controlled governments in Eastern Europe and the Far East provided a valuable asset to the Soviet side in the Cold War. These successes would not have been possible without the active participation of American Communists.

After the 1950s the Soviets no longer had as large a cadre of "Soviet patriots"—Western Communists—on hand for espionage. Western counterintelligence operations, the discrediting of the Soviet Union during the Cold War, and Khrushchev's "secret speech" denouncing Stalin combined to dry up the pool of espionage talent that had proliferated during the 1930s and 1940s. In the Cold War period (1946 to 1991) the Soviets were forced to rely on less trustworthy and less dedicated mercenary agents. The loss of most of their ideological agents—one of their most valuable assets— was a blow to the Soviets.

We should also consider the true nature of the Soviet state. That Moscow was long Washington's primary global adversary, as well as a formidable military threat, isn't in dispute. But was it correct to view the Soviet Union as the "focus of evil" in the postwar world? (This concept, first advanced in the early 1950s by *Time* magazine editor and Alger Hiss accuser Whittaker Chambers, resurfaced in the speeches of President Ronald Reagan some three decades later.) Was it valid to see Soviet Communism as an ideology no less pernicious than Nazism? Or is it now merely convenient to do so in the sense that studying triumphant moments in the half-century-long Cold War is far more compelling if America's chief foe represented genuine evil, not just impressive military might?

Preface

President Reagan was right: The Soviet Union was indeed the "focus of evil" in the postwar world. It replaced Nazi Germany as the most dangerous adversary of the free nations; its important characteristics were identical to Nazi Germany's, including mass murders, slave labor camps, and an insatiable desire for new territorial conquests.

Finally, as the taboo on honest discussion of American Communism continues to lift, it is possible to examine the extent to which domestic Communists penetrated the U.S. government and engaged in espionage. This, of course, requires reassessing the essential nature of the American Communist movement. And the 1995 declassification of the *Venona* files facilitates analysis of this issue.

The *Venona* papers, this book's subject as well as one of its main sources, render certain key facts indisputable. It is now plain, for example, that the conventional wisdom regarding two questions— "Who in America spied for the USSR?" and "What were the overriding principles that animated domestic Communists?"—has long been grounded in falsehood. Notwithstanding claims pervasive in the academy and, by extension, in standard history texts, the Communist Party USA was never a legitimate, indigenous political movement; never, in short, was the Communist Party merely a left-of-center political faction consisting of "liberals in a hurry" (to borrow a widely used, Popular Front–era concept). The Communist Party USA leadership and its rank and file were composed of Americans who willfully gave their primary allegiance to a foreign power, the USSR. As a consequence, the Party served as a natural recruiting ground—and the leadership, a vetting agency—for prospective U.S.-based Soviet spies. Before and during World War II, most of the Americans who served as Soviet spies were members of the Communist Party and were recruited with the assistance of the Party leadership.

Preface

A central goal of this book is to correct the conventional wisdom regarding American Communism—to challenge the falsehood inherent in the claim that Party members were left-wing heretics rather than disloyal conspirators. For Communists, true patriotism meant helping to make the world a better place by advancing the interests of the Soviet Union in any way possible.

From the study of *Venona*, one inescapably concludes that while this bizarre view of loyalty informed the thinking of every member, only a chosen few had the ability or opportunity to serve as spies for the Soviet Union. Though the Communists made little secret of their unwillingness to subscribe to "traditional forms of patriotism," Communist Party members managed to secure footholds in highly sensitive areas of American life. This was especially true during the New Deal years and the subsequent wartime U.S.-Soviet alliance. In this context, it is well to remember that, while the virtual taboo in intellectual circles on calling Communist Party members "Communists" was a reaction to the government's emphasis on domestic security that marked the early days of the Cold War, secrecy and concealment had long been features of the American Communist movement. The taboo on discussing who was a Communist placed violators at risk of being denounced as "Red-baiters"—an unpleasant but less-than-chilling prospect. Indeed, its effectiveness in inhibiting debate had already begun to dissipate prior to the Soviet Empire's demise. Still, even though open discourse about the moral legitimacy of the USSR and its American apologists managed finally to fight its way into the public square, a bodyguard of lies continued to protect the Communist Party USA from most academic inquiries into its espionage role.

Today, most Americans are inclined to accept the notion that monstrous crimes are intrinsic to Communism in power, and are not a mere aberration. In short, the inarguable fact that crimes against

Preface

humanity have been a feature of national life wherever Communists have seized power has implications that fewer and fewer Americans can ignore. The image of Lenin as a benevolent "tsar" whose disciples failed to grasp his political and moral instructions has lost most of its currency among serious intellectuals. In fact, American scholars were the first to note that even before Hitler, Lenin and Stalin made terror an instrument of state policy by using concentration camps, slave labor, man-made famines, and mass murder to realize political and economic goals.

Efforts to distinguish Communism from Nazism (and other manifestations of political evil) often turn on ostensible intentions. The Communists, the argument says, have good intentions; the Nazis, bad ones. Actually, the real intention—totalitarian rule—was the same. Even some of the slogans were the same.

The Nazis, like the Communists, used "peace" as a slogan to disarm their enemies. The Nazi pseudo-charity "Winter Help Work" emulated Communist "concern" for the hungry and homeless and was equally duplicitous. And both movements relied on state terror. Slogans, marketed as intentions, are less important than actions and real goals.

As for America's commitment to intelligence gathering, various factors—Communism's intrinsic evil, Moscow's ill-concealed hostility to Washington, and the USSR's military might—made it necessary both to collect information and to combat Soviet espionage efforts. The fear created by "not knowing" (from lack of timely information) has haunted ruling elites since the fifth century BC. At that time, the Chinese sage Sun Tzu argued in "The Art of War"— the first widely distributed handbook on the subject—that "knowledge is the reason... the wise general conquer[s] the enemy...."

The United States before the Second World War, however, seemed to regard itself—in this sphere as in many others—as a nation

Preface

apart, and long failed to take Sun Tzu's counsel to heart. Indeed, since the beginning of the century, the British and the Russians set the standard for intelligence gathering. Washington came late to the Great Game. Still, the key question remains: Have American efforts in this realm made a difference in the course of history?

A negative response is difficult to justify. Allied intelligence superiority played an essential role in hastening Hitler's defeat, in keeping the Cold War from escalating into a nuclear conflict—a hot war—and in preventing the global arms race from spinning out of control. In other words, despite the tendency to view intelligence as an effective weapon of war, states determined to keep the peace have long used intelligence to *deter* aggression.

As for the Soviet espionage efforts chronicled in these pages, it is clear that Moscow's agents in the United States helped prevent an earlier Nazi surrender to the Anglo-Americans—the prospect of which haunted the USSR throughout the war. As will be discussed, Assistant Secretary of the Treasury Harry Dexter White played a key role in this Soviet endeavor. White died in 1948, shortly after questioning by the House Committee on Un-American Activities and after Whittaker Chambers publicly named him as a Soviet agent. President Harry Truman had appointed the Treasury official as executive director of the International Monetary Fund two years earlier, shortly after Elizabeth Bentley had also identified him as a spy to the FBI.

Meanwhile, it has become clear that spies in the United States speeded Moscow's quest to develop and test an atom bomb—perhaps by three to five years. Documents recently released in the former USSR, moreover, demonstrate that, absent an atomic bomb, Stalin would not have unleashed Pyongyang's army to conquer the entire Korean peninsula.

All in all, it's hard not to acknowledge the importance intelli-

Preface

gence and espionage had in the half-century twilight struggle between the Soviet Union and the United States. The *Venona* files are a window through which to view Soviet activity in this realm at a time—the war years—when Moscow and Washington were military allies. It is well to recall that before the war America's "official" attitude toward covert intelligence gathering was reflected in Secretary of War Henry Stimson's suggestion that "gentlemen don't read each other's mail."

Happily, the Stimson view didn't enjoy unanimous support. And, as the Second World War ended and the Cold War began to heat up, the United States wasn't entirely unprepared. In fact, at Arlington Hall in suburban Washington, home to the Army Security Agency (ASA), the *Venona* project was already under way breaking Soviet codes.

The Soviet Union's espionage advantage turned on a unique historical circumstance: Never before had a hostile foreign power enjoyed the unadulterated loyalty of tens of thousands of Americans, many of them intellectuals, some holding senior government posts. The *Venona* files demonstrate the Communist Party USA's central role in achieving this loyalty. But the code breakers working on *Venona* helped impede the Party's achievement.

Eric and I have put together the story of Soviet espionage against the United States—espionage that took place at a time when we were "allies" in a war against Nazi Germany. For the Soviets there were no allies, only temporary cobelligerents that they spied against as they would on an enemy.

—*Herbert Romerstein*
August 2000

THE VENONA SECRETS

CHAPTER 1

What Was *Venona*?

VENONA WAS THE TOP SECRET NAME given by the United States government to an extensive program to break Soviet codes and read intercepted communications between Moscow and its intelligence stations in the West. The program was launched in February 1943 by the U.S. Army's Signal Intelligence Service, the forerunner of the National Security Agency (NSA). The effort focused on piles of coded and enciphered messages that had been sent over commercial telegraph lines. The cables in question were dispatched between 1940 and 1948. While between 1947 and 1952 most of the intercepted messages susceptible to decoding were read, the effort to crack open as many cables as possible lasted until 1980.

The Soviet foreign intelligence service, known by the acronym OGPU, was renamed the NKVD before the war. Still later, it would be known as the KGB. During the time that concerns us, some spy operations also were carried out within America and elsewhere by the NKVD's colleagues in Soviet military intelligence, later known as the GRU. The Red Army and Navy had separate agents targeting areas of special interest. But most of the espionage was conducted by the NKVD, which had replaced the GRU in the late 1930s in most intelligence collection.

Venona confirmed some of the conclusions of American counterintelligence and provided evidence for new conclusions about how Soviet espionage operated in the United States. The NKVD stations were called *Rezidenturas*. There were four of them in the United States. One was an "illegal *Rezidentura*," which we will discuss below. Three were what the Soviets called "legal *Rezidenturas*." These operated out of the Soviet embassy in Washington and the consulates in New York and San Francisco. During World War II, the *Rezident*, or chief, was Vassiliy Zarubin, who first in the New York consulate and later at the embassy in Washington used the name Vassiliy Zubilin.

Born in 1894, Zarubin joined the Cheka, Lenin's secret police, in 1920 and had a varied career in both legal and "illegal" work. In 1925 he was assigned to the Cheka's Foreign Intelligence Department and worked in China and, later, Western Europe. Subsequently, from 1934 to 1939, Zarubin worked as an "illegal" in the United States and Nazi Germany under the name Edward Herbert. He was recalled to the Soviet Union after the signing of the Nazi-Soviet Pact and assigned to the NKVD's other activity—internal repression.

In accordance with the Nazi-Soviet agreement, after the Nazi attack on Poland, the Red Army attacked the Poles from the east. The agreement with the Nazis provided the Soviet Union with almost half of Poland. By October 1939 thousands of Polish officers and enlisted men were in the hands of the Red Army. The officers were put in special camps and interrogated by the NKVD.

Zarubin arrived at one of the camps, called Kozelsk, on October 31, 1939. Although not officially the camp commander, Zarubin gave orders as if he had total control. On Zarubin's orders, some prisoners were transferred to the Lubyanka, the NKVD headquarters in Moscow, for further interrogation. His responsibility was to determine which Polish officers should be severely punished for previous anti-Soviet activity and which could be recruited for Soviet intelligence operations. He spent much of his time speaking with staff officers, former college professors, and others who might be useful.

What Was *Venona?*

Professor Stanislaw Swianiewicz was one of only a few who survived because he was removed from Kozelsk shortly before most of the others were sent to Katyn Forest to be shot. He remembered Zarubin, whom he referred to as Kombrig (Brigade Commander) Zarubin:

> [Zarubin] directed the NKVD team which investigated and recorded the history and background of prisoners.... Kombrig Zarubin was the highest Soviet authority with whom the Polish officers who were detained in Soviet POW camps could enter into direct contact, and the picture of that suave, educated, and well-mannered general is still vivid among the few survivors from those camps. There is a mystery about Kombrig Zarubin, and it is hard to tell whether he should be regarded by Poles as an enemy or as a friend.

While others did most of the interrogating, Zarubin would single out specific prisoners for discussions:

> The Kombrig was a very agreeable man to talk to. He was an educated man, he knew not only Russia, but the West as well. He spoke fluent French and German and had also some knowledge of English.... [U]sually he would offer his victim cigarettes of good quality. Sometimes also tea, cakes, and even oranges were served.

Zarubin would even lend the selected prisoners books from his library, which contained volumes in Russian, French, English, and German.[1]

The work of the NKVD interrogators in Kozelsk was over by early February 1940. Zarubin returned to Moscow in January. Later, in April and May 1940, fifteen thousand Polish prisoners of war were transferred from Kozelsk and two other camps to Katyn Forest, where they were murdered by the NKVD on orders from Stalin and Lavrenti Beria, head of the secret police.[2]

After work at headquarters in Moscow, Zarubin spent a short time in China, where he reactivated an old Soviet agent, the ex-Nazi captain Walter Stennes, who was then a military advisor to the Chinese government.[3] Accompanied by his wife, Zarubin then returned to the United States on December 25, 1941 carrying diplomatic passports. They would remain in America until August 27, 1944.[4]

Zarubin discovered he was under FBI surveillance in July 1943 and concluded incorrectly that the FBI knew of his role in the murder of the Polish officers at Katyn. In a *Venona* message to Moscow, he said, "The real reasons for surveillance of me, I think, have been accurately ascertained—the 'competitors' [the FBI] have found out about my having been at Kozelsk...." Elsewhere in the message, which was only partially broken, Zarubin referred to the Polish officers.[5]

In fact, the FBI knew nothing about his role in the murder of the Polish officers, but it suspected he was an NKVD officer from observing his activities and contacts. A month later the FBI received an anonymous letter, in Russian, identifying a number of the NKVD officers in the United States, including Zarubin. But the letter also contained some bizarre statements, such as that Zarubin was a secret agent of Japan and that his wife, also an NKVD officer, was a secret agent of Germany. Although the letter was hard to take seriously— in fact, it was eventually ascertained that the author was Mironov, an NKVD officer who, according to recent information from former KGB officers, was emotionally disturbed[6]—it did say that Zarubin and another officer "interrogated and shot Poles in Kozelsk.... All the Poles who were saved know these butchers by sight. 10,000 Poles shot near Smolensk was the work of both of them."[7] The killing of the Polish officers was well known, for the Nazis had already found

What Was *Venona?*

the bodies at Katyn, near Smolensk, and had announced this in April 1943,[8] but the FBI was not sure that Zarubin was involved—until, that is, the recent release of Soviet documents.

Zarubin's "legal" officers were all openly part of what the Soviets called the "Soviet colony" in the United States. Most used the cover of diplomats, but some were journalists for Soviet publications or the Soviet press agency TASS, or trade representatives of such Soviet companies as Amtorg. The agents they ran were Americans who used their government positions to collect secret information or to influence policy, or both. Some of the agents were so dedicated to the USSR that they were self-starters and would sometimes steal information or influence policy even without specific instructions, to the delight of their Soviet handlers.

The fourth *Rezidentura* was the "illegal" one. The *Rezident* was Iskhak Akhmerov. He and the "illegal" officers under him had no open contact with the so-called Soviet colony, although the legal *Rezidentura* provided the "illegals" with communication facilities to Moscow. "Illegal" intelligence officers had false identities and false nationalities. They worked with only the most important and sensitive Soviet agents and concealed their Soviet responsibilities from any unwitting American who might know them in their cover capacities. The only Americans who were aware that the "illegal" officers were Soviet officials were those who were themselves Soviet agents.

Zarubin worked closely in the United States with his "illegal" colleague Akhmerov, who reported to Moscow through Zarubin. Shortly before Zarubin's departure for Moscow in 1944, Stepan Apresyan, who became the New York NKVD *Rezident* in 1944, had to get Moscow's permission to maintain contact with Akhmerov. He cabled the Centre (NKVD's Moscow headquarters) with a *Venona* message: "In connection with 'Maksim's' [Zarubin's] departure how often may one meet 'Mer' [Akhmerov] and should I be the one to meet him?"9

Akhmerov subsequently held high ranks at KGB headquarters in Moscow and eventually received substantial honors: He was twice awarded the Order of the Red Banner, an important medal for heroism, as well as the Badge of Honor. He was also named an "Honored Chekist," the highest award issued specifically to KGB officers.

Born in 1901, Akhmerov joined the OGPU (foreign intelligence service) when he was twenty-nine years old. In 1932 he was assigned to the Foreign Department (INO) of the Intelligence Service. After serving in China in 1934, he was assigned to the United States as an "illegal" officer.10 The assignment was not necessarily a desirable one: A year earlier, the "illegal" *Rezident*, Valentine Markin, had died under mysterious circumstances in New York, and Akhmerov served under his successor, Boris Bazarov.11

When Bazarov left for Moscow in 1938 to be purged, Akhmerov became *Rezident*. According to his colleague at NKVD headquarters, Vitaliy Pavlov, Akhmerov directed ten American agents at this time, including people in the State Department, Treasury Department, and White House. We know from *Venona* that one of the most important agents was Harry Dexter White.

Akhmerov was at first joined in the United States by his wife, Elena, but he soon found a new love in the person of Helen Lowry, the niece of American Communist Party leader Earl Browder. Lowry, who came to New York from Kansas in 1935, was given a job in a Soviet commercial enterprise and became active in the Communist Party. The next year Soviet intelligence recruited her, and she was assigned as the assistant to Akhmerov to run a Washington "safe house"—a secure place for an intelligence officer to meet agents. When she and Akhmerov fell in love, Elena went back to Moscow. Akhmerov and Lowry married in 1939.

What Was *Venona*?

The newly wed Akhmerovs were recalled to Moscow in mid-1939, and she was given Soviet citizenship. But the Akhmerovs were sent back to the United States in September 1941 to reestablish the "illegal" apparatus that had been temporarily deactivated almost two years earlier.[12] Akhmerov's cover was a fur business; his grandfather had been in that business decades earlier. His former wife, Elena, back in Moscow, became secretary to secret police head Beria.[13]

Elizabeth Bentley, an American courier for a Soviet spy network, joined the Communist Party in New York in 1935 and became involved in Soviet intelligence activity in 1938. But, following the death of her lover and boss in the spy ring, Jacob Golos, Bentley fled the Party, confessed to the FBI in 1945, and became a highly valued source of information on Soviet espionage. She had worked with both Akhmerov, whom she knew as "Bill," and his wife, Helen, whom she had known as "Catherine" during the war.[14]

Akhmerov once told Bentley how he had courted Helen in Washington, where they worked in 1938 or 1939. When Bentley met them, they were living in New York. In the summer of 1944 Mrs. Akhmerov gave birth to a daughter, Elena, who later served as an officer at KGB headquarters,[15] and in September they moved to Baltimore.[16] Akhmerov's son with his previous wife was living with her in Moscow; in March 1945 Moscow cabled to the New York NKVD that the "son is alive and well."[17] (Young Akhmerov eventually followed in his father's footsteps and became a senior KGB officer.[18] After a KGB career in Africa, he died in the late 1980s.) Helen and Iskhak Akhmerov returned to Moscow on December 7, 1945.

Even though the Soviets had an elaborate spy mechanism functioning in America and were extremely careful to protect the identities of their agents, there were serious security problems. Early in the war the Soviets sent some messages via secret and illegal radios.

But in 1943 the Federal Communications Commission (FCC), while searching the airwaves for clandestine Nazi radio transmitters, detected unauthorized radio signals coming from Soviet consulates in New York and San Francisco. The United States government confiscated the radios,[19] thus forcing the NKVD to rely on commercial telegraph agencies such as RCA. These coded messages were routinely supplied to American wartime censors. And this, of course, made them available to the code breakers.

Still, the Soviets were confident that the Americans could not read their communications to and from their home base. The messages were not only replete with code phrases and names, but also encrypted—that is, the letters were translated into blocks of apparently random numbers. The security of this method depended on the use of what is called a one-time pad—an easily disposable booklet of thousands of groups of numbers which served to conceal the coded letter messages. The sender simply designated to the receiver which page out of hundreds in the booklet contained the right number sequences, and that page was never used again. Code breakers found "one-time pads" impenetrable because key words were not repeated by the same number groups.

But back in Moscow the exigencies of wartime led the Soviet code makers into a fatal error. The demand for one-time pads soon outstripped the production facilities, and reissuing duplicate pads became a simple necessity. Through painstaking testing of numbers and words, the Americans began to find patterns that enabled them to decrypt large portions of the dispatches.

In the end, about 2,900 Soviet messages were broken into and translated. Traffic from the New York NKVD office to Moscow during the critical war year of 1944 was the most readable; 49 percent of them were broken. By contrast, only 15 percent of the 1943 messages and less than 2 percent of the 1942 traffic were readable.

What Was *Venona*?

By war's end in 1945, the Soviets had regained their grip on security; only 1.5 percent of these cables could be decoded.[20]

The Communist Party USA and Soviet Espionage

When the *Venona* solutions began to be available to the public (between 1995 and 1997), some intelligence scholars were surprised at the extent to which Soviet intelligence had been able to penetrate the United States government. The messages also demonstrated that the overwhelming majority of Americans who spied on behalf of the Soviets were members of the Communist Party USA. Although these facts were known to the FBI and the House Committee on Un-American Activities, this was one of the most contentious issues during the long Cold War debate.

For a long time it has been an article of faith among apologists of the Left that Communist Party members were loyal citizens merely engaged in dissent and only bent on reform of the American system. *Venona* proves the opposite—their loyalty was to the Soviet Union, and many of the Party's leadership and some of the hard-core membership served as spies in the Soviet cause. *Venona* and other recently available materials help explain why American Communists betrayed their democratic country to a totalitarian dictatorship.

Although any American Communist would have been proud to be chosen to spy for the Soviet Union, only a small number of Party members had the jobs or other qualifications that the Soviets needed. When these people were recruited for espionage, their names were checked through the American Communist Party apparatus, as well as the Communist International in Moscow, to make sure that they were completely loyal and had never expressed "politically incorrect" views.

The Communists divided their followers into Party members, non-Party Bolsheviks, and fellow travelers. Party members were true believers in "my country right or wrong"—only their country was the Soviet Union, not the United States, which had provided them with educational and economic opportunities and allowed them to pursue their dreams. Party members were dedicated to the "triumph of Soviet Power in the United States."[21] Non-Party Bolsheviks had the same goal but for personal reasons did not have full Party membership. They thought and acted like Party members but lacked the membership card. Fellow travelers agreed with many Communist Party programs but were not prepared to go the whole way. Only those in the first two categories were sufficiently dedicated to the Soviet Union to be trusted to spy against their own country.

In the end, only a small percentage of American Communists were judged qualified to spy for Russia. We know of no case in which a Party member reported such an offer to the FBI. Some spies later confessed to the FBI after leaving the Communist movement for other reasons.

The Arlington Hall project was by no means the only warning American officials had of the extent of Soviet incursions into our strategic secrets. In that respect, the breaking of the *Venona* cables must be considered a validation—and a crucial one at that—of disclosures of Soviet activities that FBI investigations had already revealed.

Alarm Signal from Canada

On September 5, 1945, Igor Gouzenko, a GRU code clerk in the Soviet embassy in Ottawa, defected to Canadian authorities and brought with him documents that clearly showed the scope of Russia's spy operations not only in Canada but in the United States as well. His documents also aired the espionage role of local Communists in both countries. The case sent shock waves through the governments of Canada, the United States, and Britain. When the Canadian Royal Commission published Gouzenko's revelations,

What Was *Venona*?

Western governments and ordinary citizens became acutely aware not only of Soviet espionage but also of the activities of local Communists on behalf of Moscow.

According to Gouzenko and the documents he provided, Moscow's most important Canadian agents included Fred Rose, a Communist member of Parliament, and Sam Carr, the national secretary of the Canadian Communist Party (then called the Labor Progressive Party).

Even more alarming than the names Gouzenko provided was his evidence of the USSR's atomic espionage activities. Not everyone was appalled by his story. Joseph E. Davies, the former U.S. ambassador to the Soviet Union—and one of the American establishment's leading Stalin admirers—told the *New York Times* that Russia "in self-defense, has every moral right to seek atomic-bomb secrets through military espionage if excluded from such information by her former fighting allies."[22]

Davies had been an outstanding defender of the Moscow Purge Trials. Today, even the most dedicated Communists admit that the trials were frame-ups. But at the time, Davies and others claimed that Stalin, by purging most of the surviving leaders of the Russian revolution, had prevented a Nazi fifth column from operating in the Soviet Union. Natalia Sedova, the widow of the murdered Leon Trotsky, wrote in 1942 that "Mr. Davies has come to the fore in the role of Stalin's defender in the case relating to the frame-ups...." She commented, "It must be said that Mr. Davies is fulfilling this assignment with such shamelessness and moral irresponsibility as to cause astonishment even in our harsh epoch."[23]

Notwithstanding the benign view of Davies and others, the revelations of defector Gouzenko panicked Soviet intelligence. Although he had been a GRU (military intelligence) officer, Gouzenko also knew a good deal about NKVD (foreign intelligence) activities. Kim Philby, then working in the counterintelligence section of MI6, the British foreign intelligence service, read the still secret reports from Gouzenko in Canada and alerted his controllers in Moscow that the defector was handing over precious information.

The Soviets' first act was damage control—to protect agents who had not been disclosed by Gouzenko. At the top of the NKVD list were the two most important Soviet agents in Britain—Kim Philby, designated in *Venona* traffic as "Stanley" or "S," and Guy Burgess, whose cover name was "Khiks." Pavel Fitin, head of the NKVD's Foreign Department, sent a *Venona* cable to his station chief in London ordering him to concentrate on working with Philby and Burgess and to cut down on contacts with less productive agents.[24]

A few days later Fitin decided to insulate Philby further by dealing separately with Burgess. He ordered the London *Rezidentura* that "in view of this 'neighbor' [GRU] affair in Canada and the circumstances that have arisen on your end as a result," they must "transfer 'Khiks' [Burgess] to another officer." (NKVD/KGB and GRU officers refer to each other as "neighbors.") Fitin's instructions were explicit:

> Temporarily, until further notice, cut down meetings with "Khiks" [Burgess] to once a month. Urge "Khiks" to concentrate his attention on passing us material dealing only with large fundamental issues. The position remains the same for "Stanley" [Philby] also. If, however, you notice that, as a consequence of local circumstances greater attention is being paid to you and to our workers by the "competitors" [British intelligence], you may break off contact temporarily with the sources.[25]

What Was *Venona*?

Lavrenti Beria, Stalin's chief of intelligence and head of the Soviet secret police, added his concern on April 7, 1946, in the form of a *Venona* cable to every *Rezidentura* abroad. The Beria missive was headed: "To be deciphered personally by the *Rezident.*" The tone of the orders reflects the internal tension within the Soviet spy leadership as a result of the Gouzenko defection. "As you know from the press, the former cipher clerk of the *Rezidentura* of the GRU in Canada, Gouzenko, has betrayed our country. Gouzenko stole and passed to the Canadian authorities several dozen incoming and out-going cipher telegrams, as well as personal dossiers on a valuable agent network."

Beria explained that "Operational work in the 'neighbors' *Rezidentura* had been so organized that each operational worker had a detailed knowledge of the work of the other members of the staff, the agent network, the times and places of meetings, the nature of the tasks assigned by the Centre [Moscow headquarters], and plans for operations. Inside the *Rezidentura*, personal dossiers on the agent network were common knowledge."

Beria's cable clearly reveals the intelligence role played by local Communist Party members:

> In the work of the agent network, extensive use was made of members of the Communist Party organization who were known to the authorities of the country for their progressive activity. Thus Gouzenko's work as a cipher clerk on the head-quarters staff, and afterwards in the same post at the *Rezidentura* (where a decline in vigilance gave rise to the situation described), made it possible for the traitor to have at his disposal State secrets of great importance. Gouzenko's testimony, and a number of documents introduced by the prosecution at the initial Canadian judicial hearing, show that

Gouzenko was preparing to betray his country long before the day on which he defected.

Beria, who would make an unsuccessful attempt to succeed Stalin after the death of the Soviet dictator, noted the laxity that facilitated Gouzenko's efforts: "In the *Rezidentura*, there was no study or training of people, the most elementary principles of conspiracy were ignored, complacency and self-satisfaction went unchecked. All this was the result of a decline in political vigilance. G's defection has caused great damage to our country and has, in particular, very greatly complicated our work in the American countries. It is essential for us to draw the appropriate conclusions from the fact." Beria then laid down the law:

> In the instructions which we are sending you by the next post, rules and regulations are given to ensuring [effective] conspiracy in the work and for fostering in our comrades the qualities of Party vigilance and discipline. You are directed to observe these rules and regulations scrupulously, applying them everywhere in actual practice. Take all necessary measures to improve the organization of all agent network and operational work, paying special attention to tightening security. The work must be organized so that each member of the staff and agent can have no knowledge of our work beyond what directly relates to the task he is carrying out.[26]

Beria's demands point to a growing contradiction between the thinking of the intelligence professionals in the field and their leaders in Moscow. While the officers in the *Rezidenturas* understood the valuable role played by local Communist Party members in carrying out Soviet espionage work, Beria, a bureaucrat, knew little about foreign intelligence gathering. His expertise lay in running the USSR's massive internal repression apparatus. Beria saw the dangers inherent in using local Party members for spying. But he failed to value the access to secrets and opportunities for penetration that were obtained by the local Communist members who were animated by unquestioning ideological faith in the Soviet Union. This was quite different from the motives of those agents who were moved by money or blackmail, the usual recruitment methods used by Beria's repressive apparatus at home. He also overestimated the danger. While Western security services had penetrated the Communist parties, only very trusted Communists knew of the Soviet espionage system. No Western agents had penetrated to that level in those years. In later years most Soviet agents were recruited by mercenary lures, and their quality was much lower than the ideological agents of World War II.

Some in the West understood the espionage role of local Communist groups well before the Gouzenko affair. The FBI, for example, had already alerted government policymakers, including President Harry Truman. And on Capitol Hill, the Special Committee on Un-American Activities (the Dies Committee) had since 1938 been holding hearings on both Nazi and Soviet espionage operations.

Trotsky Exposes the Spy Network—But Few Listen

Interestingly, the most compelling information on Soviet spying during this period was virtually ignored. It was provided by Leon Trotsky, sworn enemy and rival of Joseph Stalin, who had been one of the top Soviet leaders when these operations began in 1918. In early 1940 the KGB (then OGPU) tried unsuccessfully to assassinate Trotsky in Mexico, where he was in exile, hoping to elude Stalin's long murderous arm. Later that year Moscow's agents succeeded.

After the first murder attempt, Trotsky wrote a letter to the attorney general of Mexico, which he released to the press, about the "general scheme of the GPU organization abroad." According to Trotsky, "the Central Committee of each section of the Comintern [i.e., each local Communist Party] includes a director of the GPU responsible for that country." He asserted that this individual's status was known only to the head of the Party and to one or two trustworthy officials. Others on the Central Committee "have but a slight inkling of the special status of this member." Trotsky pointed out that "as a member of the Central Committee, the country's GPU representative has the possibility of approaching all members of the Party, study their characters, entrust them with commissions [assignments], and little by little, draw them into the work of espionage and terrorism."[27]

Trotsky was even willing to tell the truth about Soviet subversion and espionage to the Dies Committee; however, he never had the opportunity (see Chapter 10).

Aborting the Communist Anti-Nazism Campaign

Most members of the American Communist Party had joined during the 1930s in response to the Party's boast of being the most effective opposition to Nazism. Many of those who later engaged in wartime espionage had joined during this anti-Nazi period. But, astonishingly, few Communist Party members and no spies fled its ranks in the wake of the 1939 Nazi-Soviet alliance, which unleashed World War II and divided Poland between Hitler and Stalin.

In 1940 André Marty, a leader of the French Communist Party who also served as the Communist International (Comintern) functionary responsible for directing the American Communist Party, boasted, "In the last fourteen months... not a single member of the National Committee... not a single... state Party leader... has turned against the Communist Party." Marty went on to report that even "the four traitors" (i.e., defectors) accorded significant publicity were "very very little people," a curious claim given that the defectors included Granville Hicks, a prominent writer, and George Wishnak, an important garment union official, who Marty said "sold out to Dubinsky." (Dubinsky was the leader of the anti-Stalinist International Ladies' Garment Workers' Union.) The other "traitors" named by Marty were Howard Rushmore, a young reporter on the CP's *Daily Worker*, and Manning Johnson, a prominent black functionary of the Communist Party and member of the Communist-infiltrated American Federation of Labor (AFL) waiters' union. Marty noted that in the course of the 1940 national election campaign, Johnson became a firm Roosevelt supporter.[28] But these few defections notwithstanding, almost all of the Party leaders and members remained loyal to Moscow.

Although many sympathizers and fellow travelers were quick to denounce the Nazi-Soviet alliance, the lack of mass defections from the Communist Party itself raised questions about the motives of American Communists. How could people who joined the Party to fight fascism and called themselves "premature anti fascists" ally themselves with Hitler?

Subsequently, apologists for the Party explained that the Soviets signed the pact with the Nazis to "buy time," which is false. Stalin never believed that Hitler would violate their agreement and attack the Soviet Union, at least as long as Britain remained a threat on the German western front. Russian researchers, moreover, have recently uncovered documents in the Soviet archives showing that Stalin refused to believe the reports by his own spies of a planned German invasion of the Soviet Union. He scrawled obscenities and "disinformation" on the reports.[29] Indeed, Western Communists, including those in America, echoed the official Soviet line that it was the British and French "imperialists," aided by President Roosevelt, who were the warmongers, while Germany, like the Soviet Union, was a force for peace.

The Hitler-Stalin pact was announced on August 23, 1939, just days before German troops invaded Poland. For Americans of all political persuasions, the alliance of the dictators added further confusion to the debate going on inside the United States between those who favored strict isolationism from the coming world conflict and those led by President Roosevelt who argued for a program of military preparedness.

Even the Western Communists were initially shocked and confused by the new situation. But a new Soviet line was quickly and secretly communicated throughout the Comintern. The war had changed the international situation. The notion that there was a difference between fascist and democratic capitalist governments had "lost its meaning." Communists abroad must now oppose their own democratic governments and their efforts to defend against the growing Nazi threat. In one message from George Dimitroff—the top Comintern official in Moscow—the Party organizations that were slow to understand the new line, "especially France, England, the USA, and Belgium," were ordered "to correct their political lines."30

It is a small irony that the militant loyalty of the American Communists to Moscow in the days leading up to the American entrance into World War II helped focus Washington's attention on the Party and its functioning, most particularly the Dies Committee hearings in the House of Representatives. Congressmen interrogated the Communist Party USA's leader, Earl Browder, and even took extensive testimony from Benjamin Gitlow, one of the brightest of the Party's former leaders, who had left the Party in 1929. Despite a decade's absence, Gitlow was able to furnish information about Soviet funding of the Party as well as about espionage carried out by American Communists on behalf of the Soviet government. Gitlow's testimony was summarized for the Comintern leadership in a memo from the American Communist Party's

What Was *Venona*?

representative in Moscow, Pat Toohey. He also reported that "at the time the Soviet-German Pact was signed and the imperialist war broke out, the bourgeois press [along with] Trotskyites, Lovestoneites, and socialists organized a wild, hysterical, anti-Soviet, and anti-Communist campaign."[31]

By this time, Hitler's ultimate intentions were scarcely a secret. Indeed, in a January 30, 1939, speech to the Reichstag, Hitler—greeted repeatedly by thunderous applause—pledged that "if the international Jewish financiers in and outside Europe should succeed in plunging the nations once more into a world war, the result will be not the bolshevization of the earth, and thus the victory of Jewry, but *the annihilation of the Jewish race in Europe*" (our italics).[32] Although it was Hitler, of course, not the Jews who started the war, the Nazis, during their alliance with the Soviet Union, abandoned antibolshevism but continued to persecute the Jews.

In this context, the willingness of American Communists to accept, repeat, and publish Soviet foreign minister V.M. Molotov's October 31, 1939, vile boast that "one swift blow to Poland, first by the German Army and then by the Red Army," eliminated "this ugly offspring of the Versailles Treaty" demonstrates conclusively that members of the American Communist Party believed that their only duty was to back Moscow. No real antifascist could approve of the Nazi conquest of Poland. In an especially infamous phrase, Molotov went on to insist that "one may accept or reject the ideology of Hitlerism as well as any other ideological system; that is a matter of political views."[33]

During this time, the American Communist Party published and widely distributed Stalin's soon-to-be embarrassing analysis of world affairs. The Soviet dictator claimed:

(a) It was not Germany that attacked France and England, but France and England that attacked Germany, thereby assuming responsibility for the present war; (b) After hostilities had broken out, Germany made overtures of peace to France and England, and the Soviet Union openly supported Germany's peace overtures, for it considered, and continues to consider, that the earliest possible termination of the war would radically improve the position of all countries and nations; (c) The ruling circles of England and France rudely rejected both Germany's peace overtures and the attempts of the Soviet Union to secure the earliest possible termination of the war. Such are the facts.[34]

Stalin and Molotov's pronouncements were read by American Communists as gospel. At the same time, they continued to receive detailed instructions from the Comintern in Moscow. One such directive was written only two days before the June 22, 1941, attack by Nazi Germany on the Soviet Union. It ordered the American Communists to continue their work to keep America disarmed and to carry out disruptive work in the armed forces. It read:

In carrying out the work of strengthening and leading the anti-war and anti-imperialist people's movement it is absolutely essential that the Party carry on a systematic ideological and political struggle against the social democratic and bourgeois reformist influence in the workers and progressive movement. It is also necessary that the Party and the communist youth organization broadly popularize the Leninist position of struggle against the imperialist war and against militarism and carry out serious work within the Army and Navy, as well as among the reserve officers of the training cadre (ROTC) and the civilian training center for the youth (CCC) and make sure that the members and cadre of the Party and the youth organization receive military training and master its art and science.[35]

What Was *Venona*?

The Nazi attack on the USSR prevented this instruction from being sent, and American Communists obediently resumed their anti-Nazi attitude and urged military support for the Soviet Union. The Comintern then switched gears and sent them a directive to accelerate their work to promote Western aid to the Soviet war effort.[36]

Clearly, Western Communists were far more comfortable as antifascists. Yet for nearly two years, they voiced the pro-Nazi political line without losing many members. They reverted to antifascism only after the Wehrmacht launched Operation Barbarossa, the attack on the Soviet Union.

But when Great Britain was standing alone against Nazi aggression, English Communists, like their comrades in the United States, actively undermined their country's defense. In addition to antiwar propaganda, the British Communists formed a unit to collect information for Soviet military intelligence (the GRU). The unit, called "Group X," was led by two high-ranking officials of the Communist Party of Great Britain. The Soviets gave them the code names "Intelligentsia" and "Nobility" (*"Znat"*). British intelligence, which was helping the Americans to decode *Venona*, learned the names of the two GRU agents, but when it released the 1940 GRU *Venona* communications, it deleted the names. Great Britain's leading expert on KGB history, Nigel West, has exposed the identity of the two Soviet agents: "Intelligentsia" was Professor J. B. S. Haldane, then chairman of the editorial board of the Communist Party's paper, the *London Daily Worker*; "Nobility" was Ivor Montagu, a leading Communist writer who would later become the president of the British Communist Party.[37]

In addition to helping lead "Group X," Haldane was assigned by the GRU to recruit additional spies. In a *Venona* message of August 16, 1940, the London GRU *Rezident* Simon Kremer ("Barch") reported that Haldane was trying to find an appropriate person to recruit in the British Military Finance Department.[38]

The British Communists provided the GRU with information that might be of only peripheral interest to the Soviets but was of great interest to their Nazi allies. For instance, in August 1940 they assessed the damage after a Nazi air raid on a factory at Filton, which produced aircraft engines.[39] A few weeks later they reported that a factory in Norwich that produced basic components for aircraft had been badly hit.[40]

In September the British Communists advised the GRU that Nazi bombings had focused on docks, railway stations, power stations, and bridges; afterwards, GRU London—the Soviet military intelligence in London—identified which docks were still intact.[41]

London GRU also provided Moscow with a significant piece of information obtained from its British Communist agents: "Warships with A.A. guns [antiaircraft guns] have been stationed in the Thames near the docks, which has not happened before."[42] A few days later, Montagu reported to his GRU handler that the British had brought six destroyers into the Thames and were evacuating Eastbourne.[43]

The British Communists further reported that an aircraft factory in Rochester had been completely destroyed and that five thousand workers transferred to Swindon to work on transport aircraft at the Phillips factory, where earlier trainer aircraft had been produced. Haldane, who was working as a scientist for the British government, reported that the British had discovered that delayed action bombs could be rendered inoperative by freezing.[44] This kind of information would, at the time, be of interest only to the Nazis.

In October Haldane reported to the GRU that "Group X" had learned from a Communist woman working in a British intelligence unit that "the British had broken some Soviet code or other and apparently she noticed in a document the following words: 'Soviet Embassy in Germany.'" GRU London advised Moscow that it had told Haldane that "this was a matter of exceptional importance and he should put to the Group the question of developing this report further."[45]

On September 7 one of the agents in "Group X" reported that in a conversation with soldiers in an antiaircraft unit, he learned that Luftwaffe pilots were using a radio beam originating in France to direct their planes to bomb Birmingham and other Midland towns.[46] On October 16 Montagu confirmed the report.[47] This radio beam, or *Knickebein*, was the Luftwaffe's unique weapon. British knowledge of it was a closely held secret because their scientists were developing electronic countermeasures to defeat *Knickebein*. From September 7 to November 13, London was bombed every night except one. Because of British countermeasures, a substantial portion of the bombs missed the targets.[48] Here again, British Communists provided the GRU with information useful only to the Nazis.

Montagu, in addition to his work as a Communist Party official and a GRU agent, served as a reporter for the Party's paper, the *London Daily Worker*. In that capacity, on October 29, 1940, he toured the 339th Battery of the Twenty-sixth Search Light Regiment of the First Anti-Aircraft Division, stationed on the northwest outskirts of London. He dutifully reported the location of the unit and told the GRU that each detachment site was twenty-five meters in diameter and that the distance between detachments was 2.5 to 2.9 kilometers.[49] It was not until *Venona* was decrypted that the British government learned of these acts of treason by British Communists. Similarly, the United States government knew few details about American Communists spying for the Soviet Union until Elizabeth Bentley's confession was confirmed by *Venona*.

THE VENONA SECRETS

The Young Code Breakers

What were the American code breakers like? They were young, in their late teens and early twenties, and mostly women. None had any experience at unraveling codes, but all had a special aptitude for math, essential to breaking the codes, and some were language specialists. Only about 10 percent were young military officers. The civilian men and women were hired as government employees at the very low level of GS-2. If they had a college degree, they could be promoted to GS-3, about the pay level of a buck private in the army. The women lived in dormitories or shared rooms in a government residence; the men scrambled for scarce space in local apartments and rooming houses.

The locale of the code breaking was Arlington Hall, a former girls' school on Route 50 in Virginia that had been taken over by the military. Temporary buildings were built on the property to accommodate them. After a two-week period of security clearance investigations, they were assigned the arduous task of decrypting secret messages.

After several years of working alone on the tedious task of deciphering, the Americans in 1945 began to cooperate with their British counterparts. Three years later the FBI began to employ the decrypted information to identify spies. FBI Special Agent Robert J. Lamphere was assigned to work with Meredith Gardner, one of the leaders in breaking through the *Venona* code barriers. Together they began to identify the cover names for spies in the messages.

Between 1948 and 1951 *Venona* helped the FBI identify a number of Soviet agents including Klaus Fuchs, Harry Gold, David Greenglass, Theodore Hall, William Perl, Ethel and Julius Rosenberg, Guy Burgess, Donald Maclean, Harry Dexter White, and later Kim Philby. Eventually—but not until 1953—the CIA joined the effort, and still more KGB agents were identified.

What Was *Venona*?

Despite U.S. efforts to keep the *Venona* project secret, the Soviets were not long in learning that their codes had been breached. As early as 1944 high officials in the Roosevelt White House were formally alerted that the army was attempting to break Soviet codes. That year, Lauchlin Currie, a close personal aide to the president and a Soviet agent, was able to report to his spy controllers, through Elizabeth Bentley, that "the United States was on the verge of breaking the Soviet code."[50]

At about the same time in 1944, Colonel Carter W. Clarke, chief of the Special Branch of G-2 (Army Intelligence), visited Arlington Hall to pass on a message to the *Venona* project directors, Colonel Harold Hayes and Lieutenant Colonel Frank Rowlett. He told them, astonishingly, that first lady Eleanor Roosevelt had learned that the army was decrypting Soviet communications—and that for unstated reasons she wanted this stopped! Having delivered the message, Clarke said that he personally felt the project should continue and that, officially, the conversation had never taken place.[51] The code breaking continued.

After the war, when two Soviet agents alerted Moscow that the code breaking project had succeeded, the Soviets changed their codes. One of the Soviet agents who reported details of the code breaking is an intelligence legend—Kim Philby, a high-ranking officer in Britain's MI6, the British equivalent of the CIA. Philby had served since the autumn of 1949 as the U.S.-based liaison between his service and the American intelligence community, and in that capacity he learned about *Venona*.

In contrast, relatively little is known by the public about the other agent, William W. Weisband, a National Security Agency employee who watched the code breaking take place. Born in Egypt in 1905, he came to the United States in 1925 and became a citizen in 1938. He joined the army in 1942 and, because he was a Russian linguist, was sent to Arlington Hall in 1945. Weisband took a particular interest in the decrypting effort, and as Meredith Gardner, one of the code breakers, recalled later, he was hovering about when an important message about atomic espionage was pulled out of the coded numbers. Later, in 1950, a former Soviet spy who confessed to the FBI identified Weisband as a fellow Soviet agent. But Weisband denied the allegation, and with only the testimony of a coconspirator, the Justice Department could not pursue the case. But when Weisband was subpoenaed to appear before a federal grand jury and failed to show up, he was jailed on contempt charges for a year. Unfortunately, evidence of his spying was insufficient to charge him.[52]

In a later damage assessment, U.S. intelligence concluded that Weisband's spying resulted in the Soviets' changing their codes, thus denying American cryptologic agencies access to vital Communist bloc communications during the early days of the Korean War. This was, in the words of historians David Hatch and Robert Louis Benson, "perhaps the most significant intelligence loss in U.S. history."[53]

Although Moscow abandoned its wartime codes, the *Venona* messages continued to yield intelligence gold dust for decades to come. Today the decryptions are more than a historical artifact. As we will see, the *Venona* cables are the mortar that holds together information from Soviet archives and U.S. government investigations. Together, they give a clear picture of Soviet World War II espionage against the United States.

CHAPTER 2

An "Agent of Influence" Makes History

IF ANYONE EMBODIED THE INTELLECTUAL LUSTER surrounding Franklin Delano Roosevelt's New Deal, it was Harvard economist Harry Dexter White. By World War II, White was considered a world-class economist, if not on the level of British superstar theorist John Maynard Keynes and Hitler's financial wizard, Hjalmar Schacht. White publicly played a leading role in planning our postwar economic strategies.

Many of White's policies came into being, and some—the International Monetary Fund and the World Bank, to name two—survive to this day. But White had another role unknown to his government colleagues: He was what intelligence professionals call an "agent of influence." He not only spied for the Soviet Union throughout the war but also sought to shape critical U.S. economic policies in obedience to the orders of his Moscow masters. As a spy, he was a rival in perfidy to Alger Hiss and to that trio of British traitors, Kim Philby, Guy Burgess, and Donald Maclean. In a sense, he trumped all of them because, as we now know, he played a major role in policy decisions that benefited the Soviet Union.

Influencing policy is an important but dangerous activity for a spy. By intervening actively in policy decisions, a spy may call attention to himself and reveal his hand. This kind of intervention is worth the risk only if the agent is placed high enough to have a reasonable chance of success. White, the assistant secretary of the treasury under Roosevelt and Truman, was a good example of this kind of spy. He also exemplified a trait difficult to understand but shown by even the most intelligent people—clinging to loyalties even after repeated proof that their loyalties were misplaced. *Venona* disclosures now make apparent that White was a very important Soviet spy—perhaps even more important than Alger Hiss.

Harry Dexter White began his strange career as a member of a prewar spy ring in the U.S. government. The ring, consisting of members of the American Communist Party, reported secret information to a Party apparatus, which in turn reported it to Soviet military intelligence, the GRU. Later it went to the NKVD, the Soviet state security service.[1]

In some respects White seemed a typical New Dealer, the sort of bright young technocrat who was drawn to Roosevelt and to his drive to use the federal government first to repair and then to radically transform American society. Born in 1892 in Boston to Jewish immigrants from Lithuania, White represented the classic American success story. He attended Columbia University, served in World War I, and obtained B.A. and M.A. degrees from Stanford prior to earning a Ph.D. at Harvard. Intelligent and personable, he quit a job teaching economics to join the New Deal, where he quickly rose to the position of assistant secretary of the treasury under Henry Morgenthau, Jr., a politically well-connected scion of a prominent banking family and personal friend of Franklin and Eleanor Roosevelt. White, in due course, became a close friend of Secretary Morgenthau as well as his most influential advisor, notably on international affairs.

But in at least one very important respect Harry Dexter White went beyond the New Deal. No one has ever determined when or where it happened, but somewhere along the line White came under the influence of Communism and, more specifically, of the Soviet

Union. While nothing in his public activity or academic work identifies him as a Marxist, he revealed his true loyalties in his secret work for the Soviet Union.

Whittaker Chambers, the liaison between the American Communist underground and Soviet military intelligence,[2] first met White in 1935. White was not a formal member of the Communist Party and did not pay dues, but he was part of a Communist underground cell, and he supplied secret Treasury Department information to Chambers, who passed it on to the Soviets. In Soviet terms White was a "non-Party Bolshevik." He was also able, through his considerable influence at Treasury, to assist other members of the underground group in getting jobs and promotions in the department.

In 1936 Chambers was assigned to work for a new Soviet boss, Boris Bykov, then head of Soviet military intelligence in the United States. When Bykov suggested paying the underground members for supplying information, Chambers was horrified. In his view, the underground consisted of dedicated Communists who helped the Soviet Union out of loyalty, not for money like mercenaries. Finally, Bykov decided that at least some of the more important people should be given an expensive present to show Soviet appreciation. He provided Chambers with money to buy four expensive Oriental rugs to give to the most valuable agents: One rug went to Alger Hiss, another to Julian Wadleigh, the third to George Silverman, and the fourth to Harry Dexter White.

The rugs were shipped to Silverman, who arranged to deliver them to the others. (Once, while visiting White's home, Chambers was shown his rug.) But the problem of providing money to the agents persisted. Innovative ways of giving financial help to agents without insulting them appear a number of times in the *Venona* intercepts.

Chambers later told the FBI that he and White never developed the friendship that Chambers had with other agents. This might have been because White, although willing to spy for the Soviet Union, never became an official member of the Communist Party. On the other hand, in 1937 Bykov asked to meet White and apparently got along with him better than Chambers had.

Chambers received information and documents from White to transmit to Soviet military intelligence from 1935 until 1938, and one document was in the batch that Chambers turned over to the U.S. government after the war. When Chambers broke with Communism, he saved samples of the documents that he had provided to Soviet intelligence as an "insurance policy." These were the famous Pumpkin Papers—documents Chambers hid one night on his farm in a hollowed-out pumpkin in fear that the Soviets might try to steal and destroy them. While most of the papers were handwritten or typed by Alger and Priscilla Hiss, one of the Pumpkin Papers was in White's handwriting. Chambers turned the papers over to the House Committee on Un-American Activities in 1948.

Soon after Chambers left the Communist underground in 1938, he contacted White in Washington. They met in front of a drug store opposite the Treasury Department on 15th Street in Washington, D.C., and it was apparent that White was not yet aware of Chambers's break. His first words were: "Have you come back to inspect the post?" Chambers revealed that he had broken with the underground apparatus and wanted White to do so as well, threatening to expose White if he continued his activity. White was terrified, and Chambers believed that he had succeeded in breaking him from the underground.[3] He was wrong.

Although after Chambers's defection the underground ring was transferred to the NKVD, it was for other reasons soon "put on ice," as the Soviets termed it. During 1939, NKVD officers throughout the world were recalled to Moscow to face demotion or death;

An "Agent of Influence" Makes History

Stalin, suspicious of his international apparatus, decided to purge most of it. White, however, was reactivated in 1941 by NKVD officer Vitaliy Pavlov in order to carry out a very important agent-of-influence operation, and during World War II he played a major role as both a Soviet spy and agent of influence.

Pavlov Joins NKVD

Vitaliy Pavlov was a twenty-five-year-old NKVD officer in 1939 when he was assigned as deputy chief of the American section of the agency in Moscow. Thus he participated with White in one of the most important influence operations of World War II. Young and inexperienced, Pavlov was assigned to the job because, as Lieutenant General Leonid Shebarshin—head of the KGB First Chief Directorate (Foreign Intelligence)—said in a newspaper interview many years later, "We suffered from the same misfortune as the entire country. As a result of repressions, the Chekists lost almost 22,000 from their ranks."[4] (Soviet intelligence officers still call themselves "Chekists" after the first name of the service, the Cheka.) The "misfortune" in question was the Great Terror—the successive waves of state-organized purges that Stalin unleashed upon the people of the Soviet Union in the 1930s. Tens of millions lost their lives as the Stalinists tried to create a Soviet Union capable of leading the World Socialist Revolution. Eventually, because of Stalin's paranoia, the killings cut deeply into the ranks of the very Communists who unleashed this vast massacre. Even the instrument of their crimes, the NKVD secret police, was caught up in the bloody turmoil. The Foreign Intelligence Department of the NKVD, which organized spying abroad, was particularly damaged. "Some departments of the NKVD," Pavlov himself recalled, "were stripped bare," an understatement, if ever there was one, for the wholesale executions of dedicated cadres.

From the point of view of a man like General Shebarshin, a professional intelligence officer, the purges, apart from the aspect of the human catastrophe, were an organizational nightmare. "A tragic result," he reminisced, "was that the foreign network—created at such risk and with such expenditures—was destroyed to a considerable degree. The entire Foreign Department leadership and practically all *Rezidents* abroad were executed...."[5] Because of the dearth of personnel, Pavlov noted that, though barely out of training school, he was propelled into an important job. His boss simply said, "This is your sector. The documents are in the cabinets. Figure them out, and work."[6]

Among the loyal Communists who were swept up in the Stalinist terror and executed in 1938 for "espionage and treason" were Boris Bazarov and Pavel Gutzeit, the NKVD "illegal" and "legal" *Rezidents*, respectively, in the United States.[7] Two of Bazarov's top intelligence officers in America, Iskhak Akhmerov and Vassiliy Zarubin, had every reason to believe that they too would be liquidated when they were brought back to Moscow to attend a large meeting in January 1940. At the meeting, Lavrenti Beria, Stalin's chief of intelligence and secret police (the original Cheka managed both functions, as did its successor organizations), denounced about two dozen of the most experienced officers present as German, British, or Polish spies. But Zarubin and Akhmerov were not killed, only demoted and assigned to low-level jobs in the American section at NKVD headquarters in Moscow. Their new boss was the young and much less experienced Pavlov, recently appointed deputy chief of the American section in Moscow. The three, Pavlov, Zarubin, and Akhmerov, would be directly responsible for reactivating White in 1941 as a Soviet agent of influence.

With the information that the *Venona* cables provided, American officials years later correctly assessed Zarubin and

An "Agent of Influence" Makes History

Akhmerov as the most successful spymasters the Soviet Union ever had in the United States. Pavlov continued his successful career, including a stint as *Rezident* in Canada, retiring as a KGB general and head of the KGB training school. By at least one significant measure—living through the Stalinist regime in its most ruthless years—the trio were surely successful, though survival in Stalin's Russia often was a matter of sheer luck. The trio performed at least one very significant service for their country: They managed to subvert various aspects of U.S. policy to Soviet ends. And Harry Dexter White was their instrument.

The penetration of the U.S. government was well under way by the time Akhmerov and Zarubin were recalled to Moscow, but most of the operation was on hold due to the shortage of intelligence officers to direct it. In the whirlwind of the purges in the late 1930s, an efficient foreign-policy-making system, complete with seasoned intelligence officers and an experienced military hierarchy, was not Moscow's priority. As the KGB leader Shebarshin later said, when war came, "the intelligence [service] had been beheaded and was in a shambles."[8] The same could be said of the military: Even as Hitler was planning to break the Nazi-Soviet Pact, Stalin was still busy purging his generals.

A Spy Can Influence Policy

During most of the Soviet-Nazi alliance, a large part of the Soviets' American agent network had been held in reserve. But in early 1941 an active agent was needed because the Soviets were concerned about Japan, which they looked upon as the eastern flank of "the capitalist encirclement of the Soviet Union." An essential element of this Stalinist theory was that, at an appropriate moment, the capitalists would unite to attack Soviet Russia. Thus the Soviet goal was to create rifts in the encirclement.

35

One tactic was to keep the Japanese militarists focused on the United States—not too difficult since the Japanese viewed America as a potential threat to their planned hegemony in the Pacific. In the high councils of the Japanese Empire, war with the United States was expected. The Imperial Navy, in particular, was spoiling for what it believed would be a quick war against a decadent democracy. But to Soviet officials, expectations and plans were not enough. They knew that important officials in the U.S. government wanted a modus vivendi with Japan in order to gain time to prepare for the coming confrontation. America's peacetime army was woefully unprepared for war in 1939-40; the draft had not been passed by Congress until September 1940, and large-scale war production—ships, planes, guns—was barely beyond the planning stages.

The Japanese could view this as an invitation for an early knockout strike—as they eventually did—or they could consider it a gift of time to concentrate on their immense western front, which included how to drive the Soviet Union out of the Far East. Already in 1938 and 1939 there had been skirmishes on the Manchurian border between Soviet and Japanese forces.

The Soviet Union's most valuable spy in Japan, Richard Sorge, reported in early 1941 that while Japan planned an attack on the United States, a Japanese-American rapprochement was possible. He warned that this could result in a Japanese attack on the Soviet Union. Joining the German Communist Party in the 1920s, Sorge was recruited into the Comintern's intelligence service and then transferred to Soviet military intelligence, the Fourth Bureau of the Red Army (later known as the GRU). On Moscow's instructions, he joined the Nazi Party and used that as a cover for his espionage work. He was sent on missions to China and began working in Japan in 1933 as a correspondent for a German newspaper. In Tokyo he

An "Agent of Influence" Makes History

maintained contact with two GRU officers, Zaitsev and Butkevich.[9] Sorge was arrested in Tokyo in October 1941, a month after he reported to Moscow that "Japan will attack America and England. The danger to the Soviet Union is over."[10] The Soviets never warned the United States.

During his interrogation, Sorge admitted to his captors that the Soviets actively opposed an easing of tensions between the United States and Japan:

> The course of the Japanese-American talks was of great importance for the Soviet Union.... First, if the Japanese-American talks had resulted in the improvement of Japanese-Chinese relations, Japan would have freed a part of her armed forces and that would have forced the Soviet Union to take precautionary measures. Second, had the Japanese-American talks succeeded, there would have arisen the danger that after their rapprochement, Japan and the USA [would] pursue a coordinated anti-Soviet policy.[11]

At this time, Akhmerov suggested that the NKVD might intervene in Japanese-American relations through an agent of influence. In April 1941, Pavlov, on Akhmerov's advice, proposed that one of the agents in the American network, Harry Dexter White, be reactivated to this end. This proposal was approved by Beria, but Pavlov and Akhmerov were concerned because many of their American agents had been recruited in the mid-1930s on the basis of Communism's supposed anti-Nazism. The Nazi-Soviet Pact, they worried, might have alienated most, if not all, of the Soviets' American agents. They needn't have worried. The American Communists remained loyal "Soviet patriots." Not one agent broke with Soviet intelligence as a result of the alliance with the Nazis.

American Communists believed what they read in Party publications—that Britain, not Nazi Germany, was the main enemy. As Communist Party chairman William Z. Foster stated in an article:

> Great Britain and France took on grave war guilt by sabotaging the peace front that the Soviet Union proposed to prevent the war. Next, Hitler went on the offensive by invading Poland. Then, as Stalin said recently, "It was not Germany who attacked France and England, but France and England who attacked Germany, assuming responsibility for the present war."
>
> The imperialist Allies assumed further responsibility by rejecting the peace proposals of Germany, the Netherlands, and the Soviet Union.... The Social-Democrats and other "labor leaders" who are seeking to enlist the workers on the side of the Allies, around the will-o-the-wisp slogan of the "lesser evil," are giving just one more illustration of the fact that they are agents of the capitalist class.[12]

As we saw in Chapter 1, up until a few days before the Nazi attack on the Soviet Union, Moscow was working on a set of instructions to the American Communist Party to continue its campaign against the Roosevelt administration and its attempt to rearm the United States. Soviet and, of course, American Communist propaganda still supported the Nazi "peace efforts" against the British "imperialist war."[13]

Communism exerted a powerful attraction across a wide swathe of American opinion in the 1930s and 1940s. Though never able to garner significant numbers of votes in more than a few local elections, American Communists, on the strength of their putative commitment to a world of peace and social justice, and riding on the prestige, in liberal circles, that the Bolshevik Revolution still commanded, were able to influence opinion makers and political activists.

An "Agent of Influence" Makes History

The Communists also, at the time, claimed for themselves the mantle of the most active and consistent opponents of Nazism. And the organizational skills of the Communist Party USA won them important positions in the labor movement, notably the new Congress of Industrial Organizations (CIO). Communist influence could, moreover, be felt in the liberal circles of the Democratic Party, and particularly among the self-styled "progressives" who joined the New Deal.

The lines between "fellow travelers" and card-carrying—though sometimes secret—members of the Communist Party were very clear, at least to the Communists. But to the public they were intentionally blurred when it suited Soviet purposes—for instance, when it was useful to have a "popular" or "united" front against "fascism." The ambiguity of these lines, to non-Communists, is one of the strongest indications of the strange attraction that Communism exerted during much of the early part of the century.

Then, too, Nazi atrocities allowed the Communists to assume a righteous anti-Nazi image, which greatly facilitated their recruitment efforts. Using the basic premise that the fight against the racist, anti-Semitic, bellicose, hateful regime in Berlin must be the first priority for all men and women of goodwill, Communist activists and sympathizers were able to convince a great many people that—at least in the short term—relatively minor disagreements about what was going on in Moscow or in the international Communist movement were secondary to fighting Hitler. In Europe as well as the United States, the Communist movement grew, in influence no less than in membership, when it made anti-Nazism (or "antifascism," as it was usually termed) its priority.

Then came the Nazi-Soviet alliance, and the ensuing pro-Nazi propaganda, in an instance, cleared the lines of demarcation between dedicated Communists and temporary fellow travelers. For this reason, young Pavlov was uncertain how he would be met by the American he had traveled halfway around the world to meet in Washington, D.C., in the spring of 1941. Pavlov remembered that since the summer of 1939, anti-Nazism had been replaced by a vociferous anti-British line and demands that the United States stay out of the "imperialist" war in Europe. Communist trade union activists went so far as to lead political strikes in defense plants, the most notable in April 1941 at Allis-Chalmers in Milwaukee. Those strikes were designed to block production of war material destined for England under the terms of the Lend-Lease Treaty, signed by President Roosevelt on March 11, 1941. Pavlov knew that with the muting of antifascism by the Communists, the now dormant networks that had been developed in America might have grown indifferent, if not hostile, to the Soviet Union. How would they react when he approached them with the notion that Japan represented a pressing threat to the United States that must be forcefully countered—a transparent maneuver, to anyone with a map handy, to deflect armed conflict between Soviet and Japanese forces in the Far East?

But Pavlov was concerned not only with the reputation of the Soviet Union in anti-Nazi circles but specifically about the views of one individual: Harry Dexter White. Pavlov had been dispatched to Washington in May 1941 to activate this "agent of influence." Officially a Soviet diplomatic courier, he became the point man for Operation Snow—the major effort to manipulate U.S. strategic policy through Harry Dexter White. A second NKVD officer went with him to provide security.[14]

Not knowing that White's devotion to the Soviet Union was that of a true believer, Pavlov approached White in the last months of the Nazi-Soviet Pact with some uncertainty. But Pavlov quickly realized that the grotesque deal between the two despotisms had not shaken the faith of the Treasury Department official.

An "Agent of Influence" Makes History

Referring to "Bill," the name under which White knew Akhmerov, Pavlov phoned White in Washington in late May 1941 and made a date for lunch at a restaurant known to White from previous meetings with Akhmerov. Pavlov recalled in his memoirs that he had told White to recognize him by his blond hair and a copy of *The New Yorker* magazine that he would be carrying. Still worried that White might have become disenchanted by the Nazi-Soviet Pact, Pavlov was prepared to give White a copy of an old Soviet, anti-Japanese forgery called the Tanaka Memorial, if he were reluctant to push the anti-Japanese policies.[15] But this proved unnecessary; White was quite willing to go along with the plan.

At the restaurant, Pavlov handed White a note outlining themes that he wanted White to promote in the high councils of American foreign policy. Among these was a firm demand that Japan stop its aggression and recall its armed forces from China and Manchuria, and further, that Japan sell a large part of its armaments to the United States. These demands, in themselves utterly excessive from the Japanese point of view, were written in extremely harsh language, obviously designed to antagonize the Japanese. According to Pavlov's recollection many years later, White tried to put the paper in his pocket, but the Russian stopped him and made him memorize it.[16]

White wrote a memorandum shortly after this meeting and sent it to Secretary Henry Morgenthau. In substance, it was an exact repetition of the points Pavlov had given him. It even contained this bizarre statement, unusual for an anti-Nazi:

> The Franco-British brand of diplomacy emulated by our own State Department appears to have failed miserably. Due to half-measures, miscalculations, timidity, machinations or incompetence of the State Departments of the United States,

England and France, we are being isolated and we find our-
selves rapidly moving toward a war which can be won by us
under present circumstances only after a costly and bitter
effort, and only with a terribly dangerous aftermath.

Morgenthau did not recognize the Soviet anti-British line
reflected in the memo, which he retained and reproduced in his
diary. The memo also demanded that Japan withdraw its military
from China, Indo-China, and Thailand. In addition, Japan was told
to lease to the United States up to 50 percent of Japanese naval ves-
sels and airplanes and to sell to the United States half of Japan's
output of war material.

Although Morgenthau did not act on White's memo at that
time, the issue would come up again. By November 1941, as war
drew nearer, the State Department was pushing for an agreement
with Japan that might delay the outbreak of hostilities. Soviet agents
in the government, as noted, were concerned that if Japan did not
go to war with the United States, it might go to war with the Soviet
Union. The last thing Stalin needed was for Japan to open a second
front in the Soviet Far East. Germany had attacked the Soviet
Union in June and, as a result of Stalin's bungling and purges, the
Wehrmacht had cut through the Red Army like a knife through
butter and had conquered vast areas of the Soviet Union.[17]

The Soviet agents in the U.S. government knew they had to do
something. Lauchlin Currie, a Soviet agent, was particularly agitated,
telling his colleagues that the State Department was planning to sell
China "down the river."[18] We've seen how the agents were often
self-starters, influencing policy or collecting information for Soviet
intelligence before their NKVD handlers had given them their
marching orders. But in this case, White had already received
instructions from Pavlov. White rewrote his hard-line memorandum

for Morgenthau, who signed it and sent it to President Roosevelt and Secretary of State Cordell Hull.

Hull used most of the harsh, demanding language in his ultimatum to the Japanese on November 26, 1941.[19] It would strengthen the hand of the war party in Tokyo, which was already prepared to attack the United States. On December 1 the final order for the attack on Pearl Harbor was given.

Recall that even the policymakers who understood that America could not stay out of the world war did not want to rush into a war with Japan. The reason was simple: American civilian and military leaders knew the country needed time to prepare for war. As Cordell Hull, FDR's secretary of state, put it in his memoirs: "I realized that there was very little possibility that the Japanese would accept a modus vivendi.... On the other hand, if by some good chance they accepted it, three more months would have been gained for the Army's and Navy's preparations, in case Japan attacked at the expiration of the temporary agreement."

During the last crucial weeks before Pearl Harbor, Hull allowed Morgenthau (who annoyed him because of his "persistent inclination to function as a second Secretary of State") to incorporate some of the points the Soviets had covertly given White into the State Department's communication to Tokyo.[20]

How important was this diplomatic maneuver in bringing about the December 7, 1941, attack on Pearl Harbor? General George Marshall, former chief of staff and no dove, observed, "Had they not attacked on December 7th, had they waited, for example, until January 1 there is a possibility that they would not have launched the attack...."[21] But most historians of World War II agree that the war party in Japan would have provoked hostilities with the United States sooner or later. What is certain is that Operation Snow was being carried out with Soviet, not American, interests in mind.

Immediately after seeing White, Pavlov, using the code name "Klim," reported to Moscow that "everything is all right, as planned." And as he would observe many years later, notwithstanding Sorge's later report that Japan had decided to make war on the United States in 1941, and not on the Soviet Union, "the possibility of a Japanese attack on our rear remained. The USA's entrance into the war [against Japan] eliminated such a threat, and therefore any actions taken to achieve such a guarantee were to our advantage."[22] Pavlov, to be sure, was congratulating himself on his work, but there is no reason to doubt that when he claimed that Operation Snow was fully justified, he expressed the view of the Soviet leadership.

The success of Operation Snow also suggested to Pavlov and other Soviet intelligence officers that the network that had been temporarily deactivated when Akhmerov returned to the Soviet Union in 1939 had probably not been affected by the Nazi-Soviet Pact. White's example made it clear that Akhmerov's American network was more pro-Soviet than it was anti-Nazi, notwithstanding its several Jewish members.

The Silvermaster Ring

Nathan Gregory Silvermaster was the leader of the spy network to which White belonged during World War II. Silvermaster was a longtime, committed Communist who had first come to the FBI's attention in the early 1920s. He had, as it were, "inherited" White from the underground Communist cell to which White provided secret government information as early as 1935. This cell, which included Alger Hiss and Whittaker Chambers, had reported to Soviet military intelligence until 1938 when the Soviets, disturbed by Chambers's abandonment of Communism, reorganized the group. Most of them were later ordered to report to the NKVD rather than military intelligence and thus became Akhmerov's responsibility.

An "Agent of Influence" Makes History

Elizabeth Bentley, an American, was a courier for a Soviet spy ring from 1939 to 1945. Bentley worked for the NKVD, which in the late 1930s took over most of the agents who had been working for Soviet military intelligence. One of these was White. Without ever meeting him, Bentley received White's information through two other Soviet agents, Silvermaster and William Ludwig Ullman. She later told the FBI that White was regarded as a valuable adjunct because of his close relationship with Henry Morgenthau, Jr., and was felt to be in a "position to secure favorable consideration for the USSR in financial matters."[23]

In her testimony before the House Committee on Un-American Activities in 1948, Bentley explained how White passed information to the Soviets through Silvermaster. Bentley had also collected Communist Party dues from some of the agents, but she did not know whether White was a formal member of the Party.[24] (Not only did the agents refuse payment, but most were willing to pay dues for the privilege of spying for the Soviet Union.)

When White was called before the Un-American Activities Committee in 1948, he flatly denied the accusations of both Chambers and Bentley, testifying that he was not a Communist "nor even close to becoming one." White denied knowing either Chambers or Bentley. He specifically denied that Chambers had asked him to break with the movement "because I never belonged to it."[25]

Whether or not he belonged to the Communist Party in a formal sense, the *Venona* intercepts reveal that White continued to supply information to Soviet intelligence throughout World War II. One of the reports from NKVD New York to Moscow revealed that White ("Lawyer") told the Soviets about a conversation between Vice President Henry Wallace and Secretary of State Cordell Hull. The Soviets were pleased to learn that Wallace suggested giving the Soviet Union a $5 billion loan.[26]

Morgenthau relied so much on White that he assigned him to be the Treasury Department representative to other agencies and to represent Treasury in the planning group at the Office of Strategic Services (OSS), America's wartime intelligence service.[27] These new duties provided rich opportunities for the Soviet spy to steal secrets and influence American policy.

A high-level NKVD official visited the United States in the summer of 1944. We do not know his true name, but his code name in the *Venona* communications was "Koltsov." During the visit, "Koltsov" had a lengthy meeting with White, which he reported to Moscow in a *Venona* message describing the information he had obtained. After discussing Germany and monetary policy, White revealed to him that a trip he and Morgenthau planned to make to Moscow had been delayed indefinitely.

In general, the Soviets believed that White was in a position to advise them on the thinking of high-level U.S. government officials. Ironically, perhaps because of his pro-Soviet bias, White sometimes misled them. He suggested, for example, that there would be little opposition to the Soviets' restoring their 1940 frontier with Finland— about 10 percent of Finnish territory. He further advised that annexing the Baltic states would not create too much opposition in the States. He was wrong—these and other Soviet expansionist moves were badly received by the U.S. government. The United States continued to allow embassies of the Baltic states in Washington and refused to recognize their incorporation into the Soviet Union.

White told "Koltsov" that he was "ready for any self-sacrifice" in his work for the Soviet Union. But he was quite rightly concerned that if his role were revealed, it would cause a "political scandal." For security reasons, White suggested that meetings be held in people's homes every four or five months and that more frequent but shorter meetings be held in his car.[28]

An "Agent of Influence" Makes History

Silvermaster was unhappy about White's meeting with "Koltsov." He complained to Akhmerov that "Koltsov" questioned White on matters on which he, "as leader of the group, in his own words, is working ceaselessly." He saw the visit from Moscow as a mark of "insufficient confidence" in his ability as leader of the spy ring.[29] Moscow responded that it made the decisions on how to handle agents and that neither Akhmerov nor Silvermaster was in a position to second-guess those decisions.[30]

This small tiff aside, Silvermaster was highly regarded by Moscow, as of course was White. Among other things, Silvermaster used White to place other agents in key government positions. In January 1945 Silvermaster reported that White was to be promoted to assistant secretary of the Treasury and that he could place Harold Glasser ("Rouble"), another Soviet agent, in his old job of assistant to the secretary. But since Glasser was a member of the Perlo ring and thus not subordinate to Silvermaster, he suggested that should Glasser get the job, he should be reassigned to Silvermaster's ring.[31] Silvermaster was always concerned about prestige and power.

The Morgenthau Plan Helps Nazi Propaganda

One of White's greatest contributions to the Soviet effort was his role in the Morgenthau Plan for postwar Germany. According to Venona, during his meeting with "Koltsov," White reported that on August 5, 1944, he and Secretary Morgenthau were heading for London and Normandy.[32] By August 7 they were at a meeting in a tent in southern England with General Eisenhower. Another Treasury official, Fred Smith, was also there and later wrote about it in an article in *United Nations World*. In the course of the discussion, Eisenhower expressed his concern that the Germans would not be punished sufficiently after their defeat. He said that all the German people were responsible for Nazism and that he would like to "see things made good and hard for them for a while." White responded, "We may want to quote you on the problem of handling the German people." Eisenhower agreed.

Encouraged by White, Morgenthau later told British officials that "I think we could divide Germany into a number of smaller provinces, stop all industrial production, and convert them into small agricultural land holders." This was the Morgenthau Plan—to convert Germany into a pasture.

At his meetings with British and American officials, Morgenthau often let White take the lead. Concerning postwar Germany, White said that if Germany were allowed to rebuild its economic power, it would again become a military threat. He suggested that the best course for the Allies was to reduce Germany to a fifth-rate power.[33]

Although first supportive, after careful study Roosevelt and Churchill rejected the plan. But a leak to the press on September 23, 1944, apparently from the Treasury Department, suggested that the Morgenthau Plan was official policy. The Nazi propaganda machine turned the story into a plot by the "Jew" Morgenthau to destroy Germany.[34] And this stiffened resistance against the American and British forces.

At the same time that White was undermining American policy and providing a propaganda weapon to the Nazis, Soviet propaganda to the German troops was telling them *"Die Hitlers kommen und gehen, aber das deutsche Volk, der deutsche Staat bleibt"* ("Hitlers come and go, but the German people, the German state remain").[35] The Soviet theme was that they planned a "soft peace" for Germany. The reality was the contrary.

Spies at the Founding Conference of the UN

Despite the rebuff of the Morgenthau Plan, White's political star within the Roosevelt administration was never higher than in

An "Agent of Influence" Makes History

1944. That summer, White was the chief American delegate at the historic conference in Bretton Woods, New Hampshire, that plotted the postwar financial rules by which the Allies intended to restore their battered economies.

In 1945 an important opportunity opened up for White and the other members of his spy ring. The founding conference of the United Nations was to take place in San Francisco in April of that year. On March 31 Secretary of State Edward Stettinius wrote to White, "On behalf of President Roosevelt and the members of the American delegation, it is my privilege to extend to you an invitation to become an official advisor to the delegation of the United States to the United Nations Conference on International Organization...."[36]

Less than a week later, a Moscow *Venona* message ordered Akhmerov to make arrangements with Silvermaster ("Robert") about maintaining contact with White, then called ("Richard"), and another member of the Silvermaster ring, William Ludwig Ullman ("Pilot") in San Francisco ("Babylon").[37] The official roster of the founding conference of the UN shows White representing the Treasury Department. Alger Hiss, an agent of the GRU, was the acting secretary general.[38] This provided the Soviets with advanced notice on how the Americans would handle questions during the deliberations.

During White's attendance at the San Francisco conference, he was handled by NKVD officer Vladimir Pravdin ("Sergej"), who served in New York but attended the conference as a Soviet news agency, TASS, reporter. White gave the Soviets information on the American delegation's internal discussions. His reports evaluated the views of Nelson Rockefeller, assistant secretary of state; Leo Pasvolsky, special assistant to the secretary of state for International Organization and Security Affairs; James C. Dunn, assistant secretary of state; Congressman Charles A. Eaton; and Senator Arthur H. Vandenberg, all of whom were members of the American delegation.

White reported that "Truman and [Secretary of State] Stettinius want to achieve the success of the conference at any price" and suggested that knowing the American position in advance "could be an effective method of counteracting the attempts of the U.S.A. to put the USSR in a disadvantageous position."[39] White also evaluated some of the Latin American delegates, his comments ranging from "good people" to "a fool."[40]

White Finally Gets Paid

In November, Stepan Apresyan, the NKVD *Rezident* in New York, advised Moscow of a new problem. White's wife, who was aware of her husband's work for the Soviet Union, complained to Silvermaster about her family's financial problems. The Whites wanted to send their daughter to a private school and lacked the money to do so. Mrs. White suggested that her husband leave the government and get a better paying job in the private sector. Silvermaster discouraged this since White was such a valuable asset.

Silvermaster explained the problem to Akhmerov, who agreed that the Soviets would provide the money for the girl's education. White would not accept payment for his work but, according to Silvermaster, would receive "gifts" as a mark of Soviet gratitude. But Akhmerov advised Silvermaster and Ullman to be very careful how they handled financial assistance to White.[41] The problem of paying agents without insulting them prevailed throughout World War II.

Elizabeth Bentley told the FBI in 1945 that White was a Soviet agent, and the FBI in turn reported this to President Truman. But White was not interviewed by the FBI until August 15, 1947, when he admitted that he had known Silvermaster since 1934. They had met as fellow government employees and frequently met at Silvermaster's home, where they played music: Silvermaster played the guitar; his wife played the piano; Ullman, who lived with Silvermaster, played the drums; and White played the mandolin.

White disingenuously said that Silvermaster had never requested that he provide information of a confidential nature to him and that "it would come as a great surprise and shock if he were to actually learn that Silvermaster was engaged in espionage."[42] Of course, Silvermaster never had to request that White provide confidential information. He was already doing so when Silvermaster began to work with him.

All that the FBI knew about White's espionage was due to Elizabeth Bentley.[43] The NSA hadn't as yet broken enough of the *Venona* intercepts to uncover all of the details of his spying, but the FBI knew enough to be confident that Bentley's story about White was true, and the bureau was concerned that White would continue supplying secret information to the Soviet Union.

In 1946 President Truman nominated White as an American representative to the International Monetary Fund. J. Edgar Hoover thereupon wrote to Brigadier General Harry Vaughan, President Truman's military aide, asking him to give the enclosed background on White to the president. Hoover described White as "a valuable adjunct to an underground Soviet espionage organization operating in Washington D.C. Material which came into his possession as a result of his official capacity allegedly was made available... to the Soviet Union." Hoover also revealed that Canadian government sources had expressed their concern to the FBI about the appointment of White.[44] The Canadians knew of White through the Soviet military intelligence defector Igor Gouzenko.[45]

A copy of Hoover's report was also sent to Secretary of State James F. Byrnes, who later revealed that he went to see President

Truman the day he read the report. Byrnes expressed his shock and asked what Truman intended to do about it. According to Byrnes, the president said that he was also surprised at the information. Byrnes suggested that White's nomination be withdrawn. When Truman checked on the status of the nomination, he was told that the Senate had already confirmed White.

At this point the president could have either refused to commission White or asked him to resign. Byrnes suggested both possible courses. But Truman did neither, and White became executive director of the International Monetary Fund.[46]

Years later, President Truman in a radio and television broadcast on November 16, 1953, challenged the revelations about White made public by the Senate Internal Security Subcommittee, which had released the Hoover letter. He claimed that he had promoted White "to keep from exposing an FBI investigation of an alleged espionage ring."[47] Defenders of President Truman's retention of White have argued that the FBI wanted him kept in the government so that they could watch him, but there is no evidence to support this claim. J. Edgar Hoover, testifying before the Senate Internal Security Subcommittee on November 17, the day after the Truman broadcast, said that the FBI had made no such recommendation and that, in fact, White's promotion made surveillance more difficult. Hoover testified: "At no time was the FBI a party to an agreement to promote Harry Dexter White and at no time did the FBI give its approval to such an agreement." He went on to say that the FBI did not object to White's firing: "No restrictions were placed upon the agencies wherein action was taken. All that we asked was that sources of information be protected."[48]

President Truman, of course, did not support retaining Communist agents in government. After all, it was he who instituted the Loyalty and Security Program. But he did not want the image of

An "Agent of Influence" Makes History

his administration and that of the New Deal to be damaged should the Republicans make a political issue of Communists in government. Truman, by not firing White in 1946, denied the Republicans a public example of a high-level Soviet agent in the government.

In 1946, however, the Republicans did not fully understand the nature and scope of Soviet espionage. They were concerned that Communists, who might be potential Soviet agents, were obtaining government employment. The reality was much worse—Communist Party members in government had been actively recruited by Soviet intelligence. By 1956 the Republicans understood much more about the role of American Communists in Soviet espionage.

In 1947, when White resigned for health reasons as U.S. executive director of the International Monetary Fund, President Truman wrote a letter to him expressing great appreciation for his work, adding that he would "feel free to call upon you from time to time for assistance...."[49]

The following year Elizabeth Bentley and Whittaker Chambers identified White as part of a Soviet network in public testimony before the House Committee on Un-American Activities. Called before the committee, White denied all charges.[50]

White would never face criminal charges. On Saturday, August 14, 1948, White returned to his home in New Hampshire from Washington and went to bed on the advice of his doctor. A few hours later, he suffered a heart attack and died on Monday, August 16.[51]

CHAPTER 3

The Making of an Apparat

THE SERVICES HARRY DEXTER WHITE rendered to the NKVD did not take place by chance. Years before the recruitment of White, the Soviets had planned to establish an apparatus in each capitalist country for espionage purposes. During the 1930s and World War II, the plans came to fruition.

In 1990 the head of the Foreign Directorate of the KGB, Leonid Shebarshin, was asked whether it was true that during World War II the Soviet Union had spied on its allies. He answered:

> Yes, we had that task then, on par with regular tasks of political intelligence and penetration behind the enemy lines. There is not, and cannot be, a full openness in relations between countries. And at that time it was necessary to be on the lookout.... We had quite good intelligence assets in the leadership of all military-political groups created by the United States. We also had good assets in the leadership of the major world powers. Someday I will tell about this line of our work, but not very soon.[1]

Even allowing for the hyperbole of a veteran proud of his service or for the continuing habits of disinformation, one thing is certain: During World War II the Soviet Union had an asset that has never been available to any other country, at any time in history— foreign supporters whose loyalty was so great that they were willing to spy against their own countries. Many worked in sensitive government agencies. These people were not the dregs of society. Intelligent and sensitive, often highly educated and sophisticated, they were willing to spy for an aggressive, totalitarian dictatorship that was responsible for the murder of tens of millions. The majority of these "Soviet patriots" had never been to the Soviet Union. Their loyalty to the Soviet dictatorship was manifested through their membership in Communist parties that considered themselves part of a "World Party," the Communist International (Comintern). *Venona* provides us with a window into the Soviet operation against the United States during its heyday.

A 1977 KGB internal history marked "top secret," which has recently come to light, states: "Valuable intelligence information was received from the foreign *Rezidenturas* of foreign intelligence organs of state security. During the war, they acquired and passed thousands of intelligence reports to the center. The *Rezidentura* 'Yunga' [the code name for Akhmerov's "illegal" *Rezidentura* in the United States] transmitted more than 2,500 photostats of documents obtained directly in leading government institutions of the USA.... The *Rezidentura* of our intelligence in London acquired 18,000 intelligence documents during the war, 90 percent of which were original. On the whole, during the war foreign intelligence obtained more than 40,000 intelligence documents, of which 1,200 were of a scientific-technical nature."[2]

During World War II the KGB was called the People's Commissariat of Internal Affairs (NKVD). Its Foreign Department ran operations outside the Soviet Union. The NKVD *Rezident* in the United States at that time was Vassiliy Zarubin, who used the diplomatic cover name Vassiliy Zubilin. In a 1943 cable to Moscow, later decoded by *Venona*, he described his heavy responsibilities. In addition to supervising the work of the other NKVD officers in the

The Making of an Apparat

United States, he reported: "I myself will retain 'Dedal'... the 'Achievement' case, and liaison with 'Rulevoj.'"[3] "Dedal," we know, was the code name for Pierre Cot, a cabinet member of the French government both before and after the war; during the war Cot was a leader of the Free French, first in the United States and then in North Africa. "Achievement," meanwhile, was the code name for a plot to help the murderer of Leon Trotsky escape from a Mexican prison. And "Rulevoj"—meaning "Helmsman"—was the code name for Earl Browder, general secretary of the American Communist Party from 1932 to 1945,[4] who assisted in the recruitment and running of Party members on behalf of Soviet intelligence.

The mind-set of the American Communists—drilled into them by their Party leaders—made it possible for them to be recruited for Soviet espionage. Frederick Vanderbilt Field, the millionaire Communist, was an agent of Soviet military intelligence. He did not admit this in his 1983 autobiography but did explain what Communists thought. He described how he would "unhesitatingly spread the gospel. Stalin was infallible; all my Communist surroundings told me so. So was Browder, although on a lower level of sanctity, and so were the other CP leaders. Whenever a newspaper headline proclaimed some startling event, we would ask the first comrade we ran into, 'Has Earl [Browder] said anything about this yet?' 'Does anyone know what Gene [Dennis] thinks?' 'What does Bill [Foster] know about it?'"[5]

In 1935 Browder had read a pledge that expressed that mind-set to two thousand new Party members in New York. They swore:

> I now take my place in the ranks of the Communist Party, the Party of the working class. I take this solemn oath to give the best that is in me to the service of my class.... I pledge myself to remain at all times a vigilant and firm defender of the Leninist

line of the Party, the only line that insures the triumph of Soviet
Power in the United States.

This was reported in the official Communist Party *Manual on Organization*, written by J. Peters, head of the Party's underground and liaison with Soviet intelligence. The manual also revealed some things about which Communists were never allowed to disagree:

> We do not question the theory of the necessity for the forceful overthrow of capitalism. We do not question the correctness of the revolutionary theory of the class struggle laid down by Marx, Engels, Lenin and Stalin. We do not question the counter-revolutionary nature of Trotskyism.
>
> We do not question the political correctness of the decisions, resolutions, etc., of the Executive Committee of the C.I. [Communist International] of the convention of the Party, or the Central Committee after they are ratified.[6]

Browder, in a rare example of veracity, explained to the Dies Committee in 1939 that members would be expelled from the Communist Party for refusal to "carry out Party decisions." He revealed that if someone's "views differ from the Party's, that means by expressing himself, he is separating himself from the Party." When asked if a Party member's disagreement with Stalin's pact with Nazi Germany would result in expulsion, Browder answered yes.[7]

Expulsion from the Communist Party was a serious matter. It did not entail simply separating the person from his former comrades. He would also be branded a Trotskyite and a spy, and Party members were instructed to "mobilize the children and women... to make his life miserable; let them picket the store where his wife purchases groceries.... Chalk his home with the slogan: 'So-and-So who lives here is a spy.' Let the children boycott his children or child...."[8]

The Making of an Apparat

In that atmosphere, no one with an independent thought was permitted to remain. The Party wanted only the most dedicated fanatics—those who would do anything, even spy against their country, in obedience to the Party's orders.

Planning Ahead

The planning for the Soviet Union's intelligence gathering operations, including the recruitment of foreigners for spying purposes, began well before World War II. In 1920 the newly created Communist International (Comintern) set in motion the forces that would provide the Soviet Union with vital intelligence two decades later. In July and August of that year, the Comintern held its Second World Congress in Petrograd and Moscow and issued twenty-one conditions for admission of any national party to the Communist International. These conditions ensured Moscow's control of the parties and divided those who would be Communists from democratic socialists.

Third in the list of Moscow's conditions was the demand that national parties should "create everywhere a parallel illegal apparatus which at the decisive moment should do its duty by the Party and in every way possible assist the revolution." It ordered "a combination of lawful and illegal work." This underground or "illegal" apparatus later provided the cadre of foreign Communists to spy for the Soviet Union.

Condition fourteen said: "Each party desirous of affiliating to the Communist International should be obliged to render every possible assistance to the Soviet Republics in their struggle against all counter-revolutionary forces. The Communist parties should carry on a precise and a definite propaganda to induce the workers to refuse to transport any kind of military equipment intended for fighting against Soviet Republics and should also by legal or illegal means carry on propaganda among troops sent against workers, Republics, etc." As the condition made evident, Communists had the duty to support the Soviet military even against their own countries.

To establish clearly where the power lay, the sixteenth condition read: "All the resolutions of the Congresses of the Communist International, as well as the resolutions of the Executive Committee, are binding for all parties joining the Communist International."[9] Thus, when foreign Communists were ordered to spy for the Soviet Union, they could not disobey, but of course they could leave the Party. But, as pointed out earlier, it is a striking fact that there is no known case in which an American Communist reported a Soviet recruitment attempt to the FBI.

American Communists had surrendered much of their political autonomy even before the Second Comintern Congress. In 1919 two rival American parties were formed: the Communist Party and the Communist Labor Party, which vied for acceptance by Moscow. Moscow sent them instructions to merge. The official statement that acquiesced in this order stated, rather poetically, in June 1920:

> Sometime recently, somewhere between the Atlantic and Pacific, between the Gulf and the Great Lakes, two groups of elected delegates assembled as the Unity Conference of the Communist Party and the Communist Labor Party. Of the former, 32; of the latter, 25 and one fraternal delegate; also a representative of the Executive Committee of the Communist International. These 59 delegates came together from all parts of the United States, held sessions for seven days, debated every issue with absolute thoroughness, [and] laid out the plan of work for the United Communist Party....[10]

The Making of an Apparat

The attendance of the unidentified representative of the Communist International was the clue that the Americans had turned their political autonomy over to Moscow. From then until after World War II, the American Communist Party made its decisions under the watchful eye and guidance of the Comintern's representative. After World War II, the International Department (ID) of the Central Committee of the Communist Party of the Soviet Union ran the foreign Communist parties and provided money and instructions through KGB channels.

In 1920 American Communists needed little encouragement to obey the instructions to set up an underground party. They hated the United States government, which had conducted a major campaign against them in the aftermath of the spy scares of World War I, during which the U.S. Justice Department tried to arrest and deport those active members who were not American citizens. The threat seemed real enough since most Party members at that time were immigrants. While the government was successful in jailing a few Communist leaders and disrupting many of the activities of the Party, relatively few were deported. Official figures show that while more than six thousand deportation warrants were issued by the Justice Department for both Communists and anarchists, only a little over four thousand were served. And of the 1,119 ordered deported, only 505 actually left.[11]

Before the merger of the two parties, the Communist Party claimed a membership of 58,000 total Communists, with about 10,000 in the rival Communist Labor Party. Meanwhile the Communist Labor Party also put the total figure at about 60,000, though it said they were evenly divided between the two parties. Theodore Draper, the American historian, estimated, somewhat more accurately, that at the time the two parties had between 25,000 and 40,000 members between them.[12]

Although the Comintern wanted every Communist Party to have an illegal apparatus, it also wanted every illegal party to have an aboveground presence. The Third Congress of the Communist International in 1921 ordered the American Communists to set up such an aboveground front. The resolution, signed by the top Soviet leaders, including Lenin, Trotsky, Zinoviev, Bukharin, Radek, and Kamenev, stated:

> American capital tries to crush and destroy the young Communist movement by means of barbarous persecution, forcing it into an unlegalised [underground] existence under which it would, according to capitalist expectations, in the absence of any contact with the masses, dwindle into a propagandist sect and lose its vitality. The Communist International draws the attention of the United Communist Party of America to the fact that the unlegalised Organisation must not only form the ground for the collection and crystallisation of active Communist forces, but that it is their duty to try all ways and means to get out of their unlegalised condition into the open, among the wide masses; that it is their duty to find the means and forms to unite these masses politically, through public activity, into the struggle against American capitalism.[13]

The orders were read and obeyed. The Workers Party of America was established in New York City, December 24–26, 1921. It had almost the same membership as the underground Communist Party. A few "radical socialists" who were not willing to go underground also joined the Workers Party. The main difference between the two parties was that the underground Communist Party was proudly a section of the Communist International while the Workers Party said nothing about its affiliation to the Comintern in its constitution, program, or resolutions. Soon American Communists referred to the aboveground party as "No. 2" and the underground party as "No. 1."[14]

The Communists were criticized in the early 1920s for their underground obsession by socialists such as Eugene V. Debs and Morris Hillquit as well as labor leader Samuel Gompers. Debs said, "There is no good reason now in this country for an underground movement." And further: "There are some of those fellows who seem to thrive on the romance of underground movements. They seem to think there is something new in all that.... It seems to me that any underground radical movement in the United States is not only foolish, but suicidal."[15]

This was answered by John Pepper, whose real name was Joseph Pogany, the Comintern representative to the American Communists at that time. Although the deportations ended in 1920, the entire American Communist Party remained underground until 1923. But according to Pepper, who ignored the three-year delay:

> These mass persecutions forced the Communist Party to orga-
> nize underground to escape annihilation. The Communist
> Party of America was prompted to lead an underground exis-
> tence for three years, not by romantic mystery or secret
> instructions from Moscow, but rather by the brutal, vindictive
> terror of the American government in the service of American
> capital. The Communists formed underground because they
> were opposed by the most formidable underground organiza-
> tion—the Department of Justice.[16]

In 1922 the Comintern considered whether to order the American Communist Party to move above ground. In explaining the idea to the Party members, Party leader Charles Ruthenberg, using the name "Damon," and Max Bedacht, using the name "Marshall," said,

"After the CPA becomes an open party it will maintain an illegal apparatus for the conduct of such work as cannot be carried on openly."[17] In 1923 the Executive Committee of the Communist International ordered the American Communists to come above ground. However, they explained, "we must by all means have in reserve an illegal apparatus...." Those Party members who were reluctant to obey the orders were told: "These are the instructions given you by the Executive.... He who refuses to adopt these tactics, let him leave the Party! The Communist International demands discipline."[18]

The underground apparatus continued to exist, and a decade later, led by Max Bedacht, it served as the link between the above-ground Communist Party and Soviet military intelligence. It was Bedacht who introduced Whittaker Chambers into the underground and recruited him for Soviet espionage.

Not only the American Communist Party, but all the sections of the Communist International were treated by the Soviets like children. The German Communist Party was the most precocious of the Comintern's wards. The Germans had the largest party, after the Russians, in the Comintern, and it was widely believed that the next Communist revolution would be in Germany. During the German Communist Party's failed 1923 uprising in Hamburg, Stalin, on behalf of the Russian Communist Party, sent the revolutionaries greetings. Published in the German Communist Party's newspaper, *Die Rote Fahne*, on October 10, 1923, it said in part:

> The approaching revolution in Germany is the most important world event in our time. The victory of the revolution in Germany will have a greater importance for the proletariat of Europe and America than the victory of the Russian Revolution six years ago. The victory of the German proletariat will

undoubtedly shift the center of world revolution from Moscow to Berlin.[19]

Although the German Communists began intelligence gathering in early 1919, they did not begin organizing a significant intelligence apparatus until 1921. The Third Congress of the Comintern, held that year in Moscow, ordered the Communist parties to establish an "intelligence department," instructing each party to organize

> a special branch in its administration for this particular work. The military intelligence service requires practice and special training and knowledge. The same may be said of the secret service work directed against the political police. It is only through long practice that a satisfactory secret service department can be created.[20]

Wilhelm Koenen, the German Communist Party official who introduced the resolution at the Congress, pointed out that a few paragraphs "had been more cautiously formulated, a few deletions had been made so that it doesn't reveal all too much to the bourgeois governments."[21] It is hard to image how this resolution could have been more revealing in its original form. On orders of the German Communist Party leadership, all Party members were made available to take part in this work if needed.[22] They penetrated government offices, opposition political parties, and the German military. The leadership of the intelligence department issued "Guidelines for Intelligence Leaders" on May 27, 1922. The instructions read in part:

> One must strive to obtain specific information, not generally obtainable by the members concerning the intentions of the authorities, of the political parties, the activities of the military counterrevolution, through the utilization of suitable Party

comrades. Further, the Party must receive, more than up to now, important political and economic material.... The prerequisite for accomplishing this work is the activity of special functionaries for information gathering, the intelligence leaders. Where, up to now, no intelligence leader has existed, one is immediately to be designated.[23]

According to a February 1925 report of the intelligence apparatus to the Party leadership: "Together with the very comprehensive military intelligence which is being received, the reports concerning internal events in the individual enemy parties and groups concerning public functions and campaigns both planned and having already taken place, concerning actions of the authorities and organizations, about political personalities, provide a prospective of the activity and intentions of the opponent without which an active party would have great difficulty."

Military intelligence was of particular use to the Soviets. As the report revealed: "The apparat did not restrict itself to obtaining information of interest only to the Party. In very many cases we were able to deliver important information and material to our friends in the Center, which also Nbg. repeatedly characterized as being quite valuable." The "Center" referred to Comintern headquarters in Moscow. "Nbg." was the abbreviation of Neuberg, the cryptonym for Tuure Lehen, a Finnish born Comintern official who was sent to Germany to run the illegal military apparatus of the German Communist Party.[24] The same intelligence service report boasted:

Since the last report it was also possible to establish a goodly number of reliable contacts. Thus there exists today to name only a few of the best connections to the office of a police chief, to a branch of the R.K. f.ö.O. [Reichskommisariat for the Preservation of Public Order] in North Germany, to the

The Making of an Apparat

Interior Ministry of a South German State, to the intelligence headquarters of the völkischen [extreme nationalist] organizations, to several international press agencies, to several very large companies, to the paramilitary police [Schutzpolizei], to organizations of employers, to important positions in the Stahlhelm [right-wing paramilitary organization], the D.N.V.P. [German National People's Party], the Democrats, and the SPD [Social Democratic Party]. At present we are developing a contact to the P.P. [Political Police]. In addition there exist a large number of connections with the Schupo [Schutzpolizei], the Reichsbanner [Socialist Defense Organization], völkischen groups, Stahlhelm, etc. Changing the individual who acted as the contact man with the agents was of great advantage.[25]

Four former officers of the East German Intelligence Service (Stasi), in a book on the history of the German Communist Party's intelligence service, commented, "In this way the political opposition was given a pretext, not so very easily dismissed, to fence off Communists and to issue prohibitions against their employment. The directives concerning the use by intelligence of Communist postal workers and telephone employees provide such an example."[26] Postal employees could and did open mail, while the telephone employees could and did tap phones. As the German example shows, the Communist movement used its members to spy on both the government and civilian political opponents. The American Communists were unable to do this until the 1930s, but by the 1940s and 1950s these activities became a serious concern of the United States government. The possibility of espionage on behalf of the Soviet Union was the justification for barring Communists from government jobs.

To the American Communists, the German Communist Party was second only to the Soviet Communist Party in prestige and respect. By 1925 the American Communists tried to emulate the Germans and set up an intelligence-gathering apparatus. In April of 1925 a meeting took place in Moscow in which all of the Communist parties were instructed to improve their intelligence gathering. John Pepper (Pogany), the Comintern representative to the American Communist Party, chaired the meeting. "Building the Information Department of the Executive Committee of the Comintern" was the cover used to instruct the Communist parties to collect information on political opponents.

According to Pepper: "In this respect, America and Germany are setting an example, being an exception to the general rule. Both parties have already taken organization measures for the purpose of keeping their CCs [Central Committees] properly informed." In attendance at the meeting were such significant Communist functionaries as Heinz Neumann, a German Communist leader; Tom Bell, a British Communist leader; and Jay Lovestone, then a leader of the American Communist Party. Lovestone used "Powers" as a cover name when the report of the meeting was published.[27]

Despite Pepper's boast, carrying out the instructions was not easy for the American Communist Party. It had few members, most of them foreign-born members of "language branches," where they spoke only their native language, not English. Even the 2,282 members in the Party's English-speaking branches included a substantial number of foreign-born. Their use as spies in the government or even in most American organizations was limited. The total number of Party members, by the Party's own estimates in 1925, was 16,325.[28]

By the early 1930s the situation of the American Communist Party was even worse. The Comintern archives reveal that in 1931 the average number of dues payers in the American Party was 8,030. A year later, the Party had recruited 19,408 new members, but membership based on dues payments was only fourteen thousand. Somehow they had lost over thirteen thousand of the new members.[29]

In 1926, on Comintern orders, the American Communist Party established a system of "worker correspondents" for industrial espionage. The German Communists were already using this information-gathering method, which they called *Betriebs-berichterstatter*, or BB for short. Workers in factories would write what were ostensibly news reports about their workplace: what the factory produced, how many workers it employed, and so on. Sometimes the information was used for stories in the Party press. More important information was vetted by the underground apparatus of the Party, and relevant material was then turned over to the Soviets, particularly when it dealt with secret formulas or blueprints.[30]

The American Communist Party issued a publication in 1926 encouraging members in factories to write reports. The publication claimed that they already had 450 members submitting them. One of the earliest recruiters of "worker correspondents" was Bill Gebert, then the editor of the Communist Party's Polish-language newspaper.[31] *Venona* identifies him as one of the Soviet operatives recruiting agents during World War II. After the war, he returned to Communist Poland. The goal, according to the Communist Party, was that in "every shop, every local union" there should be a person to collect the information.[32]

The Soviet intelligence service was, eventually, able to use some of the American Communists. In 1927 Communist Party USA leader Jay Lovestone assigned Nicholas Dozenberg, a high-ranking Party official, to leave the open Communist Party and work for Soviet military intelligence.[33] Two years afterwards, when Lovestone was in trouble with Stalin and needed to leave Moscow, Dozenberg came to his aid.[34] A few years later, after Lovestone had set up his own rival Communist group, he repaid Dozenberg by providing a member of his group, Dr. William Burtan, to assist Dozenberg in passing Soviet counterfeit American money to pay for Soviet intelligence operations. Both Burtan and Dozenberg were arrested and served long jail terms.[35]

Moscow wanted Communists as leaders of unions in basic industry—a valuable asset for Soviet intelligence. But American Communists had little influence in the trade union movement. Most of it was in light industry; almost none was in the basic industries such as steel and mining. Beginning in 1920, they had a front organization called the Trade Union Education League for the purpose of penetrating and influencing the American Federation of Labor (AFL). The Communists called this "boring from within," but its success was limited.

In 1929 a significant and disastrous decision was made in Moscow. The Red International of Labor Unions (RILU), the Comintern's labor front, headquartered in Moscow, ordered the Communist parties to establish "Red" unions to rival the legitimate trade union movement in each country. For the United States, a July 1929 letter of the RILU instructed the Trade Union Education League to set up a dual union federation to rival the AFL.[36]

The new organization, formed in August 1929, was called the Trade Union Unity League (TUUL), although its job was to split rather than unite the trade union movement. TUUL described itself as a section of the RILU, which "is the only revolutionary world union of workers. It makes war on world imperialism and its social-fascist allies of the Amsterdam International." The Amsterdam International was the non-Communist international trade union federation.[37] But the TUUL further isolated Communists, and, as a result, Party members could no longer use trade union cover to penetrate America's major industries. This project was so unsuccessful that in 1934 the Comintern instructed the American Communists to take advantage of the significant trade unions outside the AFL and set up a supposed non-Communist rival labor federation in which the Communists would play a major leadership role.

The resolution, really an order, was prepared by the Russians at a meeting of the Buro (the Moscow-based leadership) of the Anglo-American Secretariat of the Comintern held on January 13, 1934. Two American Communists were present at the meeting, William Weinstone and Leon Platt, also known as Martin Young, but they were not allowed to write the instructions. That job was done by the Soviets I. Mingulin, the head of the Anglo-American Secretariat, Otto Kuusinen, one of the top Comintern officials, and Joel Shubin, who had worked as a Communist International representative to the American Communist Party. And the decisions of the Buro were communicated not to the American Communist Party leader, Earl Browder, but to the Comintern representative to the CPUSA, "Comrade Edwards," who was in reality the German Gerhart Eisler.[38]

The American Communists were able to obey the orders to create a rival labor federation two years later, when the Congress of Industrial Organizations (CIO) was established, with Communist help. This greatly facilitated intelligence collection. For example, during World War II, Communist control of the Federation of Architects, Engineers, Chemists, and Technicians, a CIO affiliate, facilitated atom bomb espionage.[39]

The opportunity to enter the CIO at all levels was so enticing to the Communists that they neglected other essential operations. Eugene Dennis (then a representative of the American Communist Party to the Comintern), using the name T. Ryan, reported to the Comintern on the CIO project:

> For instance, in the course of the growth of the CIO movement and recent strike struggles, the Party has not only given

maximum political support to the CIO campaigns, but it has actually released hundreds of its best section and unit organisers, as well as many district functionaries, to work as CIO organisers (it has correctly made a heavy capital investment of its cadres in the industrial unions), especially in the Chicago, Detroit, Cleveland and Pittsburgh districts. This policy has not only produced excellent results and helped to widen the base and strengthen the influence of the Party in the CIO and progressive movement, but it has also had its negative effects.

The taking of large numbers of the most capable and experienced Comrades out of direct and open Party work as leaders of Party organizations, created new cadre problems which could not be immediately solved on the scale demanded. This particularly affected and weakened the work and life of scores of key sections and lower Party organizations.[40]

Despite the expenditure of manpower and money, this unique opportunity for espionage ended in 1949–1950 when the CIO expelled eleven Communist-dominated unions. When the Comintern originally instructed the American Communists in 1934 to create a new labor federation, the Americans were told to be careful not to allow real non-Communists to take control of the organization. The failure to do so allowed the American workers in 1949 to take back the unions that had been run by the Communists.

Earl Browder: Moscow's Man in America

Earl Browder was the general secretary of the American Communist Party from 1932 to 1945. Although the absolute master in his own Party, he did nothing without instructions from Moscow. He, of course, would not admit this, and in a 1938 letter to a New York state legislative committee, Browder said:

The Making of an Apparat

> A familiar charge against the Communist Party is that it
> receives "orders from Moscow," or that it is financed by
> "Moscow gold," or that it is a Party of aliens. There is no truth
> in any of these charges. The Communist Party makes its own
> decisions, it has never received orders from Moscow or any-
> where else, and if it did receive any such orders it would throw
> them in the wastebasket; the Communist Party finances itself
> entirely from its own resources within the country; its mem-
> bership is composed 99 per cent of citizens of the United
> States, and all its members must declare their intention of
> becoming citizens if they are not already citizens.[41]

The reality was quite different. In May 1933 Browder went to
Moscow to receive instructions for the American Communist
Party's Eighth National Convention, which eventually took place
April 2–8, 1934. Originally planned by the Americans for 1933, the
Comintern decided "to accept Comrade Mingulin's proposal to
postpone date of Convention for 5–6 months [and] to appoint a
commission of Comrades Mingulin (responsible), Browder and
Gerhardt [Gerhart Eisler] for the working out of the directives for
the preparation of the Convention."[42]

A few weeks prior to Browder's Moscow meeting, the Buro of
the Anglo-American Secretariat had discussed another matter of
importance to the American Communists. In an attempt to break
out of their isolation, the American Communist Party proposed
sending an open letter to its members urging them to organize outside their own ranks. The publication of the "Open Letter" was a
turning point in the history of American Communism. But the
American Communist Party could not even send a letter to its own
members without Comintern permission. After reading the draft,

the Comintern decided "to accept the draft as a basis and that a committee, consisting of Comrades Gerhardt, Browder, Weinstone, Mingulin, and Mehring be elected to rework it, to shorten it, and to include amendments proposed, according to the line of the discussion."[43] The two Americans, Browder and William Weinstone, accepted the direction of Eisler, Mingulin, and an Estonian Communist Party official working at the Comintern, "Mehring" (Richard Mirring).[44] The "Open Letter" was published in the *Daily Worker* in New York on July 13, 1933, and then as a pamphlet.[45]

The Eighth Convention of the American Communist Party took place in Cleveland in April 1934, and an agenda for the convention was prepared at the Comintern and transmitted to the American Communists in February 1934. The letter was addressed: "To Comrade E [Eisler], Copy to Comrade Browder." One of the instructions in the letter was to continue to promote the concept of a "revolutionary worker and peasant—Soviet Republic" in the United States.[46]

The main convention resolution said: "All members of the Party must in their day-to-day work, in the fight for the demands of the workers, point out convincingly and insistently that only the destruction of the capitalist system, the establishment of the dictatorship of the proletariat, of the Soviet power, can free the millions of toilers from the bondage and misery of the capitalist system."[47]

Even this resolution was vetted by the Comintern. On March 8, 1934, the Comintern Secretariat met to rewrite the draft resolution that was to be adopted unanimously at the American Communist Party Convention. It was decided that Mingulin would write a letter to "Comrade Edwards" (Eisler) to provide the instructions for the changes and additions to the resolution.[48]

In obedience to Moscow's orders, a whole series of pamphlets was issued imagining life in a Soviet America. The documents included: *In a Soviet America: Happy Days for American Youth* by Max Weiss; *Social Security in a Soviet America* by Israel Amter; *In Soviet America: The Miners' Road to Freedom* by Anna Rochester and Pat Toohey; *The Negroes in a Soviet America* by James W. Ford and James S. Allen; *In Soviet America: Seamen and Longshoremen under the Red Flag* by Hays Jones; and *Professionals in a Soviet America* by Edward Magnus.[49]

The slogan "Soviet America" had been used earlier by the Communists. When William Z. Foster ran for president of the United States on the Communist ticket in 1932, he published a book titled *Toward Soviet America* to promote the campaign.[50] During the 1928 presidential campaign, Foster, the Communist Party candidate, said:

> No Communist, no matter how many votes he should secure in a national election, could, even if he would, become president of the present government. When a Communist heads a government in the United States—and that day will come just as surely as the sun rises—that government will not be a capitalistic government but a Soviet government, and behind this government will stand the Red Army to enforce the Dictatorship of the Proletariat.[51]

This slogan did not attract many Americans. But during the sectarian period of American Communism, in the late 1920s and early 1930s, it scarcely mattered. Hardly anyone read Communist literature. After the line changed at the 1935 Comintern Congress, the American Communists finally abandoned this offensive slogan.

In the summer of 1935, when the American Communist Party sent twenty-one delegates and two alternates to the Seventh World Congress of the Communist International in Moscow, Gerhart

Eisler attended as one of the American Communist Party delegates under the name John Gerhardt.[52] In a biographical sketch Eisler prepared decades later for the Socialist Unity Party, the Communist ruling party of East Germany, he wrote: "1933/35 I worked as representative of the Comintern in the USA. In 1935 I went to the World Congress in Moscow, with the understanding of the Central Committee of the KPD [Communist Party of Germany] as a member of the American delegation. After the Congress I went back to the USA for a short time."[53]

"Earl and Edward" (Browder and Eisler) wrote a letter on January 21, 1936, to Comintern officials Dimitroff, Manuilsky, and Marty, as well as "Randolph," the name then used by Sam Darcy, the American Communist Party's representative to the Comintern. They asked, "Do you think any changes or additions are necessary to the line of our CC [Central Committee] Plenum before it goes before the Convention? If so, immediately cable us with as much detail as possible."[54]

At this convention, held June 24–28, 1936, the "Soviet America" slogan was abandoned. The Communist Party argued that "the issue now is not capitalism or socialism. It is progress or reaction, fascism or democracy."[55]

As the American Communist Party planned its Tenth National Convention, Browder wrote a letter on January 19, 1938, to Dimitroff asking for permission and for "proposals of the ECCI [Executive Committee Communist International] on the formulation of the agenda."[56]

These examples of the American Communist Party's obsequious obedience to Moscow are only a sample. The Comintern micromanaged its American section just as Stalin ran the Comintern: with an iron fist. When the Comintern was planning its 1935 congress, memos were sent to Stalin by Osip Pyatnitsky and Dimitri Manuilsky, the leaders of the Comintern. They had prepared a draft agenda and asked Stalin if he would "please give us your instructions before the first of June," as they had to issue the agenda to the public on that day. They suggested that George Dimitroff, who was well known, having confronted the Nazis at the Reichstag Fire Trial, make the main report because his renown would enhance the influence of the Comintern.[57] Stalin gave his permission.

For American Communists, even the problem of those members who weren't U.S. citizens was decided by the Comintern rather than the American Communist Party. On March 10, 1936, Mingulin wrote to the American Communist Party instructing that "a campaign must be conducted in the shortest possible period among the members of the CP so that they will do everything in their power to become citizens of the USA."[58]

At the American Communist Party's Tenth Convention in May 1938, the instructions were passed along by Browder's Soviet-citizen wife, Raisa, who used the name Irene in the United States. She said, "Following the needs and experience of our own Party, on the basis of Lenin's teachings, the new draft Constitution, which is presented to this Convention, is establishing a rule for membership in our Party, that every one who is in the Party, or is to become a Party member, must become a citizen or have intentions or [be] oriented in the direction of becoming one in the near future."[59]

An order to the Communist Party rank-and-file did not necessarily apply to its leaders. Rank-and-file members with immigration problems had to drop their membership. But Mrs. Earl Browder, who could not become an American citizen because she was an illegal alien, remained a leader of the Party, albeit in secret work. In 1944, however, the government moved to deport her, and the *Daily Worker* reported on March 21: "Free Mrs. Earl Browder of deportation charges, more educators, religious, labor and civic leaders said this week when they urged President Roosevelt to prevent the breakup of an American family. Mrs. Browder, wife of an American citizen and mother of three minor children, also citizens, is under an order of deportation because of a technical defect in her entry to this country in 1933."

Raisa already had two children with Browder when the Comintern sent her for special instruction at its training facility, the International Lenin School, to prepare her for work in the United States, where she would be the official wife of Earl Browder. According to Comintern records, in 1918 she served in the city of Kharkov as a provisional commissar of justice "with extraordinary powers," a colloquialism for the power to order executions.[60]

When Browder testified before Congress on September 5, 1939, he lied about his wife's activities on behalf of the Soviet government. He had this exchange with the committee counsel:

> Mr. Whitley: Has she [Browder's wife] ever held any official position with the Communist Party of the Soviet Government?
>
> Mr. Browder: No.
>
> Mr. Whitley: She has not?
>
> Mr. Browder: No.
>
> Mr. Whitley: Was she one of the judges of the "red" tribunal in Moscow in 1921 or 1922, or approximately that period?
>
> Mr. Browder: To the best of my knowledge and belief, no.[61]

Mrs. Browder was nevertheless ordered deported by the Immigration Service on October 31, 1940, because of her illegal entry into the United States. But in August 1943 her attorney, Carol King, wrote a letter to the U.S. consulate in Montreal, Canada, asking whether Mrs. Browder could come to Montreal and receive an immigration visa. Shortly before receiving the letter, an official at the State Department had written to the consulate that there was no objection to the issuance of an immigration visa to Raisa Browder, whom the department identified as the wife of Earl Browder. An officer in the visa section in Montreal, Julian Pinkerton, found this unusual since most such letters did not identify the husband of the potential applicant. Since she was clearly a Communist and therefore ineligible for immigration under the laws at that time, Pinkerton, after consulting with his supervisor, sent a letter advising that Mrs. Browder could come to Montreal to make the application but that if she were found to be ineligible under the law, she would not receive one. Pinkerton later explained to a congressional committee, "In common parlance that is called the brush-off. As nearly as we are permitted to state in a letter, that is equivalent to saying: 'Don't come. You won't get the visa.'"

A few days later, Pinkerton's supervisor came to him "in a somewhat flurried state of nerves" and said that he had just heard from the chief of the Visa Division of the Department of State. The Washington official "had said that the letter of the consul general in Montreal had caused concern among the friends and advisors and counsel of Mrs. Browder and that we should have known better than to send her a letter which was practically a refusal of the visa; that the visa must be issued to Mrs. Browder… a refusal of the visa at this time would be very embarrassing."

Nevertheless, when Mrs. Browder arrived, Pinkerton asked her how she had entered the United States. She answered that she had come through Canada illegally and crossed the border in an automobile. Pinkerton testified that he believed that issuing the visa to Mrs. Browder was an "unlawful procedure" and that the consulate would not have issued it without specific orders to do so.[62] Although the visa was finally issued, Mrs. Browder remained under an order of deportation and subsequent unsuccessful attempts were made to deport her.

Browder also lied to Congress about the activities of his sister, Margaret. She was an agent of the Foreign Department of the NKVD working underground in Nazi Germany. On January 19, 1938, Browder wrote a letter to Comintern General Secretary Dimitroff about his sister:

> Another personal question I must raise, because of its possible future political importance. For about 7 years my younger sister, Marguerite Browder, has been working for the Foreign Department of the NKVD, in various European countries. I am informed that her work has been valuable and satisfactory, and she has expressed no desire to be released. But it seems to me, in view of my increasing involvement in national political affairs and growing connections in Washington political circles, it might become dangerous to this political work if hostile circles in America should by any means obtain knowledge of my sister's work in Europe and make use of this knowledge in America. The political implications of such possible danger will be clear to you, being directly connected with the relations between USSR and USA, as well as to the work of our party in America. I raise this question, so that if you agree to the existence of this danger, and consider it of sufficient importance, steps can be taken by you to secure my sister's release from her present work and her return to America where she can be used in other fields of activity.[63]

Dimitroff sent Browder's letter to Yezhov, the head of the Soviet secret police and the organizer of the 1938 Purge Trial (and shortly to be replaced by Beria). Margaret was soon back home.

On September 6, 1939, in his testimony before the Dies Committee, which was investigating organizations controlled by foreign powers, Browder partook in the following exchange:

The Making of an Apparat

Mr. Whitley: Is your sister, Margaret Browder, employed in any capacity by the Soviet Government or the Communist Party?

Mr. Browder: I think not. I see her only occasionally, and I cannot say.

Mr. Whitley: Where is she residing now?

Mr. Browder: I do not know; I cannot take the personal responsibility of explaining her presence or her activities; but, to the best of my knowledge and belief, she is not and has not been—

Mr. Whitley: She has no official connection, to the best of your knowledge, and has never had any official connection?

Mr. Browder: To the best of my knowledge, she is not now and has not in the past been officially connected with any government institution.

Mr. Whitley: Or with the Communist Party?

Mr. Browder: I did not say with the Communist Party. She has been a member of the Communist Party.

Mr. Whitley: Over what period?

Mr. Browder: I do not know the exact date of her joining, but I would say it was in the early twenties.

Mr. Whitley: Was she an active Party member?

Mr. Browder: She was an active Party member.

Mr. Whitley: Is she in the United States at the present time, or do you know?

Mr. Browder: I do not know.

Mr. Whitley: Mr. Browder, do you know whether she has ever been used to travel on an illegal passport?

Mr. Browder: I do not know.

Mr. Whitley: Do you know whether she has ever been known under the name of Jean Montgomery?

Mr. Browder: I have not heard that name except as reported in the newspapers.

Mr. Whitley: Mr. Browder, does your former wife, Catherine Harris, occupy any official position with the Communist Party in the country or elsewhere?

Mr. Browder: I do not have a former wife by that name.[64]

Between Browder's letter to Dimitroff and his testimony before Congress, both his sister and his common-law wife, Kitty Harris, had been publicly identified as Soviet agents by General Walter Krivitsky, formerly a high-ranking official of Soviet military intelligence. Krivitsky, whose real name was Shmuel Ginsberg, had defected to the West in 1937 when many of his colleagues were arrested or murdered on the orders of Stalin. One in particular, Ignace Reiss, was Krivitsky's close personal friend.

Before his defection, Krivitsky's apparatus had been taken from Soviet military intelligence by the OGPU, later called NKVD and KGB. Mikhail Spiegelglass, the deputy head of the Foreign Department of the OGPU, had met with Krivitsky and had ordered him to turn over some of the more valuable agents, including two Americans. Krivitsky related in a 1939 article in the *Saturday Evening Post*:

> Spiegelglass had learned from me that a sister of Earl Browder, Margaret, was one of my operatives, and asked me to assign her to him as he had an "important job" to do in France, for which he needed the most reliable people. Subsequently, it appeared that Spiegelglass "pulled" two "important" jobs while in Paris—the kidnapping of General Miller... and the assassination of Ignace Reiss.
>
> Now that I was instructed to turn my organization over to Spiegelglass, he asked to meet my leading agents personally, and made a special point of having me present Miss Browder to him, operating on an American passport issued in the name of Jean Montgomery.

The Making of an Apparat

> Miss Browder, a woman in the late thirties, small in stature, of the school-teacher type, had been in the service of the Soviet military intelligence for quite a while. During 1936–37, she was functioning in Central Europe for us, where she had been laying the ground for the establishment of a secret radio station. Miss Browder had graduated from our special courses in Moscow as a radio operator. She lived abroad in the disguise of a student.[65]

General Krivitsky also worked with Browder's former "wife," Kitty Harris. In his articles in the *Saturday Evening Post*, he described an incident in 1937 when he was back in Moscow for consultations:

> I applied for half a dozen additional and highly trained agents, whom I needed to augment my staff abroad. A number of graduates of our secret schools for the training of men and women in military-intelligence work were sent to me to be interviewed.
>
> One of the operatives recommended to me by our director of personnel was an American woman by the name of Kitty Harris, originally Katherine Harrison. She had been described to me as the former wife of Earl Browder, Communist leader in the United States, and, therefore, as exceptionally reliable. At that time I needed a woman agent to be stationed in Switzerland, and the holder of an American passport was particularly welcome.
>
> When Kitty Harris called upon me, presenting her papers in a sealed envelope, it appeared that she was also stopping at the Hotel Savoy. She was about forty, dark-haired, of good appearance, and had been connected with our secret service for some years. Kitty Harris spoke well of Browder, and particularly of Browder's sister, who was then in our services in Central Europe.

> I approved the assignment of Miss Harris to a foreign
> post, and she left on April twenty-ninth. Others whom I had
> selected were similarly dispatched to report to my collabora-
> tors in Western Europe.[66]

The *Venona* documents show that during World War II Earl
Browder worked closely with the NKVD and supplied the Soviets
with members of the American Communist Party for espionage
work. Kitty Harris had been his "wife" in the 1920s and early
1930s[67] while Raisa remained in Russia raising his sons. Kitty
appeared again when the *Venona* documents were decrypted. She
worked for the NKVD in Mexico during World War II.

William Nowell, a former Communist Party member, attended
the International Lenin School in Moscow in 1931 and 1932. He
spoke to the FBI, who reported on July 20, 1951, that "in the latter
part of 1932... four women visited the school, one of whom was
Kitty Harris, described as the American wife of Earl Browder,
another of whom was Grace Maul, whom he [Nowell] also knew as
Grace Granich, formerly secretary to Earl Browder, a third who, to
the best of his recollection, was Jean Montgomery [Margaret
Browder], and an unidentified fourth women."

Joseph Zack Kornfeder, who attended the International Lenin
School from 1927 to 1930 and later served as a Comintern representative, advised the FBI on June 14, 1951, that Margaret Browder
"had attended the GPU [NKVD/KGB] training school at Moscow,
taking courses in radio communication and the use of code."[68]
Kornfeder was reinterviewed by the FBI on October 31, 1952.
According to the report:

> Kornfeder, a member of the Communist Party, USA, from
> 1919 to 1934 and a student in the Lenin School, Moscow,

Russia, from 1927 to 1930, was reinterviewed on October 31, 1952, regarding his knowledge of Subject's attendance at a GPU Training School in Moscow, Russia.

Kornfeder explained that to the best of his recollection Margaret Browder had been in Moscow, Russia, for an indefinite period prior to the time in 1928 that she told him she was attending a "Training School." He advised that while he had not attended any GPU Training School in Moscow with the Subject he knew that she was not attending the Lenin School or any other training school which was not conducted secretly.

Kornfeder also recalled one Kwiet, a radio operator, who had told him that the Subject was attending a GPU School to learn all communication methods used by their secret services. According to Kornfeder, Kwiet also told him that Margaret Browder had discussed the school and its methods with Kwiet.

Kornfeder reiterated that he was unable to furnish the dates of Subject's attendance at this school except that she advised him some time in the year 1928 that she was attending a "Training School." He added that it was his recollection that Margaret Browder had been in Moscow for some time prior to the date on which he met her in 1928. He also said it was his opinion, based on conversation with the radio operator, Kwiet, that this GPU school on communication methods offered courses which lasted for approximately one year.[69]

Clandestine Comintern Work

Harry Kweit, whose name was misspelled in the FBI report, was a longtime Communist Party member and a radio operator on merchant ships. Active in clandestine radio communications for Comintern intelligence, he was killed in World War II when his ship was sunk.

The Comintern ran two communications schools. One was for beginners, the other for more experienced radio operators. Harry

Kweit taught at the senior school. Some of the trainees would perform the same radio work for the NKVD during World War II.[70]

The radios were part of the communications system of OMS, the Comintern's secret International Liaison Department, after 1936 called the Liaison Service. OMS was headed by Jakub Mirov-Abramov. The radio operators were under the control of a man called David Glazer. German was the language of the Comintern, as most educated Europeans spoke it. Both Abramov and Glazer had studied in Germany.

The Comintern sent instructors from Moscow to set up, service, and repair the transmitters. The radios were secret, and ingenious technology was developed to boost the signal even when the antenna had to be strung around the walls of the room to conceal it. In the suburbs of Vienna, the Austrian Communists had a large house where an outdoor antenna could be hidden in the eaves. This provided a stronger signal than the indoor antenna. In 1934 the British Communist Party radio was in a house in the London suburbs. When problems with the signal arose, an instructor was sent from Moscow. To be able to change wavelengths and still avoid government monitoring, he devised a unique method of changing crystals between broadcasts.[71]

Nevertheless, from 1934 to 1937, the British government was able to monitor the Comintern international radio networks, including broadcasts from London. The code name used by British intelligence for these interceptions and decryptions was "MASK." The British were able to break the Comintern codes because the Party member who was used as liaison between Communist Party head Harry Pollitt and the secret radio operator was an agent of British counterintelligence, MI5. Unlike the FBI, MI5 during the early 1930s was extensively investigating the Communist Party.

Olga Gray, only twenty-three years old, had been recruited in 1928 by Maxwell Knight, an official of MI5, to penetrate the

The Making of an Apparat

Communist Party. Her intelligence and pleasing personality allowed her to rise rapidly in Party ranks, and soon she was an assistant to Pollitt. She quickly learned the basis of the code used by the Comintern radio operator and reported it to MI5. Pollitt also used her for liaison with Soviet intelligence. In 1937 her counterintelligence career came to an end as a result of a major spy trial, the Woolwich Arsenal Case. The Communist Party had instructed her to set up a "safe house" for a Soviet spy ring. When the police swept up the spies, Olga appeared as a witness for the prosecution, albeit identified only as Miss X. Since the Communist Party now knew her real identity, she dropped out of activity and eventually moved to Canada.[72] (One of the people she met at the radio site was the Comintern specialist who helped improve the radio transmission. She did not know his name, but he remembered her more than sixty years later.)

In 1936 a reserve Communist radio station was established in London. On April 15, 1936, Moscow radioed to London that the new station would receive a message every day but should not respond unless specifically requested to do so.[73]

On May 20 British Communist Party leader Harry Pollitt, using the name "West," radioed Abramov: "Necessary we close down station used up to present owing to Post Office enquiries in neighborhood regarding interference. Have we your permission operate reserve meantime? Please reply immediately." Five days later, Moscow radioed permission to use the reserve station temporarily.[74]

Moscow kept pressing the Communist parties to provide radio operator trainees and clearly specified the qualifications they needed. In a message to the Swedish Communist Party, Moscow asked for five or six candidates, half of whom should be girls. It said the students "must be 100% reliable. Desirable that they should have 2 or 3 years membership of Party or Youth, and be already proved capable of work. Interest in and love of RUBIN [radio] affairs essential.... Girls preferably stenographers or music [communications] students. Perfect health essential. Most important that their eyes, ears and hands should be in perfect order, and they should not be suffering from any contagious disease."[75]

Many Comintern messages urged that girls be sent not only to the radio schools but also to the International Lenin School, the Comintern's political and military training institute. In 1934 Pollitt radioed Abramov: "Why give me a dog's life about girl students? Sending you two by steamer leaving this week. Do you want all the women we have? Begin suspect you personally keep harem."[76] In almost 14,000 MASK messages from all over the world, only Harry Pollitt seems to have had sufficient rapport with the usually stiff-necked Abramov to joke with him.

Elizabeth Bentley, former Soviet agent, cooperated with the FBI after 1945 and reported, among other things, about Margaret Browder's activities. She told the FBI that she met Margaret Browder in the home of Earl Browder in Monroe, New York, during the summers of 1942 and 1944. Jacob Golos, her boss in the spy ring and her lover, revealed to her that Margaret Browder had been in Europe for several years as a Soviet intelligence agent but that she had ceased all such activities before 1941. Miss Browder was given several thousand dollars by her intelligence superior to establish herself in a small business.

William Browder, Earl and Margaret's brother, told Bentley that his sister's nerves were still "cracked" as a result of her experience as a Soviet agent and that it was necessary for her to withdraw from espionage activities. Margaret had worked for Zarubin in Nazi Germany as a radio operator. William Browder told Bentley the Soviets had a five-year limitation on women operators in such dangerous jobs.[77]

The Making of an Apparat

When interviewed by the FBI in 1958, Margaret Browder admitted working in underground activities in Germany from 1931 to 1938. She claimed it was to help German Communist Party members escape the country. But Hitler didn't come to power until 1933, and until then German Communists could enter and leave the country as they saw fit. The FBI report also reveals that Margaret Browder admitted that she had been in the Soviet Union for a year, returning to the United States in 1929 or 1930. She told the FBI that in 1931 or thereabouts the Communist Party gave her a passport under the name of Jean Montgomery. Margaret claimed that she could recall none of her activities or associates while in Germany. She admitted that she made three trips back to the United States while she resided in Germany. She stayed in the United States each time from one to six months to receive medical treatment. Margaret denied acting as a courier for the Communist Party or being involved in Soviet espionage during her trips from Germany to the United States.

The most significant thing she told the FBI was that on one of her visits to the United States she met two individuals whom she knew as "Poppy" and "Mommy" at the residence of her brother and sister-in-law, William and Rose Browder. "Poppy" was "a very gay person." She knew him as a talent scout for a movie studio. "Mommy" was "very quiet and reserved." Margaret remembered that the two had a small child.

When the FBI showed Margaret photographs of Vassiliy Zubilin (Zarubin) and his wife, Elizabeth, she said they were the people she knew as "Poppy" and "Mommy."

Margaret told the FBI that after her return to Germany she again met Vassiliy Zubilin and his wife, Elizabeth, but denied knowing what their activities were at that time. She said she thought he was in Germany searching for talent for an unknown movie studio.

She also revealed that she knew Zubilin by the name of "Herbert" in Germany.[78]

Vassiliy Zubilin, as we have seen, used the cover of being a Soviet diplomat in the United States from December 1941 until August 1944.[79] During that time, we know from the *Venona* documents he was the NKVD *Rezident*. His wife, Elizabeth—real name Lisa—was shown in *Venona* to be a very active NKVD officer.

On April 23, 1958, Margaret Browder again spoke to the FBI. At that time she refused to identify the photographs of the Zubilins. She began to pace the floor nervously and finally said, "I must protect myself against self-incrimination. I refuse to answer any further questions."[80]

During her April 7 interview, Browder was shown a picture of Lucy Jane Booker. She denied knowing her or having seen her either in the United States or in Germany.[81] Booker, a seasoned Communist, had worked for the NKVD during World War II as part of the Soble/Soblen espionage ring. In 1957 she spoke frankly to the FBI. In an interview on December 15, 1957, she told the FBI that she had met Margaret Browder, whom she knew as Jean Montgomery, in Berlin in 1937. She had been introduced to her by Vassiliy and Elizabeth Zubilin (Zarubin). Booker recalled a conversation she had with Margaret in Berlin, in which Booker stated that she did not have enough money to buy vitamin pills. Browder responded, "Why don't you ask for an expense account and buy some?"[82]

The FBI also talked with Louis Gibarti, a former Comintern operative who worked in the American Communist Party in the early and mid-1930s. According to the FBI, Gibarti was of unknown reliability, having provided both reliable and unreliable information in the past. Gibarti told the FBI that he had known Margaret Browder as a member of the "Women's Secretariat" of the Communist Party USA.[83]

The Making of an Apparat

At various times, the FBI had hopes that Margaret Browder could be induced to cooperate. They were particularly interested in asking her about Gaik Ovakimian, Zarubin's predecessor as NKVD *Rezident* in the United States. Browder had been seen meeting with Ovakimian.[84] But this hope evaporated when the New York FBI reported that she had died March 7, 1961.[85]

It wasn't hard for the American Communist Party's conspiratorial apparatus to get involved in Soviet espionage. It had been collecting sporadic information for the Comintern and Soviet military intelligence since the 1920s. In the early 1930s, that work was expanded. By the end of the decade, a significant apparatus existed, having been taken over by the NKVD for wartime espionage against the United States.

Espionage tradecraft was taught to dozens of American Communists at the International Lenin School in Moscow. Many more were trained in the United States. One manual for such training was obtained in 1931 in a police raid on a secret Communist headquarters in Toronto, Canada, and photostats were provided to the U.S. government. The same document was used in the United States as a training manual for American Communists.[86] Written by B. Vassiliev, the deputy head of the Organization Department of the Comintern, it explained the use of codes, ciphers, and invisible ink.[87]

The 1930s provided the American Communists with new opportunities for recruitment. The rise of the Nazis in Germany and the Great Depression in the United States caused people to turn to alternative political movements. The slogans of the fellow-traveling United Front and Popular Front allowed the Communists to create new organizations that attracted a significant number of people, including intellectuals. The Party membership grew, thus providing a larger pool of recruitment material for the espionage apparatus.

Even the American Congress was vulnerable to Communist penetration. In 1939 Dimitri Manuilsky, a top-ranking Comintern official, asked Pat Toohey, then the American Communist Party representative to the Comintern, for the names of the members of Congress who were secret Communists. Toohey responded:

> I am unable to provide you with additional and specific informa-
> tion on the question of Communist members of Congress, State
> and City legislatures. I personally do not know how many there
> are or where they are all at. This information only Comrade
> Browder, and possibly Comrades Stachel, Foster and Dennis of
> the Polburo, knows. It has never been reported to the Central
> Committee and is not discussed in Party circles....
>
> It was assumed that in the last Congress there were several
> Communists, and at present one, who may not be, for certain
> reasons, technically a card-carrying member of the Party, but is
> conscientious in following the line of the Party.[88]

Years later, John Abt, a Communist Party attorney who had been active in the espionage apparatus, revealed the names of Communist members of Congress. In his autobiography, Abt said, "The two Communists who were elected to Congress—Johnny Bernard from Minnesota and Hugh DeLacy from Washington State—were elected as Democrats. [Vito] Marcantonio, who was a friend of the Party but never a member, was elected as a Republican, a Democrat, and as the ALP [American Labor Party] candidate."[89]

Abt's sister, Marion Bachrach, had worked as the administrative assistant to Congressman Bernard. In 1942 Pavel Fitin, head of the Foreign Department of the NKVD, wrote to Dimitroff asking for a background check on potential agent Marion Bachrach.

Dimitroff asked two American Communists working in the Comintern apparatus, Nat Ross and Manya Reiss, also called Maria

The Making of an Apparat

Aerova, about their knowledge of Bachrach. The report to NKVD said that "[u]ntil 1938 Bachrach, Marion, worked as a personal secretary for Bernard, a progressive member of Congress. In 1938 Bernard was not re-elected, she was released from the job and worked as a reporter for the newspaper *PM*." She was fired from that job when she expressed her support for the Soviet Union in the Soviet-Finnish War.[90]

Even more important than the secret Communist Party members in Congress or on congressional staffs were those assigned by the Party as Soviet spies in the U.S. government's executive branch. As we shall see, in the years leading up to World War II, the Party reached into the highest ranks of federal government power and into the closely guarded laboratories of America's most vital scientific and manufacturing establishments. Instead of being a passive band of well-intentioned idealists—as Party propaganda portrayed the CPUSA—America's Communist movement had become the disciplined instrument of Moscow's global spy and covert action services. Its golden days were just ahead.

CHAPTER 4

Whittaker Chambers's Spy Ring

BEFORE THE RELEASE OF *VENONA*, much of what the American public understood about Soviet espionage in the United States, before and during World War II, came from two valuable sources, Whittaker Chambers and Elizabeth Bentley. When they broke with the Soviet intelligence service, it took time and considerable agonizing consideration before they publicly told their stories to the House Committee on Un-American Activities—only to be called liars by the Left and vilified in numerous books and articles. *Venona* proves that they told the truth.

Chambers became one of the flashpoints of the Cold War debate for his dramatic public denunciation of Alger Hiss, an important State Department official who in 1945 served as the secretary general at the founding conference of the United Nations. But Chambers was important for more than the Hiss case. His revelations, based on service as a courier for the Soviet spy apparatus during the 1930s, would be one of the most important testimonies about Soviet spycraft in America, as *Venona* decryptions show. Chambers's experience also illustrates just how tightly interlocked the American Communist Party was with the Soviet spy service.

Chambers was a twenty-four-year-old student at New York's Columbia University when he joined the Communist Party in February 1925. As we learned earlier, two years before Chambers joined, it existed as an underground organization with an aboveground front called the Workers Party. In 1923, on orders of the Communist International, the American Communists came up from the underground, merged the two organizations, and continued to call themselves the Workers Party. But a small underground apparatus continued to exist. Moscow's orders were to concentrate all main efforts on aboveground work while "[t]he illegal party shall continue to exist only as an auxiliary organization."[1]

When the plans were being made to bring the Party up from the underground, the Central Committee explained to the Party members:

> The underground machinery of the Communist Party is not merely a temporary device to be liquidated as soon as the Communist Party with its full program can be announced in the open. The underground machinery is for permanent use. It is not a machinery to be used only on emergency occasions. It is for constant use…. The Communist Party will never cease to maintain its underground machinery until after the establishment of the dictatorship of the proletariat in the form of the Workers Soviet Republic.[2]

Until Chambers joined the Workers Party, soon to be called the Workers (Communist) Party, he knew nothing about the underground machinery. It was this secret apparatus that he would join in 1932 and that assigned him to work in Soviet espionage.

Chambers was an unusual Communist—he was American-born in a Party overwhelmingly foreign-born. Only one out of seven Party members spoke English well enough to be in an English-speaking branch. The other six out of seven were members of branches that spoke their native language—three-quarters of them came from the former Tsarist Empire.[3] He was even more unusual since he was an intellectual. Most of the Party members were small shopkeepers, workers, and nonworkers, the latter consisting of the crackpots, flotsam, and jetsam that always gravitate toward extremist movements. Since the Party's founding in 1919, much of the work of its members consisted in perpetual and intensive faction fights.[4]

Intellectuals were disliked in this movement. As Chambers recounted in his autobiography, *Witness*, "The word 'intellectual' was the most lethal in the invective vocabulary of Communism." Any illiterate, he said, could win an argument by accusing his opponent of being an intellectual.[5] But, by the early 1920s, even the foreign-born faction leaders spoke English. The number of English-speaking Party members would increase in the 1930s, when the use of anti-Nazism as a Communist slogan attracted a more educated class of recruits.

The dominant Party faction was led by the dour, aloof, forty-three-year-old Charles Ruthenberg, of German Lutheran background. He was assisted by two bright young Jews in their early thirties, Jay Lovestone and Ben Gitlow.[6] Lovestone and Gitlow were called "Comrade Jay" and "Comrade Ben," but Ruthenberg, always stiff and formal, was called "Comrade Ruthenberg."[7]

The rival faction was headed by the dull, pedantic William Z. Foster, aided by Alexander Bittleman, who was brighter than Foster but lacked his major asset, an American accent. Foster was also helped by his chief stooge, Earl Browder, who in the 1930s and early 1940s would emerge as an articulate and charismatic exponent of Soviet slogans. An allied faction was headed by the even more dull-witted James Cannon. He later led a tiny group, which supported Leon Trotsky against Joseph Stalin, out of the Communist Party.

Gitlow was the hero of the Party. Bright and articulate, he bravely served a jail sentence for publicly advocating the overthrow of the government after losing a landmark Supreme Court case,

Gitlow v. *New York*. The Communist Labor Party published Gitlow's address to the jury in a pamphlet under the title *The "Red Ruby."* The title was taken from "Prosecutor Rorke's Compliment to Gitlow" when he said of Gitlow, "He would make America a Red Ruby in the Red Treasure Chest of the Red Terror."[8] Gitlow later broke with Communism and become an important government witness against the Party and its leaders.

When not fighting one another, the principal preoccupation of the American Communists at that time was how to aid the Soviet Union. That work was carried out by a front organization called Friends of Soviet Russia, affiliated with the Comintern's international front, the Workers International Relief, headed by the German Willi Muenzenberg, the preeminent Communist propaganda expert of his time.

While the Communists worked hard to help feed the starving Russians, they dreamed of bringing the American people to the glories of living in a Communist society. In 1926, a year after Chambers joined the Party, the members were proudly wearing a pin which depicted a red hammer and sickle and read, "USSR 9th Anniversary, Forward to the Soviet Republic of the USA,"[9] whereas a few years earlier they had hidden their views in the underground. Luckily for them, most Americans didn't even know that they existed.

As Earl Browder, who headed the Party during its heyday in the 1930s, would later boast:

> Entering the 1930s as a small ultra-left sect of some 7,000 members, remnant of the fratricidal factional struggle of the 1920s that had wiped out the old "left wing" of American socialism, the CP rose to become a national political influence far beyond its numbers (at its height it never exceeded 100,000 members), on a scale never before reached by a socialist

movement claiming the Marxist tradition. It became a practical power in organized labour, its influence became strong in some state organizations of the Democratic Party (even dominant in a few for some years), and even some Republicans solicited its support. It guided the anti-Hitler movement of the American League for Peace and Democracy that united a cross-section of some five million organized Americans (a list of its sponsors and speakers would include almost a majority of Roosevelt's Cabinet, the most prominent intellectuals, judges of all grades up to State Supreme Courts, church leaders, labour leaders, etc.). Right-wing intellectuals complained that it exercised an effective veto in almost all publishing houses against their books, and it is at least certain that those right-wingers had extreme difficulty getting published.[10]

While Browder's boast contained a lot of truth, he could hardly take full credit. The Communist Party USA only broke out of its isolation in 1935, when the Comintern, taking advantage of the widespread legitimate fear of German Nazism, ordered the international Communist movement to adopt an ecumenical attitude and stretch its hands out to those it previously hated, including socialists and Catholics.

When Chambers joined the Communist Party, he found himself part of this odd, foreign-oriented group that saw most of its efforts consumed by intra-Party struggles. When Ruthenberg died in 1927, Lovestone became the leader of the majority faction, which included most of the Party's few English-speaking intellectuals. Chambers gravitated toward them and became a member of the Lovestone faction.

Lovestone and his adherents led the Communist Party only with the permission of Stalin. Foster and his minority faction could appeal to Moscow only when Lovestone acted against their interests.

It hurt the Fosterites in Moscow's eyes when their factional ally, James Cannon, announced his adherence to Trotsky in 1928 and was expelled from the Party.

When Stalin summoned the leaders of both factions to Moscow in May 1929, he did not let Foster forget his former ally Cannon. At a meeting of the Presidium of the Executive Committee of the Comintern, Stalin shouted at Foster:

> Did not Comrade Foster know that he should have held aloof from the concealed Trotskyites that were in his group? Why, in spite of repeated warnings, did he not repudiate them at the time? Because he behaved first and foremost as a factionalist. Because in the factional fight against the Lovestone group even concealed Trotskyites might be useful to him. Because the blindness of factionalism dulls the Party sense in people and makes them indiscriminating as to the means they employ. It is true, such a policy is bad and irreconcilable with the interests of the Party. But factionalists as a rule are inclined to forget the interests of the Party—all they can think of is their own factional point of view.[11]

Nor was the Lovestone majority spared the lash of Stalin's tongue. Lovestone was accused of trying to play games with the Comintern or, as Stalin phrased it, treating the Comintern like a "stock market" to be manipulated. As Stalin put it, "The Comintern is not a stock market. The Comintern is the holy of holies of the working class. The Comintern, therefore, must not be confused with the stock market."

Stalin was the supreme commander not only of the Soviet government but also of the Comintern. He objected particularly to a phrase by Lovestone that there was a "running sore" in the apparatus of the Comintern.[12] This he took as a personal insult, and he decided to turn the American Party over to the Fosterites. When

Gitlow said that conscience would not allow him to obey Stalin's orders to surrender to the Foster faction, Stalin roared:

> Members of the American delegation, do you think that the conscience and convictions of Comrade Gitlow are above the conscience and convictions of the overwhelming majority of the Presidium of the E.C.C.I. [Executive Committee, Communist International]? Do you begin to understand that if each of us starts to act according to his own will without reckoning with the will of the collective, we shall never come to any decision; we shall never have any collective will, nor any leadership?[13]

Stalin decided that if the American Communists could not stop the factionalism, he would. He ordered Lovestone and Alexander Bittleman, the brightest of Foster's followers, to give up their posts in the American Party and be placed at the disposal of the Comintern for assignment abroad. Stalin insisted that the Lovestone group could retain its majority only if it obeyed his orders. He said, "At present you still have a formal majority. But tomorrow you will have no majority and you will find yourselves completely isolated if you attempt to start a fight against the decisions of the Presidium of the Executive Committee of the Comintern. You may be certain of that, dear comrades."[14]

Lovestone and the even more outspoken Gitlow defied Stalin and were removed from the American Communist Party leadership. They not only lost their majority overnight, but some of their most active supporters also abandoned them and joined the Foster faction—among them Robert Minor, Jack Stachel, Max Bedacht, and J. Peters. All of them remained leaders of the Communist Party for many decades, and the last two worked for the Soviet intelligence service recruiting American Communists for espionage.[15]

A troika—the word comes from the Russian three-horse sleigh—took over the Party leadership. Two were former Lovestoneites, Minor and Bedacht. The third was Foster's closest friend and supporter, Earl Browder. Although Bedacht was for a time the acting general secretary, the troika was soon dissolved, and Browder became the general secretary, or head of the Party. This direct insult to Foster came about because even though he did not resist Stalin's orders, he was considered an incorrigible factionalist.

Chambers was not expelled with the hundreds of other Lovestoneites, but dropped out when he became disgusted with the Party. He later told the FBI, "During this period, I was never formally expelled by the Communist Party. I still considered myself a Communist but other members of the Communist Party refused to have anything to do with me. This was the common treatment for heretics."[16]

During his time in the Party, Chambers divided his life between his political activities and the advancement of his literary career. His former classmate at Columbia, Clifton Fadiman, was associated with the publishing house Simon and Schuster, and he got Chambers a job translating Felix Salten's wonderful children's book *Bambi* from German into English.[17] The book was first published in 1929, and recent editions still use the Chambers translation. Chambers later translated Salten's *Fifteen Rabbits*, which was published by Simon and Schuster in 1930.

In 1931 Chambers married the sweetheart he had met in the Communist movement, Esther Shemitz, and they would remain husband and wife for the rest of their lives. She was not actually a Communist Party member but a dedicated fellow traveler who spent all her time with her friends in the Party.[18] In 1929 a Party member named Grace Hutchins wrote a book for International Publishers

Whittaker Chambers's Spy Ring

called *Labor and Silk*. The illustrations for the book were by her friend Esther Shemitz.[19]

Hutchins, the closest friend of Esther Chambers, was a witness at their wedding, but when Whittaker Chambers finally broke for good with the Communist Party in 1938, she visited his brother-in-law Reuben Shemitz and told him to advise Chambers to report to the Communist Party "or else." When he didn't do so, she returned and told Reuben that he must "surrender [Chambers] to the Communist Party" and that she, Hutchins, "would guarantee the safety of his sister and her children."[20] Chambers still did not turn himself in, and his brother-in-law eventually turned notes that he had received from Hutchins over to the FBI. In 1943, still involved in Communist underground work, Hutchins organized the funeral of Jacob Golos, a high-ranking Soviet espionage operative.[21]

In those days, even if activists dropped out or were expelled from the CPUSA, their link with Soviet intelligence often continued. Moscow continued to dominate their thinking despite their disenchantment with the local scene. Moscow's spy services regularly used such people, who would pay their debt to the Comintern for earlier ideological deviations by undertaking dangerous underground work and espionage. After Lovestone and his followers were forced out, Lovestone maintained contact with the GRU (Soviet military intelligence) and in 1931 attempted to bring his group back into the Comintern fold through those contacts. But his bid was rejected, and he later revealed, in his 1940 Dies Committee testimony, that the representative he met was Moishe Stern, then the GRU chief in the United States, who used the cover name Mark Zilbert. Stern wrote for the Comintern organ *Communist International* under the byline M. Fred[22] and was later known as General Kleber when in 1936 he headed the International Brigades in Spain, successfully leading the defense of Madrid. As a result of a disagreement with the Comintern's representative in the International Brigades, Andre Marty, he was ordered back to Moscow in 1937 and spent the rest of his life in a Soviet slave labor camp.[23]

Chambers Returns to the Communist Party

The Browder-dominated Communist Party did not mind losing Lovestone and many of his fellow factionalists in the 1929 expulsions but was not happy about losing the talented young intellectual Whittaker Chambers. Soon Party activists tried to reestablish their friendship with him and invited him to write for a Party magazine, *New Masses*. In 1930 and 1931, Chambers wrote some short stories for the magazine, including the very popular *Can You Hear Their Voices?* and *Our Comrade Munn*.[24] The former was subsequently published under that title in pamphlet form.[25]

By the spring of 1932, Chambers was back in the Party's favor and was assigned as editor of the *New Masses*. But he had put out only three issues when he received a phone call from Max Bedacht, who had abandoned Lovestone at the 1929 Moscow meeting with Stalin in order to gain a leadership position in the Party. Bedacht for a short time was acting general secretary of the Party but was soon replaced by Browder. Bedacht remained on the Politburo and handled "special work" for Soviet intelligence.

Born in 1883 to a Catholic family in Munich, Germany, Bedacht came to the United States in 1908. He became a citizen in 1914 and was a charter member of the Communist Party in 1919.[26] After Bedacht betrayed the Lovestone faction in 1929 when Stalin denounced it, he went to work with Earl Browder in the Party leadership. But Browder did not like Bedacht and soon exiled him to be the leader of the International Workers Order, a Communist front with many foreign-born members. This gave Bedacht access to members' personal documents such as foreign birth certificates, naturalization certificates, and other paperwork that could help obtain false passports for Soviet intelligence operatives.

Bedacht's daughter, Elsa, married a Soviet citizen and worked at the Comintern headquarters in the 1930s and during World War II. In 1944, after the Comintern was supposedly dissolved, Bedacht asked a Soviet diplomat about his daughter. The question reached George Dimitroff, who still ran the now secret Comintern as part of the Central Committee of the Soviet Communist Party. Elsa was working at Institute 205, the code name for the secret Comintern. Dimitroff did not tell Bedacht where his daughter was working but did say that she "works in Moscow, she and members of her family are in good health, and she copes with her work quite well."[27]

In 1948 Bedacht was expelled from the Communist Party for criticizing Eugene Dennis, the leader who replaced Browder.[28] Called before the grand jury investigating Soviet espionage in 1949, Bedacht nevertheless evaded telling the truth. He claimed to the press that, while he may have met Whittaker Chambers, he knew nothing about espionage.[29]

But now back to 1932. As one of the senior Party people, Bedacht had never spoken to the lower-rank Chambers before his phone call to the young intellectual. Bedacht set up a meeting at which he told Chambers that he, Chambers, had been assigned to do "underground work." Chambers did not think it was a good idea since he had just returned to a public Party position at the *New Masses*, and it might seem peculiar if he suddenly disappeared. Bedacht allowed him to discuss the matter with his wife overnight. The next day, when Chambers told him that he and his wife decided that he should not do "underground work," Bedacht told him that he had no choice.

Bedacht took him to see John Sherman, who had been expelled from the Party for Lovestoneism but had come back to do "underground work." When Sherman took him to meet a Russian whom he knew only as "Herbert," Sherman's superior, Chambers soon realized that "underground work" really meant working directly for the Soviets.[30]

Chambers was not sure why Sherman had recommended him for the underground assignment. It may have been due to his excellent knowledge of German, the language often used in both the Comintern and Soviet intelligence. Chambers also noted that he, Bedacht, and Sherman were all former Lovestoneites and sensed he was being tested for forgiveness and readmission.

At any rate, Chambers acquiesced, and Sherman explained that Chambers's job was to act as the liaison between the underground apparatus and Max Bedacht of the open Communist Party. Sherman used the German word for liaison man: *Verbindungsmensch*.[31] During the first month of Chambers's underground work, Sherman introduced him to the Russian who would be his superior in the apparatus. He was called "Ulrich." Chambers later identified him from an FBI photograph as Alexander Ulanovsky.[32] He was an officer of Soviet military intelligence, the Fourth Bureau of the Red Army, later called GRU.

Enter George Mink

When members of the American Communist Party had secret information for the Russians, they would send the material by courier to Bedacht, who would give it to Chambers to pass on to Ulrich. On one occasion, when material concealed in a small mirror was being brought by a Communist merchant seaman, the courier failed to make contact. The courier passed the message to George Mink, the Communist Party waterfront organizer, who brought it to Bedacht for Chambers to pass to the Russians. When the backing of the mirror was removed, it revealed six frames of 35mm film, which contained the message.[33] Chambers never knew what the messages said—he had no need to know. He continued to work for Ulrich until 1934, when the Russian was assigned other duties.

Mink was also deeply involved in underground operations. Born in the Russian Empire in 1899, Mink, whose real name was Godi Minkowsky, came to the United States at the age of twelve. In 1921 he joined the aboveground Workers Party and the underground Communist Party. A member of the Foster faction, Mink came under attack by the Lovestoneites.[34] He was accused of having ties with a recently expelled Trotskyite,[35] and, while Mink was later exonerated, the confrontation may have convinced him to try to prove himself by undertaking intelligence work for the Soviets.

In 1935, Ulrich—using an American passport with the name "Shirman"—Mink, and another Party underground worker, Leon Josephson, went to Europe on false passports in an operation for Soviet military intelligence. In March, Comintern headquarters in Moscow learned that a group had been arrested in Copenhagen, so the Comintern used its secret radio on March 15, 1935, to order the Danish Communist Party to "telegraph who has been arrested." Three days later Moscow learned that it was Mink and his group and asked Copenhagen to "make cautious inquiries" to find out more details.[36]

On March 27 the Comintern ordered the Danish Communist Party to "hasten to arrange for a suitable lawyer for the Mink affair in Copenhagen" and to make sure the lawyer was a "non-Party person, who has nothing to do with Communist affairs.... Wire how much he should be paid. Do not let the affair fail because of money difficulties." Moscow ordered further that no one connected with "our illegal work must come in contact with the lawyer."[37]

There was considerable concern in Moscow over this matter, and on April 25 the Comintern radioed to Copenhagen: "What is being done in the Mink affair by the Party or anyone else? Is any news of this matter to hand [sic]? Please telegraph reply." Although the underground people were ordered not to make contact with Mink's attorney, information about the case was obtained through Richard Jensen, a high-ranking secret Comintern operative head-quartered in Copenhagen,[38] who learned that the defendants were to be released.[39]

On May 18 the Danish Communist Party radioed Moscow: "Mink has received his passport and has already been let go, while the others have not received their passports, but on Monday May 20th at 24 hours [midnight] they will be allowed to go and can then travel in one of our ships." But no Soviet ship was immediately available for them, so they had to wait in Copenhagen.[40] A year later Mink was back doing underground work, and Moscow ordered the Danish Communist Party to give him fifty American dollars and instructed, "Inform us of Mink's [false] passport name."[41]

It turned out that Mink had attempted to rape a chambermaid at his hotel. His arrest led to the discovery of his false passports and identification and to the arrest of his companions.[42] Neither the Danes nor Moscow knew that British intelligence intercepted the messages on the case. After his release, Mink made a reputation for himself as a GPU executioner in Spain during the Civil War. His reward was to be killed in one of Stalin's purges later in the decade. Mink's fellow GPU executioner in Spain, Vittorio Vidali, also known as Carlos Contreras, reported Mink's death in his book *Diary of the Twentieth Congress of the Communist Party of the Soviet Union.* Vidali served in the postwar period as head of the Communist Party of Trieste.[43]

The arrest of Mink and his coworkers in Copenhagen has become part of a disinformation story spread by the current Russian intelligence service, the SVR. A series of books being published in Moscow under the editorship of Yevgeny Primakov, former head of

SVR and later Russian prime minister, on the history of the Russian foreign intelligence, presents the official viewpoint. Despite the overwhelming evidence to the contrary, one of the disinformation themes in the books is that the Soviets did not use members of the foreign Communist parties for espionage. Even after the release of *Venona*, which showed that during that period almost all of the agents were Party members, Russian intelligence is still trying to sell the false story. For example, Volume 3 of the official history says:

> Did intelligence use the foreign Communist parties in its activities? It is hard to unequivocally answer this question, which has been often asked in the intelligence literature. Formally there was a strict prohibition of higher Party authorities and the intelligence leadership to use members of local Communist parties abroad for intelligence work. However, in practice there were cases when the *Rezidenturas*, without notifying the Center, would recruit Communists for collaboration.
>
> Interesting in this regard is a memorandum from A. Kh. Artuzov, who at the time performed the duties of chief of military intelligence, to the USSR People's Commissar for Defense K. Ye. Voroshilov regarding the reasons for the exposure of the *Rezidentura* in Denmark. Artuzov wrote, "Comrade Ulanovsky [the *Rezident*] was arrested because he violated the order prohibiting recruitment of Party members. All three of the Danes that he recruited are Communists. Comrade Ulanovsky concealed from us the fact that they were Communists."[44]

This is pure myth: Both Mink and Josephson were members of the American Communist Party, and the Comintern's concern about Mink showed it was fully aware of his Party membership. Both the Comintern archives and *Venona*, moreover, show that the NKVD headquarters authorized the use of Party members. One of the authors of this book had the opportunity in late 1998 to discuss the issue with retired KGB General Vadim Kirpichenko, the deputy editor-in-chief of the official book series, and pointed out that most of the agents during the 1930s and World War II were members of the Communist parties and were recruited with the cooperation of the Soviet intelligence and Party leadership. After first denying this, Kirpichenko finally admitted that it was true but said it was because of the Jews. The NKVD *Residents* were Jews and recruited their friends in the Communist parties. The author responded that neither Zarubin nor Akhmerov, the two *Residents* in the United States during the war, nor most of their officers were Jewish. Kirpichenko shrugged this off and said that this was how he and his colleagues wanted to explain the matter. This tells us more about the accuracy of official information released by the KGB and of the continuing attitude toward the Jews than it does about the history of the service.

The Burglary of Jay Lovestone's Files

During the late 1930s, the struggle against expelled rival Communists had broken into open warfare. Leon Josephson continued his work in the Communist underground when he returned to the United States and was soon involved in a burglary. In 1938 Pat Toohey, the American Communist Party representative to the Comintern, sent a memo to George Dimitroff, the Comintern general secretary. He reported:

> The entire archives of the notorious Jay Lovestone have come into the possession of our Central Committee. These archives are the complete records of Lovestone's letters, documents, addresses and financial dealings for the past 10 years....
>
> These records include documents revealing Lovestone's close connection with notorious anti-working class and

bourgeois forces in America and in Europe. There are considerable documents relating to Lovestone's international deal-
ings, plus letters and addresses of his European cohorts. Some
of these documents refer to certain persons in the USSR who
are mentioned in letters which discuss the trials of the
Trotskyist-Bukharin spies. Others of these letters deal with
some shady munitions deal which Lovestone was engaged in.

Some of these documents indicate that Lovestone maintains very close connection with one Mendelsohn [*sic*] of
Canada, whom comrade Browder believes to be a Soviet
employee of an important branch. [At this point, the Russian
letters OGPU—the Soviet intelligence service at that time—
are handwritten.] Lovestone seems especially close to Mrs.
Mendelsohn according to these records.[45]

The Mendelsons, still Soviet secret agents in the late 1930s,
remained close friends of Lovestone for decades. During World
War II, Lovestone became an anti-Communist, an official of the
American trade union movement, and later collaborated with the CIA
in anti-Soviet trade union and human rights activities.[46] The
Mendelsons, close friends of Lovestone, were involved in Communist
underground and Soviet intelligence operations, including the production of false passports, when Lovestone headed the American
Communist Party.[47] As we shall see, they continued in this work long
after Lovestone's expulsion.

Toohey told Dimitroff in his memo that Browder wanted to
ship documents relating to international affairs to Moscow but was
concerned about sending them through the GPU representative in
the United States, whom he called "Smith," "but bearing in mind
the Mendelsohns [*sic*] matter and if there are others like him,
Comrade Browder will transmit these materials via his own methods
if he is notified to 'send special materials yourself.'" At the top of the

memo appear the letters OMS in Russian, designating the secret and illegal work department of the Comintern, where apparently the memo was sent.

Lovestone talked about the loss of his files in testimony before the Dies Committee. He was not too happy to appear before this committee, which he felt was too right-wing. But he answered its questions truthfully:

> In July 1938, in the height of the fight against Communist Party domination of the United Automobile Workers, C.I.O., an attempt was made to get me. The attempt was made on a Sunday, because generally I would be staying home on Sundays to work, but that Sunday I happened not to be at home. I was not gotten, but my home was rifled and confidential documents of all sorts and sundry were stolen. I immediately knew that that could be performed by only one of two agencies, either the Gestapo, because of my vigorous fight against the Nazis, and because of my visiting Germany and organizing the underground revolutionary movements in Germany after Hitler took power, or by the G.P.U.
>
> I must confess I was wrong in thinking it was more likely the Gestapo, because a couple of weeks after that the *Daily Worker* came out with full photostatic copies of quite a number of documents rifled from my home, documents pertaining to the struggle against Communist Party manipulation and domination in the United Automobile Workers. When I saw that I knew it was a G.P.U. job. Through our own channels we began to investigate and we learned that it was a G.P.U. job, directed by a G.P.U. agent in this country by the name of Mr. Leon Josephson.[48]

Lovestone's information was corroborated in 1944 when the FBI made a surreptitious entry into the property of Philip Levy, who was involved in the false passport operation of the American Communist Party. FBI agents found the personal files of Leon Josephson, which were hidden for him by Levy. In the file was a collection of the material stolen from Lovestone in 1938. Levy was a business associate of Soviet military intelligence officer Arthur Adams in 1939. They both served as officers of Technological Laboratories in New York, a cover company for Soviet espionage. When Mink, Josephson, and Ulanovsky were arrested in Denmark, in addition to their false passports, the latter two had business credentials issued by Philip Levy's earlier business, the Intercontinental Oil Company.[49]

In 1947 Josephson appeared as a witness in the case of Gerhart Eisler, who had used a false American passport in 1934. Josephson admitted that he had filed a false application to obtain a passport for Eisler at the request of Harry Kweit.[50] Josephson had no hesitation in naming Kweit, who had died on a ship that was sunk during World War II. As noted, Kweit was a Comintern radio expert during the 1930s.

From Communist Study Group to Spy Ring

Less than a year after Bedacht began using Chambers as a courier, he was replaced by a new control officer known as J. Peters. Soon Chambers was put in contact with an underground Communist apparatus that Peters was running in Washington. Since the group was providing secret government information, Peters instructed Chambers to set up a location in Washington or Baltimore to photograph the documents.[51]

Chambers learned that the leader of the Washington cell, Harold Ware, had recently returned from the Soviet Union, where he ran an agricultural cooperative. When Chambers met him, Ware had a job in the Agricultural Adjustment Administration, a United States government agency, where he recruited some colleagues into his cell.

The Communist interest in U.S. agriculture stemmed from one of Moscow's bizarre concepts. The Soviets believed that the American "peasants" would be a revolutionary force along with the American factory workers. At a conference of CPUSA leaders in July 1933, the Party's farm work director, Henry Puro, whose real name was John Wiita, pointed out that Stalin believed it was an error to ignore organizing farmers.[52] The CPUSA jumped to obey. It set up a front to recruit farmers and penetrated the Agriculture Department. The Party's front was called the United Farmers League, and it published a newspaper, *The United Farmer*. It called conferences in which members pretended to be non-Communists, but as Puro pointed out, the conferences were "politically initiated, inspired and organized by our Party...."[53] Henry Puro himself served as national secretary of the United Farmers League.[54]

At an American Communist Party Politburo meeting on April 12, 1934, Donald Henderson reported on meetings that he had with Harold Ware and Jack Stachel to discuss the farm operations of the Party and the instructions for Puro.[55] Stachel remained a high-ranking official in the Communist Party apparatus while Henderson went on to become the leader of the Food, Tobacco, Agricultural, and Allied Workers of America, which was expelled by the CIO in 1949 for being Communist-controlled.[56]

When Chambers met Ware in 1934, the underground group Ware led consisted mainly of employees of the Agricultural Adjustment Administration (AAA). Chambers called it "Apparatus A." Among the members were Lee Pressman, Alger Hiss, Donald Hiss, Henry Hill Collins, Jr., Victor Perlo, John Abt, Nathan Witt, and Charles Krivitsky, who later called himself Charles Kramer. Chambers told the FBI that "Ware then quickly realized that the possibilities for the Communist Party far exceeded this little group in AAA."[57]

Whittaker Chambers's Spy Ring

The Party members fanned out into other agencies, and each set up additional cells, first organized as study groups, which evolved into Communist Party units. Leaders of the units identified those members who would be willing to collect information from their agencies for the Communist Party national leadership. They were soon collecting information for Soviet military intelligence. "The leaders of Apparatus A were known to each other," Chambers told the FBI, and, "The leaders of Apparatus A also knew the identities of the members of the other cells. However, the individuals who made up the various cells did not, or at least in practice were not supposed to know the identities of the other leaders of Apparatus A or the identities of the persons that made up the other cells."[58]

Alger Hiss soon left AAA and took a job with the Nye Committee, a congressional committee investigating the armaments industry. He became the first member of a parallel group, Apparatus B, whose purpose was to penetrate "old line agencies" such as the Navy and State departments.[59] Hiss served as legal assistant to the committee and participated in the questioning of such distinguished Americans as Bernard Baruch, who had helped organize the war effort during World War I.[60] Hiss's brother, Donald, was also transferred to Apparatus B and worked first in the Labor Department and then in the State Department. Chambers said he received documents only from Alger Hiss, not from Donald, who was never charged with any crime.

Although Apparatus A was primarily interested in influencing government policy rather than in espionage, Chambers pointed out to the FBI that Alger Hiss was soon able to obtain secret documents. Hiss himself reported that the committee was receiving important State Department documents, and Peters instructed Chambers to photograph any of the sensitive documents.[61]

The Soviets took a great interest in the work of the Nye Committee, both because of the secret government documents and because of its propaganda value. In September 1934 the Comintern radioed the Swiss Communist Party that the information coming out of the Nye Committee was of "great importance" in a propaganda campaign against Western armaments. The Swiss were also told that Browder had been instructed to send the Comintern information on other subjects. The propaganda campaign would claim that Germany and Japan were planning an attack on the Soviet Union and that other countries, including the United States, were selling them arms.[62]

In 1936 Alger Hiss served for a short time in the office of the solicitor general and then in September went to work for the State Department. According to Chambers's statement to the FBI, each of those career moves had to be cleared by J. Peters.[63]

In late 1935 or early 1936 Lee Pressman left his government job to be general counsel of the CIO. He told Chambers that there was some concern in the Communist Party Central Committee about this move. Chambers assured him that it was not a problem.[64] Control of a future significant union, such as the CIO, was so important to the Soviet Union that even an underground worker like Pressman had to be used for that work. Eugene Dennis, the American Communist Party representative in Moscow, told the Comintern in 1937 that the numerous Party functionaries assigned to work in the CIO left a shortage of experienced personnel in the Party apparatus.[65]

Enter Boris Bykov

In the fall of 1936 yet another Russian controller appeared on the scene. J. Peters introduced him as "Peter," the operative who would in the future give Chambers his orders. Chambers later learned from Walter Krivitsky, a former GRU general, that "Peter" was Boris Bykov.[66]

Colonel Bykov's arrival had a dramatic effect on the Communists in the underground apparatus. Before he came, Chambers had received documents on only three occasions. One batch was from Alger Hiss at the Nye Committee; the second came from two members of a subcell in Apparatus A, Julian Wadleigh and Ward Pigman; the third came from Harry Dexter White, handed over to Chambers by Robert Coe, another member of a subcell in Apparatus A.[67]

With the arrival of Bykov, the demand for and supply of documents increased dramatically. Bykov thought that the members of the underground might be induced to obtain even more documents if they were given money. Chambers objected, saying that this would insult them—they were loyal Communists, not mercenaries. Bykov then suggested that some be given an expensive present. Chambers agreed, and, as we've seen, four expensive Bokhara rugs were given to George Silverman, Harry Dexter White, Alger Hiss, and Julian Wadleigh.[68]

Bykov demanded to meet some of the important members of the underground personally. Thus, in the spring of 1937, Alger Hiss traveled to New York to meet Bykov. Chambers picked Hiss up near the Brooklyn Bridge station of the elevated train and took him by train to Brooklyn. They met Bykov in the Prospect movie theater. The three of them then took a subway and later a taxi, to make sure they weren't being followed, to Manhattan's Chinatown. They ate dinner and discussed matters at the Port Arthur Restaurant. Since Bykov spoke poor English, Chambers interpreted Bykov's German for Hiss. After Bykov finished making the long and unnecessary speech about the need to struggle against fascism and help the Soviet Union by providing secret information, he got down to business. Hiss agreed to provide more State Department documents to be copied and the originals returned.[69]

Chambers later told the FBI:

> Shortly after this New York meeting between Bykov and Alger
> Hiss, the latter began producing material. At this time, Alger

Hiss was employed in the State Department as assistant to Francis Sayre, the then Assistant Secretary of State.

The method of transmitting this material was as follows. Alger Hiss would bring home original documents from the State Department over night as "a matter of custom." On an agreed night, I would go to the 30th Street house and Alger would then turn over to me a zipper case containing these documents. I might state that it is also entirely possible that I brought a zipper case and placed the documents therein to avoid carrying or using Alger's case. I would then take these documents by train to an apartment which was located on the corner of Calvert and East Madison Streets in Baltimore, Maryland....

I had previously brought a Leica camera and other photographic equipment, given me by Bykov, to this apartment.... I used the apartment for photographing documents.[70]

Chambers would return the original documents and give the microfilm to Bykov. When he decided to break with the Soviets, he kept a collection of original documents and microfilms as an "insurance policy," which he later turned over to the U.S. government.

On Bykov's orders, Chambers asked Harry Dexter White to provide documents more readily, rather than only sporadically, as was his custom. Bykov then decided that he had to meet White. The meeting was arranged in Washington, and after a conversation that Chambers was not in on, Bykov appeared satisfied.[71]

The other members of the ring also provided secret government documents. Chambers set up the methods by which the documents could be photographed and copies turned over to Bykov.

The Robinson/Rubens Case

Before Bykov took over in 1936, J. Peters had introduced Chambers to a man called "Richard," who was involved in producing false passports. The events that followed from this introduction started Chambers on the path to breaking with the Soviets. "Richard's" real name, although Chambers never knew it, was Arnold Ikal; Ikal was a Latvian Communist who had been sent to the United States by Soviet military intelligence (the GRU) to obtain false passports for their officers and agents. J. Peters told Chambers that "Richard" was upset by the purges in the Soviet Union. He had heard that his close friend and compatriot General Jan Berzin, head of the GRU, had been shot. "Richard" was therefore relieved when he received a message to return to Russia signed "Starik," which was the code name for Berzin. When "Richard" returned to Russia with his wife in December 1937, they each carried two passports, one in the name of Robinson, the other in the name of Rubens.[72] The Russians arrested him on his arrival and arrested her a few days later. In the interim, she had been contacted by the American embassy. The disappearance of an American citizen alarmed the American diplomats, especially when they discovered that the couple's passports were illegally obtained.

Two American officials were allowed to meet with Mrs. Rubens on February 10, 1938, in her Soviet prison cell, where they established that she was indeed an American citizen. But they could do nothing for her. She was not placed on trial until June 1939, when she was convicted of entering the Soviet Union with false documents and sentenced to eighteen months in jail. As she had already been in jail that long, she was soon released. She then visited the embassy on June 19, 1939, and said that she intended to remain in the Soviet Union to be of possible assistance to her husband, who was still under arrest. The embassy learned in November that she had taken Soviet citizenship and gone to Kiev.[73]

Actually, there was much more to this case than the American officials understood. Chambers knew her husband, Ikal, was a Soviet military intelligence officer. Part of the NKVD file on Ikal's case was obtained from the Soviet archives by Chambers's recent biographer, Sam Tanenhaus. From this we learn that Ikal was one of the many Latvians recruited as spies by Soviet military intelligence, the Fourth Bureau of the Red Army. He was particularly close to its head, Jan Berzin. Under torture, Ikal falsely confessed that he and Berzin were agents of the intelligence service of the then independent Latvia. He claimed that Berzin had sent him to the United States in May 1933 to work for Latvian intelligence and a Latvian nationalist organization.[74] Among other Latvian agents, Ikal identified Alfred Tilton, Dick Murzin, Boris Devyatkin, and Nicholas Dozenberg. Dozenberg was lucky. Unlike the hapless Soviet intelligence officers Tilton and Merzin, who were executed in the Moscow purges, he was sitting in an American prison, having been caught in a bizarre counterfeiting scheme ordered by Moscow to finance Soviet military intelligence operations. Dozenberg was a Latvian-born official of the American Communist Party who in 1927 was relieved by Lovestone of Party work and assigned as an agent to Alfred Tilton, then head of Soviet military intelligence in the United States.[75]

On December 22, under torture, Ikal also confessed to being an agent of Germany. He falsely identified Dr. Philip Rosenbliett, a dentist, as a go-between for "Berzin's Latvian national fascist organization and the US Trotskyites." Rosenbliett was the brother-in-law of American Trotskyite leader James Cannon. Chambers knew Rosenbliett as part of the Soviet spy ring and also knew that he was vehemently opposed to his brother-in-law.[76] Rosenbliett returned to the Soviet Union and disappeared.

Ikal also said falsely that in 1933 Rosenbliett had put him in touch with Nathan Mendelson, a Canadian, who, together with his wife, worked with Jay Lovestone.[77] Two days later, Ikal claimed that he maintained contact with Lovestone through the Mendelsons.[78] As we saw earlier, the burglary of Lovestone's files revealed to the

Comintern that as late as 1938 he was still in contact with the Mendelsons. Ikal's story, for its part, shows that years after Lovestone's expulsion from the Communist Party, his friends the Mendelsons were still working for Soviet intelligence.

By January 1939, Ikal recovered his courage and denied all the false statements he had made about himself and his fellow Soviet intelligence officers. Asked on January 29, "You confirm your previous testimony of your anti-Soviet activities and anti-Soviet contacts?" he answered, "No, I renounce my previous testimony." Asked, "Why did you give false testimony?" he answered, "The testimony that I gave was the kind that was demanded of me." He specifically denied any relationship to German or Latvian intelligence organizations or Trotskyites or Lovestoneites.[79] The Ikal couple was never heard from again.[80]

Chambers Breaks with Communism

The Robinson/Rubens disappearance came as a big shock to Chambers. Already upset by the purges of leading Soviet officials whose names he knew well, the disappearance of his comrade "Richard" was too much for him. Chambers began to ponder how he could extricate himself from Soviet espionage. One move was to contact an old school friend, Herbert Solow, who was a democratic socialist. He wrote two articles explaining the Soviet false passport operations and gave them to Solow. The articles, which were never published, were retained by his friend. Chambers signed the articles "Karl," the name by which the Washington spy ring knew him. Written in 1938, almost a year before the Nazi-Soviet Pact of August 1939, Chambers's first article contained the clairvoyant statement, "Soviet Russia is Hitler's natural ally...." Fully expecting the two articles to be published, Chambers opened with a threat to his former comrades:

This pseudonym will be recognized by my former Russian, Latvian and American comrades, especially the military Communists. Let it be a sign to them that if the usual campaign of slander and denial begins, I shall publish material omitted here and the identities of "Barber" and "Sandor." It is time that we threw open the windows at no matter what cost and let out the stench of 1,000,000 bodies, victims of Stalinism's Purge....[81]

"Barber" was the name Chambers used for Max Bedacht, who once practiced that profession. "Sandor" was his name for J. Peters, who sometimes used the name Alexander or Sandor Goldberger. Peters, whose real name was Isidor Burstein, was born in Austria-Hungary in 1894. Chambers wrote about the false passport work of Ikal, the man he knew as "Richard" and the press knew as Robinson/Rubens. Chambers revealed that all of the information the American embassy in Moscow was sending back to Washington on this case was available to Soviet military intelligence through photostatic copies obtained by the spy ring in Washington. He wrote, "The Americans, of course, did not know that by putting their coded confidences on the wire or in the diplomatic mail, they were automatically putting them into the hands of the Soviet secret service and ultimately of Stalin himself...."

Concerning "Comrade Barber"—Bedacht—Chambers wrote that "one of his posts in the American [Communist] Party gave him special access to naturalization and other personal papers." Bedacht headed the International Workers Order, a Communist front with many foreign-born members, who had the type of papers useful for Soviet intelligence—foreign birth and baptismal certificates and naturalization papers. These helped obtain false passports for Soviet intelligence officers and agents who spoke with a foreign accent. Although the American Communist Party had demoted Bedacht in the Party leadership, "the Russians," Chambers said, "insisted that Comrade Barber, as their rascal, continue in the lesser post that gave him control of naturalization papers." Chambers revealed that the Canadian false passport operation was also under the control of "Richard."[82] This was the Canadian apparatus of Lovestone's friend, Mendelson.

In his second article—"Welcome, Soviet Spies!"—Chambers revealed that the false passports used by George Mink, Leon Josephson, and Nicholas Shirman (Ulanovsky), when they were arrested in Copenhagen in 1935, also came from this spy ring.[83] Chambers's friend Herbert Solow was very interested in the Ikal case. Solow, without revealing Chambers as his source, went to see Lovestone for whatever further information he might have. But Lovestone told him to forget about it. Solow, not knowing about the Mendelsons or of Lovestone's involvement with them, refused and, in an April 16 letter, complained that Lovestone had given no explanation for his curious reluctance to provide information about another "reactionary criminality" of the Stalinists.[84]

Chambers Fears for His Life

Chambers now lived in fear that the GPU would kill him as it had killed other defectors from the Soviet service. Solow insisted that to save his life, Chambers had to reveal what he knew. He compared Ignace Reiss, the former Soviet intelligence officer murdered in Switzerland before he could tell what he knew, with General Walter Krivitsky, who revealed all and was still alive. Chambers, he said, had to decide whether to be "the American Reiss or the American Krivitsky."[85]

Chambers's fear for his life was triggered when his friend Paul Willert of Oxford Publishers told him that Richard Childs of Modern Age Books had asked him for Chambers's address.

According to Solow, "Chambers thinks Childs was inquiring for the GPU, although Childs may not be aware of that."[86] At about the same time, Chambers wrote a letter to his friend Robert Cantwell. Willert, he said, had told him that "Modern Age Books called up the other day and wanted your address. Childs called. I told him, any mail would be forwarded. Childs said that he must see you that day and mail wouldn't do and he's been phoning every day since. I told him I thought you lived somewhere in Baltimore." According to Chambers, Childs was a Party member.[87]

Chambers knew that Modern Age Books had been set up by the Communist Party on orders of the Comintern. A document in Comintern files contained the 1936 orders to the American Communists "to establish a 'library' of 50 cent paper-covered books, to be published under 'neutral' publishing auspices...."[88] A short time later, Modern Age Books, a paperback publishing house, appeared and published a whole series of books, most of which followed the Communist propaganda line.[89] In 1942 Alfred K. Stern, a Soviet agent, filed an application for federal employment. He identified himself as the vice president of Modern Age Publishing Company.[90]

Then came August 1939 and the Hitler-Stalin pact. It was the final straw. Chambers decided to break cover. Isaac Don Levine urged Chambers to accompany him on a visit to Assistant Secretary of State Adolph A. Berle. The date was September 1, the day the German invasion of Poland shocked the world. The stated purpose was to provide the U.S. government with information that Chambers had on Soviet espionage activities in America and information he believed the Russians probably would now share with their new Nazi friends.

Berle headed his notes "Underground Espionage Agent." Chambers told him about Lee Pressman, John Abt, Charles Krivitsky (Charles Kramer), Lawrence Duggan, Julian Wadleigh,

Eleanor Nelson, and Donald and Alger Hiss. Berle wrote in his memo, "When Loy Henderson interviewed Mrs. Rubens his report immediately went back to Moscow. Who sent it?—Such came from Washington." When Chambers was later interviewed by the FBI, he did not remember mentioning the Henderson report to Berle.[91] In his unpublished articles, Chambers knew that the Robinson/Rubens/Ikal information had been made available to the Soviets through his underground apparatus. One of the reports, handwritten by Alger Hiss, was among the documents that Chambers would later turn over to the U.S. government.

Levine contacted Chambers and reported that Berle had given the information to President Roosevelt, who simply laughed. When Berle tried to press the issue, Roosevelt responded in a colorful phrase that Chambers felt he should paraphrase: "Go jump in a lake."[92]

Disappointed by the lack of interest of government officials, Chambers decided to forget the matter and concentrate on his career; thus, he soon became a senior editor of *Time* magazine.

At the same time, Alger Hiss's career also advanced rapidly, for the threat of American involvement in the war had galvanized official Washington into action. He eventually rose in the State Department to the post of director of the Office of Special Political Affairs,[93] a position that enabled him to order up important documents relating to military strategy. His highest post was secretary general of the founding conference of the United Nations. But his career was dogged by rumors and reports concerning his loyalty. Finally, on December 10, 1946, Hiss resigned from the State Department to become president of the Carnegie Endowment for International Peace.[94] He had been handpicked for the post by one of his establishment patrons, no less a figure of Republican rectitude than John Foster Dulles.

Unfortunately, Dulles was unaware of what Secretary of State James Byrnes and Hiss's friend and later secretary of state Dean Acheson already knew. Testifying in 1949 at a secret hearing of the Senate Foreign Relations Committee, Acheson said that in late 1946 Byrnes told him that he had received continual reports from various sources, including the FBI, that Hiss had been involved in Communist activities. The information had come from Chambers, but the FBI did not want the source identified. A short time later, Hiss told Acheson that he had been offered the job at the Carnegie Endowment but was concerned about leaving government while he was under some sort of cloud. Acheson said, "My advice to you is take this job. This is the kind of thing which rarely, if ever, gets cleared up. The Government has to protect its sources of information; there is no way of having any final adjudication of this matter. People will continue to raise these doubts about you so long as you are in a position where you are subject to this sort of attack, and if I were you, I would just leave and go to New York."[95] Hiss took the advice, and for a time, it appeared that he might remain masked forever.

Chambers Is Discovered by Congress

Chambers, too, hoped that his role in espionage would be forgotten, but he discussed it with some friends. On March 20, 1945, Raymond Murphy visited Chambers's home in Westminister, Maryland, where Chambers told him about the spy ring. Murphy made copious notes, which he showed to a number of people. In 1947 Father John F. Cronin, the assistant director of the National Catholic Welfare Conference, sent those notes to the FBI.[96] Other conservatives heard rumors about Chambers's allegations as well.

By 1948, ten years after he had left the underground, the House Committee on Un-American Activities learned about Whittaker Chambers. The most important agent that Chambers had worked with was Alger Hiss. He was also the man Chambers considered his closest friend in the underground. When Chambers testified before the committee on August 3, 1948, he did his best to protect Hiss, who was already known to the congressmen. Chambers did not tell Congress that the Hiss group was supplying secret government documents. He said, "The purpose of this group at that time was not primarily espionage. Its original purpose was the Communist infiltration of the American government. But espionage was certainly one of its eventual objectives."[97] But nuance was lost on the congressmen, and the printed hearings carried the title across the top of each page, "Communist Espionage."

In its Interim Report, the committee listed the names of the government officials identified by Chambers as members of the underground group:

> Harold Ware (deceased), Department of Agriculture
>
> John J. Abt, Department of Agriculture; Works Progress Administration; Senate Committee on Education and Labor; Justice Department
>
> Nathan Witt, Department of Agriculture; National Labor Relations Board
>
> Lee Pressman, Department of Agriculture; Works Progress Administration
>
> Alger Hiss, Department of Agriculture; Special Senate Committee Investigating the Munitions Industry; Justice Department; State Department
>
> Donald Hiss, State Department; Labor Department
>
> Henry H. Collins, National Recovery Administration; Department of Agriculture
>
> Charles Kramer (Krevitsky), National Labor Relations Board; Office of Price Administration; Senate Subcommittee on War Mobilization

Victor Perlo, Office of Price Administration; War
Production Board; Treasury Department

Chambers identified J. Peters as his supervisor in the apparatus and Harry Dexter White as a member of the group but not a Party member. In his subsequent discussions with the FBI, he identified more Soviet agents, including George Silverman, Harold Glasser, and Lawrence Duggan, although he knew the last only through talks with Peters. Chambers also mentioned Lauchlin Currie as a person close to Silverman and White but did not know him as an agent.[98]

When the *Venona* messages became available, they confirmed many of those named by Chambers as Soviet agents, including John Abt, Alger Hiss, Charles Kramer, Victor Perlo, Harry Dexter White, George Silverman, Lawrence Duggan, Harold Glasser, J. Peters, and Lauchlin Currie.

Alger Hiss testified before the Un-American Activities Committee on August 5; brother Donald Hiss, Lauchlin Currie, and Harry Dexter White testified on August 13. All denied ever having been Communists or having had any involvement with the underground group, except Duggan, who committed suicide before he could testify.[99] Duggan had been a valuable NKVD asset during World War II, and his information was transmitted in a number of *Venona* messages.[100] In 1944 he advised Akhmerov that he was resigning from the State Department for personal reasons, and in a *Venona* message Akhmerov told Moscow that the Soviets would continue to use him in another capacity.[101]

The others named by Chambers all invoked the Fifth Amendment on membership in the Communist Party. The committee then heard further testimony by Alger Hiss and Chambers in which the two men continued to contradict each other. Although Hiss claimed that he never knew Chambers, in each session Chambers added more details

Whittaker Chambers's Spy Ring

that only a close friend of Hiss could know. The committee members who initially believed the patrician-looking, handsome, and well-dressed Hiss soon found the overweight, disheveled Chambers more credible. Outside the committee room, Hiss told the press that if Chambers were to repeat his charges without the immunity conferred by testimony before a congressional committee, he would sue.

Chambers was invited to appear on *Meet the Press*, a program presented by the Mutual Broadcasting System in association with the *American Mercury*. During the program, there was this exchange with Edward Folliard of the *Washington Post*:

> Folliard: Mr. Chambers, in the hearings on Capitol Hill you said over and over again that you served in the Communist Party with Alger Hiss. Your remarks down there were privileged; that is to say, you were protected from lawsuits. Hiss has now challenged you to make the same charge publicly. He says if you do he will test your veracity by filing a suit for slander or libel. Are you willing to say now that Alger Hiss is or ever was a Communist?
>
> Chambers: Alger Hiss was a Communist and may be now.
>
> Folliard: Mr. Chambers, to go back to that opening question, you accepted Alger Hiss's challenge and publicly said that he had been at least a member of the Communist Party. Does that mean that you are now prepared to go into court and answer to a suit for slander or libel?
>
> Chambers: I do not think Mr. Hiss will sue me for slander or libel.
>
> Tom Reynolds of the *Chicago Sun-Times*: Would you charge Alger Hiss with an overt act as a Communist, as you said he was? Did Alger Hiss at any time, to your knowledge, do anything that was treasonable or beyond the law of the United States? That, I believe, brings you the opportunity to accept the Hiss challenge.

> Chambers: Whether or not it brings me the opportunity to
> accept the Hiss challenge, I am quite unprepared to say whether
> he did or did not. I am not familiar with the laws of treason.

In answer to another question, although exposing Hiss as a Communist, Chambers continued to protect him from the truth about his espionage. Chambers said, "I think that what needs clarification is the purpose for which that group was set up to which Mr. Hiss belonged. That was a group, not, as I think is in the back of your mind, for the purpose of espionage, but for the purpose of infiltrating the government and influencing government policy by getting Communists in key places."[102]

Hiss sued, and Chambers answered by producing the original documents that he had saved as an "insurance policy." He turned additional microfilms over to the House Committee on Un-American Activities after famously hiding them overnight in a hollowed-out pumpkin. Some were in Hiss's handwriting, others typed on Hiss's typewriter, and at least one was in the handwriting of Harry Dexter White.

Hiss Is Indicted for Perjury

Hiss was indicted for perjury and on December 16, 1948, pleaded not guilty. His first trial, presided over by Judge Samuel Kaufman, ended in a mistrial on July 10, 1949. He was retried, and on January 20, 1950, Hiss was convicted of perjury and sentenced to five years in prison.[103]

During the second trial, before Judge Henry W. Goddard, former State Department official Julian Wadleigh testified that he knew Whittaker Chambers as a Soviet courier and admitted that he had funneled four hundred to five hundred secret documents from the State Department to the Soviets. None of them was among the documents turned over to the U.S. government by Whittaker Chambers, which he testified were given to him by Alger Hiss. Wadleigh said that he had been recruited by a friend, Eleanor Nelson.[104] This confirmed what Chambers had told the FBI—that Eleanor Nelson headed a separate spy ring.[105] The Comintern archives show that in 1933 the Communist Party USA Organizational Department received information that in Washington, D.C., some members of the Young People's Socialist League were very close to the Communist Party. One of them was Eleanor Nelson, 2412 Pennsylvania Avenue, NW.[106] Eleanor Nelson went from Communist sympathizer while a Young Socialist to member of the executive board of the CIO and secretary treasurer of the Communist-controlled United Federal Workers of America.[107] More important, she became the head of a Soviet spy ring based in Washington. The position she held in the United Federal Workers gave her access to the records of government employees, which the Soviets could use to recruit agents. This opportunity ended in 1949, when the CIO expelled the union, renamed United Public Workers, as a Communist-dominated organization.[108]

Noel Field: "The Other Hiss"

Judge Kaufman, in the first trial, had not permitted testimony from former Soviet spy Hede Massing. Massing, Gerhart Eisler's former wife, had been involved in Soviet espionage in the United States since the early 1930s. In her testimony at the second Hiss trial, she repeated what she had admitted to the FBI in an interview on December 7, 1948. She revealed that Noel Field, then a State Department colleague of Hiss, worked for her and had supplied her with information that she turned over to her Soviet superior. According to the FBI:

> After about a year, and possibly in the winter of 1935–36, Noel
> Field told Hede that someone else was also recruiting him to do

the same work and he did not know just what to do. Hede told Noel that she would like to meet this person that was trying to recruit him so that they could have it out. Field said that he would arrange to have Hede meet the person. According to Hede, approximately a week later Field had a dinner party at his apartment in Washington. Hede recalls that Herta Field, Noel's wife, was present, along with Noel, herself, and Alger Hiss.... Noel Field told Hede that Hiss was the person that was trying to recruit him.

Hiss had asked which apparatus she worked for, and Hede told him it was none of his business. Then one of them said, "What difference does it make who gets Noel? We're working for the same boss." Hede retained her agent.[109]

Chambers also told the FBI about Hiss's attempt to recruit Noel Field. Hiss failed because Field was already working for another apparatus headed by Hedda Gompertz, another name for Hede Massing. Later when Field left the State Department and went to work in Geneva, he told Hiss, who repeated it to Chambers, that Lawrence Duggan was now carrying on his work with Gompertz.[110]

The story told by Hede Massing and Whittaker Chambers was confirmed when the East European Communist archives were opened after the fall of the Soviet Union. The authors of this book were able to obtain documents from the Czech Secret Police archives through the cooperation of Karel Skrabek, a leader of the Czech human rights movement, who was researching Communist repression in Czechoslovakia.

Skrabek helped us obtain a report from the Czech Ministry of National Security dated March 30, 1955. The investigation, by a commission of the Central Committee of the Communist Party of Czechoslovakia, concerned "The Case of Field and His Accomplices."

Field had been convicted in Communist Hungary on false charges of being an American spy, and a number of Czechs were convicted in their country of conspiring with him. But on November 17, 1954, the Hungarian government announced that their new investigation revealed that Field was not an American spy.

The Czech investigation, for its part, revealed that although Field was severely tortured, he did not confess to spying for the United States but insisted that he was a spy for the Soviet Union in the United States. His revelations confirmed those of Massing and Chambers. The Czech report said:

> Noel Field said that he was a friend of [Alger] Hiss at the time he worked at the State Department and that Hiss worked for the USSR as a spy. He knows it, allegedly, from a discussion with him in which Hiss tried to convince him to work with him. Of course, at the time Noel Field already worked for Soviet intelligence through the Massings. Massing, who later was a traitor, testified about Hiss in front of the Committee on Un-American Activities and Mrs. Massing Gumperz testified against him in front of a New York Federal Jury which convicted Hiss [and sentenced him] to a five-year prison term.

The Czech report said that Field, who was born in 1904, entered the State Department in 1925 and worked in the West European Division. In the early 1930s he met Paul Massing and his wife, Hede, the former wife of Gerhart Eisler. They recruited Field for Soviet espionage and instructed him not to follow his inclinations and openly join the Communist Party. He provided them with secret State Department reports and other documents. In 1935 he left the State Department and in February 1936 went to work for the League of Nations in Geneva to aid Loyalist refugees from the Spanish Civil War.

The Massings met with Field in Geneva in the spring of 1937 on their way to the Soviet Union. They put him in touch with two Soviet intelligence officers, Ignace Reiss and Walter Krivitsky. He reported to them until Krivitsky advised him that he had betrayed the Soviet Union and was in hiding. Field attempted to find Reiss but soon learned from the newspapers that he was dead. The Czech report neglected to mention that Reiss had been murdered by the NKVD.

Soon Krivitsky, too, left the Soviet service and obtained asylum in the United States, but he was later murdered in Washington. Eventually, the Massings broke with Communism. It was Field's connection with these four that was used against him at his trial in Hungary.

In May 1938 Field visited Moscow and asked the American Commission of the Communist International to allow him to become a member of the Communist Party. The Party accepted him as a secret member and told him that he would be contacted by someone using the code word "Brooks" to activate him. But, possibly due to a shortage of Soviet intelligence officers because of the earlier purge, he wasn't contacted until 1944, in Switzerland, and the contact was not followed up. In the meantime, the Swiss Communist Party advised him that he had not been accepted for membership. Field was working for a humanitarian organization called the Unitarian Service Committee, which took care of refugees from Nazi-occupied Europe. In this, he worked closely with the OSS and knew Allen Dulles, the OSS chief in Switzerland. Although he never revealed his Soviet connections to OSS, his American connections were used against him in the Hungarian trial.

When Chambers testified about Alger Hiss in 1948, Field decided not to return to the United States. In 1949 he was lured to

Prague, arrested, chloroformed, and turned over to the Hungarians. In addition to Field's contact with the four NKVD people who defected, his relationship to Allen Dulles was also used against him. The Czech file contained a letter he wrote to Max Horngacher, a Swiss Communist who wanted OSS help to get into Yugoslavia in April 1945. In the letter, Field suggested that he contact Allen Dulles. According to the Czech file, Horngacher was an NKVD *Rezident* in Switzerland during World War II under the name "Braun."[111]

Hungarian scholar Maria Schmidt found similar information on the Field case in the Hungarian archives. She quoted from an interrogation of Field in Hungary in which he said, "In Fall 1935 Hiss at one point called me to undertake espionage for the Soviet Union.... I informed him that I was already doing such work." During a trip to the United States in 1939, he again met Hiss. Field said, "From the press I learned that Krivitsky was hanging around in Washington and I had to be prepared that he might reveal me. Since Hiss, in theory, knew all about me, I could inform him without much breaching the law of secrecy, that I was in danger because of a grass [informer]. We agreed that if he got any information about it, he would send me [a] warning, but I never received such [a] warning."[112]

Field, upon his release from prison, opted to remain in Communist Hungary. During the 1956 Hungarian uprising, he opposed the Hungarian Freedom Fighters and supported the Soviet invasion. In an article explaining his views in an American Communist magazine, he defended even those who tortured him in prison. He said that since they believed him guilty, he "approve[d] their detestation" because "they hate the same things and the same people I hate."[113] Noel Field never returned to the United States and died in Hungary on September 12, 1970.[114]

If Judge Samuel Kaufman had had his way, the jury would never have heard the truth about Alger Hiss and his relationship with Noel

Field. The first Hiss trial was severely criticized by those who believed Hiss guilty. Even before the trial ended, the press learned that Kaufman had manipulated the calendar so that he could be made the judge in the case.[115] Congressman Frank Keefe, a Republican from Wisconsin, placed in the *Congressional Record* of July 18, 1949, serious allegations of misconduct and corruption by Judge Kaufman, some directly linked to New York congressman Emanuel Celler. Kaufman had allegedly received bribes on behalf of Celler from companies that wanted his influence with executive branch agencies.

Hiss in *Venona*

Hiss was released from prison in November 1954 and, until his death in 1996, continued to insist that he was innocent. But evidence in the trial and some developed after his conviction showed the opposite. In August 1969 the NSA finished breaking a March 30, 1945, *Venona* message from the Washington, D.C., *Rezidentura* to Moscow headquarters. It reported a meeting between the Soviet "illegal" *Rezident* Akhmerov and an agent of Soviet military intelligence called "Ales." In reading the message, one sees clearly that "Ales" was Alger Hiss.

The message said that "Ales" had been working for military intelligence since 1935. (While most of the others were transferred to NKVD in 1938, Hiss remained with military intelligence.) "Ales" maintained a small group "for the most part consisting of his relations." Akhmerov's report went on to say that "the group and "Ales" himself work on obtaining military information only. Materials in the State Department allegedly interest Soviet military intelligence very little and he does not produce them regularly."

"Ales" (Hiss) told Akhmerov that he and his group had recently received Soviet medals. He reported "Ales" as saying that "after the Yalta Conference when he had gone on to Moscow, a Soviet personage in a very responsible position (Ales implied that it was Comrade Vyshinsky) allegedly got in touch with Ales and at the behest of the military intelligence passed on to him their gratitude...."[116]

Hiss had been at the Yalta Conference and had then flown to Moscow with Secretary of State E. R. Stettinius, Jr. He worked first as deputy and then as head of the Office of Special Political Affairs, which received a considerable amount of military information.

When this *Venona* message was partially broken back in 1950, the FBI tentatively concluded that "Ales" was Alger Hiss. A May 15, 1950, FBI memorandum said, "It would appear likely that this individual is Alger Hiss in view of the fact that he was in the State Department and the information from Chambers indicated that his wife, Priscilla, was active in Soviet espionage and he also had a brother, Donald, in the State Department. It also is to be noted that Hiss did attend the Yalta Conference as a special advisor to President Roosevelt, and he would, of course, have conferred with high officials of other nations attending the conference."[117] The information that Hiss flew on the State Department plane from Yalta to Moscow confirmed the identification.

Hiss's Last Report

On September 12, 1946, columnist Drew Pearson wrote an article based on a classified U.S. military study of British military operations against the Greek Communist insurgency. Although Pearson misquoted the report, it was clear that he had seen a copy. This created great concern in State Department security since the document also contained highly classified information on the British order of battle in Greece. The document had been in the office of Alger Hiss.

The investigation showed that the document, prepared at the request of the State Department, was missing. It also showed a serious security laxness in Hiss's Office of Special Political Affairs. The office had frequently ordered extra copies of classified documents which then went missing. When Hiss was questioned about this, he immediately denied responsibility. In the days before Xerox machines, a spy had to copy, retype, or photograph a document. If extra copies were lying around, it was relatively easy to steal one. The investigation indicated that the document had reached Drew Pearson, thanks to his reporter David Karr.[118]

A sensitive document, such as this report, would first be used by the KGB for its intelligence value and then passed to a different agent to exploit in a disinformation operation. David Karr was the other agent. Starting in the 1930s as a reporter for the *Daily Worker*, and therefore a member of the Communist Party, Karr worked his way into the legitimate newspaper business. After World War II, the poor boy from New York turned reporter suddenly had a new career as an international financier and wheeler-dealer, with access to important Western political figures. Cynics suspected that he was working for the KGB and that his vast wealth was supplied by the Soviet government.

The cynics were proved right when in 1992 one of Russia's best journalists, Yevgenia Albats, found an important KGB document in the Soviet archives. It showed that Karr had been regularly providing the KGB with information that was in turn relayed to the Central Committee of the Communist Party of the Soviet Union. The 1978 document, which showed the extent of Karr's political connections in the United States, stated:

> In 1978, American Senator Edward Kennedy appealed to the KGB to assist in establishing cooperation between Soviet organizations and the California firm Agritech, headed by former Senator J. Tunney. This firm in turn was connected to a French-American company, Finatech S.A., which was run by a

competent KGB source, the prominent Western financier D. Karr, through whom opinions had been confidentially exchanged for several years between the General Secretary of the Communist Party and Sen. Kennedy. D. Karr provided the KGB with technical information on conditions in the U.S. and other capitalist countries which were regularly reported to the Central Committee.[119]

Venona also provided information on Karr's work for the Soviets. In 1944 Soviet agent Samuel Krafsur relayed to Soviet intelligence officer Vladimir Pravdin information that he had received from Karr.[120] One of Karr's last business deals—he died July 7, 1979—was with Armand Hammer to market 1980 Soviet gold Olympic coins.[121] President Carter decided to boycott the Olympics because of the Soviet invasion of Afghanistan, but the coins were marketed anyway.

Despite his conviction, Alger Hiss's defenders have tried in every which way to discredit the evidence against him, as, for example, in 1962 when United Press International reported: "Attorney General Robert F. Kennedy said yesterday that new claims of innocence by convicted perjurer Alger Hiss are not supported by the facts."[122] But successive American governments and courts have repudiated all of them.

The last attempt to exonerate Hiss took place in 1992. The most active supporter of Hiss, John Lowenthal, contacted the highly respected Russian Colonel General Dmitry Volkogonov, who had been assigned by President Boris Yeltsin to oversee the Russian archives. He asked that the archives be checked to find material on Alger Hiss.

Volkogonov asked Yevgeny Primakov, then head of the Russian Foreign Intelligence Service (SVR), to examine the KGB archives and see if anything on Hiss could be found. Primakov responded that no documents in the KGB archives indicated that Hiss was a spy for the Soviet Union. When Lowenthal released the Volkogonov statement to the press, major stories in the *New York Times* and *Washington Post* claimed that Hiss was innocent.[123] But the story soon fell apart.

On November 11 Volkogonov visited Washington, and one of the authors of this book, Herbert Romerstein, was able to talk to him. When Romerstein pointed out that Hiss was an agent not of KGB (NKVD) but of military intelligence (GRU) and that he worked in an American Communist Party underground unit reporting to the GRU, Volkogonov said he needed to look in the files of the Communist International, as the GRU files were closed even to him.

Upon his return to the Soviet Union, Volkogonov sent a letter to the Moscow newspaper *Nezavisimaya Gazeta* in which he said:

> This year I received several fax appeals from Alger Hiss and his lawyer asking for help in elucidating whether this person acted as an agent of Soviet special services in the 1930s and 1940s. Of course, I sent them on to the Foreign Intelligence agency. But the requests continued. When I found out that Hiss was 88 years old and that he only wanted to die peacefully without being branded a "spy," I telephoned Ye. M. Primakov. He reasonably said that they give out no information about who is or is not a spy. However, he agreed to help determine the truth of the matter.
>
> I was able to visit the foreign intelligence archive several times. Its employees, on Primakov's instructions, said that A. Hiss was not registered in the documents as a recruited agent. I reported this to Hiss's lawyer, adding that perhaps the American's official contacts with Soviet diplomats had been considered espionage. After all, the Cold War was then at its height…. As to whether A. Hiss was or was not a "spy" I can render judgment only as a historian. The more so as, as far as I know, the agency

in which those documents from the 1950s were reviewed was not the only one which was involved in intelligence. Furthermore, there are no guarantees that they all survived.[124]

Three weeks after the article appeared in the Moscow newspaper, the *New York Times* got around to the story. Having devoted a half page on October 29 to exonerating Hiss, it carried one column on December 17 headed, "Russian General Retreats on Hiss." The *Times* interviewed General Volkogonov in the meantime. He admitted that "the Ministry of Defense also has an intelligence service, which is totally different, and many documents have been destroyed. I only looked through what the KGB had. All I said was that I saw no evidence." Volkogonov said that he never met Hiss, but "the attorney, Lowenthal, pushed me hard to say things of which I was not fully convinced."[125]

When General Volkogonov died in 1995, the *New York Times* in an obituary reported, "In 1992, he wrote a letter saying there was no evidence in KGB archives that Alger Hiss was a spy, which was read as an exoneration by the defenders of Mr. Hiss. The attendant furor in the United States forced the historian to retract his statement and concede that he had not examined all the files."[126]

When Alger Hiss died in 1996, the authors of this book wrote an article in *The New Republic* citing the recently released *Venona* documents exposing Hiss as an agent of one Soviet intelligence service, the GRU, and stating that he wanted to provide additional information to another Soviet service, the NKVD. Our article was entitled "Hiss: Still Guilty."[127]

The intertwined lives of Whittaker Chambers and Alger Hiss demonstrate how closely linked American Communists were to their Soviet spymasters and what a dangerously small and incestuous world it was. The Elizabeth Bentley case tells us even more.

CHAPTER 5

The Elizabeth Bentley Spy Rings

WHITTAKER CHAMBERS'S DEFECTION could not have come at a worse time for Soviet intelligence. Two other major disasters, both ordered by Stalin, took place at the same time. The first was the transfer of most intelligence collections from military intelligence—the GRU—to foreign intelligence—the NKVD. The second was the purge, which decimated both the GRU and the NKVD. Many of the victims were Stalin loyalists, but this mattered little to Lavrenti Beria, Stalin's chief of internal repression and foreign intelligence, who carried out the killings.

Because of Whittaker Chambers's defection, the Soviets had to make significant changes in their intelligence operation in the United States. J. Peters was removed as leader of the underground—replaced by Rudy Baker—and allowed to run a small ring in the government that provided information only to the American Communist Party leadership. The lack of trained intelligence officers due to the purge forced the NKVD temporarily to break contact with, or, in its words, "put on ice," many of the agents. That notwithstanding, the American Communist Party was able to maintain its underground apparatus. This state of affairs continued until 1941, when, after the Nazi attack on the Soviet Union, Vassiliy Zarubin returned as the NKVD *Rezident* and Iskhak Akhmerov as the "illegal" *Rezident*.

When Rudy Baker was in Moscow in January 1939 to report to the Comintern on the "work of the Conspiratorial Apparatus" of the

American Communist Party, he said that he had taken over the underground apparatus from J. Peters on June 13, 1938.[1] In the late 1920s Baker had been a Communist Party district organizer in Detroit and from 1927 to 1930 attended the International Lenin School in Moscow. From 1930 to 1931 he directed the American CP Organizational Department and then conducted illegal work for the Comintern in Korea, England, and Canada. In 1931 he lectured on the history of the Communist International for the Workers' School, the CPUSA training school in New York City.[2]

During World War II, Baker monitored the radio communications from the Comintern to the American Communist Party. The messages to Moscow from the CPUSA were transmitted through the NKVD. One revealing message was sent to Dimitroff, head of the Comintern, by the NKVD Foreign Department head, Fitin, in 1942. Fitin wrote, "We are sending you a telegram we received from Rudy [Baker] addressed to you from New York. 'The reception is good 8-9. One of your new chauffeurs is often negligent in his work.'" It was signed "Son," Baker's code name.[3] It is clear from the context that the chauffeur meant radio operator. It was another NKVD play on words, for in Russian the word chauffeur is spelled "schofer" and "cipher" is spelled "schifer."

On October 2, 1941, the American Communist Party representative to the Comintern, Pat Toohey, using the code name "Brother," sent a clandestine radio message to Baker. Toohey advised that "one of our friends named Cooper, who works in your country and whom we trust, is authorized to establish contact with you.... We gave him the address of Hannover, meet him there. The password for the meeting: 'I have something for you from Brother, some greetings.' After you establish direct contact with him, continue this contact not directly, but through one of your secret comrades."[4] "Hannover" or "Hanover" was the code name for a Communist Party underground safe house.

The Elizabeth Bentley Spy Rings

On October 25 Baker responded in a radio message to Toohey: "In future instead of Hanover meeting place use: Dr. R. Wasserman, 226/30 East Twelfth Street, New York. Should ask for Adams.... Cooper has not shown up."[5] "Cooper" was the code name for the recently returned Zarubin.

Dr. Rubin Wasserman was an old-time, trusted Communist, who had been at that address as early as 1939, when he signed a Communist Party Nominating Petition. He remained involved in Communist Party underground activities for many years. In 1953 Party member Edward Wolkenstein, assigned to penetrate the Bethlehem Steel Company in Buffalo, New York, gave Wasserman's name at the same address as a reference. Wolkenstein was assigned to clandestine penetration of basic industry by the CPUSA.[6]

In a message Baker sent to Toohey in Moscow on microfilm in January 1943, signed "Son" and addressed to "Brother," Baker revealed that during the year 1942 communications between the American Communist Party and Moscow were being handled by "Cooper." When Zarubin met with Steve Nelson, head of the Communist Party underground in California, he identified himself as "Cooper."[7] The message also referred to "Father," the code name for Earl Browder.[8] Two 1944 *Venona* messages from the NKVD New York *Rezidentura* referred to messages to and from "Son."[9] The NKVD was still carrying messages between the American Communist Party and the Comintern, which supposedly had been abolished in 1943. Later some radio communications between the American Communist Party and Moscow were handled by the GRU.

Jacob Golos

In order to maintain some spy work before the return of Zarubin and Akhmerov, the Soviets reactivated Jacob Golos, one of the most senior NKVD agents in the United States. KGB records recently released in Moscow reveal that Golos was born in 1890 in tsarist Russia as Jacob Raisen and worked in an underground Bolshevik organization until 1907 or 1908, when he was arrested and spent two years in prison in Siberia. He fled to the United States around 1910 and in 1915 joined the Socialist Party. In 1919 he was a founder of the American Communist Party and lived in the Soviet Union from 1926 until 1929.

In 1930, after returning to the United States, Golos began his work for the NKVD. Early messages from Soviet intelligence officers to the Moscow headquarters refer to him as our "reliable man in the U.S." In 1936 Golos sent his wife and son back to the Soviet Union, but he remained in the United States.

During the 1930s Golos made numerous trips to the Soviet Union on false passports, including one in 1937 when he led a delegation to celebrate the twentieth anniversary of the Soviet Revolution. At that time, he was honored by being taken to meet A. Slutsky, the head of the Foreign Department of the OGPU. Golos received no money from the Soviets for his work, but in 1937 Pavel Gutzeit, the NKVD *Resident* in New York, insisted that he be given $100 to $150 a month to pay the expenses of his cover business, World Tourists, Inc., a travel agency used by the NKVD and the American Communist Party to handle secret trips between the United States and the Soviet Union. On his return to the Soviet Union, Gutzeit became another victim of the purge.

In 1939 one of the few NKVD officers still in the United States, Gaik Ovakimian, was ordered to contact Golos and instruct him to reestablish an agent network. In NKVD terms, Golos was called both a group leader and a *Resident*. Although the latter term usually referred to the Soviet officer who headed the NKVD *Rezidentura*, it was also sometimes used for senior agents who ran networks. In May 1941 Ovakimian, who used the Soviet trade organization Amtorg as his cover and therefore did not have diplomatic immunity, was arrested by the FBI and in July was deported.

In 1940 the overworked Ovakimian had turned Golos over to his deputy, Pavel Klarin—*Venona* code name, "Luka"; real name, Pavel Pastelnyak. Klarin did not like Golos. In April 1940 he complained that Golos was the "Achilles heel" of the *Rezidentura* and that working with him would cause its operations to collapse. Golos had been arrested by the FBI in October 1939 for failing to register the public activities of World Tourists under the Foreign Agents Registration Act. He pleaded guilty and paid a fine. As a result, the FBI began surveillance of Golos, and Klarin was concerned that he would inadvertently lead the American investigators to the NKVD operations. KGB files show that Soviet spies provided the NKVD with FBI reports revealing that Golos and Ovakimian had been seen together on February 18, 1941. Klarin's concern was real, but he overstated it, and Moscow, trusting Golos, ignored him.

When Ovakimian was arrested in May 1941, Klarin broke contact with Golos. But a few months later, when Zarubin arrived back in the United States as *Rezident*, he took over the Golos operation and continued to work with him until Golos's death in November 1943.[10] Even though Moscow had recommended that an NKVD officer gradually take over the Golos operations, there were not enough Soviet officers to handle all of the work, so Klarin remained in New York under cover of vice consul and worked under Zarubin until November 1943.

The code name of Golos was "Zvuk," the Russian word for sound, a play on his adopted name Golos, the Russian word for voice. By July 1940 Golos had twenty possible agents under cultivation. The official KGB history book said that only after Golos's death "did it suddenly become clear [to the NKVD] what colossal work Golos had done, and consequently how much he knew about the affairs of the Soviet special services."

In October 1939 a message from the New York *Rezidentura* reported, "Recently through 'Zvuk' [Golos] we have obtained ten blank forms signed and stamped by [New York] City, which can be used to obtain birth certificates and then to apply for passports as American citizens, as well as similar forms without signature. More than seventy naturalization certificates for persons of different nationalities, and twenty-seven birth certificates which may also be used to obtain passports."[11] It was through his friend Bedacht and the other agents in the International Workers Order that Golos was able to obtain such documents.

In December of 1940 Golos learned that he was being investigated by the Dies Committee, the Special Committee on Un-American Activities. He brought a large package to his girlfriend, Elizabeth Bentley, because she had a fireplace in her apartment where he could burn incriminating documents. As she helped him burn the documents, she could see what they were and later told the FBI:

> I observed [that] a great amount of this material consisted of letters and pamphlets in Russian.... I also recall definitely that he burned a small folder that appeared to be either an identification card or credentials. His photograph was on one side of the flap with his signature and on the other side was something in Russian, and in the middle there appeared the letters OGPU in bold type. Although I did not have a thorough knowledge of the Russian language, I had studied this language for about one month and was able to distinguish the various letters of the alphabet, and I am quite sure that I recognized those letters to be OGPU. I asked him what this folder was and he informed me that those were his credentials which he used in Russia and

his replies indicated that he was connected in some manner with the Soviet Secret Police.

Bentley revealed to the FBI that as a member of the Communist Party, she became involved in NKVD operations when she fell in love with Jacob Golos, who was eighteen years her senior and had a wife and son in the Soviet Union. She became both his mistress and his most important coworker.

Born in Connecticut in 1908, Bentley joined the Communist Party in 1935 while at Columbia University. She studied Italian, visited fascist Italy, and, horrified by what she saw, volunteered to do "antifascist work." She was introduced by Pauline Rogers, a fellow Communist Party member, to Juliet Stuart Poyntz, an old Communist Party apparatchik who was recruiting people for "underground work." She was not recruited at that time but later heard in the Party that Poyntz had disappeared. When she later mentioned this to Golos, he told her that Poyntz was a traitor and had been liquidated by the Soviet intelligence service.

In June 1938 the Columbia Placement Bureau arranged a job for her with the Italian Government Library in New York. Pauline Rogers put her in contact with a man who used the name F. Brown in the open Communist Party and Mario Alpi in the underground. He was actually one of the Communist International's representatives in the United States and was assigned to the Italian bureau of the Party. In October 1938 Brown introduced her to Jacob Golos, and she began to supply him with information on Italian fascist activities. In March 1939 she was fired by the Italians when they found she had written an antifascist article for the *Columbia Spectator*, an official college newspaper.[12]

Bentley and Golos soon became lovers, and she became his "good right arm." His affectionate nickname for her was

"Umnista," the Russian word for "smart girl," or, in teacher language, "pet female student." When NSA discovered that "Umnitsa" was a *Venona* code name, it translated the name as "good girl" or "clever girl," which was almost right. After the death of Golos, Bentley's *Venona* code name was changed to "Myrna."

The Silvermaster Ring

In late June 1941, Golos's old friend Earl Browder contacted him and said that a group of government employees in Washington wanted to help the Soviet Union, which had just been attacked by Nazi Germany. The information these government employees could garner could be very valuable.[13] This group, Nathan Gregory Silvermaster's group, was one of those "put on ice" when the Soviet "illegal" intelligence officer Iskhak Akhmerov returned to Moscow in 1939. Browder put him in touch with Jacob Golos.

Golos had a problem—Ovakimian was under arrest, and, as noted, Golos did not get along well with his deputy, Klarin. In addition, Zarubin had not yet arrived in the United States. Nevertheless, an opportunity like this could not be ignored. Golos met with Silvermaster and learned the details about his group of Communist government employees. In August 1941 Golos was sick and sent Bentley to meet with the Silvermaster group. The National Security Agency, in its release of the *Venona* intercepts, commented, "In *Venona* we also see some persons who appear to fall somewhere in between agent and officer. American Communists Jacob Golos, Elizabeth Bentley, and Greg Silvermaster, veteran controllers of agent networks, could be placed in this category. In fact, Silvermaster was at one time the only American citizen in the KGB Hall of Fame in Moscow."[14]

Silvermaster was not recruited in the 1930s on the basis of anti-Nazism, as were other members of his ring. He was an old-time Communist. The earliest reference to Silvermaster in the FBI files

The Elizabeth Bentley Spy Rings

was a report from Seattle dated April 11, 1922, stating that "Nathan Silvermaster, a young Communist of the University District Seattle... [a student] at the University of Washington had left April 9, 1922, for San Francisco." According to the FBI, "Silvermaster was stated to be a known Communist...." In the San Francisco Bay area, Silvermaster taught economics at St. Mary's College from 1926 to 1931. He was also identified as a close associate of Isaac Folkoff,[15] who was to reappear during World War II as part of the Soviet spy ring involved in atomic espionage.

The FBI said that "the files of the Department of Agriculture contain a report which revealed that Silvermaster in 1935 contacted Sam Darcy, head of the Communist Party of California. This report further states, 'By virtue of his associations and his affiliations and particularly by virtue of his thesis, it can be easily concluded that Silvermaster is an active radical.'" The FBI did not reveal the original source of this information. It was American Legion member Pat Silberstein, who had penetrated the Communist movement on behalf of the Legion. Until the late 1930s, the FBI had no penetration of the Communist Party. When the FBI was ordered by President Roosevelt to watch the Communists, it had to play catch-up. The local police and the American Legion supplied it with much of its information. But most of their sources, such as Silberstein, were at low levels in the Communist movement, and it was only by coincidence that they might stumble on information concerning espionage agents.

In early 1934 Silberstein joined a Communist front, the Workers Ex-Servicemen's League, which gave him access to some of the Communist leaders in California. In a report for the American Legion written in 1936, Silberstein stated:

> My first contact with Mr. Gregory Silvermaster was the early
> part of July, 1934. I was sitting in the office of Sam Darcy who

is head of the Communist Party in California and candidate for Governor on that ticket. I was then in the confidences of the higher-ups of this Party. While in his office a telephone message came which was answered by Mrs. Catherine McGee. She came into the office and said that Silvermaster was on the phone. Darcy answered the phone and said "Hello, Gregory" and made a later date with him. This aroused my suspicions and I immediately checked up on Silvermaster and found that he was then in charge of the Research and Statistical Department of the S.E.R.A. [California State Emergency Relief Administration].

Silberstein also reported that Silvermaster had gone to Washington to take a job in the Agriculture Department. On October 9, 1935, based on the Silberstein report, the California American Legion wrote to the Legion's National Americanism Commission in Washington with information on Silvermaster. The Washington headquarters confirmed that Silvermaster had been appointed to a job in the Agricultural Adjustment Administration (AAA) on August 15, 1935.[16]

FBI files reveal that after his AAA job, Silvermaster transferred to the Maritime Labor Board in November 1938. He returned to the Agriculture Department in July 1940 but later transferred to the Board of Economic Warfare and subsequently to the Treasury Department.[17]

According to the FBI, Silvermaster's wife was born in Russia and was the daughter of Baltic baron Peter Witte, an influential counselor to the tsar. Although arrested by the Bolsheviks, he was later released and allowed to head a scientific institute. The FBI also reported that William Ludwig Ullman, another member of the spy ring, resided with the Silvermasters during the war.[18]

The Elizabeth Bentley Spy Rings

In August 1941 Bentley visited Helen Silvermaster in Washington and again two weeks later, when she was given secret U.S. government documents and introduced to Ullman.[19]

Silvermaster was a rich source for Soviet intelligence. He collected some of the information himself, but most was provided by his agents, including Ullman, Harry Dexter White, and Lauchlin Currie, an important White House official. In May 1942 *Venona* messages were sent by the NKVD New York to Moscow with detailed information about American airplane and artillery production. This information was provided by Silvermaster, then code-named "Pel."[20] Military production figures were obviously closely guarded secrets during wartime.

In 1942 U.S. military counterintelligence reported to the War Department its suspicions that Silvermaster was a Communist and should therefore not have access to secret and confidential information. When Silvermaster was shown the report by his superiors, he wrote a memorandum denying the allegations. His denial was believed by Robert P. Patterson, undersecretary of war, who wrote to Silvermaster's employer, the Board of Economic Warfare: "I am fully satisfied that the facts do not show anything derogatory to Mr. Silvermaster's character or loyalty to the United States, and that the charges in the report of June 3rd are unfounded."[21]

In September 1943 the New York *Rezidentura* reported to Moscow in a *Venona* message that Golos said the FBI had resumed its investigation of Silvermaster—a few days earlier two FBI representatives had visited Lauchlin Currie and asked him whether Silvermaster was a Communist Party member.[22] Currie told the FBI that he did not believe that Silvermaster was a Communist, according to the FBI's report.[23]

Bentley reported to the FBI in 1945 that although she had never met Currie, she had been told by Silvermaster and George

Silverman, another member of the ring, that he furnished them with secret information. She recalled that on one occasion Currie had passed the information that "the United States was on the verge of breaking the Soviet code."

After the death of Golos, Silvermaster, according to Bentley, discussed with "Bill" (what the agents called Akhmerov) the advisability of introducing Currie and White directly to a Russian contact. Silvermaster mentioned this to Bentley and indicated that he was against the idea.[24]

Bentley of course knew nothing of *Venona*, but her account of the request from Akhmerov for direct contact with the agents was confirmed in a *Venona* message of February 15, 1945. Moscow headquarters asked New York to "find out from Akhmerov ["Albert"] and Silvermaster ["Robert"] whether it would be possible for us to approach Currie ["Pazh"] direct."[25]

Silvermaster felt that he was important enough to have personal contact with the agents—the Russians were not needed. He was a valuable agent, and he knew it; the information he passed to the NKVD was a serious threat to American security. New York NKVD reported to Moscow via *Venona* on July 1, 1944, that, according to Silvermaster, Ullman ["Polo"] and an unidentified agent, code name "Tur," reported that "ANVIL has been postponed until 15 August."[26] "Anvil" was the American-British code name for a plan to invade southern France and thus take pressure off the troops at Normandy. The plan had been postponed a few times, and the Americans were pressing the British to launch it on August 15. The final decision was taken shortly before July 2,[27] and the Soviets had the information by July 1. This was extremely dangerous information. If the Nazis had learned of it through poor Soviet communications, American and British lives would have been put at risk. But the spy ring supplying classified American information to the

Soviets had little concern about compromising American secrets. Its only interest was in helping the Soviet Union.

When the United States began making plans for the postwar military, Silvermaster immediately passed the secret information to the Soviets.[28] He also obtained a fifty-page top secret report of the War Production Board. Because of its length, it could not be communicated by *Venona* and was sent to Moscow by courier.[29]

Silvermaster was also able to provide the Soviets with reports from the OSS, the U.S. intelligence service.[30] Moscow responded by instructing NKVD New York to obtain detailed information on OSS employees through Silvermaster.[31]

Moscow was very concerned about non-Communist, anti-Nazi opposition groups in Germany. Such people in the future Soviet occupation zone might create difficulties. Silvermaster came to the rescue by providing information on these people, some of whom had been in touch with American intelligence. The OSS had provided the U.S. Army with twenty thousand names of reliable, anti-Nazi Germans. The British had compiled a similar list of Austrians.[32]

At times, Silvermaster's spy ring collected so much classified information that it was cumbersome. The documents were photographed by Ullman, and the microfilms turned over to the NKVD. In October 1944 Silvermaster handed over fifty-six undeveloped films. These included economic warfare reports and a memorandum for the president on Lend-Lease to France.[33]

On Moscow's instructions, Silvermaster's material was in the future to be broken into small packages and carried by courier to New York for shipment. It was handled by the NKVD "illegal" group headed by Akhmerov. Three agents were assigned as couriers to collect information from Silvermaster and his wife (code name "Dora"). The couriers were instructed to bring the packages to Olga Khlopkova, a clerk at the Soviet consulate in New York.[34] In January

1945 Khlopkova had been assigned as liaison with Akhmerov. In March she was given permission by Moscow to meet with Helen Lowry, the American wife of Akhmerov, to coordinate the operation.[35] Lowry, remember, was the niece of American Communist Party leader Earl Browder.

Based on Bentley's information, the FBI began a physical surveillance of Silvermaster on November 17, 1945, and identified one of the couriers. On December 1 the bureau saw Alexander Koral enter Silvermaster's car and drive around for a long time. Afterwards Koral was followed back to New York. This confirmed Bentley's explanation to the FBI of how Soviet agents transferred documents while driving.[36]

Koral was called before the House Committee on Un-American Activities in 1948. The committee believed that he would provide significant information on the Soviet spy ring. Information leaked to the press generated headlines such as "Key Spy Witness on Stand, Koral May Tell Inside on Ring" (*New York Journal American*, August 9, 1948). Instead, he invoked the Fifth Amendment on Communist Party membership and on whether he knew Silvermaster. After his testimony, committee investigator Louis J. Russell took the witness stand and revealed information that could have come only from Koral. According to Russell, in 1939 Koral was approached by a man called "Frank" who offered him money to serve as a courier. Koral was in need of funds at the time for medical bills for his son. Koral would meet with unidentified people and bring back the package to give to "Frank." In October 1945 Koral was told by "Frank" to travel to Washington and meet with "Greg." His meeting in Washington was with Gregory and Helen Silvermaster.

Russell reported that in December 1945 Koral returned to Washington and advised Silvermaster that he would no longer be meeting with him. He received a package from Silvermaster which he later turned over to "Frank."[37] Koral later testified before a grand jury and appeared at a closed session before the House Committee on Un-American Activities. At a later public session, it seemed that Koral had "confessed" his espionage activities. But if Koral had, he apparently did not tell the whole story. He made no reference to the female officer with whom Khlopkova worked, nor did he mention Akhmerov, whom he knew as "Bill." The FBI did not learn about Khlopkova until the *Venona* messages were broken years later.

Because he invoked the Fifth Amendment, Koral was dismissed from his job as an engineer for the New York City school system. Koral sued to regain his job, but the suit failed. State Supreme Court Justice Ferdinand Pecora upheld Koral's dismissal, ruling: "The questions directed to petitioner by the congressional committee, which he declined to answer, concern espionage activities by him. Spying on the government is incompatible with an obligation of loyalty to that government."[38]

Apparently Koral's comrades believed he was cooperating with the government and did little to defend him when he was fired. The board of education subsequently used the legal finding in the Koral case as part of the basis for ousting teachers who invoked the Fifth Amendment when asked about their Communist Party membership.

Although the FBI did not begin physical surveillance of Silvermaster until November of 1945, the NKVD was concerned that an investigation might identify other agents. As early as January 1945, it decided to remove the filming facilities from Silvermaster's home, to which Silvermaster agreed when he was assured that he would not lose control and that the change was for security reasons only. In addition, he would not lose Ullman, who lived in the Silvermaster home and had been doing the photography.

Bela and Sonia Gold, a husband-and-wife team of Communist Party members, were given the job of photographing the documents.

But Gregory and Helen Silvermaster were concerned about the reliability of the Golds. Akhmerov, however, assured them that there was no problem, that they were loyal Communists. Akhmerov reported to Moscow, "Being their leader in the Communist Party line [apparatus] Silvermaster could give them orders."[39]

To keep both the officers and the agents happy, Moscow authorized awarding medals to show appreciation. Lavrenti Beria, Soviet head of intelligence and security, wrote to Stalin himself requesting permission to give medals to "the most distinguished employees of the 1st (Intelligence) Directorate, NKVD/NKGB, USSR...." The Russian officers received the Order of the Red Banner, a medal awarded for courage in combat against the enemy, and some of the agents received a medal for courage only slightly less significant, the Order of the Red Star. Among those who received the Red Banner medals were Akhmerov and Apresyan. Among the agents who received the Red Star were Silvermaster, Elizabeth Bentley, and the courier for the atomic spy ring, Harry Gold.[40]

Akhmerov reported in a *Venona* message that Silvermaster was overjoyed with his medal: "[H]e says his work for us is the one good thing he has done in his life." Silvermaster considered the award not only a personal honor but also an honor to his group. He asked if he could show the medal and the award book that accompanied it.

In the same message, Akhmerov and his wife, code name "El" and "Eliza," also thanked Moscow for his medal. The message was signed by Apresyan.[41] On February 10 Apresyan told Moscow that his wife, Alexandra, code name "Zoya," and he "express sincere gratitude to our government for the high award it has bestowed upon us...."[42]

The Perlo Ring

In May 1944 a new group of agents came under the jurisdiction of Golos and Bentley. This group had been working with J. Peters and supplied its information only to the American Communist Party leadership. Peters and Golos were old friends. In 1932, when J. Peters was the American Communist Party representative to the Comintern, Golos visited Moscow, and Peters arranged for his contacts. [43]

Peters, sometimes called Peter, had fallen on hard times in the Party, although he retained contact with the NKVD and was carried on its books as a *Rezident* or group leader. His *Venona* code name was "Storm."[44] On March 5, 1943, a GRU official named Ilyichev sent a memo to Comintern head Dimitroff. He wrote: "Our representative in the US has advised us that a Communist group is active in Washington to provide the CPUSA leadership with information. The group is headed by the Central Committee worker 'Peter.' Our representative further informs us that some members of the group are unhappy with 'Peter' as he hardly pays any attention to the work of collecting information and takes no interest in the information he receives. Please inform us if this is your group."

Receiving no answer, an official of the GRU, Bolshakov, wrote to Dimitroff on May 5: "I ask that you instruct your people to speed up the reply to our letter of March the 5th... concerning the group of workers selected by the Central Committee of the CPUSA for information work and headed by the Central Committee worker 'Peter.' We are interested in whether it is your group."[45] The authors of this book could not find an answer from Dimitroff in the Moscow files but know that the case was taken over by the NKVD.

Elizabeth Bentley told the FBI in 1945 how she had inherited the "Perlo group" from Jacob Golos. She said:

> Approximately one or two months prior to the death of Golos in November 1943, he remarked to me that he had very recently made contact with another group in Washington and he seemed to regard this acquisition as valuable.... It is my

recollection that he indicated to me that he had been placed in contact with this new group by Earl Browder.... I learned nothing further... until early in 1944 when Browder mentioned to me that Golos had been contacting the group in Washington and had been unable to keep an appointment with them as the date for such meeting came on the Sunday after Golos' death on Thanksgiving Day, 1943. He told me he was anxious for me to meet this group and that he might make necessary arrangements for such meeting. Approximately two months after this conversation between Browder and myself early in 1944 he informed me that he had been able to make appropriate arrangements and directed that in order to meet this group I should go to the apartment of Mr. John Abt, on Central Park West near 90th Street... in New York City.

On the date specified I went to the apartment of John Abt, was admitted by him to his apartment and there met four individuals none of whom I had ever seen before. They were introduced to me as Victor Perlo, Charlie Kramer, Henry Magdoff and Edward Fitzgerald. They seemed to know, at least generally, that they could talk freely in my presence and I recall some conversation about their paying Communist Party dues to me, as well as my furnishing them with Communist Party literature. There followed then a general discussion among all of us as to the type of information which those people, except Abt, would be able to furnish. It was obvious to me that those people, including Abt, had been associated for some time and that they had been engaged in some sort of espionage for Earl Browder.

I recall that Perlo, who at that time had a position in the War Production Board, declared he would be able to supply statistical data in the aircraft field generally; that Kramer, who I believed at that time was associated with Senator Harley Kilgore's Committee [the Subcommittee on War Mobilization] in Washington, said he would be able to pass along Capitol Hill gossip; that Magdoff, who had just returned from a period of approximately six months' hospitalization, expected to return to the War Production Board but was uncertain as to what specifically he would be able to furnish; and that Edward Fitzgerald, at that time also in the War Production Board, indicated he would be able to furnish me with miscellaneous statistical information coming to his attention in the War Production Board.[46]

Perlo and the rest told her about other members of their group, including Donald Wheeler at OSS and Harold Glasser. Bentley could provide no documentary evidence, but her story was consistent with other information developed through FBI investigation. It was only after the decoding of *Venona* messages during the 1960s and research in Soviet archives in the 1990s that Bentley's revelations were fully confirmed.

In 1943, while the Perlo group was still reporting to the American Communist Party leadership, two partially broken messages indicated that the NKVD should get in touch with Communist Party official Eugene Dennis in regard to some project.[47] Dennis, a longtime Comintern apparatchik, was also involved in the penetration of OSS.[48]

Bentley didn't know it yet, but the NKVD planned to take direct control of this group, despite Browder's having put Golos and Bentley into the loop. A *Venona* message in April 1944 told Moscow that the New York *Rezidentura* also wanted to take over direct contacts with the Silvermaster group. Akhmerov reported in the message that on April 27 Bentley had told him that, after the death of Golos, Browder had assigned her to deal with the group. She was, of course, passing on the information she received to Akhmerov. Bentley said that before meeting with her, Silvermaster would first meet with Browder and that her meetings with Silvermaster required Browder's permission. Even Golos, she said, met with Silvermaster only once every six months. Akhmerov was not satisfied with her claim that she needed Browder's permission for each meeting and reported to Moscow, "Possibly she is making this up and exaggerating" in order to maintain exclusive control over contacts with the agents. He referred to Bentley's "unreasonable fear that we would contact them directly." Akhmerov suggested that either Zarubin, the *Rezident*, or he should see Browder and come to some agreement about this matter and Bentley's role.

Further along in the message, Akhmerov referred to the Perlo group, which had been contacted through John Abt. He gave the agents' true names: "Kramer, Perlo, Flato, Glasser, Edward Fitzgerald and others in a group of seven or eight Communist Party members." Bentley had spoken to Abt and Perlo, and "they told her that this group was neglected and that nobody was interested in them. Kramer is the leader of the group. All occupy responsible posts in Washington." In a partially broken portion of the message, Akhmerov referred to Soviet military intelligence, which had been in contact with the group earlier, and said, "For more than a year 'Maksim' [Zarubin] and I tried to get in touch with Perlo and Flato. For some reason or other 'Rulevoj' [Browder] did not come to the meeting and just decided to put 'U' [Bentley] in touch with the whole group. If we work with this group, it will be necessary to remove her...." Akhmerov continued, "Recently I met Perlo by chance in 'Arena's' [Mary Price's] flat." Interestingly, Akhmerov told Moscow that he had never met Browder, his wife's uncle.[49] Other messages show that the direct contact with Browder was being handled by the legal *Rezident*, Zarubin.

On May 13, 1944, the New York *Rezidentura* sent a *Venona* message from Akhmerov explaining the background of the case to Moscow: "On 'Rulevoj's' [Earl Browder's] instructions 'Umnitsa'

The Elizabeth Bentley Spy Rings

[Bentley] contacted through 'Amt' [John Abt] a new group in Washington D.C." One of them, Harry Magdoff, appeared in the message in his true name and with his new *Venona* code name, "Kant." Bentley's impressions of the group were reported by Akhmerov: "They are reliable Communist Party members, politically highly mature; they want to help with information. They said that they had been neglected and no one had taken any interest in their potential...." J. Peters ("Storm") had maintained contact with the group, but the new arrangements required that four members of the group take turns traveling to New York every two weeks to provide information. The four were "Raider" (Victor Perlo), "Plumb" (Charles Kramer), "Ted" (Edward Fitzgerald), and "Kant" (Magdoff). Kramer and Fitzgerald already knew Silvermaster, according to Akhmerov, who promised Moscow background information on them.[50]

On May 30 the promised background information on the agents was sent to Moscow in a *Venona* message, based on the personal history the agents had provided:

> "Ted" [Edward Joseph Fitzgerald]—old Communist Party member, capable, reliable, works in the Civilian Allocation Division of the War Production Board.
>
> "Kant" [Harry Samuel Magdoff]—became a Communist Party member a long time ago, works in the Machine Tool Division of the War Production Board.
>
> "Raider" [Victor Perlo]—an old Communist Party member, reliable, capable, works in the Airplane Allocation Division of the War Production Board. [A partially broken section of the message referred to his contacts with "Arena" (Mary Price) and "Storm" (J. Peters).]
>
> "Plumb" [Charles Kramer]—an old Communist Party member, works in the Kilgore Committee. [In 1944 Charles Kramer served as an economic advisor to Senator Harley M.

Kilgore's Subcommittee on War Mobilization of the Senate Committee on Military Affairs.]

"Izra" [Donald Wheeler]—has been a Communist Party member for several years, a trade union official, capable, works in the Labor Division Research and Analysis Branch of the Office of Strategic Services.

Harold Glasser, who was temporarily abroad, was identified as an old Communist Party member whom J. Peters knew well. In a partially broken section of the message, Jacob Golos is mentioned, as is the use of trade unions and other contacts by the CPUSA.[51]

A document in the Comintern archives shows that in September 1944 Pavel Fitin, head of the Foreign Department of the NKVD, sent some of the same names of the Perlo group to George Dimitroff, head of the Comintern—which continued to function although it had allegedly been dissolved a year earlier—to be checked out for political reliability.

The Fitin memorandum stated:

Top Secret

Com. Dimitroff

Please communicate information regarding these members of the Communist Party of America:

1. *Charles Flato*, in 1943 worked at the Board of Economic Warfare USA.

2. *Donald Wheeler*, works in a department of the Office of Strategic Services.

3. [*Charles*] *Kramer*, works in Washington in a government office.

4. *Edward Fitzgerald*, works in War Production Board.

5. [*Harry*] *Magdoff*, works in War Production Board.

The Elizabeth Bentley Spy Rings

6. *Harold Glasser*, on assignment abroad.

7. *[Victor] Perlo*, works in War Production Board.

Fitin

28/29 September, 1944[52]

In Moscow, Fitin asked the New York *Rezidentura* about the channels used by the NKVD in the United States to obtain information from agents. A February 1944 message says it clearly: "The Silvermaster material goes through Bentley" and is processed for shipment to Moscow by Akhmerov.[53]

By July 1944 Akhmerov had established personal contact with Silvermaster, which made Bentley very unhappy. Akhmerov wrote a lengthy report about the problem, which was sent by pouch to Moscow. We have a summary of the report because it was transmitted via *Venona*. It read, "Bentley has very much taken to heart the fact of Akhmerov's direct contact with Silvermaster, evidently supposing that we do not trust her. She is offended by Browder consenting to our liaison with Silvermaster."[54]

Mary Price was one of the Communist Party members reporting to Moscow through Bentley. She had been assigned as an undercover Soviet agent in the office of Walter Lippmann, the well-known non-Communist journalist.[55] As a result of a July 1944 meeting with Bentley, the New York *Rezidentura* reported:

Some weeks ago Bentley ["Umnitsa"] told Akhmerov ["Mer"] that Browder ["Rulevoj"], as a result of a conversation with Mary Price ["Dir"], had apparently decided that Price must be withdrawn completely from our work in order to employ her fully in Communist Party USA work. In Browder's opinion Price's nerves had been badly shaken and her health is poor, which renders her unsuitable for our work. In Akhmerov's opinion it is possible to get Browder to change his opinion about the advisability of this decision, which Akhmerov suspects was made under pressure from Bentley, who for some reason dislikes Price. Akhmerov has informed Bentley that if Price is really ill she will need rather to be withdrawn for a rest, but afterwards be used in liaison with a conspirative apartment [NKVD safe house], etc. She has been working for a long time and has acquired considerable experience. Akhmerov proposes that she should not be employed in active Communist Party work. Telegraph your opinion.[56]

That Browder had this kind of influence over the way the NKVD used its agents showed the extent of his power. Akhmerov did not suggest ordering Browder about how to handle Price but believed that he could be convinced to change his mind. Further on in the message, Akhmerov raised a different question with Moscow. He felt that it would be useful to provide military information to the GRU (Soviet military intelligence), which he referred to as "the neighbors," because "the lack of exchange of information with the neighbors here does not contribute, in my view, to our friendly relations...." Akhmerov suggested that if the NKVD were given permission to provide the information, it should conceal the identity of the sources because of "the danger of [GRU] people possibly being sent to check our sources."[57]

Despite the conflict between Bentley and her Soviet handlers over who would maintain contact with the agents, Bentley remained important to the NKVD. In November 1944 the honorary chairman of Russian War Relief, Allen Wardwell, wrote a letter to a Soviet official suggesting that an organization be set up to send parcels to Russia. This did not sit well with the NKVD *Rezidentura* because World Tourists, run since the death of Golos by Bentley, did just that kind of work, and it was the cover Bentley used for her espionage activity. Bentley, whose *Venona* code name had been changed to "Myrna," was still working for the Soviets, and they still had plans for her. Thus, to undermine Wardwell's plan, the New York *Rezidentura* suggested that he be told to contact Anastas Mikoyan, the Soviet commissar for foreign trade in Moscow. Mikoyan would be advised to turn Wardwell down.[58]

The NKVD was doing well—the information that Moscow wanted was flowing regularly. In June 1944, for example, the New York *Rezidentura* reported to Moscow that at Akhmerov's request Silvermaster had obtained copies of the pilots' operating manual for the most important American fighter planes and bombers, including the B-25G.[59]

Harold Glasser, a member of the Perlo group, was another valuable asset. In May 1944 he was promoted to assistant director of monetary research for the Treasury Department. He had earlier been temporarily loaned to the War Production Board. He was highly regarded in his job and had access to a considerable amount of sensitive information.

Later, Glasser was transferred from the Perlo to the Silvermaster group. Glasser's secretary, Sonia Gold ("Zhenya"), was already working for Silvermaster.[60]

Charles Kramer, who was named a Soviet agent by Whittaker Chambers, was also named by Elizabeth Bentley as a member of the Perlo group. He invoked the Fifth Amendment on both when asked by the Senate Subcommittee on Internal Security but said he had worked for Senator Kilgore's subcommittee doing "research on the influence of cartels on mobilization and the war effort."[61]

Lauchlin Currie, for his part, worked at the White House as a spy and as an agent of influence and was one of the most important sources of information for the Silvermaster ring. He passed his information on to the Soviets through Silvermaster and George Silverman.

Currie's help to the Soviets included using a political fixer to protect a State Department official who had passed classified information to a pro-Communist magazine, *Amerasia*, which was owned and edited by Earl Browder's friend Philip Jaffe. On June 5, 1945, six people, including State Department official John Stewart Service, were arrested by the FBI on espionage charges. The evidence against them consisted of copies of classified documents found in the office of *Amerasia* by OSS investigators in a surreptitious entry to determine how the magazine was able to quote classified information.

On June 11 Currie contacted the Washington wheeler-dealer and fixer Thomas (Tommy the Cork) Corcoran and told him that he wanted the charges against Service to be dropped. Corcoran said that this might get him into trouble with other clients, so he would try to do it "on the side," but "if I have to, I may even come out front, but… I would rather not have to." After a number of contacts between Corcoran, Currie, and Service, Corcoran assured Service, "I did want you to know I'd gone right up to the top on the damn thing" and that he was sure he could get Service's name "cut out" of the case. When contacting Justice Department officials, Corcoran told them that he was helping Service for someone else but didn't mention the name Currie. Among those he spoke to was Attorney General Tom Clark. The fixer succeeded with the help of the Justice Department attorneys, and the grand jury did not indict Service for espionage. Philip Jaffe paid only a small fine. The FBI knew all about this because it had a wiretap on Corcoran and heard his conversations with Currie, Service, and the Justice Department officials.[62]

The value to the Soviets of the *Amerasia* espionage operations protected by corruption and special favors was grasped only after the decryption of the *Venona* messages. In this case, they were GRU rather than NKVD communications. Even though only a few GRU messages could be decrypted, those that were provide valuable insights. In June 1943 the GRU *Rezident* in New York, Pavel Mikhailov, reported to Moscow that one of his agents, Joseph Bernstein, had found a new recruit. Bernstein, who worked for *Amerasia*, had recruited T. A. Bisson,[63] who had just joined the staff of the Institute for Pacific Relations (IPR) and was the associate editor of IPR's magazine, *Pacific Affairs*.[64] Bisson had recently lost his job as principal economic analyst with the Board of Economic Warfare after admitting in a closed session before the Dies Committee that he was involved in some groups that the committee identified as Communist-controlled.[65]

Bisson's real name was revealed in *Venona*, as was his new cryptonym, "Artur." Bisson, Moscow had learned, turned over to Bernstein four reports that he had taken from the Board of Economic Warfare. One of them was a report that Bisson had written which revealed to the Soviets that "because of transport difficulties it is necessary finally to give up the idea of sending American troops to China; instead of this it is better to send arms to the Chinese army."[66]

Bisson joined the editorial board of *Amerasia* but in October 1945 was sent to Japan by the U.S. government to participate in the strategic bombing survey until March or April 1946.[67]

Currie was also helpful to another person identified by the FBI as a Soviet agent. He was a strange refugee from Nazi Germany who called himself Paul Hagen—real name Karl Frank. Hagen was under investigation by the FBI in an internal security case in 1945. During the investigation, the FBI learned that Lauchlin Currie, who was then being investigated in the espionage case, had once appeared as a sponsor for a visa application of Hagen. According to the FBI, "Hagen... has been alleged on numerous occasions to be a secret agent of the Soviet government. Hagen is an Austrian-German refugee who, since his arrival in the United States, has been active in the American Friends of German Freedom movement, a Communist inspired and infiltrated organization, and has also carried on the work of his group known as the 'New Beginning.' Hagen, at the time he was questioned in connection with his visa application, admitted being a member of the Communist Party in Europe from 1919 to 1929. He further admitted being a leader in this movement, but stated he had no contacts with Communists since his arrival in the United States. Investigation to date has indicated this statement is false as he has contacted numerous known Communists."[68]

Hagen had been a charter member of the German Communist Party but had left during a faction fight in 1929. Since 1915 he had been a close friend and associate of Gerhart Eisler, who remained in the Communist Party and later held high-level posts in the Comintern and in postwar East Germany. During the 1930s Hagen was the head of a left-socialist group called "New Beginning" which advocated collaboration with the Communists. The German Communist Party penetrated the group and supplied many of its internal documents to the Comintern. The documents, which are now in the archives of the German Communist Party, show that some were supplied by Hagen.[69]

Hagen attempted to gain employment with the OSS in 1942. In a report titled "Autobiographical Data," he told the agency that "during the later part of 1937 (July) I visited Spain, where several of my friends who had been active with the Loyalists had disappeared. I returned to Prague in August."[70] He neglected to mention his March 1937 trip to Spain, where he met with Gerhart Eisler. In a card sent from Barcelona to the members of his Paris organization, he wrote, "Much better than we anticipated!... Very pleasant discussion this morning with the Communist Party. Tomorrow I will be seeing Gerhard [in Valencia]!" "Gerhard" was

Gerhart Eisler. The card also said that Mark Rein, who was also involved in New Beginning, had just left Barcelona. The card was dated March 19, 1937.[71]

Rein was the son of Raphael Abramovich, a leader of the Russian Mensheviks who was considered by the Communists to be a major enemy, but Rein, his son, advocated collaboration with them. During the night of April 9–10, Mark Rein was abducted from his hotel in Barcelona by the Communist secret police. He was never seen again. Although he was not a danger to the Communists, he was the son of an enemy of the Soviet Union. The murder of his son was Raphael Abramovich's punishment.

Despite Hagen's claim that he had gone to Spain to investigate the disappearance of his friends, Abramovich felt that he had done little to clear up the disappearance of Rein, who, said the father, had gone to Spain on behalf of Hagen and had come in contact with the Communists as a result.[72]

In 1937 Hagen went to the United States to raise money for the New Beginning Group. In May he reported to his comrades in Europe that he had found a valuable and wealthy contact. Of all the wealthy anti-Nazi Americans that Hagen might encounter, the one he did find was the Soviet agent Alfred K. Stern, to whom Hagen gave the code name "Stone."[73] Some of the FBI's information on the Communist and Soviet espionage connections of Hagen came from the German Labor Delegation, an organization of social democrats and trade unionists who had escaped from Nazi Germany.

Target: Eleanor Roosevelt

In August 1943 the New York NKVD *Rezidentura* reported to Moscow that Paul Hagen "is close to the wife of President Roosevelt."[74] This message related to an earlier one in May in which the *Rezident* in New York, Zarubin, reported to Pavel Fitin, the head of the Foreign Department of NKVD, that the *Rezidentura* was planning the "processing" (a KGB term for developing and recruiting an agent) of Eleanor Roosevelt. This was quite unrealistic and showed little understanding of the American political scene. The plan was for Mrs. Roosevelt to be put in touch with Zarubin's wife, Elizabeth, also an NKVD officer (code name "Vardo"), through Trude Pratt, who later became Mrs. Joseph Lash.[75] Hagen had been introduced to Mrs. Roosevelt in 1939 by Joseph Lash, her close friend and, later, biographer.[76] When the *Venona* intercepts were released, Mrs. Lash spoke to the Associated Press and claimed that she knew nothing about this incident or of any plan by the Soviets to use her to influence Mrs. Roosevelt.[77]

Joseph Lash was a leading young socialist in 1935 when he organized the merger of the Student League for Industrial Democracy, a Socialist group, and the National Student League, a Communist organization, into the American Student Union (ASU).

Although Lash denied having ever joined the Communist Party, he was the closest collaborator the Communists had in the socialist youth and student movement. In 1936 he wrote a book with his close friend James Wechsler, who was then a leader of the Young Communist League. The book, *War—Our Heritage*, reflected the straight Communist Party line and was published by the official Communist publishing house, International Publishers.[78]

In 1937 Lash asked Communist Party head Earl Browder for financial assistance to the ASU. He explained that the Socialist Party financially supported Socialist youth organizations and that the Communists should do the same. (The Young Communist League was fully subsidized by the Communist Party.) The matter was taken up by the Political Bureau, which passed a resolution that the Communist Party would "obligate itself to make a direct contribution of $1,000 to [the] work of ASU." During the Politburo meeting, it was reported that the Socialist Party had brought charges against Joseph Lash and George Edwards for violating discipline by their collaboration with the Communists.[79] In September 1937 Lash resigned from the Socialist Party.

When the Nazi-Soviet alliance was announced in the summer of 1939, Lash began having second thoughts about Communism. And he later spoke out against the Soviet invasion of Finland. This undermined his standing with the Communists. However, on December 1, 1939, when he was called as a witness before the Dies Committee, he gave evasive answers and refused to acknowledge the Communist control of the ASU.[80] Within a few weeks, all that changed when the Communists decided to get rid of Lash.[81] In December 1939 the Fourth National Congress of the ASU ousted Lash. This was dutifully reported to the Comintern by an unnamed Young Communist International instructor sent by Moscow to survey student movements in the West.[82]

In light of Lash's new views, his friend Mrs. Roosevelt requested that Congressman Martin Dies again bring him before the Un-American Activities Committee. At that session Lash testified that "with the Nazi-Soviet Pact certain things were proven to me which made it crystal clear that I could not get along or go along with the Communists...."[83] Although Lash's views on the Communists had changed, the NKVD continued to think it might recruit the first lady through Lash's girlfriend.

The plan to recruit Mrs. Roosevelt was totally bizarre. Although she was extremely naive and often fooled by the Communists, she was certainly not one of them. When warned that an organization she supported was a Communist front, she could sometimes be moved to withdraw.

Benjamin Mandel, a former Communist Party official who left with the Lovestone faction and later became a conservative and research director of the Senate Subcommittee on Internal Security, wrote to Mrs. Roosevelt on December 16, 1940. Mandel was at that time working closely with the Dies Committee. He called her attention to the fact that she was a sponsor of the "First American Rescue Ship Mission," supposedly organized to help Spanish refugees. But he identified the group as a Communist front and said that it was being used to bring Soviet agents into the United States. Mandel enclosed articles in the Socialist newspaper *New Leader* for December 7 and December 14, 1940, in which the refugee ship mission was exposed as a Communist front.

Mrs. Roosevelt responded to Mandel on December 21, 1940: "I have read your letter and the article. Since giving my name I have found out that the committee Miss [Helen] Keller asked me to join is not under good auspices and have resigned." Mandel wrote her again on December 26, enclosing a clipping from the *New Leader* of December 21 announcing that other liberals had also withdrawn from the organization.[84]

A letterhead of the American Rescue Ship Mission dated December 14, 1940, showed the names of Mrs. Roosevelt, Helen Keller, and Josephine Truslow Adams, among others. The *New York Times* of January 7, 1941, reported that Mrs. Roosevelt had resigned from the group. The *Washington Times Herald* reported on January 8, 1941, that Henry Morgenthau, Sr., the father of the secretary of the treasury, had resigned from the organization because of its Communist involvement. The *Washington Star* reported on February 8, 1941, that Helen Keller had also resigned. A letterhead of the American Rescue Ship Mission of March 6, 1941, was considerably shorter than the previous one. Most of the liberals had followed Mrs. Roosevelt in leaving.

Intercontinent News was a Soviet-funded news agency in New York. It provided Soviet propaganda stories for the American Communist press, and it sent lengthy texts to Moscow on developments in the United States. On January 9, 1941, Intercontinent News cabled Moscow about "the resignation of Eleanor Roosevelt and a few others from the Rescue Ship Mission and attempts by the press to discredit the organization…."[85] This was a matter of great concern to Moscow.

Mandel's letter had helped erase Mrs. Roosevelt's name from the Rescue Ship Mission project. But it was not all clear sailing. When Mandel wrote Mrs. Roosevelt on March 18, 1941, exposing the China Aid Committee as a Communist front, she wrote back, "I do not understand what you are trying to bring to my attention. Will you please be clear and tell me what you want to know from me?"

Mandel didn't want to know anything from her but only wished to advise her that the Communists were again using her. He explained that she was lending her name to a group "whose purpose it is not to aid China—with which I am in full sympathy—but to raise money for Communist ends both here and in China and to carry out the aims of Soviet diplomacy in both countries." Mrs. Roosevelt responded, "I do not think that the Washington Committee to Aid China is Communist. It is true that this country has aided Japan. The other statements you quote are extreme but I doubt if they are Communist." One of the quotations in Mandel's original letter was from the Communist Party member and Soviet agent Frederick V. Field, a leader of the China Aid Committee. Field accused the United States of aiding Japan and—this was during the Soviet-Nazi alliance period—urged "withdrawal of aid from England" and "full cooperation with the Soviet Union."[86] But even that failed to alert Mrs. Roosevelt to the true nature of the China Aid Committee.

The Mayflower Communist and the Roosevelts

The Soviets did not understand Mrs. Roosevelt—she was a loyal, if sometimes fallible, American. They might have been misled because she had been duped by a Communist activist named Josephine Truslow Adams, a descendant of America's second and sixth presidents. Adams was a leader of the Descendants of the American Revolution, a Communist-front doppelganger of the legitimate Daughters of the American Revolution and Sons of the American Revolution.[87] Adams used her organization to agitate against the draft during the Soviet-Nazi alliance.[88]

Adams boasted to her Communist associates, including Earl Browder, that she had the ear of Eleanor Roosevelt and even of the president. A leading historian of Communism during the 1930s, Harvey Klehr, has written about the case and argues that the Communists should not have taken Adams seriously, for by the 1950s she was clearly insane. But this is too simple. She was certainly insane later when she forged letters and pretended to have a closer relationship to Roosevelt than she actually had. But documents in the Roosevelt Library show that during World War II she did indeed have some influence on Eleanor Roosevelt—and, through her, the president—regarding some policies.

Adams established a relationship with Mrs. Roosevelt at the behest of Earl Browder, but the Soviets appear not to have played a role. In July 1943 the GRU *Resident* in New York, Pavel Mikhailov, said in a *Venona* cable to his director in Moscow that Theodore Bayer, a Communist Party functionary and GRU agent, had reported on a woman "from an aristocratic family, [who] has known the President and his wife for a long time, evidently a secret member of the Communist Party."[89]

In August 1944 GRU official Bolshakov wrote to Comintern head George Dimitroff asking about Adams. Bolshakov reported that "on Browder's assignment [she] systematically meets the President of the United States, Roosevelt." He asked Dimitroff, "Please inform us whether it is true and whether you have any information on the subject." The top secret letter was addressed to Dimitroff at the Central Committee of the All Union Communist Party (Bolsheviks).[90] As mentioned, the Comintern had supposedly been dissolved in 1943, and its leaders, including Dimitroff, had been assigned to the Soviet Communist Party Central Committee to continue its work secretly as "Scientific Institute 205."

Adams had been very active in the campaign to get President Roosevelt to commute the prison sentence of Earl Browder, who had been convicted of passport fraud. A December 8, 1941, mass meeting demanding Browder's release had as its chairman Josephine Adams and as speakers and sponsors a whole list of "Mayflower" names. The meeting also featured "Old American Songs."[91]

Roosevelt finally gave in to the considerable pressure to free Browder. The pressure came from Communist-dominated CIO unions and from people with "important names" such as Congressman Vito Marcantonio, Dashiell Hammett, Rockwell Kent, Max Lerner, Harlow Shapley, and Richard Wright, not to mention petitions and letters that poured into the White House thanks to the Citizens' Committee to Free Earl Browder, which had been set up by the Communist Party. Roosevelt's action did not go over well with everyone. The Social Democratic Federation of New York—moderate Socialists closely associated with the trade union movement, which supported the president's policies—wrote to the president on May 17, 1942, protesting the commutation.[92]

In another related incident, previously mentioned, the Soviets were very concerned about the American government's plan to deport Earl Browder's wife, Raisa, known as Irene in the American Communist Party. A secret Comintern memo reported: "In December 1943 the Immigration Department of the USA took a decision in accordance with which Raisa Browder must be deported from the country. The Immigration Department decision was based on the fact that she entered the USA illegally. This decision can be canceled only by President Roosevelt." The memo went on to say that American newspapers from January 1944 indicated that a major campaign was being conducted to pressure Roosevelt on her behalf.[93]

Josephine Adams thereupon wrote a letter to Mrs. Roosevelt on July 4, 1944, asking her to assist Raisa Browder, and the letter was sent on to Earl Harrison, the commissioner of the Immigration and Naturalization Service.[94] Astoundingly, Mrs. Browder's problem was resolved. The following month, an official in the U.S. consulate in Montreal, Canada, received instructions from Washington to issue a visa to Mrs. Browder so that she could go to Canada and reenter the United States legally.[95]

Commissioner Harrison did not mind cooperating with the Communists. On May 9, 1942, he spoke at the Sixth National Conference of the American Committee for Protection of Foreign Born, a Communist front. President Roosevelt sent a message of greetings to the same meeting. The chairman of the organization was Hugh De Lacy of Washington, a Democratic member of Congress from 1945 to 1947.[96] According to John Abt, an important Communist Party functionary who was shown by *Venona* to be involved in Soviet espionage, De Lacy was a member of the Communist Party during the time he served in Congress.[97]

In 1943 Earl Browder made direct contact with President Roosevelt. Browder was advised by Dimitroff in Moscow, via clandestine radio, that his old colleague, Comintern apparatchik Victorio Codovilla, who was in Argentina, had been arrested and was going to be deported to Spain. Browder was ordered to use influence on the American government to defend him.[98] Browder therefore cabled Roosevelt on June 14, 1943, asking him to intervene because of his concern that Codovilla might be executed in

Spain. Codovilla, using the name Medina, had been the Comintern representative in Spain in the 1930s.

Roosevelt responded on June 23, saying that although this was a matter "within the exclusive jurisdiction of the Argentine Government," he was asking America's ambassador to Argentina to keep him informed about Codovilla's case. On June 26 Roosevelt wrote another letter to Browder informing him that Ambassador Armour had advised him that Codovilla would not be deported. On July 12 Browder wrote back thanking the president.[99]

Browder reported back to Dimitroff via NKVD channels, and Pavel Klarin, the NKVD *Rezident* in New York, cabled General Fitin, head of the Foreign Department of the NKVD, on July 18, 1943, with the information. The cable in *Venona* is only partially broken, but Fitin sent a fuller text with some deletions to George Dimitroff. Combining both texts, we get a fuller understanding of the message.

Klarin reported Browder's correspondence with the president. Browder gave the message to Klarin through Jacob Golos, code-named "Zvuk." According to Golos, Roosevelt told Browder that he approved of how the American Communists were carrying out the "party line" of support to the Roosevelt administration. Roosevelt did not trust former Republican presidential candidate Wendell Willkie, who he suspected would revert to the old Republican position of opposition to the New Deal when opportune. (During the war, Willkie publicly supported the president.)

The NKVD message reported that the president told the American Communists to understand that the Allies' invasion of Sicily was the prelude to a major invasion of Europe, although Churchill was an obstacle. According to the message, Roosevelt also told Browder that he favored the poll tax because this would allow him to break the power of the "southern political machine." The

NKVD message, but not the memo to Dimitroff, referred to America's southern population as "fascist."

Roosevelt was particularly pleased, according to Browder (through Golos), with the work of Communists in New Jersey who helped unify the Democratic Party and opposed the creation of a Labor Party, which would only have split the vote and helped the Republicans.[100]

Meanwhile, Josephine Adams remained active on the political scene. In October 1944 she wrote to Mrs. Roosevelt, "Last evening it was requested through [presidential assistant] D. [David K.] Niles that E. B. [Earl Browder] withdraw from the radio debate with [George] Sokolsky on the election." Filed with the letter in the Roosevelt Library was an unidentified newspaper clipping reporting that Browder had canceled the debate with Sokolsky. The letter was marked to be shown to the President.[101] The election was a month away. The Communists actively supported Roosevelt's reelection, but public support from Earl Browder was not an asset in most of the country.

Niles, a mysterious political operative for President Roosevelt, had other associations with the Communists. An NKVD *Venona* message from New York to Moscow reported on a plan to send a husband and wife team of NKVD "illegals" to Mexico. The message said, "Through Roosevelt's advisor David Niles—will take three-four days will cost $500.... [A]round Niles there is a group of his friends who arrange anything for a bribe. Through them Michael W. Burd ["Tenor"] obtains priority and has already paid them as much as $6,000. Whether Niles takes a bribe himself is not known for certain." Burd was a Soviet agent and an officer of the Midland Export Corporation in New York City.[102]

On August 2, 1944, the New York *Rezidentura* reported to Moscow that "Niles refused to intervene in the case explaining that he had only recently interceded for one refugee and recommended approaching Congressman [Arthur] Klein." When this did not work, Niles intervened. And although the project was held up because Niles was busy with the Democratic convention, the matter was finally taken care of—Burd handled the paperwork.[103]

Whittaker Chambers reported to the FBI an odd story about Niles that he had heard from a fellow Soviet agent named John Hermann in 1934 or 1935. A Soviet agent named Silverman (not George Silverman) was living in the next building from Alger Hiss. This Silverman apparently had an obviously homosexual affair with David Niles. Silverman had told Niles of the work of the underground apparatus in Washington, and Niles later threatened to expose the activities of the Communist group unless Silverman left his wife. To solve the problem, J. Peters, the head of the American Communist underground, ordered Hermann and Harold Ware to get Silverman to leave Washington, D.C., immediately.[104]

While the best agents were loyal Communists, sometimes corrupt officials could be bribed to help the Soviets. The climate of opinion in wartime Washington, moreover, treated Communists as just another political group, and Eleanor Roosevelt's naiveté helped the Communists to exert influence. In the final analysis, she was a very poor choice as a recruit to serve a foreign power. She was neither a Communist nor corrupt. Only a dedicated Communist would agree to spy for the Soviet Union, never an American who would sometimes agree with the Communists on a particular issue.

Bentley Confesses

The Soviets understood little about Americans; they certainly didn't understand Eleanor Roosevelt. And they didn't even understand Elizabeth Bentley, who had done so much on their behalf. They were shocked when she went to the FBI and even more when she told what she knew to the House Committee on Un-American Activities.

On November 5, 1945, Elizabeth Bentley contacted the FBI and told them about her espionage work for the Soviet Union. She did not retain any documents on espionage, but the FBI investigation confirmed significant parts of her story. *Venona* confirmed most of the rest.

On July 31, 1948, Bentley appeared in a public session of the House Committee on Un-American Activities and, like Whittaker Chambers, who testified three days later, told a shocking story of Soviet espionage at high levels in the U.S. government. While most of the congressmen understood and believed what she was saying, one clearly did not. He was John Rankin, who supported Alger Hiss long after the other members had concluded that Chambers was telling the truth. Rankin, a Mississippi Democrat, was a racist and an anti-Semite. He was not prepared to believe the testimony of former Communists that high-ranking officials, particularly if they were not Jews, were Soviet spies. In 1950, when the controversial Anna Rosenberg was named assistant secretary of defense, Rankin showed his colors. He said on the House floor, "Anna Rosenberg, a little Yiddish woman from Austria-Hungary, will now become Assistant Secretary of National Defense, if confirmed by the Senate, and will have more power over the lives of the American people than was ever exercised by any American President."[105] Despite the hyperbole about Mrs. Rosenberg's supposed vast power, Rankin was really concerned only because she was Jewish.

One of the most important pieces of information Bentley received from Silvermaster came from Lauchlin Currie, Bentley testified. Silvermaster reported that "Currie came dashing into Mr. Silverman's house, sort of out of breath, and told him that the Americans were on the verge of breaking the Soviet code." Silverman reported this to

Silvermaster, who contacted Bentley to transmit the information to the NKVD. This appears to be the information given to the White House about the work being done on the *Venona* intercepts.

Rankin was not so much concerned about the breach of security as he was that Bentley had accused a high White House official and fellow Democrat—who was not Jewish—of being a Soviet agent. Rankin said, "Now, the thing that disturbs me is that you take the testimony, the statement of two men, Silverman and Silvermaster, relayed from one to the other, about what this Scotchman in the White House, Mr. Currie, said about Communism." Silverman and Silvermaster were, of course, Jewish names, but Currie was a Scotsman, and Rankin came to his defense.[106]

When an August 10, 1943, *Venona* message was decoded, it provided direct evidence that Bentley was truthful and that Rankin was wrong again. In this case, Currie provided Silverman with a sensitive memorandum on U.S. policy that had gone from the White House to the State Department.[107] In June 1944 Currie reported to the NKVD that President Roosevelt was reluctant to recognize the government of Charles de Gaulle until the French were willing "to take a more liberal position with respect to the colonies." Currie also said that he would try to influence the non-Communist Poles to acquiesce to Soviet territorial demands.[108]

In February 1945 NKVD headquarters ordered Akhmerov to try to set up direct contact with Lauchlin Currie rather than through Silvermaster.[109] Actually, Akhmerov had already met with Currie. An October 1944 *Venona* message revealed a meeting attended by Currie, Silverman, Silvermaster, and Akhmerov.[110] As most of the message could not be decrypted, it is not possible to know what Currie, the two Soviet agents whom he had previously used to transmit his information to the NKVD, and the senior Soviet "illegal" intelligence officer discussed. By March 1945

General Fitin was concerned that Akhmerov had pressed too hard to maintain a direct relationship with Currie. He pointed out that Currie had a good personal relationship with Silvermaster and that if Currie was uncomfortable working directly with a Soviet officer, Silvermaster should continue his relationship.[111]

After Currie denied the allegations in hearings before the House Committee on Un-American Activities, he left the United States for Colombia. In 1956 he applied for Colombian citizenship, stating that he had lost his American citizenship by staying out of the country more than five years. Born in Canada, Currie was a naturalized American citizen.[112]

Bentley identified the following people as members of the two spy rings:

SILVERMASTER GROUP

Nathan Gregory Silvermaster, director of Labor Division, Farm Security Administration; detailed at one time to Board of Economic Warfare.

Solomon Adler, Treasury Department; agent in China.

Norman Bursler, Department of Justice.

Frank Coe, assistant director, Division of Monetary Research, Treasury; special assistant to United States ambassador in London; assistant to the executive director, Board of Economic Warfare and successor agencies; assistant administrator, Foreign Economic Administration.

Lauchlin Currie, administrative assistant to the president; deputy administrator of Foreign Economic Administration.

Bela Gold (known to Miss Bentley as William Gold), assistant head of Division of Program Surveys, Bureau of Agricultural Economics, Agriculture Department; Senate Subcommittee on War Mobilization; Office of Economic Programs in Foreign Economic Administration.

The Elizabeth Bentley Spy Rings

Mrs. Bela (Sonia) Gold, research assistant, House Select Committee on Interstate Migration; labor-market analyst, Bureau of Employment Security; Division of Monetary Research, Treasury.

Abraham George Silverman, director, Bureau of Research and Information Services, United States Railroad Retirement Board; economic advisor and chief of analysis and plans, assistant chief of Air Staff, Matériel and Services, Air Forces.

William Taylor, Treasury Department.

William Ludwig Ullmann, Division of Monetary Research, Treasury; Matériel and Service Division, Air Corps Headquarters, Pentagon.

Perlo Group

Victor Perlo, head of branch in Research Section, Office of Price Administration; War Production Board; Monetary Research, Treasury.

Edward J. Fitzgerald, War Production Board.

Harold Glasser, Treasury Department; loaned to government of Ecuador; loaned to War Production Board; advisor on North African Affairs Committee in Algiers, North Africa.

Charles Kramer (Krevitsky), National Labor Relations Board; Office of Price Administration; economist with Senate Subcommittee on War Mobilization.

Solomon Leshinsky, United Nations Relief and Rehabilitation Administration.

Harry Magdoff, Statistical Division of War Production Board and Office of Emergency Management; Bureau of Research and Statistics, WPB; Tools Division, WPB; Bureau of Foreign and Domestic Commerce.

Allan Rosenberg, Foreign Economic Administration.

Donald Niven Wheeler, Office of Strategic Services.[113]

Bentley listed other agents who were not attached to these two rings, some of whom will be discussed in Chapter 9, on the penetration of the American intelligence community.

Perlo and Abt continued to work in open Communist activities. In 1969 Perlo wrote a pamphlet that was mailed to all members of the Senate and House of Representatives in which he identified himself as chairman of the National Economics Commission of the Communist Party USA.[114] When almost half of the few remaining Communist Party members left in 1991 in protest against Gus Hall's dictatorship in the Party and his receipt of Soviet money, Perlo remained a Communist Party member. Most of the group that left the Party formed the Committees of Correspondence, sometimes referred to as "Communism with a human mask." But Perlo remained an unreconstructed Stalinist until his death in 1999.

John Abt also remained a Party member until his death in 1991. Abt married Jessica Smith after her first husband, Harold Ware, who had set up the original Communist underground group in the government, was killed in an accident. In a posthumously published autobiography, Abt admitted the existence of the underground group. He claimed, however, that "we were simply providing [the Communist Party with] political analysis of New Deal policy, based on our positions as insiders in various government agencies. Our purpose was not to help foreign governments but to help our own...." He admitted that "it is conceivable that the commentary and analyses we provided to the national Party leadership may have reached the Soviets...."[115] Abt was being disingenuous; he knew quite well during the 1930s that the information being supplied was for the Soviets. More important, he organized the 1944 transfer of the Perlo ring from supplying information to the Party leadership to supplying it to Soviet intelligence.

Bentley died on May 18, 1959. She had defected to the FBI and ultimately testified before the House Committee on Un-American

The Elizabeth Bentley Spy Rings

Activities because she feared, after the death of Golos, that the NKVD wanted to run the agents without her and because of the expulsion of her friend, Earl Browder, from the American Communist Party. These disappointments caused her to rethink her ideological commitment to the Soviet Union. As a result, her appreciation of the United States was reignited, and she regained her religious faith. She became one of the most valuable American counterintelligence sources.

The Comintern Goes Underground

On May 15, 1943, the Communist International announced that it had dissolved itself. The statement, signed by George Dimitroff and other members of the Executive Committee of the Comintern,[116] was used by the Soviet propaganda machine to convince the West that it was no longer threatened by Communist plans for world conquest. But, as we've seen, the Comintern did not dissolve, and messages continued to be sent through NKVD channels between the American Communist Party and Dimitroff, who headed the now secret Comintern—code-named "Scientific Institute 205." In September 1943 Moscow ordered the *Rezidenturas* in a number of countries, including the United States, to cease personal contact with leadership of the local Communist parties and to forward their material to the supposedly abolished Comintern. (Apparently the last part of the orders was canceled, for the messages continued to come.) The orders said that meetings between NKVD officers and local Communists could take place only with "special reliable conspiratorial contacts of the Communist Party organizations who were not suspected by the... local authorities." Each such meeting required the permission of Moscow and could only be used for significant intelligence purposes.[117]

The meetings continued, and in February 1944 the New York *Rezidentura* reported that there had been several between the

Rezident, Zarubin, and Earl Browder's brother, Bill. Bernie Chester, head of the New York State Communist Party Control Commission, continued to meet with NKVD officers and checked out the names of Communist Party members recruited for espionage. In the course of one such meeting, in February 1944, Chester insisted to Akhmerov that Browder's new political line was correct.[118]

Browder had gone beyond Moscow's apparently soft political line; he had dissolved the American Communist Party and replaced it with the Communist Political Association. The NKVD New York *Rezidentura* reported to Moscow that the change made no difference in light of "the rather insignificant influence which their votes have hitherto had in the elections."[119] The Communist vote was indeed insignificant; the Communists were useful only as suppliers of espionage agents and propagandists for the Soviet Union.

But Browder nevertheless got into trouble with Moscow for dissolving the Communist Party into the more nebulous "political association." In April 1945 Jacques Duclos, a Comintern and French Communist Party official, wrote an article in the French Party's theoretical magazine, *Cahiers du Communisme*, condemning Browder's new line.[120] Browder, who had been treated by his comrades as the American Stalin, suddenly lost their support. He was removed from his post of general secretary and soon expelled from the Party. Browder was replaced by Eugene Dennis as head of the Party.

Browder later claimed that he had developed the soft line with the "knowledge, consent, and support" of "the whole international leadership of Communism...."[121] He was not telling the truth. The Comintern archives contain a March 8, 1944, message from Dimitroff to Browder which said, "I am somewhat troubled by the new theoretical, political and tactical positions being developed by you. Are you not going too far in accommodating the changing international situation, even going so far as the denial of the theory and practice of the class struggle and the necessity for the working class to have its own independent political party?" This matter was considered so important that Dimitroff had to get the permission of Molotov to send the message.[122]

Browder, though expelled from the Communist Party, never told the truth about his role and the role of other CPUSA officials in Soviet espionage.

Bentley did enormous damage to the Soviet espionage apparatus in the United States, despite the efforts of the KGB's historians to minimize her role. Vitali Pavlov, the World War II *Rezident* in Canada, is one of the retired KGB officers presently writing intelligence history in order to improve the image of the KGB. Like his colleagues, Pavlov provides some true information but tries to conceal much more. He insisted in his autobiography that

> as a result of the betrayal of one of the agents in the illegal group that was led by J. Golos, American counterintelligence obtained the opportunity in 1946 of uncovering a number of our valuable agents. However, timely measures taken by Moscow and the New York *Rezidentura*, as well as the extremely inept exploitation of the traitor by American counterintelligence, made it possible to preserve our most effective intelligence capabilities. But, both Zarubin and Akhmerov had to leave to avoid unjustified risk. By the end of 1946 both of them ended up in Moscow at almost the same time as I did.[123]

Pavlov—who was recalled to Moscow because of the 1945 defection of Igor Gouzenko, an important GRU cipher clerk in Canada—explained that because Golos was "swamped with work," he turned over some of his agents to "his messenger Bentley." When Golos fell ill, he allowed Bentley to meet with more agents and told her the names of some of the others. Bentley provided those names to the FBI in 1945 and to the House Committee on Un-American Activities in 1948.

According to Pavlov, "The majority of the valuable sources of information who worked for [Soviet] foreign intelligence on an ideological basis were true American patriots. They viewed their assistance to Soviet Russia in the battle against Hitler's Germany as a duty to democratic America, since the U.S. and USSR were fighting together against the common enemy."[124]

Apparently Pavlov forgot that he came to the United States in 1941 to reactivate Harry Dexter White as a Soviet agent during the Soviet-Nazi alliance. He expressed concern at the time that White, an antifascist, might refuse his services to Nazi Germany's Soviet ally. As it turned out, White was willing to resume work for Soviet intelligence even under those circumstances.[125] The American Communists were not "American patriots," as described by Pavlov, but Soviet patriots.

Pavlov maintains that many of the agents not known to Bentley continued to spy. Indeed, *Venona* shows that other Soviet agents were never identified by the FBI. But *Venona* does make clear that the most important agents were identified and neutralized by the information provided by Elizabeth Bentley and Whittaker Chambers.

CHAPTER 6

Atomic Espionage

CAN IT BE THAT JOSEPH STALIN WAS WELL INFORMED about the American development of the atomic bomb long before President Harry Truman? *Venona* and other recently available sources tell us that Soviet intelligence was regularly reporting to the Kremlin on the top secret British-American atom bomb project as early as 1941. Truman was not briefed on it until April 1945, shortly after he was sworn in as president.

Truman met Stalin for the first time in July of 1945 at the Potsdam Conference, where they discussed the nature of postwar Europe, including Soviet control of the newly conquered countries of Central Europe. The Americans and British also urged the Soviets to enter the war against Japan.

In mid-1944 military strategists had agreed on a two-phase invasion of the Japanese home islands to begin in November 1945. Even the most optimistic early estimates predicted horrifying American casualties—as many as one-third of the American invasion force of over three-quarters of a million troops. By the early summer of 1945 the outlook had become even more grave. Despite heavy saturation bombing, the Japanese had successfully moved massive numbers of troops to the home islands. Washington was suddenly aware that its initial attack wave might be defeated and that American dead and wounded might prove prohibitively high.[1]

All this changed when the United States successfully tested an atomic bomb on July 16. The planned invasion might be avoided altogether if Japan surrendered when exposed to the powerful new weapon. The closely guarded secret of the bomb could now be shared with our Soviet ally. As one of the sessions ended, Truman walked over to Stalin. Churchill was standing nearby. The president later recounted the incident: "On July 24, I casually mentioned to Stalin that we had a new weapon of unusual destructive force. The Russian Premier showed no special interest. All he said was that he was glad to hear it and hoped we would make 'good use of it against the Japanese.'"[2]

Stalin exhibited no surprise because he already knew about the American atom bomb test from Soviet intelligence. Two weeks earlier, an NKVD message to Beria reported that the Americans had scheduled the first atomic bomb test. The message identified the spies who provided the information by their *Venona* code names "Mlad" and "Charles." The latter was Klaus Fuchs, a German refugee who was part of the British team sent to work on the A-bomb. "Mlad" was a teenage employee at Los Alamos named Theodore Hall. The *Venona* message had not yet been decrypted when Truman met Stalin, and in any event, despite FBI attempts to educate him, Truman paid little attention to Soviet spying in the United States. The special value of the *Venona* decryptions is that they confirmed the FBI's concern that the Soviets had mounted a full-scale intelligence offensive against the American atomic program.

We now know that the first word the Soviets had about American and British work on the atomic weapon came from the NKVD *Rezidentura* in London on September 25, 1941, which reported on a meeting nine days earlier held by the British Uranium Committee. It had concluded, incorrectly as it turned out, that an atomic bomb could be developed within two years. (It took almost four.)

Atomic Espionage

The NKVD report to the Soviet leadership was signed "Potapov." Apparently, Yelena Potapova, a researcher at NKVD headquarters whose excellent knowledge of English and science helped her write many of the memos on atomic espionage for Beria and Stalin, wrote the summary of the message from the London *Rezidentura*.[3]

The source of the information, as shown in the report, was an agent code-named "List," real name John Cairncross, a Soviet spy who served as private secretary to Lord Hankey, chairman of the British Uranium Committee.[4] In his memoirs, Cairncross denied being the source.[5] He argued, disingenuously, that he was merely the secretary to Lord Hankey and that his listing on the purloined document as secretary to the committee was erroneous.

On March 10, 1942, Beria suggested to Stalin that a committee of scientists, political officials, and intelligence officers be set up to work on the atomic bomb. Pavel Sudoplatov, a senior NKVD officer, was later appointed to head the intelligence work on the project. His job was to coordinate the data on the atom bomb project gathered by Soviet agents in the United States, England, and Canada.[6]

The Canadian Connection

In the early 1940s the atomic bomb program was America's most closely guarded secret. America was principally concerned that the Nazis might steal this American technology and also feared Soviet espionage. But the nature and extent of the Soviet espionage efforts were neither known nor understood by the Western allies. Their "wake-up call" came on the night of September 5, 1945, with the defection of Igor Gouzenko, a Soviet military intelligence (GRU) cipher clerk in Canada, where the GRU—not the NKVD, as in the United States—did most of the significant espionage. When Vitali Pavlov arrived in Canada in August 1942 as the NKVD

Rezident, his main complaint was that "a number of people, who seemed to me to be the most promising sources of information, were already 'grabbed by my military "neighbors" '—workers in the GRU *Rezidentura*...."[7]

Since atomic spying was a GRU responsibility in Canada, Gouzenko's information was particularly valuable because he had a large collection of GRU messages between Moscow and Ottawa that he had removed from the safe of the *Rezident*. Some of Gouzenko's documents show that the GRU worked through two longtime intelligence agents, Fred Rose, a Communist member of the Canadian Parliament, and Sam Carr, the organizing secretary of the Canadian Communist Party, then called the Labor Progressive Party.

In August 1943 the GRU in New York sent a *Venona* message to its director in Moscow that directly confirmed Gouzenko's information. The report boasted that "Fred [Fred Rose] our man in Canada has been elected to the Canadian Parliament." While this improved the opportunities available to the agent, New York GRU suggested that Moscow warn Sergei Kundryavtsev, the GRU officer in Canada handling him, "about increasing caution to the maximum." The New York message was signed by Pavel Mikhailov, the GRU *Rezident*.[8] But the Soviets were not cautious enough—Gouzenko was able to obtain documents showing that Fred was a Soviet intelligence agent.

Born in Poland in 1907, Fred Rose came to Canada at age thirteen. During World War II, he told the Canadian authorities, who were checking on the foreign-born, that he had joined the Young Communist League (YCL) in 1925 at age seventeen and the Communist Party in 1927. He rose rapidly in the Party; by 1929 he was a member of its Central Executive Committee and the national secretary of the YCL and then spent six months in Moscow during 1930 as a member of the Executive Committee of the Young Communist International.[9]

Atomic Espionage

A notebook in the handwriting of GRU *Rezident* Zabotin was obtained by Gouzenko. It referred to the agent "Fred" as having worked for the "neighbors" since 1924. Each Soviet intelligence organization referred to the other as the "neighbors." Since this was a GRU notebook, the "neighbors" were the NKVD. This contradicted what he would later tell Canadian authorities, for he would maintain that he had joined the YCL a year later, in 1925. The notation said that "Fred" had contacted one of the GRU officers, Major Sokolov, in May–June 1942 and offered to resume his work for the Soviets. He was checked out through the GRU *Rezident* in the United States, Pavel Mikhailov, who decided to reactivate him.[10]

In light of Rose's work as a Soviet spy, a statement about him in the 1938 YCL yearbook is amusing. It stated that he "likes to read spy stories...."[11] When Rose was arrested, as a result of the Gouzenko revelations, his friends asked for a delay in the trial so that a British attorney could come to Canada to represent him. This turned out to be D. N. Pritt,[12] the paid Soviet propagandist who in his writings supported the Moscow purge trials and later defended the atomic spies in the United States. Rose was convicted of espionage and given a six-year sentence. When he was released from prison in 1953, he went first to Czechoslovakia and then to Poland, where he lived out his life.

Rose's closest friend in the Communist Party and Soviet espionage was Sam Carr, who was born in eastern Ukraine, a colony of the tsarist empire, in 1906, and came to Canada in 1924 at age eighteen. During the World War II inquiries, he told the Canadian authorities that his real name was Schmil Kogan and that he had joined the YCL in 1925 and the Party in 1927. Carr studied at the Lenin School in Moscow in 1929. In 1937 he was appointed organizing secretary of the Communist Party.[13]

Information that Carr provided to the Communist International in 1937 was different from that which he gave the Canadian government and tells us much about this experienced espionage agent. In a form he filled out for the Executive Committee of the Comintern, he gave his real name as Arthur Ross and his Party name as Sam Carr. He said he had joined the YCL in 1924, not 1925, and the Party in 1925, not 1927. When asked who in the Executive Committee of the Comintern could recommend him, he answered Comrade Moskvin.[14] This was the Comintern name of Moishe Trillisser, the organizational secretary of the Comintern who had previously served as head of the Foreign Department of the OGPU. Even as a young man, Carr had close connections with the leadership of Soviet foreign intelligence.

Gouzenko obtained a card with notations on Carr from the GRU files. It gave his code name as "Frank" and said that, while he was financially secure, he "takes money." It also revealed that "detailed material on his biography is available in the Center of the Comintern. Has an excellent knowledge of the Russian language, he graduated from the Lenin School in Moscow."[15]

It appears that Carr was dispatched to Canada at age eighteen for Comintern and intelligence work. His newfound Canadian friend, Fred Rose, one year his junior, joined him in this activity. When Rose was arrested, Carr fled Canada and hid in the United States with the help of Morris Childs, whom he knew from the Lenin School, and other American comrades, until he was arrested by the FBI and deported to Canada.[16]

Convicted of espionage and sentenced to six years in jail, Carr was released in 1954. Unlike Rose, Carr remained in Canada until his death in 1989 at the age of eighty-three.[17]

Most importantly, documents obtained by Gouzenko and supplied to Canadian authorities identified other GRU agents, including David Gordon Lunan, an army officer working in the Wartime Information Board and later the Canadian Information Services,

Atomic Espionage

Dunford Smith, Edward Mazerall, and Raymond Boyer of the National Research Council of Canada. Significantly, another of the agents named was Allan Nunn May, a British civil servant in Canada who had access to information on the atomic bomb.

Gouzenko's documents showed that on March 29, 1945, Lunan reported to GRU Major Rogov, the Soviet assistant military attaché, that Dunford Smith, a National Research Council employee code-named "Badeau," informed him that secret work was being done on nuclear physics (bombardment of radioactive substances to produce energy). "This is more hush-hush than radar and is being carried on at the University of Montreal and at McMaster University at Hamilton," Badeau reported. It was Badeau's view that the purchase of a radium-producing plant by the government was connected with this research.

The next month the *Rezidentura* in its "organizational directives" instructed Rogov to "ask 'Badeau' whether he could obtain Uran[ium] No. 235, [but] let him be cautious. If he can, let him write in detail about the radium-producing plant."

Instead Lunan tried to get another member of his spy ring, Israel Halperin, to steal the uranium sample at the request of the GRU. Halperin, a research scientist who was serving as a major in the Canadian Directorate of Artillery, either wouldn't or couldn't obtain it.

The job was then given to Allan Nunn May, an active Communist, who had come to Canada from Britain to work on the atomic bomb project in Montreal. In July 1945, Nunn May reported that he might soon be ordered to return to England. Moscow instructed the *Rezidentura* to obtain as much information from him as possible before he left Canada. On August 9 Zabotin reported to the NKVD Center that agent "Alek" (Allan Nunn May) had handed over a sample of uranium and information on the bomb dropped on Japan.

In September, Nunn May returned to England. He was given orders to contact a GRU officer there so that he could continue his espionage. Moscow instructed the GRU *Rezident* in Canada, Zabotin, to make the arrangements for the contact. Zabotin suggested a meeting on October 7 at 11 PM in front of the British Museum. Moscow answered that at 11 PM it would be too dark and that the meeting should take place at 9 PM. Nunn May would be carrying a copy of the *Times* under his left arm. while his GRU contact would carry the magazine *Picture Post* in his left hand.[18]

The meeting never took place. Moscow had been warned by Kim Philby, *Venona* code name "Stanley," of the extent of the information that Gouzenko had provided the Canadians. One story holds that Philby arrived at the MI6 headquarters in London at the same time that it received a detailed report from Canada on the Gouzenko revelations. He grabbed a copy of the cable and left the building.

The *Venona* intercepts show that on September 18 Moscow instructed London to take security precautions because of "Stanley's" information "about the disruption of our work in Canada."[19]

The British authorities were watching for the Nunn May meeting. When it failed to take place, they arrested him. He soon confessed:

> About a year ago whilst in Canada, I was contacted by an individual whose identity I decline to divulge.... He apparently knew I was employed by the Montreal laboratory and he sought information from me concerning atomic research.
>
> I gave... very careful consideration to... making sure that development of atomic energy was not confined to the USA. I took the very painful decision that it was necessary to convey general information on atomic energy and make sure it was taken seriously. For this reason I decided to entertain [the] proposition made to me by the individual who called on me.

Atomic Espionage

After this preliminary meeting I met the individual on several subsequent occasions whilst in Canada.... [He requested a] sample of uranium from me and information generally on atomic energy.

At one meeting I gave the man microscopic amounts of U.233 and U.235 (one of each). The U.235 was a slightly enriched sample and was in a small glass tube and consisted of about a milligram of oxide. The U.233 was about a tenth of a milligram and was a very thin deposit on a platinum foil and was wrapped in a piece of paper.

I also gave the man a written report on atomic research as known to me....

The man gave me some dollars (I forget how many) and a bottle of whiskey and I accepted these against my will.

Before I left Canada it was arranged that on my return to London I was to keep an appointment with somebody I did not know. I was given precise details as to making contact but I forget them now. I did not keep the appointment because I had decided that this clandestine procedure was no longer appropriate in view of the official release of information and the possibility of satisfactory international control of atomic energy.

The whole affair was extremely painful to me and I only embarked on it because I felt this was a contribution I could make to the safety of mankind. I certainly did not do it for gain.[20]

Even while confessing, Nunn May failed to tell the whole truth—that he was a longtime Soviet agent who had stolen whatever his handlers instructed him to steal. Allan Nunn May was sentenced to ten years' imprisonment for his spying. He was never contrite and argued that he had a right to spy because it helped our Soviet ally.

The Nineteen-Year-Old Spy

The Canadian evidence alerted American authorities to Soviet atomic spying. They soon learned that the Soviets had made a major effort to obtain atomic secrets in the United States. An NKVD officer with scientific training, Leonid Kvasnikov, *Venona* code name "Anton," was assigned to New York to coordinate the spying. Myriad agents were used as spies, recruiters, and couriers.

The youngest Soviet agent in the atomic bomb project was nineteen-year-old Theodore Hall. In a bit of Soviet humor, his *Venona* code name was "Mlad," the root of the Russian word for "young." Ted Hall was a brilliant undergraduate student at Harvard University in 1944 when his roommate, Roy Glauber, and another friend were invited by the government to work on a supersecret military project. Ted asked if he, too, could be recommended for the project. Glauber, to his later regret, recommended him. Glauber was unaware that Hall was a member of the Young Communist League and was shocked in 1995 when the release of *Venona* disclosed that his ex-roommate had been a Soviet spy. While at Harvard, Glauber also met a friend of Hall's named Saville Sax, who one day began roasting eggs in the fireplace in their room. Glauber found Sax eccentric, but he didn't pay him much mind. Such eccentricities were not uncommon among Harvard students at that time.

Glauber, Hall, and another student were taken to Los Alamos in 1944 and learned that despite their youth they would be working on a very important secret weapon, an atomic bomb. In November 1944 Hall was given leave and returned to his home in New York, where he saw his friend and fellow YCL member Saville Sax. When Hall explained his new job, Sax convinced him to provide the Soviet Union with the developments at Los Alamos.

But neither of them knew how to contact Soviet intelligence. Sax's first idea was to see Earl Browder, the head of the Communist

Party. Browder was indeed deeply involved in Soviet espionage, but a visit from a teenager with important secrets was a little unusual and could have been an FBI provocation, so Browder's secretary turned the boy away. Sax's mother, a member of the Communist Party, was active in Russian War Relief, as was Nicholas Napoli, the president of Artkino Pictures, Inc., which distributed Soviet films in the United States. So Hall and Sax contacted Napoli, who was a good choice—he was a Communist Party member and was himself involved in Soviet espionage.[21]

Sax told his story to Napoli and was sent to Sergei Kournakoff, the military correspondent of the *Daily Worker*, also a Soviet intelligence agent.[22]

Kournakoff had an unusual background. He didn't start his political life as a Communist. Born in Russia in 1892 into a family of landed noblemen and army officers, he volunteered for the army in 1914 at the outbreak of World War I. After the Bolshevik Revolution, Kournakoff served in the White Army fighting against the Bolsheviks. Fleeing Russia, he came to the United States in 1921 as a stateless person. Wishing to return to the Soviet Union, he paid his dues by collaborating with the American Communists, writing for the newspaper *Rusky Golos* in Russian and the *Daily Worker* in English.[23] When Soviet intelligence later demanded his services, he acquiesced.

He was extremely active spying on Russian émigré organizations and became so important to the NKVD that when he missed his son, who had returned to the Soviet Union, the boy was brought to the United States illegally under the cover of a Soviet merchant seaman. But he could remain only a few days, arriving June 14, 1943, and leaving on June 16.[24] Kournakoff's code name at that time was "Cavalryman," a reference to his previous experiences in the tsar's army. In October 1944, under his new code name, "Bek," he expressed concern that he had not heard from his son for some time.

The New York *Rezidentura*, anxious to please him, requested that Moscow have the son send a letter "by the next post."[25]

Kournakoff returned to the Soviet Union in 1946 and died there in 1949. Eulogies were published in the American Communist press at the time of his death, but no mention was made of his work for Soviet intelligence.[26]

The New York *Rezidentura* reported in a *Venona* message to Moscow that "Bek" (Kournakoff) had met with Theodore Hall. In an example of poor tradecraft, Hall's true name was spelled out in the message—the NKVD was sure that its "one-time pad" codes could not be broken. Hall was described as follows: "19 years old, the son of a furrier. He is a graduate of Harvard University. As a talented physicist he was taken on for government work." Hall had not yet graduated from Harvard, but the rest of the message was accurate. It identified him as a *"Fizkul'turnik,"* or "gymnast." It was a play on words; the Russian word for high school boy is *"gimNazist."* *"Fizkul'turnik"* was the code word for Young Communist League members. On October 15, 1943, the Young Communist League had changed its name to the nicer sounding American Youth for Democracy.

Hall and Sax gave Kournakoff a report on Los Alamos and a list of the key personnel working on the atom bomb project. Hall also provided a photograph of himself in case a different Soviet officer needed to recognize him at a secret meeting. The two youths were not yet sure that they had made the proper contact. In fact, they had, but they continued their search. The next day, Sax went to the Soviet consulate, where he met a Soviet vice consul, Anatoli Yakovlev, in reality the NKVD officer Anatoli Yatzkov. Sax gave him a second copy of Hall's report.[27] Yatzkov took over the case, bypassing Kournakoff.

The job of checking out the bona fides of the two young new agents was given to Bernie Chester, the Communist Party USA's liaison with the NKVD, who was also ordered to check out Bluma Sax, Saville's mother. According to a *Venona* message, Kournakoff was angry that Yatzkov had taken over the handling of Sax. In another Soviet joke, Sax was given the code name "Star," the root of the Russian word for "old"—he was only about a year older than Hall. Since only Kournakoff, not Yatzkov, had met Hall, who had returned to Los Alamos and been inducted into the army,[28] Sax was assigned as the courier to obtain Hall's information.[29]

Sam Cohen, another young scientist, was Hall's friend at Los Alamos. He had no idea that Hall was a spy. Cohen was a patriotic American who was later credited with inventing the neutron weapon for use against Soviet tanks in the event of a Soviet invasion of Western Europe during the Cold War. Cohen remembered Hall well and described him as the most disheveled and eccentric GI in the camp. Most of them were out of uniform and a little peculiar, but Hall stood out. When author Romerstein spoke to Hall in 1995, he appeared to be the same brilliant airhead he had been as a teenage spy years earlier.

In March 1945 Moscow reported to the New York *Rezidentura* that Hall's report on the work at Los Alamos had been received with great interest at the NKVD Center.[30] In May the *Rezidentura* sent Moscow another report from Hall on atom bomb research. It revealed the locations of work being done and the names of the heads of each research group. All of the names were clearly written out except one, that of J. Robert Oppenheimer,[31] who was listed as "Veksel," the head of Los Alamos. Although having a cryptonym did not prove that someone was a spy, for this reason and others Oppenheimer remains a controversial figure.[32]

In July, Moscow sent an angry message to New York about a security breach which was blamed on Yatzkov. Apparently an incident took place in front of Roy Glauber which they thought might expose Hall.[33] Fifty years later Glauber could not remember such an incident.

The FBI knew nothing about Theodore Hall's spying until the *Venona* messages were broken in 1950. At the time, *Venona* was its only evidence against him unless someone else in the spy ring could be induced to talk. But this didn't happen. Both Hall and Sax lied when the FBI interviewed them. Without the use of *Venona*, the FBI could not challenge their stories. In 1950, mail covers, in which the return address was reported to the FBI, were placed on all incoming letters to Hall and Sax, both of whom were living in Chicago.[34]

Hall, questioned by the FBI on March 16 and 19, 1951, as a result of the *Venona* message, falsely denied recognizing a photograph of Kournakoff. He was also shown photographs of Yatzkov and the Rosenbergs. He truthfully denied knowing any of them but falsely stated that he had never heard of Yakovlev, the name under which Sax knew Yatzkov.[35]

Hall moved to England with his family in 1962. Neither Hall nor Sax was ever indicted. Their names became known only after the release of the *Venona* intercepts in July 1995.

Without the cooperation of Hall or Sax, federal prosecutors did not have a live witness to use against this ring. The *Venona* information was "close hold" and could not be used in open court. In addition, it might have been difficult to explain the complicated work of the code breakers to a jury.

In the fall of 1995 author Romerstein and *Reader's Digest* senior editor Ralph Bennett met with Hall in Cambridge, England. Hall had seen only the *Venona* document that mentioned him by name, but now Romerstein and Bennett showed him the rest of the *Venona* information relating to his spy activities. While Hall would not confirm that he was engaged in World War II espionage, he did make comments acknowledging the truth of some of the information and expressed concern that even at that late date he might be prosecuted.

Atomic Espionage

(Bennett and Romerstein described their meeting with Ted Hall in the *Reader's Digest* of September 1996.)[36]

Hall promised to write a statement for Bennett and Romerstein by late November or early December 1995, which he never sent, but instead wrote one for journalists Joseph Albright and Marcia Kunstel. While he did not specifically admit to espionage, he said that when he was nineteen he was "immature, inexperienced and far too sure of myself." He nevertheless expressed no shame at his earlier activity but insisted "that brash youth had the right end of the stick."[37] All that aside, *Venona* proved without a doubt that he had been a Soviet atomic spy.

A reporter for the British left-of-center *Guardian* newspaper visited Ted Hall and his wife in early 1996. He reported that they still "read a variety of leftist journals" and had been members of the British Campaign for Nuclear Disarmament.[38]

The 1992 release in Russia of atomic espionage documents revealed that "Mlad" and "Charles" had alerted the Soviets to the first American atom bomb test.[39] *Venona* identified them as Hall and Fuchs.

For a time, Sax remained the courier between Hall and Yatzkov. Later, Lona Petka Cohen, a legendary Soviet spy, became Hall's courier. Her husband, Morris, had been recruited by the NKVD while serving in the International Brigades during the Spanish Civil War. Cohen's pseudonym in Spain was Israel Altman. When the real Israel Altman was interviewed by the FBI, he revealed that he had volunteered for service in Spain and filled out papers concerning his background, but he had been turned down for service. However, a passport with his name was used by Cohen.[40]

After being wounded at the front, Cohen was assigned to the NKVD training school in late 1938. An evaluation of him by the Communist Party unit at the spy school, found in the Comintern archives in Moscow, stated that he was "a very good comrade" who showed "great initiative and activity in our political work." While similar evaluations for other soldiers were signed by the full name of the political commissar, Cohen's evaluation was signed only with first names—Wilhelm, Heinrich, Bill, and Jim.[41] The Comintern records show that in 1935 Morris joined the Communist Party, where he was a unit organizer and a member of the Section Committee.[42]

When Cohen returned to the United States, he married Lona Petka and recruited her for espionage. In another example of poor tradecraft, the Soviets used Morris and other Spanish Civil War veterans, some of whom had been trained for espionage, as guards at the Soviet Pavilion of the 1939 New York World's Fair.

Pavel Pastelnyak was in charge of the guards. His experience had been with Soviet border troops, and he had little experience in foreign intelligence. Even worse, he knew almost no English. When the Soviets decided to withdraw from the World's Fair in 1940, Pastelnyak was assigned to the NKVD *Rezidentura* in New York.[43] There was little work to do since most of the agents had been temporarily deactivated due to the demotions or executions of most of the experienced Soviet intelligence officers, so Pastelnyak's lack of English was unimportant. When Gaik Ovakimian, the *Rezident*, was arrested by the FBI in April 1941, Pastelnyak assumed his position.[44] But he remained in that post only until December, when Vassiliy Zarubin returned as *Rezident* and reactivated some of the agent network.

Morris Cohen worked at the Soviet trade organization Amtorg and was part of the reactivated network. When Morris was drafted into the U.S. Army, Lona continued her work for the NKVD, assigned as a courier for agents at Los Alamos, and continued after the war. In 1948 a senior KGB officer was sent from Moscow to work with her. He was forty-five-year-old William Fischer, later known to us as Colonel Rudolf Abel. After only one year in the

United States, he was awarded an important Soviet medal for bravery, the Order of the Red Banner, for his work in atomic espionage.[45]

Morris Cohen came from a Communist family. His parents, Harry and Sarah, enrolled with the election board in New York as members of the Communist Party in 1936.[46] In 1940 they both signed nominating petitions to put the Communist Party on the ballot.[47] An FBI investigation revealed that Cohen's mother, Sarah, was an active member of the Communist Party.[48] Lona Petka Cohen was born to Polish Catholic parents, became estranged from her family at an early age, and became an atheist and a Communist before she met Morris.[49] The NSA never identified the *Venona* code names for Morris and Lona Cohen, but we now know that Morris was called "Volunteer" and Lona was called "Lesley."

Soviet television broadcast an interview with the Cohens in 1989. Lona recalled that one of her wartime agents worked for American intelligence; she had never met him, but he sent her coded letters through his brother.[50] An August 1944 *Venona* message reported information that "Volunteer's" wife had received from the agent "Link" through his brother.[51] This appears to be the same case that Lona spoke about on Moscow television. The NSA identified the agent "Link" as William Weisband. Weisband joined the U.S. Army Signal Security Agency in 1942 and worked overseas. When he returned to the United States, he was assigned to the Arlington Hall code-breaking facility and watched the decryption of *Venona* messages. Meredith Gardner, NSA's ace cryptologist, later recalled that Weisband watched him as he broke a December 1944 *Venona* message dealing with atomic espionage.

Although Weisband was stationed at Arlington Hall in Virginia in 1945, he was handled by Alexander Feklisov, an NKVD officer operating out of New York. Weisband would periodically visit New York to turn over information, including the fact that the Americans had broken a Soviet code and were reading Amtorg messages.[52] But since the wartime messages were already in American hands, the *Venona* code breaking continued despite Weisband's information. Weisband's spying helped the Soviets protect later coded messages.

Five years later, in 1950, the FBI arrested and turned in a Soviet agent named James Orin York. He identified Weisband as one of his Soviet contacts to whom he had passed classified information. Weisband was never prosecuted for espionage, which he denied, but was convicted of contempt after refusing to appear before a grand jury and was sentenced to a year in prison. Weisband, who died in 1967, was one of two agents who reported to the Russians on the *Venona* decryptions. The other was Kim Philby.[53]

In October 1951 the FBI received a report from the British with concern about possible Soviet espionage activities at the Hanford, Washington, plutonium plant. The FBI had no evidence at that time of such activity but knew that some of the Soviet agents, including Hall, had access to information regarding the Hanford atomic energy project.[54]

The KGB allowed its former officer Vladimir Chikov to use information on the espionage work of the Cohens in a book to be published in the West, written with the help of a bright and knowledgeable American researcher, Gary Kern. Some of the information related to an agent that Lona had worked with at Los Alamos and later Chicago. This agent provided the names of two potential recruits for the KGB who were working at the Hanford atomic research facility. Morris Cohen also met with him, and Rudolf Abel observed one of the meetings in Chicago. Chikov claimed the cryptonym of the agent was "Perseus," the name used in the book.[55] After examining *Venona* messages, Kern realized that Chikov had deliberately mixed together the activities of a number of Soviet agents under the phony code name "Perseus." Under pressure from

Kern, Chikov admitted that these particular incidents actually related to an agent code-named "Mlad." He would not provide the real name, but we know from *Venona* that it was Ted Hall.

Morris and Lona Cohen continued their work in the United States for Soviet intelligence until 1950; the FBI knew nothing of their espionage activity. But in June 1950, warned by their Soviet superiors of the arrest of David Greenglass, the Cohens threw a farewell party for themselves on July 5, told their neighbors that they were departing for California,[56] and fled to the Soviet Union. Less than two weeks later, the Rosenbergs were arrested.[57]

The FBI became interested in the Cohens in 1953 when many Communist Party functionaries were going underground. An informant advised the bureau that the Cohens were Communists, that they had disappeared a few years earlier, and that they could be part of the CP underground. In 1955 Morris's father told the FBI that he knew nothing of his son and daughter-in-law's whereabouts but that he was still receiving small Veterans Administration disability checks for his son. He added that "his son's long unexplained absence had been the cause of considerable concern and sorrow to his late wife and himself and that it was also likely a contributing factor to his late wife's death and his own broken health."[58]

The FBI's first break in the case came on June 21, 1957, with the arrest of Rudolf Abel, whose real name was William Fischer. FBI agents found in his possession a package with $4,000 and photographs of a man and a woman. The photographs bore the names Morris and Shirley. Abel claimed that these were just two people he had met in the park one day and did not know their full names, but phrases used for agent recognition were written on the pictures. The FBI realized that the pictures were the kind that enabled a KGB officer to recognize agents when he met them for the first time and that the phrases were the "parole," or code words, to establish the contact.[59]

FBI sources soon identified the individuals in the photos as Morris and Lona Cohen.[60] In 1961 the Cohens were arrested in England as part of a Soviet spy ring, using the names Helen and Peter Kroger. The FBI was able to identify them to the British, and they were convicted and sentenced to long prison terms. In 1969 they were exchanged for a hapless young Englishman who had been arrested in the Soviet Union for mailing anti-Soviet leaflets for the Russian émigré organization NTS. A year later the FBI office in Switzerland requested copies of their photographs and finger-prints,[61] but by this time the Cohens were living in the Soviet Union under the protection of the KGB. Lona Cohen died in 1992 and Morris in 1995.[62] The Soviet government honored each of them with important medals, the Order of the Red Banner and the Order of People's Friendship. Shortly after Morris's death, President Yeltsin, considered a friend of the West, awarded him and Lona the highest Russian medal for bravery, the Gold Star, Hero of the Russian Federation—the new version of the Soviet Gold Star, Hero of the Soviet Union—for their heroic work against the United States and Great Britain.[63]

Harry Hopkins—Soviet Spy

Leonid Kvasnikov, a scientist in the New York *Rezidentura*, coordinated the collection of atomic information with the help of many officers and agents. On February 1, 1943, an American company received a request from the Soviet government to obtain 220 pounds of uranium oxide, 220 pounds of uranium nitrate, and 25 pounds of uranium metal. The company, Chemator, Inc., in New York City, had obtained small amounts of other chemicals for the Soviets as part of Lend-Lease. But this was the first time that the Soviets had asked for uranium. Although the company knew nothing about the secret atom bomb development, it asked the appropriate U.S. government authorities for permission, which was granted under Lend-Lease, but the uranium metal could not be obtained.

By March the Soviets were ordering tons of uranium, but Chemator, Inc., still could not to obtain it. Lieutenant General Leslie Groves, head of the Manhattan Project, was, moreover, concerned about Soviet espionage and later told Congress that he complained to the Lend-Lease executives, but they said that "there was a great deal of pressure being brought to bear on Lend-Lease, apparently to give the Russians everything they could think of. There was a great deal of pressure brought to give them this uranium material." According to General Groves, "We didn't want this material shipped, yet they [Lend-Lease] kept coming back and coming back."[64] The man who ran Lend-Lease was President Roosevelt's close friend and advisor Harry Hopkins.

General Groves was asked by the committee to testify because two days earlier it had taken testimony from Major George Racey Jordan, who had helped ship Lend-Lease material to the Soviet Union, first from Newark, New Jersey, and then from Great Falls, Montana. Jordan, however, had alerted the committee to the shipments of uranium and testified that Harry Hopkins had told him on the phone to expedite the shipments.[65] (He later wrote a book claiming that Hopkins had helped the Soviets against the interest of the United States.)[66] At the time of his testimony, 1950, no one thought that Hopkins might be a Soviet agent—that information surfaced years later from *Venona* and a report by an important KGB defector.

Hopkins was an expert on welfare. He headed the New York State welfare program until Governor Franklin Roosevelt became president and brought him to Washington. There he expanded his interest to include foreign policy and became President Roosevelt's major advisor. Others identified as spies by Chambers also found their way into the foreign policy establishment. Alger Hiss moved from the Agriculture Department to the Nye Committee investigating the armament industry. From there he went to the State Department, where he rose to a very high level. Harry Dexter White in the Treasury Department was given responsibility for all of that department's foreign policy activity. And John Abt went from Agriculture to the Justice Department, while Charles Kramer ended up in the Senate Subcommittee on War Mobilization.

Robert E. Sherwood, the friendly biographer of Roosevelt and Hopkins, began his book: "During the years when Harry Hopkins lived as a guest in the White House, he was generally regarded as a sinister figure, a backstairs intriguer, an Iowan combination of Machiavelli, Svengali and Rasputin. Hostility toward him was by no means limited to those who hated Franklin Delano Roosevelt. There were many of Roosevelt's most loyal friends and associates, in and out of the Cabinet, who disliked Hopkins intensely and resented the extraordinary position of influence and authority which he held."[67]

In the early 1960s Oleg Gordievsky, a KGB officer, attended a lecture by the veteran Chekist Iskhak Akhmerov, who, as we have seen, had been the "illegal" *Rezident* in the United States during the war. Akhmerov mentioned his contact with Alger Hiss, but the man he described as "the most important of all Soviet wartime agents in the United States" was Harry Hopkins. Gordievsky became one of the most knowledgeable defectors from the KGB. Even more to the point, for ten years before his defection, Gordievsky had been an agent in place for British intelligence (MI6) until he was exposed by CIA traitor Aldrich Ames.

In the lecture, Akhmerov described his contacts with Hopkins, which he said began before the American official's first visit to Moscow.[68] Akhmerov returned to the United States in late September 1941. Hopkins was dispatched to Moscow right after the Nazi attack on the Soviet Union, June 22. Akhmerov must have worked with Hopkins in the 1930s before Akhmerov returned to the Soviet Union in 1939.

When Gordievsky discussed Akhmerov's revelations about Hopkins with KGB colleagues and later with British intelligence and CIA officers, all agreed that Hopkins clearly had been a very important agent indeed. But after Gordievsky's discussions with his coauthor, British historian Christopher Andrew, he would say only that Hopkins was "an unconscious… agent."

The idea that Hopkins was "unconscious" is unrealistic. He was certainly conscious of the fact that he was dealing with the Soviets. More importantly, he was dealing with Akhmerov, the "illegal" *Rezident*. Some have argued that Hopkins was only serving as Roosevelt's "back channel" to Stalin. If this were true, his contact would not have been Akhmerov but any one of the many Soviet officials he saw regularly. Konstantin Oumansky, whom Hopkins frequently visited, was the Soviet ambassador until December 1941. He was replaced by Ambassador Maxim Litvinov, not only a very important Soviet official but also a cultured and intelligent contact of many Americans, including Hopkins. Litvinov's British-born wife, Ivy, traveled in the best social circles in Washington, although she, too, was a dedicated and experienced Communist and could have served as a "back channel." In 1943 Hopkins was in close official contact with Soviet general A. I. Belyaev, an official of the Soviet Purchasing Commission. Two *Venona* messages from Belyaev to the Soviet leadership contained messages to them from Hopkins,[69] who was also in direct contact with the dour but intelligent Andrei Gromyko after he replaced Litvinov as ambassador in August 1943. An October 1944 message from Gromyko to Molotov transmitted notes of a conversation with Hopkins on a variety of matters, including the forthcoming presidential election. Vassiliy Zarubin was assigned to the Washington embassy from the consulate in New York and could have acted as a "back channel." With such Soviet contacts, there was no need for Hopkins to meet with Akhmerov. More importantly, Akhmerov had no reason to break his "cover" as a middle-class businessman and reveal his identity as a Soviet intelligence officer to Hopkins unless Hopkins were an agent himself.

Direct evidence in *Venona* confirms Akhmerov's statement of his connection with Hopkins. A May 1943 *Venona* report signed by Akhmerov reveals that Soviet agent "19" reported discussions, during which he was present, between Roosevelt and Churchill during a May 1943 conference in Washington, D.C.[70] While the dates of the meetings are in State Department files, there are no official U.S. government records of the discussion at some of them. The Soviet report is the only one we have on one such meeting!

Eduard Mark, a military historian, after carefully examining *Venona*, concluded that agent "19" was Harry Hopkins.[71] Only Hopkins had a close enough relationship with Roosevelt to allow agent "19" to attend the secret meetings with Churchill. Mark referred to former KGB general Sudoplatov's claim that Hopkins had a confidential "back channel" relationship with Ambassadors Oumansky and Litvinov.[72] That is probably true, but if they indeed served as "back channels" for Hopkins, it does not explain the role of Akhmerov, who stayed away from the Soviet embassy to maintain his cover.

General Vadim Kirpichenko of the KGB headed the "Illegals Directorate" from 1974 to 1979. In a 1992 interview with the official Soviet army newspaper, he described the responsibilities of an "illegal" officer. He said, "The main nucleus of illegal intelligence consists of our fellow countrymen who have undergone special training and traveled abroad disguised as foreigners. They have a perfect knowledge of foreign languages and a thorough knowledge of the country in which they are to work." He pointed out that the KGB officer using the cover of "some official post in an institution abroad" may be known to the opposing counterintelligence service. But, he said, "an illegal can go where he likes. Unless, of course, he behaves stupidly and 'blows his cover.'"[73]

Akhmerov was not stupid. As an "illegal" *Rezident*, he kept his identity as a Soviet intelligence officer secret from the American government. He certainly would not identify himself to President Roosevelt's right-hand man. It was decades after the war before American intelligence agents were able to identify the Soviet spy chief they called "Elizabeth Bentley's Bill" as Akhmerov. In short, since Akhmerov was Hopkins's Soviet contact, Hopkins was a Soviet spy. It explains, among other things, why Hopkins was adamant about shipping uranium to the Soviet Union despite the objections of the military authorities.

There is also evidence of Hopkins's contact with the Communist underground in the early 1930s. Whittaker Chambers testified in 1948 that the secret Communist apparatus in the U.S. government consisted of a leading group of seven men, each of whom was the leader of a separate cell.[74] One of those cell leaders was Lee Pressman. The procedure was for each cell leader to organize a study group in his own government agency. The members of the group would then be evaluated and some chosen to join the underground apparatus of the Communist Party, later to be used for Soviet espionage.

Pressman established such a study group in the Department of Agriculture in late 1933. One of the members of the group was Harry Hopkins. None of the other members, all of whom were fellow travelers, has ever been connected to Soviet espionage.[75] When Pressman was questioned by the House Committee on Un-American Activities in 1948, he invoked the Fifth Amendment on questions relating to the Communist underground apparatus.[76]

In 1950 Pressman again appeared before the committee and admitted membership in a Communist Party cell in the Agriculture Department. He identified as other members of the cell John Abt, Nathan Witt, and Charles Kramer. Pressman testified that he was recruited into the Communist Party by Harold Ware, who also met with the group. After Ware's death, J. Peters met with the group. Pressman, who was evasive during much of his testimony, said nothing about the study group that included Hopkins.[77] Those identified by Pressman had already been publicly named by Chambers.

Pressman was deputy to Jerome Frank, general counsel to the Agriculture Department and another member of the study group, until 1935 when Harry Hopkins hired Pressman as general counsel to the Federal Employment Relief Administration, later the Works Progress Administration. In 1936 Pressman left the government and became general counsel of the CIO.[78]

On a number of significant issues relating to the Soviet Union, Hopkins unsurprisingly pressed for pro-Soviet solutions. The postwar future of Poland was an important area of disagreement between the Western allies and the Soviet Union. In September 1944 the Red Army was approaching Warsaw. The Polish underground Home Army, with the support of the government in exile in London, organized an uprising against the Nazi occupation. Although this would help the Red Army by undermining Nazi resistance, it also meant that the Poles would have a say in their country's future. So the Red Army halted its offensive long enough for the heroic Poles to be slaughtered.

Earlier, Roosevelt and Churchill planned to send allied planes to drop supplies to the beleaguered Poles and asked Stalin to allow the planes to land on Soviet territory:

> We are thinking of world opinion if anti-Nazis in Warsaw are
> in effect abandoned. We believe that all three of us should do

the utmost to save as many of the patriots there as possible. We hope that you will drop immediate supplies and munitions to the patriot Poles of Warsaw, or will you agree to help our planes in doing it very quickly? We hope you will approve. The time element is of extreme importance.

Stalin refused in a blistering letter:

> Sooner or later the truth about the handful of power-seeking criminals who launched the Warsaw adventure will [come] out. Those elements, playing on the credulity of the inhabitants of Warsaw, exposed practically unarmed people to German guns, armour and aircraft. The result is a situation in which every day is used, not by the Poles for freeing Warsaw, but by the Hitlerites, who are cruelly exterminating the civil population....
>
> I can assure you that the Red Army will stint no effort to crush the Germans at Warsaw and liberate it for the Poles. That will be the best, really effective, help to the anti-Nazi Poles.[79]

Unfortunately, some of the American military failed to understand the significant morale and political issues involved and opposed risking planes to supply the Poles. General F. L. Anderson, deputy commanding general for operations, U.S. Strategic Air Force in Europe, met with Hopkins on September 11, 1944. He told Hopkins that he thought the air drops were a bad idea, both because of the risk and because they might jeopardize our relations with Russia. Hopkins agreed and said that he would relay this to the president immediately. More significantly, according to Anderson, Hopkins said "that he would see that any cablegrams whether they came from Mr. Churchill or from Mr. Winant [U.S. ambassador in

London] would be held in abeyance and that we would not be committed to do this job."[80] That Hopkins would admit to a visitor that he was holding back cables to President Roosevelt that came from Churchill and the U.S. ambassador in London is amazing, but it indicates his incredible power.

After Roosevelt's death, President Truman sent Hopkins to Moscow in May 1945 to meet with Stalin. Assistant Secretary of State Charles Bohlen took minutes of the meeting. The American position was in favor of free elections in Poland. But Bohlen's notes showed that instead of pushing the American position, Hopkins told Stalin "that the United States would desire a Poland friendly to the Soviet Union and in fact desired to see friendly countries all along the Soviet borders." Stalin replied, "If that be so we can easily come to terms in regard to Poland."[81] The result was a Communist puppet government in Poland as repressive as that of the Soviet Union.

Hopkins also promoted his friends, including Colonel Philip R. Faymonville, who had been military attaché in Moscow from 1933 to 1938. Faymonville's colleagues considered him to be extremely pro-Soviet, calling him the "Red Colonel." When Hopkins in 1941 suggested sending him back to Moscow to expedite Lend-Lease, army intelligence objected. Hopkins said only, "You might as well get his papers ready, because he's going over." Hopkins arranged for Faymonville to be promoted to brigadier general and later to major general.[82]

To the Soviets, Faymonville's sympathetic attitude was not enough. They wanted him under control. According to a top secret official Soviet intelligence history, in 1942 the NKVD assigned an agent with the code name "Electric" to "develop" (a Soviet term for recruit) Faymonville. He arranged to meet the general at a concert at the Bolshoi Theatre. Faymonville was attracted to the young man and invited him to his apartment. Later that night the general drove the young man home, taking evasive turns to shake off anyone tailing them. He didn't know that his lover was an NKVD agent. He gave the young man his telephone number and arranged future trysts.[83] Faymonville was trapped—Hopkins, by forcing the army to send Faymonville back to Russia, had delivered the vulnerable American officer into Soviet hands.

Not everything Hopkins promoted was successful. In April 1944 Victor Kravchenko, an official of the Soviet Purchasing Commission, defected to the United States. The Soviets were furious and conducted a major operation to spy on him and try to get him back. Hopkins, for his part, urged the president to return the defector to the Russians. Roosevelt said that it would be easier to return the man if he were sure that the defector would not be shot. Since Hopkins could not supply such assurance, Kravchenko was not returned.[84]

In short, Hopkins frequently intervened with President Roosevelt in support of the Soviets. His covert relationship with Akhmerov is the best explanation of this activity.

"Kvant"—Mercenary

Venona messages to Moscow in June 1943 reported on a different kind of Soviet spy. He was a mercenary Soviet agent whose code name was "Kvant." Unlike most of the other agents during this period, "Kvant" was mainly interested in money. He requested a meeting for June 14 in the Soviet embassy, where he was received by Andrei Gromyko, then the deputy to Ambassador Maxim Litvinov and chargé d'affaires in Litvinov's absence. When he learned it was an intelligence matter, Gromyko handed "Kvant" over to an NKVD officer. "Kvant" explained that he had turned over valuable information on the atomic bomb to Semen Semenov, an NKVD officer in New York, using as cover the Soviet trade organization Amtorg. "Kvant," said the message, "is convinced of the value of the material and therefore expects from us a similar recompense for his labor—in the form of a financial reward." He was given $300.

"Kvant" provided the Soviets with highly technical information on the experiments and formulas that led to the development of the atomic bomb.[85] The decrypted messages contain no further reference to "Kvant." He has never been identified, although it appears that he was a significant scientist and well enough known to be received at the Soviet embassy by such a high-level official as Gromyko.

Arthur Adams—A Veteran Spy

Unlike Canada, where atomic espionage was handled by the GRU, Soviet military intelligence, in the United States the NKVD was in charge. The GRU assisted the NKVD with atomic espionage and assigned its most experienced intelligence officer, Arthur Adams, to assist in the efforts. Adams had been the first Soviet intelligence officer ever to operate in the United States. He served on the staff of Ludwig C. A. K. Martens, the Soviet pseudo-ambassador from 1919 to 1921—the United States did not recognize the Soviet Union until 1933. Martens opened up an office in New York rather than Washington, and he claimed it was an embassy. But the United States would not recognize his diplomatic claims, and he was deported in January 1921. Adams returned with him to the Soviet Union.

Adams's job was to steal technology from American firms. To accomplish this, he made numerous trips to the United States. Adams's real background is a mystery; we know only what he told the U.S. government in visa applications, some of which may be false. Calling himself Arthur Alexandrovich Adams, he first entered the United States from Canada in 1915, telling the Immigration Service officers that he had lived in the United States since 1910 and had spent only a few months in Canada. There are no records to confirm or refute his claim. All we know is that he was a Russian revolutionary before the Communist takeover in Russia.

When he tried to bring his wife into the United States in 1915, he produced Juliet Stuart Poyntz as a character witness. Poyntz later served as a Soviet agent but disappeared when she began to express doubts about the Soviet Union.[86]

Adams returned to the United States in 1928–1929 and again in 1932–1933 under cover of the Soviet trade organization Amtorg. At that time, he claimed to have been born in Sweden in 1885. In 1937 Adams was in Canada and attempted to reenter the United States. Samuel J. Novick, a businessman active in Communist underground operations, wrote a letter to the Immigration and Naturalization Service requesting permission for his "Canadian representative, Arthur Adams," to come to the United States to work for his company, Wholesale Radio Service Company, Inc. He claimed that Adams had been employed by him for ten years in Canada, where he said Adams had been born. The application was turned down.

When Novick was asked by the House Committee on Un-American Activities about his relationship with Adams, he said that he had met him in 1938 when Adams was a customer of his firm in Canada. When confronted with his 1937 letter to the Immigration Service, Novick claimed that he couldn't remember whether what he had written was true. In fact, it was not. During most of the time that Novick claimed Adams was his employee in Canada, Adams was in the Soviet Union. Novick had a hard time keeping his lies straight.

Adams finally got into the United States in May 1938 and in 1940 filed a Declaration of Intention to become an U.S. citizen. He registered for the draft and also under the Alien Registration Act, giving Canada as his place of birth in the year 1890. This would have made him over fifty years old, a little old to be drafted into the army.

As a cover for his espionage activities, Adams used supposed employment with the Electronics Corporation of America, headed by Samuel J. Novick, and Keynote Recordings, headed by Eric Bernay, another businessman in the Communist underground. Novick told the Un-American Activities Committee that the last time he had seen Adams was in 1945 at the office of Keynote Recordings. He claimed, "I went there to discuss record manufacturing possibilities with Mr. Bernay." Novick's company received classified contracts during the war in connection with radar installations.[87]

Adams was assigned to the GRU's support for the NKVD's atom bomb espionage project in 1944. He traveled to Chicago to meet with Clarence Francis Hiskey, a Communist Party member working on atomic research at the University of Chicago. Hiskey began his research on the atom bomb in September 1943 at Columbia University. The following month, he was transferred to the University of Chicago. There he made contact with the Communist Party district leadership. He appears to be the agent called "Ramsey" in *Venona*.[88]

Meanwhile, the NKVD, using the apparatus of the Communist Party USA, tried to take Hiskey away from the GRU. A *Venona* message on May 4, 1944, regarding "Ramsey," refers to "Olsen… district leader of the Communist Party in Chicago." "Olsen" was a code name. The Illinois district leader of the Communist Party was Morris Childs, whose brother Jack and sister-in-law Roz were active in the Party in New York. According to the message, Childs's wife, "who has been meeting 'Ramsey,' is also an active Communist Party member and met 'Ramsey' on the instructions of the organization." "Ramsey" was leaving the Chicago area and the *Rezidentura* suggested that Bernie Chester, the Communist Party liaison with the NKVD, get a letter from Childs which could be used by one of "our people" who would meet with the agent.[89] Hiskey testified before the House Committee on Un-American Activities that he worked at the University of Chicago's metallurgical laboratory until about May 1, 1944, when he was inducted into the army.[90]

In the spring of 1944, Hiskey, still working for GRU, traveled to Cleveland to meet with a colleague, John Chapin, who was temporarily assigned to work in Ohio. He told Chapin about his contact Arthur Adams, who, he said, was a "Russian agent," and asked whether Chapin would be willing to meet with him. Chapin agreed and gave Hiskey an ordinary house key that Adams could use to identify himself when he made contact.[91] In July, Roz Olsen (Roz Childs, sister-in-law of Morris and wife of Jack) wrote to Hiskey asking him to arrange to have someone put in contact with his "friend."[92]

In September 1944 Adams met with Chapin in Chicago and gave him the key. They then arranged to meet in Adams's room at the Stevens Hotel. During that meeting, Adams asked Chapin to provide him with information about his work on the atom bomb project. Chapin, in testimony before the House Committee on Un-American Activities in 1948, revealed the story but insisted that he never supplied classified information to Adams.[93] Chapin, although never prosecuted, was removed from his job handling classified information.

In December 1944 the New York *Rezidentura* advised Moscow that Bernie Chester, whose new code name was "Dick," was in contact with Jack Childs but not with Roz, whose code name was "Floks." As in many cases, the agents operated through "cut outs" and never personally met a Soviet intelligence officer. As a result, NKVD headquarters often knew little about the agents other than that they had been personally recommended by Communist Party USA officials. The *Rezidentura* planned to send Jack Childs, who knew Hiskey, to Hawaii to meet with Hiskey, who was stationed there in the army.[94]

Jack and Roz Childs had worked through Bernie Chester and, indirectly, with a Soviet intelligence officer. In March 1945

Moscow advised the New York *Rezidentura* that it would permit a meeting between the Childs family and an intelligence officer. But Moscow ordered NKVD New York first to report on what Chester had told the Childs couple about the scope of Soviet intelligence operations.[95]

In 1951 Morris, Jack, and Roz Childs were recruited by the FBI. For the next three decades, the family worked as FBI undercover agents in the Communist Party underground and in the KGB. Together with Morris's new wife, Eva, they made many trips to the Soviet Union gathering information for the FBI. But it appears that they were asked little about their World War II activity, which would have provided substantial information about Soviet wartime espionage. Possibly because of the compartmentalization of information in the FBI, special agents working on *Venona* were not told about the secret work of the Childs family and did not realize that they were the Olsens. The story of the Childs family and their often dangerous work for the United States has been documented in John Barron's exciting book *Operation Solo*.[96]

In December 1945 the press carried stories revealing that Arthur Adams was a Soviet intelligence officer. He disappeared and presumably went back to the Soviet Union. Soviet "illegals" such as Adams maintained contact with Moscow through a Soviet intelligence officer working as a "diplomat"—in Adams's case, Pavel Mikhailov, the GRU *Rezident*. On December 13, 1945, after the exposure of Adams, Mikhailov quickly left the United States.[97]

Klaus Fuchs—Spy from Germany

Klaus Fuchs had been sent by the British to help the Americans develop the atomic bomb and was not identified as a spy until after his return to England. In September 1949, based on FBI analysis of *Venona* traffic, the British arrested him.

Atomic Espionage

Fuchs, the son of well-known Protestant theologian Emil Fuchs, was born in 1911 in Russelsheim, Germany. A member of the Communist Party since 1930, he fled to England after Hitler took power.[98] In 1941 Fuchs was invited by Rudolf Peierls, an important physicist, to assist him with research work for the British government. Fuchs later confessed, "When I learned about the purpose of the work [an atomic bomb] I decided to inform Russia and I established contact through a member of the Communist Party."[99] The "member of the Communist Party" was soon identified as Jurgen Kuczynski, a longtime German Communist Party apparatchik who served as the leader of the German Communists in London.

A *Venona* GRU message from London to Moscow revealed that "On 8th August 'Barch' [Simon Kremer, officially the secretary to the Soviet military attaché in London, in reality the GRU *Rezident*] had a meeting with a former acquaintance of Dr. Fuchs...."[100] The message was only partially broken but appears to be the report to Moscow stating that Kuczynski had offered the services of his friend Fuchs to Soviet military intelligence. Using Fuchs's real name in a message was again poor tradecraft or, to use the Russian term, *konspiratsiya*.

In his confession, Fuchs revealed that after he had been put in contact with the Soviets, he often met with persons he would not name to pass on information to the Soviet Union. He said, "At this time I had complete confidence in Russian policy and I had no hesitation in giving all the information I had. I believed the Western allies deliberately allowed Germany and Russia to fight each other to death. I tried to concentrate on giving information on the result of my own work."[101]

Despite his desire to protect his comrades, Fuchs's information helped British counterintelligence to identify some of them, which Soviet sources later confirmed. The woman assigned by Kremer to be Fuchs's courier was Ruth Kuczynski, Jurgen's sister.[102] Under the code name "Sonia," she had served Soviet intelligence for many years and twice was awarded the Order of the Red Banner.[103] Fuchs even identified a picture of his courier in the United States, which was shown him by the FBI in England. The FBI knew the man in the picture as Harry Gold. Fuchs worked for Soviet military intelligence in England, but his spy work in the United States was run by the NKVD. Gold was an NKVD agent.

An early Fuchs-Gold meeting took place in New York City, where some of the theoretical work was done on the A-bomb. Later meetings were held in New Mexico when Fuchs was at Los Alamos. From *Venona* and the testimony of Gold, we learn more of the details of Fuchs's spying on behalf of the Soviet Union.[104] Fuchs's first meeting with Gold was reported to Moscow in February 1944:

> On 5th February a meeting took place between "Gus" [Harry Gold] and "Rest" [Klaus Fuchs]. Beforehand [Gold] was given a detailed briefing by us. [Fuchs] greeted him pleasantly but was rather cautious at first; during the discussion [Gold] satisfied himself that [Fuchs] was aware of whom he was working with. [Fuchs] arrived in the United States in September as a member of the British mission on "Enormous" [the atomic bomb project]. According to him the work on the atomic bomb in the United States is being carried out under the direct control of the United States Army represented by General [Brehan] Somervell and [Secretary of War Henry] Stimson: at the head of the group of British is a Labour Member of Parliament, Ben Smith. The whole operation amounts to the working out of the process for the separation of isotopes of Uranium. The work is proceeding in two directions: the electron method developed by [Professor Ernest] Lawrence... [part of the message missing].

Atomic Espionage

The message was signed by Leonid Kvasnikov, *Venona* code name "Anton,"[105] who was in charge of atomic spying in the New York *Rezidentura*.

Gold was sent to the meeting by his NKVD control officer, "Sam," later identified as Semen Semenov, whose cover was the Soviet trading organization Amtorg. According to Gold, "He was the most American of all of the Soviet agents. That is, in New York City he would very well pass for a native New Yorker. His accent, if you listened to it, was a little off."

The first Fuchs-Gold meeting took place on Manhattan's East Side near the Henry Street Settlement. To recognize each other, Gold carried an extra pair of gloves and a book, and Fuchs carried a tennis ball, which, although ordered by Semenov, struck Gold as a little peculiar. Gold took the scientist uptown to Manny Wolff's restaurant on Third Avenue and 49th Street.[106]

In June 1944 Fuchs provided Gold with a copy of a June 6 report he had written entitled "Fluctuations and the Efficiency of a Diffusion Plant." A *Venona* message reported it to Moscow only nine days after it was written.[107]

Robert Lamphere of the FBI was brought into the *Venona* project on October 19, 1948. Copies of decrypted messages were made available to the FBI but were very closely held. Lamphere's job was to help the cryptologists identify the agents that were known only by code names. One of the first messages he worked on was about the meeting between "Rest" and "Gus." When he discovered that the highly classified report given to the Russians only a few days after it was published was written by Klaus Fuchs, he became suspicious. Soon he linked it to other reports, including one mentioning Fuchs's sister by name. Lamphere's work was relayed to British counterintelligence.

In a September 26, 1949, report on the case, Lamphere outlined the evidence against Fuchs. Captured German documents identified

Fuchs as a Communist Party member. Fuchs's sister, Kristel, lived in the United States and was in contact with the unidentified Soviet agent "Gus." Kristel's husband, Robert Heineman, was reported to the FBI as a member of the American Communist Party in 1947. Klaus Fuchs's address was found in the address book of Israel Halperin, one of the people arrested as a result of the Gouzenko revelations. While he was pretty sure that Fuchs was "Rest," Lamphere could not identify "Gus."[108] FBI agents with pictures of spy suspects traveled to England to interrogate Fuchs.

In May 1950 Fuchs identified Harry Gold to the FBI as the contact he knew by the street name "Raymond."[109] The Americans now could identify him as the spy called "Gus" in *Venona*. Moscow changed Gold's code name on October 5, 1944, from "Gus" to "Arno."[110]

Harry Gold's contact with Fuchs's sister, Kristel, after a missed meeting with Fuchs was reported in a *Venona* message, which in another instance of poor tradecraft gave her true name. In August 1944 the New York NKVD *Rezident* Stepan Apresyan reported to Moscow that a month earlier, after hearing that Fuchs was leaving for England, the New York *Rezidentura* had instructed Gold to contact him. The instructions were passed through NKVD officer Anatoli Yatzkov, who also worked with the Rosenbergs. Yatzkov was Gold's new NKVD control officer. Gold knew him as "John."

Gold was instructed to meet with Fuchs and give him the password he would need for contact in England. But Fuchs didn't make the meeting. A few weeks later, Gold, still looking for Fuchs, was told that he had left for England. In fact, as the NKVD later learned, he had been transferred to Los Alamos. Yatzkov ordered Gold to find Fuchs's sister in order to resume his contact with the scientist.[111]

Kristel Fuchs Heineman, Klaus Fuchs's sister, had been away from her home in Cambridge, Massachusetts, and Gold could not contact her until September. (The progress of the attempt was duly reported to Moscow.)[112] When Gold finally visited her, Kristel advised him that her brother had been transferred to the Southwest. Gold gave her the phone number of an NKVD "safe house" in Manhattan to call when her brother came to visit her. When Fuchs called, Gold was sent to Cambridge to meet him. At this point they established a routine for contact in New Mexico.[113] When these *Venona* messages, which contained the real name of Fuchs's sister, were deciphered, they helped provide Lamphere with the links in the chain of evidence that identified Fuchs and led to Gold.

Fuchs served nine years in a British prison, after which he went to East Germany, where he lived for the rest of his life. According to an official East German publication, "Since 1959 he has played a leading part in GDR nuclear research and since their creation in 1973 and 1979 he has been chairman of the scientific councils of the Academy of Sciences for problems of basic research in energetic and microelectronics." More important, he was made a member of the Central Committee of the East German Communist Party, called the Socialist Unity Party of the German Democratic Republic.[114] Apparently, he had been forgiven for confessing to the British and identifying Gold to the FBI. Fuchs died on January 28, 1988, in East Berlin.[115]

But he was not forgiven by Kim Philby, one of the Soviet Union's most successful spies, who argued that when a spy is caught he should keep his mouth shut. As Philby explained in his KGB authorized autobiography, "Fuchs not only confessed his own part in the business, but also identified from photographs his contact in the United States, Harry Gold. From Gold, who was also in a talkative mood, the chain led inexorably to the Rosenbergs, who were duly electrocuted."[116]

CHAPTER 7

Atomic Espionage—The Rosenberg Case

HARRY GOLD, BETRAYED BY KLAUS FUCHS, was arrested by the FBI; he in turn told the bureau everything he knew, which ultimately led FBI investigators to Julius and Ethel Rosenberg. Gold was an unusual Soviet spy for this era. Although totally loyal to the Soviet Union, he was, unlike most of his fellow spies, not a Communist Party member but a "non-Party Bolshevik." He was recruited for Soviet espionage in 1934 by his friend Thomas Black, who was active in industrial espionage for the Soviets. Gold was sympathetic toward the Soviet Union, but, more importantly, he was concerned about anti-Semitism, particularly in Nazi Germany. First Black and then his Soviet control officers explained to Gold that anti-Semitism was a "crime against the state" in the Soviet Union— and that the Soviet Union was the main enemy of Nazi Germany. Even during the Nazi-Soviet Pact, Gold was told by one of his Soviet bosses that soon the Soviet Union would attack Germany, "and we will wipe Nazism from the face of the earth."[1]

In reality, there was considerable and official anti-Semitism in the Soviet Union in the 1930s, and it was Hitler, not Stalin, who broke the Soviet-Nazi alliance in 1941. But despite these distortions, the promises of fighting against anti-Semitism and Nazism were powerful weapons in keeping Harry Gold working as a Soviet spy.

Gold's early work for the Soviets was industrial espionage, stealing chemical formulas from American firms with his friend Black, a

Communist Party member since 1931 and a Soviet spy since 1933. Later, Black was transferred to the operations against the Trotskyites, and Gold was occasionally called upon to assist Black in surveying supposed Trotskyites in Philadelphia[2] under the new NKVD control officer, Dr. Gregory Rabinowitz, whose cover in the United States was as representative of the Russian Red Cross.[3]

During World War II Black was transferred back to industrial espionage. A March 1945 *Venona* message from the head of Soviet foreign intelligence in Moscow, Pavel Fitin, instructed the New York *Rezidentura* to use Black, then code-named "Peter," to gather information on the National Bureau of Standards.[4] When the FBI confronted Black in 1950, he told everything he knew. Black's information confirmed that the apparatus created to operate against Trotsky and his followers also provided some of the agents involved in atomic espionage. Black's recruit, Gold, evolved into a highly trusted agent who was awarded the important Soviet medal for bravery, the Order of the Red Star, in 1943.[5]

But the NKVD made an important mistake when Gold was put in contact with one agent too many—David Greenglass. Although the New York *Rezidentura* said, in one *Venona* report to Moscow, "We consider it risky to concentrate all the contacts relating to 'Enormous' [the atom bomb project] on 'Arno' [Harry Gold] alone,"[6] it nevertheless took that risk and sent him to Greenglass because no other courier was available.

Julius Rosenberg Identified

Greenglass, who worked on the A-bomb project at Los Alamos, was Julius Rosenberg's brother-in-law. (Ethel Rosenberg was David's older sister.) The Rosenbergs were members of the Communist Party and had convinced David to join the Young Communist League during the late 1930s.[7] When Greenglass was identified by the FBI from information Gold gave, Greenglass, to save himself and his wife, Ruth, told the FBI about Ethel and Julius Rosenberg.

As a Soviet spy, Julius Rosenberg couldn't attend Communist Party branch meetings, fearing that too many of his comrades would get to know him. Rosenberg maintained his membership in the Party through Bernard Schuster—Party name: Bernie Chester—the head of the New York State Control Commission of the Communist Party. The Control Commission was the Party's internal security apparatus, and Chester was the Party's liaison with Soviet intelligence.

A September 1944 *Venona* message to Moscow described Rosenberg's activity: "In the Communist Party line 'Liberal' [Julius Rosenberg] is in touch with Chester. They meet once a month for the payment of dues. Chester is interested in whether we are satisfied with the collaboration and whether there are not any misunderstandings. He does not inquire about specific items of [Soviet intelligence] work. Inasmuch as Chester knows about the role of 'Liberal's' group we beg consent to ask Chester through 'Liberal' about leads from among people who are working on 'Enormous' and in other technical fields."[8]

Rosenberg was eager to recruit new people for Soviet espionage. He and his wife, Ethel, suggested recruiting his sister-in-law, Ruth Greenglass, to set up a "safe house" for the spy ring. The New York *Rezidentura* reported the Rosenbergs' suggestion to Moscow: "Lately the development of new people has been in progress. 'Liberal' [Julius Rosenberg] recommended the wife of his wife's brother, Ruth Greenglass, with a safe flat in view. She is 21 years old, an American citizen, a member of the Young Communist League since 1942. She lives on Stanton Street. 'Liberal' and his wife recommend her as an intelligent and clever girl."[9]

It was bad tradecraft to put Ruth's real name in the message, but then the NKVD believed its code couldn't be broken. The American

code breakers proved the Soviets wrong. The 1995 release of the first
Venona messages by the NSA sent shock waves through the ranks of the
Rosenberg defenders. Walter and Miriam Schneir, whose 1965 book
argued that the Rosenbergs were innocent,[10] found the *Venona* messages "amazing, sad, disturbing material...." The Schneirs admitted
that the messages reveal that Julius Rosenberg was a spy and that the
American Communist Party and particularly its leaders were involved
in the recruitment of Party members for espionage. But they clutched
at a straw to argue that "Ethel Rosenberg was not a Soviet agent."[11]

What the Schneirs ignored was that both Julius and Ethel had
recommended Ruth Greenglass as an agent. The Soviet intelligence
officers did not take recommendations from just anyone, only those
of a "trusted comrade." Since the spies were run in rings rather than
individually, Moscow sometimes knew little about the agents, other
than that they were part of a group, whereas the NKVD officers in
the field were often well versed on an agent's background. On
receiving the Ruth Greenglass recommendation, Moscow wanted to
know more about Julius Rosenberg's wife. The New York
Rezidentura responded: "Surname that of her husband, first name
Ethel, 29 years old. Married 5 years. Finished secondary school. A
Communist Party member since 1938. Sufficiently well developed
politically. Knows about her husband's work and the role of 'Metr'
[Joel Barr] and 'Nil' [unidentified]. In view of delicate health does
not work. Is characterized positively and as a devoted person." The
message was signed "Anton"—Leonid Kvasnikov, the Soviet intelligence officer in charge of atomic spying.[12]

Poor health, however, did not stop Ethel, who was devoted to
the Soviet Union, from helping her husband's espionage.

The Schneirs and other defenders of the Rosenbergs now argue
that Julius was merely a Soviet spy—not an atomic spy. In fact, Julius
Rosenberg organized the theft not only of atomic secrets but also of

other important military technology. In a September 1944 *Venona* message, the New York *Rezidentura* reported that Rosenberg provided information on a "robot" bomb that would be mounted on aircraft carriers for use against Japan.

The key to the government's case against the Rosenbergs was what David Greenglass had supplied the Soviets, through the Rosenbergs: a diagram of the lens that would be used to detonate the bomb. David testified that while on leave in New York, Julius introduced him to a Russian who asked specifically about the "high explosive lenses" and the "formula of the curve of the lens."[13]

This meeting appears to have been in response to a request from Rosenberg that an intelligence officer with scientific knowledge meet with Greenglass. A December *Venona* message from the New York *Rezidentura* said:

> "Osa" [Ruth Greenglass] has returned from a trip to see "Kalibr" [David Greenglass]. "Kalibr" expressed his readiness to help in throwing light on the work being carried on at Camp-2 [Los Alamos] and stated that he had already given thought to this question earlier. "Kalibr" said that the authorities of the Camp were openly taking all precautionary measures to prevent information about "Enormous" [the atomic bomb project] falling into Russian hands. This is causing serious discontent among the progressive workers…. [In] the middle of January "Kalibr" will be in "Tyre" [New York City]. "Liberal" [Julius Rosenberg], referring to his ignorance of the problem, expresses the wish that our man should meet "Kalibr" and interrogate him personally. He asserts that "Kalibr" would be very glad of such a meeting. Do you consider such a meeting advisable? If not, I shall be obliged to draw up a questionnaire and pass it to "Liberal." Report whether you have any questions of priority interest to us.[14]

The security arrangements at Los Alamos notwithstanding, Greenglass prepared a diagram of the crucial lens that caused the bomb to detonate. Julius Rosenberg, by requesting that a Soviet intelligence officer speak directly to Greenglass, set in motion a chain of events that would result in the death sentence for both Julius and Ethel.

The Rosenbergs also introduced the Greenglasses to Ann Sidorovich, who planned to meet them in New Mexico to pick up the atomic information. David and Ruth had not met Ann before but knew her husband, Mike Sidorovich. In case Ann could not make the trip, Julius provided David with half of a Jell-O box. If an unknown person approached David with the other half, he would be the courier.[15] When Ann could not make the trip, a man arrived at the Greenglass apartment in Albuquerque and produced the other half of the Jell-O box. David would later identify that man during the Rosenberg trial as Harry Gold. David admitted giving Gold sketches and descriptive material on the atom bomb. At the request of Julius Rosenberg, David compiled a list of people at Los Alamos that he thought might be vulnerable for recruitment and gave it to Gold.[16]

Gold confessed in the Rosenberg trial that he had met with Greenglass in Albuquerque and had obtained the information on the bomb project. He explained that he had been given half of a Jell-O box, which he described as "a piece of cardboard, which appeared to have been cut from a packaged food of some sort," from the Soviet intelligence officer Yatzkov, whom he knew as "John." Yatzkov instructed Gold to tell Greenglass, "I come from Julius."[17]

Other Members of the Rosenberg Ring

Ann Sidorovich, whose failure to make the trip caused the fateful meeting between Gold and Greenglass, was a close friend of the Rosenbergs. Her husband, Michael, had worked for Soviet intelligence earlier but had dropped out of activity. In October 1944, when Rosenberg recommended him for the spy ring, the New York *Rezidentura* told Moscow that Sidorovich was a member of the Communist Party:

> He was a volunteer in Spain. He lives in the Western part of New York State; for the past three years has not carried on active political work. "Liberal" [Rosenberg] has known him since childhood; during the last 10 years has known him in political life. He characterizes him and his wife as devoted and reliable people. The wife by profession is a dressmaker and can open a shop in the city for cover. Let us know whether you consider "Linza" [Michael Sidorovich] more suitable to go to "Yakov" [William Perl]. A reply for communicating to "Liberal" is necessary before 23 October. At the meeting with "Liberal," "Linza" expressed readiness to renew contact with us.[18]

As Sidorovich's code name implied ("Linza" translates as "lens"), he was a photographer. The New York *Rezidentura* was asking Moscow for instructions on whether he should be used to assist Rosenberg or be sent to help William Perl, another member of the ring, who was then in Cleveland.

Moscow soon authorized the recruitment, and Sidorovich's first assignment was to help Rosenberg photograph stolen classified documents.

In late December the New York *Rezidentura* reported to the NKVD Center that "Michael Sidorovich and his wife have left for 'Yakov's' [William Perl's] town [Cleveland, Ohio]." At the end of December, Julius Rosenberg was scheduled to go to Cleveland and put Sidorovich in touch with Perl. The NKVD provided $500 to help Sidorovich with expenses.[19]

William Perl, Sidorovich's espionage colleague in Cleveland, was very important to the Soviets. In September 1944 the New York *Rezidentura* reported to Moscow that while Perl had been reimbursed for his travel to bring stolen material to New York, he received no pay. New York held that his material was "no less valuable than that given by the rest of the members of 'Liberal's' group who were given a bonus by you." The *Rezidentura* suggested that Moscow authorize a bonus to him of $500.[20]

Although members of the Rosenberg ring, like other Soviet agents, were loyal Communists and did not expect to be paid, the NKVD wanted to give them "awards." Some of those "awards" were in cash, some were expensive gifts. In March 1945 the Moscow Center, in a *Venona* message to New York, ordered the payment of an "award" of $1,000 to Rosenberg; other members of the group were given "valuable gifts." The New York *Rezidentura* was instructed to invent "well thought-out cover stories" to explain to the agents why they were receiving the money or gifts, because the agents did not want to feel like mercenaries: They were revolutionaries working to assist the Soviet Union, the base of the world revolution. The instructions were signed by Lieutenant General Pavel Fitin, the head of NKVD foreign intelligence.[21]

Julius Rosenberg was a direct link between Soviet intelligence and the leadership of the American Communist Party, and in a *Venona* message in April 1945, the Moscow Center referred to information "reported by 'Liberal' himself to the leadership of the 'fellow countrymen' [Communist Party USA]."[22]

Recruiting new agents was one of Julius Rosenberg's most important jobs for his Soviet handlers. In July 1944 the New York *Rezidentura* reported to Moscow in a *Venona* message that earlier in the month Rosenberg had been sent by his employer, the U.S. Army Signal Corps, to Washington for ten days.

Atomic Espionage—The Rosenberg Case

Rosenberg viewed his former classmates at City College of New York as potential recruits. While in Washington, he visited one such classmate, Max Elitcher. In yet another example of poor tradecraft, NKVD New York used Elitcher's true name in the message. Elitcher, Moscow was told, worked for the Bureau of Standards as head of the "fire control section for warships [which mount guns] of over five-inch caliber. He has access to extremely valuable material on guns." The *Rezidentura* reported that Elitcher had a Master of Science degree and, since finishing college, had been a member of the Communist Party. Rosenberg recommended him to Soviet intelligence, characterizing him as "a loyal, reliable, level-headed and able man. Married, his wife is a Communist Party member. She is a psychologist by profession, she works at the War Department. Max Elitcher is an excellent amateur photographer and has all the necessary equipment for taking photographs." New York asked the Moscow Center to check Elitcher out and give consent to his recruitment.[23]

Elitcher's recruitment would prove a costly error for Rosenberg, for Max later appeared as a witness in the Rosenberg trial and implicated not only Julius but also codefendant Morton Sobell.[24] (Elitcher was identified in 1948 when the July 1944 *Venona* message was decoded.[25]) The NKVD error in using Elitcher's true name in the message was even worse than Julius Rosenberg's; together it ended in helping to send Julius Rosenberg to the electric chair.

In June 1944 another of Rosenberg's potential recruits was reported to the Center, but the National Security Agency deleted his name from the released *Venona* messages.[26] The new recruit was another school friend of Julius Rosenberg, and NKVD New York planned to use Bernie Chester, the Communist Party official, to maintain contact with him. The New York *Rezidentura* asked Moscow's permission to recruit him and reported that the potential agent graduated from City College of New York and was active in the Federation of Architects, Engineers, Chemists, and Technicians (FAECT).[27] FAECT was a union controlled by the Communist Party.[28]

The unidentified recruit may have been Aaron Coleman, who was employed by the U.S. Army Signal Corps at Fort Monmouth, New Jersey, until September 1953. He lost his job when he was accused by the army of removing classified documents from the fort, some of which had been found in his home. On December 8 and 19, 1953, he testified before the McCarthy Committee and gave long and convoluted answers to the committee's questions. The chief military intelligence officer at Fort Monmouth, Andrew J. Reed, testified that Coleman, after denying the removal of classified documents, admitted it and allowed a search of his home, where the classified documents were indeed found.

Coleman testified that he knew Julius Rosenberg and Morton Sobell at City College in New York. He admitted having seen Sobell later, and he allowed his name to be used as a reference in 1947 on Sobell's application for a job. He claimed that he was not a member of the Young Communist League while in college but that Rosenberg had taken him to one meeting. Another classmate, however, testified that Coleman had in fact been a YCL member.

Coleman denied ever seeing Julius Rosenberg while he was employed at Fort Monmouth,[29] but during his trial Rosenberg testified that he had met with Aaron Coleman at the fort. Rosenberg also said that Coleman was a fellow member of the FAECT.[30] Coleman was never prosecuted, only fired from his position with the Signal Corps.

Alfred Sarant, a member of the Communist Party, was also recruited by the Rosenberg spy ring in May 1944. In the message from New York asking Moscow's permission for the recruitment, the *Rezidentura* carelessly included his true name in the transmission. Sarant was described as "25 years old, a Greek, an American citizen who lives in [New York City]. He completed an engineering course at Cooper Union in 1940 [and] worked for two years at the Signal Corps Laboratory at Fort Monmouth." He was fired from Fort Monmouth for what the NKVD in the Venona message described as "past union activity" and then worked for two years at Western Electric.[31]

The New York *Rezidentura* reported to Moscow that Rosenberg was in contact with Sarant, who was given the *Venona* code name "Khyus." As he was a good friend of Joel Barr, *Venona* code name "Metr," and already a member of the Rosenberg ring, the *Rezidentura* decided to "pair them off and get them to photograph their own materials." Although Sarant was a good photographer and had his own darkroom, he did not have a Leica, a high-quality German camera that was ideal for photographing documents, so the *Rezidentura* proposed giving him one. The plan was for Barr to give the developed film to Rosenberg, who would be responsible for supervising the team.[32]

While the Rosenbergs were awaiting trial, Julius met a kindred soul in the Federal House of Detention, who turned out to be a valuable source of information for the FBI. It was only after obtaining the *Venona* messages that we can see just how valuable his information was. Jerome Tartakow, a former member of the Young Communist League, was asked to contact Rosenberg by another prisoner, Eugene Dennis, general secretary of the American Communist Party. Tartokow was a common criminal, but he easily made friends with other Communists in the jail, including Dennis and William Perl, a member of the Rosenberg spy ring.

Initially Tartakow was reluctant to cooperate with the FBI, but by February 1951 he had agreed, with the stipulation that he would neither testify in court nor receive any compensation. Tartakow was placed in the same cell as Rosenberg, who told him that he and his wife would not confess and would go to the electric chair rather than reveal anything. Tartakow reported to the FBI that "Rosenberg is fanatically devoted to the cause of Communism and is prepared to die for it."

Rosenberg revealed to Tartakow that he had stolen a "proximity fuse" to detonate antiaircraft shells when they got close to enemy planes, then a highly guarded secret, and had provided it to the Russians. Rosenberg also admitted to Tartakow that when the FBI questioned him, he had $7,000 in cash and a Leica camera in his home. Ethel, Julius said, put the money and the camera in a shopping bag and gave it to a Communist Party member living in New York's Knickerbocker Village to hide for him. When Tartakow told this to the FBI, the bureau had no way to confirm this part of his story until the *Venona* files were decrypted.

In May 1944 the New York *Rezidentura* was worried about how to handle the large amount of secret documents provided by the agents. They were being photographed at the home of Yatzkov, but a *Venona* message revealed that this was considered dangerous. The NKVD decided that Julius Rosenberg, who then had the code name "Antenna," should photograph the material himself.[33]

In July 1944 the New York *Rezidentura* asked Moscow to instruct the Mexico City *Rezidentura* to buy two cameras and send them to New York immediately. One of the cameras was for Rosenberg, the other for the office of the *Rezidentura*. The cameras were sent from Germany to Mexico and cost $200—because of the war they were not available in the United States.[34] A few weeks later, the Moscow Center sent instructions to the Mexico City *Rezidentura*: "Buy two Leica cameras. A sum of money amounting to 2,400 pesos was transferred on 27 July addressed to [Ambassador Konstantin] Oumansky."[35]

Soon there was a shortage of film. Kvasnikov, the head of atomic spying in the New York *Rezidentura*, thereupon requested that Moscow instruct the *Rezidentura* in Mexico City to supply New York with one hundred 35mm cassettes.[36] Rosenberg was running eight agents, and until he got the help of Sidorovich, he was doing all the photography himself. He was working so hard that Kvasnikov advised Moscow, "The state of 'Liberal's' [Rosenberg's] health is nothing splendid. We are afraid of putting 'Liberal' out of action with overwork."[37]

Tartakow was providing valuable information on the Rosenberg spy ring, and in March 1951 he hinted that he would like to be compensated for his information. The FBI agreed. Tartakow then went on to report to the FBI that Rosenberg had told him that the Sidorovichs, members of his ring, had an identical Leica camera given to them by the Russians. Rosenberg told Tartakow that he did not expect the Sidorovichs, who were as deeply involved in espionage as he was, to testify against him because if they did, "they would have to cut their own throats."[38]

In April 1951 Rosenberg revealed to Tartakow that Sarant had "two excellent friends, namely Professors 'Beta' and 'Morris or Morrison.'" The FBI realized that Rosenberg was talking about two professors at Cornell University, Hans Bethe and Philip Morrison, both involved in atomic research.[39] The bureau wondered why Bethe and Morrison should be so close to Sarant, who was not on their intellectual level.

Bethe had been interviewed by the FBI in 1950, when he told the special agents that he knew Sarant through the latter's father-in-law, Victor Ross, described by Bethe as holding "opinions very close to [the] Communist Party line."[40] Ross had written a character reference on a job application for Joel Barr, a member of the ring, and the FBI was already interested in him.[41]

Based on the Tartakow information, the Albany FBI office asked permission to interview Bethe and Morrison. But headquarters responded, "Inasmuch as Dr. Bethe has previously been interviewed concerning this matter on July 28, 1950, and he is presently under investigation as a subject of a separate [redacted] matter, it is not desired that he be re-interviewed at this time. With respect to Dr. Philip Morrison, he is likewise the subject of a separate [redacted] investigation and, in view of his past critical attitude toward the Bureau at the time of his previous interviews in applicant and other routine matters, it is not desired that he be interviewed in connection with this matter."[42] The redacted words could have been espionage, but apparently the FBI was concerned that the vocal Morrison would cause it some bad publicity.

The FBI proceeded to interview Communist Party members that it suspected of being members of the Rosenberg ring. Alfred Sarant was interviewed by the FBI in July 1950 and was vague on every significant issue. But he admitted knowing Julius and Ethel Rosenberg and said that he thought he might have been introduced to them by Joel Barr. Sarant, however, made a significant admission, according to the FBI report: "Sarant, after denying that he had ever engaged in espionage activities with Julius Rosenberg, was asked, 'Did Rosenberg ever proposition you?' He replied that Rosenberg did and that he believed this took place at one of their meetings under the following circumstances. He and Rosenberg were alone and walking one evening some place in NYC's Lower Eastside.... [He] believes it possible that they met earlier in the evening at a meeting of the FAECT union...." Sarant said that Rosenberg was "sounding him out politically," but "I did not bite." He also told the FBI that he was a close friend of both Joel Barr and William Perl.[43]

Sarant and Barr Flee

When Tartakov told his story to the FBI, Sarant and Barr had both disappeared, and the FBI knew nothing about their whereabouts, except Tartakow's report that Rosenberg said that Sarant was in Europe. The FBI believed that the pair was somewhere in the Soviet bloc. It wasn't until 1983 that Mark Kuchment, a Jewish refugee from the Soviet Union working as a historian at the Russian Research Center of Harvard University, revealed that he had discovered the whereabouts of the two fugitives. Sarant, Kuchment reported, lived first in Czechoslovakia and then moved to Leningrad, where he lived and worked under the name Philip Staros. Under that name, he engaged in computer research for the Soviet military and died in 1979. Barr, an electronics engineer, was still alive and working in Leningrad as Joseph Berg.[44]

The files of the Czech Ministry of the Interior provide additional information on the activities of the two before they reached the Soviet Union. During the hysteria against Jews in Czechoslovakia in the aftermath of the anti-Semitic Slansky Purge Trial of 1952, a complaint was made to the secret police that Barr and Sarant were suspicious foreigners too interested in the work of the institute where they were employed.[45] The complaint was reported in a letter to the Czech minister of the interior, Rudolf Barak, from the Communist Party Central Committee, Department of State and Defense Administration:

> In July 1953 the Central Committee of the Communist Party got a report from workers of the Military Technical Institute about Philip Staros of Greek nationality and about Joseph Berg of English nationality, who suspiciously were interested in production in this technical Institute. These people were placed in the Institute in 1950 through the Central Committee of the Communist Party of Czechoslovakia and through the Secretary Slansky.
>
> We submitted this warning on July 21, 1953, to be inves-

tigated by the Ministry of Interior from which we got an
answer in 1953 that this is really a very important matter and
that it is being investigated by the proper department of the
Ministry of Interior....

Since the suspicious activity of the above named is
observed from the time they entered this job and since it is a
very important production facility we asked you to express
yourself on whether our approach was all right.[46]

Even though they had been placed in their jobs by Slansky, the
main victim of the anti-Semitic purge trial, the secret police found
them innocent of any wrongdoing, possibly because the KGB
vouched for them. On May 20, 1954, the minister of the interior
reported to Antonin Novotny, the first secretary of the Communist
Party, that "the activity of both named above... is all right from the
viewpoint of State Security." After being vetted in Czechoslovakia,
Barr and Sarant moved to the Soviet Union, where they performed
valuable services for their hosts.

Barr was interviewed in Leningrad in 1992 by the *Los Angeles
Times* and said, "I am ready to confess, or whatever the word is, to say
that really I made a tremendous mistake.... Knowing what I do now
it was a tremendous mistake to have done what I did."[47] What he did
was help design the first Soviet computer and become a pioneer in
the Soviet microelectronics industry. He also built the first Soviet
radar-guided antiaircraft gun, which was used against American
planes in the Vietnam War. He claimed that he never meant to "put
the United States in peril" but wished only to help Communism
thrive in Russia so that one day it would spread to America.

Barr insisted that his work on the antiaircraft gun was justified
because Vietnam was a bad war which was opposed by millions, but
Robert Lamphere, also interviewed by the paper, disagreed.

Atomic Espionage—The Rosenberg Case

(Lamphere had been the FBI agent assigned to work with the code breakers on *Venona* to identify the Soviet agents.) Lamphere said, "I think he's a spy and a traitor, and I feel very angry about the fact that he can come back to America and get a US passport."

Barr made a number of trips back to the United States and resumed contact with friends and relatives. His brothers, however, refused to speak with him. Barr died in Moscow on August 1, 1998.[48]

With some of the atomic spies in Europe, beyond the reach of the government, and others unable to be tried without live witnesses, the most promising case was that of Julius and Ethel Rosenberg.

The Rosenberg Defense Campaign

Julius and Ethel Rosenberg's case was largely ignored by the Communist Party until after their conviction. The Party, for example, made no attempt to provide the couple with first-class lawyers. Instead, they had the decidedly third-class Communist lawyer Emanuel Bloch as their counsel. Though the evidence against them was overwhelming and a better lawyer would probably have also lost the case, Bloch didn't help. The Party, moreover, knew that Bloch was a poor lawyer. In 1949, a year before the Rosenberg indictment, Bloch had been accused of mishandling a civil rights case by Ann Rivington, who had worked as a reporter for the *Daily Worker* since the 1930s. The experienced Rivington made her accusation in a letter to William Patterson, a Communist Party national leader and head of the Civil Rights Congress, a Communist front. He in turn sent it to the Communist Party's New York State Control Commission. Rivington, an unpaid *Daily Worker* employee, said that when she spoke to Bloch about his poor handling of the civil rights case, he countered by offering to use his influence in the Communist Party to get her a paying job. She "took this as a veiled and astute attempt at a bribe."[49]

Bloch's defense of the Rosenbergs was, indeed, poorly conducted. The Rosenbergs were convicted and received the death penalty. Judge Irving R. Kaufman, in sentencing them on April 5, 1951, said:

> I consider your crime worse than murder.... I believe your conduct in putting into the hands of the Russians the A-bomb years before our best scientists predicted Russia would perfect the bomb has already caused, in my opinion, the Communist aggression in Korea, with the resultant casualties exceeding 50,000 and who knows but that millions more of innocent people may pay the price of your treason. Indeed, by your betrayal you undoubtedly have altered the course of history to the disadvantage of our country. No one can say that we do not live in a constant state of tension. We have evidence of your treachery all around us every day for the civilian defense activities throughout the nation are aimed at preparing us for an atom bomb attack.[50]

Morton Sobell was sentenced to thirty years in prison; David Greenglass, despite testifying truthfully about his own activities and those of his sister and brother-in-law, was sentenced to fifteen years.[51] Sobell, who declined to testify in his own defense, served eighteen-and-a-half years in federal prison. He still denies his guilt but admits his leftist sympathies. In 1979 he visited Communist Cuba and when he returned tried to organize a shipment of electronics, books, and magazines for Cuban institutions.[52]

For a time, while the Rosenbergs sat on death row, the Communists continued to ignore the case because it showed a too obvious link between the American Communist Party and Soviet espionage. Without the open support of the Communist Party, the defense campaign started in low key with the publication in August 1951 of a series of articles by leftist journalist William A. Reuben. Published in the *National Guardian,* a New York weekly edited by Cedric Belfrage, a British citizen exposed in *Venona* as a Soviet agent, the case did not receive much attention. No *Daily Worker* stories appeared on the Rosenbergs until after the death sentences were pronounced. Even then, for months there were only occasional stories, mainly citing other people's views that the death penalty was too harsh. It was not until January 3, 1952, that the official voice of the Communist Party, the *Daily Worker,* in a small story on page 3, announced the formation of the National Committee to Secure Justice in the Rosenberg Case.

Soon thereafter a major Communist campaign was launched on behalf of the Rosenbergs. There was a reason. The Rosenberg case was needed to distract attention from the case of Rudolf Slansky, the general secretary of the Czech Communist Party, who was arrested in December 1951. He was Jewish, as were most of his codefendants in the purge trial that the Czech Communist secret police ran a year later. To counter the bad image created throughout the world by the Czech Communist anti-Semitic purge, the Rosenberg defenders stressed the Rosenbergs' Jewish origin to accuse the United States of anti-Semitism. They ignored the fact that the judge, Irving Kaufman, was also Jewish, as was the prosecutor, Irving H. Saypol, and much of his staff.

A 1952 leaflet of the Rosenberg Committee argued the anti-Semitic line with a headline that read: "People Rallying to Save Rosenbergs, Religious and Other Leaders Protest Death Sentence of Young Jewish Couple—Urge President Grant Clemency." A similar headline appeared in a leaflet in newspaper format called *To Secure Justice.* A postcard to President Truman issued by the National Labor Committee for Clemency for the Rosenbergs, an affiliate of the Rosenberg Committee, claimed that clemency "would be greeted throughout the world by the Jewish people." Another leaflet aimed at black Americans was entitled "Stop the Legal Lynching of Ethel and Julius Rosenberg" and made reference to blacks' being framed in the South.[53]

The false accusation of anti-Semitism in the United States in respect to the Rosenbergs distressed American Jewish leaders. They issued a statement in mid-1952:

> For some months the Anti-Defamation League has been alert to an intensive propaganda campaign being promoted by a Communist-inspired group which seeks to create the false impression that Ethel and Julius Rosenberg, convicted atom spies, have been the victims of an alleged anti-Semitic frame-up. This campaign has been slanted to agitate Jewish people throughout the US and the world in an effort to gain adherents and thereby give the entire project an appearance of being promoted by Jews as such. The following statement has just been released by all the Jewish agencies constituent to the National Community Relations Advisory Council, alerting American Jewry to this "fraudulent" effort.
>
> Any group of American citizens has a right to express its views as to the severity of the sentence in any criminal case. Attempts are being made, however, by a Communist-inspired group called the National Committee to Secure Justice in the Rosenberg Case, to inject the false issue of anti-Semitism into the Rosenberg case. We condemn these efforts to mislead the people of this country by unsupported charges that the religious ancestry of the defendants was a factor in the case. We denounce this fraudulent effort to confuse and manipulate public opinion for ulterior political purposes.[54]

A Jewish leader provided a copy of the statement to the CIA in order to alert the agency to the possibility of a similar propaganda

Atomic Espionage—The Rosenberg Case

campaign abroad. The CIA in turn sent the statement to the FBI for the information of J. Edgar Hoover.

The concern was well founded. In late 1952, as the anti-Semitic hysteria generated by the Slansky case was reaching its height in Czechoslovakia, the agitation about the Rosenberg case spread to Europe. Before November 1952 there had been little activity in Europe, but on November 27, 1952, a Rosenberg Committee appeared in London and another in Paris on December 3. The false accusation that anti-Semitism was behind the conviction of the Rosenbergs had been a major propaganda theme. French Communist leader Jacques Duclos said in the Paris Communist newspaper *L'Humanité* of December 9, 1952, that the Rosenbergs were convicted because they were Jews, whereas the Slansky trial victims were convicted because they committed crimes.

Rabbi S. Andhil Fineberg, director of Community Service of the American Jewish Committee, exposed the real reason for the campaign in his 1953 book *The Rosenberg Case: Fact and Fiction*:

> The explanation for the sudden feverish activity of the international Communist network on behalf of the doomed American pair can readily be understood when one recalls that the trial of Rudolf Slansky and thirteen co-defendants took place in Prague, Czechoslovakia, on November 20–21, 1952, and ended with the hanging of eleven defendants on December 3. Reports of what was transpiring at that trial sent a wave of revulsion through the free world. It appeared that even the hypnotized worshipers of the Kremlin would not be able to stomach the Prague trials. Eleven of the fourteen defendants were Jews by birth who were completely devoted to the Communist cause. They had been hostile to their own religious group, anti-Zionist and entirely servile to Moscow yet in this trial the Communist leadership, which had prided itself on having "outlawed" anti-Semitism and

on having been the exponent of perfect equality regardless of race or religious origin, indulged in unmistakable anti-Semitism.[55]

Czech archives show that in 1953 an American Communist Party official, William Patterson, who also headed the front organization Civil Rights Congress, contacted the Czech ambassador in Washington to suggest that his government offer to exchange the American journalist William Oatis, who had been arrested in 1951 in a spy frame-up, for the Rosenbergs. The Czech Communists agreed but asked permission from the Russians. The Russian answer, if any, has not been found.[56] Oatis was released in 1953 before the Rosenbergs were executed.[57] It's possible that the Soviets found the Rosenbergs more useful as martyrs than as two more Communist mouths to feed in Prague. In a moving plea to President Eisenhower in June of 1953, Ethel Rosenberg pointed to the release of Oatis as a reason for the president to commute the Rosenbergs' sentences.[58] President Eisenhower did not respond.

The Rosenberg apologists published numerous books and pamphlets to try to defend the atomic spies. Some of them were by well-known Soviet-line propagandists. The Rosenberg Committee, for example, published two pamphlets by the notorious D. N. Pritt, England's leading Soviet-paid propagandist. One of the pamphlets was then reprinted by the *National Guardian*.[59] Pritt, who in the 1930s defended the Moscow purge frame-ups, looked harshly on the American judicial system.[60]

In April 1953 Leon Josephson and John L. Spivak, two experienced operatives of the Communist Party USA underground apparatus, burglarized the office of David Greenglass's attorney, O. John Rogge, and removed notes on the attorney's interviews with Greenglass and other documents. They were photostatted and returned to the attorney's files.[61]

Atomic Espionage—The Rosenberg Case

The photostats of the purloined documents were taken to France, where they were released by the French Rosenberg Committee. The Rosenberg Committee in the United States then distributed selected excerpts from them in an attempt to discredit the Greenglass testimony. Rogge wrote to Emanuel Bloch, the Rosenberg attorney, in May protesting the violation of attorney-client privilege. Bloch returned copies of some of the photostats, but on June 4 the Rosenberg Committee held a press conference to promote its distorted analysis of the documents.[62]

Nathan Glazer, a former associate editor of *Commentary*, published by the American Jewish Committee, wrote a fitting answer to the Rosenberg defenders in 1956. After making a study of the case under a grant from the Fund for the Republic, he pointed out that "the defenders of the Rosenbergs and Sobell believe the whole story has not been told. They are quite right. *But the story that has not been told is of espionage more extensive than we now know.*"[63] The *Venona* messages provide much more information about the extent of Soviet atomic spying, which was not available to Glazer.

When Judge Kaufman concluded that the Rosenbergs' spying helped the Soviets get the atom bomb and was one of the factors that precipitated the Korean War, he was right on the mark. A document found in the archives of the Central Committee of the Communist Party of the Soviet Union shows that in 1948 the North Korean dictator Kim Il Sung asked Stalin's permission to attack South Korea. Stalin wanted the invasion to take place, but he pointed out that "such a large affair in relation to South Korea... needs much preparation." When the attack did take place, Stalin, in support of the future attack, provided all of the arms and equipment needed by the North Koreans.

On August 29, 1949, the Soviets tested their first atom bomb. America no longer had a nuclear monopoly and was therefore less of a threat to the Soviet Union. At the end of May 1950, Stalin decided that the invasion of South Korea should take place, which it did on June 25, 1950.[64]

CHAPTER 8

Atomic Espionage—California Phase

EARLY IN WORLD WAR II, the NKVD learned from its agents in the American Communist Party that the Radiation Laboratory, University of California at Berkeley, was doing theoretical calculations to develop an atomic bomb. Moscow assigned the San Francisco *Rezident*, Gregory Kheifitz, to exploit this knowledge for espionage.

Kheifitz assigned his assistant Peter Ivanov, Soviet vice consul in San Francisco, to the project. His contact was Steve Nelson, a member of the Communist Party's National Committee and head of the Alameda County organization of the California Communist Party. Nelson was also the head of the West Coast section of the secret underground apparatus of the Communist Party. He worked for Rudy Baker, who ran the underground from his base in New York.[1]

In late March 1943 Nelson met in his Oakland, California, home with an atomic scientist, Joseph Weinberg. The FBI had a microphone in Nelson's home and overheard the conversation. William Branigan, who later headed the FBI's Soviet Counter-Intelligence Section, was the young FBI agent who had the burdensome job of listening to the conversations in Nelson's home.[2] Branigan heard Nelson instruct Weinberg to gather and send him information from other Party members working with him on the atom bomb project at the University of California at Berkeley. He told Weinberg that the Party members working there should destroy their membership books, refrain from using liquor, and use extreme caution in gathering and supplying atom bomb information. Weinberg, in response, reported on experiments that had been conducted to develop the atomic bomb, reading aloud a complicated formula which Nelson copied down.

A few days later, Nelson phoned Kheifitz's subordinate Peter Ivanov and requested that they meet somewhere secretly. Ivanov suggested "the usual place." The FBI followed Nelson and saw him meet Ivanov in the middle of an open park on the grounds of San Francisco's St. Joseph's Hospital. Nelson handed a package to the Soviet intelligence officer.[3]

Both Weinberg and Nelson were subpoenaed by the House Committee on Un-American Activities in 1949 and questioned together. Weinberg claimed he had never met Nelson, while Nelson invoked the Fifth Amendment when asked if he knew Weinberg.[4] At a subsequent hearing of the committee, Weinberg was shown pictures of Nelson and again claimed never to have met him. When asked whether Nelson had come to his home in August 1943, he claimed not to remember such an occasion. He also denied that Communist Party functionary Bernadette Doyle was in his home at the same meeting.[5] But two special agents of the army's Counter-Intelligence Corps assigned to the atom bomb project provided the committee with sworn statements that directly contradicted Weinberg's testimony.

James Murray, the officer in charge of the unit handling security at the atom bomb research project at the University of California, testified that a "highly confidential informant"—in reality, the FBI—had advised his office that a scientist at the radiation laboratory had disclosed secret information about the A-bomb project to a member of the Communist Party, who later passed it on to the Russian consulate in San Francisco. FBI investigators identified the scientist as Joseph Weinberg and the Communist Party functionary as Steve Nelson.

Atomic Espionage—California Phase

While Murray and his colleagues were conducting a physical surveillance of Weinberg in August 1943, the "highly confidential informant" advised them that there would be a meeting that evening in Weinberg's home and that both Nelson and Bernadette Doyle were expected.

Murray and two other intelligence officers, on the roof of an apartment house next door to the Weinberg home, could observe the dining room of his second-story apartment. They saw Nelson, Doyle, Weinberg, and about five other people seated around the table. According to Murray, they could also see Weinberg and Nelson attempting to adjust the window. When the meeting appeared to be breaking up, the intelligence officers ran down to the street and observed Nelson and Doyle leaving together.[6]

Weinberg was indicted for perjury, was tried—and was acquitted. The inability or unwillingness of the FBI to air the wiretap evidence hobbled the espionage case. But the wiretap on Nelson proved to be a rich source of information for the counterintelligence officers.

On April 10 Branigan listened as a man with a Russian accent, who identified himself as "Cooper," visited Nelson. FBI investigators identified the man as Vassiliy Zarubin, the NKVD *Rezident* in Washington. During the meeting, Zarubin counted out ten packages of American bank notes, and Nelson commented, "Jesus, you count money like a banker." Zarubin said, "Well, you know, I used to do it in Moskva." Zarubin provided the money that Nelson needed to finance his espionage apparatus.

Zarubin and Nelson also discussed the work of Gregory Kheifitz and Louise Bransten, an important agent in the apparatus. At the time, the very wealthy Mrs. Bransten was the mistress of Kheifitz and used her large house for soirées which allowed Kheifitz and other NKVD officers to meet and recruit important Americans.

But some Party officials, Nelson told Zarubin, were concerned that Party members were being recruited directly by Soviet intelligence officers without going through the Party apparatus. William Schneiderman, the head of the California Communist Party, was reluctant to use Party members for Soviet espionage. Nelson's solution was to assign one Communist Party functionary in each important city or state as liaison with an NKVD officer. That member would handle the assignment of other Party members for espionage or "special work," as the Communists phrased it.[7]

Schneiderman's reluctance to participate in espionage activities indicated his timidity at that time. Schneiderman had served as the American Communist Party representative to the Comintern in 1934 and 1935 and in that capacity worked with Soviet intelligence. He was also the ex-husband of Peggy Dennis, the wife of Comintern functionary Eugene Dennis, both deeply involved in the Communist underground and Soviet intelligence operations before and during World War II.

But Schneiderman had a problem. In 1939 the U.S. government began a case to cancel his citizenship, obtained in 1927, and to deport him to his native Russia. After numerous courts upheld his denaturalization, the case finally made it to the United States Supreme Court and was pending when Nelson and Zarubin discussed him at their meeting. The Supreme Court ruled in Schneiderman's favor, but the four-year court case frightened him. He had lived in the Soviet Union and worked in the Comintern for two years, and many of his friends had died in the purges. He certainly didn't want to leave America and live in that dangerous environment.

Now, freed from the fear of deportation, Schneiderman changed his mind about working with the NKVD. In April 1945 Isaac (Pop) Folkoff, a veteran Communist and Soviet agent with the *Venona* code name "Uncle," told the NKVD that the local head of the Communist Party, Schneiderman, *Venona* code name "Nat,"[8] would work with them. In February 1946 the NKVD San Francisco

Atomic Espionage—California Phase

Rezident, Stepan Apresyan, reported to Moscow that he was in "Liaison with 'Nat.'"[9]

When Steve Nelson recounted his life to two sympathetic academics in 1980, he said, "I never had any links with Soviet espionage in the United States." And, "There may have been a Soviet espionage network operating in this country, but common sense would dictate against recruiting prominent Party officials."[10]

It might have been "common sense" not to use CPUSA members and leaders in espionage, but that is precisely what happened. *Venona* shows that most of the agents working for the NKVD during World War II were members of the Communist Party; some were Party officials. The top leadership of the Party not only was aware of the activity, but it also provided the Party members to the Soviets. These espionage rings were closely associated with the Communist Party underground, which Nelson ran in California.

The NKVD code name for Nelson could have been "Butcher." An agent with that *Venona* code name but unidentified by NSA had the responsibility, as did Nelson, of recruiting new people.[11] In January 1944 a San Francisco *Venona* message to Moscow reported the recruitment by "Butcher" of a Shell Oil Company chemist, Leo Levanes, code name "Al'ma," and said, "Among Butcher's contacts there are also some interesting targets in the aviation plants in Los Angeles." The message is signed "Kharon," the *Venona* code name for Gregory Kheifitz.[12]

The Comintern files in Moscow reveal that Steve Nelson was born in Yugoslavia in 1903 and came to the United States in 1920. He joined the Communist Party in 1924 and was a Party functionary in 1930. The next year he was sent to the Lenin School in Moscow for two years of training.

From July to October 1937, Nelson served in the International Brigades in Spain as brigade political commissar, replacing Dave

Springhall.[13] Although he served for less than a year—others were summarily shot for complaining that they had served their full time and should be sent home—Nelson was treated as a great hero by the Communists.[14] Springhall was national organizational secretary of the British Communist Party when he was arrested for Soviet espionage by the British authorities in 1943. He served five years in prison and died in Moscow in 1953.[15]

Using Trade Unions

Many of the spies involved with atomic espionage were members of the Federation of Architects, Engineers, Chemists, and Technicians (FAECT). Communist control of this union provided a valuable contact point for NKVD recruitment of agents. In August 1943 the GRU in New York reported in a *Venona* message to its Moscow headquarters that experimental work in Sacramento, California, was being conducted for the War Department at the Radiation Laboratories and that a "progressive professor" who worked there might be recruited through Communist Party member Paul Pinsky. The NSA deleted the name of the professor but left in that of Pinsky, who was the head of the FAECT in the area.[16] In 1941 Pinsky represented the FAECT as a sponsor of the Citizens' Committee to Free Earl Browder, who was in jail for passport fraud.[17]

In 1944 the NKVD decided to recruit one of the officials of the union, *Venona* code name "Larin." As usual, the potential recruit was checked for political reliability through the Communist Party. The New York *Rezidentura* reported in a message to Moscow that Bernie Chester had provided a character sketch of "Larin" obtained from the Communist Party. According to the *Rezidentura*, "They do not entirely vouch for him. They base this statement on the fact that in the Federation 'Larin' does not carry out all the orders received from the leadership [of the Communist Party]. He is stubborn and self-willed.

Atomic Espionage—California Phase

On the strength of this, we have decided to refrain from approaching 'Larin' and intend to find another candidate in FAECT."[18]

Marcel Scherer, vice president of the FAECT and possibly "Larin," was not a favorite of the Communist Party leadership, even though he had been a member since 1919.

In the early 1940s Scherer participated in organizing the FAECT at the Radiation Laboratory of the University of California, which was involved in early atomic research. But in 1944 he was removed by the Communist Party from his job in the FAECT and assigned to work at a lower level in another Communist-controlled union, the United Electrical Workers. (In 1950 Scherer was cited for contempt for invoking the Fifth Amendment before the House Committee on Un-American Activities but was acquitted in May 1951.)[19]

The FAECT was formed in New York City in the late 1920s by a Communist splinter group in the AFL, though it did not become really active until the 1930s. A Communist Party letter to all district organizers sent out in May 1934 pointed out that the Party "fraction" (secret cell) in the FAECT had asked for help in organizing outside New York for the purpose of "establishing Party contacts in these professions...." According to the letter, of the three thousand members of the FAECT in New York, only ninety were Communist Party members; another 250 were sympathizers. The Communist Party nevertheless controlled the organization.[20]

Less than a year later, the FAECT expanded nationwide. In a letter to all Party districts, the Organization Commission urged that more Party members be assigned to the organization because in many cities there were none to direct the chapters.[21] In 1946 the FAECT became part of the United Office and Professional Workers, CIO (UOPWA).[22] In 1949 the CIO expelled UOPWA for being a Communist-dominated organization,[23] and the Soviets lost another valuable intelligence asset.

Isaac Folkoff was Kheifitz's agent and close friend in the American Communist Party. Known affectionately by his fellow Communists as "Pop," Folkoff was a charter member of the Party and handled its secret funds in California. In February 1944 he requested $500 from the NKVD to pay mercenary agents who were working at Standard Oil.[24]

One of Folkoff's recruits was a U.S. government official who worked at the Office of Censorship in San Francisco. James Walter Miller, although sympathetic to Communism, was not a member of the Communist Party. Folkoff reported to Kheifitz that Miller, who was given the code name "Smutnyj," which means "vague," was an "honest man," but "talkative." Kheifitz asked Moscow for permission to recruit Miller as an agent, to be handled by NKVD officer Byacheslav Misluk, *Venona* code name "Mazhor." But should Moscow have doubts, said Kheifitz, he could be handled by a member of the American Communist Party in order that he think that the information was going to the Party rather than to the Soviet Union.[25] About a week later, Miller was being handled by Harrison George, editor of the Party's West Coast newspaper, the *People's Daily World*. The NKVD suspected that Miller could be an American agent since he pushed himself on the Communists, but the CP insisted that this was impossible and that he could provide valuable information through his work. Nevertheless, for security reasons, Miller was not told that his information was going to Moscow.[26]

Harrison George was a longtime Comintern operative. In 1934, under the code name "Fisher," he headed the San Francisco office of the Pan-Pacific Trade Union Secretariat of the Red International of Labor Unions. Ostensibly a trade union group, this was in reality the cover for secret Comintern operations as well as for Soviet military intelligence. On July 2, 1934, Japanese

Atomic Espionage—California Phase

Comintern official Sanzo Nosaka praised "Fisher's" work in a report to Moscow.[27]

Through Harrison George, James Miller reported in December 1943 that in examining letters sent to Moscow by some Soviet officials in San Francisco, the Office of Censorship had discovered "secret writing." The *Rezidentura* suggested that this was probably a message from naval GRU.[28] Later that month Miller reported that the FBI was watching the transmittal of funds from Moscow through the Bank of America.[29] Overall, because of Miller, Folkoff's spy ring was able to supply valuable information to the NKVD. An intelligence service operating on hostile territory needs to know whether its communications are being intercepted and the transferral of money for operations observed.

FBI agents watched numerous meetings between Kheifitz and Folkoff, after which Kheifitz would carry off a package or envelope given him by Folkoff. The FBI also watched Folkoff's secret meetings with agents Steve Nelson, William Schneiderman, and Louise Bransten.[30]

Kheifitz was the NKVD *Rezident* in San Francisco from 1941 until July 1944, when he was replaced by Grigori Kasparov. Then, in early 1945, Stepan Apresyan was transferred from New York to take over as the San Francisco *Rezident*.[31]

As a result of these rapid changes, the NKVD lost contact with Folkoff. In April 1945 Apresyan tried to reestablish it and asked Moscow for "Uncle's" (Folkoff's) picture, so he could recognize him. But the password for needed contact had become confused.[32]

Apresyan finally reached Folkoff by phone, but the aging Communist had forgotten the password. When he finally recalled it, he told Apresyan that he couldn't remember when and where he was supposed to meet, so Apresyan had to run the risk of visiting Folkoff at his home.

During this time, Apresyan asked Moscow for the name of the California Communist Party leader. He received no answer, but a few weeks later when meeting with Folkoff he was told the name was Bill Schneiderman. Apresyan gave Schneiderman the *Venona* code name "Nat," and "Uncle" was back to recruiting Communist Party members for Soviet espionage.[33]

Folkoff had a network of Communist Party members who assisted him in "special work"—Soviet espionage activities and the closely related underground operations of the American Communist Party. Among the operatives in this network was Rudy Lambert, the head of the California Communist Party Control Commission, the West Coast equivalent of the job held by Bernie Chester in New York.

In November 1945 NKVD San Francisco reported in a *Venona* message to Moscow that one of its agents, Callahan (the NSA identified him as Jerome Michael Callahan, a ship's clerk), had advised them that Rudolph Lambert had obtained information concerning uranium deposits in Nevada, Utah, and Arizona. Moscow was asked whether it wanted additional information.[34]

The J. Robert Oppenheimer Case

Referring to a "reliable confidential informant"—FBI code for its own wiretaps—the bureau offered this summary:

> A reliable confidential informant advised that J. Robert Oppenheimer was contacted on October 3, 1941, by Isaac Folkoff, an important functionary of the Communist Party, San Francisco, who advised Oppenheimer that he would be unable to attend to a matter with him over the weekend and he had made arrangements for Steve Nelson, a member of the National Committee of the Communist Party, to see Oppenheimer for

him at that time. According to the informant an individual who was believed to be Steve Nelson contacted Isaac Folkoff on October 6, 1941, at which time Folkoff was informed that while in the East Bay, Alameda County, on the preceding day which was October 5, 1941, he got $100 from "him" and arranged for Leo Baroway, important functionary of the Communist Party, San Francisco, to hand it to Folkoff. The informant further advised that around October 14, 1941, J. Robert Oppenheimer contacted Isaac Folkoff and requested him to arrange for Rudy Lambert, a functionary of the Communist Party in San Francisco, to contact him. The informant advised that during the same meeting, Oppenheimer advised Folkoff that an individual whom he identified as Steve had contacted him and had given him a message for Folkoff.[35]

Oppenheimer testified during his loyalty hearing in 1954 that he was also connected with another member of Folkoff's apparatus, Dr. Thomas Addis, who contacted Oppenheimer in the winter of 1937–1938 to ask him to contribute money to the Spanish Republican cause. Addis explained to Oppenheimer that although he was contributing money to Spanish relief organizations, he could really "do good" by providing money "through Communist Party channels, and it will really help." Oppenheimer testified that he was providing as much as $1,000 a year of his $15,000 income to this cause.

Oppenheimer explained that he met Addis and Rudy Lambert "through Spanish relief efforts," but the Communists were not the only channels for funds to help the Spanish Republicans. Oppenheimer could have as easily contributed to the socialist and humanitarian organizations that were also raising funds for Spanish refugees.

Oppenheimer gave the money for the Communist Party to Addis, but soon Addis told him to give it directly to Isaac Folkoff, who was in charge of the secret fundraising.[36] In 1935 Addis had visited the Soviet Union as a representative of Stanford University Hospital to attend the International Physiological Congress in Leningrad. The California District of the Communist Party wrote to the Central Committee in New York requesting that, because Addis had "been effective in bringing a large number of professional people close to the Party," he be given a "silk credential" to use on the trip.[37]

A "silk credential" was a red ribbon signed by the head of the Communist Party. Sewn into a jacket, it was taken out in Moscow and shown to the proper authorities to identify the bearer as a trusted comrade. These "silk credentials" can actually be seen today in the Comintern archives in Moscow.

Through Addis, Oppenheimer met Louise Bransten and attended "parties" in her home at which Communist officials such as William Schneiderman tried to explain "what the Communist line was all about." Oppenheimer testified that he didn't know whether Bransten, the mistress of Kheifitz, was a Communist.[38] Bransten, who set up these "parties" to enable her lover, Kheifitz, to spot potential recruits for Soviet espionage, was the ex-wife of Richard Bransten, Party name Bruce Minton. According to Elizabeth Bentley, Minton supplied Jacob Golos with two people in the U.S. government who could be useful in Soviet espionage.[39]

An FBI wiretap on February 26, 1941, revealed that Folkoff was attempting to arrange a meeting between J. Robert Oppenheimer, Rudy Lambert, and an individual known only as "Tom." It is not known whether the meeting took place, and the FBI was never able to identify "Tom," but there is an intriguing possibility—that "Tom" was the code name of the experienced NKVD officer Leonid Eitingon, who was in San Francisco at that time. According to Eitingon's superior, Pavel Sudoplatov, Eitingon "traveled across America to Los Angeles and San Francisco and sailed for China in

Atomic Espionage—California Phase

February 1941. Eitingon took advantage of the trip to resume contacts with two agents he had planted in California in the beginning of the 1930s. They were to become couriers in the network obtaining American atomic secrets from 1942 to 1945." Sudoplatov described one of Eitingon's "moles" as the "owner of a medium-sized retail business"; Folkoff, a charter member of the Communist Party, owned a retail clothing business, the Model Embroidery and Pleating Company in San Francisco.[40] Eitingon was also an old friend and colleague of Kheifitz. According to Sudoplatov, Kheifitz, when he was assigned to San Francisco, was given funds to support "the two moles established by Eitingon…. From this seedbed we made our first contacts with Robert Oppenheimer and the builders of the American atomic bomb."[41]

In 1945 a "reliable confidential informant" gave the FBI an address book belonging to Vladimir Pozner, a Russian/French filmmaker, that contained the name and address of J. Robert Oppenheimer.[42] While we don't know how Oppenheimer knew Pozner, we do know that Pozner was another NKVD agent. The New York *Rezidentura*, in a July 1943 *Venona* message to Moscow, reported that it was "planning to use" Vladimir Alexandrovich Pozner in its work. It gave him the *Venona* code name "Platon" and described him as "a Jew born in Leningrad no earlier than 1897." Until 1925 he had lived in Germany and then until 1941 in France. He had been in the United States since May 1941. In 1943 Pozner, a Lithuanian citizen, requested Soviet citizenship.

Pozner had worked in France for Paramount Studios and MGM as a recording engineer. In 1943 he was head of the Russian section of the film department of the United States War Department. According to the *Rezidentura*, "He has contacts in the United States which are of interest to us," and so the *Rezidentura* asked for permission to use him as an agent on the recommendation of NKVD officer Alexandr Fomin.[43] By November 1943 Pozner was being used by the *Rezidentura* to contact other agents and to provide his address for agents to communicate secretly with the NKVD.[44]

Oppenheimer lost his security clearance in 1954 after hearings before the Atomic Energy Commission's Personnel Security Board, headed by Gordon Gray. Conventional wisdom has it that Oppenheimer was punished because he had many Communist friends. But while most members of the American Communist Party and many functionaries were not involved in Soviet espionage, evidence shows that any Party member capable of aiding Soviet intelligence was invited to do so—and did. And most of the Communists close to Oppenheimer were involved in espionage.

The FBI's interest in Oppenheimer started long before the scientist became involved in the atom bomb project. According to a March 28, 1941, FBI report from San Francisco, a wiretap revealed that in the fall of 1940 Oppenheimer had been at a meeting at the home of Haakon Chevalier, a member of the Communist Party. Identified at the meeting were Party officials Isaac Folkoff and William Schneiderman. The FBI investigation continued until 1943, when army intelligence advised the FBI that because Oppenheimer was an important official of the atom bomb project and under investigation, the army "had a full-time technical and physical surveillance of Oppenheimer." The FBI thus closed its case and did not resume the investigation until 1946, when Oppenheimer left the atom bomb project.[45]

Although the case was closed, information about Oppenheimer kept appearing in other FBI investigations. The FBI's "technical surveillance," or microphone, in Steve Nelson's home provided an interesting bit of information. On March 23, 1943, Nelson told the young scientist Joseph Weinberg that he had previously approached Oppenheimer to secure information about the work done at the

Atomic Espionage—California Phase

Radiation Laboratory of the University of California at Berkeley. According to Nelson, Oppenheimer refused to provide the information. (Weinberg gave Oppenheimer's name as a reference when he obtained employment at the Radiation Laboratory.)[46]

Oppenheimer's refusal of Nelson's request appears to relate to an incident in the winter of 1942–1943 when Oppenheimer's friend Haakon Chevalier visited him at his home and mentioned that a mutual friend, George Eltenton, had been approached by an official of the Soviet consulate to obtain technical information on the atom bomb project for the Soviet Union. Chevalier asked Oppenheimer to provide the information, and Oppenheimer later testified that he had refused.

On August 26, 1943—months after the incident—Robert Oppenheimer decided to report it to security officers. He was interviewed by Lieutenant Colonel Boris T. Pash and Lieutenant Lyall A. Johnson of the area intelligence office at the Radiation Laboratory, but at first he refused to identify the person who had contacted him on behalf of Eltenton and the man from the Soviet consulate. But under pressure from the security officers, Oppenheimer finally named Chevalier on December 14, 1943.

When Chevalier was contacted by the FBI in June 1946, he admitted the incident with Eltenton and said he had mentioned it to Oppenheimer only to find out if secret information about the project should be made available to Russian scientists.[47] Eltenton was also interviewed by the FBI and revealed much more than either Oppenheimer or Chevalier, such as that in late 1942 Peter Ivanov of the Soviet consulate had asked him to obtain information concerning research being conducted at the University of California's Radiation Laboratory. Ivanov specifically mentioned Oppenheimer's having such information,[48] and the FBI knew that Ivanov was helping Kheifitz on atomic espionage.

When Oppenheimer testified before the Personnel Security Board of the Atomic Energy Commission, his recollection of the story had changed. He now claimed that Chevalier told him only that Eltenton had a "means of getting technical information to Soviet scientists" and that he, Oppenheimer, thought this was terrible.[49] Oppenheimer's minimizing of the incident was directly contradicted by Eltenton in his statement to the FBI.

Oppenheimer also testified that he knew Steve Nelson through his wife, Kitty Oppenheimer, who had been a member of the Communist Party and had been in contact with Chevalier as late as 1946 and 1947.[50] Her previous husband, Joe Dallet, was a Party organizer who was killed in the Spanish Civil War. When Joe wanted Kitty to visit him in Spain, he wrote her to "get in touch with Jack in Paris" in order to organize the trip. Jack was Jack Reid, whose real name was Arnold Reisky, the head of the American section of the secret Communist apparatus in Paris that organized the supply of troops to the International Brigades. He had earlier done underground work for the American Communist Party and in 1935 worked on the secret radio that broadcast coded messages between the American Communist Party and Moscow.[51] At his own request, Reid, an old friend and comrade of Dallet, was assigned to a combat role in Spain, where he was killed. Kitty's friendship with Steve Nelson dated from his Spanish Civil War connection with her late husband.

Nelson and Bernadette Doyle, the organizational secretary of the Alameda County, California, Communist Party, were rather talkative in the Party office, unaware that the FBI had a microphone planted there. In December 1942 Steve Nelson said that a Party member who was very friendly with J. Robert Oppenheimer, Dr. Hannah Peters, told him that Oppenheimer could not be active in the Party at that time "because of his employment on a special project." Doyle remarked that the matter should be taken up with the Party State Committee since the "two Oppys" were well known as Communist Party members.

In May 1943 John Murra, a Spanish Civil War veteran suspected by the FBI of being a Soviet intelligence agent, arrived at Alameda Party headquarters to talk to Doyle. Murra wanted to get in touch with Kitty Oppenheimer, and Doyle helped him make the contact. She told him that Robert and Kitty Oppenheimer were "comrades," that Robert was working on a special secret project at the Radiation Laboratory at the University of California, and that therefore his name must be removed from any of Murra's mailing lists.[52] Murra knew Kitty Oppenheimer from his days in the Spanish Civil War. (Murra, together with Jack Reid, had been in the Communist secret apparatus in Paris.)[53]

Many of Kitty Oppenheimer's friends, like her husband's, had connections to Soviet espionage. In 1936, when Kitty Oppenheimer applied for a passport, she requested that it be mailed to her in care of Zelma Baker (later Mrs. Benjamin Miller) in Philadelphia. In December 1946 the FBI interviewed the Millers because of their association with the veteran GRU officer Arthur Adams, who was assigned to steal atom bomb secrets. Dr. Miller told the FBI that he first met Adams in 1940 in Chicago when another doctor, whose name he couldn't recall, suggested that he treat Adams for a cold. From then until 1943 they met six or seven times in Chicago, and in 1944 Adams visited the Miller family at their home in Bethesda, Maryland.

Adams, the GRU officer, was under constant FBI surveillance, and some of his mail, opened by the FBI, revealed that in 1944 Zelma Miller had written him a number of times. In one of the letters, in the summer of 1944, she expressed her love for Adams and told him how anxious she was to see him. She suggested that a good time for him to visit would be the weekend of September 30 or October 14. An FBI surveillance team saw Adams contact Mrs.

Miller while she was in New York City between trains en route from Bedford Hills, New York, to Washington, D.C. When she was questioned by the FBI, Mrs. Miller insisted she knew little of Adams, having seen him only a few times.[54]

In November 1945 the San Francisco *Rezidentura* reported to the Moscow Center that Oppenheimer's brother, Frank, also took part in atomic research but warned that "scholars who have taken part in these pursuits are under the surveillance of the American counterintelligence." Robert Oppenheimer, it reported, was one of the two "chief scientific leaders on the atomic bomb."[55]

Robert Oppenheimer's brother, Frank, and sister-in-law, Jacquenette, called Jackie, were also members of the Communist Party. Frank Oppenheimer worked on the atom bomb project at the Radiation Laboratory at the University of California from 1941 to 1947, and during that time he also worked on and off at Oak Ridge (1944–1945) and at Los Alamos (1945). Frank and Jackie testified before the House Committee on Un-American Activities in 1949, at which time he admitted that he had been a member of the American Communist Party from 1937 to 1941 and that he knew a Communist Party functionary named Isaac Folkoff.[56] Frank Oppenheimer also said that he had left the Communist Party in late 1940 or the first months of 1941—a year and a half into the Soviet-Nazi alliance—and admitted he knew Steve Nelson but said that he had only met him at social gatherings.

Jackie Oppenheimer, who testified at the same time, also admitted being a member of the Communist Party from 1937 to 1941 and knowing that Folkoff was a Party functionary. She remembered getting a Communist Party card but didn't remember what it looked like or whether it had a seal with a hammer and sickle. She testified that she just threw it into a dresser drawer. In fact, her 1937 membership card #56370 (actually a small book) does have a hammer and sickle stamp on the cover and, moreover, shows that she paid dues every month from February to November and received a dues stamp which she pasted in her Party card monthly.[57] During her testimony, she said she thought that the American Communist Party might at an "earlier" time have belonged to the Communist International,[58] and yet her Party card and that of her husband showed quite clearly "Communist Party of the USA (Section of the Communist International)" and contained an "International Solidarity" stamp for money they contributed for international Communist operations.

Two years before his testimony before the House committee, Frank Oppenheimer issued a statement to the press: "The allegation made by the *Washington Times Herald* that I had been a member of the Communist Party is a complete fabrication." The Washington newspaper had listed the numbers of his Communist Party card for 1937, 1938, and 1939.[59] The numbers were the same as those cited by the committee in 1949.

We learn more about the Oppenheimer brothers from the *Venona* messages. In December 1944 Ruth Greenglass returned to New York from a visit to her husband at Los Alamos. She reported that "Oppenheim" from California was working at the camp.[60] This appears to refer to Frank Oppenheimer, since brother Robert was the director at Los Alamos.

In May 1945 the New York *Rezidentura* sent Moscow a list of places, provided by Ted Hall ("Mlad"), where research on the atom bomb was taking place and the names of the head of each. The names of all except one were given as real names. The exception was the director at Los Alamos, where the code name "Veksel" was given for Oppenheimer.

In March 1945 the NKVD Center in Moscow ordered the New York *Rezidentura* in a *Venona* message that it should send its agent "Guron" (who could not be identified by the NSA) to Chicago to "re-establish contact with 'Veksel'… as soon as possible."[61] This incident was significant, for it revealed earlier NKVD contact with Oppenheimer and that the contacts continued while he was working on the atom bomb project. The NSA in releasing the messages commented, "The role played by the person cover named 'Veksel' remains uncertain but troubling."[62]

Perhaps we would have more answers to questions about Oppenheimer if the FBI had realized that the Illinois Communist Party head, Olsen, who worked with the NKVD, was in fact Morris Childs. From 1951 on, Childs worked as a secret agent of the FBI in the Communist underground in liaison with the KGB. If he had been asked about the wartime NKVD operations in Chicago, the Oppenheimer case might have been solved.

The evidence is clear that the NKVD had contact with Oppenheimer and that the nuclear scientist and his wife were surrounded by people with Soviet intelligence connections. But since this was only circumstantial evidence, it did not prove that Oppenheimer provided secret information to the Soviets. The direct evidence was given by Pavel Sudoplatov, Moscow-based overseer of Soviet atom bomb espionage, who claimed in his 1994 book, *Special Tasks*, that Oppenheimer supplied the Soviets with classified reports on atom bomb development. He also said that some of the information came through the wife of the NKVD *Rezident* in the United States, Zarubina, who traveled frequently to California and was in direct contact with Oppenheimer's wife, Kitty.[63]

Sudoplatov's claims created a firestorm in the American press. The American Physical Society held a press conference in which five "experts" denounced the statements about Oppenheimer "as wildly inaccurate and probably fictitious." And the organization's forty-member council expressed "profound dismay" at the accusations "made by a man who has characterized himself as a master of deception and deceit."[64] Numerous other scientists, journalists, and others with no direct knowledge of the case joined the protest.

The old KGB operative Sudoplatov might possibly have lied to his coauthors, Jerry and Leona Schecter, who were experienced journalists, but the Schecters found documentary evidence to back his story. Sudoplatov had been jailed in 1953 by the Soviet government because of his close association with the then-discredited Lavrenti Beria. In 1968 he was released and tried in succeeding years to get a Communist Party hearing to rehabilitate him and restore him to the good graces of the Soviet leadership. In 1982, for example, he sent an appeal to Yuri Andropov and the Politburo outlining his career and asking for rehabilitation. In this secret document, Sudoplatov boasted that he had "rendered considerable help to our scientists by giving them the latest materials on atom bomb research, obtained from such sources as the famous nuclear physicists R. Oppenheimer, E. Fermi, K. Fuchs, and others."[65] It would have made no sense for Sudoplatov to lie to Andropov, the former head of KGB and dictator of the Soviet Union, who would have easily found him out.

Until Sudoplatov's testimony, even *Venona* could not prove that Oppenheimer had collaborated with Soviet intelligence; the only conclusion had to have been a Scotch verdict—unproved—or, as the NSA commented, "troubling." But with Sudoplatov's information we can say for certain that Oppenheimer did in fact knowingly supply classified information on the atom bomb to the Soviet Union.

In May 1995 Les Aspin, former U.S. defense secretary and then chairman of the president's Foreign Intelligence Advisory Board, reopened the issue. He held a press conference on May 1 in which he released a letter from Louis J. Freeh, the director of the FBI, which stated, "The FBI is not in possession of any credible evidence that would suggest that Niels Bohr, Enrico Fermi, Robert Oppenheimer, or Leo Szilard engaged in any espionage activity on behalf of any foreign power to include that involving atomic bomb secrets. Indeed, the FBI has classified information available that argues against the conclusions reached by the author of *Special Tasks* [Sudoplatov]. The FBI, therefore, considers such allegations to be unfounded."[66]

Aspin explained at the press conference that he had "negotiated" the text of the letter with FBI director Freeh. He did not explain why a simple statement of the truth needed to be negotiated, unless it wasn't exactly true. A number of the people present at the press conference, including Jerry Schecter and Herb Romerstein, challenged Aspin's conclusions. Aspin responded, "You can believe what you want…. This is not, I presume, the last word on this subject." He was right. Schecter then asked whether *Venona*, which had not been released, would lead to Aspin's conclusion. Aspin said yes but that *Venona* was too sensitive ever to be released. He was wrong. In less than a year, Senator Pat Moynihan succeeded in getting it released. (Aspin said at the press conference that Sudoplatov had confused code names and identities. After so many years, Sudoplatov did not remember which code names identified which agents, but he did remember clearly the names of the agents, and he gave the same names to Jerry Schecter that he had earlier written in his secret letter to Andropov.)

The reaction in Moscow to Sudoplatov's revelations was mixed. In December 1993—before the book came out—at a celebration of the anniversary of the KGB held in the headquarters of its successor, the SVR, there was a standing ovation for Sudoplatov as "the living history of the service."[67] But when the book was released, the SVR denied any responsibility for it. As late as March 1998, spokeswoman Tatyana Samolis issued a statement denying that Oppenheimer had ever provided any atomic bomb information to the Soviet Union.

Atomic Espionage—California Phase

But other KGB retirees leaked information to the Russian press that bolstered Sudoplatov's story. In 1996 *Pravda* carried an article based on SVR sources saying that documents obtained from Oppenheimer and other important Western scientists are still in the secret Soviet archives. The *Pravda* article went on:

> It is no secret that first-hand information on [a] nuclear reaction experiment performed in 1942 by the Italian physicist E. Fermi in Chicago was obtained through scientists close to Oppenheimer. The source of this information was a former staff member of Comintern, G. Kheifitz, our *Rezident* in California and a former secretary to N. Krupskaya [Lenin's wife]. He was the one who informed Moscow of the fact that the development of the nuclear bomb is a practical reality. By this time, Kheifitz had established contact with Oppenheimer and his circle. In fact, the Oppenheimer family, in particular his brother, had links with the then illegal Communist Party of the U.S. on the West Coast. One of the locations for illegal meetings and contacts was the house of the socialite Madam Bransten in San Francisco. It is precisely here that Oppenheimer and Kheifitz met. For our intelligence, people who were sympathetic to Communist ideas were extremely valuable for establishing contacts.... Madam Bransten's salon lasted from 1936 to 1942. The Soviets supported it. Kheifitz helped transfer the funds for its financing.[68]

Sudoplatov died in September 1996.[69] For most of his life, he used espionage, assassination, and repression against the West and any Russians who might oppose the Soviet dictatorship. It is ironic that only two years before his death, he provided the world with significant evidence about the Soviet agents who stole the secrets of the atom bomb.

Einstein and Atomic Espionage

Oppenheimer is not the only one recently to come under renewed scrutiny; others of the bomb project scientists have been found to be equally tainted. One of the more intriguing names in the spotlight these days is the acknowledged father of atomic physics—Albert Einstein, who hitherto has been portrayed as naive and otherworldly.

After escaping from Nazi Germany in 1933, Einstein took American citizenship in 1940. However, in 1947 he said, "I came to America because of the great, great freedom that I heard existed in this country. I made a mistake in selecting America as a land of freedom, a mistake I cannot repair in the balance of my life."[70]

The 1995 Russian edition of the Sudoplatov book had additional information about atomic spying. A woman named Margarita Konenkovo, who was identified by Sudoplatov as a Soviet spy, had introduced Albert Einstein to Pavel Mikhailov, the GRU *Rezident* in the United States, to provide the Soviet Union with atomic information. In 1998 some of Einstein's love letters to Mrs. Konenkovo dated 1945 and 1946 were sold at auction by Sotheby's auction house. An article in the *New York Times* referred to the Sudoplatov book and pointed out that Einstein's letters to Mrs. Konenkovo make reference to Mikhailov. Paul Needham, a consultant to Sotheby's, after consulting a number of scholars, argued that Einstein had little technical information to offer the Soviets.[71]

General Yuri Kobaladze, the spokesman for the KGB successor organization, SVR, told the press that he had no evidence that Konenkovo worked with Soviet intelligence.[72] He was not lying when he said that nothing could be found in the KGB files—she did not work for the NKVD, later called the KGB; she worked for military intelligence, the GRU.

Before Einstein escaped from Nazi Germany, his personal secretary, Helen Dukas, was involved in Soviet underground work.

Atomic Espionage—California Phase

According to information gathered by U.S. Army intelligence and made available to the FBI:

> Prior to 1933, the Comintern, and other Soviet Apparats, were active in gathering intelligence information in the Far East. The agents who gathered this information sent it to agents in other countries in coded telegrams. These agents then recoded the telegrams and forwarded them to addresses in Berlin, one of which was the office of Albert Einstein.... Einstein's personal secretary turned the coded telegrams over to a special apparat man, whose duty it was to transmit them to Moscow by various means....
>
> It was common knowledge, especially in Berlin, that Einstein sympathized with the Soviet Union to a great extent. Einstein's Berlin staff of typists and secretaries was made up of persons who were recommended to him (at his request) by people who were close to the Klub Der Geistesarbeiter (Club of Scientists), which was a Communist cover organization. Einstein was closely associated with this club and was very friendly with several members who later became Soviet agents. Klaus Fuchs, who was associated with the club as a student in the early 1930s, was jailed in England for giving atomic bomb information to the Soviets. Einstein was also very friendly with several members of the Soviet Embassy in Berlin, some of whom were later executed in Moscow in 1935 and 1937.[73]

In 1950 another important atomic scientist from the American project, Bruno Pontecorvo, defected to the Soviet Union. He later worked on the Soviet atom bomb project and was a close friend of Klaus Fuchs. Another of Pontecorvo's friends was Frederic Joliot-Curie, who was removed as chairman of the French Atomic Energy Commission because of his membership in the French Communist

Party.[74] Russian researchers recently found a 1946 document showing that Joliot-Curie advised a Soviet diplomat that "French scientists... will always be at your disposal without asking for any information in return."[75]

Soviet scientists probably would have eventually come up with an atomic bomb on their own, but the NKVD/KGB speeded up the process considerably. The NKVD not only stole the secrets but also controlled the slave laborers who built the facilities that produced the bomb. Soviet acquisition of the atom bomb of course changed the relationship of forces in the postwar world, for the Soviets used it as a threat repeatedly in order to blackmail the West into acquiescing to their demands. Everyone remembers the Cuban missile crisis and other occasions when the Soviets used the atomic threat. The American and other Western Communists who helped the Soviet Union build its atomic arsenal made all this possible. That it did not always work was due to the diplomacy and resolve of Western leaders.

In 1989 *Moscow News* published an interview with Professor Igor Golovin, assistant to Igor Kurchatov—the father of the Soviet atom bomb, who worked directly under Lavrenti Beria. Golovin, referring to Beria, said:

> Today everyone knows, of course, that he was a bloodthirsty butcher. But at that time Kurchatov addressed a Politburo member, a person commanding immense power and wielding influence on Stalin. And the fact that Stalin subordinated all work on the atomic project to Beria himself attests to the importance which he attached to it.... All construction projects, mines, "atom-towns," even our Institute in Moscow [then Laboratory No. 2, now the Kurchatov Institute of Atomic Energy]—all these facilities employed the labour of prisoners.

Did you see our club? This building used to be a prison, it was surrounded with a tall bare wall, with submachine gunners in its corner towers. All the buildings, including the one in which the first atomic reactor (boiler as it was called at the time) was commissioned, were built by prisoners and the present-day International Center of Nuclear Research in Dubna. Its first builders were also prisoners.... There were many thousands of them at our construction sites.

Golovin pointed out that Beria continued to run the Soviet atomic energy program until the day of his arrest and murder by his colleagues on the Politburo in 1954: "The instructions given by him the day before were still being fulfilled, when the lightning bolt hit him."[76]

CHAPTER 9

Target: OSS

UNDER NORMAL CIRCUMSTANCES, the hardest target for any intelligence service to penetrate is the rival intelligence service in another country. The exception was the CIA's predecessor, the Office of Strategic Services (OSS), America's World War II intelligence service. Established on July 11, 1941, when President Roosevelt named William J. Donovan coordinator of information, America's first attempt at centralized intelligence suffered from both inexperience and misperceptions about Soviet intentions.[1] *Venona* reveals how easily the NKVD penetrated OSS.

The United States was not yet at war when Donovan was first given his assignment—to collect information for the president of the United States and, in the event of war, to drop people behind enemy lines for intelligence gathering and sabotage.

Known as "Wild Bill" for the World War I combat exploits that had earned him a Congressional Medal of Honor, Donovan saw his original mandate from FDR as just a starting point. Before his covert spies and saboteurs could wreak havoc inside the Third Reich during World War II, the OSS had to be turned into a world-class service that could gather and interpret information on all phases of the war—military, economic, and political. Donovan and his top aides, London station chief David K. E. Bruce and his Swiss-based chief spy, Allen Dulles, both agreed: They would do business with the devil himself to become the main source of President Roosevelt's strategic planning. Military intelligence inside the War Department hated the notion, but the OSS nevertheless began to grow beyond anything in the original plans.

Even before the first covert agents were sent to be trained by British commandos at a hastily established secret camp in Canada known as Camp X, Donovan set out to recruit the best and brightest minds from American universities and from the crowded émigré community of European intellectuals who had managed to flee Hitler's persecutions. He was blissfully unconcerned that some of these recruits to the OSS's elite Research and Analysis section were unabashed leftists, a high proportion of whom had actually been Communist Party members in their home countries. Having Europeans who made no secret of their leftist sympathies in high-ranking positions within the OSS made it easier for American Communists, such as Latin American chief analyst Maurice Halperin (an NKVD agent), to keep their covers as earnest antifascists while they gathered secrets for Moscow.

In November 1941 Donovan decided that it would be useful to have men with military training for behind-the-lines operations in the war he knew would soon come. His search for such men opened the door to Communist infiltration. Hundreds of American Communists had recently returned from the Spanish Civil War with military experience. Approximately three thousand Americans, 60 percent of them members of the Communist Party or Young Communist League, had been sent to Spain by the Communist Party. Approximately 1,200 returned, half of them wounded.[2] These combat-experienced activists were motivated to fight against the Nazis, who had attacked the Soviet Union in June 1941. Donovan contacted Milt Wolff, the commander of the Veterans of the Abraham Lincoln Brigade (VALB), in November and asked for a list of available men.

Target: OSS

Such a request would have been impossible before June 1941. The American Communist Party and its front, the VALB, had no interest in fighting Nazi Germany until it directly threatened the Soviet Union. In fact, from May 30 to June 2, 1940, the American Communist Party held a special antiwar conference during its Eleventh National Convention in New York City.[3] Milt Wolff spoke at that convention and attacked the Spanish Civil War veterans who supported the Allies—he called them "deserters" who "under the care of the Socialist Party and the ILG [International Ladies' Garment Workers' Union] [were] attempting to set up an international brigade to help the Allies." Instead, he said, the VALB "planned an intensive program of activity for the present period and are going full force in the campaign for peace and to keep America out of the war."[4]

A year later Wolff spoke at the Chicago convention of the VALB. His public speech was no different from the earlier secret speech he had made at the Communist Party convention. Wolff labeled Franklin Roosevelt a "red-baiting, union-busting, alien-hunting, anti-Negro, anti-Semitic" president who was on a "jingo-istic road to fascism in America." Referring to the president as "Franklin Demagogue Roosevelt," Wolff said that the VALB would oppose "Roosevelt and the war-mongers" and would fight against American involvement in the European war.[5] And a VALB special convention newspaper issued by the *Chicago Post* was headlined "Lincoln Veterans Convention Fights Convoy Plan," followed by "No Convoys No A.E.F."—a reference to the American Expeditionary Force that joined the Allies during World War I.

The refusal of American Communists to support the Allies against Nazi Germany, particularly among those who had served in the Spanish Civil War, was an obedient response to orders the Communist International had sent to the Communist parties shortly after the outbreak of the war.[6]

On September 15, 1939, a secret meeting of the Secretariat of the Executive Committee of the Communist International took place in Moscow. The subject under discussion was the plan of the British and French to organize military legions composed of refugees from Germany and the occupied countries to fight the Nazis. Among those in attendance were men who would serve as postwar Communist dictators in their own countries—George Dimitroff of Bulgaria, Klement Gottwald of Czechoslovakia, and Wilhelm Pieck of Germany—as well as the Soviet official Otto Kuusinen. Secret instructions were then issued to the Communist parties on September 21, 1939:

> The fact that the present war is an imperialist war which cannot be supported by the working class of any country, also determines the attitude of the Communists toward the so-called National Legions: the Communists, irrespective of from what nation, decisively reject such Legions and expose the dangerous swindle of the English-French imperialists in presenting the matter as if these Legions were an instrument of the struggle against fascism, for democracy and for the liberation of oppressed peoples. In reality they are an instrument in the hands of the imperialists and enemies of the Soviets and, in the end, are supposed to be utilized for the suppression of the revolutionary movement of its own people, similar to the last war in the case of the Polish and Czech Legions.

Based on the above, the orders were as follows:

> 1) On no account may Communists actively participate in the building up of the National Legions (signing of appeals, propaganda, publicity, etc.); on the contrary, they must openly come out against the formation of such Legions and on a political basis.

2) It is particularly to be avoided that former Spanish fighters make statements in support of the forming of Legions and in support of the voluntary entry into the same or into the English or French armies.

3) Voluntary entry of Communists into the Legions or into the English-French Army is absolutely inadmissible, irrespective of how much moral pressure is exercised on the part of the authorities. Even in the event that Communists are placed before the alternative of voluntary entry into the Legion or army, or forced labor, or concentration camp, Communists may not voluntarily join.

A copy of these orders was given to Pat Toohey, the American Communist Party representative to the Comintern.[7]

The Communists Become "Patriotic"—But...

When Donovan spoke to Milt Wolff in November 1941, the situation had changed drastically—the Nazis had attacked the Soviet Union. Wolff forgot his earlier isolationism. He now wrote a pamphlet for the Veterans of the Abraham Lincoln Brigade demanding that the United States open a Western front in Europe, though America wasn't even in the war.[8] Wolff reported Donovan's request to Eugene Dennis, a member of the Communist Party Politburo who had recently returned from Moscow. Dennis gave Wolff tentative permission but, remembering the earlier orders, asked for Moscow's authorization.

Meanwhile, Donovan put Wolff in contact with Colonel S. W. (Bill) Bailey of Britain, who was in charge of recruiting men for the British training school in Canada known as Camp X. Wolff first provided a number of non-American Spanish Civil War vets, including twelve Yugoslavs, three Czechs, and an Italian. After America entered the war in December 1941, Wolff added ten Americans, a Greek, and three Yugoslavs.

In late December 1941 the American Communist Party leadership officially assigned Dennis to maintain links with American intelligence. Dennis used his contact with the NKVD to ask whether Wolff's activity was permitted by Moscow. Soon Donovan spoke to Dennis directly and asked for a contact with the underground Communist Party organization in France. Dennis falsely replied that he didn't know how to establish such a contact.

On May 13, 1942, Pavel Fitin, head of the Foreign Department of the NKVD, sent a top secret memo to George Dimitroff at Comintern headquarters. He stated that the NKVD believed that "this [Wolff] affair is a political mistake of the CPUSA leadership, due to which the American and English intelligence got a chance to enter the channels of not only the American CP, but other Communist parties as well. Comrade Ryan [Dennis] asks for your instructions as soon as possible on all matters touched upon to be given to the American, Spanish, Italian, and Canadian Communist parties."[9]

Dimitroff answered the same day, giving Fitin a top secret message to be sent to the American Communist Party:

> On the question of Wolff, the following directive is given to the American friends:
>
> We consider permission given to Wolff to recruit people for English and American intelligence to be a political mistake. This would give the intelligence services a chance to penetrate the American and other Communist parties. We propose a serious discussion of the most expedient measures and forms of stopping this recruitment and all contact with these intelligence services. Warn the Spanish and Italian comrades about this also.[10]

Target: OSS

On June 1 Fitin passed a message from Dennis to Dimitroff. Dennis reported that he had discussed the instructions with Browder and that "we agree fully with your proposal regarding the activity of Wolff. We have taken all necessary measures to halt this activity and to prevent his influencing leftist organizations to join with him." Dennis suggested that Communists be allowed to join the OSS as individuals, as well as other cooperation, but not in situations where the OSS would be in control of the situation.[11]

Wolff was only twenty-six years old in 1941 and had been a member of the Young Communist League before going to Spain. He joined the Spanish Communist Party while there,[12] and after returning to the United States he transferred to the American Communist Party. After closing down his OSS project, Wolff enlisted in the army in June 1942 and was eventually assigned to work in the OSS. He was commissioned a second lieutenant on June 6, 1944.[13] A number of other Communists, as Dennis had suggested to Moscow, also joined OSS as individuals. Jack Bjoze, secretary-treasurer of the New York VALB post and head of the organization during the war,[14] later told journalists Joseph Albright and Marcia Kunstel that he had attended the Soviet intelligence school in Barcelona with Morris Cohen when they served in Spain.[15] He is not one of those identified in *Venona*, but Cohen, who was called "Volunteer" in *Venona*, was deeply involved in Soviet espionage after World War II in both the United States and England.[16]

William Donovan was, of course, not a Communist. He was fully aware that Communists were active in the OSS, but he considered them allies in the war against Nazi Germany and failed to consider the other implications. Some in Congress saw the matter differently. When Donovan was questioned on March 13, 1945, before the Special House of Representatives Committee on Military Affairs, he lied. When asked by Congressman Charles Elston (R-Ohio),

"Would you take a person into your organization who you knew had been a Communist?" Donovan answered, "I have never done so." He also said, "No man has been taken in with my knowledge who was a Communist...." He specifically defended Milt Wolff and George Wuchinich, OSS officers and Spanish Civil War vets.[17]

A *Venona* message in August 1943 revealed that Wuchinich (also spelled Vuchinich) had supplied secret OSS information to Toma Babin ("Breme"), an agent of Soviet military intelligence and a Communist Party official. The message said:

> (a) The Yugoslav Government is getting ready to move to Cairo. (Thereafter they plan to go to Yugoslavia together with the allied troops.) A large group of Yugoslav reactionaries from the USA is about to go to the same place, in particular many members of the "Royal Officers' Club." They are all hostile to the Partisan movement in Yugoslavia.
>
> (b) In Cairo there are military units formed from Yugoslav prisoners of war freed by the Allies in Africa. These units are under the control of the American Command.[18]

After the war, when he returned to Pittsburgh, Wuchinich continued to work for the Communist Party and became a member of the Party's western Pennsylvania Nationality Commission and western Pennsylvania's executive secretary of the American Slav Congress, a Communist front.[19] In June 1953 Wuchinich and Wolff both invoked the Fifth Amendment on Communist Party membership and other matters before the Senate Subcommittee on Internal Security.[20]

Babin was an important agent of the GRU. In July 1943, as reported in a *Venona* message, he provided an extensive report on a U.S. shipment of military equipment to England and North Africa.[21]

Target: OSS

Donovan Goes to Moscow

Donovan traveled to Moscow in December 1943 on an official mission to organize OSS/NKVD cooperation in the war effort. Two days after a meeting with Molotov on December 25, Donovan met with Pavel Fitin. Donovan offered to advise the NKVD of the identities of OSS agents in Nazi-occupied Europe so that if the OSS were "dealing with an individual or group which the Soviet government knew to be untrustworthy... it would be of utmost value to have the benefit of their advice and counsel...." Providing the names of agents to another intelligence service would never have been done by a more experienced intelligence official. General Fitin naturally liked this idea and suggested that American facilities be used to send Soviet agents into Germany, France, or other areas far from the Soviet Union. General Donovan said that the OSS "would be glad to help in any way they could."[22] This helped Fitin solve a serious problem. As a result of a Comintern decision in 1938 to disband the Communist Party of Poland and liquidate its leaders in Moscow, which had falsely accused them of being "agents of Polish fascism,"[23] almost no reception committees were available to help airdropped agents, such as safe houses and transportation.

The agreement's aftermath also had serious consequences. Due to Stalin's paranoia, many of the Central European Communists who worked with the OSS on the orders of the Comintern were persecuted after the war as alleged American agents.

Donovan seemed to care little about the Communist penetration of OSS, even though a list secretly supplied to the NKVD by Donovan's assistant, NKVD agent Duncan Lee, showed that OSS security was aware of the identities of many of the Communists. But Donovan was unaware that a number of these Communists were spying on the OSS for the NKVD. His aim was to protect the image of his organization and of the Roosevelt administration, and his lies to Congress about Communist infiltration of his agency were based on that, not on any sympathy for the Communist cause. This myopic view nevertheless allowed the Soviets to penetrate and spy on American intelligence and endanger the missions and the lives of OSS officers and agents.

Bentley and the Agents in OSS

Venona messages decoded after the war reveal a number of reports that the NKVD received from Maurice Halperin, the chief of the Latin American Division of OSS Research, whose code name was "Zayats," and Donovan's close friend and assistant, Duncan Lee, code name "Koch." Elizabeth Bentley told the FBI that Halperin, Lee, and Donald Wheeler of the Perlo spy ring were Communist Party members and had supplied her with OSS information.[24] Bentley had no documents to back her story, only her word.

Duncan Lee, testifying before the House Committee on Un-American Activities, admitted that he knew Bentley but denied that he was a Communist Party member or that he had divulged classified information.[25] Halperin invoked the Fifth Amendment on Communist Party membership when called before the Senate Subcommittee on Internal Security in 1953 but, while denying he committed espionage, refused to say whether he had given Bentley OSS information.[26] Donald Wheeler, for his part, invoked the Fifth Amendment on almost everything in his 1953 testimony before the House Committee on Un-American Activities.[27]

Venona later proved that Bentley was truthful in all three cases. In May 1943 Lee reported to the NKVD that he expected to go to Chungking, China, in the middle of June on behalf of the OSS, and the New York *Rezidentura* asked Moscow if it wished to maintain contact with him there. If so, New York would provide him with a password. In the message, Zarubin, the New York *Rezident*, reported, "We discussed with [Lee] the question of his removing documents for photographing. [Lee] said that in some cases he agrees to do this, but as a rule he considers it inexpedient." Lee promised to think of less dangerous ways of providing the NKVD with OSS information.[28]

In September 1944 Lee advised the NKVD that the Security Division of OSS had prepared a list of employees known to be Communist Party members or sympathizers. Four were suspected of providing information to the Russians, among them Wheeler and Halperin. A *Venona* message from New York to Moscow reported that Lee promised to get a copy of the list for the NKVD.[29]

Five days later, on September 20, a *Venona* message from Moscow to New York ordered Lee to get hold of the list and Bentley to cease temporarily her liaison with Wheeler and Halperin. Moscow also ordered Lee to prepare a report on the Security Division of OSS.[30] Two days later, NKVD New York, in a *Venona* message, provided the list of nineteen Communist Party members that the OSS Security Division had identified.[31]

A September 1944 message reported: "'Koch' [Duncan Lee] advises that 'Diktor' [William Donovan] will soon return and decide the question of his [Lee's] trip. The 'Izba' [OSS] intends to send him to India or China for 5-6 months. From what 'Myrna' [Elizabeth Bentley] says, [Lee] agrees that we should get in touch with him there. We are giving [Bentley] the task of getting exact data on when and where exactly [Lee] is going [and] with what mission."[32]

In October a *Venona* message from New York reported that Lee had been appointed by Donovan as head of the Japanese section of a secret department of the OSS:

> [Lee] advises that his section has men in China working with a
> little group of Japanese Communist Party members in

Communist territory on the problem of dispatching people to Japan. The plan consists in the use of Korean Communist Party members and of the situation that Japan is importing Korean manpower. Details are being ascertained.

According to a communication of Lee the OSS is very much concerned about the fate of its people in territories occupied by the Red Army particularly in Germany where the concentration of the OSS's people is higher than in other countries. The OSS fears that its people will be shot....[33]

Back in June, Duncan Lee had reported to the NKVD:

Dewitt Poole, Head of the Nationalities Branch of the [OSS], compiled a report on the activities of the Roman Catholic priest Orlemanskiy. In February of this year O[rlemanskiy] met him and communicated his desire to go to Moscow with a view to ascertaining the position of the USSR on the religious question and trying to clarify the relations between the two countries. On returning to the [USA] he handed over all the documents he had brought to the representative of the Vatican who thanked him and sent the documents to the Pope.[34]

It was of great interest to the NKVD that a Catholic priest who had visited the Soviet Union had reported on that visit to the OSS.

One *Venona* message from NKVD *Rezident* Zarubin to Moscow listed a number of agents in the OSS, including "Zayats" (Maurice Halperin), "Koch" (Duncan Lee), and "Ostorozhnyj" (Julius J. Joseph). He described Joseph as working in the Far Eastern section of the OSS.[35] Joseph, in testimony before the Senate Subcommittee on Internal Security, invoked the Fifth Amendment on questions relating to his membership in the Communist Party.[36] An October 1944 message to Moscow from the New York *Rezidentura* identified

Target: OSS

Julius J. Joseph's sister, Emma Harriet Joseph, code name "Ivy," as a Soviet agent who had been accepted for work in the OSS and was scheduled to be sent to Ceylon. According to the report, "'Ivy' is a young Communist Party member who was highly spoken of by 'Myrna' [Elizabeth Bentley]. If we wish to establish a liaison with her in Ceylon, Bentley will make up the password."[37]

Zarubin also listed another agent in OSS, "Kollega," who worked in the photographic section. Although not identified by the code breakers, this appears to be Carl Marzani. A filmmaker and, later, a publisher who after the war was convicted of concealing his Communist Party membership while employed by the government, Marzani spent 1949–1951 in a federal penitentiary. Later, in 1956, he invoked the Fifth Amendment on Communist Party membership when testifying before the House Committee on Un-American Activities,[38] but Marzani was exposed as a paid KGB agent by retired KGB general Oleg Kalugin in his 1994 autobiography. Kalugin revealed that Carl Marzani had received KGB money in the early 1960s to finance his publishing house, Marzani & Munsell.[39]

One Soviet agent planted in the OSS was recruited by Martha Dodd, who worked for the Soble/Soblen spy ring (about which we will learn more in Chapter 11). A June 1942 *Venona* message from the New York *Rezidentura* told Moscow that on the recommendation of "Liza" (Martha Dodd) "we are cultivating the American Jane Foster with a view to signing her on [that is, recruiting]. She is about 30 years old and works in Washington…. Foster is a 'Zemlyachka' [member of the Communist Party]."[40] This was an NKVD play on words. "Zemlyachka" can be translated as "compatriot," and the Russian contraction for Communist Party is "ComPartiya."

Jane Foster, born in 1912, was employed by the OSS from 1943 to 1946. Her husband, George Zlatovski, served in the International

Brigades in the Spanish Civil War and in the United States Army during World War II.[41] A 1960 FBI report stated:

> Jane and George Zlatovski, American citizens currently residing in France, served under Jack Soble's supervision from 1945 to 1951. In a report [to NKVD] intercepted by Boris Morros, Jane Zlatovski claimed that while employed by the U.S. Army in Austria in 1947-1948, she obtained through her Army employment names, photographs and biographies of agents of the Counter Intelligence Corps and the Central Intelligence Agency, similar information concerning their "native agents" and "practically every scheme they hatched." Only disruption of contact with her superiors prevented successful delivery of such information to the Soviet Intelligence Service.
>
> Jane Foster Zlatovski and George Zlatovski were indicted on July 8, 1957, for conspiring to commit espionage. The Zlatovskis could not be arrested as they had escaped to France.[42]

Foster wrote an autobiography in 1980 in which she denied her role in Soviet espionage and even claimed that if she returned to the United States her life would be in danger.[43] The truth was that she had confessed to the French intelligence service and provided it with information concerning Soviet espionage in France. She also spoke to the FBI Paris office about espionage activities in the United States by Earl Browder's brother, William. But the FBI could not use the information in a criminal case against him because Foster refused to return to the United States and testify.[44]

A Longtime Communist in the OSS

Another Soviet agent in the OSS was a longtime member of the Communist Party, Leonard Emil Mins, code name "Smit." While working as a research analyst in the OSS in 1943, Mins was called before an executive session of the Special Committee on Un-American Activities (the Dies Committee). Questioned by J. B. Matthews, the committee's director of research, he denied that he had ever been a member of the Communist Party but did admit to teaching a course at the Communist Party Workers' School in 1937. He also admitted living in the Soviet Union for a time and returning to the United States in 1936.[45] The last two statements were true, the first was false. Comintern records in Moscow show that he was a charter member of the Communist Party USA.

In January 1935 the Comintern sent a message to the American Communist Party asking the Party to confirm Mins's personal history in its files, which showed that he had joined the Communist Party in 1919 and in 1920 began full-time work for the Party. In 1921 he transferred to the German Communist Party. Then from 1924 to 1925 Mins worked as a translator for the Executive Committee of the Communist International in Moscow, after which he returned to Germany and worked in the German Communist Party until 1927. He thereupon transferred back to the Communist Party USA and did Party work in the Agitprop (Agitation and Propaganda Department) and the Organizational Department of the Central Committee until 1932. His membership was transferred to the Soviet Communist Party in August or September 1934, when he returned to Moscow.[46]

After verifying his bona fides, the Comintern at a subcommittee meeting of the Anglo-American Secretariat on August 23, 1935, ordered Mins to return to the United States.[47] He did so in 1936, and the New York Communist Party's Workers' School catalog for January–March 1937 listed him as an instructor.[48]

Mins was a spy in the OSS, but he worked not for the NKVD but for Soviet military intelligence, the GRU. In July 1943 he reported to the GRU that in a talk he had with John Morrison, deputy chief of the

Russian section of the OSS, he learned that a group of military officers was promoting the idea of war with the Soviet Union. He also
reported that at an unnamed American university a group of eighty-
one army officers had completed Russian language training and would
be used in a special code-breaking unit.[49]

In August of 1943 Mins reported to the GRU that beginning on
August 13 the Russian division had worked day and night to complete an urgent report, though he did not know the subject and
could not obtain a copy.[50] And in September Mins tried to learn the
identity of a person who gave a lecture at the U.S. General Staff on
war with Russia but again failed.[51]

As a result of an investigation of Mins by the Dies Committee,
the OSS charged him with being a Communist. A GRU *Venona* message to Moscow on August 17, 1943, reported that the day before,
Mins had had a hearing before a civil service appeals board to avoid
being fired. Six of his OSS colleagues appeared as character witnesses,
but Mins nevertheless lost his job.[52]

On June 11, 1953, Mins testified before the Senate Subcommittee
on Internal Security and invoked the Fifth Amendment about whether,
while employed by the United States government, he had also been
employed by or in "the Soviet military service." He also invoked the
Fifth on whether he had taught at the Workers' School, written for
Communist Party publications, or advocated the overthrow of the government by force and violence.[53]

Helen Tenney also served the NKVD as an agent in the OSS
and was also identified to the FBI by Elizabeth Bentley in 1945.
According to Bentley, Tenney supplied information in 1942 to Jacob
Golos that she had obtained while working for an organization
called Short Wave Research, a covert affiliate of the OSS. When
Short Wave Research closed down, Golos convinced her to get a
job officially with OSS. Although he wanted her in the Latin

Target: OSS

American Division, where she could work with Maurice Halperin, she was assigned to a very secret Spanish Division, which received reports from OSS agents in Spain. After the death of Golos, she turned her information over to Bentley. Along the way, she was able to supply large amounts of official OSS reports marked secret and confidential.

Tenney also gave Bentley "a considerable quantity of written data reflecting the activities of OSS personnel in virtually all sections and all countries of the world...."[54] The authors of this book found documents in the Comintern archives that confirmed Bentley's allegation. On October 19, 1944, Pavel Fitin wrote a top secret message to George Dimitroff, who continued to function as head of the supposedly dissolved Communist International: "We request that you send immediately any information that you have about the following American citizens: Coplon (Kompid), Judy, works in the Department of Justice USA, [and] Tenney, Helen, works in the Office of Strategic Services." Dimitroff responded on October 31 that there was no information in the file.[55] Many of the American Communists recruited by the NKVD were checked for ideological purity through the Comintern files.

The authors also found in the Comintern archives a microfilm copy of a secret OSS report on Spain, stolen from Tenney's section, dated July 8, 1943. The document concerned Communist operations in Franco's Spain and was very sensitive at the time it was sent to Moscow, as it indicated that the OSS had informants both in the Spanish government and in the opposition. It is available today in the U.S. National Archives.[56]

The OSS penetration gave the NKVD valuable information about the agency's operations, but the Soviets needed a better understanding of its structure. This was handled in November 1944, when, *Venona* intercepts revealed, Bernie Chester, the American

Communist Party liaison with the NKVD, was given a special assignment to write a report on the structure of the OSS.[57]

Spies in the Justice Department

In addition to the OSS, the Justice Department was an important target of Soviet intelligence. During the intramural power struggle that went on when the OSS was set up, the duties of conducting both intelligence and counterintelligence activities in the western hemisphere were jealously preserved by FBI director J. Edgar Hoover. Indeed, the joint operations mounted by the FBI and Britain's covert service against Nazi spy rings in Latin America were one of the unalloyed American covert victories of the war. In consequence, the Soviets had a special appetite for FBI reports on hemisphere operations that circulated in the Justice Department. Other agencies also reported significant information to Justice.

Judy Coplon was an NKVD spy, code name "Sima," in the Department of Justice. In July 1944 the New York *Rezidentura* reported that she worked in the department's Economic Warfare Section. The New York *Rezidentura* requested Moscow's permission to recruit her if the NKVD Center was interested in the type of material she could provide.[58] She was approved, and in December the *Rezidentura* reported that Coplon had been transferred to the Foreign Agents Registration Section of the Department of Justice.[59]

Coplon was only twenty-two in 1943 when she went to work in New York for the Department of Justice. In January 1945, at her request, she was transferred to Washington. In 1949 the FBI, while watching a suspected KGB officer, Valentine Gubitchev, saw him meet Coplon. Gubitchev and Coplon were arrested during a later meeting on March 4, 1949. In Coplon's purse were confidential FBI reports that she had brought along to pass to Gubitchev. Coplon was tried for espionage in Washington and on July 1, 1949, was sentenced to ten years in prison. She and Gubitchev were also tried in New York City on a separate charge of conspiring to commit espionage. They were convicted, and on March 9, 1950, both were sentenced to fifteen years in prison. Gubitchev's sentence was suspended with the provision that he leave the United States and not return.

Coplon's conviction was reversed on a technicality, and the court also held that she was entitled to a new trial in the Washington, D.C., case. She was freed and not retried, but Learned Hand, the judge in the case, stated that, although he was reversing the conviction, her guilt was plain.[60] Coplon has spent her remaining days placidly running a small restaurant in New York.

Another Soviet agent in the Justice Department, Norman Bursler, was identified by Elizabeth Bentley during her 1948 testimony before the House Committee on Un-American Activities.[61] The authors found documents in the Comintern archives that confirm Bentley's identification. A November 5, 1944, memo from Fitin to Dimitroff asked that the Comintern "please check and inform us about Norman Bursler, former member of the CPUSA currently working in the Department of Justice of the USA."[62] As with the memo on Tenney and Coplon, the Bursler message was typed but the names were handwritten in Russian by Fitin. Even the NKVD secretaries were not supposed to know the names of the agents.

A *Venona* message from the New York *Rezidentura* in November 1944 reported information supplied by Bursler through Gregory Silvermaster on Felix Somary, an advisor to a number of U.S. government agencies, concerning Nazi economic activity. Bursler was identified in the message as a member of the American Communist Party.[63]

British Intelligence in New York

Well before America's forced entry into the war, Britain had created a special intelligence division, known as British Security

Coordination (BSC). It was at first charged with mounting a propaganda campaign to combat the dominating isolationist strain in American public opinion. After Pearl Harbor, agents for BSC worked jointly with the FBI throughout the southern hemisphere and provided the original training and equipment for Donovan's OSS recruits. From the start, BSC proved as easy for the Soviets to penetrate as the OSS. Bentley, for example, identified Cedric Belfrage, an employee of BSC, as a source of information to the Soviets through Jacob Golos.[64] Once again, Bentley's information was confirmed by *Venona* messages decoded long after her testimony.

An April 1943 *Venona* message reported that Belfrage had provided the Soviets with an OSS report on the Yugoslav partisans (Communists) and the Mikhailovic (Nationalist) movement, both of which were fighting against the Nazis. In May, Belfrage reported to the Soviets that Sir William Stephenson, the BSC director in New York, had returned from England together with Winston Churchill. Belfrage also told Jacob Golos that he might be transferred to England and would continue working for the Soviets there. Golos provided him with the password "Greetings from Molly" to be used in making contact with the Soviet officer in England.[65] After the war, Belfrage was a founder and editor of the leftist *National Guardian* in New York. He was deported to England in 1953.

In a May 29 *Venona* message, Zarubin told Moscow that Belfrage had reported that the FBI was unhappy with the "subversive activity" of British intelligence inside the United States, apparently referring to unilateral intelligence and influence operations conducted by Stephenson and his unit. Despite such protests, recently released British security documents show that Stephenson's operation continued clandestine intelligence gathering against American targets and conducted covert operations against prominent isolationists throughout the war.[66]

Target: OSS

The French Connection

In addition to gathering information about U.S. intelligence, the penetration of the OSS was extremely valuable for the NKVD for another reason. It gave the Soviets information on the non-Communist resistance movements in Nazi-occupied Europe that hoped to form democratic governments after the war. These movements were also penetrated where possible. The NKVD through the American Communist Party was able to recruit Pierre Cot, a minister in both the prewar and postwar French governments and an important figure in General Charles de Gaulle's Free French resistance movement.

In November 1940 Earl Browder communicated to the NKVD that Pierre Cot had met with him and asked that the Soviet Union be notified that he supported an alliance between it and France. Cot explained that although he supported England in its fight against the Vichy (pro-Nazi) government in France, he would be willing to reverse his position if the Soviet Union so wished. He was, in fact, prepared to carry out any task the Soviet government assigned to him.[67] Cot, who had arrived in the United States in September 1940 after escaping from France,[68] had a long record of collaboration with the Comintern's international front apparatus, headed by Willi Muenzenberg, but was not himself a Communist Party member. At the time, part of France was occupied by the Nazis; the rest was the domain of the puppet government in Vichy. Cot's American friends would have been shocked to learn that the supposed anti-Nazi was so pro-Soviet that he was prepared, if the Soviets so desired, to give political support to the pro-Nazi puppet government. But he didn't have to embarrass himself by openly supporting the Nazis; the Soviets had better use for him in the anti-Nazi resistance movement.

Cot's information on the French resistance movement was passed to the Soviets through Earl Browder until 1943. Then

Moscow wanted direct contact, and Vladimir Pravdin, an NKVD officer under cover as a journalist for the TASS news agency, contacted Cot in June 1942 while he was making a public speech. He was later officially recruited, with Moscow's permission, as an agent of the NKVD and allocated the code name "Daedalus" ("Dedal," in Russian).[69] But this took some time.

In February 1943 Pavel Fitin sent a message to Comintern head Dimitroff reporting information from Cot which had been obtained by the NKVD through Browder.[70] In June 1943 Zarubin personally took over the handling of Cot from Browder.[71]

The next month Cot suggested that he transfer to Algiers to work directly with General de Gaulle. Zarubin asked Moscow's advice, saying that whatever NKVD decided, Cot "will obey unquestioningly."[72] In the meantime, the NKVD checked out prospective new agents among the Free French through Cot.[73]

The Soviets had another longtime agent operating in the French Resistance: André LaBarthe, code name "Jerome," who was director general of armament and scientific research in de Gaulle's movement. *Venona* shows that LaBarthe was an agent of Soviet military intelligence, working in London for the French Resistance. Another agent closely associated with him was Alta Martha LeCoutre, code name "Martha," who was Pierre Cot's former mistress and LaBarthe's secretary.

LaBarthe and LeCoutre worked for the GRU as early as 1940, during the Soviet-Nazi alliance. Information they provided at that time about the resistance movement might well have found its way through the Soviets to the Nazis. In July 1940 LeCoutre reported to the GRU that LaBarthe was working closely with the British war industry and members of the British cabinet. LeCoutre was described in the *Venona* report as a former member of the German Communist Party who had worked earlier in the Moscow-controlled

Red International of Labor Unions; LaBarthe was described as not being a member of the Communist Party but as "sympathetic toward us," having served in Spain with the International Brigades.

LaBarthe told the GRU that he would continue working with de Gaulle until he received Soviet instructions to do otherwise, and "he will go where you instruct him to go." He was able to collect information for the Soviets under the pretense of writing a book on the defeat of Germany. According to the GRU *Resident* in London, Simon Kremer, "Last night [LeCoutre] passed me some material [on] an invention by a French engineer for the improvement of bombing. This material is due to be handed over to the British. This morning the material was returned after being photographed. The material is in French and is accompanied by the appropriate drawings."

LeCoutre received only a small salary as LaBarthe's secretary, although in the past she had gotten some financial help from French Communist Party official Marcel Cachin. The GRU, however, was paying LaBarthe for his help and agreed to provide money for LeCoutre as well because "politically she is stronger than [LaBarthe] and influences him." The contacts took place through LeCoutre because LaBarthe spoke poor English.[74]

In an August 1942 *Venona* message, the *Rezidentura* advised Moscow that LaBarthe had reported that the British were planning to send Free French troops to Dakar, French West Africa, but General de Gaulle opposed the plan because his troops were poorly armed and, moreover, would have to fight against other Frenchmen. On Moscow's instructions, the GRU *Rezidentura* ordered LaBarthe to stay in London with de Gaulle.

LaBarthe also offered to provide forged French passports for the GRU.[75] In late September he reported that de Gaulle and his troops were in Sierra Leone ready to attack Dakar from the landward side.[76] This information would have been of great value to the Nazis if their Soviet ally had shared it with them, but, although we know that the Soviets were supplying the Nazis with oil and other war materials, we do not know the extent of intelligence sharing between the two totalitarian states.

In early September 1940, LaBarthe reported to the GRU that he was very concerned because someone had told the British that he was a left-winger and had served in Spain. Kremer reported to Moscow that he had advised LaBarthe not to be concerned and to improve his work for the British and de Gaulle. At the same time, LeCoutre reported that LaBarthe felt that he was not getting enough money, and Kremer said the Soviets would increase his pay, but "the amount of intelligence [collected by the pair] must be increased."[77]

The resistance movements throughout Nazi-occupied Europe, including that of the French, were the basis for OSS and British intelligence penetration of the Reich. That these clandestine organizations were also targets of Communist penetration was a serious problem but one that was not fully understood by the West. The prevailing attitude among the leaders of the Anglo-American alliance was to fight one war at a time. There was, moreover, a division of opinion about what policies to adopt toward the Soviet Union once victory was assured, but again, most leaders from FDR and Churchill down hoped the Russians would be pacified if Stalin could learn to trust the Allies.

The Soviet leadership was under no such illusion. Moscow, from the start, looked beyond immediate war aims toward the long-term advance of the Communist cause. The Soviets' extensive collection of information on American, British, and French military and intelligence activities was dangerous in wartime. Even during the anti-Nazi alliance, the possibility that their communications could be read created a significant problem. During the Nazi-Soviet alliance, the possibility that the Soviets might share intelligence with their Nazi partner was far more dangerous.

The NKVD penetration of the OSS and the liberation organizations that fought against the Nazi occupation of Europe had significant postwar implications. During the Cold War, the CIA supported democratic political groups in formerly Nazi-occupied Europe. But the KGB, through its agents recruited during the war and its information about American and British intelligence, did its best to impede these prodemocracy movements. Non-Communist wartime operatives who had been recruited by the Allies in target countries now behind the Iron Curtain were ruthlessly hunted down and exterminated. Prodemocracy movements supported by the Anglo-American intelligence services were compromised and, in the early years of the Cold War, suppressed. The dark night of totalitarianism remained over half of Europe and threatened other governments around the world for almost half a century. In the long run, democracy won, but the NKVD's work during the war was extremely useful to the postwar KGB. The blind dedication of well-placed Americans who, like their British and French counterparts, served Moscow's spymasters gave the USSR a crucial advantage in those early days of the conflict.

CHAPTER 10

Hunting Down "Polecats"

ALTHOUGH THE SOVIET UNION WAS FIGHTING for its life during World War II, it allocated an inordinate amount of espionage resources and manpower against those referred to in the *Venona* code as "Polecats" (Trotskyites) and "Rats" (Jews).[1] The Soviets' concern had little to do with the war effort and much with what Moscow wanted in soon-to-be-conquered Eastern and Central Europe—a hegemony that would not be challenged by rival political or national movements.

Americans whose radical political views rivaled the Communists', such as the Trotskyites, or whose concern for their coreligionists in Nazi-occupied Europe might threaten future Communist control, such as the Jews, were targets for Soviet espionage.

This was consistent with the history of Soviet intelligence. When the Soviet secret service was established on December 20, 1917, by order of the first Soviet dictator, V. I. Lenin, it targeted ordinary Russians whose political or religious views displeased the Communist hierarchy. It was originally called the All Russian Extraordinary Commission of the Council of People's Commissars to Fight Against Counterrevolution and Sabotage, or Cheka for short. The Council of People's Commissars assigned Polish-born Felix Dzerzhinsky to head the new organization.[2]

The Cheka, Lenin's secret police, had "extraordinary powers," which meant the power of summary execution. Its victims included not only supporters of Russia's previous governments, such as monarchists or democrats, but even revolutionary groups that had fought the tsar, such as the Mensheviks and Social Revolutionaries, as well as Orthodox clergymen and Zionists.[3] The Russian Communist Party used the Cheka to repress any opposition. On February 8, 1919, a decree of the Communist Party revealed that "the Extraordinary Commission [Cheka] was created, exists and works as a direct organ of the Party through its directives and under its control."[4]

On December 20, 1920, the Foreign Department of the Cheka was established on the orders of Dzerzhinsky and instructed to work closely with the intelligence directorate of the Red Army, which at that time was mainly responsible for foreign intelligence.[5]

The Russian Communist Party gave the Cheka another responsibility—to create disinformation to confuse and undermine its enemies—and thus on January 11, 1923, the Politburo ordered the establishment of a disinformation section. An official KGB history reported that, over the years, Soviet disinformation was also called "actions to influence," "operational disinformation," "active measures," "operational games," and "assistance measures." "Despite the variation in terms," the history reported, "all of these were and are definite, purposeful actions to confuse an actual or potential enemy regarding one's true intentions or capabilities, as well as to obtain an advantageous reaction from the 'object of influence' that would be practically unattainable using open methods."[6]

The Hunt for Enemies of the State

Hunting down and kidnapping or killing enemies who had escaped abroad was an important function of the Cheka, then called GPU and later NKVD. The leaders of the White Army veterans who had fought the Bolsheviks in the Russian Civil War and were active in Western Europe with their dreams of overthrowing the Soviets were prime targets. The 1937 kidnapping in Paris and murder of the leader of the White Army veterans, General Yevgeny Miller, was organized by the former White Army general Nikolai Skoblin and his wife, the well-known Russian singer Nadezhda Plevitskaya. They were paid Soviets agents, receiving $200 a month.[7]

The Soviet government had a major problem in parts of the former tsarist empire: Nationalist movements were demanding independence. Ukraine, in particular, was a hotbed of agitation. Not only were Ukrainian nationalists active in eastern Ukraine, but Zionists were organizing the Jewish youth there, as well as in western Ukraine, which remained under Polish control until the 1939 Nazi-Soviet Pact. These were true Zionists—those who wanted to establish a Jewish homeland in Palestine—not simply Jews, whom the Soviets misnamed "Zionists."

The official KGB history boasted that state security was struggling against

> the Zionist underground, which was conducting active subversive work against Soviet power, especially in Ukraine and Byelorussia. Thus, at the end of April 1922, Chekists in Ukraine halted an attempt by the Zionists to conduct their second, illegal congress in a Kiev synagogue. On the suggestion of the Odessa provincial department of the GPU, the Odessa *gubispolkom* [provincial executive committee] was forced temporarily to shut down recreation and reading rooms in the city, which local Zionists had taken control of and turned into centers of anti-Soviet activity. Over the course of 1923-24, state security organs exposed and neutralized countless underground anti-Soviet Zionist organizations, and conducted strikes against their channels of communication with foreign anti-Soviet Zionist centers and foreign intelligence organizations.[8]

In 1928 and 1929 the GPU was still conducting "significant work for the breakup and liquidation of Zionist organizations. A number of leaders were repressed, and many were exiled to Palestine. This had some influence on several other leaders and active members of these organizations, and they emigrated from the USSR."[9] During World War II, Zionism would again become a major concern of the Soviet security and intelligence apparatus.

In the early 1920s the Ukrainian independence movement was led by Symon Petlura, who had headed the short-lived government of independent Ukraine at the end of World War I. After their defeat by the Red Army in 1920, having been weakened by combat against the Russian White Army, some Ukrainian units continued their armed struggle in the underground while Petlura organized political support abroad.

In 1926 Colonel Evan Konovaletz succeeded Petlura, who had been murdered, possibly at Soviet instigation, as the leader of the Ukrainian independence movement. In May 1938, according to Ukrainian sources, he was contacted by a supposed Ukrainian nationalist courier named "Walluch," who had just arrived from the Soviet eastern Ukraine. They met in Rotterdam at the Atlanta Café, where the visitor gave Konovaletz a package of material supposedly from the Ukrainian underground. "Walluch" left first. A few minutes later, the package exploded, killing the Ukrainian leader. The courier left that afternoon on a Soviet ship.[10]

"Walluch" was the NKVD officer Pavel Sudoplatov, who had penetrated the Ukrainian nationalist movement. He would later become the foremost KGB organizer of murders abroad. According to Sudoplatov, Stalin himself gave him the order to murder Konovaletz. (He added that the bomb was in a package of chocolates, not documents, and that he left Rotterdam by train, not by ship.)[11]

Hunting Down "Polecats"

The Bolsheviks and Mensheviks were two factions of the Russian Social Democratic Labor Party at the turn of the century. They had split into two parties when the Mensheviks advocated both internal democracy in the Party and political freedom in the future Russia. When the Bolsheviks took power in 1917, the Mensheviks were among their first victims. Some of the Menshevik leaders escaped abroad, where they continued their political campaign against Bolshevik repression.

Of all the Mensheviks living abroad, the Communists most hated Raphael Abramovich, an articulate and outspoken critic of Bolshevik repression. American Communists considered anyone opposed to Soviet Russia their enemy. In February 1925 the American Communist Party, then called the Workers Party of America, issued a pamphlet entitled "The White Terrorists Ask for Mercy." The Mensheviks were neither Whites—that is, pro-tsarists—nor terrorists. According to the Communist pamphlet:

> International Menshevism has sent a special representative to the United States, Raphael Abramovich, member of the central committee of the Menshevik Party of Russia and member of the executive committee of the Second International.... Since the Russian Proletariat has made the task of saving capitalism an unsafe profession at best within that part of the world controlled by the Soviets, the Russian Menshevists have made their living by painting most terrible pictures of Bolshevism, to the edification of big capital and to the terror of the international petty-bourgeoisie. Seeing these pictures losing their terror the Mensheviks are preparing to paint them over anew. Citizen Abramovich is entrusted with the task of accomplishing this in the United States. Abramovich raises the demand of release of political prisoners in Soviet Russia. Who are the "politicals" in Soviet Russia? "Socialists," answers citizen Abramovich;

"Socialists, who are persecuted for interpreting Socialism different from the interpretation of the Bolsheviks; Socialist brothers
of the Bolsheviks incarcerated by them only because their idea of
socialism differs just a little from that of the Bolsheviks."[12]

The Central Executive Committee of the Workers Party issued
secret instructions that in whatever city Abramovich spoke, the
Communists should organize demonstrations in support of Soviet
Russia and disrupt the meeting.[13] Demonstrations took place at
some of the Abramovich meetings, and at others the Communists
tried to organize boycotts, but in general they were unsuccessful.
Abramovich was a credible opponent of the Bolshevik regime and as
such received much attention in the press.

Abramovich, in short, was considered a dangerous man by the
Soviets. Their method of neutralizing him, since he was not within
their reach, was to try to discredit him. In 1931 the Soviet government
organized a trial of supposed Russian Mensheviks who would impli-
cate Abramovich in a plan not only to overthrow the Soviet government but even to support foreign military intervention to this end. In
fact, though the Mensheviks wanted to establish democracy in Russia,
they opposed any intervention by foreigners. Most of the defendants
at the trial had not been part of the Menshevik Party; another few had
been at one time but had dropped out during the Soviets' severe
repression of the party. The defendants testified that Abramovich had
come to Moscow in the summer of 1928 to prepare for the alleged
foreign intervention. One of the defendants testified about a meeting
with Abramovich during which he said that it was important to
destroy the Communist Party of the Soviet Union and Soviet power.
In the defendant's words: "From this, Abramovich drew the conclusion that it was necessary to begin with active sabotage methods in the
various branches of the Soviet economic system.... The second basis

of the struggle against the Soviet power was military intervention, declared Abramovich. The foreign delegation of the RSDP [Russian Social Democratic Labor Party—the official name of the Mensheviks] was of the opinion that intervention must be supported as the only serious and practical weapon for the overthrow of Soviet power."[14]

The Menshevik Party was an active section of the Socialist International, which immediately began a campaign to expose the falsity of the trial. Their best weapon was the evidence that Abramovich was never in Russia in the summer of 1928; indeed, he had been at a congress of the Socialist International in Brussels, Belgium, at precisely that time. His photograph was taken among the delegates, and the Socialist International published it on the front cover of a pamphlet that contained articles by leading Socialists—Abramovich, Friedrich Adler, Leon Blum, and Emil Vandervelde. Abramovich in his article poked fun at the GPU for its sloppiness, such as placing him in Russia when he was at a major public meeting elsewhere. The terrible thought had come to him, he said, that a "Menshevik damager" had infiltrated the OGPU and was deliberately making it look stupid![15]

Another faction to suffer persecution was the Trotskyite movement. Stalin believed that the Trotskyites were a serious political threat to his regime. Thus they, too, became a major target of Soviet foreign intelligence, and the NKVD spent enormous amounts of time and energy infiltrating their ranks and disrupting their activities. Although they were very weak, a few, including Trotsky himself, possessed important information about Soviet activities and even about intelligence operations. Stalin wanted these people killed not only to preserve the Soviet Union's secrets but also because of his personal animosity against his former rival, Trotsky. Even so, the intensive spying seems excessive considering how small and ineffective the movement was.

Trotsky was born Lev Davidovich Bronstein in a small Ukraine town in 1879, the same year as the Georgian-born Iosif Dzhugashvili, who took the nom de guerre Stalin—"man of steel"—during his years as a clandestine operator for the Bolsheviks. They shared a ruthless faith in the idea that the ends of Communism justified any means to attain it but otherwise were quite different. Stalin was a political insider, a bureaucratic in-fighter. Trotsky was a rigidly dogmatic theoretician who was capable of charismatic leadership, which he demonstrated while leading the Red Army, but he was ultimately an inefficient political organizer. By the mid-1920s Stalin established his power base in all the viable institutions of the young Soviet state, most notably the Communist Party itself, where the real power resided.

Politically defeated by Stalin by the late 1920s, Trotsky tried to organize his followers abroad into a political movement but garnered only small groups of supporters in a few countries. His worldwide organization, the Fourth International, was not formed until 1938 and had few adherents. Stalin therefore needed an excuse to annihilate the Trotskyite opposition within the Soviet Union and its contacts abroad. The opportunity came on December 1, 1934, when a young Communist named Nikolayev shot Sergei Kirov, the Leningrad Communist Party boss, at the historic Smolny Institute, where Lenin had his headquarters before moving the Soviet government to Moscow.

The first reaction of the Soviet government was to arrest "White Guards," a Soviet term for monarchist opponents of the regime. Added to those already in prison, 103 were sentenced to death and executed. Actually many of these victims were not White Guards at all but Ukrainian democrats and other dissidents.[16] Within a month, Stalin's accusatory finger was pointing at the opposition Communists Trotsky and Zinoviev, a former Comintern head. On January 1, 1935, the Young Communist International, using the

Hunting Down "Polecats"

Comintern radio, provided instructions to its sections in each country. It is worth quoting at length:

> The enquiry into the murder of Kirov has disclosed a horrible picture of the counter-revolutionary work of the remainder of the former Zinoviev-Trotsky opposition, which had lost all hope of the support of the masses, and had prepared to murder Stalin and his colleagues, and aimed at the fall of Soviet power through imperialist intervention.
>
> Trotsky, one of the chief organizers and ideological leader of this criminal fascist group, bears the full responsibility for the murder of Kirov.
>
> Enlighten everywhere the workers, youth, especially the Socialist youth, as to the counter-revolutionary fascist character of the role of Trotsky and the Trotskyites.
>
> Attain active results, resolutions of youth, rouse hate and disdain against Trotsky and the Trotskyites.
>
> Try for the complete expulsion of Trotskyites from the workers movement.
>
> Continually explain Stalin's useful works and great role as the successor of Marx-Lenin, as the ingenious organizer of the victories of socialism in the U.S.S.R. and as the beloved leader of the world proletariat.
>
> Show Stalin as the greatest leader, friend, human being, who is surrounded by the love of hundreds of millions.[17]

An information bulletin with similar rhetoric was distributed by the Comintern to headquarters in Moscow, where the purge had already begun. The orders were clear: "We must increase our vigilance in our own ranks. Among the staff of the Comintern there were two members of the Zinoviev-Trotskyite Group, among them Magyar [Ludwig Magyar], who maintained connection with a leader of the Zinoviev group, Safarov [Georgi Safarov], even after the murder of comrade Kirov and, after the arrest of Safarov by the organs of the proletarian dictatorship, attempted to support him materially."[18]

On January 28 the Comintern radioed its parties abroad: "Stop all advertising and sale writings Magyar and Safarov."[19] Magyar and Safarov were old Comintern apparatchiks with expertise on the Far East. Magyar had also been sent to Germany as a Comintern instructor and advisor to the German Communist Party Central Committee. He fled to France when Hitler took power and was recalled to Moscow in time to be arrested. Safarov was an old colleague of Lenin who accompanied him on the sealed train used by the German General Staff to send Lenin and his coworkers into Russia in 1917 in order to undermine the tsarist government's military capability.[20]

Extreme rhetoric by the Soviet and Comintern apparatus was by now a staple of anti-Trotskyite propaganda and was readily, even automatically, picked up by Communists outside the Soviet Union. Thus, when in 1935 Moshe Katz, a staff member of the Yiddish-language American Communist newspaper, *Morning Freiheit*, produced a pamphlet defending the coming purges, he wrote, "The fact that the terrorists came not only from the sewer of the White Guard counter-revolution, but also from the scum of the Trotzky-Zinoviev opposition, tended to confuse some of those friends of the Soviet Revolution who do not know how bitterly Trotzky, Zinoviev, Kamenev, and their followers fought against the Party and against the policies of the Soviet government since the first days of the October Revolution...."[21]

In a similar vein the Swiss Communist Party was ordered by the Comintern to attack the Trotskyites in connection with the Kirov murder. The Swiss were told to "expose Trotskyite opposition to Soviet [Union], explain story of Trotskyite tendency towards fascism, [and how Trotskyites] have become direct agents of fascism in every country."[22] The message was signed by Wilhelm Knorin, who headed the Comintern Secretariat for Central Europe. His opposition to Trotskyism didn't help him. He was arrested in June 1937 and died in the Gulag slave labor camps in 1939.[23]

Zinoviev, the first head of the Comintern, and eighteen others were also arrested. During their trial, all of them confessed. The court concluded that they were not directly responsible for the assassination of Kirov by their Leningrad colleagues but that they "were aware of the terroristic tendencies of the Leningrad group and that they promoted these tendencies." They were all sentenced to prison. Safarov was a witness against them and was not tried with the others.[24] This did not help him. He was held in custody and finally died in 1942.[25]

The purge constantly needed new victims. Not only former supporters of Trotsky but even his political enemies were accused of "Trotskyism," arrested, and finally killed. Zinoviev had supported Stalin against Trotsky. When Stalin turned on Zinoviev, Bukharin sided with Stalin. Soon he too was ousted.

The Purge Trials

In August 1936 Zinoviev and several of his codefendants were taken out of jail and put on trial again, this time for being directly involved in Trotskyist "sabotage" and in espionage for foreign intelligence services. After torture and threats to their families, they confessed to the false charges—the usual procedure in Soviet trials. New defendants appeared, and they, too, were turned into witnesses and accusers against Zinoviev and Trotsky (the latter, of course, was living outside the USSR).

One of the defendants, Konon Berman-Yurin, testified that he had been assigned by Trotsky to murder Stalin. "He [Trotsky] said that the terroristic act should, if possible, be timed to take place at a plenum or at a congress of the Comintern, so that the shot at Stalin would ring out in a large assembly. This would have a tremendous repercussion far beyond the borders of the Soviet Union and would give rise to a mass movement all over the world. This would be an historical political event of world significance." But, he added, when he could not gain admission to such a high-level meeting, he did not carry out the plan.[26]

The cleverest of Trotsky's American followers, Max Shachtman, commented wryly, "It wouldn't do to shoot Stalin in a hallway, in his office, on the street, at his home, or while he was riding to hounds. It had to be done during a Congress, or at the very least during a Plenum. Otherwise, you understand, the shot and his death might not be noticed at all. It might be given a 2-line item on the back page of *Pravda*, and the whole effect of the assassination would be lost."[27]

Valentine Olberg was also a witness/defendant. He testified about a supposed close relationship between the Trotskyites and the Gestapo. Olberg claimed that he had obtained a false Honduran passport with the aid of a Gestapo agent and with the permission of Leon Sedov, Trotsky's son. Sedov, he said, also provided him with the 13,000 Czech kronen to pay for the passport.[28]

Sedov responded from his exile in Paris that the story was untrue and that Olberg was not even a member of the Trotskyite movement.[29] Moreover, the Gestapo involvement in the passport was disproved by another source. A British Communist reported to the Comintern on a discussion he had had in London with a member of the New Beginning Group. This organization of left-socialists had been infiltrated by secret Communist agents. The New Beginning member revealed that his organization had information on Olberg, who was well known in the non-Stalinist left, and that "we only know that Ohlberg [sic] lied when he said he had been given his passport by the Gestapo. We knew Ohlberg [sic]. He was a meek and modest man...." While looking for a job, Olberg learned that he might get one in Russia, but the Soviet embassy said he needed a valid passport. So Olberg went to Prague, where he bribed someone in the Honduras legation to get it for him. "The sum agreed upon was 7,000 K.C. [Czech kronen] (appr. £60).... The bulk of it came from the sale of his own books which he had managed to bring out with him from Germany; he sold them to the Massaryk [sic] Library."30

Another witness/defendant, E. S. Holtzman, testified that in 1932 he went to Copenhagen to meet with Trotsky and Trotsky's son, Leon Sedov. He said, "I arranged with Sedov to be in Copenhagen within two or three days, to put up at the Hotel Bristol and meet him there. I went to the hotel straight from the station and in the lounge met Sedov. About 10 AM we went to Trotsky. When we arrived Trotsky first of all asked me about the feelings and the attitude of the mass of the Party members towards Stalin. I told him that I intended to leave Copenhagen that day and would leave for the USSR within several days.... Throughout this conversation I was alone with Trotsky. Very often Trotsky's son Sedov came in and out of the room."

Holtzman claimed that Trotsky told him it was necessary to remove Stalin and "also said that the only means of removing Stalin was terrorism."31 In Paris Sedov immediately answered with a *Red Book* that exposed the lies of the "witnesses." He pointed out that he had never been to Copenhagen. His father had been there only from November 14 to December 2, 1932, during which time Trotsky had no more than one Russian-speaking visitor, Abraham Senine (who later worked for the NKVD in the United States under the name Jack Soble). Trotsky, not knowing that Senine was a GPU agent, thought he was wavering ideologically and tried to convince him to stay in the Trotskyite movement.

Sedov exposed something even more important—there was no Hotel Bristol in Copenhagen. The hotel where Holtzman claimed to be staying and where he said he met Trotsky no longer existed. There *had* been a Hotel Bristol, but it was closed in 1917, and the building was torn down.[32]

The official book of the trial summary, published in English in Moscow, contained this embarrassing claim. But when, on Comintern instructions, it was reprinted in Great Britain, that part was missing. The British version had a preface by D. N. Pritt, a Labour member of Parliament.[33] Pritt was also the author of an eyewitness account of the trial, published by the American Communists, which defended the Soviet position.[34]

On October 23, 1936, the Comintern in a secret radio message to the British Communist Party ordered the latter to "arrange with Pritt and Gollanz for publication of pamphlet Zinoviev trial in French, German, Czech, Spanish, Dutch, Scandinavian languages. All our publishers are informed. Arrange for suitable honorarium."[35] Gollanz was a leftist British publisher with secret Comintern ties who broke with them during the Soviet-Nazi alliance. The Comintern had previously radioed the Communist parties of Sweden, Denmark, and Holland that money had been remitted to pay for such publications.[36] The "honorarium" was of course the payment to Pritt.

(D. N. Pritt continued to write disinformation on behalf of the Communists. In 1952, for example, he wrote an introduction to a publication of the International Association of Democratic Lawyers, a Soviet front, that contained false charges of atrocities by American troops in Korea and China, including the fantastic claim that the United States used germ warfare.)[37]

The NKVD was embarrassed by the Hotel Bristol fiasco. As in the case of Raphael Abramovich in 1931, it had again framed a case without checking the details. This had to be rectified. So the Danish Communists opened a café next to a hotel and put up a sign, "Café Bristol." They then carefully photographed the Café Bristol sign with part of the hotel sign so as to suggest that there really *was* a Hotel Bristol. The American Communists published the picture in the *Daily Worker*. It was also used in a leaflet advertising a speech by Mauritz A. Hallgren, a fellow-traveling writer for the *Baltimore Sun*.

The leaflet advertised a "Solidarity Meeting" under the slogan "The Soviet Union Marches On!" In addition to Hallgren, who served the Communists as part of a significant disinformation campaign against the Trotskyites, there was another speaker, James Waterman Wise, son of Rabbi Stephen S. Wise. The Comintern was elated when the rabbi, possibly influenced by his fellow-traveler son, issued a statement denouncing Trotsky.[38] The chairman of the meeting was Malcolm Cowley, literary editor of *The New Republic*.[39] In 1932 Cowley had urged Americans to vote for the Communist Party presidential ticket of William Z. Foster and James W. Ford[40] and remained a fellow traveler until the Nazi-Soviet Pact.[41]

The Trotsky case and the Moscow trials had by now taken on international dimensions. The Stalinists had to discredit the Trotskyites overseas while at the same time destroying them in the Soviet Union, not so much because they were really competing with the Communist parties but because they were revealing too much and could undermine the relations the Soviets were beginning to form with non-Communists in order to further their foreign policy objectives.

The Trotskyites in turn established the American Committee for the Defense of Leon Trotsky in 1937. Attracted to the committee's demand for a fair trial for Trotsky, many non-Communist liberals voiced their support. This dismayed Soviet strategists, who were in the midst of building "popular front" movements in the Western democracies and trying to attract many of the same liberals. According to documents in the Comintern archives, the American Communist Party responded by establishing a special subcommittee of its Politburo. It was headed by William Z. Foster, the Party's national chairman. In a report to a Politburo meeting of February 11, 1937, Foster characterized the establishment of the Trotsky Defense Committee as "the little defeat which we suffered...." In response, the Party decided to publish a series of pamphlets to refute the Trotskyites, and Party members were ordered to check their personal libraries and "clean out all libraries of Trotskyist Literature."[42]

The American Committee for the Defense of Leon Trotsky was extremely active. It succeeded in getting a significant number of liberals and socialists to raise the question of a fair trial and political asylum in a Western country for Trotsky. Trotsky was living in Norway when the 1936 Moscow trial took place, and, shortly before, a gang of fascists had raided his home on the pretext of finding "incriminating evidence of illegal activities."[43]

The Soviets put substantial pressure on Norway to expel Trotsky to a country where they could get their hands on him. On December 4, 1935, for example, the Comintern radioed secret orders to the Communist Party of Sweden: "Demonstrate that Trotsky is agitating for the murder of comrade Stalin. Organize a wide campaign under the slogan: —'Trotsky must leave Norway.'"[44]

Stalin's instrument in applying pressure was the Norwegian minister of justice, Trygve Lie, a future secretary general of the United Nations (1946 to 1953). Lie had a long career on the extreme Left. In 1921 he was secretary of a delegation of Norwegian Socialists who brought their organization, the Norwegian Labour Party, into the Communist International. And while in Moscow, Lie and other members of the delegation issued a declaration urging Norwegian trade unionists to join the Moscow-based Red Labor Unions International (also known as the Red International of Labor Unions or the Profintern).[45] The Norwegian Socialists, as it turned out, soon left the Comintern.

On August 26, 1936, Norwegian policemen came to Trotsky and told him that on the orders of Lie he would not be permitted to make public statements or even to answer the charges against him at the Moscow trials. When he remonstrated, he was placed under house arrest. Lie thereupon pressured Trotsky to sign an agreement to be silent, but Trotsky continued to refuse. In December 1936 Trotsky was put aboard a steamship and deported to Mexico.[46]

Writing in December 1937, Trotsky commented on Trygve Lie: "This minister of justice was a member of the Third International just a few years ago and, in this sense a comrade of mine? I cannot conceal the fact that [while] I am thinking of this I spat in the Atlantic Ocean."[47]

Mauritz Hallgren was one of the liberals who joined the Trotsky Defense Committee. Whether he was sent by the Communist Party or joined on his own is not known, but Hallgren sent a letter of resignation on January 27, 1937, and he wrote that the Trotskyites had

> but one purpose and that is to use the committee as a spring-board for new attacks upon the Soviet Union. I do not intend under any circumstances to allow myself to become a party to any arrangement that has for its objective purpose (whatever might be its subjective justification) the impairment or destruction of the socialist system now being built in Soviet Russia. You will, therefore, withdraw my name as a member of the committee.[48]

Hallgren pointed out that since Trotsky had found asylum in Mexico, he no longer needed it in any other country, such as the United States. This was important to the Communists, for in 1937 Stalin ordered the NKVD to murder Trotsky.[49] And if Trotsky were to go to the United States, not only would he propagandize for his cause, but it would be also much harder to kill him.

At a February 4, 1937, meeting, the Politburo of the Communist Party, which important American Communists attended, decided to publish Hallgren's letter as a pamphlet that would be "sent out to a large list of people—editors of papers—say a list of 1,000 people." William Z. Foster commented during the discussion, "One angle that we have to pay more attention to is the question of Trotsky coming into the U.S. I think this is a very serious danger. These Trotskyites and their sympathizers are putting this right at the head of their agitation. We have to take up seriously this fight against Trotsky coming here. We have to meet their demand with some real resistance. In making this fight we have to show that the issue of asylum is not involved, that that question as MH [Mauritz Hallgren] says, is out."

Another discussant, probably Earl Browder, said at the meeting that Hallgren's "letter represents the most conscious and developed form of the whole trend of thought, particularly in intellectual circles." He went on to say, reflecting the paranoia of Stalin:

> I think the point that Comrade Foster made of the campaign of the Trotskyites to bring Trotsky into the U.S. is an important point which must receive increasing attention now. We must make it clear that what is actually being worked for is to give Trotsky a free hand to organize the campaign for the coming war, and as a part of that to disrupt the anti-war forces, the anti-fascist forces everywhere, which means disrupt the trade union campaign, People's Front campaign, FLP [Farmer Labor Party] efforts, etc. and that Trotsky is a real danger in this respect and his entrance into the U.S. would be a real danger because he comes in not just as Trotsky, but as the spearhead of the concentration of reactionary forces of Americans and of the world.

Hunting Down "Polecats"

One of the decisions made at the February 11 meeting was to get letters from Vicente Lombardo Toledano and other Mexican labor leaders to American trade union officials, such as John L. Lewis, denouncing Trotsky.[50] As we shall see, *Venona* messages from Mexico City identify Lombardo Toledano as an NKVD agent.

On February 21, at a meeting of the New York State Committee of the Communist Party, Israel Amter instructed the Party "to spread the Hallgren pamphlet, especially among liberals."[51]

In an evaluation of the *Baltimore Sun*, I. Mingulin, who headed the Anglo-American Secretariat at Comintern headquarters, wrote that "in the editorial board of the newspaper there are such, sometimes very left bourgeois elements, as Hallgren, the instigator of the campaign against the 'Trotsky Defense Committee,' sympathizing with socialism and refusing to participate in any kind of statement if it is aimed against the USSR."[52]

It has always been known that there was a systematic Communist campaign against Trotsky and that special efforts, such as these, were made to prevent him from defending himself. What was not clear until the opening of the Comintern archives in Moscow was the degree to which these efforts occupied the leadership's time and the extent to which they were micromanaged directly from Moscow.

The Third American Writers Congress, a Communist front, took place in New York on June 2–4, 1939, and used Hallgren's name as a sponsor in its call to Congress. In April 1941, after the signing of the Nazi-Soviet Pact, the Fourth American Writers Congress no longer carried Hallgren's name.[53] Hallgren appears to have dropped out of most pro-Communist activity when the pact with the Nazis was signed. In any event, having used him to disrupt the Trotsky Defense Committee, the Communists no longer needed him.

A pamphlet reprinting editorials from the international labor and liberal press was published for the Trotsky Defense Committee by the Trotskyite publishing house Pioneer Publishers.[54] The same publishing house printed for the Socialist Party of the United States *The Witchcraft Trial in Moscow* by Friedrich Adler, secretary of the Labor and Socialist International, with a preface by American Socialist leader Norman Thomas.

The Trotskyites had in fact joined the Socialist Party in June 1936. Many Socialists, who had strong feelings about fairness, would have defended Trotsky's rights in any event. Now, the proximity of Trotskyites in the party focused their attention on the issue but also exposed the manipulative, destructive activity of this small Marxist-Leninist group, and the Trotskyites were pushed out in December 1937.

The Socialists never had any illusions about Trotsky. They knew he was no democrat. They were simply demanding human rights for their dissident Communist leader even though he had persecuted their comrades when in power in Russia. Friedrich Adler, in one of the most forthright statements of the period on the dividing line between democratic socialists and Communists, pointed out:

> We were never Trotskyists, not when the Communists of all countries had to walk in awe of the supreme leader of the Red Army, nor when six months after Lenin's death Stalin presided jointly with Trotsky over the Fifth Congress of the Communist International (1924), nor later when the struggle for the succession had led to Trotsky's proscription. The defendants in the Moscow trial and their alleged "spiritus rector," Trotsky, were not our friends when they were great rulers in the Soviet Union, nor were they when they went into opposition in order to replace the dictatorship of Stalin by their own. We had no reason whatever to expect from Trotsky or Zinoviev that the development of the

Soviet Union towards the Socialist democracy for which we are hoping, would be accelerated if they returned to power.[55]

The American Committee for the Defense of Leon Trotsky held a meeting in New York's Hippodrome on February 9, 1937, to hear a speech by Trotsky telephoned from his home in Mexico. But the telephone call could not be put through. Max Shachtman announced that the telephone wires had been cut north of Mexico City in an apparent act of Stalinist sabotage. In the end, Trotsky's speech had to be read to the meeting by Shachtman. In the speech, Trotsky demanded to appear before a public, impartial commission of inquiry, saying, "If this commission decides that I am guilty in the slightest degree of the crimes which Stalin imputes to me, I pledge in advance to place myself voluntarily in the hands of the executioners of the G.P.U."[56]

The Dewey Commission

Under the leadership of prominent seventy-eight-year-old philosopher John Dewey, a commission was established in 1937 by Socialists, liberals, and Trotskyites to look into the truth about the Moscow trials. Clarence Hathaway, the editor of the *Daily Worker*, reported to a Communist Party Politburo meeting on April 2, 1937, that the Communist Party had received a telegram from John Dewey announcing a preliminary hearing in Mexico City on whether Trotsky was guilty of the charges in the Moscow trials. He invited the Communists to send an attorney to participate. The Communists decided not to reply but instead to attack Dewey in the *Daily Worker*. They also sent someone secretly to Mexico City to work with Vicente Lombardo Toledano to organize opposition to the Dewey tribunal.[57]

Although the Communists refused to send official participants or even observers to the hearings, one of their agents was present. Ben Stolberg, a knowledgeable and incorruptible liberal, suggested that his friend Carleton Beals be invited to serve on the Commission of Inquiry. Sidney Hook, who worked on the commission, commented later that Stolberg was "unaware apparently of Beals' close association with Toledano, the head of the Mexican Communist Union organization."[58]

Led by Lombardo Toledano, the Mexican Confederation of Labor had opposed Trotsky's asylum in Mexico and participated in propaganda operations against him.[59] Lombardo Toledano and his union also provided the thugs used by the NKVD for the ensuing physical attacks on Trotsky and his followers.

Predictably, instead of trying to learn the facts, Carleton Beals acted as the "prosecuting attorney" when the former Soviet leader testified. He tried to force Trotsky to reveal the location of his archives, some of which had already been stolen in Paris by Soviet agents. He also tried to embarrass Trotsky by asking, "How many workers of the Soviet Union support your doctrines?" Trotsky answered that finding the answer to that would require "Soviet democracy."

At one session, Beals and Trotsky volleyed accusations at one another. Beals accused Trotsky of sending Soviet official Mikhail Borodin to Mexico in 1919 or 1920 to establish the Communist Party. This charge was intended to embarrass Trotsky and perhaps force the Mexicans to expel him. Trotsky answered that he had no part in sending Borodin to Mexico, that he was only attending to the military situation in Russia at that time. Beals countered by saying that the statement had come from Borodin. If so, Trotsky said, Borodin was a liar.

In a closed session, the commission told Beals his question was improper, and Beals resigned.[60] Beals played the same disruptive role in the Dewey Commission that Hallgren had played in the American Committee for the Defense of Leon Trotsky—to disorder Trotsky's defense through controversy and confusion.

Hunting Down "Polecats"

Despite the efforts of Beals, any objective evaluation of the Moscow trials could conclude only that they were crude frame-ups. The contradictory testimony, dearth of documents, and lack of opportunity to present a defense case made this clear. The Dewey Commission's findings, published under the title *Not Guilty*, made a compelling argument.

When the *New York Times* reported the findings on December 12, 13, and 14, 1937, Moscow was very upset. Sidney Bloomfield, an American Communist working at the Comintern in Moscow, was assigned to write a report on "Recent Trotsky Propaganda in the USA." The *Times* had reported a radio broadcast on the findings by Professor Dewey and an answer by the Soviet apologist Corliss Lamont. Bloomfield complained:

> While the *Times* gave a number of columns including front-page publicity to the Trotskyist poison campaign, quoting elaborately, it gave only two small paragraphs to Corliss Lamont, head of the Friends of the Soviet Union, who followed Prof. Dewey over the radio immediately the same evening upon the conclusion of Dewey's speech. Lamont's address is published in the *Daily Worker* of December 14th. In this statement Lamont takes issue with Dewey on the important questions and quotes Carleton Beals, the journalist who has resigned from Trotsky's Investigation Commission while in Mexico City because "my questions were considered unfortunate because Trotsky answered badly and it should not be publicly stated I was told that most of his documents were merely copies." Lamont cited the consistent poisonous campaign of Trotskyism against Spain and China and called for American sympathy to be continued "towards the heroic efforts of the Soviet Republic to construct a new world whose basic ethical principle is loyalty to the welfare and progress of all mankind."[61]

Enter Ambassador Davies

While Trotsky's defenders made some small inroads in leftist intellectual circles, they had little effect on the liberal establishment. Joseph E. Davies, the U.S. ambassador to the Soviet Union, attended some of the Moscow trial sessions. He came away convinced. His best-selling book, *Mission to Moscow*, shows that Davies, a New Deal activist, knew little about Russia and less about Communism. He was convinced by the staged show trials because he was ignorant of the facts. He became a one-man apologist for everything Soviet.

In a December 1941 article, Davies argued that the purge trials eliminated the Nazi "fifth column" in Soviet Russia:

> A few days after Hitler's attack on Soviet Russia, I was asked the question, "What about Fifth Columnists in Russia?" Off the anvil, I replied, "There aren't any—they shot them...." Much of the world construed the famous treason trials and purges from 1935 to 1938 to be outrageous examples of barbarism, ingratitude, and hysteria. But it now appears that they indicated the amazing farsightedness of Stalin and his close associates.[62]

Davies's propaganda brought about a pro-Soviet surge in the United States. In 1943 his book was made into a major motion picture. The film, a box office flop, cost two million dollars, and another half million was spent on publicity—four thousand dollars in newspaper ads[63] that contained such ridiculous slogans as "The greatest one-man mission since Paul Revere's ride!"[64]

Those knowledgeable about the Soviet Union, among them Max Eastman, Sidney Hook, Dwight Macdonald, A. Philip Randolph, Bertram Wolfe, Eugene Lyons, Lionel Trilling, and Edmund Wilson, signed a statement exposing the film's support for the appalling Moscow trials of 1936–1938.[65] The Socialist *New Leader* and the Republican National Committee both issued reprints of news stories critical of the film. Nevertheless, Davies's movie had its defenders. Not only the Hollywood Left but also the Veterans of Foreign Wars denounced critics of the movie. Victor E. Devereaux, national chairman of Americanism for the Veterans of Foreign Wars, told the *Daily Worker* that the movie had been the target of "subversive influence" of "renegade Communists."[66] In a May 28 press release, Devereaux called these critics of *Mission to Moscow* "a lunatic fringe of emotional crackpots."[67]

In July 1943 Davies contacted a respectable journalist to ask that he publish compromising information about the Trotskyites, according to NKVD agent Jacob Golos. Pavel Klarin reported this to Moscow in a *Venona* message. He suggested that the New York *Rezidentura* give Davies information in order to calumniate Trotsky.[68]

Trotsky's closest collaborators were his wife, Natalia Sedova, and his son, Leon Sedov. The rest of Trotsky's family, with the exception of his young grandson, had all been killed or forced to commit suicide in Stalin's USSR. Leon Sedov died on February 16, 1938, at age thirty-two. He had an operation for appendicitis, and while the operation was successful, the patient died. Trotsky knew that his son had been murdered and in his grief wrote:

> The first and natural supposition is that he was poisoned. It presented no serious difficulty for the agents of Stalin to gain access to Leon, his clothing, his food. Are judicial experts, even if untrammeled by [diplomatic] considerations capable of arriving at a definitive conclusion of this point? In connection with war chemistry the art of poisoning has nowadays attained an extraordinary development. To be sure the secrets of this art are inaccessible to common mortals. But the poisoners of the G.P.U. have access to everything. It is entirely feasible to

conceive of a poison which cannot be detected after death, even with the most careful analysis.[69]

Referring to the Stalinists, Trotsky wrote in his characteristic style filled with revolutionary and even biblical references: "Before they killed him they did everything in their power to slander and blacken our son in the eyes of contemporaries and of posterity. Cain Djugashvili [Stalin] and his henchmen tried to depict Leon as an agent of fascism, a secret partisan of capitalist restoration in the USSR, the organizer of railway wrecks and murders of workers. The efforts of the scoundrels are in vain. Tons of Thermidorian [counterrevolutionary, in the Marxist lexicon] filth rebound from his young figure, leaving not a stain on him. Leon was a thoroughly clean, honest, pure human being."[70]

Trotsky was right; his son was murdered by the GPU. Its agent Mark Zborowski was a man who worked closely with Sedov and later came to the United States, where he worked in the Soble/Soblen spy ring. When Zborowski's role as a GPU agent was exposed, he was called before the Senate Subcommittee on Internal Security. Asked about his role in the assassination of Sedov, he answered, "I don't know that it had to do with assassination. The assignment was given to find out from Sedov his relationship with the Hitler movement—that is what I was told, that Trotsky prepared with the Germans a plot against the Soviet Union—and that was my assignment."

Prodded about Sedov's death, Zborowski remembered that "maybe" he had called the ambulance that took Trotsky's son to the hospital. But Sedov, he claimed, died of peritonitis. In the course of the questioning, Zborowski became flustered and blurted out, "May I state, Senator, that I was not given an assignment to lure Sedov to a place for assassination. The idea was at the time it was told to me, the idea was to lure him to a place where he and me together would be kidnapped and brought to Soviet Russia, that was the idea that was explained to me." The kidnapping ended in murder.

Although Zborowski was responsible for the theft of some of Trotsky's archives from the Nicolaevsky Institute in Paris, he claimed during his testimony not to remember the incident. The committee also learned that Zborowski had provided information to the Soviets about the whereabouts of NKVD defector Ignace Reiss, who was in contact with Sedov. Using Zborowski's information, the Soviets located and murdered Reiss. Zborowski also provided information about another NKVD defector, Walter Krivitsky. But this time, the NKVD could not locate its victim, and Krivitsky was able to flee to the United States.[71] But later, after testifying before the Dies Committee in 1941, Krivitsky was murdered in Washington, D.C.

In 1939, after the murder of his son, Trotsky took every opportunity to reveal what he knew about Stalin's dictatorship and the role of the NKVD in murders abroad and to answer Stalinist charges. One opportunity came for a major propaganda opening. The House Special Committee on Un-American Activities, or the Dies Committee (named for its chairman, Martin Dies), invited Trotsky to testify. He received a call from the committee's research director, J. B. Matthews, and then a telegram asking him to come to the United States for the hearing. The telegram read:

> DIES COMMITTEE OF THE UNITED STATES HOUSE
> OF REPRESENTATIVES INVITES YOU TO APPEAR AS
> WITNESS BEFORE IT IN THE CITY OF AUSTIN
> TEXAS A CITY DESIGNATED WITH A VIEW TO
> YOUR PERSONAL CONVENIENCE stop DATE OF
> YOUR APPEARANCE TO BE APPROXIMATELY FOUR
> WEEKS FROM NOW stop DIES COMMITTEE AGREES

TO ARRANGE FOR YOUR ENTRY INTO THE UNITED STATES FOR THE PURPOSE OF TESTIFY-ING BEFORE IT stop WILL ALSO ARRANGE FOR PROPER PROTECTION stop THE COMMITTEE DESIRES TO HAVE A COMPLETE RECORD ON THE HISTORY OF STALINISM AND INVITES YOU TO ANSWER QUESTIONS WHICH CAN BE SUBMITTED TO YOU IN ADVANCE IF YOU SO DESIRE stop YOUR NAME HAS BEEN MENTIONED FREQUENTLY BY SUCH WITNESSES AS BROWDER AND FOSTER stop THIS COMMITTEE WILL ACCORD YOU OPPORTU-NITY TO ANSWER THEIR CHARGES stop YOU WILL PLEASE TREAT THIS INVITATION AS NOT FOR PUB-LICITY FOR THE PRESENT.

Trotsky received the telegram on October 12 and answered the same day:

I ACCEPT YOUR INVITATION AS A POLITICAL DUTY stop I WILL UNDERTAKE NECESSARY MEA-SURES IN ORDER TO OVERCOME PRACTICAL DIF-FICULTIES stop PLEASE ARRANGE UNDER THE SAME CONDITIONS ENTRY FOR MY WIFE stop SHE IS INDISPENSABLE FOR THE PURPOSE OF LOCAT-ING THE NECESSARY DOCUMENTS' QUOTATIONS DATES IN MY FILES stop NECESSARY TO HAVE YOUR QUESTIONS AS SOON AS POSSIBLE IN ORDER TO SELECT THE NECESSARY DOCUMENTS stop ALSO DESIRE EXACT QUOTATIONS FROM DEPOSITIONS OF FOSTER AND BROWDER CON-CERNING ME PERSONALLY.[72]

James Burnham, then one of Trotsky's most intelligent followers and later a leading conservative, opposed Trotsky's appearing before the committee. He felt that the Stalinists would use an appearance before a "conservative" congressional committee as a propaganda weapon against Trotsky.[73] Trotsky never appeared, but for other reasons.

J. B. Matthews told Herbert Romerstein in the 1960s that the State Department had prevented Trotsky's entry into the United States, thus killing all chances of his testifying. Matthews commented that the department was allowing all sorts of Communist aliens into the United States in violation of our law, but this was the only one it kept out. Trotsky's willingness to expose Stalin in any forum might well have encouraged Stalin to have him killed.

The Assassination of Trotsky

An attempt to kill Trotsky took place on May 24, 1940. On that day, a band of thugs led by the artist David Alfaro Siqueiros, a member of the Mexican Communist Party, appeared at Trotsky's residence in the Mexico City suburbs dressed in police uniforms. The thugs disarmed and tied up the police guards outside the building and kidnapped one of Trotsky's American bodyguards, twenty-five-year-old Robert Sheldon Harte.

When Harte disappeared some of his friends suspected that he might have been a Stalinist agent—until his body turned up in a lime pit a few days later. But Julian Gorkin, a Spanish anti-Stalinist leftist, then close to the Trotsky circle, continued to suspect Harte because he had opened the door to the attackers, possibly, too, because Harte knew the leader of the group. In addition, he argued, Harte's family thought he was a Stalinist, not a Trotskyite.[74]

The argument has not been definitely resolved, but Pavel Sudoplatov, who directed the murder operation from Moscow, claimed that a GPU officer named Joseph Grigulevich, code name "Padre," had met Harte and gained his confidence. On May 24 Grigulevich knocked on the gate when Harte was on guard duty. Seeing someone he knew, Harte began to open the gate, and the Siqueiros group stormed in. Since Harte could identify Grigulevich, the attackers took him away and murdered him.[75]

Leonid Eitingon, who ran the assassination team on the scene, told a different story. Eitingon, a cohort of Lavrenti Beria, was in the Soviet Gulag in 1954. Beria himself was killed when he tried to take power after Stalin's death. Eitingon was questioned by the KGB about various incidents in his career. Along the way he said that Sheldon Harte had been recruited by the NKVD in New York and had the code name "Amur." In due course he was sent to Mexico to penetrate the Trotsky household. During the attack

> it was found that Sheldon was a traitor. Although he did open the door of the gate, the room to which he led the participants in the raid contained neither the archive nor Trotsky himself. When the raid participants opened fire Sheldon told them that if he had known all this, he as an American would never have agreed to participate in the affair. This behavior was grounds for the decision to eliminate him. He was killed by the Mexicans.[76]

In other words, the attackers apparently expected to find either Trotsky or his archives in the part of the house they entered. When they discovered that the Trotskys were in another part of the house, they blamed Harte. His complaint that he did not expect this kind of violent attack sealed his fate. Eitingon's account appears to be the most accurate explanation of the death of Robert Sheldon Harte.

After machine-gunning the house, the attackers entered Trotsky's bedroom. In the darkness they mistook a pile of bedclothes for the husband and wife and fired into the empty bed while Trotsky and Natalia watched from a dark corner.

The Trotskys had been awakened by the sound of shooting. Natalia jumped out of bed and dragged her husband to a corner of the room. When she tried to shield Trotsky with her body, he forced her to lie flat on the floor. Bullets tore into the wall just over their heads. Their concern was for their fourteen-year-old grandson, Seva, who was asleep in a nearby room. They heard the child's door open, and by the light of an incendiary bomb thrown by one of the attackers they could see that one of them was in the boy's room.

Hearing the shots, Seva got under his bed. One of the assailants then fired into his bed, and a bullet grazed Seva's toe. When they left his room, he ran out trailing blood and shouting "Grandfather." His grandmother ran to his room and found it empty. Her first thought was that Seva had been kidnapped, but they soon found him hiding. The young boy thought that his grandparents had been killed.

Aided by sources in the Mexican non-Communist Left, the police began the search for Siqueiros and the other Mexican Communists involved in the assassination team. Among them were Luis and Leopoldo Arenal and Antonio Pujol, who participated in the assault, and David Serrano, who had obtained the police uniforms. Serrano was a member of the Politburo of the Mexican Communist Party. Luis Arenal, like Siqueiros, was an artist and member of the Communist Party. Some of his drawings had appeared in the Communist Party's *New Masses*.[77]

Immediately after the attack, Trotsky's American followers in the Socialist Workers Party reported the attempt on his life in a fund-raising appeal. The money, they said, would "help strengthen the guard and defense equipment."[78] His followers improved the defense of his home: The guard was increased and better armed, bulletproof doors and windows were installed, and bombproof ceilings and floors were added.[79] In the meantime, Trotsky was fighting back with the weapon he knew best, the pen.

Infuriated by the assassination attempt, Trotsky became all the more determined to reveal his knowledge of Stalinist operations. First, he wrote a letter to the attorney general of Mexico, the chief of the federal police, and the foreign minister:

> It is *first* of all necessary to affirm that the attempted assassination could only be instigated by the Kremlin; by Stalin through the agency of the GPU aboard. During the last few years, Stalin has shot hundreds of real or supposed friends of mine. He actually exterminated my entire family, except me, my wife, and one of my grandchildren. Through his agents abroad he assassinated one of the old leaders of the GPU, Ignace Reiss, who had publicly declared himself a partisan of mine. This fact has been established by the French police and the Swiss judiciary. The same GPU agents who killed Reiss trailed my son in Paris. On the night of November 7, 1936, GPU agents broke into the Scientific Institute of Paris and stole part of my archives. Two of my secretaries, Erwin Wolff and Rudolf Klement, were assassinated by the GPU; the first in Spain, the second in Paris. All the theatrical Moscow trials during 1936–37 had as their aim to get me into the hands of the GPU.

Trotsky laid out in detail how the Comintern financed and controlled the Communist parties of each country. He showed how the Soviet intelligence service used the Comintern apparatus and the leadership of the national Communist parties to recruit agents for both espionage and terrorism.[80] He then wrote a lengthy article on the subject quoting extensively from General Walter Krivitsky, a GPU defector, and Benjamin Gitlow, a former American Communist member of the Presidium and Executive Committee of the Communist International, to prove his points.[81] But Western governments paid little attention to Trotsky's revelations. He was, after all, a foreign revolutionary with an animosity toward Stalin, and despite the Nazi-Soviet Pact, some of the pro-Soviet euphoria continued and would intensify during the American-Soviet alliance. It was only after World War II that the West began to learn the lessons that Trotsky had tried to teach it years earlier.

After the failure of the attack on Trotsky's home, the NKVD activated its fall-back plan. Two years earlier, an NKVD agent who was a member of the Spanish Communist Party had been assigned to work his way into the Trotsky entourage. Pretending to be a Belgian named Jacques Mornard, the handsome young Spaniard was introduced to a Trotskyite girl who was not terribly popular with boys. After a whirlwind romance, she had complete trust in her lover, who used that trust to get to know Trotsky. And once again, despite the earlier attempt on his life, the guard around Trotsky was ineffective.

On August 20, 1940, in the late afternoon while sitting at his desk, Trotsky was struck in the head by a small pickaxe. The murderer was the dashing Spaniard, who was visiting on the pretext of showing the "old man" an article he had written.

Hearing "a terrible, heart-rending cry," Natalia rushed to the room, where Trotsky was standing in the doorway, his face covered with blood and his arms hanging limply at his side. His wife helped him to lie down on a mat and put a piece of ice on his wound. He said, "Seva [their grandson] must be kept out of all this."

When a doctor arrived, he said that the wound was not too serious. But Trotsky said to Joe Hansen, one of his assistants, pointing to his heart, "I feel it there... that it is the end. This time, they've succeeded." Trotsky was taken to the hospital, where he lost consciousness. He was operated on but died without regaining consciousness.[82]

But previously, though grievously wounded, Trotsky had prevented the assassin from escaping, and he was apprehended by thirty-year-old Joseph Hansen and twenty-nine-year-old Charles Cornell, two of Trotsky's assistants. They wanted to kill the assailant, but Trotsky, speaking slowly and with difficulty, said, "No, they mustn't kill him, but must make him talk." A document was found on the killer which stated that he was a Trotsky supporter and that Trotsky planned to send him to Russia to assassinate Stalin and other Soviet leaders. He later claimed that he was also to commit sabotage in the Soviet Union. All of this was palpably false.[83] The assassin insisted that his name was Jacques Mornard. Investigation in Mexico and the United States provided his true identity. He was Ramon Mercader, a member of the Spanish Communist Party.

The death of Trotsky did not, however, end the NKVD operations against the Trotskyites. A significant NKVD apparatus that had been built in the United States to spy upon them continued to function. Even during World War II, when spying on "Polecats" did nothing to aid the war effort, Stalin and Beria continued the campaign.

The forces that led to the death of Trotsky were set in motion in December 1934, when the American Trotskyites, after consulting with the "old man" himself, merged their organization, then called the Communist League of America, with a small Marxist group called the American Workers Party and became the Workers Party of the United States. The Trotskyites had entered into partnership with A. J. Muste, a pacifist, semisocialist minister whose organization contained prolabor people with a variety of views. Among them were Louis Budenz and Arnold Johnson, both of whom leaned ideologically toward the Communist Party. They refused to participate in the merger and publicly joined the Communist Party instead. Budenz was assigned as labor editor of the CP newspaper, the *Daily*

Worker. He would later tell the Un-American Activities Committee how he became involved in NKVD operations and the murder of Trotsky. The story follows.

In late 1936, shortly after joining the Communist Party, Budenz was called to a meeting with Jack Stachel, a CP Politburo member. Here Budenz met Jacob Golos, chairman of the Party's Control Commission and secretly an officer in the Soviet intelligence service. Golos in turn introduced him to a number of Soviet intelligence officers.

Some months later Budenz was introduced to a man called "Roberts." He soon learned that this was Dr. Gregory Rabinowitz, head of the Russian Red Cross in the United States. Rabinowitz was a physician and a surgeon, and the Red Cross was a good cover for his NKVD activities. According to Budenz, "This man was a very intelligent person, fatherly in his manner, and immediately proceeded to organize new activity on my part. He instructed me to introduce him to various Stalinists who were penetrating the Trotskyites or might be useful along that line because of their work or associations."

Among those Budenz introduced to "Roberts" was Ruby Weil, whom he knew from the Muste group. She had secretly joined the Communist Party and been sent to a special training school by Bernard Schuster, also known as Bernie Chester. Chester was responsible for Communist underground work in New York and New England. He would, of course, reappear during World War II working with Julius Rosenberg in atomic espionage. He was also assigned by the NKVD to check the background of Communist Party members whom they intended to use for espionage.[84]

Weil had some very valuable contacts. She was friendly with three Trotskyite sisters who were fellow members of the Workers Party, Ruth, Hilda, and Sylvia Ageloff. Ruth had served as Trotsky's secretary, but Ruby's particular friend was Sylvia, a Brooklyn social worker who could devote her vacation and other free time as a courier for the Trotskyites.

"Roberts" wanted to meet Ruby Weil and told Budenz to introduce him as "John Rich." Before meeting him, Budenz gave Weil a considerable sum of money, which came from "Roberts," to pay for clothes, telephone, and other expenses in her operations against the Trotskyites. Weil was reluctant to take the money, but when Budenz explained that she needed to be well dressed for the project, she agreed.

Budenz learned from Weil that she had arranged to accompany Sylvia Ageloff on a trip to Paris, where Sylvia would attend a Trotskyite congress. Ruby told Sylvia of her interest in Trotskyism and her desire to visit her sister in England.

In 1950 both Sylvia Ageloff and Ruby Weil testified before the House Committee on Un-American Activities. According to Sylvia, while in Paris, Ruby introduced her to a man she called Jacques Mornard, who claimed to be a Belgian. Weil testified that Mornard had been sent to her by a person she knew as "Gertrude" who was living in Paris.

Sylvia was not a very attractive girl, yet the handsome Mornard paid her great attention and became very important in her life. After being together for more than six months in Paris, Sylvia returned to New York in early 1939, and Mornard followed in September. He said he was in the United States illegally using a forged passport in the name Frank Jacson to avoid service in the Belgian army.

When Mornard went to Mexico, where he claimed that he had a job waiting, Sylvia went to meet him in January 1940, and they lived together for three months.[85] Mornard, the murderer, used Sylvia's name to gain access to Trotsky.

Hunting Down "Polecats"

Trotsky was killed in a country where the NKVD was well prepared to kill him. Mexico was an important base for its activity. Some of the Spanish Communists recruited for espionage during the Spanish Civil War had taken refuge there; but more important, it was a base for operations against the United States. Among the American Communists assigned to that base was Earl Browder's former common-law wife, Kitty Harris. She had accompanied Browder to China in 1928 and 1929 while Raisa, the mother of Browder's children, was still in Moscow. Kitty was born in London to Russian revolutionary émigré parents who moved to Canada when she was eight. After the Russian Revolution, she moved to the United States and joined the Communist Party, and in 1931 she was recruited by Soviet military intelligence to work as a courier.[86]

In the late 1930s Kitty Harris served as a courier for Donald Maclean, a Soviet spy in the British Foreign Office. The pair soon became lovers, and Maclean brought Harris secret Foreign Office documents, which they would photograph in her room.[87] In November 1941 she was sent on a ship from Vladivostok to San Francisco on her way to an assignment in Mexico.[88]

Harris's particular assignment was to work with Mexican labor leader and Soviet agent Vicente Lombardo Toledano, which she did for a number of years. But in April 1944 the NKVD began to worry that Harris might be homesick and try to contact her relatives and endanger the operation. Thus in May, Moscow sent a *Venona* message to Mexico City for Harris:

> Tell "Ada" [Kitty Harris] that we have got in touch with her relations and that they are all alive and well. One of her sisters works, as before, in Amtorg, earning 180 dollars a month and another works in the [Soviet] Purchasing Commission in Washington DC. A third sister formerly worked for the newspaper *PM* [a

leftist New York City daily] but recently transferred to work in TASS [the Soviet news agency].... The mother lives with a female relative and yet another sister and is feeling well. Instructions have been given to our *Rezidentura* in New York about regularly forwarding to "Ada," through you, letters from her relatives. "Ada" may write letters through you to her sister who works for Amtorg. Address letters received from "Ada" to "Sergej" [Vladimir Pravdin, whose cover was as a TASS representative in New York] for "Knopka" [Harris's sister, Nancy Bell] and send them by the first regular mail.[89]

Harris was obviously so important that even in wartime the Soviets were willing to supply her with news of her family.

One of Harris's jobs was to use Lombardo Toledano to obtain visas and identity documents for Soviet underground operatives in or passing through Mexico. In a May 1944 message the Mexico City *Rezidentura* advised Moscow that Harris had refused to carry out one such request on the grounds that Lombardo Toledano had told her not to contact a certain corrupt Mexican official that the Communists had previously used. Moscow was extremely angry and ordered the Mexico City *Rezidentura* to "tell her that we require our orders to be carried out without any discussion. Explain to her that she receives instructions and tasks only from you and carries them out at your request." It repeated the order to get the documents.[90]

Kitty's health was not good. In December 1943 NKVD Mexico City sent a *Venona* message to Moscow reporting that Kitty had become seriously ill and had been taken to the hospital, where she had undergone two operations, one for appendicitis and the other to remove a large tumor.[91]

Because of her heath problems, the NKVD ordered Kitty to return to the Soviet Union in July 1946. She obtained Soviet citizenship in June 1947 and was sent to live in Riga, Latvia.[92] But she was unhappy and kept demanding that she be returned to intelligence work. Her demands became so annoying that she was arrested and spent two years in prison, most of the time in the prison hospital. She was released after Stalin's death in 1953 and lived in the Soviet Union until her death in 1966.[93]

Much of Harris's work in Mexico revolved around the attempt to free Trotsky's murderer from a Mexican prison, as well as operations against the Trotskyite movement. So it was ironic that she, like so many Trotskyites and others, eventually found herself in a Soviet prison.

The architect of the Trotsky murder was Leonid Eitingon, a senior GPU official experienced in assassinations. His supervisor was Pavel Sudoplatov, Stalin's maestro of assassinations. In his autobiography Sudoplatov revealed that after a March 1939 meeting with Stalin, he was promoted to deputy director of the NKVD Foreign Department and put in charge of the operation against Trotsky.[94]

It took a number of years to determine the real name of Trotsky's murderer. Finally, Julian Gorkin, a leader of the Spanish Marxist organization POUM, learned that he was Ramon Mercader, the son of an old member of the Spanish Communist Party and agent of the GPU, Caridad Mercader.[95]

When Mercader was arrested for Trotsky's murder, his passport, bearing the name Frank Jacson, was discovered. It had been altered by changing the name and the picture; it had originally belonged to Tony Babich, a member of the Canadian battalion in the International Brigades during the Spanish Civil War. The officers of many American and Canadian brigade members took their passports and gave them to the Soviets for use by their intelligence agents. The loss of hundreds of passports forced the United States to reissue them in a different color.[96]

Mercader was convicted of the murder and remained in prison until his term expired. On May 6, 1960, a representative of the Czech embassy met him on his release, and he was put on a plane to Havana. There he was immediately placed on a ship to the Soviet Union, where his name was changed to Ramon Lopez.[97] He received the highest Soviet medal for heroism, the Gold Star, Hero of the Soviet Union, as well as the Order of Lenin from Alexander Shelepin, then head of the KGB. In 1974 he returned to Cuba as an advisor to Fidel Castro. After his death in October 1978 of lung disease, his body was returned to Moscow. Mercader's mother died in Paris in 1975.[98]

But while Mercader was still in a Mexican prison, his NKVD colleagues plotted his escape. The *Venona* intercepts show that the orders came from Lavrenti Beria, Stalin's secret police chief. The senior intelligence officer in charge of the operation was Leonid Eitingon, *Venona* code name "Tom." His assistant was Pavel Klarin, *Venona* code name "Luka," who served as deputy *Rezident* in Mexico City from November 1943 to May 1944.[99] He had been deputy *Rezident* in New York prior to that and later returned to that post. His real name was Pavel Pastelnyak.[100]

Soon after his arrival in Mexico City, Klarin established a group to carry out the escape. On December 23, 1943, he told Moscow that the escape could take place in four days but asked for $20,000 for "urgent requirements." The message was sent by the Mexico City *Rezident*, Lev Tarasov—"Yurij"—and addressed to "Petrov," Lavrenti Beria.[101]

On December 29 Moscow received a report from Mexico City with excuses for inaction. Beria was told that, having arrived in Mexico City, Klarin attempted to contact the agents, American Communist Jacob Epstein, code name "Harry," and Mexican Communist Juan Gaytan, code name "Juan." Epstein, however, said he had been out of contact and therefore could not make the necessary preparations.

The escape was delayed, but new plans were soon set up—neutralize the guards, whereupon Mercader would be driven to a safe location.[102] The conspirators finally decided that April 8, 1944, would be a good day for the escape, for "conditions will be eased, the vigilance of the warders will be relaxed...." This was the day before Easter Sunday, when the prison officials would be distracted by personal matters. The Soviet intelligence officers, moreover, had consulted with an unidentified agent in the prison administration about the possibility of using a senior warder in "effecting the escape...." Since their unidentified agent for some reason could not help them in the near future, the April 8 date seemed better than ever.[103]

A few days before the planned escape, Gaytan reported that he had learned from a Mexican newspaper journalist that Mercader had obtained special privileges at the prison, which might complicate the plan. Julian Gorkin, who later investigated the case, reported that Mercader "occupied a large cell, very calm, well-ventilated and sunny. He was smartly dressed, ate very well, drank coffee and liqueurs, smoked best-quality cigarettes. He had a good library and a wireless set at his disposal and money in abundance, or rather super-abundance." Gorkin asked, "Where did this money come from?"[104]

In June the plan for the escape was on again. A prison doctor, Esther Chapa, *Venona* code name "Lata," was to be used in the new attempt. Moscow was advised that "she is an old Communist Party member, a prominent doctor and bacteriologist, and keeps in touch on scientific matters with our [Soviet] scientists through Voks [All-Union Society for Cultural Relations with Foreign Countries—a cover operation for the NKVD]. She is about 40 years old and is the first wife of 'Volk' [an NKVD agent named Rosendo Gomez, editor of the magazine *Tiempo*], who speaks very highly of her."[105]

This plan didn't work either, but Gorkin learned that "the Communist Dr. Esther Chapa, Chief of the Prison Delegation for the Prevention of Crime up to May, 1947, nominated him [Mercader] as her secretary—that is to say, as her delegate in the prison. As such he was able to move about freely and at the same time had a great deal of influence over the warders and the prisoners." With the complicity of the prison secretary, another Stalinist agent, the prison had become a dangerous Communist center. Dr. Chapa, Mornard (Mercader), and the prison secretary, in fact, exercised a veritable dictatorship. The scandal went so far that many of the prisoners complained, and, after a brisk intervention by the Mexican authorities, the situation was remedied. Dr. Chapa was dismissed, and Mornard lost the privileges he had enjoyed—and abused.[106]

Because of the continued failures of the much planned escape, various NKVD officers tried to put the blame on anyone else: Lev Tarasov, the Mexico City *Rezident*, tried to blame Zarubin, and Klarin complained about Tarasov's failures. Specifically, Klarin said that Tarasov's "light-hearted approach to the Mercader case does not inspire any confidence in his ability to cope with the task set him. Working jointly with him has shown that the case is in inexperienced and far from firm hands." Tarasov frequently left the embassy early and took a few days off to drive to his country cottage sixty miles away.

In addition to Tarasov's interference with the rescue attempt, Klarin complained that Tarasov "is living in grand style" with two servants and a house with large grounds. Tarasov, it appears, was also rude and tactless and alienated his colleagues.[107]

Klarin had his own troubles. He had been in Mexico City only a few months when Moscow complained that he had sent telegrams to his wife "in clear"—that is, not coded.[108] This was a serious matter, as this could reveal secrets of the NKVD operations.

By August 1944 Jacob Epstein, an American NKVD agent working in Mexico, had been sent home to the United States and was suspected by the NKVD of having indiscreetly revealed information
about the plan to free Mercader.[109] It is possible that Klarin, by then
back in Moscow, was still spreading the blame for the escape failure.

Jacob Epstein was an American Communist Party member who
served in the International Brigades in the Spanish Civil War. He
was there for only about six months in 1938, but his wife, Ruth
Wilson Epstein, served as a nurse with the brigades from May 1937
until the end of 1938.[110] Jacob was born in 1903, and Ruth was
three years his junior. They were both members of the Communist
Party in New York.[111]

In an example of incredibly poor tradecraft, the NKVD in
Moscow sent a *Venona* message to the New York *Rezidentura* with a
password and details about making contact with "Nona." In its
answer, New York said, "'Nona' is Jacob Epstein's wife; that is to say,
Ruth Wilson."[112] By revealing the real names of persons, together
with their code names, the NKVD provided a valuable tool to the
NSA in identifying Soviet agents.

Jacob was a 1924 graduate of Cornell University. He was very
vague when asked questions by the House Committee on Un-
American Activities during a hearing on the Trotsky assassination.
He couldn't even remember signing his own passport applications.
But he could remember enough to take the Fifth Amendment on
Communist Party membership, on whether he had met with Pavel
Klarin, and on any meetings with Anna Colloms.[113]

In February 1943 NKVD New York advised Buenos Aires to
cancel the use of another mail drop address and use only the
address of Anna Colloms.[114] Colloms, a teacher at Washington
Irving High School in New York City, left New York for Mexico
City on August 12, 1943, during her summer vacation. She carried

with her a box of apparently blank stationery. Five of the sheets were completely covered by writing in secret ink. U.S. Customs took the box of stationery from her and gave it to the FBI, who developed the secret writings. Customs returned the box when she arrived back in the United States.

Colloms tried to contact Epstein in Mexico City but failed. Upon her return to New York on September 16, 1943, she gave the box to her sister-in-law, Ethel Vogel, also a member of the ring. Vogel passed it on to Ruth Wilson, the wife of Jacob Epstein.[115]

Two weeks after her return to the United States and her report to her superiors on the incident with the box of stationery, NKVD New York cabled Buenos Aires: "Do not write any more to the address of An[n]a Colloms. Warn 'Aleksandr' about this. I shall send a new address in the very near future."[116] "Aleksandr," an unidentified NKVD agent also known as "Alex," operated in Chile. In July of 1942, NKVD Buenos Aires provided an address for "Alex" in Santiago, Chile, and suggested secret writing using the Pocket Book Edition of *Defense Will Not Win the War* as a code book.[117] Knowing which book was used helped the American cryptologists to break into yet more Soviet messages.

When Anna Colloms testified before the House Committee on Un-American Activities on October 19, 1950, she admitted knowing Jacob and Ruth Wilson Epstein but used the Fifth Amendment to decline answering questions about the Communist Party as well as about the box of stationery containing the ciphered messages.[118]

In December 1942 the Buenos Aires *Rezidentura* expressed concern that some of its letters had been intercepted by the American wartime censors' office. The NKVD New York was asked to warn Lydia Altschuler, who was handling one of the mail drops.[119] Altschuler was the education director of the Consumers Union, Inc., and invoked the Fifth Amendment before the House Committee on

Hunting Down "Polecats"

Un-American Activities when asked about her acting as a mail drop and her membership in the Communist Party. She testified that her parents lived in the Soviet Union and that her father had worked for the Soviet trading organization Amtorg prior to moving to the Soviet Union in the early 1930s.[120]

In December 1942, to assist in handling the secret communications, the Comintern prepared Spanish Communist Party member Victor de Frutos for transfer back to Argentina, where he had been born. He had lived in Spain since 1927 and joined the Young Communist League in 1931, at age twenty-five, and the Communist Party in 1933. A Spanish Civil War veteran, de Frutos was trained in cryptography and microphotography. At the training school, he was evaluated as "politically developed, party-devoted."[121]

By October 1944 de Frutos was in trouble with headquarters. His friend, Spanish Communist exile and NKVD agent Francisco Anton, had asked him to get information about his family in Moscow. De Frutos added a postscript to a letter he sent to Lydia Altschuler by ordinary mail in which he revealed Anton's address. Anton's father in Moscow wrote him a letter at that address and, through Altschuler, advised him that his wife had died. On learning of this, NKVD headquarters ordered the Mexico City *Rezidentura* to "point out to 'Anton' that his action is a wholly impermissible breach of elementary conspiracy [konspiratsiya].... Tell 'Anton' that his father is still working in the same place and that his children are well. He and the children are fully provided for by us."[122] About six months later, Moscow advised Montevideo that de Frutos had been arrested in Argentina.[123]

The plot to free Mercader, Trotsky's murderer, continued, but Moscow urged the Mexico City *Rezidentura* to proceed with caution. The *Rezident* was told that he could meet with agents himself "only in exceptional cases." In early 1945 a new complication emerged.

Mercader's mother, Caridad, *Venona* code name "Klava," arrived in Mexico City. Moscow told Mexico City in a *Venona* message that it must consider Caridad's safety "and this complicates our work," particularly the work of freeing her son.[124]

Meanwhile, Caridad's other son, Jorge, who was in the Red Army, had been captured in combat with the Germans. In May 1945 Moscow asked the Mexico City *Rezidentura* to transmit a message to Caridad advising her that Jorge was alive and well and had been liberated from a German POW camp.[125] Since she was still in Mexico in August, the *Rezidentura* asked for and received Moscow's permission to establish her as a foreigner living in Mexico.[126] But the *Rezidentura* had to keep her away from its operations and use an intelligence officer under cover as a diplomat to maintain contact with her.[127]

And so it ended. Trotsky's murderer was never rescued. In 1954 he admitted to reporters that he was an ardent Communist and not the dissident Trotskyite that he had claimed.[128] Caridad, Sudoplatov, and Eitingon also received medals for their roles in the Trotsky assassination.

After her son's release from prison, Caridad lived in Moscow with him during the 1960s. Eitingon, despite his long service to the Soviet regime, was arrested twice, once for supposed involvement in the Jewish "doctor's plot" and the second time for his involvement with Lavrenti Beria. Eitingon commented later, "There is one small guaranteed way not to end up in jail under our system. Don't be a Jew or a General in the State Security Service."[129] Eitingon, a senior intelligence official, had connections with Beria, who headed the intelligence service during the Stalin era. He also had no control over the fact that he had been born to Jewish parents. But for the Soviet regime, both of these facts were sufficient excuses to throw him in the Gulag.

CHAPTER 11

The Jack Soble/Robert Soblen Ring

ON SEPTEMBER 13, 1962, a lengthy article appeared in the Soviet government newspaper *Izvestiya* under the caption "Robert Soblen's Tragic Death—American Secret Police Hounds Innocent Man to Death." According to the Communist newspaper, the dead man was a victim of FBI harassment and the U.S. marshals office, persecuted in American, British, and Israeli courts, and guilty only of "holding leftist views."[1]

Soblen had died two days earlier in a hospital in Great Britain. He was about to be deported to the United States, where, several months earlier, he had been tried and convicted of espionage. Jumping bail two days before he was due to begin serving his life sentence, Soblen had gone to Israel with a Canadian passport issued to one of his brothers. Concluding that he had entered their country illegally and unimpressed by his appeal to the "law of return" granting citizenship to Jews, the Israelis expelled him, and while on the flight to London, from where he would have been sent to the United States, Soblen attempted suicide.[2] While he lay in a hospital with slashed wrists and a knife wound in the abdomen, the British government rejected his appeal for asylum. "[Dr. Soblen] is not in danger of persecution in his own country for his political opinions or on racial grounds," the British home secretary stated in the House of Commons on August 2. "[He] is a convicted spy...."[3]

The end of Robert Soblen's career ranks as little more than an obscure footnote in the history of the Cold War. Yet the Soviets' vehement protest of his innocence shows the importance they attached to his activities. What Soblen really did would not be fully understood until the insights contained in the *Venona* files were aired.

Robert Soblen and his brother, Jack Soble, ran an extensive Soviet spy network in the United States. They started their careers as Soviet intelligence agents operating against the Trotskyites in the early 1930s. During that time their target was pre-Hitler Germany, where the Trotskyites were a small but significant group. Trotsky's most valuable supporter was Kurt Landau. Born in Vienna in 1903, Landau had been active in Austrian and German revolutionary politics in the 1920s. But then he left the German Communist Party and found his way into the Trotskyite movement, where he was a valued organizer, highly regarded and trusted by Trotsky himself, who, after being expelled from Russia, went first to Turkey, then to Norway, and finally to Mexico, where he was assassinated.

Soon, two particularly active and energetic members appeared in the Trotskyite movement in Germany. They were Ruvelis Sobolevicius and Abromas Sobolevicius, known in the movement as "Roman Well" and "Abraham Senine." We would later know them as Robert Soblen and Jack Soble. There is no evidence that their comrades realized these two Lithuanian-Jewish revolutionists were brothers, and they certainly did not know that the brothers were Soviet agents. In the late 1920s they entered the "Left Opposition," as the dissident faction that supported Trotsky within the international Communist movement was known. They devoted most of their time from 1929 to 1931 to disrupting the tiny organization. They managed to isolate Landau and by mid-1931 succeeded in alienating him from Trotsky and driving him out of the movement. The operations against him can be discerned by reading the internal bulletin of the Trotskyites, intended for their members only.[4] In 1937 Landau was murdered by the Soviet secret police in Spain.

The Sobolevicius brothers came to America in 1941 as Robert Soblen and Jack Soble. In addition to their other spying chores for the NKVD, the brothers took over an active operation against the Trotskyites that had taken years to build. Investigation by the governments of the United States and Mexico, as well as by some of the Trotskyite victims, revealed much of the picture. But, as noted, only when *Venona* was released did the whole picture emerge.

Robert Soblen was forty-one years old when he arrived in America with a degree in medicine and surgery from the University of Leipzig in Germany. From 1942 to 1944 he worked in hospitals in Boston and New York and from 1944 to 1946 for the United Nations Relief and Rehabilitation Administration. Later he practiced medicine in New York City.[5] But his professional work was only a cover for his espionage activity.

His brother Jack had a less impressive cover career running small businesses funded by the NKVD. In 1944 and 1945 he and his brother-in-law, Arnold Wolston, were ordered by the NKVD to operate the S & V Cafeteria on 38th Street and 5th Avenue in New York City—"For this we gave him the authorized advance of 2,000 [dollars]," the NKVD message read. When the cafeteria was established, the New York NKVD *Rezident* reported to Moscow that "cover has been fixed up for 'Abram' [Jack Soble]."

Soble persuaded a friend, Sam Appel, to help him run the business in order to allow him more time for his espionage work. Appel, who knew nothing about the espionage, was a bad choice. With his experience and relatives in the restaurant business, Appel took increasing control of the business, and Sobel, worried that Appel was trying to steal the business from him, decided to get rid of him.[6]

The Soble/Soblen brothers' superior was Vassiliy Zarubin, the NKVD *Rezident* in the United States. Zarubin signed messages to Moscow as "Maxim."

Zarubin assigned an old agent he had recruited in 1936 to be the courier for the spy ring, Hollywood film producer Boris Morros. The colorful Morros had a significant Hollywood career. Starting out as a music director, Morros became an independent producer in 1939, responsible for such pictures as *Flying Deuces* with Laurel and Hardy and *Second Chorus* with Fred Astaire, Paulette Goodard, and Artie Shaw's band. In 1936, when Morros was trying to send packages to his parents in Moscow, Zarubin appeared and introduced himself as Edward Herbert, someone who could help. Zarubin himself was in the United States from 1934 until 1937 working as an "illegal" intelligence officer with a false passport under the name Edward Joseph Herbert.[7] After helping Boris Morros send a few packages to his parents in Russia, Zarubin had a request. He told Morros that he was going to Germany to help fight against Hitler. (He spoke German well, but with an obvious accent, just as his excellent English was heavily accented.) Zarubin needed a good cover to explain why he, a foreigner, was in Nazi Germany and suggested that Morros provide him with a letter identifying him as a talent scout for Morros's film business.

Morros gave him a letter of introduction on the stationery of Paramount Studios, Hollywood, California, signed "Boris Morros, General Music Director." Part of the agreement was that Zarubin leave a sum of money with Morros. It would be sent back to him in Germany in monthly installments of $50. Morros agreed and would occasionally reply to letters sent to him from Germany by the fictitious "Edward Herbert."

During the summer of 1937 Morros was visited by another Russian, who identified himself as an Samuel Shumovsky, an assistant

The Jack Soble/Robert Soblen Ring

to Edward Herbert. The new contact berated Morros for not writing often enough to Herbert, a failure that could cost Herbert his life: "He writes you two or three letters for every one you send him. You must keep the agreement you made with him." Morros claimed that he stopped writing letters to his "talent scout" after this encounter. Again in early 1939 another Russian appeared to complain about his failure to write Herbert, but Morros continued to ignore the request.

Then in 1942 Zarubin reappeared in New York. He told Morros to forget the name Edward Herbert; he was now Vassiliy Zubilin, an official of the Soviet consulate, and he could arrange to have the producer's father brought to the United States. Zarubin kept his promise: The aged father of Boris Morros was brought by ship from Vladivostok, across the Pacific, to Seattle, Washington.

The quid pro quo was that Morros would provide cover for Soviet agents through his film business. They could be talent scouts, salesmen, or film crew. The contact for Morros to use in communicating with Zarubin was a woman in New York named Leah Melament. When Morros came to the city, he would contact her to arrange meetings with Zarubin.[8] He was also to serve as a courier.

In the spring of 1943, the FBI, watching Zarubin, saw him meet with Boris Morros. The bureau opened an investigation of the film producer and soon discovered that he was working as an agent for Soviet intelligence. The FBI confronted him in July 1947, and, although he still had brothers in Russia, Morros agreed to operate as a double agent for the FBI in the Soviet spy ring.[9] He continued in that role for ten years, finally providing the evidence that destroyed part of the Soviet espionage apparatus. While he was working for the FBI, he was able to identify many of the agents run by Zarubin, particularly those in the Soble/Soblen spy ring.

One of the Soviet agents planted among the American Trotskyites and run by the Soble/Soblen brothers, who were by then working as a team, was Sylvia Franklin, known to the Trotskyites as Sylvia Caldwell. She was one of the Communists provided to the NKVD by Louis Budenz, Communist Party Central Committee member and editor of the *Daily Worker*. After his 1945 break with the Communist Party, Budenz explained to the FBI the indispensable role the CPUSA played in facilitating Soviet spying in the United States. Specifically, in a statement to the House Committee on Un-American Activities, Budenz revealed that the NKVD "illegal" intelligence officer, Dr. Gregory Rabinowitz, had ordered him to recruit more infiltrators into the Trotskyite movement.

Budenz contacted Jack Kling, the leader of the Young Communist League in Chicago, "to get hold of some Stalinist agent infiltrating the Trotskyites who could be moved to New York and put into the Trotskyite national office." Kling introduced him to Sylvia Franklin, who had already infiltrated the Trotskyites in Chicago. Her husband, Irving Franklin, one of the many Spanish Civil War veterans working for Soviet intelligence, was active for the NKVD in Canada. Franklin's true name was Zalmond David Franklin; his *Venona* code name was "Chen."

Budenz set up a meeting between Sylvia Franklin and Rabinowitz in Chicago, after which Rabinowitz paid her expenses and brought her to New York. He also brought her husband down from Canada, and they were both set up in a Bronx apartment, although Sylvia told the Trotskyites she was unmarried and living in a separate apartment.

Budenz went on: "By first volunteering to do secretarial work in the national Trotskyite offices in New York, Sylvia Franklin under the direction of Roberts-Rabinowitz, gradually made herself indispensable to James Cannon, then head of the American Trotskyites. She became his secretary and served in that capacity for some time. Roberts-Rabinowitz advised me that she had proved to be invaluable in bringing copies of all of Trotsky's mail and other Trotskyite communications to him for his information." But Budenz had no further personal contact with Sylvia after turning her over to "Roberts."

Dr. Rabinowitz left the United States in 1939, and Budenz did not know his replacement. Shortly before he left, he sent a message to Budenz through Jacob Golos with instructions to meet him in the Bronx apartment of Irving Franklin, where he said good-bye.[10]

Sylvia Franklin—*Venona* code name "Satyr"—regularly turned over the letters she found in the Socialist Workers Party office to the NKVD. One 1943 letter was of particular importance, as it dealt with activities in Mexico in connection with Trotsky's murderer, Mercader. A summary of the letter was sent to Moscow in a *Venona* message by Pavel Klarin, *Venona* code name "Luka."[11]

In 1954 the FBI located Franklin, who had remarried and was now Sylvia Doxsee. When she refused to answer questions, she was brought before a grand jury. Her testimony on October 7, 1954, was vague and unresponsive. She gave her date of birth as October 5, 1914, and admitted marrying Franklin in 1935 and divorcing him in 1943, but as soon as the questions zeroed in on her penetration of the Socialist Workers Party or details about her former husband, she invoked the Fifth Amendment.

Sylvia was called back before the grand jury on June 18, 1958. Soble was by then in custody and talking, so the government was better armed with information. Sylvia now testified more truthfully. Shortly after her marriage to Irving Franklin, she joined the Young Communist League and was sent by it to penetrate the Young People's Socialist League (YPSL), of which the Trotskyites were then a faction. When the Trotskyites were pushed out of the Socialist Party and the YPSL in 1937, she joined them in the new Socialist Workers Party.

Sylvia described how she had volunteered to work in the Socialist Workers Party office, finally becoming secretary to the leader, James Cannon. She revealed that she would bring material from the Trotskyite office to her husband's apartment, where she would turn it over to a man she called "Jac," the same man she had originally met in Chicago, introduced by Louis Budenz. He was Dr. Rabinowitz.

After a while Sylvia began going to the apartment of another Soviet agent, Lucy Booker, where she would type copies of some of the documents obtained in the Socialist Workers Party office. It was in Booker's apartment that she met a man she knew as "Sam," who was Jack Soble. "Sam" later introduced her to another man, whose picture she identified for the FBI. He was Robert Soblen.[12]

When Irving Franklin returned to New York, he continued to work for the NKVD all during World War II. He was involved as a courier for the New York *Rezidentura* to a group of Czech exile officials who had been recruited by the Soviets. These included Vasili Sukhomlin of the Czech Information Service and Jan Fierlinger, the information officer at the Czech consulate in New York. Franklin garnered information from these sources on the State Department and even on conversations between Roosevelt and Churchill concerning the Baltic states and Eastern Europe. In one report, he revealed that the U.S. State Department was concerned with the Soviet creation of the National Committee for a Free Germany, believing that it could be used by the Soviets to help control Germany after the war.[13]

But Irving Franklin talked too much, and in 1944 it got him into trouble with his Soviet bosses. After divorcing Sylvia, he married Rose Richter and confided to his new brother-in-law, Nathan Einhorn, that he worked in Soviet espionage. Einhorn, a fellow Communist Party member, immediately reported this lapse to Bernard Chester, the New York State Communist Party liaison with the NKVD, and the

NKVD decided to remove Franklin from intelligence work and told him "to put an end to his criminal chatter about liaison with us...." Chester was ordered to continue watching Franklin.[14]

Einhorn was an active Communist. He recruited Charles Grutzner into the Party in 1937 when both were reporters for the *Brooklyn Eagle*.[15] Grutzner later was a reporter for the *New York Times*. From 1939 until 1946, Einhorn was the executive secretary of the New York Newspaper Guild, the union to which many reporters belonged. In 1949 he took employment with the Polish Information Service, an official agency of the Communist Polish embassy in Washington, D.C. When questioned before a Senate committee in 1953, he said he had not been a member of the Communist Party since 1949, when he took the job with the Polish government, but he used the Fifth Amendment when asked about any earlier time.[16]

The Trotskyites were the first defendants under the Smith Act in 1941, accused of advocating the violent overthrow of the United States government. The Communist Party leadership was the second in 1948. Ironically, it was the Communist Party that helped the Justice Department prosecute the Trotskyites by supplying the department with some incriminating internal documents. Years later, Philip Jaffe, a close friend of Earl Browder, received from him a collection of material against the Trotskyites that the Communist Party had turned over to the Justice Department.[17] Some of this information was collected by the NKVD infiltrators, including Sylvia, in the Trotskyite movement.

It was not farfetched for the NKVD to make agents devote the better part of their time to activities that would seem, in hindsight, to be arcane Marxist family quarrels. The *Venona* documents have helped to clarify this aspect of Stalinism—namely, projection to foreign countries of the Soviets' politics and of course their political style, which included slander, thuggery, and murder.

Examples of Stalinist methods used abroad were particularly striking in the Spanish Civil War, during which the NKVD hunted down and murdered political opponents. But the activities of the Soble/Soblen brothers were, in a smaller way of course, equally significant and would help American investigators understand with whom and with what they were dealing. One of the most instructive cases was that of Mark Zborowski.

The brothers Soble/Soblen handled a number of agents, including those operating against the Trotskyite and Jewish organizations. One such was Mark Zborowski, the man who had assisted in the murder of Trotsky's son, Leon Sedov, in Paris in 1938. In his covert activity as an NKVD agent, Zborowski had become a close associate of Sedov, another of whose close associates was a Russian woman named Lola Estrine. She would later marry the Menshevik (Russian socialist), anti-Communist writer David Dallin and live with him in the United States.

After the fall of France, Zborowski hid in a small town in the south where he received a letter from Mrs. Dallin offering to help him immigrate to the United States. He arrived in this country on December 15, 1941, and the Dallins found him an apartment in Brooklyn and helped him get a job. In 1943 he suddenly told the Dallins that he had found an apartment in their building in Manhattan, and the two families became very close.

After the murder of Trotsky, Mrs. Dallin dropped out of Trotskyite activity. Her husband, David Dallin, had never been a Trotskyite, but both still had friends in the movement. Zborowski, on NKVD instructions, became active in the Trotskyite organization in New York, and in July 1943 he reported on the activities of Jean van Heijenoort, the secretary of Trotsky's Fourth International organization. Others in his circle were Terry Mangan; Sarah Weber, a Fourth International activist and Trotsky's secretary in Mexico; and

The Jack Soble/Robert Soblen Ring

Albert Goldman, who had served as Trotsky's attorney and was active in the Socialist Workers Party.[18] All were Zborowski's targets.

Mark Zborowski was the kind of individual—part intellectual, part thug, part true believer—that the Communist movement knew how to use. It was not by accident that he was involved in one of the most famous post–World War II scandals, the one that went down in the annals of the Cold War as the Kravchenko affair. Kravchenko, a Soviet defector, provided an insider's knowledge of the Stalinist state and "blew the whistle" on the Stalinist Terror and the Gulag. A spectacular trial ensued in Paris, which became one of the first occasions after World War II when a public line was drawn between Communists and anti-Communists.

The Plot Against Kravchenko

In the spring of 1944 Victor Kravchenko, an official of the Soviet Purchasing Commission in Washington, decided to defect. He had confided in David Dallin, who encouraged him. One day, on his way to visit Dallin, Kravchenko asked for directions from a stranger on the street. By fantastic coincidence, the stranger was Zborowski. A little earlier Zborowski had heard from Dallin that one of the old Bolsheviks working in the United States was planning to defect. Zborowski, recognizing the stranger's accent, reported to Jack Soble that he had seen the "old Bolshevik" who hoped to defect. Soble reported the matter to Zarubin, who said it was impossible—there were then only three old Bolsheviks in the United States. His concept of an old Bolshevik was someone who had belonged to the Party in Russia before the revolution. Kravchenko had not joined the Party until 1921. This confusion impeded the NKVD from aborting his defection.

Kravchenko defected in April 1944. It was Zarubin's fault that the defection had not been impeded, but he was not one to take blame. Jack Soble later described to FBI special agent Dick McCarthy how Zarubin screamed at him in Russian that it was Jack's fault. This incident took place on crowded upper Broadway, and years later Soble was still upset about it. "We were supposed to be sophisticated intelligence officers," he said. "He yelled at me in the street. It was a scandal! A scandal!"[19]

As the *Venona* materials later revealed, the NKVD then swung into action. Lavrenti Beria took personal control of the case. The New York *Rezidentura* reported in a *Venona* message that Zborowski was instructed to get close to Kravchenko but to be careful not to arouse the suspicion of the Dallins by pressing too hard. Zborowski reported back to the NKVD that he expected to have a long talk about the Kravchenko affair with David Dallin in a few days.[20] Other NKVD sources, meanwhile, were reporting that Kravchenko had contact with well-known anti-Communist journalists, notably Joseph Shaplen, labor reporter for the *New York Times*, and Eugene Lyons, a *Reader's Digest* editor.[21]

An NKVD agent named Christina Krotkova, *Venona* code name "Ola," was assigned to learn more about Kravchenko. She was employed by the U.S. government in the Office of War Information. In a *Venona* message to Moscow, the New York *Rezidentura* reported that Krotkova had learned that Shaplen was deeply involved in the defection of Kravchenko. Disgust with the Soviet system combined with the desire for a better life had led Kravchenko to ask Shaplen for his help, and the journalist put him in touch with the American government.

The NKVD *Rezidentura* then instructed Krotkova to develop close relations with both the Dallins and Shaplen.[22] Krotkova, who already knew Mrs. Dallin, made it a point to meet Shaplen. Within a few days, Krotkova reported that Kravchenko was living out of town but sometimes came to New York. She said that Shaplen and

The Jack Soble/Robert Soblen Ring

Vladimir Zenzinov, an editor of a Russian-language newspaper who was close to the former head of the Russian Provisional Government, Alexander Kerensky, often went to see Kravchenko. Shaplen had promised Krotkova that he would introduce her to the defector.[23] She also spent time talking to Zenzinov, who told her that Kravchenko was in a depressed state and in fear for his life but had an article scheduled to appear in late May in the magazine *Cosmopolitan*.[24] Kravchenko provided some of the most chilling illustrations of Soviet operations against private (nongovernmental) individuals in the United States.

Zarubin received information from Vasili Sukhomlin, *Venona* code name "Mars," a Soviet agent working in the Czech Information Service, that Kravchenko was living in Kerensky's cottage in Connecticut.[25] Sukhomlin may have been involved in Soviet espionage for the money rather than for ideological motives. According to the New York *Rezidentura* he was receiving about $20 a week ($250 for three months) from the Soviets.[26]

In the meantime, Zborowski was also busy working for the NKVD. A *Venona* message from New York to Moscow reported on information that he had learned from Mrs. Dallin. Kravchenko was dictating his book to her while consulting with David Dallin and Isaac Don Levine.[27] Well-informed and prolific, Levine was one of the leading American writers on Soviet affairs, including espionage. On June 24 Mrs. Dallin introduced Zborowski to Kravchenko. The two men talked from 9 PM until noon in the Dallin apartment and then moved to Zborowski's apartment, where they continued the conversation until four in the morning.

Zborowski learned that Kravchenko had been put in touch with Lola Dallin by a woman who worked with him for the Soviet government in Washington. Moscow was anxious to learn who she was, and the New York *Rezidentura* reported that the woman had been acquainted in Berlin with Mrs. Dallin.[28] The NSA later concluded that the woman in question was Sara Judey, formerly Veksler, who was with Kravchenko on March 30, 1944, when he contacted the Dallins. If the Soviets had made the connection, she would have been in serious trouble. Apparently, they did not.

Zborowski also reported that Kravchenko told him about an NKVD officer in Russia named Karlov who had revealed to Kravchenko the names of some agents, including Kravchenko's mistress. We know nothing more about Karlov, but his revealing the names of agents could not have helped his career. Zborowski also learned about Kravchenko's disagreements with Levine and his desire to work with another writer, Max Eastman, whom the NKVD also considered an important enemy of the Soviet Union.[29]

Kravchenko testified before the House Committee on Un-American Activities in 1947 and produced two books—*I Chose Freedom*, about his experiences in Russia, and *I Chose Justice*, about his lawsuit against a Communist newspaper in Paris that libeled him.[30] In his second book he described how the KGB had tracked him down and threatened his life.[31] He did not know that he had Zborowski to thank for this.

Kravchenko died in 1966. His death was ruled a suicide, although after firing a bullet into his temple, he supposedly put the pistol back in his pocket.[32] His friends believed that the long arm of the KGB had finally pulled the trigger, but until the KGB files are opened, no one will ever know.

Further Adventures of Mark Zborowski, Cultural Anthropologist

While working the Kravchenko case, Zborowski also tried to become a member of the International Secretariat of the Trotskyite Fourth International, recently vacated by Jean van Heijenoort. He

The Jack Soble/Robert Soblen Ring

didn't get it. When the New York *Rezidentura* reported the failure to Moscow, it softened the disappointment by saying that Zborowski was working for Moscow against Kravchenko "and is carrying out the task very diligently."[33]

In 1945, when van Heijenoort was planning to go to France to head the French Trotskyite organization, Zborowski reported it to Moscow. Moscow reponded:

> 1) How are things going as regards to Van's departure?
>
> 2) By what route does Van intend to travel to France?
>
> 3) From whom is he counting on receiving assistance during his trip?
>
> 4) What is the extent of "Kant's" [Zborowski's] knowledge about the plan for Van's trip? If Van's trip remains realizable and can be decided upon definitely, get "Kant" to take up this question in real earnest so that he knows all the details of the preparation for the trip.[34]

If Moscow wanted the information in order to do physical harm to van Heijenoort, it did not succeed. Van Heijenoort left the Trotskyite movement in 1946. (He had joined the movement in the late 1920s and was a secretary for Trotsky from 1932 to 1939.) After leaving the movement, van Heijenoort went back to teaching philosophy and mathematics, and in 1978 he published his book, *With Trotsky in Exile: From Prinkipo to Coyoacan*, when he was professor emeritus of philosophy at Brandeis University.[35]

In September 1944, on Moscow's orders, Zborowski's code name was changed from "Tulip" to "Kant."[36] In late 1944 Zborowski asked Moscow for permission to join the American Communist Party. This was not good tradecraft, for he was still collecting information for the NKVD and had a relationship with the

American Trotskyites. Membership in the American Communist Party would allow some Communists who were not "in the loop" to know his identity. But for some reason, Moscow agreed. The New York *Rezidentura* spoke to Bernie Chester, their liaison with the American Communist Party, who said that as long as the Soviet comrades would vouch for Zborowski, he could be admitted to the American Communist Party with two sponsors. Chester was one and would secure another. Zborowski would have to submit an application and fill out a questionnaire.[37] Since Zborowski was a known Trotskyite, there would have been no way for him to join the Communist Party without the sponsorship of Chester, who was in charge of security for the New York State Communist Party, in addition to his work for the NKVD.

In December, control of Zborowski was taken over by NKVD officer Stepan Shundenko, and Zborowski joined the American Communist Party.[38]

Zborowski was a busy agent. In November 1944 he had a discussion with Elsa Reiss, the widow of the NKVD officer murdered in Europe when he tried to defect to the Trotskyites, who was unaware that Zborowski had been responsible for his murder.[39] She told Zborowski of the existence of Camp Ritchie, a training school for American intelligence. She had been recommended for employment at the school by the Menshevik leader Raphael Abramovich. Zborowski reported that this was a school to train cadres for a new war.[40] In fact, it trained people in connection with the war against Nazi Germany.

The NKVD had in fact heard over a year earlier about the military intelligence school at Camp Ritchie, Maryland. Details of the camp were provided to the Soviets by a member of the Soble/Soblen ring, Ilya Wolston, who was a student at the school and the nephew of Jack Soble and Robert Soblen.[41]

The Jack Soble/Robert Soblen Ring

Zborowski continued to provide information about Kravchenko. Although still in contact with the defector, he got most of his information from Mrs. Dallin. Another NKVD agent, Christina Krotkova, was also involved in this work. She and Zborowski were instructed to get closer to Kravchenko, and Krotkova soon became his translator and typist. In January 1945 Zborowski reported that Kravchenko and Dallin were in a "great panic" because Kravchenko was being shadowed by unknown persons. In addition, they had been warned that the U.S. government was preparing to turn Kravchenko back over to the Soviets.[42]

Kravchenko and Dallin had good reason to be concerned. In late December and early January, discussions were going on in the White House about returning Kravchenko. Harry Hopkins, the president's close friend and advisor and a Soviet agent,[43] had heard from his friend Joseph Davies, the former ambassador to Russia and a notorious Soviet sycophant, that American intelligence was trying to recruit Kravchenko. The Soviets asked that he be returned to them as a "deserter from the Red Army," and Hopkins suggested to Roosevelt that they grant the request. But Roosevelt was reluctant, saying that it would be easier to return him if the Soviets promised not to shoot him. Hopkins said cold-bloodedly that once he was in Russian hands, no one could know whether he had been shot or not. Roosevelt refused to return the fugitive.[44]

Zborowski was finally exposed in 1954 by NKVD defector Alexander Orlov. Leon Feldbin, later known as Alexander Orlov, was born in 1895 to Jewish parents in a town near Minsk, Russia. He joined the Bolshevik Party in May 1917, and after the October Revolution he became involved in military operations and intelligence work. His cousin Zinoviy Katsnelson was even higher in the Soviet intelligence apparatus, but Orlov himself carried out a number of important intelligence operations abroad.

Assigned by the NKVD as head of Soviet intelligence in Spain in September 1936, Orlov served there during Spain's Civil War. He was still there when the Soviet purge of intelligence officers began. Earlier he had been warned by Abraham Slutsky, chief of the Foreign Department of the NKVD, that he was in danger, particularly because he was a Jew. In February 1938 Slutsky, who was also a Jew, died. It was rumored that Beria later called him an "enemy of the people," which implied that Slutsky had been purged. But the Russian Foreign Intelligence Service, the successor to the KGB, denies this. It insists that he died of a heart attack.[45]

Orlov, however, suspected that Slutsky had been murdered. His own cousin, Katsnelson, was also a victim of the purge. On July 9, 1938, Nikolai Yezhov, Stalin's head of intelligence, who ran the purges, ordered Orlov to return to the Soviet Union. Two days later, Orlov, with his wife and daughter, left Spain, but not to return home. They took a ship from France to Canada and went into hiding.

Orlov was a very important Soviet intelligence officer, so important that six years after his defection, his fellow NKVD officers in a *Venona* message from Mexico City to Moscow still treated him with respect. Reporting on Vitoria Sala, a member of the Spanish Communist Party then in Mexico, with the *Venona* code name "Khota," they said that this agent's "work was so important that liaison with him was maintained by 'Shved' [Alexander Orlov] himself and not by 'Tom' [Leonid Eitingon]."[46] Eitingon had been Orlov's deputy in Spain and replaced him after his defection.

Orlov had learned about Zborowski when he visited NKVD colleagues in Paris in 1937. He had seen the agent and knew his name was "Mark." He did not know "Mark's" family name, but only that his pen name among the Trotskyites was "Etienne." In

The Jack Soble/Robert Soblen Ring

December 1938 Orlov wrote an anonymous letter to Trotsky warning him about the agent:

> This agent provocateur had for a long time assisted your son L. Sedov in editing your Russian "Bulletin of Opposition" in Paris, and collaborated with him until the very death of Sedov....
>
> The provocateur's name is "Mark." He was literally the shadow of L. Sedov; he informed the Cheka about every step of Sedov, about his activities and personal correspondence with you which the provocateur read with the knowledge of L. Sedov. This provocateur wormed himself into the complete confidence of your son and knew as much about the activities of your organization as Sedov himself. Thanks to this provocateur several officers of the Cheka have received decorations.[47]

Mrs. Dallin visited Trotsky in Mexico in the summer of 1939, and he showed her the letter accusing "Mark" of being an agent. Realizing that "Mark" was Zborowski, Mrs. Dallin defended her friend, saying, "That is certainly a definitely dirty job of the NKVD, who wants to deprive you of your few collaborators that you have in France." When she returned to Paris, she told Zborowski about the letter. He laughed and said, "You know how the NKVD works."[48]

In 1954 David Dallin contacted Orlov to discuss the book on Soviet espionage that he was writing. In the course of the discussion, Orlov mentioned the agent "Mark," but Dallin made only a vague response. However, during a second meeting in Dallin's home, Mrs. Dallin said that she and her husband had brought Zborowski to the United States in 1941, and she admitted that it was she who had advised Trotsky that his anonymous letter was a Soviet provocation. A few days later, Orlov reported to the United States Attorney's Office that a Soviet agent, Mark Zborowski, was living in New York.

The FBI began an investigation and interviewed the widow of Ignace Reiss. She could not believe that Zborowski was an agent and that he had betrayed her husband, so she warned Zborowski that the FBI was investigating him based on information from Orlov.[49]

When Zborowski was interviewed by the FBI, he admitted some of his activities in Europe but denied working for the NKVD in the United States. He then reported the FBI interview to his NKVD controller, Jack Soble. In early 1956 the Senate Subcommittee on Internal Security held hearings on Zborowski. It heard testimony from Orlov, Zborowski, and Mrs. Dallin. Zborowski was a little more frank than he had been with the FBI. He admitted some of his work for the NKVD in Europe and even blurted out that the plan was only to kidnap Trotsky's son, Sedov, not kill him, making clear his role in the murder. But Zborowski continued to deny any spy activities in the United States.[50]

Zborowski's testimony panicked Soble, who reported it in a letter to Zarubin in Moscow. He believed that Zarubin still headed the "illegal" directorate at the KGB headquarters, but Zarubin had already retired.

Soble sent the letter to Moscow through his courier, Boris Morros, who had been "turned" by the FBI in 1947 and was operating as a double agent—J. Edgar Hoover read the letter before it ever reached Moscow. It was used in a perjury trial of Mark Zborowski, who was convicted and in December 1958 sentenced to five years in prison. The conviction was overturned, but he was convicted again in a second trial and this time served a prison sentence.[51]

After his release from prison, Zborowski got a job teaching sociology at the University of California, Berkeley. But he was once again exposed as a former Soviet agent in February 1969 by the university's Independent Socialist Club. The same year, he published a book with the title *People in Pain*, a study of how different ethnic groups respond to pain—an incredible subject for a KGB murderer to study. The foreword to the book was written by the well-known sociologist Margaret Mead. She had earlier written the foreword to Zborowski's book *Life Is with People*, which he wrote with Elizabeth Herzog, who had no ties to Soviet intelligence. The book has become the classic study of Jewish life in the little towns of Eastern Europe.[52] Zborowski pointed out in the preface to *People in Pain* that the book "is the result of several years of research to investigate pain as a cultural experience. This project was undertaken under the sponsorship of the United States Public Health Service and The Institute for Intercultural Studies at the American Museum of Natural History." He identified Margaret Mead as "my guide, consultant, and informant at all stages of the study. No words can adequately express my feelings of indebtedness to her for years of friendship, scholarly advice, and moral encouragement."[53] It is hard to imagine how a government agency and serious academics could welcome such a person into their midst and sponsor his work.

Mark Zborowski died on April 30, 1990, in a California hospital at age eighty-two. He had retired in the early 1980s, but his academic colleagues continued to honor him.[54]

Zarubin's Stern Gang

One day in December 1943, while Boris Morros was working for Zarubin's espionage apparatus, he received a call at his Hollywood office. Morros was ordered to travel east immediately to consult with Zarubin. When he arrived, Zarubin told him that in order to expand Morros's music business, worth $6,000, and use it as cover for Soviet espionage agents, an investor had been found who would provide between $100,000 and $200,000—the actual amount was $130,000. The investor turned out to be Alfred K. Stern and his wife, Martha.[55]

Stern was born in 1897 in Fargo, North Dakota. His wife, Martha Dodd, was born in 1908 in Ashland, Virginia.[56] Zarubin told Soble that Alfred Stern worked for the Soviet Union in the 1930s, possibly in operations related to Germany. [57]

Martha Dodd had been recruited for Soviet espionage in Berlin while her father was the American ambassador there from 1933 to 1937. Her recruiter was Boris Vinogradov, the press attaché at the Berlin Soviet embassy. Martha met him on January 20, 1934, at a party in the home of her friend Sigrid Schulz, Berlin correspondent for the *Chicago Tribune*. Although married with children in Moscow, Vinogradov romanced the American ambassador's daughter and started her career in Soviet espionage.

The embassy staff knew of Martha's reputation for "sleeping around" long before she got to Germany. When she arrived in Berlin, she worsened her reputation by sleeping with Nazi storm troopers, Hitler's bully boys. Later, one of the embassy officials speaking about this to the FBI repeated a joke bandied about by the staff of the embassy: "We used to refer to her as the first Nazi penetration of America."

Soon she found for a lover a much more intellectual Nazi, Ernst Udet, an early supporter of Hitler who helped build the Luftwaffe. In June 1936 he became the chief of the Technical Office of the Nazi air force. Since Martha's affair with Vinogradov had begun earlier, during 1934,[58] her affair with Udet may well have been on orders from the Soviets. One of the people who knew Martha in Berlin commented that she was surprised at her affair with Udet "in view of Martha's known anti-Nazism."

The FBI deleted the names of most of the people it interviewed who knew Martha Dodd in Berlin when their statements were released under the Freedom of Information Act. But some could easily be identified by the surrounding descriptive material. One such was Louis Lochner, the longtime Associated Press bureau chief in Berlin. According to Lochner, Martha's father, Ambassador William Dodd, incompetent and dull-witted, "blundered his way through the years that he served in Germany.... He did the United States absolutely no good because of his ignorance of the situation that prevailed in Germany in the 1930s."

Dodd often consulted Lochner, who found that it was hard to "draw a picture" for the ambassador, who was unable to follow the simplest explanation. It was common knowledge, Lochner went on, that Martha was having an affair with someone at the Russian embassy. Moreover, according to Lochner's sources in the American embassy, there was concern "that items that were told to Dodd in confidence were finding their way into Russian hands."

The FBI also interviewed Agnes Walker, the widow of well-known American journalist and expert on Germany H. R. Knickerbocker. She remembered meeting Martha Dodd at a luncheon in Berlin in 1934 and related that Martha had been "on friendly terms with a member of the Nazi Party" but broke off that relationship and "took up" with "the Russians." Martha had been particularly close to the press attaché of the Soviet embassy in Berlin, Vinogradov. Walker said that she believed this relationship had begun in the spring of 1934.[59]

Vinogradov, who was Jewish, died in the Soviet purges in the late 1930s. Martha later wished to know more about his fate.[60] In 1957 she wrote a letter to the Soviet writer Ilya Ehrenberg, whom she had met in Mexico earlier, about Vinogradov. Martha told what she knew about her former lover:

> I have learned since I was here that he was shot around 1938, supposedly after he confessed to "collaborating with the Nazis." I have no way of verifying this report but I am sure that

he was not guilty and I cannot believe it until the evidence can be examined anew by some objective person in these days. Also in the light of what has been revealed by Khrushchev it is possible that the confession was extorted from him by torture. Have you any way of looking into this matter without embarrassment to yourself or to me? To repeat the facts: He was in Berlin from 1931–35 as press attaché and first secretary to the Embassy; then in Bucharest from 1935–37; and finally in Warsaw as Counselor of Embassy in 1937–38.[61]

Martha married Stern in 1938 and the next year wrote a book called *Through Embassy Eyes* describing her life in Berlin. Vinogradov was not even mentioned, but, interestingly, Udet was. Martha devoted six pages to him, referring to her relationship with him as "friendly intimacy."[62] She asked her friend Bennett Cerf to publish her book through Random House. Cerf, a well-known humorist and author, was president of the publishing house at that time. He refused, and the book was taken up by Harcourt Brace. When the book received good reviews in the press, Martha telephoned Cerf and asked how many copies of the book he thought might be sold. He answered "that if each man she had been to bed with had bought a copy the book would be a great success." A few minutes later, Martha's husband, Alfred Stern, called and threatened to punch him in the nose. Cerf told this story to the FBI.[63]

Alfred Stern had a lot of money from a divorce settlement with his wealthy former wife. He also had good political connections. Stern served as an important advisor to the pro-Communist New York congressman Vito Marcantonio. For a number of months, beginning in February 1949, the FBI had a wiretap on the Sterns' home. The wiretap was probably due to Boris Morros, who revealed to the FBI that Stern was a member of a Soviet spy ring. Frequent phone calls were recorded between Stern and Marcantonio, and in one fascinating conversation, on March 7, 1949, Marcantonio told Stern of his fight against legislation that supported the Central Intelligence Agency, a matter of great interest to the Soviets.[64]

When Zarubin left the United States in 1944, he handed over both Morros and the Sterns to Jack Soble. Earlier, Zarubin unwittingly set in motion the downfall of the Sterns when he introduced Alfred to Boris Morros in December 1943. Although Morros had not yet been "turned" by the FBI, he was a difficult person to deal with. Soon Stern and Morros were arguing about money and the business, in which the Sterns were the principal investors.

A year after the partnership was established, Alfred Stern complained to Moscow that things were not going well. Rather than submit his report through Soble, a good friend of Morros, Stern used another Soviet intelligence channel. He wrote a memo and sent it with a letter addressed to Zarubin's wife, Elizabeth. Stern gave the letter and memo to Rose Browder, the wife of Bill Browder, Earl's brother. She in turn passed the material to her niece Helen Lowry, *Venona* code name "Elsa," the wife of Iskhak Akhmerov, the NKVD "illegal" *Rezident*. Akhmerov thereupon turned the messages over to the New York NKVD *Rezident*, Stepan Apresyan, who transmitted them to Moscow. This long chain was necessary in order to bypass Soble and Morros.

Stern's memo went into detail about Morros's shortcomings and the derogatory things others were saying about him. He also complained that the business was being mishandled. He wrote, "The business, in which we all had great hopes, has reached the stage when immediate intervention on an authoritative level is required.... The 130,000 [dollar] investment is exhausted; in view of the poor business management and misguided artistic temperament unsuitable for conducting a very systematic business this sum is not enough, which allows one to envision future prospects as very dubious in this case."[65]

After their role in Soviet intelligence was exposed, the Sterns insisted that Boris Morros was lying about them because of a failed business deal. They conveniently forgot that the business provided a cover for Soviet intelligence and that Stern in writing to Moscow referred to it as "the business in which we all had great hopes...."

When Bill Browder was interviewed by the FBI in 1959, he was no longer a member of the Communist Party. His brother, Earl, had been removed as Party leader in 1945 on Moscow's instructions and was expelled from the Party a year later. Bill left the Party at the same time. Browder admitted that Stern contributed five or six thousand dollars a year to the Communist Party but said he was not a Party member. He said nothing about his knowledge of the Sterns' espionage activities or that his own wife was a conduit for Alfred's report to Moscow.[66]

Jack Soble was arrested in January 1957. He and his wife confessed to the FBI and, on April 10, 1957, pleaded guilty to espionage.[67] Jack Soble's confession implicated his brother, Robert Soblen, in Soviet espionage. Jack and other witnesses testified against Robert at his trial, where he was convicted of conspiracy to commit espionage and was sentenced to life in prison.

The Waning of the Sterns

By late 1946 the activities of the spy ring had diminished considerably. Alfred Stern told Jack Soble that he was tired of working for the Soviets and would like to join the open Communist Party. Soble put him in touch with Esther Rand. She in turn put him in touch with a Communist Party functionary whose name was unknown to Soble. Soble, however, remembered that the person was associated with the Communist weekly *New Masses*.[68] At that time,

The Jack Soble/Robert Soblen Ring

Rudy Baker, who headed the American Communist Party's underground apparatus, worked out of the *New Masses* office.

In 1953 the Stern family moved to Mexico. They were still there in 1957 when Jack Soble was arrested. He soon confirmed the story told ten years earlier to the FBI by Boris Morros about the role of the Sterns in espionage. In July 1957 the Sterns left Mexico for Czechoslovakia, where they lived out the rest of their lives. Martha continued to write for the Communist press, including *The Worker*, an American Communist Party newspaper. She wrote one article denouncing the imprisonment in Mexico of David Alfaro Siqueiros, whom she called a "great revolutionary artist," but neglected to mention that Siqueiros had been the head of the murder squad that had attacked the home of Leon Trotsky in an unsuccessful assassination attempt in 1940.[69]

The Sterns were under indictment for espionage when they arrived in Prague in September 1957. They held a press conference, but only the Czech press was invited. There the Sterns insisted that "the accusations by Boris Morros that we are or were Soviet agents are fantastic inventions of a Hollywood impostor, a part and parcel of his lurid career. Character assassination by publicity is one of the vicious techniques Morros and the agencies of the U.S. government and Committees of Congress are employing to try to destroy or silence those people who dare to dissent."[70]

The American embassy reported to the State Department that after the closed press conference, Alfred Stern accidentally met correspondents from Reuters and Agence France Presse. He was very curt with them and told them that he was in Prague as a "tourist." He thereupon stepped into a large official Tratra automobile and was driven off.[71]

While living in Mexico, Martha wrote a novel opposing the loyalty oaths that some American universities demanded of those who had the privilege of teaching students. Her friends on the Left loved the book, which had jacket blurbs by Albert Einstein and Robert Hutchins.[72] In May 1960, after the Sterns had been exposed as Soviet agents, Martha inscribed a copy of her book in Prague to the well-known millionaire leftist Cyrus Eaton, who, she wrote, was "a great democrat, in appreciation of your wisdom and courage. With warm regards, Martha Dodd Stern."[73]

By 1971 the Sterns were hinting that they would like to return to the United States but only if the indictments were dropped. The two key witnesses against them, Boris Morros and Jack Soble, were dead. The Sterns applied for U.S. passports at the embassy in Prague on July 30, 1971.[74] The FBI consulted with the U.S. attorney for the southern district of New York, Whitney North Seymour, Jr., who said he would "be willing to dismiss this indictment but only if the Sterns were willing to make full disclosures."[75]

The FBI wanted to question them, first of all, about Martha's involvement with Soviet espionage when she was in Germany as the ambassador's daughter; second, about the Sterns' World War II activities with Boris Morros and Jack Soble, particularly the people the Sterns had recruited; and third, about Alfred Stern's second channel of information to the Soviets. We now know that this was through Rose Browder and Akhmerov, the "illegal" *Rezident*. The fourth area was anything that they could provide about their contacts with Soviet intelligence after leaving the United States.[76]

Negotiations with the U.S. government were conducted on behalf of the Sterns by Victor Rabinowitz, an attorney who later admitted having been a Communist Party member.[77] One suggestion was that the Sterns go to a non-Communist country where they would be interviewed by the FBI. The Sterns opted for Yugoslavia, but the FBI preferred Austria, Italy, or France.[78]

The Jack Soble/Robert Soblen Ring

The negotiations went on and on. On January 22, 1974, Assistant U.S. Attorney Thomas Edwards advised Rabinowitz that the Sterns would be arrested or prosecuted unless they were willing to talk to U.S. government authorities concerning their involvement in Soviet espionage. Rabinowitz insisted that if they went to a Western country, the U.S. government would try to have them extradited.[79]

The next year another Communist attorney entered the picture. Rabinowitz's partner, Leonard Boudin, contacted the Justice Department to suggest that his clients be interviewed by an American representative in a neutral country. He was told that if they went to a neutral country, the Justice Department would proceed from there.[80] But in July Rabinowitz changed his story. Now he wanted the meeting to take place in August at the American embassy in Prague.[81] The FBI responded wryly, "Czechoslovakia does not appear to fall within the definition of an interview in a neutral country."[82]

The negotiations continued until Jimmy Carter became president, when the pressure intensified. Don Edwards, an extreme left-wing Democratic congressman from California, became involved in the case at the request of Sylvia Crane, a friend of the Sterns. Edwards wrote to Attorney General Griffin Bell that "a reliable friend of mine" had visited the Sterns and reported that they were anxious to return to the United States.[83] When Crane had been interviewed by the FBI on April 4, 1957, she had claimed no knowledge of any espionage activity on the part of the Sterns but did say that the Sterns "were such strong individualists that their membership in the Communist Party was inconceivable to her." She described the Sterns as her "friends."[84] Two years later, the FBI interviewed another friend of the Sterns who had been in the Communist Party from the late 1930s to the mid-1940s and had met the Sterns through William Browder. She identified Sylvia Crane as a member of a Communist Party branch that met on 106th Street in Manhattan.[85]

The first Justice Department response to Edwards was from Robert Keuch, deputy assistant attorney general, who advised him that it was inappropriate for the Justice Department to discuss the case with anyone other than the Sterns' attorney.[86] This didn't stop Edwards. In December he wrote to President Carter's counsel, Robert Lipshutz, suggesting that the indictments against the Sterns be quashed because they were based on unreliable testimony by Boris Morros.[87]

In March 1978 Edwards wrote again to Attorney General Bell complaining about the letter he had received from the Justice Department almost a year earlier. He wrote, "Naturally the attorneys for the Sterns have been in touch with the Justice Department but with no success whatsoever. Justice is 'going by the book,' and that would include these old sick folks returning, being interviewed by the FBI, court proceedings, etc. A glance at your file would indicate, I think, that the indictment would fail. All ten witnesses are dead, and it wasn't much to begin with more than 20 years ago. Alfred Stern is 80 years old and could not possibly withstand the strain of a drawn-out court proceeding. Sometimes justice includes being kind and generous. Although I don't know the Sterns, perhaps their case is one of these."[88]

But the Justice Department continued to insist that it would negotiate the matter only with the Sterns' attorney.[89] Edwards tried the White House again, writing to Anne Wexler, an assistant to the president.[90]

In August 1978 the FBI reiterated to the Justice Department its opposition to dropping the indictment against the Sterns unless they provided truthful information to the U.S. government about their espionage activities.[91] The FBI then heard from someone in the U.S. Attorney's Office that "the [Justice] department made some type of commitment to Victor Rabinowitz or his partner, Leonard

Boudin, concerning the Stern case without prior consultations with the [U.S. attorney, southern district of New York]."[92] On September 11, 1978, Robert Keuch advised the U.S. attorney in New York that a decision had been made to dismiss the indictment against the Sterns. The FBI could do nothing and advised the Justice Department that since it "had decided against our recommendation we would therefore abide by the Department's position."

On March 22, 1979, the charges against the Sterns were dropped. Congressman Edwards and Sylvia Crane were interviewed by the *Washington Post*. Edwards neglected to mention that he had begged the Justice Department to drop the indictments of the two old people. Instead, he crowed that his research showed that Boris Morros was of "doubtful integrity," while Sylvia Crane said she thought that the indictments of the two were "part of a McCarthy dirty tricks campaign."[93]

The Sterns were indicted three years after Joe McCarthy had been discredited. As for Representative Don Edwards, an FBI memorandum on his quote stated "that it was his opinion 'Morros was of doubtful integrity.' We [the FBI] have no reason to question Morros' integrity based on his relationship with us for a number of years. Further, the article states that the FBI was reluctant to let the Sterns return without a ten-hour interrogation. As was indicated above, we only stated our position in favor of an interview, and the article's statement is a hyperbole."[94]

The Sterns were overjoyed. In a letter to her old friends George and Eleanor Wheeler, Martha said, "You've probably heard about our vindication at last. The case was dismissed for lack of evidence by the U.S. government. It does come very late in our lives, true, and we've suffered plenty in the last 20 years, but at least we kept our honor and decency and did not have open or secret sessions here, or anywhere else, with the CIA and FBI or any other agencies and did not 'blabber-mouth' to anyone, though in fact there was nothing to blabber about."[95]

That year, the Sterns contributed $500 to Congressman Don Edwards's election fund. He sent them a letter of thanks and said, "I hope that you two will soon be coming to the United States."[96] The Sterns never did come home. The real reason for all the activity generated by their friends was to have the indictment dropped so that they could boast of their vindication.

Alfred Stern died in Prague in June 1986.[97] Martha Dodd Stern died there a few years later.

The arrests of the Soble/Soblen brothers ended the work of their spy ring. While they were involved in a number of operations for the NKVD, a good deal of their time and energy was directed against nongovernmental Americans—particularly Trotskyites and, as we shall see, Jews. Stalin's obsessions drove NKVD activities even when they distracted the spy service from more important duties.

CHAPTER 12
"Polecats" and "Rats":
Spying on Dissidents and Jews

AS THE WAR IN EUROPE WAS WINDING DOWN in 1945, the NKVD became increasingly concerned about possible postwar rivals. In addition to the usual Soviet anti-Semitism, it feared that American Jewish organizations that had developed contacts with fellow Jews in Nazi-occupied Europe might interfere with Soviet control in the newly conquered territories. The Soviets were also concerned about their traditional enemies now living in the United States. A *Venona* message from Moscow to *Rezidenturas* in various parts of the world, including New York, ordered the intensification of work on "old and new Russian and nationalist émigrés, the Russian, Armenian and Mohammedan clergy, Trotskyites and Zionists...." They were ordered to provide specific proposals for dealing with these groups and, in regard to agent penetration, to "advise by telegraph about persons ear-marked for recruitment, in order to obtain permission."[1] The Ukrainians were a particular target.

Again in April 1946 Beria, head of the Soviet Intelligence and Security Service, cabled the *Rezidenturas* to "intensify surveillance of the activity of White émigré, Nationalist, Trotskyite, Zionist and ecclesiastical organizations...."

Although Jews were a constant target, Moscow was also concerned that Armenians abroad might influence the Communist-controlled Armenian Church based in the Soviet Union. In 1945, when a synod was scheduled by the church in Soviet Armenia to elect a new leader, the NKVD was very interested in the foreign delegates and ordered the *Rezidentura* in Mexico City, which coordinated spying in Latin America, to investigate them.[2]

A few weeks later, the *Rezidenturas* in Mexico City, Bogota, and Montevideo were ordered to identify all of the South American delegates scheduled to go to the meeting.[3]

Jack Soble ("Czech"), who headed the apparatus directed against "Polecats" (Trotskyites) and "Rats" (Jews), transferred the leadership of this work to his brother, Robert Soblen ("Roman") in May 1945.[4] As Chapter 11 explained, both were experienced operatives who had worked for Soviet intelligence since the early 1930s.

Stalin: Jews and Negroes Are Not Americans

The NKVD's obsession with Trotskyites came from Stalin's paranoid belief that this tiny political group was somehow a threat to the Soviet Union. The same paranoia had fueled the Soviet mass purges of the late 1930s. The targeting of Jews stemmed from another of Stalin's misconceptions. He believed that in the United States, Jews and blacks were not Americans but other nationalities. Reflecting Stalin's thinking, a 1938 Comintern report identified the members and candidates of the American Communist Politburo as four Americans, four Jews, one German, and two Negroes.[5] This concept had its origin in the experience of the Soviet Union, where members of many nationalities were Soviet citizens. Jews, regardless of where in the Soviet Union they were born, did not share the nationality of their neighbors but carried the word "Jew" on their internal passports. This reflected Russian history. In tsarist Russia, known at that time as a prison house of nations, all non-Russians had an inferior status, but Jews were particularly vulnerable.

The Soviet leaders understood that Jewish intellectuals played important roles as thinkers and organizers in socialist and

Communist movements, and they had no hesitation in using them. Yet they had little affection or even respect for them.

Because Stalin believed that blacks were not Americans, the Communist International sent instructions to the American Communists to promote the idea that Negroes in a crescent-shaped area of the southeastern United States, as far north as part of Virginia and as far south as part of Texas, should demand the right to secede and establish a separate government. The Communists called this "Self-Determination in the Black Belt." The instructions, moreover, referred to black farmers as "peasants," another East European concept totally unknown in the United States.[6]

This slogan, however, gained little support even in the 1930s, when racial violence in the South and discrimination throughout the United States were routine. The demands of black Americans were for their full rights as Americans, not for an independent, segregated black country.

In 1961 W. E. B. DuBois, at age ninety-three, became a Communist Party member,[7] but thirty years earlier he had condemned Communist misuse of Negroes. As editor of the NAACP magazine *The Crisis*, DuBois wrote, "The Communists, seizing leadership of the poorest and most ignorant blacks, head them toward inevitable slaughter and jail-slavery, while they hide safely in Chattanooga and Harlem. American Negroes do not propose to be the shock troops of the Communist Revolution, driven out in front to death, cruelty, and humiliation in order to win victories for white workers."[8]

Only a handful of black Americans were attracted to the Communist Party, and they did not stay long. Eugene Dennis in a report to the Comintern written in April 1941 revealed that there were only twenty-five Negroes in the Detroit Communist Party compared to 450 a few years earlier. Most of these losses had occurred even before the announcement of the Soviet-Nazi alliance in August 1939.[9]

Later, as a result of the Nazi-Soviet Pact, the Party lost Manning Johnson, one of its most talented black leaders. In 1935 he ran for Congress on the Communist Party ticket. In 1938 the Comintern authorized the American Communists to make Johnson a candidate (alternate) member of the Party's Central Committee. It warned, however, that although he was "capable and energetic, [and] a good mass worker," he had a tendency to deviate from the Party line.[10] His opposition to the Nazi-Soviet Pact was a major deviation. After resigning from the Party, he became an active anti-Communist.

As soon as the Soviet Union was attacked by Germany, the American Communist Party abandoned any concern about anti-Negro discrimination. Herbert Hill, then an assistant field secretary of the NAACP, in a 1951 article, gave an example of Communist disregard for Negro rights during World War II. He said, "Some wounded Negro soldiers were left unattended and without medical care at Fort Devens in 1945. When four Negro WACs stationed at the fort learned of these outrages they protested. For this they were court-martialed. But widespread protest from churches, labor unions, and civil rights organization forced Army officials to reverse themselves." But, Hill went on, the Communist response to this incident was to reprimand the WACs instead of support them. Black Communist leader Ben Davis responded in the *Daily Worker* on April 8, 1945, "We cannot temporarily stop the war until all questions of discrimination are ironed out." And then when A. Philip Randolph, a prominent civil rights leader, protested against anti-Negro discrimination, he was accused in the *Daily Worker* of being a "fascist helping defeatism."[11] Human rights for blacks was far less important to the Communists than devoting everything to the defense of the Soviet Union.

As for the Jews, despite the pogroms and persecutions in the

Soviet Union, American Jews played an important role in the Communist Party USA. According to Alfred Kutzik, the chairman of the National Jewish Commission of the Communist Party from 1989 to 1992, during most of the CPUSA's existence, almost half of its membership and a quarter of its leadership were Jewish.[12] At its height, the Communist Party had fewer than 100,000 members, of whom about half were Jews. Clearly, the Jewish Communists represented only a tiny fraction of the several million Jews in America, and according to Kutzik, by 1989, during the decline of the Party, when over a million-and-a-half Jews lived in New York City, only about 300 were members of the Communist Party.[13]

The Comintern did not like having Jews in the Party leadership and, after the "Bolshevization" of the Party in 1929,[14] made every effort to replace them with those whom Moscow considered "Americans." A 1937 Moscow evaluation complained that the Party's Agitprop (Agitation and Propaganda) Commission consisted of seven members, but "not one of these comrades is an American. Here, we have no reference to the formal side as to their place of birth, but [only] that none of these comrades was raised with the American masses...." All those named were Jews. The report went on to speak about the "understanding of the American masses which Comrade Browder shows is native to him...."[15] To Moscow only a non-Jew like Browder could understand American thinking.

The Comintern's disdain for Jews reflected Stalin's own anti-Semitism. In 1907 Stalin, who almost never traveled abroad, attended the London Congress of the Russian Social-Democratic Labor Party. Referring to the Party's main factions in his report on the congress, Stalin noted that the majority of the Menshevik delegates were Jews, but the majority of Bolshevik delegates were Russians. He recounted a Bolshevik joke: "The Mensheviks constituted a Jewish group while the Bolsheviks constituted a true Russian group and, therefore, it wouldn't be a bad idea for us Bolsheviks to organize a pogrom in the Party."[16] Two years earlier, Russia had experienced a series of anti-Semitic pogroms that left thousands of Jews dead or injured. Stalin's jocular anecdote is revealing. When he became dictator of Russia, he pursued anti-Semitic policies that culminated in a mass persecution of Jews shortly before he died.

Beyond this, the widespread Jewish opposition to Soviet policies provided a strong motive for mistrusting Jews. As early as 1929 American Communists had to mobilize forces to defend the office of their Yiddish-language newspaper, the *Jewish Daily Freiheit*, from Jewish demonstrators who protested its editorial support for Arab pogroms against the Jews in Palestine.[17]

While the Comintern promoted the ethnic pride of minorities in countries not under its control, it disparaged such feelings among Jews. At the Communist Party USA's 1938 convention, Phil David, the Bronx County executive secretary, made a speech filled with Jewish pride, suggesting that Jews played an important and positive part in colonial America and during the Revolutionary War. David boasted accurately that "the Jews have participated in the major struggles for the creation of democracy, extension of democracy, and the preservation of democracy in the United States as have all other nationalities and groups making up the American people."[18]

In short order, a Comintern instructor at the convention, Ferruccio Marini, alias Mario Alpi and "F. Brown," criticized David's speech as "bourgeois nationalism."[19] The ethnic pride of other groups could be a useful weapon for the Communists, but the ethnic pride of Jews had to be condemned.

Sam Darcy (*né* Dardek), who served in Moscow as the American Communist Party representative to the Comintern from 1935 to 1937, witnessed the show trials that Moscow conducted to "prove" to the world that leading Communists who disagreed with Stalin were "Nazi agents."[20] There were also a number of secret trials, including those of General Mikhail Tukhachevsky, the legendary Soviet military leader, and seven other generals. Among them was General Ion Yakir, the commander of the Kiev (Ukraine) Military District, an old Communist and one of the most distinguished and highly decorated Jewish Soviet generals. Many of the victims were Jews, and the idea that they could be Nazi agents was ridiculous.[21]

The trials so shocked even seasoned American Communist Party members that Darcy was asked uncomfortable questions when he returned to the United States. In June 1937 he complained at a Central Committee meeting that comrades had asked him, "How is it that most of the eight generals are amongst the national minorities?" Darcy understood that this referred to the executed Jewish generals and responded that the question implied doubt that the Soviets had solved the "nationality question"; he assured them that the Soviets had. But, he added, Nazi agents had concentrated on recruiting agents in the western part of the Soviet Union, Ukraine and White Russia, where many Jews lived.[22]

As noted earlier, during the 1930s the Communist Party recruited some Jewish intellectuals who saw the CPUSA as an anti-Nazi movement. Nevertheless, most Jewish Americans were indifferent to the Party, while some were strongly anti-Communist. In 1938 and 1939 Jewish concern focused on the mortal danger Jews faced in Nazi-controlled territory. Moreover, the governments of the United States and Britain showed little desire to rescue them. But then neither did the Soviet Union, which, even before the Soviet-Nazi alliance, was not interested in taking in Jewish refugees. Theodore Bayer, an American Communist Party member and a Soviet agent (code name "Simon"), wrote in the *Soviet Russia Today*: "The USSR up to now has never undertaken to receive mass immigration, and this would hardly be a propitious time to tackle this new and difficult problem. It would run, of course, the danger of importing purposely planted spies and saboteurs of all kinds, as has happened in the past. Further, there would be the practical difficulty of fitting a group made up largely of non-working class, non-farming people into a Socialist and collectivized economy...."[23] Bayer's point was that since Jews didn't fit into Soviet society or in its plans for the future, it was not wise to rescue them from the Nazis.

Targeting Jewish Organizations

The Soviets' disdain for Jews and concern about "Zionists" did not impede their desire to penetrate Jewish organizations. On June 1, 1936, the Polish Communist leadership in Moscow ordered its underground Party to penetrate the World Jewish Congress (WJC). Two weeks later the Comintern Secretariat ordered the British Communist Party to infiltrate a WJC meeting in Geneva, "despite [its] reactionary Zionist character."[24]

The Soviet-Nazi alliance, which strengthened the dangerous anti-Semitic Hitler regime, was not expected to be popular among Jews. In March 1940 William Z. Foster, the American Communist Party's national chairman, speaking at a meeting of the National Council of Jewish Communists (formerly the Jewish Buro of the Communist Party), tried to explain:

> We all know the world policy that the Jewish bourgeois leaders and their Social Democratic aids [sic] have worked out in the name of their people in connection with the present imperialist war. Briefly, this consists of active support of Great Britain and France against Germany, combined with an attempt to turn the war against the Soviet Union.... By identifying themselves with British imperialism, as their conservative leaders have done, the Jews can only go from one defeat to another.... The war and all the terrors that it brings immediately and

threatens eventually to humanity in which the Jewish people will be the greatest sufferers cannot be overcome merely by fighting Hitler.[25]

This insensitive speech was acceptable only to Communist Party members. Many Jews who joined the front organizations or read the Communist Party newspaper *Morning Freiheit* dropped away. The *Freiheit* circulation had been growing and as early as 1934 reached 22,000 readers, rising until 1938, when it reached 36,000. By 1940 it had dropped to 17,000.[26]

Communist disregard for vital Jewish interests was mirrored in the Party's support for the gains the Soviet Union reaped from its cynical alliance with Nazi Germany. On June 27, 1940, less than a year after joining in the Nazi destruction and partitioning of Poland, the Soviet Union sent an ultimatum to Rumania, demanding that it cede Bessarabia and the neighboring northern part of Bucovina to the Soviet Union. Rumania asked Germany, with whom it was ideologically aligned, for help. Nazi Germany, the Soviet ally, answered, "In order to avoid war between Rumania and the Soviet Union, we can only advise the Rumanian government to yield to the Soviet Government's demand."[27]

Although this takeover, with Nazi complicity, was undertaken not to help Jews but to expand the Soviet Empire, the American Communist Party issued a leaflet in Chicago proclaiming, "Celebrate the Bessarabian Liberation/500,000 Jews Saved!" It spoke of the "grandeur [of] the peaceful, liberating policy of the Soviet Union...." The leaflet went on to attack the largest Yiddish-language newspaper of that time, the *Jewish Daily Forward*:

And what do these "gentry," the *Forward* group, have to say about the great Bessarabian Liberation? Nothing but slander, sneers, innuendoes, back biting against the great Soviet Union. Once and for all—let's ask the *Forward*! Which road? Roumanian fascism, anti-Semitism OR SOVIET FREEDOM, and liberation? Once and for all—we must realize that the *Forward* and Zionist leadership, or any group which slanders and attacks the Soviet Union, such groups are traitors to the Jewish race—the enemies who must be DRIVEN OUT. Yes, there is hope for the Jewish people—there is a road to freedom. This path does not mean support for British Imperialism, for 'fifth columnist' Chamberlain! This path does not mean support for the Roosevelt administration which is rushing headlong into war. No, the road forward for the Jewish masses lies in alliance with the working class; Support the peace policy of the Soviet Union![28]

While attempting, through their own media or front organizations, to rally support for Soviet policies, the Communists, as stated, also sought to penetrate Jewish organizations in order to keep an eye on them and, where possible, inflict their positions useful to the Soviet Union.

Esther Rand, an experienced Communist Party member, was one of the agents assigned to penetrate Jewish groups. She was handled by veteran Soviet intelligence officer Jack Soble. Rand was known to the FBI as a member of the Communist Party, and on January 16, 1947, an FBI surveillance of Soviet "illegal" Jack Soble observed him meeting with her.[29] On April 15, 1957, Soble, who by then had been arrested, confessed to the FBI that "Esther Rand furnished him with reports on Jewish matters which he in turn furnished to the Soviets."[30]

In May 1944 NKVD New York sent a *Venona* message to Moscow advising that it had decided to expand Rand's work. Employed by the United Palestine Appeal, where she could spy only on the Zionists, she would now be placed as administrative secretary of the American Committee of Jewish Writers, Artists, and Scientists, "where she will be able to expand her opportunities for using Jewish organizations and prominent figures."[31] In those jobs, she provided the NKVD with information on Jews in soon-to-be Soviet-occupied Eastern and Central Europe who had contact with American Jewish relief organizations. In 1948 Rand went back to her work for the United Jewish Appeal, which evolved into the major fund-raising organization for Jewish charities that helped in both the United States and countries abroad.[32]

Although the American Committee of Jewish Writers, Artists, and Scientists had many non-Communist members, Albert Kahn, a Soviet agent identified by Elizabeth Bentley, was on the executive committee.[33]

The honorary president of the organization was Albert Einstein. In 1949, when the American committee published a vile pamphlet that denied the existence of Soviet anti-Semitism, Einstein signed the introduction.[34] Einstein also served as honorary president of the American Birobidjan (Ambidjan) Committee, another Communist front, which promoted the segregated Jewish area in an isolated part of Siberian Russia as an alternative to Zionism. While Soviet agent Joseph Bernstein was the national organizer, Soviet agent Albert Kahn was a member of the National Committee.[35] Melech Epstein, the leading expert on Jewish Communist history, exposed the American Birobidjan Committee as the "middle-class counterpart of the ICOR," a more obvious Communist front that raised funds for Birobidjan.[36] Ambidjan was somewhat more sophisticated, recruiting unsuspecting dupes; ICOR was a crude Communist front that used insulting rhetoric against the very Jews that it wanted to influence. A 1932 pamphlet, for example, claimed that a "covert war against the construction of the

USSR is carried on by a black united front of 'Yarmulke' Jews, Zionists and social fascists."[37] These referred to three different groups: religious Jews,[38] supporters of a Jewish state, and socialists, then referred to by the Communists as "social fascists."

Birobidjan, the supposedly Jewish Autonomous Region of the Soviet Union, was, of course, a fraud, and most of the people living there were not Jewish. But this was not immediately apparent, and for a number of years Birobidjan had a certain value as a kind of vast Potemkin village that garnered sympathy for the Soviets in Jewish circles. The Soviets went to considerable length to conceal this fraud. In 1936 the American Communists organized a delegation of prominent Jews to visit Birobidjan. When the proposed list arrived in Moscow, it was discovered that one of the delegates was Charles Zimmerman, a leader of the International Ladies' Garment Workers' Union. Zimmerman, a former Communist Party member, had left in 1929 and now fought against Communist infiltration of his union. Sam Darcy, using the name "Randolph," wrote a memo to Comintern official Dimitri Manuilsky reporting that the American Communists were being instructed to reduce the size of the delegation to make sure that Zimmerman was excluded.[39] No way could so knowledgeable a Jewish leader as Zimmerman be permitted to visit Birobidjan! He might grasp the truth and expose it.

Duping Albert Einstein

Einstein, despite his brilliant mind, was a frequent victim of Communist manipulation. In the 1920s and early 1930s, he was enticed to support the front apparatus organized by Comintern leader Willi Muenzenberg. Einstein served as one of the "presidents" of Muenzenberg's International Congress Against Colonial Oppression and Imperialism, held in Brussels on February 10, 1927. On February 21 Muenzenberg wrote to Osip Piatnitsky, head of the Organizational Department of the Comintern, requesting Soviet payment for the costs of the congress. On June 15 Muenzenberg reported to Piatnitsky that "the secretary of the well-known professor Albert Einstein with the name Jacoby, a member of the Communist Party of Germany," was carrying out a secret Communist assignment in the Balkans.[40]

Another of Muenzenberg's fronts, the Workers International Relief (*Internationale Arbeiter Hilfe*), boasted that Einstein had written them: "All honor to the Workers' International Relief for the work it has done! All hand and brain workers should realize the importance of this organization and seek to strengthen it."[41] As we have seen, the Soviets continued their interest in Einstein when he became involved in the American atom bomb project.[42]

America's entrance into World War II made it possible to garner support among American Jews for the Soviet Union and concretely for the Soviet war effort against Nazi Germany. In 1942 Jewish groups joined to pledge one million dollars for Russian War Relief.[43] New opportunities also opened up for Soviet penetration of Jewish organizations and propaganda. The Soviet propaganda apparatus arranged for twenty-five leading Soviet Jews, including Solomon Mikhoels, a prominent Jewish Soviet actor, to issue a statement urging Jews throughout the world to support the Soviet war effort.[44]

The Murder of Erlich and Alter

In September 1941 the Soviet government decided to establish a Jewish Anti-Fascist Committee to mobilize international Jewish support for the Soviet war effort. An NKVD officer, Aron Volkovisky, asked two leaders of the Jewish socialist trade union movement in Poland, Henryk Erlich and Victor Alter, to head the effort. In prewar Poland, they had been leaders of the General

Jewish Workers' Union, known as the "Bund," which was affiliated with the Labor and Socialist International. Both Erlich and Alter had been arrested by the Soviet secret police in September 1939, when the Red Army invaded Poland. Immediately after the Nazi attack on the Soviet Union in June 1941, they were sentenced to death. A few weeks later, their sentences were commuted to ten years of hard labor in the Gulag. But in September 1941 they were released, so that they could meet with foreign Jews, and were offered the leadership of the newly formed Jewish Anti-Fascist Committee.

Erlich was to be chairman, Solomon Mikhoels vice chairman, and Alter the general secretary. They met with Lavrenti Beria to plan their committee, which was created by the NKVD, but Erlich and Alter were nevertheless ordered to write to Stalin asking for official permission to set it up. In their October letter, the two wrote explaining the purpose of the committee, which was "to stimulate, organise, and direct the energies of the Jewish masses and, if possible, entire Jewish communities of all countries, in the supreme fight against Hitlerism."

They were then taken by the NKVD to the town of Kuibishev, where the committee would be headquartered, but after midnight on December 4 at a restaurant, they were summoned by telephone and ordered to report to the NKVD headquarters. They were never seen again.

Erlich and Alter were known throughout the world as leaders of the socialist, trade union, and Jewish movements, and leading Americans from each group protested their disappearance. After over a year of unanswered appeals, yet another cable was sent to Soviet foreign minister Molotov asking for "release of these outstanding courageous fighters against Fascism and Nazism." Among the signers were William Green of the AFL, Philip Murray of the CIO, David Dubinsky of the International Ladies' Garment Workers'

Union, and even such fellow travelers as Albert Einstein and Leo Krzycki of the American Slav Congress, a Communist front.

The answer came almost a month later in a letter from the Soviet ambassador, Maxim Litvinov, to William Green. Writing on behalf of Molotov, Litvinov reported:

> For active subversive work against the Soviet Union and assistance to Polish intelligence organs in armed activities, Erlich and Alter were sentenced to capital punishment in August, 1941.
>
> At the request of the Polish Government, Erlich and Alter were released in September, 1941.
>
> However, after they were set free, at the time of the most desperate battles of the Soviet troops against the advancing Hitler army, they resumed their hostile activities including appeals to the Soviet troops to stop bloodshed and immediately to conclude peace with Germany.
>
> For this they were rearrested and, in December, 1942, sentenced once more to capital punishment by the Military Collegium of the Supreme Court. This sentence has been carried out in regard to both of them.[45]

When mass meetings of trade union and Jewish organizations took place in England and the United States to protest the murders, the American Communists organized a group of one hundred trade unionists to sign a statement condemning the protesters for "helping the Nazi strategy to divide and conquer."[46]

American Communist Party leader Earl Browder, in a speech in New York City on April 1, 1943, claimed that those who protested the murders were part of "a conspiratorial effort of American citizens, organized on American soil, to overthrow the government of the Soviet Union, an ally of the United States...." He went on: "We do not know the evidence upon which a Soviet court condemned

Erlich and Alter. But we have enough evidence of the conspiracy in the United States, of which Erlich and Alter were agents, to confirm the findings of the Soviet court." The "conspirators" accused by Browder were Nathan Chanin, the head of the Jewish Labor Committee, trade union leader David Dubinsky, and Abraham Cahan, editor of the *Jewish Daily Forward*.[47]

For its part the Polish government in exile, from its London headquarters, protested the murders to the Soviet government on March 8, 1943. The answer from the Soviet government on March 31 rejected the protest and again falsely claimed that the two socialists had appealed to "the Soviet armies to cease this bloodshed and to conclude an immediate peace with Germany...."

Although the denials and rationalizations by the Soviet government and the American Communists in the Erlich and Alter affair should have been insulting to any person of normal intelligence, American involvement in the war put the burden on the anti-Communists to demonstrate why they were apparently distracting the public from the great task of helping America's ally beat the enemy. This line of reasoning was apparent a few weeks later when, on April 26, 1943, a Soviet note to the Polish government in exile severed relations between the two countries. The Poles, it appeared, had asked for an investigation of the German claim that the Soviets had murdered thousands of Polish officers at Katyn Forest.[48] This request came only after the Poles had exhausted all other channels in their attempts to find out what had happened to their officers and following an accumulation of evidence showing that the blame the Soviets placed on the Germans for the massacre was not credible, most notably because the Germans had not been in control of Katyn when the massacres occurred.

But the same appeal to rally behind an ally during the war, which had dimmed the outrage in the Erlich and Alter affair, was again

"Polecats" and "Rats": Spying on Dissidents and Jews

helpful in the Katyn affair. It allowed a Soviet sympathizer, Corliss Lamont, to write brazenly in the introduction to a *Soviet Russia Today* pamphlet published May 1943:

> Soviet Russia's severance of relations with the Polish Government-in-Exile, over the Nazi-inspired charge that the Russians murdered 10,000 Polish army officers, shows clearly the danger to the United Nations [that is, the Allies] of the splitting tactics engineered by Hitler and definitely helped along by the general campaign of anti-Soviet propaganda carried on during recent months in Britain and America. According to the London Bureau of the *New York Herald Tribune*, "It is a safe assumption that the Poles would not have taken so tough an attitude toward the Soviet Government if it had not been for the widespread support Americans have been giving them in the cases of Henry Ehrlich and Victor Alter" [Erlich's name was sometimes spelled Ehrlich].

The foreign editor of the *Herald Tribune* at that time was Joseph Barnes, who had a long relationship with Soviet intelligence.[49]

The pamphlet contained the National Council of American-Soviet Friendship's full-page ad in the *New York Times* of May 18, 1943. It was an "Open Letter to the American People on American-Soviet Friendship" with a long list of signatures, some of them innocent dupes but many of them the usual signers of Communist-front manifestos. A few Soviet agents, such as Frederick Vanderbilt Field and Maxim Lieber, were also on the list.

True to form, the "Open Letter" complained about those in the United States who voiced any criticism of the Soviet Union. It said, "They prejudge and play up every new accusation leveled at the Soviet Government by the diehard Russophobes among the Polish émigrés, deliberately provoking disunity over such issues as the

Ehrlich-Alter case and the Nazi-inspired charge that the Russians murdered 10,000 Polish officers."[50]

This letter included the name of Albert Einstein, who had earlier protested the murders of Erlich and Alter. When the American representatives of the Jewish-Polish "Bund" wrote to him about this, Einstein answered, "I have always been convinced that the execution of the two Polish Jewish labor leaders was a fatal political error and that the accusations are very improbable in themselves. I would never have signed any statement containing assertions to the contrary. In the 'Open Letter' I signed, there was only said that an obnoxious misuse has been made of this case by the adversaries of honest collaboration with Russia. There was, therefore, no reason for me to refuse to sign this Open Letter."[51]

Within a short time, the Communists in England were circulating the rumor that Einstein had withdrawn his name from the cable of protest to Molotov in the Erlich and Alter case. He responded in a letter to a Jewish group, "I have never believed in the guilt of Henryk Erlich and Victor Alter and I have never concealed this conviction."[52]

But the harm was done. By cleverly putting prestigious individuals like Einstein in the position of feeling that "political errors" weighed little against the value of "honest collaboration" between the allies in the war against Nazi Germany, the Communists were able to divert attention from actions that revealed their nature and their real war aims. Crude as the Soviet denials of the Katyn crimes were, they worked—not until many years later did incontrovertible evidence show that Katyn was a Soviet, not a Nazi, crime. Similarly, as crude as the Jewish Anti-Fascist Committee operation was, it served its purpose: Famous Jews (and others) restrained their indignation over the fate of courageous Jewish democratic leaders (whom the Communists wanted to eliminate in anticipation of their postwar strategy) so as not to distract from the fight against the greater threat to the Jews represented by the Nazis.

Erlich was replaced as chairman of the Jewish Anti-Fascist Committee by Solomon Mikhoels. He was soon joined in the leadership by the Soviet Jewish poet Itzik Feffer. In July 1943 they visited the United States and in September, England. Their visits received widespread support from Jews in both countries; they appeared at public meetings, met with leaders of the Jewish communities, and raised money to aid the Soviet Union.[53]

In May 1944 NKVD New York reported to Moscow headquarters in a *Venona* cable that the *Rezidentura* had a copy of an eighteen-page report written by Mikhoels on the activities of Jewish organizations in the United States and of the Jewish leaders he had met.[54] The fact that he was an informer for Soviet intelligence was kept secret from his American friends. Feffer had been a secret police informer since 1944. But their roles did not prevent the KGB from murdering them—Mikhoels in January 1948 and Feffer in August 1952.[55]

Mikhoels and Feffer sent a letter in June of 1946 to M. A. Suslov, director of the Foreign Policy Section of the Central Committee of the Communist Party of the Soviet Union. They boasted of the visits of foreign Jews and their work in promoting Soviet views:

> Recently Mr. B. Z. Goldberg (Waife), the son-in-law of Sholem Aleichem, visited the Soviet Union. He is a prominent public figure in the United States, a member of the executive committee of the Soviet-American Friendship Society (headed by Lamont), chairman of the Committee of Jewish Scientists, Writers, and Artists of the United States (Albert Einstein is president of the Committee), vice-president of Ambidjan, the

All-American Society for Aid to Birobidzhan.... Mr. Goldberg is also a major American journalist, a contributor to the newspapers *Toronto Star, St. Louis Dispatch, New York Post,* and *Today,* and to the magazine *New Republic.* Mr. Goldberg stayed in the Soviet Union from January 11 to June 8, excluding one month when he traveled to Finland, Sweden, and Denmark.

During his stay in the Soviet Union, Mr. Goldberg was received in Moscow by M. I. Kalinin and S.A. Lozovsky; he attended all meetings of the Supreme Soviet of the Soviet Union; and he had a series of meetings with Soviet writers (including a banquet at the Union of Writers), with representatives of the Soviet Jewish community (at the Jewish Antifascist Committee in the USSR headquarters), with leaders of the State Jewish Theater, with the chief rabbi of the Moscow Jewish congregation, Shliffer, and with leaders of the Red Cross, among others.

Mr. Goldberg visited Riga, Tallin, Leningrad, Minsk, Vilnius, Kaunas, Kiev, Odessa, Lvov, Uzhgorod, Mukachevo, Brody, and Stalingrad. He was received by the leading workers and writers in the capitals of the union republics.

During his stay in the Soviet Union, Mr. Goldberg dispatched via the Soviet Information Bureau 33 articles to the American, Canadian, English, Palestinian, Polish, and Yiddish press. The articles were extremely friendly toward the Soviet Union.

Before his departure, Mr. Goldberg began to write a book in English entitled *England, the Opponent of Peace,* and a book in Yiddish entitled *Jewish Culture in the Soviet Union.*[56]

Goldberg was a well-known Communist sympathizer; the Soviet Union could do no wrong. Years later, when Goldberg learned that his friends in the Jewish Anti-Fascist Committee had been tortured and murdered by the Soviet secret police in a 1948 purge, he modified his views.[57]

"Polecats" and "Rats": Spying on Dissidents and Jews

What Goldberg did not know was that he and Paul Novick, charter member of the Communist Party and editor of the *Freiheit*, had been accused at a secret trial of the Jewish Anti-Fascist Committee leaders of being "American spies" who conspired with the Soviet Jews against the Soviet government. The KGB officer in charge of secretly running the Jewish Anti-Fascist Committee was himself a Jew, Gregory Kheifitz.[58] He had previously been the NKVD *Rezident* in San Francisco and was active in atomic espionage.[59] But even this did not spare him from being arrested in 1948 during the KGB campaign against the Jewish Anti-Fascist Committee.[60]

Solomon Lozovsky, an old Bolshevik Jew active in the Jewish Anti-Fascist Committee, was accused of being the ringleader of the conspirators and was also shot. Lozovsky had been head of the Red International of Labor Unions from 1921 until the late 1930s. During the war, he headed the Soviet Information Bureau and was responsible for worldwide propaganda activities.

According to a 1957 official Soviet study of the case by General Cheptsov which was sent to Marshal Zhukov, "At the preliminary investigation Feffer maintained that when he and Mikhoels traveled in the USA in 1943, at the instigation of Lozovsky and JAC, they entered into relationships with certain American capitalists, agreed with them on financial aid and support of nationalistic activity in the USSR, and handed them espionage information. However, in court he denied this and stated that all their meetings in the USA with Americans had been controlled by employees of the USSR embassy and he named them, but none of them was questioned during the investigation."

Cheptsov learned from the case file that Feffer himself had been a KGB agent since 1944. When he asked the KGB officers in charge of the case for evidence that Goldberg and Novick were "American spies," they could not provide it.

General Cheptsov's report on the frame-up was translated and printed in full in a book by the Russian Jewish historian Arkady Vaksberg, who had been working in the Soviet archives to document the persecution of Soviet Jews.[61]

Novick, too, was not aware that he had been named a spy in the secret trial of the Soviet Jews, but the more he learned about Soviet anti-Semitism, the more critical he became of the Soviet Union. In 1971 he was accused of "Jewish nationalism" by the leadership of the American Communist Party and expelled. Documents concerning his case were circulated to Party branches to be read to the membership.[62] There was little opposition within the Party to his expulsion, although he had been a leading figure in Communist activities for many decades.

While the Soviets manipulated and eventually destroyed the Jewish Anti-Fascist Committee for their own ends, American Jewish organizations, focused as they were on basic issues of Jewish survival, concentrated their wartime activities on supporting the Allied war effort. By any measure, they provided substantial help to the Soviet Union, either because they were sincerely deluded about the Soviets' true attitude toward Jews or because they felt they simply had no choice, given the overriding goal of defeating Nazi Germany and rescuing Jews in areas under Nazi control.

In 1943 an organization was established to press the United States government to organize specific activities to protect the Jewish victims in Nazi-held Europe. Called the Emergency Committee to Save the Jewish People of Europe, it was organized by Peter Bergson, a supporter of the right-of-center Zionist Revisionist Movement, and attracted widespread support. Among its original honorary chairmen were Arthur Garfield Hays of the ACLU, Herbert Hoover, William Randolph Hearst, and Harold Ickes, a member of Roosevelt's cabinet.[63]

"Polecats" and "Rats": Spying on Dissidents and Jews

President Roosevelt, in a message to the organization's founding conference in July, insisted that Hitler's defeat was all that was needed to save European Jews.[64] Pressure from the Jewish organization, however, changed his mind, and on January 22, 1944, the president announced the creation of a War Refugee Board to rescue European Jews.[65]

The American Communists were not happy about the Emergency Committee because it distracted from all-out support for the Soviet Union. In addition, the committee had attracted a wide range of people from right to left, many of whom were anti-Communist. In the *Daily Worker* of July 12, 1943, Communist functionary Abraham Chapman complained about the appearance of Herbert Hoover's name among the initiators of the committee. The name of William Randolph Hearst was even more offensive to the Communists. According to Chapman, "The invitation of Hoover and Hearst to this conference is a scandal. It is a disservice to the Jewish people and to the war effort...."

Chapman further complained in the *Daily Worker* on July 28 that among the speakers at the founding conference were Isaac Don Levine, Bertram D. Wolfe, Suzanne LaFollette, and Lawrence Spivak, all knowledgeable people who had spoken out against the Moscow trials and other Soviet atrocities. But according to Chapman, the way to save European Jews was to promote the Anglo-Soviet-American coalition and to open a second front.[66] The United States was building up forces for the Normandy invasion, but the Communists were pushing for an earlier invasion, notwithstanding the added cost of American lives.

Continuing their campaign against the Emergency Committee, the Communists planted a rumor in October 1944 that Eddie Cantor, actor and national cochairman of the committee, had resigned.[67] The Emergency Committee issued an immediate denial.[68] (Indeed, an ad published by the committee as late as January 22, 1945, and signed by Cantor protested the terrible conditions facing the Jews, not only in Soviet "liberated" territory such as Poland and Rumania, but even in France.)[69]

Target: Jewish Telegraphic Agency

Along with distrusting and trying to discredit Jewish rescue organizations which they did not control, the Soviets attempted to subvert sources of accurate, independent information on Jewish affairs. A particular target was Jacob Landau, the managing editor of both the Overseas News Agency and the Jewish Telegraphic Agency. The Overseas News Agency was established in 1940 by Jewish groups to provide the world press with accurate information about the Nazis. The Jewish Telegraphic Agency in turn provided news about Jewish activities to the world press. An experienced journalist, Landau had founded an earlier Jewish telegraphic agency in February 1917 in Holland.[70]

Landau and his colleagues collected a considerable amount of information about Jewish life. Some of it was made available to the press, but some concerning Jewish underground activities in Nazi-occupied Europe had to be kept secret. Landau was dangerous to Soviet interests because they could not control him, and they feared that he might interfere with their plans for postwar Europe. In January 1944 NKVD Mexico City reported that an agent named Elena had advised it that Landau had arrived in Mexico City. Thanks to the NSA work on *Venona*, she was identified as Elena Vazquez Gomez, a known Soviet agent.[71]

Two weeks later another agent told NKVD that Landau had "liberal tendencies" and that, while he supported the policies of the British government, he sometimes published critical articles by the British Labourite Harold Laski.[72]

"Polecats" and "Rats": Spying on Dissidents and Jews

When the Jewish Telegraphic Agency attempted to send a representative to Moscow in May of 1944 to make contact with the Jewish Anti-Fascist Committee, NKVD New York, in its report to Moscow, suggested that an intelligence officer be put in contact with the journalist, presumably to watch him.[73] In September 1944 NKVD Mexico City reported in a *Venona* message to Moscow that it had been able to place an agent in what it called "the intelligence organization which is being set up by Landau." The agent had the cryptonym "Seda," which NSA identified as Elena Vazquez Gomez, earlier referred to by her real first name. In addition, the NKVD was planning for a male agent to give it information on Landau's activities in Mexico.

NKVD agent Kitty Harris, the former mistress of Earl Browder who was now working in Mexico, was assigned the job of developing a detailed business and political biography of Landau with the help of another NKVD agent, the trade union leader Vicente Lombardo Toledano.[74] Toledano was extremely valuable in the campaign against Leon Trotsky that ended with his murder.[75]

In 1945 Beatrice Heiman became a Washington reporter for the Jewish Telegraphic Agency, which gave her access to the White House and other government departments. She was also present at off-the-record background briefings given to correspondents by top government officials. Her previous job was with the Soviet press agency TASS, and during the 1930s she worked in the Soviet embassy as secretary to the ambassador. She also had a relationship through her father, Julius Heiman, with the legendary Soviet espionage officer Arthur Adams, a specialist in the theft of industrial secrets who worked on atom bomb espionage in World War II.[76] Heiman was another Soviet agent in the Jewish Telegraphic Agency who not only spied on Jewish groups but also used the agency as cover for spying on the American government.

Although Jews, as we have seen, were a particular target of Soviet spying for political reasons, they were also considered enemies for religious reasons. In the early 1930s, the American and British Communist parties published a translation of a Soviet book explaining the Communist attitude toward all religion. It was particularly vehement on the Jews: "What about the Jewish religion? It is of very great value to the Jewish capitalists, who, with the help of the rabbis, and the ancient 'sacred' Hebrew tongue (which throws glamour over their innumerable mummeries) hold the people in bondage. All the other religions perform similar services for their respective capitalist masters."

The Catholic Church was another major target of their hatred. The Communists wrote in the same book: "The Catholic Church, with the Pope in its van, is now an important bulwark of all counter-revolutionary organisations and forces. It is the good and faithful servant not only of the old capitalist landowning bourgeoisie, but also of the new bourgeosie—the industrial and financial barons of today. The Catholic Church aids and abets the fascists in their struggle against the revolutionary workers' movement, and it joins the chorus of all the other churches who are clamouring for war against the U.S.S.R. But the Catholic Church does not stand alone. Every other ecclesiastical organisation—Lutheran, Anglican, Jewish, Buddhist, Mohammendan, and other—likewise helps the capitalists and landowners of its country to exploit and stupefy the masses, and keep them steeped in the delusion that the long-suffering of the people, their humiliation on earth, their starved and aching lives will receive an ample reward in heavenly bliss."[77]

The Communists nevertheless thought to benefit by pretending friendship toward Jews—while simultaneously, of course, spying on them. In June 1938 they began the same game with the Catholics. Earl Browder, the CPUSA leader, addressed a message to Catholics blithely claiming that Communists and Catholics had the same goals, adding piously, "We extend the hand of brotherly cooperation to the great mass of democratic Catholics."[78]

The real reason for the "outstretched hand" was explained by Louis Budenz at a secret meeting of the Communist Party Central Committee in December 1938. "We can see what this Catholic question means," he said, "in the building of the democratic front, when we consider the Catholics in the Democratic Party. The overwhelming majority of Catholics of all national origins are Democrats. This is further emphasized when we note their important position in the leadership of the Democrats and in the Democratic apparatus. We cannot begin to touch the Democratic Party at any point, particularly in the industrial centers and also in its progressive wing, without being confronted with active Catholic leaders."[79] The report was sent to Moscow and the authors of this book found it in the Communist International archives. Ironically, Louis Budenz left the Communist Party in 1945 and soon became an active Catholic and anti-Communist. After his conversion, he explained to his fellow Catholics how the Communists used "the outstretched hand" to infiltrate and manipulate them.

Another document in the Comintern archives prepared for Moscow by the American Communists in 1937 was titled "Confidential report on work in religious and non-religious Catholic organizations." The reason for the outstretched hand, it explained, was that "a real race is on as to which force will win over the Catholic people in this country—the forces of reaction and fascism as represented by the Catholic church or the forces of progress and democracy." The report revealed that the Communist Party had sent agents into such Catholic organizations as the Holy Name Society. In one parish, the Communists boasted, "We have a Party comrade who is secretary of the Holy Name branch in this parish, which is one of the largest branches in the city. In addition, this branch is most important because of the fact that it gives leadership and shapes the policies of most of the reactionary and anti-Communist campaigns that are now developing in the Catholic world. This comrade is well known in conservative Irish Catholic circles, and the many offices which he holds in various Catholic organizations...."

The report discussed "one of the most outstanding leaders in the anti-Communist campaign—a Paulist priest, Father Ward. Father Ward is also the editor of a monthly anti-Communist paper entitled *Wisdom*." The publication had a circulation of twenty thousand, but the Party boasted, "We have two Party members now on the editorial staff...." While the Communists didn't identify those Party members, they provided enough information to identify one of them as Jeremiah F. O'Carroll, described as "secretary of the Catholic missionary order, president of the Irish Emergency Relief organization in 1930, widely known as a conservative in Irish circles, staff correspondent on the leading anti-Communist publication *Wisdom*, secretary of the Paulist Holy Name Society...."[80]

O'Carroll's true affiliations were eventually revealed to the Catholic organizations by a young Catholic, William Harmon, who had been enticed into the Communist Party by fellow members of the Transport Workers Union. Although he remained a Communist for only a short time, he was made secretary of his Party unit in September 1937. In testimony in September 1938 before the Dies Committee, Harmon identified O'Carroll as a member of the Communist Party unit: "This is a man who was an organizer in Brooklyn, sent there by the Central Committee [of the Communist Party]. He had connections with the various Catholic organizations in this city; he was a member of the Association of Catholic Trade Unionists, and worked for the Paulist Fathers, and, I understand, was working for them at the time and living with them. He was a member of the Holy Name Society and the Knights of Columbus. He was brought to Brooklyn for the expressed purpose of beating down Communist propaganda.... However, he was transferred out of Brooklyn shortly after that. I exposed him to the Association of Catholic Trade Unionists, and they canned him. He denied it, but he never showed up again in any meeting. I understand he was expelled from various organizations he belonged to."[81] The March 1939 issue of *Wisdom* nevertheless describes J. F. O'Carroll as a "staff correspondent."

The International Workers Order and Espionage

While the NKVD and the Communists used propaganda to undermine their political enemies in various ethnic groups, they also utilized their front, the International Workers Order (IWO), to penetrate those communities. The IWO, with tens of thousands of foreign-born members, divided into nationality groups, was a valuable source of citizenship papers as well as birth and baptismal certificates, all of which could be used to obtain passports for Soviet agents.

From its founding in 1930, the IWO was completely controlled by the Communist Party. The IWO began when a Communist-led group split with the Socialist-led Workman's Circle, a Jewish fraternal organization. The Communists accused the Workman's Circle of being "social-democratic defenders of democracy" and called it the "social-democratic petty bourgeoisie." The 5,000 splitters were soon joined by 6,000 Hungarians, 4,000 Slovaks, and 9,000 Russians, all in groups led by the Communists to form a front organization much larger than the Communist Party.[82]

In a report to the Comintern in 1932, S. Gusev, who had been the Comintern's representative in the United States, referred to the IWO as "a mass organization under our control...."[83] A pamphlet issued to its members that same year explained that "you as a member of the I.W.O. ought to support the Communist Party, which is the only party that stands four-square back of the Soviet Union and is trying to organize and lead the workers in a manner that will bring about the workers' rule also in this country."[84]

In 1933 Max Bedacht, a charter member of the American Communist Party, headed the IWO. It was Bedacht who in 1932 ordered Whittaker Chambers to go into the Communist underground and work for Soviet intelligence.[85]

In the late 1930s Boleslaw Gebert took over the leadership of the Polish section of IWO. Like Bedacht a longtime Party member, he had represented the American Party at the Twelfth Plenum of the Executive Committee of the Communist International using the name "Jack Pringle."[86] Gebert was a Soviet agent with the *Venona* cryptonym "Ataman." One of his jobs for the NKVD was to control Oskar Lange, a supposed non-Communist Polish leader who put himself under Soviet control.

The NKVD decided that Lange would henceforth be given the *Venona* cryptonym "Friend." Since the Soviets believed that he would "undoubtedly play a political role in Poland in the future," it was necessary to use him. Lange was an American citizen but was appointed Polish ambassador to the United States in 1945 by the Polish Provisional Government. He was known to be pro-Soviet but not a member of the Communist Party. According to Arthur Bliss Lane, former U.S. ambassador to Poland, Lange advised him that his appointment had been urged by Joseph E. Davies, the fervently pro-Soviet former U.S. ambassador to the Soviet Union. Lane later learned that Stalin himself had suggested to Harry Hopkins in June 1945 that he promote the Lange appointment.[87]

Lange advised the NKVD in August 1944 that Polish democratic leader Stanislav Mikolajczyk could be brought into the Communist-controlled Provisional Government and that it was not necessary for the Communists to make "serious concessions" to achieve this.[88]

Gebert had meanwhile requested in May 1944 that Moscow supply information that would be useful when Lange visited the Soviet Union.[89] Ten days later Gebert reported to Moscow that Lange had been helpful in the propaganda campaign against the murdered Henryk Erlich and that he had significant contacts in socialist, Czech, and American political circles.[90]

The following month Gebert was turned over to an unidentified NKVD officer with the cryptonym "Selim Khan," who would henceforth run him.[91] By July Gebert reported to his new NKVD handler that a journalist introduced to him by Lange had revealed details of a conversation with Stanislav Mikolajczyk, the non-Communist Polish leader whom the Soviets were attempting to manipulate. Lange also gave Gebert a copy of the report that he had given to the State Department concerning his trip to the Soviet Union and his conversations with Stalin.[92]

In August Gebert reported that Lange had been recommended to Mikolajczyk by Czech leader Eduard Benes as a worthy member of the future Polish government. It was later revealed that Benes, a non-Communist, had been manipulated by Lange to make this recommendation.[93]

Gebert was also used as a conduit for clandestine NKVD funding of Polish-language propaganda books in the United States. In October 1944 NKVD New York reported in a *Venona* message to Moscow that Gebert had been promised a thousand dollars to pay for the publication of a book in Polish. He had received only five hundred when Pavel Klarin, *Venona* cryptonym "Luka," was transferred from New York to Mexico City. Gebert was waiting for the rest of his money.[94] After the war, Gebert returned to Poland, where he served the Communist regime as a trade union official.

Michael Tkach, another Soviet agent, was the longtime leader of the Ukrainian section of IWO and the editor of the *Ukrainian Daily News*, a Communist newspaper. His *Venona* cryptonym was "Perch." In July 1943 Tkach was assigned to manipulate a Ukrainian émigré, Vladislav Biberovich, who was working for the Canadian Department of National Defense. Biberovich had been a Ukrainian nationalist but had switched and become pro-Soviet. The NKVD had plans for him.[95]

In June 1944 Tkach, like Gebert, was turned over to the NKVD officer with the code name "Selim Khan," who apparently was responsible for work among ethnic groups in the United States. Later that month the contact with Tkach was stopped, and he was put temporarily in "cold storage."[96]

But in February 1945 the NKVD decided to reactivate Tkach. He had been the responsibility of NKVD officer Konstantin Shabanov, *Venona* cryptonym "Shakh," who left the United States in September of 1944, but was now reassigned to Aleksandr Saprykin, *Venona* cryptonym "Boris."[97] But Shabanov forgot to hand over the password for the contact, and Saprykin did not know the agent's real name. When he requested that Moscow give him the password and "Perch's" real name,[98] Moscow replied in an incredible breach of security that "Perch's" real name was Tkach.[99]

Elizabeth Bentley later identified Michael Tkach to the FBI as one of Jacob Golos's agents who had supplied information on Ukrainian nationalists to the Soviets.[100]

An even more important agent, Eugene Kahn, was also involved in Jewish circles. Albert Eugene Kahn was born May 11, 1912, in London, England. He was identified to the FBI as a Communist Party member during the 1940s, became president of the Jewish section of the IWO called the Jewish Peoples' Fraternal Order in 1944,[101] and was seen attending a special New York State Convention of the Communist Party in 1945.[102]

In March 1940 Kahn's name began to appear on the masthead of an "anti-Nazi" newsletter, *The Hour.* By June he was listed as its managing editor, and in September he became its editor, replacing Russian-born Dr. Albert Parry. The non-Communist Parry explained to OSS in 1942, "*The Hour* had its inception as the organ of the League Against Nazi Propaganda, with Kahn as Executive Secretary of the League. When it became unfashionable for Communists to be against Nazi propaganda before June 22, 1941, Kahn dropped the League and it went out of business. *The Hour* remained largely as Kahn's own organ, under Communist control, when the others [non-Communists] resigned." He further revealed that "the Anti-Defamation League, which originally helped finance *The Hour,* is no longer doing so because Kahn has followed the Communist line."

When Parry, a journalist and historian, decided to resign from the newsletter in 1939, Kahn threatened "reprisals against his family in Russia should he attack Communism." Although Kahn later told him that the threat had only been "rhetorical," three years later Parry was still terrified and asked the OSS to keep his name secret.

In a June 2, 1942, letter to the OSS, Parry wrote, "The fight never came into the open, mainly because I feared for the safety of my relatives in Russia." He revealed that the American Council Against Nazi Propaganda was controlled by Kahn and Alfred K. Stern, who dissolved it after the Nazi-Soviet Pact.[103] Stern, of course, was later revealed to be a Soviet agent.[104] Parry dutifully wrote a pro-Soviet book in 1944 but told the OSS secretly of his distrust of Communists.[105]

Kahn, for his part, was the coauthor with Michael Sayers of three books that promoted the Soviet party line. The most egregious of these was *The Great Conspiracy*, written in 1946, which claimed that the United States government had been involved in a conspiracy since 1917 to overthrow the Soviet Union. The Soviet disinformation that Trotsky was a Nazi agent was also repeated extensively in the book.[106] The Communist Party USA promoted the book, and in 1947 CPUSA general secretary Eugene Dennis instructed "all State and District secretaries" of the Communist Party to organize the sale of an updated paperback version of it.[107]

Back in 1945 Elizabeth Bentley had revealed to the FBI that Kahn was part of the Jacob Golos spy ring. Kahn had rifled through the files of the Anti-Defamation League, she told the FBI, for information for Golos and the Soviets. Bentley, Golos's lover, had served as his courier. She had been introduced to Kahn in January of 1942 and thereafter collected his Communist Party dues, although he was working in the Communist Party Jewish Bureau and paid dues there as well.[108] In explanation, some Soviet agents paid dues not only to their Party branch but also to the underground Communist unit affiliated with the Soviet intelligence apparatus. One of Kahn's services to the Soviets, according to Bentley, was to collect information about anti-Soviet Ukrainians in the United States.

A Soviet agent with the code name "Boets" (Fighter) appears to have been Albert Kahn. In June 1943 he reported to the New York NKVD that from June 22 to June 24 a congress was scheduled in Winnipeg, Canada, of the Ukrainian Canadian Committee, an umbrella organization for Ukrainian religious and political organizations in Canada. NKVD New York transmitted this information in a *Venona* message.[109]

Golos died in November 1943, but Kahn's information continued to flow to Moscow. In February 1944 New York NKVD reported that "Fighter" had provided information on Jacob Landau, who was a target of Soviet surveillance.[110] When Golos died, his most important agents were transferred to Elizabeth Bentley, but some, like Kahn, who was described in a June *Venona* message as providing only sporadic information on the "Second Line" (émigré matters), were transferred to the unidentified Soviet officer with the code name "Selim Khan."[111] Later that month Kahn and other Golos agents were put into "cold storage," temporarily deactivated until an officer was found to handle them.[112]

By 1946 Kahn was still out of contact with Soviet intelligence. Stepan Apresyan, the former NKVD *Rezident* in New York, was then in San Francisco in the same capacity. In a *Venona* message to Moscow and to his colleagues in New York, he said, "We recommend that you take an interest in the author of *The Great Conspiracy* and former editor of the journal *The Hour,* Albert Kahn...."[113] Apresyan understood Kahn's value as a Soviet agent.

Years later, in June 1960, then-KGB head Alexander Shelepin recommended in a memo to the Central Committee of the Communist Party of the Soviet Union that Albert Kahn, who was in Moscow, be commissioned to write a pamphlet attacking Allen Dulles, head of the CIA. According to Shelepin, the KGB "considers it advisable... to carry out the following measures targeted at further discrediting CIA activity and compromising its leader Allen Dulles." When the document was found in Soviet archives, the Cold War International History Project in Washington contacted Kahn's son, Brian, who stated that "to his knowledge his father was never approached to write a publication ridiculing Allen W. Dulles and never did so, and that, while sympathetic to Socialism and the USSR, he would never have written anything at the direction of Soviet intelligence."[114]

A son should have faith in the integrity of his father, but in this case, the faith was misplaced. Albert Kahn did not write this particular pamphlet, but he did author a good deal of Soviet disinformation. The anti-CIA pamphlet was signed by Bob Edwards, a prominent maverick Labour member of the British Parliament, and Kenneth Dunne, a journalist, and was published in 1961. In 1965 the CIA said that although the ostensible authors were the Labour member of Parliament and the British journalist, "it is now known that the manuscript was researched in Moscow by a senior KGB disinformation officer, Col. Vassily Sitnikov, and then served up for final polish and printing in the United Kingdom."[115]

Although Kahn didn't write this particular smear for the KGB, he had participated in a similar KGB disinformation campaign almost a decade earlier. In 1951 the KGB decided to discredit Major General Robert Grow, the military attaché of the American embassy in Moscow. His personal diary was photographed by Soviet agents working in the American embassy, but in order to conceal where it was copied, the diary was sent to the Ministry of State Security (Stasi) of East Germany.[116] The Stasi used its agent, a former British serviceman named Richard Squires, to release selected portions of the diary for a disinformation book. To conceal the Russian source of the diary, Squires pretended that it had been obtained while General Grow was in the Allied Zone of occupied Germany, and Frankfurt was given as the scene of the photography. This also helped the case against General Grow since it indicated that he had violated security by carrying his diary into Germany rather than leaving it securely at the Moscow American embassy.

Squires's book distorted the material in Grow's diary, added other disinformation themes, and was published in East Germany, but no indication of this is revealed in the book. Squires instead claimed that he had received the diary from an unnamed old friend who was the Berlin correspondent of a London newspaper. The fictional British journalist supposedly received the diary from an equally fictional American officer in Frankfurt. The real source, the Stasi, got the diary from the KGB.

"Polecats" and "Rats": Spying on Dissidents and Jews

The central theme of Squires's book was that General Grow was plotting a war against the Soviet Union. The book was supposedly translated from an English edition called *On the War Path*.[117] But there never was an English edition.

In July 1952 Kahn issued a pamphlet entitled *The Diary of General Grow, as exposed by Major Richard Squires, Introduction by Albert E. Kahn*. It was apparent that Kahn had never even seen the German-language book. It was called, he wrote, *On the Road to War*, a mistranslation of *Auf Dem Kriegspfad*, or *On the War Path*. What Kahn had was an English translation of part of the book and photocopies of small clippings from the diary. Kahn referred to "General Grow's espionage operations in the Soviet Union and... his feverishly eager efforts to promote a third world war."[118] As military attaché, Grow was responsible for collecting public information about Soviet military activity. Soviet military attachés do the same but also often run espionage agents. Grow was not accused of running agents. The quotations that indicated a desire to start a third world war were not only out of context but also inconsistent with both the general's view and American policy.

After General Grow was court-martialed and convicted, he retired from the army.[119] The Soviets benefited from destroying the career of an American officer and, more importantly, from damaging America's image with false charges of warmongering. And Albert Kahn played an important role in assisting this KGB disinformation operation.

One of the single most important Communist underground apparatchiks surfaced in 1944 as a member of the General Council of the IWO.[120] But his real job was "general director of organization of the IWO." He was Sam Milgrom,[121] who in 1947 was elected executive secretary of the organization.[122] This was a good place for an experienced Communist underground worker to put his hands on the identity documents of many foreign-born members, which could be used to provide cover for Soviet "illegal" officers and agents. (The IWO was ordered dissolved by the New York State Courts in 1951 when an extensive trial revealed that money supposedly used to provide insurance for its members had been illegally channeled for Communist Party purposes.)

At the time of Milgrom's death in 1977, the Communist Party newspaper *Daily Worker* revealed that he was "known in the Party as A. W. Mills."[123] Louis Budenz, the former Communist Party official, testified in a court case against the IWO that "at a National Committee meeting as early as 1937, I was introduced to Mr. Mills by Jack Stachel as a veteran member of the Communist Party underground in this country—those are the exact words he used."[124] Milgrom used the Mills pseudonym when he worked in Paris during the Spanish Civil War in the late 1930s in the secret apparatus of the American Communist Party that provided manpower and support to the International Brigades.[125]

In the post–World War II period, the reason for the Soviets' interest in the activities of American Jewish organizations and their connections with Jews in wartime Europe became clear. The major Soviet campaign against Jews in formerly Nazi-occupied Europe took shape and provided, in retrospect, the best explanation for the wartime murders of Erlich, Alter, and the Polish officers at Katyn. They wanted no competition in their new imperial domains and considered Jews with contacts in the West a threat.

Viewed in this perspective, the disappearance of Raoul Wallenberg, which caused years of anguish to his family in Sweden and to the thousands of Jews whom he had saved from the Nazis, can be explained as a chapter in the Soviet strategy to eliminate all sources of opposition to their rule. Wallenberg was the Swedish diplomat who, when working with President Roosevelt's War

"Polecats" and "Rats": Spying on Dissidents and Jews

Refugee Board, rescued Hungarian Jews from the Nazis. On January 17, 1945, when the Red Army captured Budapest, Wallenberg was arrested by SMERSH, the Soviet unit charged with eliminating potential enemies in the newly conquered territory.[126] The word SMERSH was a contraction of the Russian words for "Death to Spies." Wallenberg disappeared in the Soviet Gulag, where he died.

The anti-Jewish campaign in Eastern Europe culminated with the trial in Czechoslovakia of leading Communist officials, most of whom were Jews, in November of 1952. The charge against the victims, chiefly Rudolf Slansky, was of being "Trotskyite-Titoite, Zionist, bourgeois-nationalist traitors and enemies of the Czechoslovak people, of the people's-democratic system and of Socialism, and being in the service of the American imperialists."[127] It was quite an indictment—and totally false.

Of course, the defendants confessed and were convicted by the kangaroo court; most were executed. The trial shocked Western Jews. A study of the trial by the American Jewish Committee stated: "The trial of Rudolf Slansky and thirteen co-defendants which took place in Prague November 20-27, 1952, and ended with the hanging of eleven defendants on December 3, 1952, has very serious implications for the security of the Jews throughout the world."[128]

The Jewish Communist victims in Eastern Europe were not Zionists and were certainly not American agents. Most were in the anti-Nazi underground during the war and had contact with American officials who were helping these operations and Jewish groups in the West who were helping to rescue Jews in the occupied areas. These contacts were Stalin's excuse to wipe out many Communists who had not been in the Soviet Union during the war. Non-Communist Jews who were active in democratic movements in these areas were also persecuted for their contact with Western Jews. Persecution and personal repugnance notwithstanding, Soviet intelligence continued to try to use Jews as agents. A secret study was made by the KGB in 1986 on the subject *The Peculiarities of Recruit Development of Foreign Jews Who Are Ethnically Tied to the USSR*. Prepared by Colonel A. A. Ivanov, the study noted:

> In many instances, Jews living in the West who are ethnically tied to the USSR possess vital intelligence information by nature of their positions and type of work. Some of them occupy prominent social-political positions and play a notable role in financial, economic, business and scientific technical areas; they serve in government and state agencies; they work in commercial and diplomatic representations, in military organizations, in important scientific-technical centers, and in mass media organizations; and they have access to valuable intelligence information.
>
> Of particular interest in this vein are Jewish immigrants to the USA from the "first" (the end of the 19th and beginning of the 20th centuries) and second (the 20s-30s) emigration, and their descendants who continue to maintain ties with relatives living in the Soviet Union. As a rule, they occupy a firm position in industrial, financial, and scientific-technical circles of the country, and also in large American-Jewish organizations. Many of them work in places that are targets of primary intelligence interest: in the State Department, Congress, the National Security Agency, the White House, the Defense Department, and others.

Some of Colonel Ivanov's analysis of Jews had a positive, if somewhat condescending, flavor. He noted, for example, that when attempting to recruit Jews, the process should not be drawn out but done quickly because "Jews have a trait that is undesirable for us, openness in their relationships with their compatriots and their wives." Further, the Jewish potential recruit "must be convinced that he is dealing with an intelligent, educated, erudite, well-rounded person. This is obligatory because the operative's level of intellectual development is one of the determining factors of his authority in the eyes of a Jewish RDT [recruitment development target]."

On the other hand, Ivanov's suggestion that KGB officers read the old anti-Semitic book signed by Henry Ford, *The International Jew*, indicates the source of some of his conclusions.[129] He referred to elements in the Jewish character such as "vanity, haughtiness, self-aggrandizement, and an increased self-appreciation." He claimed further, "This striving for material wealth, a passion for money, and the predominance of personal egotistical interests in the hierarchy of moral values are factors which, as a whole, could play a positive role in attracting Jews to cooperate with KGB foreign intelligence."[130]

It is interesting to note that among the many Americans who were arrested or identified as mercenary agents of the KGB during the 1980s and early 1990s, virtually none were Jews. Apparently Colonel Ivanov's tendentious evaluation of Jewish vulnerabilities for KGB recruitment was as bizarre as Stalin's view of the Jews as non-Americans.

CHAPTER 13

Target: Journalists

JOURNALISTS CAN BE A TWOFOLD ASSET for an intelligence service. They not only often have sensitive information from government sources, but they can "spin" their articles to promote a specific viewpoint. The KGB always appreciated these traits, and during World War II, when it was called the NKVD, it successfully used Communist journalists in the West to carry out its subversive tasks.

In the years leading up to World War II, a ready pool of likely recruits was developed among veterans of the International Brigades in the Spanish Civil War. One of them, Samuel Krafsur, worked for the Soviet TASS news agency after returning from Spain. In May 1944 the New York *Rezidentura* reported in a *Venona* message to Moscow:

> After many months of study we propose to use an employee of TASS, Samuel Krafsur, henceforth "Yaz," for cultivating newspapermen's circles in Washington. "Yaz" is a "Zemlyak" [member of the Communist Party], was in the International Brigade in Spain. He is absolutely devoted to the USSR, always zealously carries out minor tasks set by [NKVD officer] Vladimir Pravdin in connection with obtaining information. Systematic work among "Yaz's" extensive connections will provide opportunities for obtaining valuable information and also of studying individual subjects for signing on [recruitment].

One of Krafsur's contacts was Joseph Berger, the personal secretary of the chairman of the Democratic National Committee. The *Rezidentura* suggested that, since Krafsur's NKVD boss, Pravdin, was in Washington, a New York–based NKVD officer be put in contact with him so that information he obtained could be received in New York promptly.[1] Although more details about Berger, who wrote under the pen name Jeremiah Digges, were sent to Moscow on May 25, 1945, including his close relationship with the American Communist Party, there is no evidence in *Venona* that Berger himself was ever recruited for Soviet espionage. Nevertheless, Krafsur, through this contact, was able to give the NKVD a priceless window on the inside doings of the Roosevelt administration during wartime.

By September 12, 1944, NKVD Moscow got around to checking Krafsur out with the Comintern. In a message to Dimitroff, Pavel Fitin asked that the Comintern archives be checked on "Samuel Krafsur, born in 1913 in Boston, member of the CPUSA since 1934, who was in Lincoln Brigade in Spain in 1937." As with other such typed messages, a blank space was left and filled in by hand with the name of the agent. Even NKVD secretaries were not supposed to know the real names of agents. Dimitroff responded on September 23 that there was no derogatory information on Krafsur.[2]

Krafsur, as an American, could circulate among other journalists and sometimes attend off-the-record press conferences. On August 17, 1944, he attended one such press conference where Secretary of State Cordell Hull made some off-the-record comments, which Krafsur dutifully reported to the NKVD. Hull condemned groups that were trying to isolate the Soviet Union, which no doubt pleased the Soviets, and they had to be amused by some of his other comments: "What you think about the Russians' temperament, customs, and manners should play no part in these questions.... The methods and system of the USSR may be shocking in questions of its internal policy. However, if you try to oust the USSR from the international arena, it will lead to serious consequences." He went on to refer to "the repulsion which is felt toward individual Russian internal questions."[3]

Soviet intelligence officers were trolling the waters of American journalists, trying to hook even bigger prey. NKVD officer Vladimir Pravdin maintained his own contacts with journalists, including Walter Lippmann, a leading opinion maker, with whom he met regularly. Sometimes Lippmann would tell Pravdin something the Soviets considered important. But the NKVD wanted more from him, so, as we shall soon see, it planted an agent in Lippmann's office.

In September of 1944 Lippmann told Pravdin that there were disagreements between Roosevelt and Churchill on the question of the future of Germany and the role of Britain in the occupation.[4] On September 9, and repeated again on September 14, the *Rezidentura* reported to Moscow that Krafsur had spoken with *Baltimore Sun* reporter Paul Ward, who confirmed Lippmann's statement about Roosevelt/Churchill disagreements. At the same time, Joseph Bird, a *Washington Star* reporter, told the same thing to Lawrence Todd, another employee of TASS.[5] Ward and Bird thought they were sharing information just with other American journalists, not with Moscow via the NKVD.

In October, Krafsur obtained a statement made by Averill Harriman, U.S. ambassador to the Soviet Union, before a closed meeting of American correspondents only. Harriman explained the Soviet plans to establish a puppet state in Poland: "The USSR wants to have friendly disposed neighbors and will not allow the seizure of power by the professional elements in the backward countries."[6] This view of an important American diplomat encouraged Soviet expansion and the takeover of these "backward countries," which had achieved independence years earlier and had a higher culture and living standards than the Soviet Union.

The Recruitment of I. F. Stone

Krafsur continued his attempts to recruit American journalists in the fall of 1944. When Pravdin tried three times, unsuccessfully, to contact I. F. Stone, an openly pro-Communist journalist, Krafsur was told to sound him out. Stone did not respond, and Bernie Chester was then ordered by the NKVD to check out his relationship with the Communist Party.[7]

Meanwhile, Pravdin and the New York *Rezident*, Stepan Apresyan, felt a personal antagonism. Each complained to Moscow about the other. On October 10 Apresyan sent a *Venona* message to Moscow outlining the dispute, saying that although Pravdin had brought Krafsur into the NKVD's work, he was not utilizing the agent efficiently. Pravdin, undeterred, insisted that he had good contacts who "provide useful comments on the foreign policy" of the United States; nevertheless, he asked Moscow to transfer him to Washington so that he could recruit more "valuable people." He suggested that he needed to make more use of the Communist Party USA in NKVD operations, including those against the FBI, and in setting up "safe houses." According to Pravdin, "Without the help of the Communist Party USA we are completely powerless. Apresyan rushed in to add to the same message:

> In this note Pravdin has put in a nutshell his whole conception of the reasons why he has made no real progress, and his approach to the next few months. His view that without [his moving to] Washington and [the help of] Earl Browder, we are doomed to vegetate is mistaken. It is not true that everything of value is in Washington and it is doubly untrue that without Browder we are "powerless." I consider that in any case we shall have to have recourse to the help of the Communist Party USA,

but they ought not to be the one and only base especially if you take into account the fact that in the event of Thomas Dewey's being elected [president], this source may dry up.[8]

This *Venona* message makes clear both the importance of the American Communist Party to Soviet espionage and, in particular, the role of the Party's leader, Earl Browder. Those who argue that the American Communist Party was not a significant factor in Soviet espionage are clearly wrong. Even more, and equally clear, those Russian writers who claim that headquarters was unaware of the use of Party members are concealing the truth. This message, and many others, show that the *Rezidentura* reported to headquarters whenever it used Communist Party members—the majority of its agents. The documents in the Comintern archives disclosed that Fitin, head of the Foreign Department of NKVD, was fully aware of the use of American Communists in espionage and personally checked their ideological purity with the Comintern.

Further on in the same message Pravdin reported that he was planning to recruit I. F. Stone and Joseph Barnes, foreign news editor of the *New York Herald Tribune*. Apresyan responded in the message to Moscow, "The signing up of Barnes is obviously not only inadvisable but unrealizable; however, it is desirable to use him without signing him up."[9] The message does not make clear why it was "obviously" inadvisable and unrealizable to recruit Barnes to the NKVD. One explanation may be that he was already working for the GRU. Whittaker Chambers, the 1930s liaison between the GRU and the American Communist Party underground, told the Senate Subcommittee on Internal Security on August 16, 1951, that his superior, J. Peters, introduced him to Frederick Vanderbilt Field to assist in the recruitment of State Department official Lawrence

Duggan for Soviet espionage. Peters told Chambers that Field was a member of a Communist Party underground cell together with Joseph Barnes and that "some difficulty had arisen between the two men about their wives." The Communist Party's underground apparatus gathered information which J. Peters provided to the GRU. Field's recruitment of Duggan failed because he was already working for the NKVD. Barnes later married Field's wife.[10]

The recruitment of I. F. Stone was reported to Moscow headquarters in subsequent *Venona* messages. In October 1944 Pravdin advised Moscow that he had finally met with Stone. He said that he had tried to contact Stone several times previously, both personally and through Krafsur, but Stone had been avoiding both of them. Stone told Pravdin when they finally met that he had avoided them, "fearing the consequences," because the attempts to contact him had been made with "insufficient caution." When Pravdin then attempted to recruit him, Stone "gave him to understand that he was not refusing his aid but one should consider that he had three children and did not want to attract the attention of the FBI." Stone, in the end, agreed to work for the NKVD and meet regularly with an officer, but as he seldom went to New York, Pravdin suggested assigning someone to work with him in Washington. Although Stone explained that he was doing well financially, he said that "he would not be averse to having a supplementary income." Pravdin suggested to Moscow that if it agreed to this "business" relationship, Stone had to do his part and really produce.[11]

The NKVD "business" relationship with Stone worked out, as shown by a December 1944 *Venona* message which reported that a group of journalists, including Stone, provided Pravdin with information about the plans of the U.S. General Staff to cope with the German counteroffensive in the Battle of the Bulge and resume the Allied offensive.[12] Though the other journalists identified, Walter Lippmann and Raymond Gram Swing, did not know that Pravdin was an intelligence officer rather than a fellow journalist, Stone knew full well.

Stone's *Venona* code name was "Blin," the Russian word for "pancake" (similar to "blintze"). Stone complained in his column of November 11, 1951, that the *New York Herald Tribune* had reported on his leftist activities. He joked that he would not be surprised if he read in the *Herald Tribune* "that I was smuggled in from Pinsk in a carton of blintzes...."[13] Intelligence tradecraft requires that agents not know their code names, but as *Venona* revealed, in a number of cases it seems that some did, and Stone was one of them. His inside joke was odd. You might talk about smuggling something from Russia in a vodka bottle or caviar jar or some other normal Soviet export, but blintzes?

In 1992 a British journalist reported a speech at Exeter University by retired KGB general Oleg Kalugin. According to Andrew Brown, writing in *The Independent*:

> Mr. Kalugin said that at the end of the Second World War people would come in dozens to volunteer to work for the Soviets, especially in France and Italy. But it was also true that in the United States the KGB "maintained very serious sources until the late-40s." The crucial year was 1956. Khrushchev's secret speech denouncing Stalinism (which leaked to the West and revealed the horrors of mass executions) revolted the whole world. After 1956, the intelligence service simply could not recruit people on ideological grounds. The invasion of Czechoslovakia in 1968 was another almost mortal blow. "We had an agent—a well-known American journalist—with a good reputation, who severed his ties with us after 1956. I myself convinced him to resume them. But in 1968, after the invasion of Czechoslovakia... he said he would never again take any money from us."[14]

In articles published at the time, authors Breindel and Romerstein identified I. F. Stone as the agent Kalugin had discussed.[15] Despite the controversy that ensued, it is clear from the evidence that Stone was indeed a Soviet agent.

When the Soviet army crushed the Czechs' attempt to organize what they called "Communism with a human face," I. F. Stone wrote in his newsletter of September 23, 1968, that "the hopes of democracy under Communism have been destroyed...." But his main concern was that "the strengthening of the hard-liners in Moscow will strengthen the hard-liners in Washington."[16]

In the years before the invasion of Hungary, Stone was an enthusiastic Stalin fan. In 1949, when Stalin reached his seventieth year, his disciples wrote special pamphlets in his honor. His closest associate, the director of the mass murders and slave labor camps, Lavrenti Beria, set the tone for KGB participation in promoting the Stalin cult: "On this memorable day, the words of greeting to our leader sound with new force in the world's every tongue and dialect: Glory to Comrade Stalin. On to new victories, under the leadership of the great Stalin."[17]

Stone used his column to honor Stalin's birthday and compare him to those he called "pigmies," such as Truman and Attlee, who then led the governments of the United States and England. Stone was also enamored with "the newly victorious Mao Tse-tung, Nehru and Tito." But, he said, "They have a long way to go before they can match the tough and crafty old revolutionary who has ruled Russia for a quarter of a century."[18] Stone failed to mention the purges, the mass murders, the slave labor camps, and the increasingly obvious anti-Semitic campaign that symbolized Stalin's rule.

A KGB officer in the Stalin era was sure to earn considerable praise from his bosses if he could place an article honoring Stalin on his birthday in an American newspaper. The Soviet Union used this to bolster KGB chief Beria's claim that in "every tongue and dialect" Stalin was greeted on his birthday.

Two days after Stone's panegyric to Stalin, he wrote another nasty little piece about Harry Truman, complaining that the American president had invoked the name of God at a memorial to the war dead at Arlington Cemetery. According to Stone, "There is some doubt as to whether and how much Mr. Truman himself believes in God."[19] Stone found only good in Stalin and only bad in the American president.

Many other examples show how Stone promoted Soviet disinformation themes. Perhaps the most outrageous was his book *The Hidden History of the Korean War*. As everyone knows, on June 25, 1950, the North Korean army, unleashed by Stalin, invaded South Korea. The Soviet Union and its supporters predictably claimed that the South Koreans attacked North Korea. In his book, Stone used bizarre reasoning to back this bit of information. One example was his quotation from John Foster Dulles, who had predicted that "positive action" would help preserve peace in the Far East. Stone implied that he was referring to the Korean War, which began three days later.[20] The book was filled with this sort of deliberate misinterpretation of statements designed to conceal the fact that the Communist side started the war. Some of the false statements supporting the Soviet line were traceable to Soviet disinformation, but others appeared to be Stone's own inventions.

During the Vietnam War, Stone again did his part for Soviet propaganda. In his newsletter of September 26, 1966, he reported a story about an American airman shot down in Vietnam who had escaped from a POW camp and was rescued:

> Dengler said the villagers were friendly. No one asked him how
> they felt about U.S. bombings, or what kind of gas we were

dropping on them—at a press conference 3 days earlier in San Diego, Dengler said that when he heard a plane overhead and smelled the gas it was dropping, he said to himself, "Man, that is Uncle Sam's gas. That is real" and came out of hiding and laid down an SOS.[21]

The truth was that the Americans were not dropping gas on the Vietnamese, and Dengler hadn't said that they were. Dengler told the story, misquoted by Stone, in testimony before the Senate Armed Services Committee. He described how the helicopters jettisoned gasoline while coming in for the rescue. He smelled the gas and knew they were coming down for him.[22] When the story was exposed, Stone's defenders argued that he had just made a mistake. Oddly, all his mistakes were anti-American; he never made mistakes in favor of the United States.

One technique used by the KGB was to release a disinformation story through overt channels, such as the official Soviet press. This would then be replayed not only in the legitimate Western press but also by Soviet agents, who would emphasize the particular disinformation themes. In January 1968, before the invasion of Czechoslovakia, which caused the KGB to lose Stone again, the Soviets released an interview with Kim Philby, the KGB agent who had escaped before the British could arrest him. In the interview Philby attacked the former deputy director of the FBI, D. Milton Ladd, saying, "This astonishingly dense personage tried to convince me in all seriousness that Franklin Roosevelt was a Comintern agent."[23] The story was false but was repeated by Stone as part of a program to denigrate the FBI. On the same page, Stone printed a quotation from Soviet dissident Vladimir Bukovsky, then in a Soviet prison. Of all statements by Bukovsky condemning the Soviet slave labor camps and other atrocities, Stone sought fit to print a statement in support of freedom of speech and in the Communist Party's right to exist in the United States.

Target: Lippmann

Walter Lippmann was one of the most serious and respected American journalists during World War II. While many disagreed with Lippmann's syndicated column, most were aware that he had good sources of information in the Roosevelt administration. The NKVD also knew and thus sought to take advantage of Lippmann's government connections. While Lippmann was willing to meet and have discussions with the NKVD officer Pravdin, who he believed was simply a TASS correspondent, he certainly would not knowingly have given him sensitive information. But that problem had already been solved by planting an agent as Lippmann's secretary.

Mary Price, Lippmann's secretary, had been turning over information from his files to Soviet agent handler Jacob Golos since 1941.[24] A June 1943 *Venona* message shows that not only was Price, code name "Dir," supplying information, but when making a trip to Mexico to visit her brother, she also carried NKVD messages to an agent in Mexico City.[25]

Communist Party leader Earl Browder had decision-making power about how to handle the agents, which made the NKVD's job difficult. In June 1944, for example, Elizabeth Bentley, who took over some of Golos's agents, met with Browder and brought him together with Mary Price. When the two women were alone, Mary said that "she had informed Browder that she wanted to get out of the whole business and that he had said he would think it over and let her know." A few days later, Browder told Bentley that he had decided to let Price go and that she should advise Price to that effect.[26]

When Bentley told this to the FBI in 1945, she had no documentary evidence to uphold her story. But once again, Bentley's word was confirmed years later when a *Venona* message was decoded. As discussed earlier, New York reported to Moscow:

> Some weeks ago Bentley ["Umnitsa"] told Akhmerov ["Mer"] that Browder ["Rulevoj"], as a result of a conversation with Mary Price ["Dir"], had apparently decided that Price must be withdrawn completely from our work in order to employ her fully in Communist Party USA work. In Browder's opinion Price's nerves had been badly shaken and her health is poor, which renders her unsuitable for our work. In Akhmerov's opinion it is possible to get Browder [who was Akhmerov's wife's uncle] to change his opinion about the advisability of this decision, which Akhmerov suspects was made under pressure from Bentley, who for some reason dislikes Price. Akhmerov has informed Bentley that if Price is really ill she will need rather to be withdrawn for a rest, but afterwards be used in liaison with a conspirative apartment [NKVD safe house], etc. She has been working for a long time and has acquired considerable experience. Akhmerov proposes that she should not be employed in active Communist Party work. Telegraph your opinion.[27]

Akhmerov didn't want to lose Price, who could provide sensitive information from Lippmann gleaned from government officials, but Browder had the last word. By September 1945 Mary Price was working in Greensboro, North Carolina, for the Communist-front Southern Conference for Human Welfare.[28]

Mission in Moscow

Journalists, even if they were known Communists, were sometimes trusted by other Americans. As a result, they could obtain information of interest to NKVD that no Soviet citizen could hope to get. This was true even in Moscow. Janet Ross, a member of the American Communist Party, worked in the Comintern in the 1930s and 1940s with her husband, Nat Ross. On August 11, 1939, the Secretariat of the Executive Committee of the Comintern decided that the American Communist Party should assign a *Daily Worker* correspondent to work in the press section of the Comintern. The orders were issued to the American Communist Party.[29]

Although Nat and Janet Ross were already in Moscow, on October 10 Pat Toohey, the American Communist Party representative, suggested that they be sent back home to the United States, where they were needed because of the increased tension due to the Nazi-Soviet Pact.[30] He was overruled, and the two were kept in Moscow. In August 1940 Nat and Janet were assigned to a special training school of the Comintern.[31]

From the Comintern's viewpoint, it was good that they remained in Moscow. Janet Ross, calling herself Janet Weaver, became the *Daily Worker* correspondent in Moscow, which gave her access not only to the other American journalists but also to the diplomats in the American embassy.

Janet would report to George Dimitroff on her conversations with American diplomats and journalists, and he in turn would send her reports to Foreign Minister Molotov. A number of the reports and Dimitroff's transmittal memos to Molotov are still in the Comintern archives. A few, unfortunately, have been lost in the intervening years, but those that still remain tell a shocking story.

Dimitroff sent Molotov a report on August 8, 1942, from Janet Ross based on a meeting at the American embassy between American journalists and General Omar Bradley. Dimitroff's note was marked top secret, but Ross's report has been lost. On August 26 Dimitroff sent Molotov another of Janet's reports. This one was preserved, and it concerned an informal party in honor of Ambassador William

Standley given by the American correspondents in Moscow. Also present were military attachés. As a result of this discussion with the ambassador, the correspondents concluded that the Soviet demand for a second front in Europe would not take place soon. This helped confirm the official statements made to the Soviets themselves by the U.S. government.

In September of that year Wendell Willkie visited Moscow. Although a Republican who had run for president against Roosevelt in 1940, he had become a strong supporter of the president. Janet was able to get directly from Willkie, and indirectly through other journalists, further valuable information for the Soviets. According to Willkie, Roosevelt wanted to open a second front, but Churchill was delaying it. She also overheard part of a conversation between Willkie and Ambassador Standley in which they seemed to be arguing, but she couldn't determine about what.

On November 27 Janet reported to Dimitroff that she was present at a dinner at the American embassy to which only Americans had been invited. She reported what she had heard there from the American military people and journalists. One of the military babbled that American successes in the Pacific war were due to something so secret that only a few people knew about it. We know now that it was the breaking of the Japanese codes—a most closely held secret.

On March 8, 1943, Janet was able to clue in the Soviets on the views of Ambassador William Standley about how the Soviets were concealing the extent of American Lend-Lease help. Janet's secret report to Molotov, via Dimitroff, revealed that the ambassador had firsthand experience meeting Russians who did not know that the war materials they were using were American-supplied. The Soviets had been concealing this. At a closed meeting with a small group of American journalists, Standley suggested that although Soviet censorship would try to prevent it, the journalists should do their best to report the story to the American people. Janet's report, of course, helped harden official Soviet attitudes toward the ambassador.

Two days later, Harry Hopkins pressed for the removal of Ambassador Standley on the grounds that the ambassador had lost Stalin's confidence as a result of his complaint to the American journalists. Hopkins enlisted the support of former ambassador Joseph Davies to help him convince the president to fire Ambassador Standley. When the decision was made, Standley resigned and was replaced by Averill Harriman.[32]

On June 30, 1943, Dimitroff sent Molotov a secret report from Janet on a meeting between American and British correspondents with Arthur Hays Sulzberger, owner of the *New York Times*. The conversation was wide-ranging, covering the second front, Japan, and even the forthcoming 1944 presidential elections. Ross treated Sulzberger's views as coming from a well-informed American journalist but was unhappy that he was critical of the Soviet Union. She reported with glee that when *New York Times* foreign correspondent Cy Sulzberger, Arthur's nephew, was leaving the meeting, he had said, knowing that she was a *Daily Worker* reporter, "It is well known to you that your newspaper hates my uncle. This talk is strictly unofficial. Do not disclose it, please." Janet said she responded that she understood, adding that she would in any case be ashamed to "repeat such stupidity." She did not tell Sulzberger that she reported everything to Dimitroff and Molotov.[33]

As soon as the NKVD received Janet's report (all such material, even if sent to Molotov, went to the NKVD) it asked the New York *Rezidentura* for a report on Sulzberger. The *Rezidentura* reported back immediately that he had been born in 1891, had graduated from Columbia University, and was a member of the Democratic Party. It also reported that he was connected with "reactionary circles in the State Department," citing specifically

Sumner Welles, undersecretary of state, and Loy Henderson, an expert on the Soviet Union.

It was extremely valuable for the Soviet Union to have an American available who could understand other Americans and had access to the U.S. embassy and to Western journalists in Moscow. Janet had joined the Communist Party in 1934, when she was twenty-five years old. Nat Ross had joined the Communist Party in 1928, when he was twenty-four. They were well-trained Communists and served the Soviet Union well. Nat Ross left the Communist Party in 1957 after reading Khrushchev's secret speech denouncing Stalin but has refused to discuss what he knows about the Communist Party USA and its secret relationships with the Soviet Union.

With the end of World War II and the start of the Cold War, the Soviets lost most of their ideological assets. But of those that remained, journalists were considered very important. The KGB trained its subordinate intelligence services, such as the East German Stasi, to use journalists as agents and for "active measures"—that is, influence operations. In a 1992 book, two former Stasi officers described how their service was taught its tradecraft by the KGB. They quote from a speech of the head of the active measures section of Stasi, Colonel Rolf Wagenbreth, at a lecture at the Stasi training school:

> A journalist who is competent most of the time has a good reputation in society. Politicians esteem him, stiff-necked brass hats loosen up in his presence, vain artists seek contact with him, industrial bosses want to win him over for their own purposes.... Once he has been recruited as a spy or as a channel for disseminating certain types of information, he can and may do almost anything in the eyes of the public: He may question sensitive personnel with access to classified information without being suspected.... He may carry tiny cameras with him.... He

can drive and jet all over the world.... He can also spread disinformation, he can try to trip up a political opponent, he can generate sympathy or aversion and mobilize the public for or against something. I am talking here, of course, about Western journalists. For all of these reasons, we work with this "media" target from the very beginning and, if I might say so, not without success.[34]

A few journalists remained agents of the KGB out of conviction and some for money. But most journalists in the West became increasingly critical of Communist ideas and Soviet reality. The KGB, for its part, increased the activity of its disinformation service and continued to prey on often unwitting journalists to spread its message. As for Soviet Communist journalists, they lost their credibility in the West.

CHAPTER 14

Conclusion

BEGINNING IN 1938 and continuing well into the 1970s, a number of government institutions concerned with subversion and espionage sought to understand the nature and purpose of Communist activities in the United States and the relationship of the Communist Party USA to Soviet espionage. These institutions included law enforcement and counterintelligence agencies, such as the FBI, and legislative committees, such as the House Committee on Un-American Activities and the Senate Subcommittee on Internal Security, which were charged with developing legislation to protect the nation's security.

The information accumulated and analyzed by the people involved in this work led both elected and executive branch officials to conclude that the Communists did not represent just another political party. Their loyalty was to a foreign power, the Soviet Union, and their goal was nothing less than the subversion and destruction of American democracy. To advance that goal, the leadership of the Communist Party conscripted whichever of its members were capable of espionage to assist the Soviet intelligence service.

It was not really difficult to demonstrate Communism's subversive intentions; after all, the Party's literature, oratory, and organizational style scarcely attempted to conceal its ultimate objective. In their most sectarian period, the Communists didn't hesitate to heap scorn on what they called sham "bourgeois" democracy and openly to propose leading the way toward a "Soviet" America. Even in periods when it sought to project a mainstream face and its leaders referred to Communism as "20th Century Americanism," the Communist Party did not deny that it viewed capitalism as fundamentally unreformable; nor did it deny that, for the Party, meaningful change required the forceful overthrow of the American government.

Dissent, in the American constitutional system, is viewed as a legitimate activity; the reformist tradition, for instance, has always been respected in the United States. Loyalty to a foreign power is something else altogether. It is treason.

The Communists, of course, never admitted to being traitors who placed the interests of America's principal adversary (after the defeat of Nazi Germany) ahead of their own nation's. Yet over and beyond Cold War findings, documentation that has come to light since the breakdown of the Soviet Union has provided additional proof that a significant part of the U.S. Communist Party's energy was devoted to infiltrating the American government to obtain information useful to the Soviet Union. This is called spying, and citizens who engage in it are customarily called traitors.

The new documentation available since 1991 has been, broadly, in two categories—(1) the archives of the Communist International, which were kept in Moscow, and the files of other Communist parties in Eastern and Central Europe; and (2) the *Venona* papers, which were kept in Fort Meade, Maryland. The former were not available for the obvious reason that the rulers of the Soviet Union did not want their activities known. The latter, though no longer sensitive since they concerned activities that had taken place in the mid-1940s, were nevertheless considered inviolate for what they might reveal to an adversary about American cryptologic capabilities.

But finally made public, the material from east and west combined shows that the U.S. Communist Party was extensively and

Conclusion

fruitfully involved in Moscow's espionage infrastructure in America. The Party's leading personalities, including General Secretary Earl Browder, were active participants in recruiting and vetting Party members on behalf of Soviet intelligence. Indeed, most of the wartime Soviet agents in the United States were members of the Communist Party. Through the Party, the USSR was able to draw prospective agents from a pool of ideologues loyal to Moscow, a circumstance unique in history. This reality, which was clear to U.S. government investigators and many others for decades but which was—and is—disputed by liberal historians, is now a known fact.

Fact: There existed in important agencies of the U.S. government networks of American spies under the control of Soviet military intelligence and NKVD officers. These included individuals whose disloyalty has been acknowledged for years by almost all serious students of the subject. Alger Hiss, Harry Dexter White, and the Rosenbergs through the years have had a shrinking pool of defenders. Others, until the *Venona* documents were aired, were considered heroes of American liberalism.

Fact: *Venona* has shown conclusively that the highest-level American government official working for Soviet intelligence was Harry Hopkins, the close friend and advisor of President Roosevelt. His clandestine contact with "illegal" Soviet intelligence officer Iskhak Akhmerov, to whom he provided secret government information, alone makes the case against Hopkins. Only a Soviet agent would be permitted to know that an "illegal" intelligence officer such as Akhmerov was connected with the Soviet Union.

Fact: Atomic scientist J. Robert Oppenheimer performed work on behalf of the Soviet Union. Although it has long been known that several of the scientists involved in the Manhattan Project believed the world would be safer if the secrets of atomic energy were shared with the Soviet Union, it had been considered bad manners even to suggest that the sensitive Oppenheimer could possibly be so crude as to be a conscious collaborator with the Soviet secret police. But he was.

Fact: The Left liked to use one of the right wing's favorite complaints as evidence of its inanity—its belief that American journalists, including some of the best known, had been deliberately enlisted in the Soviet cause. The *Venona* documents leave no room for doubt that this was exactly the case, in particular regarding the loyalty of I. F. Stone to the Soviet Union and, in his case, to his bank account.

Fact: The NKVD spied on American citizens who were not involved with the government. They were targeted because the Soviets considered them rivals or impediments to their operations in the United States or in postwar Europe.

Fact: The Communist movement displayed systematic and consistent anti-Semitism. Following Moscow's example, the Communist parties denigrated Jewish aspirations and cynically worked with the openly anti-Semitic Nazis when it served Moscow's interests. The *Venona* files reveal a total cynicism in the manipulation of Jewish interests by the Communists. The anti-Semitism that is flagrantly displayed by contemporary Russian Communists is a product not of the present political confusion and near-anarchy in the ex-Soviet Union but of an anti-Semitic tradition that remained rampant during the dictatorship of the Party "of all the workers of the world."

Beyond a rereading of certain key events in twentieth-century American history, the new documentary evidence demands a reconsideration of the way government officials and politicians, as well as private citizens, reacted to the Communist problem. The conventional wisdom, of course, claims that there was an unfortunate overreaction to Communism abroad and even more so at home in the late 1940s and 1950s that resulted in terrible policy mistakes which have haunted America for decades—from enhanced loyalty requirements for civil

Conclusion

servants to excessive rearmament and the Vietnam War. The short-hand term for this "overreaction" has entered our language: "McCarthyism."

One of the most interesting aspects of the new documentary evidence of Soviet intelligence activities in the United States is that it demonstrates to what a very great degree Senator Joseph R. McCarthy was, in fact, irrelevant to the anti-Communist cause. McCarthy's maiden speech on Communist infiltration of the U.S. government was made in February 1950. While he added little to our knowledge, he did force public discussion of the issue—something that the Left did not appreciate. Ultimately, the attack on McCarthy did substantial damage to the cause he championed. His influence in Congress lasted only during his tenure as chairman of the Government Operations Committee's Permanent Subcommittee on Investigations—a period of little more than a year.

The series of political decisions, backed by legislation, to rid government agencies of Communist infiltration and influence was the work not of the Republican senator from Wisconsin but of the Democratic administration of Harry Truman and a bipartisan majority in Congress.

Although he would often try to cover up Soviet espionage for partisan political reasons, Truman was ironically, in the long run, a more effective foe of Soviet subversion than McCarthy. One of the brightest of the Communist Party functionaries in the 1950s, Philip Frankfeld, the head of the Party in Maryland, pointed out in a 1951 pamphlet that the danger to the Communist Party was not from McCarthyism but from Trumanism. Frankfeld cited the facts: "Truman is President of the United States and not Joe McCarthy. Truman is in the driver's seat and has had governmental power concentrated in his hands since Roosevelt's death in April 1945. Truman determines both foreign and domestic policies—and not

Joe McCarthy." It was the Truman administration that enforced Congress's anti-Communist legislation.

Frankfeld suggested that the Communist Party "direct its main blows against Trumanism as the main enemy of the American people today."[1] Frankfeld should have known better; he had been an experienced Party and Young Communist League functionary since the 1920s. While he was factually correct, he was, to use a term coined by the Communists, "politically incorrect." He should have remembered the old Stalinist tactic of demonizing an opponent and then using his vilified name in a broad-brush smear against anyone who challenged Communist views or activities.

This tactic had been effectively used against Trotsky. In the incredibly named pamphlet *Defects in Party Work and Measures for Liquidating Trotskyites and Other Double-Dealers*, Stalin falsely accused the Trotskyites of being "a gang of wreckers, diversionists, spies, assassins, without principles and ideals, working in the pay of foreign intelligence services." He dubbed them "Trotskyite-fascist agents of the foreign intelligence services."[2] Soon dissidents in the Communist parties and opponents outside the parties were accused of "Trotskyism" and even "Trotskyite-fascism." And this despite the fact that Trotsky not only was not a fascist but also was a strong believer in the "unconditional defense of the U.S.S.R., the first workers' state, against the inside and outside foes of the proletarian dictatorship!" Trotsky even argued that "to defend the U.S.S.R., as the main fortress of the world proletariat, against all the assaults of world imperialism and of internal counter-revolution, is the most important duty of every class-conscious worker."[3] In the Soviet Union, and after the war in Eastern Europe, millions were arrested and imprisoned in slave labor camps or executed for the crime of "Trotskyism," although few of them were actually supporters of Trotsky.

Conclusion

In the postwar period, Frankfeld knew that in 1948, when Stalin had a falling out with Yugoslavia's Marshal Tito, the same tactic was used. People were executed in the newly conquered countries of Eastern and Central Europe for being "Tito-fascists."[4]

Thus, in like manner, McCarthy's name became the equivalent of Trotsky's and Tito's in earlier years. It was too useful a weapon to waste by substituting "Trumanism." Frankfeld was punished for telling the truth—he was expelled from the Communist Party.[5]

In 1953, when the Republicans won a majority in the Senate, McCarthy became chairman of the Senate Government Operations Committee's Subcommittee on Investigations. He soon hired the experienced and knowledgeable J. B. Matthews as staff director. Matthews, a fellow traveler in the 1930s, broke with the Communists and became the leading authority on Communist operations. From 1938 to 1944 he was the research director of the Special Committee on Un-American Activities. The Democrats on the Senate committee objected to the appointment, charging that Matthews believed all Protestant ministers were pro-Communist. They quoted from an article he had written in the *American Mercury* saying, "The largest single group supporting the Communist apparatus in the United States today is composed of Protestant clergymen."

Matthews's detractors failed to mention either his unequivocal declaration that "the vast majority of American Protestant clergymen are loyal to the free institutions of this country" or that he went on to ask why any clergyman would become involved in Communist fronts insofar as "Communist dogma is diametrically opposed to every tenet of Judeo-Christian theology and philosophy."[6]

Matthews, a mature and cautious expert on Communist history, might have been able to curb McCarthy's rhetorical excesses and rein in the flamboyant, inexperienced subcommittee staff, notably Roy Cohn, David Shine, and Robert Kennedy. But Matthews was concerned that the attacks on him would embarrass McCarthy, and he resigned soon after the attacks were leveled, despite McCarthy's efforts to persuade him to stay.

Some of the McCarthy Committee's probes produced important and damning information, such as Communist infiltration of the army and waste and mismanagement in the Voice of America. In the latter investigation, a Democratic member of the committee, Senator Henry Jackson, played an important role. But the far more knowledgeable and competent House Committee on Un-American Activities, which existed from 1938 to 1974, and the Senate Subcommittee on Internal Security, which existed until 1976—McCarthy played no role in either—produced an immense body of evidence, collected at hearings and set down in reports. The printed hearings of these two committees remain an invaluable resource, particularly in the continuing efforts to place new revelations in perspective.

The political Left spawned the term "McCarthyism" and infused it with dire and even evil connotations and then used it effectively to define an entire period. But President Truman's Executive Order 9835 was issued in March 1947, three years before McCarthy's notoriety began. It was this measure that instituted loyalty and security checks and effectively barred most Communist Party members from government employment.

The president believed that by ensuring that Communists could not serve in government, he could impede Soviet espionage efforts, but he was not thrilled by the prospect of a Republican Congress investigating this issue and used the loyalty order to restrict congressional access to security information. Truman recognized that any such inquiry would reflect unfavorably both on his administration and on the New Deal. Thus, in 1948, Truman—who certainly knew better—took it upon himself to characterize the House committee's Alger Hiss investigation as a "red herring."

Conclusion

Indeed, in the very month of Hiss's federal perjury indictment (the statute of limitations on espionage had lapsed), Truman asked his attorney general to "get a statement of facts from the FBI about the meddling of the House Committee on Un-American Activities and [about] how they dried up sources of information which would have been useful in the prosecution of spies and Communists." The president went on to claim that the House committee's "meddling" was an effort to deflect attention "from the shortcomings of the 80th Congress...." Truman even suggested that the committee be accused of "contributing to the escape of certain Communists who should have been indicted."

No such FBI statement was issued. In this, FDR's successor was animated solely by partisan considerations. In reality, the USSR's extensive North American intelligence apparatus started retrenching—and even withdrawing agents—as early as 1945, when the Igor Gouzenko case broke in Canada. But much of the apparatus was soon restored, and Soviet intelligence continued to use a selected group of American Communists as agents for almost a decade more.

One contemporary left-of-center historian, Melvyn P. Leffler, argues that Truman surrendered to the Republicans by initiating his loyalty program and his campaign to deport alien Communists. Leffler even suggests that Truman "collaborated with the House Committee on Un-American Activities."

This interpretation is bizarre in view of Truman's war on what he called the Republican "do-nothing 80th Congress." The president opposed the Republican-led House Committee on Un-American Activities and wanted to fight Soviet espionage and subversion his own way, without GOP help.

Ironically, even after the term "McCarthyism" was forged, implying demagogic methods, the Communist threat—notably Communist efforts to infiltrate and manipulate institutions and organizations—was widely taken to heart. Even liberal non-governmental organizations like the NAACP and the American Veterans Committee (AVC) expelled Communists from their ranks. As early as 1940 the ACLU banned Communists from leadership posts, a policy that continued well into the Cold War era. The ACLU's reasoning was not complicated: In its view, the Communists' commitment to the Bill of Rights was highly selective and decidedly unprincipled.[7] Similarly, an official of the AVC, testifying on the Federal Employees Security Program before the Senate Post Office and Civil Service Committee in June 1958, argued that his group was "probably the only completely voluntary general membership organization which successfully defeated a deliberately organized Communist attempt to infiltrate and capture its organization."

Even while arguing against the scope of the loyalty and security program, AVC leader Lincoln Lauterstein contended "that no member or supporter of an organization controlled by an essentially foreign power or of an organization dedicated to the overthrow of the Government by force or violence should hold a Government job. Such a person is disloyal in the proper sense of the word...." Lauterstein went on to suggest that if such folks hold government posts, it is appropriate to deem them "security risks" if their work involves classified information.[8]

As late as March 15, 1955, Joseph L. Rauh, Jr., the national vice president of the Americans for Democratic Action (ADA), testified that "the real danger is one of espionage and sabotage, not one of ideas." Said Rauh, "We can defeat the Communist idea, but we need strong measures to defeat their espionage and sabotage attempts." According to Rauh, both major political parties had failed to make the "public aware of the danger of sabotage as distinguished from the danger of Communist ideas."[9]

Conclusion

Rauh confused membership in the Communist Party, which was an act, with belief in Communist ideas. Views can be combated with better ones, but membership in the Communist Party required loyalty to a hostile foreign power. The ADA itself, to be sure, played an active role in the battle of ideas. It had been formed in 1947 precisely in order to counter the "Progressive Citizens of America" and similar Communist fronts.

During this period, a powerful blow to American Communists, and to Moscow's espionage apparatus, was the expulsion of eleven Communist-dominated labor unions from the CIO. The Party had played an important role in building the CIO, which had come to serve as a crucial cover for Communists seeking to infiltrate national political life—some of whom, not surprisingly, worked for Soviet intelligence.

But in 1949 the CIO brought charges against eleven unions, held hearings, and expelled them from the organization. The report containing the evidence used by the CIO to expel these unions was published in 1951 by the United States Senate Committee on Labor and Public Welfare, at the request of a member of the committee, Senator Hubert H. Humphrey. The CIO set up rival, democratic unions, and those controlled by the Communists withered.[10]

In England, the British Labour Party had long fought attempts at Communist penetration. Even during the war, Labour rejected various CP affiliation proposals. This, recall, took place at the height of wartime Anglo-Soviet amity. In a telling 1943 letter, the Labour Party told the Communists that their affiliation application had been rejected; according to the Labourites, "(a) The Constitution and Rules of the Communist Party, as laid down by the Communist International, cannot be reconciled with those of the Labour Party. (b) The Communist Party, being a Section of the Communist International, is unable to accept of its own free will the decisions of the Annual (Labour) Party Conference [because] it is subject to its over-riding commitments to the International. The Communist Party has no authority within itself to enter into or, having entered into, to remain within the Labour Party, if the Communist International determines otherwise. (c) Officers and representatives of the Communist Party held their positions in the name of the Communist International and, if admitted to the Labour Party, would remain bound to carry out, within the Labour Party, the directions of the Communist International."[11]

In 1946 the Labour Party published a pamphlet by famed leftist economist Harold J. Laski, "The Secret Battalion." Laski wrote:

> They [the Communists] act like a secret battalion of para-troopers within the brigade, whose discipline they have accepted. They meet secretly to propose their own line of action; they have one set of rules to regulate their conduct to one another, and a different set of rules to be observed towards those who are not in the battalion.[12]

Laski understood that the dedication and duplicity of the Communist Party members permitted them to penetrate the Labour Party in order to carry out Moscow-directed subversion and disruption. The *Venona* decryptions showed American counterintelligence officers that the Communists were using the same method of operation to penetrate the U.S. government.

With insights gained from *Venona* and a formula gleaned from the Soviet intelligence service's defectors, such as Chambers, Bentley, and Gouzenko, the FBI realized that its penetration of the Communist Party, while valuable for identifying potential spies, was inadequate. To pierce the activities of the KGB required a much higher level of penetration of the Communist Party. This became

Conclusion

possible only in 1951 after the KGB had diminished its use of ideological agents. The FBI conducted a program called by the special agents "cage rattling." FBI agents would confront Party functionaries on the street and ask if they wanted to talk. Most of the time, they were answered with obscenities. But, in a few cases, they struck gold.

When FBI agents confronted Jack Childs, to their surprise, he said, "What took you so long?" They knew that Jack was not only a Communist Party functionary but also an experienced underground operative. He was trained in Moscow and during the 1930s penetrated Nazi Germany for the Comintern. His wife, Roz, had worked in Moscow for the Red International of Labor Unions. When the FBI agents spoke to Jack, he said they really should talk to his brother. His brother, Morris Childs, was a graduate of the International Lenin School and, in the late 1920s, had been recruited in Moscow by the Soviet intelligence service. When he returned to the United States, he held high-level jobs in the Party, including editor of the *Daily Worker*. But now, after a severe heart attack, he was bedridden and had dropped out of Party activities. One of the reasons for Morris's heart attack was a trip to Moscow in 1946 when he learned that many of his friends had died in the purges. Most were Jews, and Morris realized that the Soviet Union had become openly anti-Semitic.

When the FBI saw him, Morris agreed to help in any way he could but said that his physical condition prevented him from real work. He was wrong about that—a stay at the Mayo Clinic and a new reason to live brought him back to health.

When Morris returned to the Communist Party, his close association with Soviet intelligence operations convinced the Party leadership to assign him as the liaison with the Soviets to organize the smuggling of Soviet money to the American Communist Party. He continued in that role until the early 1980s, frequently traveling to Moscow and meeting with the highest-level Soviet political and intelligence officials. Their frank discussions with him, his brother, Jack, and their wives, Eva and Roz, were fully reported to the FBI. The four of them had become American agents, penetrating the KGB's secrets. Their story was told in a recent book by John Barron, senior editor of the *Reader's Digest* and expert on the KGB.[13]

With the help of the Childs family, the FBI penetrated the innermost circle of the Communist Party USA and discovered its relationship with the KGB and the Soviet Communist Party. If this had occurred a dozen years earlier, it would have been impossible for the NKVD to have had much success in penetrating the U.S. government and in spying on Americans.

APPENDIX A

The Documents

THE RELEASE OF THE *VENONA* documents, beginning in 1995, afforded historians the opportunity to see at last the unvarnished truth about Soviet espionage in the United States. The *Venona* papers render key facts indisputable. To take just one example, we now know for certain that what Whittaker Chambers told American authorities—at the time so controversial—was true.

Yet *Venona* alone does not tell the whole story. Only by comparing the decrypted Soviet cables with other material can we understand the scope of the Soviets' spying apparatus and what that meant to the course of World War II and the ensuing Cold War. Essential to the study of Soviet espionage are documents from the Moscow archives, material the FBI has released about its investigations, and the results of congressional inquiries into these matters.

The pages that follow offer just a small sampling of the thousands of documents the authors examined in assembling this book. Yet in this collection we see the clear signs of a vast, carefully orchestrated espionage campaign that the Soviet Union waged against the United States, its ostensible ally in the fight against Hitler's Germany.

Appendix A

WORKERS PARTY OF AMERICA

GENERAL SECRETARY
C. E. RUTHENBERG
ACCOUNTS AND SUPPLIES DEPT.
N. DOZENBERG
ORGANIZATION DEPARTMENT
JAY LOVESTONE
AGITPROP DEPT.
MAX BEDACHT
RESEARCH DEPT.
EARL R. BROWDER

NATIONAL OFFICE

1113 W. WASHINGTON BLVD.. ROOM 301

CHICAGO. ILL.

PHONE MONROE 4714
290

"DAILY WORKER"
OFFICIAL DAILY ORGAN
J. LOUIS ENGDAHL.
WILLIAM F. DUNNE.
EDITORS

IN CHICAGO BY MAIL $6.00 PER YEAR
OUTSIDE OF CHICAGO 6.00

January 9th.1926.

TO ALL PARTY UNITS.

Comrades,Greetings:

Every live member of our party knows and understands the
significance of holding **L E N I N   M E M O R I A L**
M E E T I N G S. The dates have been set by the Agitprop
Department as Jan.21.to 30th.inclusive.

To propagandize,to popularize leninism among the working
masses of this country,aside from the educational and
propaganda value of speeches,leaflets,party papers and
literature generally,- THE LENIN MEMORIAL BUTTONS ,are the
best for that purpose. These must be sold and distributed
among the workers everywhere,in the shops,mills,mines,
factories and other places of employment. Have the unemployed
wear the button to remind them what Leninism has built
for the workers in Russia,etc.etc.

SAMPLE OF THE BUTTONS HEREWITH. Place your order for them
at once. If there is no funds in the treasury of your
nucleus or branch - borrow the money and pay it back after
the meeting of the nucleus or branch,and after the buttons
are sold. In fact,you can make some money for your treasury
from the sale of the buttons.If you have time you can place
an appropriate ribbon to the button and make it look like
a regular badge and sell them for 25 cents each or more.

The price is $6.00 per 100 or $25.00 for 500 or more.
PAYMENT MUST BE SENT WITH THE ORDER. We can send them
C.O.D.if you desire. Use the order blank,if convenient.

Please do not delay action.There is no time to be lost.
It takes time to get the order to you.

Fraternally yours,

N. Dozenberg

Accounts & Supplies Dept.

Could you furnish us with an address of a secretary of a
nonparty organization which would be interested to use
these buttons for the intended purpose ? Write at once.

The most notable aspect of this 1926 letter is the letterhead itself, which lists the officers of the
Workers Party (which would later become the Communist Party USA). They included:
Nicholas Dozenberg, who later went to work for Soviet military intelligence; Jay Lovestone,
who maintained a relationship with Soviet intelligence after he was expelled from the
Communist Party in 1929 (he later became an active anti-Communist); Max Bedacht, who
recruited Whittaker Chambers into Soviet espionage; and Earl Browder, who had a long relationship with Soviet intelligence. *(1 page)*

Appendix A

June 3rd, 1932.

Comrade Mekhlis,
"Pravda".

Dear Comrade Mekhlis,

The bearer of this note, Comrade Golos, has for
several years been in charge of the printing of our Party
papers in New York, particularly the "Daily Worker".
The American Party would like to utilise his stay in the
Soviet Union to have him acquaint himself with the technique
and methods of newspaper printing here. We would be very
much obliged if arrangements could be made for the comrade
to see the "Pravda" printing plant.

Fraternally,

J.Peter,
Representative CP USA,
ECCI.

In this 1932 letter, J. Peters (also known as J. Peter), the American Communist Party representative in Moscow, asks for a favor for his friend Jacob Golos. Like Peters, Golos was a Soviet
intelligence agent. *(1 page)*

Appendix A

22 [Вх. № 256 /.]
"28" I 1939 г.

Секретно.

КРАТКИЙ ДОКЛАД О РАБОТЕ КОНСПИРАТИВНОГО
АППАРАТА КП. США.

Конспиративный аппарат КП. США существует около 4 лет. В продолжении всего этого периода работой конспиративного аппарата руководил тов. ПИТЕРС. 13 июня 1938г. он был освобожден от этой работы и назначен на другую работу, а спец-работа была поручена т. БЕЙКЕРУ.

Тов. ПИТЕРС организовал связь между Центральным Комитетом и Штатами и ввел подобную систему связи в наиболее важных округах, для этой цели недавно послав двух товарищей для развертывания этой работы в Чикаго и Кливленде.

Этот отдел создал также вполне удовлетворительное и безопасное хранение особо важных документов Центрального Комитета. Безопасное хранение секретного архива Центрального Комитета проводилось по меньшей мере в продолжении 15 лет с различной степенью безопасности документа. Секретные документы хранятся в частных домах/ на частных квартирах/. Спец. Стделом также были произведены опыты по установлению радиосвязи специально воспроизводящего аппарата, электрического прибора для определения противника. Для этой работы были найдены средства. Для финансирования этой работы созданы группы из людей не являющимися прикрепленными ни к какой парторганизации и т.о. являющиеся засекреченными.

Недостаток этой работы заключается в том, что всем стало известно, что эту работу проводит ПИТЕРС.

Отдел не ставил перед собой проблему разоблачения врагов внутри партии. Этот вопрос разрешался непосредственно т. БРАУДЕРОМ от центра и дисциплинарными комиссиями в боль-

Memo from the Moscow archives on the 1939 report of Rudy Baker, head of the Communist Party USA conspiratorial apparatus. Baker explained that in 1938 he had replaced J. Peters in the job. *(1 page)*

Appendix A

W 112

From: New York
To: Moscow
No.746,747,748   25 May 1942

To VICTOR(1).
     PAL(2)[PEL] reports the distribution of planes by
types for the first [B% week] of May:

Heavy bombers - U.S. Army 28;
  [11 groups unrecovered];
                    USSR 7
Light 2 motored - X(a) [1 group unrecovered];
                    USSR 35
Light 1 motored - Navy 18;
                    X(a) 8.
2 motored fighters - Army 43.
1 motored fighters - Army 44;
                      Navy -1U-;
                      X(a) 49;
                      USSR 3.
Transport - [3 groups unrecovered]
Training -   Army 340;
             Navy 10;
             X(a) 2;
             China 14
[110 groups unrecovered]
displacement 139630, deadweight 221562. Passenger - volume
displacement 11812, deadweight [11 groups unrecovered] 1%
of Roosevelt's program for 1942.

Construction [1 group unrecovered] by months:
     January 123000 gross tons;
     February 196000;
     March   194000.

     According to data of the U.S. Army, representatives of
the army in the air industry [1 group unrecovered] issue to
the USSR of priority on fighter planes. [3 groups unrecovered]
the United States is trying to produce for the USSR 45000
fighter planes during the next two months. [110 groups
unrecovered] factory [2 groups unidentified] output of planes
for the USSR.
           [765 groups unrecovered and unrecoverable]

                         No.493

                        MAKSIM(3)

(1) Lt. Gen. P.M. Fitin
(2) Nathan Gregory Silvermaster
(3) Vassili Zubilin
(a) An unidentified country, possibly Great Britain.

~~TOP SECRET EIDER~~ BRIDE

A May 1942 report from the New York *Rezidentura* to Moscow on U.S. air strength. *(1 page)*

Appendix A

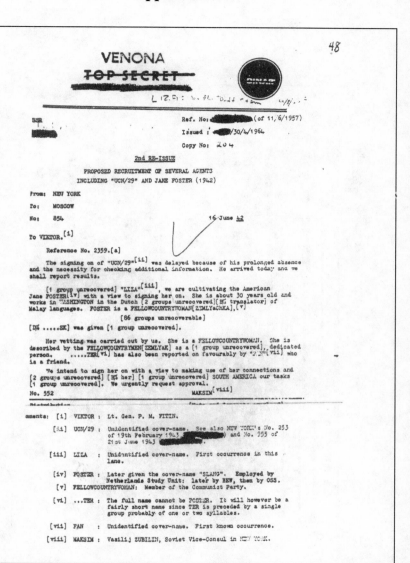

A June 1942 message from the New York *Rezidentura* to Moscow reporting that "Liza"—later identified as Martha Dodd—was recruiting Jane Foster of OSS. *(1 page)*

Appendix A

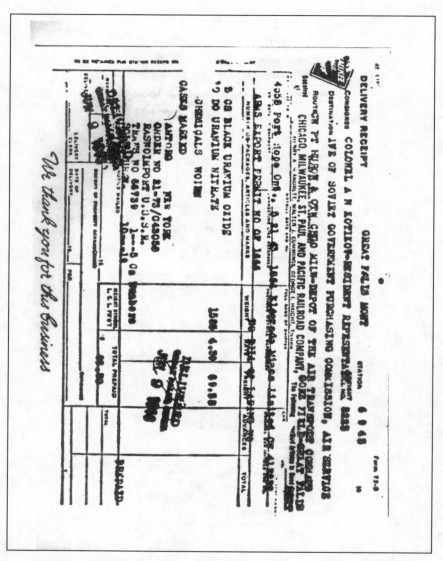

The receipt for a 1943 shipment of uranium oxide and uranium nitrate ordered by Harry Hopkins, President Roosevelt's close friend and advisor. Against the objections of American military authorities, Hopkins—a Soviet agent—insisted that the uranium be sent to the Soviet Union. *(1 page)*

Appendix A

299

Reissue

From: NEW YORK

To: MOSCOW

No: 1061,1062,1063

3 July 1943

[Part I]   According to information of the Administration of the
Army Air Forces of the "COUNTRY"[i] of 21 April this year
which was received from "AILERON [ELERON]"[ii] through "PAL
[PEL]"[iii] 3 groups unrecovered] : Numerical strength of the
Army Air Forces of the COUNTRY (the first figure in the COUNTRY,
the second abroad):

   1.   Commissioned personnel including warrant officers (the
senior non-commissioned rank):

      Pilots   39096; 12 [2 groups unrecoverable]
      Bombardiers   5742; 1882.
      Navigators   4690; 2168.
      Observers   410;   165.
      Those responsible for armament 987; 3613.
      Bombardiers   1214; 910.
      Meteorologists 669; 434.
      [1 group unidentified] 1594; 877.
      [1 group unidentified]   487; 162.

      [41 groups unrecovered]

      ---- gunnery 3021; 0.
      [9 groups unrecovered]

      Total officers and warrant

      [15 groups unrecoverable]

      aviation school 11 [2 groups unrecovered]; 0.

   2. Enlisted personnel:
      Pilots   609; [2 groups unrecovered].
      Radio operators 4236; 502.
      Flight

      [36 groups unrecoverable]

[Part II]

      Armourers trained in gunnery   10025; 4136.
      Armourers untrained in gunnery 24104; 8581.
      Radio operators trained in gunnery 3616; 3663.
      Radio operators untrained in gunnery 25803; 8599.
      [3 groups unrecovered]   1900; 83345.
      Persons undergoing government training 32102; 0.

      [51 groups unrecoverable][a]

      ----chief [1 group unidentified] 445; 0.
      Office of Coast Artillery   64; 0.
      Engineer corps   3246; 1333.
      Chaplains   866; 0.
      Office of Chemical Warfare   1274; 72.
      Financial Department

      [25 groups unrecoverable]

This report, sent from the New York *Rezidentura* to Moscow in July 1943, details the
strength of the U.S. air corps. George Silverman obtained the data and passed it through
Nathan Gregory Silvermaster. *(2 pages)*

469

Appendix A

Medical corps 1513; 383.
Veterinary corps 296; 0.
Military police 333; 115.
Armament department 3137; 477
Quartermaster 3527; 562.
Communications corps 6136; 1690.
Women's Army Corps 138; 0.
Others 15; 221.
Total officers 35944; 7682.

[Part III]
2. Enlisted personnel:
Coast artillery   841; 0.
Engineer corps   45527; 32713.
Office of Chemical Warfare   14680; 1072.
Financial department   5675; 79.
Medical corps   60921; 1439.
Veterinary corps   701; 0.
Military police   30247; 2905.
Armament department   40404; 10256.
Quartermaster   7980; 500
Communications corps   71528; 31810.
Women's Army Corps   2496; 0.
Others   110562; 15007
Total enlisted personnel of the Air Forces 463662[??];

[6 groups unrecovered]

No.588   [Signature unrecoverable]

T.N.[a] Within these 51 unrecoverable groups the enlisted
personnel are probably totalled and a new "paragraph
1 - Officer personnel" started.

Comments:
[i] COUNTRY: U.S.A.

[ii] AILERON: Abraham George SILVERMAN.

[iii] PAL: Nathan Gregory SILVERMASTER.

(page 2)

470

Appendix A

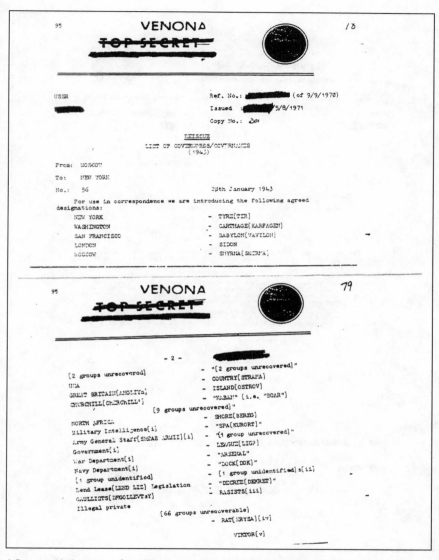

A January 1943 message from Moscow to the New York *Rezidentura* listing important code words, among them the designations for major cities, nations, and even Prime Minister Winston Churchill of Great Britain. *(1 page)*

Appendix A

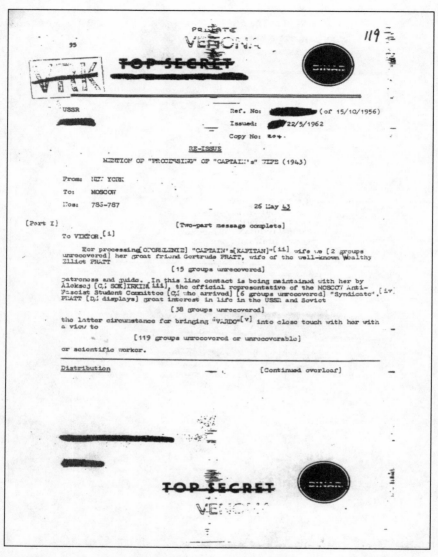

In this May 1943 message, the New York *Rezidentura* tells Moscow of the bizarre plan to recruit (or "process," in the Soviet argot) Eleanor Roosevelt through her friend Gertrude Pratt. The first lady was to be put in touch with Elizabeth Zarubin ("Vardo"), an experienced Soviet intelligence officer. Needless to say, the plan didn't work. *(1 page)*

Appendix A

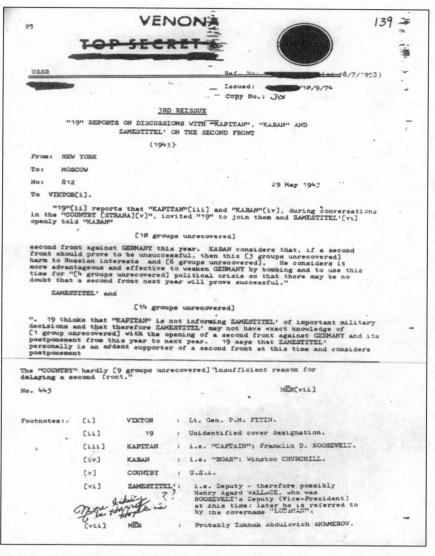

A May 1943 message from "illegal" *Rezident* Iskhak Akhmerov to Moscow revealing that agent "19," later identified as Harry Hopkins, had reported on a meeting between Roosevelt and Churchill at which he was present. *(1 page)*

Appendix A

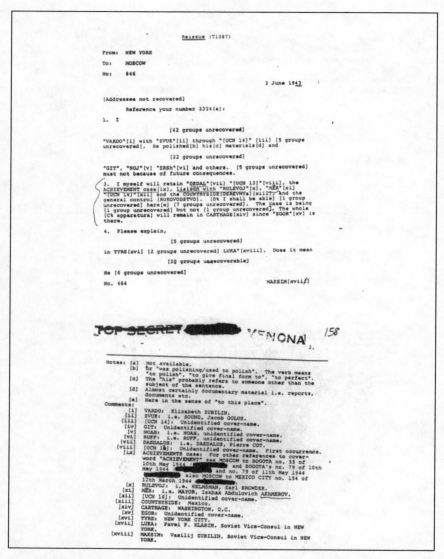

Reissue (T1087)

From: NEW YORK

To: MOSCOW

No: 846

3 June 1943

[Addressee not recovered]

    Reference your number 2324[a]:

1. I

              [42 groups unrecovered]

"VARDO"[i] with "ZVUK"[ii] through "[UCN 14]"[iii] [5 groups unrecovered[. He polished[b] his[c] materials[d] and

              [22 groups unrecovered]

"GIT", "NOJ"[v] "ERSh"[vi] and others. [5 groups unrecovered] must not because of future consequences.

3. I myself will retain "DEDAL"[vii] "[UCN 13]"[viii], the ACHIEVEMENT case[ix], liaison with "RULEVOJ"[x], "MER"[xi] "[UCN 16]"[xii] and the COUNTRYSIDE[DEREVNYa][xiii?] and the general control [RUKOVODSTVO]. [bt I shall be able] [1 group unrecovered] here[e] [7 groups unrecovered]. The case is being [1 group unrecovered] but not [1 group unrecovered]. The whole [C% apparatura] will remain in CARTHAGE[xiv] since "EGOR"[xv] is there.

4. Please explain,

              [5 groups unrecovered]

in TYRE[xvi] [2 groups unrecovered] LUKA"[xviii]. Does it mean

              [20 groups unrecoverable]

He [6 groups unrecovered]

No. 464   MAKSIM[xvii]

TOP SECRET ████ VENONA 158

2.

Notes: [a]   Not available.
     [b]   Or "was polishing/used to polish". The verb means "to polish", "to give final form to", "to perfect".
     [c]   The "his" probably refers to someone other than the subject of the sentence.
     [d]   Almost certainly documentary material i.e. reports, documents etc.
Comments: [e]   Here in the sense of "to this place".
     [i]   VARDO: Elizabeth ZUBILIN.
     [ii]   ZVUK: i.e. SOUND, Jacob GOLOS.
     [iii] [UCN 14]: Unidentified cover-name.
     [iv] GIT: Unidentified cover-name.
     [v]   NOAH: i.e. NOAH, unidentified cover-name.
     [vi] RUFF: i.e. RUFF, unidentified cover-name.
     [vii] DAEDALUS: i.e. DAEDALUS, Pierre COT.
     [viii] [UCN 13]: Unidentified cover-name. First occurrence.
     [ix] ACHIEVEMENTS case: For other references to cover-word "ACHIEVEMENT" see MOSCOW to BOGOTA no. 55 of 10th May 1944 ████ and BOGOTA's no. 79 of 10th May 1944 ████ and no. 79 of 11th May 1944 ████ also MOSCOW to MEXICO CITY no. 154 of 12th March 1944 ████
     [x]   RULEVOJ: i.e. HELMSMAN, Earl BROWDER.
     [xi] MER: i.e. MAYOR, Iskhak Abdulovich AKhMEROV.
     [xii] [UCN 16]: Unidentified cover-name.
     [xiii] COUNTRYSIDE: Mexico.
     [xiv] CARTHAGE: WASHINGTON, D.C.
     [xv] EGOR: Unidentified cover-name.
     [xvi] TYRE: NEW YORK CITY.
     [xvii] LUKA: Pavel P. KLARIN, Soviet Vice-Consul in NEW YORK.
     [xviii] MAKSIM: Vasilij ZUBILIN, Soviet Vice-Consul in NEW YORK.

In June 1943 Vassiliy Zarubin (Zubilin), the NKVD *Resident* in the United States, told Moscow of his assignments. Zarubin was the liaison for Pierre Cot, a leader of the Free French, as well as Earl Browder, general secretary of the American Communist Party. He also handled "Achievement," the plot to free Leon Trotsky's murderer. *(1 page)*

Appendix A

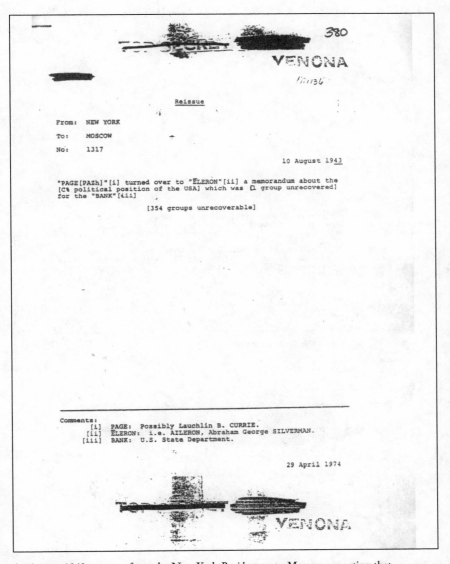

Reissue

From: NEW YORK

To: MOSCOW

No: 1317

10 August 1943

"PAGE[PAZh]"[i] turned over to "ÉLERON"[ii] a memorandum about the [C% political position of the USA] which was [1 group unrecovered] for the "BANK"[iii]

[354 groups unrecoverable]

Comments:
[i]   PAGE: Possibly Lauchlin B. CURRIE.
[ii] ÉLERON: i.e. AILERON, Abraham George SILVERMAN.
[iii] BANK: U.S. State Department.

29 April 1974

An August 1943 message from the New York *Rezidentura* to Moscow reporting that Roosevelt aide and Soviet agent Lauchlin Currie had turned a classified State Department document over to George Silverman. *(1 page)*

Appendix A

Reissue (T331)

From: New York

To: Moscow

No: 1328

12 August 1943

To the Director.

1. FRED [i], our man in LESOVIA [ii], has been elected to the LESOVIAN parliament. His personal [D% opportunities] [1 group garbled] undoubtedly are improving, but warn LION [iii] about increasing caution to the maximum.

2. In SACRAMENTO, California, in Radiation Laboratories [a], large-scale experimental work is being conducted for the War Department. Working there is a progressive professor ████████ [a] [iv], whom one can approach through the KORPORANT [v] PINSKY [a] [vi] -- one of the directors

[24 groups unrecoverable]

No. 213   MOLIÈRE [MOL'ER] [vii]

T.N.: [a] Given in the Latin alphabet.

Comments:
   [i]   FRED: Fred ROSE, M.P.

   [ii]   LESOVIA: Canada

   [iii] LION: Sergej N. KUDRYaVTsEV, First Secretary of the Soviet
                 Embassy, Ottawa.

   [iv]   ████████████████████████████████

   [v]   KORPORANT: Member of the Communist Party.

   [vi]   Paul George PINSKY, research director of CIO in California.

   [vii] MOL'ER: Pavel P. MIKhAJLOV.

In August 1943 the GRU (Soviet military intelligence) informed Moscow that Fred Rose, "our man in 'Lesovia' [Canada]," had been elected to the "Lesovian" parliament. Despite warnings to be more careful, Rose was identified as a Soviet agent and served a jail term before returning to his native Poland. *(1 page)*

Appendix A

VENONA

~~TOP SECRET~~

USSR

Ref. No.:

Issued : 25/6/1973

Copy No.: 301

MEETING BETWEEN "GUS'" AND "REST"; WORK ON ENORMOUS
(1944)

From: NEW YORK

To: MOSCOW

No.: 195   9th February 1944

Personal to VIKTOR[i].

    In reply to No. 302[ii].

    On 5th February a meeting took place between "GUS'"[iii] and "REST"[iv]. Beforehand GUS' was given a detailed briefing by us. REST greeted him pleasantly but was rather cautious at first, [1 group unrecovered] the discussion GUS' satisfied himself that REST was aware of whom he was working with. R.[iv] arrived in the COUNTRY[STRANA][v] in September as a member of the ISLAND[OSTROV][vi] mission on ENORMOUS[ENORMOZ][vii]. According to him the work on ENORMOUS in the COUNTRY is being carried out under the direct control of the COUNTRY's army represented by General SOMERVELL[SOMMERVILL][viii] and STIMSON[ix]: at the head of the group of ISLANDERS[OSTROVITYaNE][vi] is a Labour Member of Parliament, Ben SMITH[x].

[Continued overleaf]

VENONA

~~TOP SECRET~~

- 2 -

    The whole operation amounts to the working out of the process for the separation of isotopes of ENORMOUS. The work is proceeding in two directions: the electron method developed by LAWRENCE[LAURENS][xi.]

[71 groups unrecoverable]

separation of isotopes by the combined method, using the diffusion method for preliminary and the electron method for final separation. The work

[46 groups unrecovered]

18th February, we shall report the results.

The New York *Rezidentura*'s account of a February 1944 meeting between Klaus Fuchs, a Soviet spy who was part of the British team sent to work on the atomic bomb, and Harry Gold, the courier for the atomic spy ring. *(1 page)*

Appendix A

<u>Reissue</u> (T91ø)

From: NEW YORK

To: MOSCOW

No: 687

13 May 1944

On HELMSMAN's[RULEVOJ][i] instructions GOOD GIRL[UMNITsA][ii] contacted through AMT[III] a new group [C% in CARTHAGE][C% KARFAGEN][iv]:

[53 groups unrecoverable]

MAGDOFF - "KANT"[v]. GOOD GIRL's impressions: They are reliable FELLOW-COUNTRYMEN[ZEMLYaKI][vi], politically highly mature; they want to help with information. They said that they had been neglected and no one had taken any interest in their potentialities

[29 groups unrecoverable]

"STORM[ShTORM]"[vii]. RAIDER[REJDER][viii], PLUMB[LOT][ix], TED[x] and KANT will go to TYRE[TIR][xi] once every two weeks in turn.

PLUMB and TED know PAL[PEL][xii]. We shall let you have identifying particulars later.

No. 373   MAYOR[MER][xiii]

Comments:
[i]   HELMSMAN: Earl BROWDER.
[ii]   GOOD GIRL: Elizabeth BENTLEY.
[iii]   AMT: Presumably a mistake for John ABT. See also NEW YORK to
        MOSCOW No. 588 of 29 April 1944. (S/NBF/T11ø).
[iv]   CARTHAGE: WASHINGTON, D.C.
[v]   KANT: Henry Samuel MAGDOFF.
[vi]   FELLOW COUNTRYMEN: Members of a Communist Party.
[vii]   STORM: Unidentified.
[viii] RAIDER: Victor PERLO.
[ix]   PLUMB: Possibly Charles KRAMER.
[x]   TED: Probably Edward Joseph FITZGERALD.
[xi]   TYRE: NEW YORK CITY.
[xii]   PAL: Nathan Gregory SILVERMASTER.
[xiii] MAYOR: Probably Iskhak Abdulovich AKhMEROV.

25 July, 1968

103.

As Akhmerov told Moscow in May 1944, Elizabeth Bentley of the American Communist Party contacted a new group of agents through Party attorney John Abt and on the instructions of Earl Browder. Names included Harry Magdoff ("Kant"), Edward Fitzgerald, and Charles Kramer. (*1 page*)

Appendix A

17 May 1944

After a study lasting many months, we propose to use an employee of the Editorial Office [REDAKTsIYa][i], Samuel KRAFSUR[ii], henceforth "IDE[YaZ']", for cultivating newspapermen's [C? circles] in CARTHAGE[KARFAGEN][iii]. IDE is a FELLOW COUNTRYMAN[ZEMLYaK][iv], was in the International Brigade in SPAIN. He is absolutely devoted to the USSR, always zealously carries out minor tasks set by SERGEJ[v] in connection with the obtaining of information. Systematic work among IDE's extensive connections will give opportunities for obtaining valuable information and also of studying individual subjects for signing on [KONTRAKTATsIYa]. Of the more than [B? 20] leads of IDE's which could be used on the basis of I.'s[Ya.] personal relationships with them [the following][a] deserve special attention: Joseph BERGER[b][vi] - personal secretary of the Chairman of the National Committee of the Democratic Party. ████████████[vii] - brother of the well-known journalist ███████████[viii]. IDE is very friendly with them both. In future, if the development of IDE's work requires it, [C% we shall provide] him with an active contact [ZhIVAYa SVYaZ'] so that informa- tion will be received in TYRE[TIR][ix] promptly. We await your sanction.

No. 381

T.N.   [a]   Inserted by translator.

       [b]   For some unexplained reason the text broke off here at the end of
             a line of cipher and the remainder of the message was sent as a
             repeat in NEW YORK's No. 738 on 23 May 1944. The repeat gives
             the internal serial number, but not the signature of the message.

Comments: [i]   REDAKTsIYa: TASS, the Soviet Press Agency.

             [ii]   KRAFSUR: Simon Samuel KRAFSUR

             [iii] KARFAGEN: WASHINGTON, D.C.

             [iv]   ZEMLYaK: Member of the Communist Party

             [v]   SERGEJ: Vladimir Sergeevich PRAVDIN.

             [vi]   BERGER: Joseph Isadore BERGER. Wrote under the
                    pseudonym of Jeremiah DIGGES.

             [vii] ████████████████████████ Journalist, born in 1899.

             [viii] ████████████████████████ Newspaper correspon-
                    dent born in 1897, brother of ████████████

27 May 1968

~~TOP SECRET TRINE~~ VENONA
117.

In May 1944 Moscow learned of New York's efforts to recruit journalist Samuel Krafsur. *(1 page)*

479

Appendix A

95

USSR

Ref. No: 3/NBF/T521 (of 28/5/1954)

Issued: 8/8/1965

Copy No: 204

3RD RE-ISSUE

PERSONAL HISTORIES OF THE PROBATIONERS OF A NEW GROUP (1944)

From: NEW YORK

To: MOSCOW

Nos.: 769, 771   30 May 44

[Two-part message complete]

[Part I] To VIKTOR[i].

    The probationers[STAZhERY] of the new group have given the following personal histories of themselves:

1. "TED"[ii], an old FELLOW COUNTRYMAN[ZEMLYaK][iii], capable, reliable, works in the Civilian Allocation Division of the DEPOT[DEPO][iv].

2. "KANT"[v] became a FELLOW COUNTRYMAN a long time ago, being [8 groups unrecovered], works in the Machine Tool Division of the DEPOT.

3. "RAIDER[REJDER]"[vi], an old FELLOW COUNTRYMAN, reliable, capable; works in the Aeroplane Allocation Division of the DEPOT [4 groups unrecovered] ARENA[vii] through [8 groups unrecovered] STORM [ShTORM])[viii].

[Continued overleaf]

DISTRIBUTION

3/NBF/T521, Re-issue
(3 pages)

160.

Akhmerov's May 1944 message to Pavel Fitin, head of the Foreign Department of the NKVD, related the code names of a new group of agents. *(3 pages)*

Appendix A

TOP SECRET

— 2 —

3/NBF/T521, Re-issue

4. [B´ PLUMB [LOT]][ix], an old FELLOW COUNTRYMAN, reliable, works on the KILGO...[x] Committee

[62 groups unrecoverable]

ARENA's apartment.

[64 groups unrecovered]

Donald WHEELER "IZRA"[xi], has been a FELLOW COUNTRYMAN for several years, [B¼ a Trade-Union] official, capable, works in the Labor Division Research and Analysis Branch of IZRA[xii]

[Part II]   [6 groups unrecovered]

[34 groups unrecovered]

he did not[a] maintain contact with

[53 groups unrecovered]

about this group from SOUND [ZVUK][xiii] [3 groups unrecovered] material on them.) CHAR...[xiv].

[39 groups unrecoverable]

.   (He is everywhere in

[14 groups unrecovered]

For this purpose the Trade Unions [8 groups unrecovered] Trade Unions, working class and [G¼ progressive] contacts of the local FELLOW COUNTRYMEN.

[9 groups unrecovered]

[B¼ He] maintains a close friendship with MUSE[MUZA][xv] and has repeatedly tried to marry her. He is a close friend of [B¼ SLAN[G] [B¼ SLEN[G]][xvi] [3 groups unrecoverable] and often comes to TYRE[TIR][xvii] with her[( ][b] SLANG[SLENG] has spoken very well of him). Harold GLASER[xviii] an old FELLOW COUNTRYMAN. Temporarily abroad (evidently STORM knew him well). Concerning the remaining members of the group we will advise later.

MAYOR[MER][c][xix]

No. 419
30th May

Notes: [a]   The original suggests that this clause was introduced by some such phrase as "if" or "provided that".

            [b]   Inserted by the translator.

            [c]   The signature, sent at the end of Part I in accordance with normal practice, was sent as MAJ, but was corrected in a service footnote at the end of Part II to MER.

[Continued overleaf]

3/NBF/T521, Re-issue

TOP SECRET

161.

(page 2)

Appendix A

VENONA

~~TOP SECRET~~

- 3 -

3/NBF/T521, Re-issue

Comments: [i] VIKTOR: Lt. Gen. P. M. FITIN.

[ii] TED: Probably Edward Joseph FITZGERALD.

[iii] FELLOW COUNTRYMAN: Member of the Communist Party.

[iv] DEPOT: War Production Board.

[v] KANT: Harry Samuel MAGDOFF.

[vi] RAIDER: Victor PERLO.

[vii] ARENA: Probably Mary Wolfe PRICE.

[viii] STORM: Unidentified cover-name.

[ix] PLUMB: Possibly Charles KRAMER.

[x] KILGO: Senator KILGORE was Chairman of the War Mobilisation Sub-Committee of the U.S. Senate Military Affairs Committee.

[xi] IZRA: Also mentioned in MOSCOW's No. 954 of 20th September 44 (3/NBF/T1068), NEW YORK's 582 of 28th April 44 and 1244 of 31st August 44 (not published) and NEW YORK's 1325 of 15th September 44 (3/NBF/T21) and 1389 of 1st October 44 (3/NBF/T96).

Donald WHEELER

[xii] IZRA: Office of Strategic Services.

[xiii] SOUND: Jacob GOLOS.

[xiv] CHAR...: Unidentified. May be a cover-name or a real name.

[xv] MUSE: Unidentified cover-name.

[xvi] SLANG: Jane ZLATOVSKY.

[xvii] TYRE: NEW YORK, N.Y.

[xviii] Harold GLASER: Harold GLASSER.

[xix] MAYOR: Possibly Iskhak Abdulovich AKhMEROV.

3/NBF/T521, Re-issue

~~TOP SECRET~~

VENONA

162.

(page 3)

Appendix A

A 1944 memo, in Russian, from Pavel Fitin to George Dimitroff, head of the Comintern, asking for information on new agents referred to as "Members of the Communist Party of America." The memo is typed, but Fitin filled the names in himself, since secretaries were not allowed to know the identities of agents. The names are given as: Charles Flato, Donald Wheeler, [Charles] Kramer, Edward Fitzgerald, [Harry] Magdoff, Harold Glaser, and [Victor] Perlo. These names track closely with those Akhmerov provided in his May messages. *(1 page)*

Appendix A

USSR

Ref. No: S/NBF/T509 (of 12/4/1954)

Issued: 12/6/1957

Copy No: 205.

RE-ISSUE

POSSIBLE REFERENCE TO MATERIAL OBTAINED BY "PAL" AND
REFERENCE TO "ZhENYa" (1944)

From: NEW YORK

To: MOSCOW

No: 918   28 June 44

To VIKTOR.[i]

   PAL[PEL].[ii] at MAYOR's[MER][iii] request has obtained by way of specimens:
Pilots Operating Instructions for the aeroplanes Army B25 H5 and 10, B25G, A36
A1 NA and Navy Models BG1G, BG 1H, BG 1G and British Mitchell.

                    [59 groups unrecovered]

aeroplanes.

No. 502

   In reply to your telegram No. 2828[a], SONYa is a real name. Her cover-
name is ZhENYa[iv] [3 groups unrecoverable][b].

                    [30 groups unrecovered]

. No. 50[BX 5]
28 June 1944   MAY[MAJ][v]

Distribution   [Notes and Comments overleaf]

244.

Silvermaster ("Pel") and Akhmerov ("Mer") obtained classified operating instructions for
American and British planes, as Moscow learned from this June 1944 communication. *(1 page)*

Appendix A

Reissue (T511)

From: NEW YORK
To: MOSCOW
No.: 927

1 July 1944

To the 8th Department.

According to information of PAL [PEL][i] TUR[ii] POLO[iii]:

1. "ANVIL"[iv] has been postponed until 15 August.

The Allies [1 group unrecovered] to delay the operation, so that [4 groups unrecovered] VOGELKOP, PALAU and HALMAHERA but [3 groups unrecovered] LUZON and FORMOSA.

2. [10 groups unrecovered]

[50 groups unrecoverable]

4. RAS[v] refuses to accept the conditions of the Allies

[28 groups unrecovered]

have to do with RAS but

[84 groups unrecovered]

review in order to have an opportunity

[8 groups unrecoverable]

Comments:
[i] PEL: Nathan Gregory SILVERMASTER.

[ii] TUR: Unidentified

[iii] POLO: Probably William Ludwig ULLMAN.

[iv] "ANVIL" was the code-word given to the Allied invasion of the south of France.

[v] RAS: Gen. Charles de GAULLE.

~~TOP SECRET DINAR~~ VENONA

246.

On July 1, 1944, Soviet spies Nathan Gregory Silvermaster and William Ludwig Ullman reported that the Americans and British had decided to postpone Operation Anvil until August 15. "Anvil" was the code name for the plan to invade southern France and thus take pressure off the troops at Normandy. Had the Nazis intercepted this information, it could have cost many American lives. *(1 page)*

Appendix A

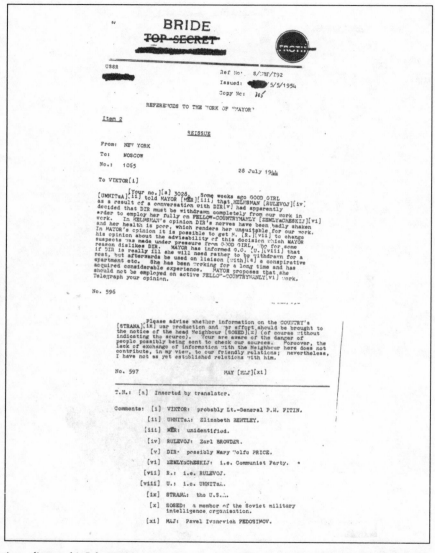

According to this July 1944 report to Moscow, Elizabeth Bentley had told Akhmerov ("Mer") that Earl Browder was removing agent Mary Price from intelligence work. That he could make such a decision indicates Browder's significant authority with the NKVD. *(1 page)*

Appendix A

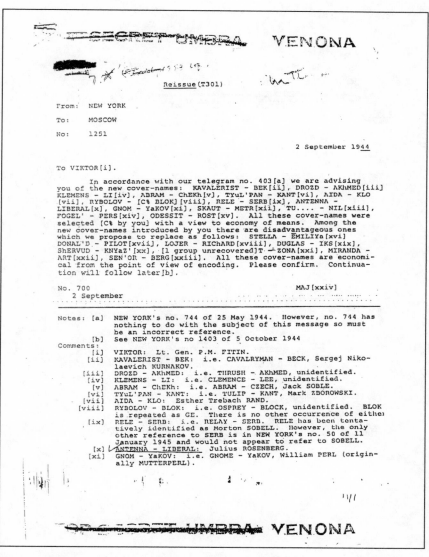

VENONA

Reissue(T301)

From: NEW YORK

To: MOSCOW

No: 1251

2 September 1944

To VIKTOR[i].

In accordance with our telegram no. 403[a] we are advising you of the new cover-names: KAVALERIST - BEK[ii], DROZD - AKhMED[iii] KLEMENS - LI[iv], ABRAM - ChEKh[v], TYuL'PAN - KANT[vi], AIDA - KLO [vii], RYBOLOV - [C% BLOK][viii], RELE - SERB[ix], ANTENNA - LIBERAL[x], GNOM - YaKOV[xi], SKAUT - METR[xii], TU.... - NIL[xiii], FOGEL' - PERS[xiv], ODESSIT - ROST[xv]. All these cover-names were selected [C% by you] with a view to economy of means. Among the new cover-names introduced by you there are disadvantageous ones which we propose to replace as follows: STELLA - ÉMILIYa[xvi] DONAL'D - PILOT[xvii], LOJER - RIChARD[xviii], DUGLAS - IKS[xix], ShERVUD - KNYaZ'[xx], [1 group unrecovered]T -L ZONA[xxi], MIRANDA - ART[xxii], SEN'OR - BERG[xxiii]. All these cover-names are economical from the point of view of encoding. Please confirm. Continuation will follow later[b].

No. 700   MAJ[xxiv]
    2 September

Notes: [a] NEW YORK's no. 744 of 25 May 1944. However, no. 744 has
            nothing to do with the subject of this message so must
            be an incorrect reference.
       [b] See NEW YORK's no 1403 of 5 October 1944
Comments:
       [i]   VIKTOR: Lt. Gen. P.M. FITIN.
       [ii] KAVALERIST - BEK: i.e. CAVALRYMAN - BECK, Sergej Niko-
             laevich KURNAKOV.
       [iii] DROZD - AKhMED: i.e. THRUSH - AKhMED, unidentified.
       [iv] KLEMENS - LI: i.e. CLEMENCE - LEE, unidentified.
       [v]   ABRAM - ChEKh: i.e. ABRAM - CZECH, Jack SOBLE.
       [vi] TYuL'PAN - KANT: i.e. TULIP - KANT, Mark ZBOROWSKI.
       [vii] AIDA - KLO: Esther Trebach RAND.
       [viii] RYBOLOV - BLOK: i.e. OSPREY - BLOCK, unidentified. BLOK
             is repeated as GE. There is no other occurrence of either
       [ix] RELE - SERB: i.e. RELAY - SERB. RELE has been tenta-
             tively identified as Morton SOBELL. However, the only
             other reference to SERB is in NEW YORK's no. 50 of 11
             January 1945 and would not appear to refer to SOBELL.
       [x]   ANTENNA - LIBERAL: Julius ROSENBERG.
       [xi] GNOM - YaKOV: i.e. GNOME - YaKOV, William PERL (origin-
             ally MUTTERPERL).

SECRET UMBRA VENONA

The NKVD frequently changed the code names of intelligence officers and agents. This message from New York to Moscow provided a list of changes. *(2 pages)*

Appendix A

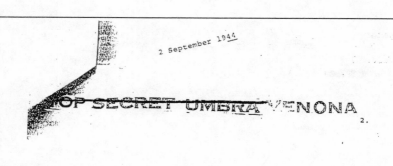

TOP SECRET UMBRA VENONA

2.

Comments (cont'd.)

[xii]	SKAUT – METR: i.e. SCOUT – METRE, probably either Joel BARR or Alfred SARANT.
[xiii]	TU.... – NIL: Unidentified.
[xiv]	FOGEL' – PERS: i.e. VOGEL – PERSIAN, unidentified.
[xv]	ODESSIT – ROST: i.e. ODESSITE – GROWTH, unidentified.
[xvi]	STELLA – ÉMILIYa: Unidentified.
[xvii]	DONAL'D – PILOT: i.e. DONALD – PILOT, William Ludwig ULLMAN.
[xviii]	LOJER – RIChARD: i.e. LAWYER – RICHARD, Harry Dexter WHITE.
[xix]	DUGLAS – IKS: i.e. DOUGLAS – X, Joseph KATZ.
[xx]	ShERVUD – KNYaZ': i.e. SHERWOOD – PRINCE, Laurence DUGGAN.
[xxi]	....T – ZONA; i.e. ....T – ZONE, unidentified.
[xxii]	MIRANDA – ART: Probably Helen KORAL.
[xxiii]	SEN'OR – BERG: i.e. SENOR – BERG, unidentified.
[xxiv]	MAJ: i.e. MAY, Stepan APRESYaN.

20 May 1975

(page 2)

Appendix A

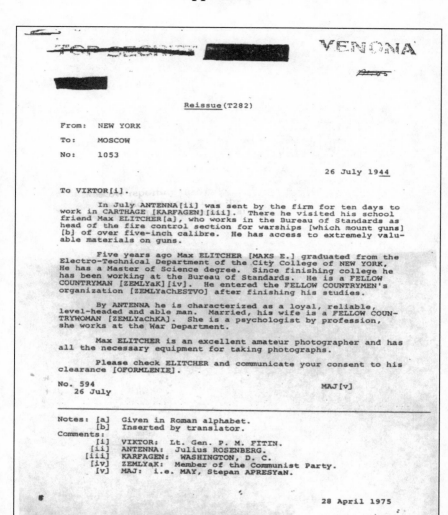

VENONA

Reissue (T282)

From: NEW YORK
To: MOSCOW
No: 1053

26 July 1944

To VIKTOR[i].

In July ANTENNA[ii] was sent by the firm for ten days to work in CARTHAGE [KARFAGEN][iii]. There he visited his school friend Max ELITCHER[a], who works in the Bureau of Standards as head of the fire control section for warships [which mount guns] [b] of over five-inch calibre. He has access to extremely valuable materials on guns.

Five years ago Max ELITCHER [MAKS E.] graduated from the Electro-Technical Department of the City College of NEW YORK, He has a Master of Science degree. Since finishing college he has been working at the Bureau of Standards. He is a FELLOW COUNTRYMAN [ZEMLYaK][iv]. He entered the FELLOW COUNTRYMEN's organization [ZEMLYaChESTVO] after finishing his studies.

By ANTENNA he is characterized as a loyal, reliable, level-headed and able man. Married, his wife is a FELLOW COUNTRYWOMAN [ZEMLYaChKA]. She is a psychologist by profession, she works at the War Department.

Max ELITCHER is an excellent amateur photographer and has all the necessary equipment for taking photographs.

Please check ELITCHER and communicate your consent to his clearance [OFORMLENIE].

No. 594   MAJ[v]
   26 July

Notes: [a]   Given in Roman alphabet.
       [b]   Inserted by translator.
Comments:
       [i]   VIKTOR: Lt. Gen. P. M. FITIN.
      [ii]   ANTENNA: Julius ROSENBERG.
     [iii]   KARFAGEN: WASHINGTON, D. C.
      [iv]   ZEMLYaK: Member of the Communist Party.
       [v]   MAJ: i.e. MAY, Stepan APRESYaN.

28 April 1975

TOP SECRET   VENONA

In July 1944 the New York *Rezidentura* reported to Moscow that Julius Rosenberg had recruited his school friend Max Elitcher. Elitcher would eventually appear as a prosecution witness against Rosenberg and Morton Sobell. *(1 page)*

Appendix A

```
From:  NEW YORK

To:    MOSCOW

No:    1340
```

                                                    21 September 1944

To VIKTOR[i].

    Lately the development of new people [D% has been in progress]. LIBERAL[ii] recommended the wife of his wife's brother, Ruth GREENGLASS, with a safe flat in view. She is 21 years old, a TOWNSWOMAN [GOROZhANKA][iii], a GYMNAST [FIZKUL'TURNITsA][iv] since 1942. She lives on STANTON [STANTAUN] Street. LIBERAL and his wife recommend her as an intelligent and clever girl.

          [15 groups unrecoverable]

[C% Ruth] learned that her husband[v] was called up by the army but he was not sent to the front. He is a mechanical engineer and is now working at the ENORMOUS [ENORMOZ][vi] plant in SANTA FE, New Mexico.

          [45 groups unrecoverable]

detain VOLOK[vii] who is working in a plant on ENORMOUS. He is a FELLOWCOUNTRYMAN [ZEMLYaK][viii]. Yesterday he learned that they had dismissed him from his work. His active work in progressive organizations in the past was the cause of his dismissal.

    In the FELLOWCOUNTRYMAN line LIBERAL is in touch with CHESTER[ix]. They meet once a month for the payment of dues. CHESTER is interested in whether we are satisfied with the collaboration and whether there are not any misunderstandings. He does not inquire about specific items of work [KONKRETNAYa RABOTA]. In as much as CHESTER knows about the role of LIBERAL's group we beg consent to ask C. through LIBERAL about leads from among people who are working on ENORMOUS and in other technical fields.

    Your no. 4256[a]. On making further enquiries and checking on LARIN[x] we received from the FELLOWCOUNTRYMEN through EKhO[xi] a character sketch which says that they do not entirely vouch for him. They base this statement on the fact that in the Federation LARIN does not carry out all the orders received from the leadership. He is stubborn and self-willed. On the strength of this we have decided to refrain from approaching LARIN and intend to find another candidate in FAECT [FAKhIT][xii].

No 751   MAJ[xiii]
  20 September

    Comments:
        [i]   VIKTOR: Lt. Gen. P. M. FITIN.
       [ii]   LIBERAL: Julius ROSENBERG.
      [iii]   GOROZhANKA: American citizen.
      [iv]   FIZKUL'TURNITsA: Probably a Member of the Young
            Communist League.
       [v]   i.e. David GREENGLASS.
      [vi]   ENORMOZ: Atomic Energy Project.
     [vii]   VOLOK: ███
    [viii]   ZEMLYaK: Member of the Communist Party.
     [ix]   CHESTER: Communist Party name of Bernard SCHUSTER.
      [x]   LARIN: Unidentified.
     [xi]   EKhO: i.e. ECHO, Bernard SCHUSTER.
    [xii]   FAKhIT: Federation of Architects, Chemists, Engineers
           and Technicians. See also NEW YORK's message no. 911
           of 27 June 1944.
    [xiii]   MAJ: i.e. MAY, Stepan APRESYaN.

                                                    28 April 1975

A September 1944 message from New York to Moscow reporting that Julius and Ethel Rosenberg had recommended that their sister-in-law Ruth Greenglass be recruited as an agent. Moscow accepted recommendations for agents only from highly trusted sources. Both Rosenbergs were trusted agents. *(1 page)*

Appendix A

VENONA

40

Reissue(T9.2)

From: NEW YORK

To: MOSCOW

No: 1657

27 November 1944

To VIKTOR[i].

Your no. 5356[a]. Information on LIBERAL's[ii] wife[iii].
Surname that of her husband, first name ETHEL, 29 years old.
Married five years. Finished secondary school. A FELLOWCOUNTRYMAN
[ZEMLYaK][iv] since 1938. Sufficiently well developed politically.
Knows about her husband's work and the role of METR[v] and NIL[vi].
In view of delicate health does not work. Is characterized posi-
tively and as a devoted person.

No. 922

Advise on the possibility of using in our work the engineer
MAZURIN Vladimir N. [viii]. He worked as deputy to the constructor
of Plant 155. He graduated from MAI[viii] in 1936. Is now working
at ARSENIJ's[ix] plant [x]. [2 groups unrecovered] [D% I request
your decision on the question].

No. 923   ANTON[xi]

Notes: [a]   Not available.
Comments:
       [i]   VIKTOR: Lt. Gen. P. M. FITIN.
       [ii]   LIBERAL: Julius ROSENBERG.
       [iii] Ethel ROSENBERG, nee GREENGLASS.
       [iv]   ZEMLYaK: Member of the Communist Party.
       [v]   METR: Probably Joel BARR or Alfred SARANT.
       [vi]   NIL: Unidentified.
       [vii] Vladimir Nikolaevich MAZURIN.
       [viii] MAI: i.e. MOSKOVSKIJ AVIATSIONNYJ INSTITUT, Moscow
              Aviation Institute.
       [ix]   ARSENIJ: Andrej Ivanovich ShEVChENKO.
       [x]   Bell Aircraft Plant, NIAGARA FALLS, N.Y.
       [xi]   ANTON: Leonid Romanovich KVASNIKOV.

1 May 1975

VENONA

A November 1944 report on Ethel Rosenberg. During World War II, Moscow knew little about individual agents in its espionage networks. But the New York *Rezidentura* knew and trusted Mrs. Rosenberg.

Appendix A

Another memo from Fitin to Dimitroff, this time asking for background on Judy Coplon of the Justice Department and Helen Tenney of OSS. *(1 page)*

Appendix A

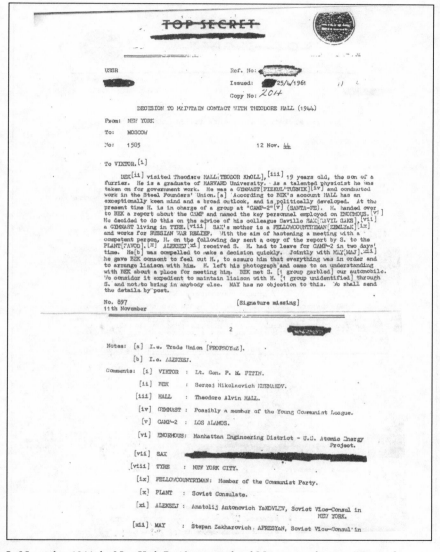

In November 1944 the New York *Rezidentura* updated Moscow on the recruitment of nineteen-year-old Theodore Hall, the youngest spy at Los Alamos. *(1 page)*

Appendix A

~~TOP SECRET~~

USSR

Ref.No.: S/NBF/T294
Issued: ██/22/1/1953
Copy No.: 205

FINANCIAL ASSISTANCE FOR "RICHARD"

From: NEW YORK
To: MOSCOW
No.: 1634   20 Nov. 1944

To VICTOR[i].

According to advice from ROBERT[ii] RICHARD's[iii] wife has complained recently about [D% financial]

[65 groups unrecoverable]

in particular with business [BIZNES] since this would relieve them of heavy expenses.

ROBERT told RICHARD's wife, who knows about her husband's participation with us, that we would willingly have helped them and that in view of all the circumstances would not allow them to leave CARTHAGE [KARFAGEN][iv]. ROBERT thinks that RICHARD would have refused a regular payment but might accept gifts as a mark of our gratitude for

[7 groups unrecovered]

daughter's expenses which may come to up to two thousand a year.

ALBERT said to ROBERT that in his opinion we would agree to provide for RICHARD's daughter's education and definitely advised ROBERT, PILOT[v] and the rest against attempting to offer RICHARD assistance.

[Continued overleaf]

- 2 -   S/NBF/T294

While sharing ALBERT's opinion about the necessity for assistance we draw your attention to the fact that RICHARD has taken the offer of assistance favourably. Please do not delay your answer.

No. 912
21st November   MAY [MAJ][vi]

Comments: [i]   VICTOR: possibly Lieut.-General Pavel M. FITIN.
          [ii] ROBERT: Nathan, Gregory SILVERMASTER.
          [iii] RICHARD: ~~possibly~~ Harry Dexter WHITE.

A November 1944 message from New York to Moscow about providing financial assistance to Soviet agent Harry Dexter White, President Roosevelt's assistant secretary of the treasury. *(1 page)*

Appendix A

~~TOP SECRET~~

USSR ▬▬▬▬▬

Ref.No.: S/NBF/T296

Issued: ▬▬ 22/1/1953

Copy No.: ⅔

"OLD" AND "YOUNG"

From: NEW YORK
To: MOSCOW
No.: 94   23 Jan 1945

To VICTOR[i].

Your nos. 316 and 121[a]. The checking of OLD [STAR][ii] and YOUNG [MLAD][iii] we entrusted to ECHO [EKhO][iv] a month ago, the result of the check we have not yet had. We are checking OLD's mother[v] also.

BECK [BEK][vi] is extremely displeased over the handing over of OLD to ALEKSEJ[vii]. He gives a favourable report of him. ALEKSEJ has met OLD twice [but][b] cannot yet give a final judgement. YOUNG has been seen by no-one except BECK. [C% On the 8th January] YOUNG sent a letter but never [C% made arrangements] for calling to a meeting. He has been called up into the army and left to work in the camp [viii].

OLD intends to renew his studies at Harvard University at the end of February.

No. 67   [1 group unrecoverable]

[T.N. and comments overleaf]

- 2 -   S/NBF/T296

T.N.: [a] Neither message is available.
      [b] Inserted by translator.

Comments: [i]   VICTOR: possibly Lieut.-General Pavel M. FITIN.
          [ii]   STAR: Saville Savoy SAX.
          [iii] MLAD: Theodore Alvin HALL.
          [iv]   EKhO: Bernard SCHUSTER (Communist Party name CHESTER).
          [v]   Mrs. Bluma SAX.
          [vi]   BEK: Sergej Nikolaevich KURNAKOV.
          [vii] ALEKSEJ: Anatolij Antonovich YaKOVLEV.
          [viii] Probably Camp 2, i.e. the LOS ALAMOS Laboratory, NEW MEXICO.

In January 1945 New York told Moscow that Bernard Chester, the Communist Party USA liaison with the NKVD, was checking out Ted Hall, his friend Saville Sax, and Sax's mother. Soviet intelligence agent Sergei Kournakoff ("Bek") was unhappy that NKVD officer Anatoli Yakovlev had bypassed him and taken over the handling of Sax. *(1 page)*

Appendix A

MGB

From: MOSCOW

To: NEW YORK

No: 143

15 February 1945

Your No. 136[a].

Telegraph immediately the text of the memorandum, the expansion of AR4, which ACHESON it is that you are talking about, the English title of the sub-committee for DEKRET[DEKRET][i] matters and its

[33 groups unrecovered]

No. 899

Your No. 131[b].

PERCH's[OKUN'] surname .. TKACH[ii].

No. 933

Your No. 134[a]. We agree with your proposal for using ShURIN[d].

No. 901

Find out from "ALBERT"[iii] and "ROBERT"[iv] whether it would be possible for us to approach "PAGE, PAZh"[v] direct.

State what you [D] know, [..] groups unrecovered].

No. 902
** February

VIKTOR[vi]

Notes: [a] NEW YORK-MOSCO- No. 294 of 10 February 1945.

[b] NEW YORK-MOSCOW No. 292 of 10 February 1945.

[c] Probably NEW YORK-MOSCOW No. 293 of 10 February 1945.

[d] If ShURIN is not a surname, it could be treated as an ordinary noun (meaning "wife's brother") and refer to someone mentioned in the NEW YORK message to which this message is replying; it could be a cover-name.

Comments: [i] DEKRET: Lend-Lease.

[ii] TKACh: Mikhail TKACh, editor of the "Ukrainian Daily News".

[iii] ALBERT: Probably Iskhak Abdulovich AKhMEROV.

[iv] ROBERT: Nathan Gregory SILVERMASTER.

[v] PAZh: Possibly Lauchlin B. CURRIE.

[vi] VIKTOR: Lt. Gen. P. M. FITIN.

27 May 1968

With this message, dated 15 February 1945, Moscow instructed the New York *Rezidentura* to find out from Akhmerov and Silvermaster if the Soviets could approach Lauchlin Currie directly. Currie, of course, had already passed classified data through Soviet agents. *(1 page)*

Appendix A

VENONA

USSR

Ref. No: 3/NBF/T2278

Issued : A265/16/08/1979

Copy No: |

MOSCOW REQUESTS MORE DETAILS ON "IZBA" WORKERS LISTED IN NEW YORK MESSAGE

From: MOSCOW

To : NEW YORK

No : 173   22 February 1945

Your No. 137 [i].

1) Try to obtain through ROBERT [ii] more detailed information on the workers of the "IZBA" [iii], whom you list.

[16 groups unrecovered]

"DIKTOR" [iv]

No. 1098   VIKTOR [v]

Footnotes: [i] NEW YORK's No. 205 of 10 February 1945 (3/NBF/T16)

[ii] ROBERT: Nathan Gregory SILVERMASTER

[iii] IZBA : The Office of Strategic Services

[iv] DIKTOR: is RADIO-ANNOUNCER: William J. DONOVAN

[v] VIKTOR: Lt. General Pavel Mikhajlovich FITIN

Distribution

Copies
1-2   NSA (A265)
3   FBI
4   CIA
5   Security Service
6
7   (via CIA)
8   ASIO (via NSA)
9   Security Service ████ Representatives - WASHINGTON
10

• 3/NBF/T2278

TOP SECRET **VENONA**   107.

CLASSIFIED BY NSA/CSSM 123-2
DECLASSIFY ON Aug 70 2009

A February 1945 message from Moscow asking that Silvermaster obtain information about employees of the OSS. *(1 page)*

Appendix A

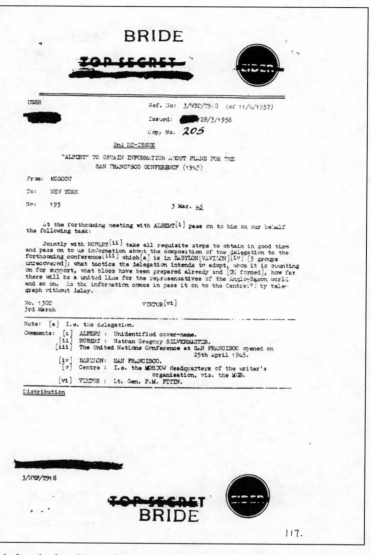

BRIDE

~~TOP SECRET~~   EIDER

USSR   Ref. No: 3/NBF/T918 (of 11/4/1957)

                        Issued: 28/3/1958

                        Copy No. 205

2nd RE-ISSUE

"ALBERT" TO OBTAIN INFORMATION ABOUT PLANS FOR THE
SAN FRANCISCO CONFERENCE (1945)

From: MOSCOW

To: NEW YORK

No: 195   3 Mar. 45

    At the forthcoming meeting with ALBERT[i] pass on to him on our behalf
the following task:

    Jointly with ROBERT[ii] take all requisite steps to obtain in good time
and pass on to us information about the composition of the delegation to the
forthcoming conference[iii] which[a] is in BABYLON[VAVILON][iv] [5 groups
unrecovered]; what tactics the delegation intends to adopt, whom it is counting
on for support, what blocs have been prepared already and [ON formed], how far
there will be a united line for the representatives of the Anglo-Saxon world
and so on. As the information comes in pass it on to the Centre[v] by telegraph without delay.

No. 1302   VIKTOR[vi]
3rd March

Note: [a] I.e. the delegation.
Comments: [i]   ALBERT : Unidentified cover-name.
          [ii] ROBERT : Nathan Gregory SILVERMASTER.
          [iii] The United Nations Conference at SAN FRANCISCO opened on
                                25th April 1945.
          [iv] BABYLON: SAN FRANCISCO.
          [v]   Centre : I.e. the MOSCOW Headquarters of the writer's
                                organisation, viz. the MGB.
          [vi] VIKTOR : Lt. Gen. P.M. FITIN.

Distribution

3/NBF/T918

~~TOP SECRET~~   EIDER
              BRIDE

                                                            117.

Several weeks before the founding conference of the United Nations, held in San Francisco
in April 1945, Pavel Fitin instructed Akhmerov and Silvermaster to gather as much information on the conference as possible. *(1 page)*

Appendix A

VENONA

TOP SECRET

USSR	Ref. No.: 3/NBF/T1268 (of 14/3/1960)
	Issued: ___/17/2/75
	Copy No.: 301

2ND REISSUE

1. GURON TO VISIT CHICAGO TO RE-ESTABLISH CONTACT WITH VEKSEL' AND MEET ___
2. GOLDSMITH AND GREGORY BREIT WORKING ON ENORMOUS
3. RAMSEY; PETER AND OTHER AGENT NETWORK

(1945)

From:	MOSCOW
To:	NEW YORK
No.:	259 21 March 1945

To ANTON[i].

VENONA

TOP SECRET

2

3/NBF/T1268

1. In our Nos. 5823[ii] of 9 December 1944, 749[iii] of 17 January 1945 and 606[iii] of 1 February 1945 instructions were given to send GURON[iv] to CHICAGO to re-establish contact with VEKSEL'[v]. Carry these out as soon as possible. GURON should also make use of his stay in CHICAGO to renew his acquaintance with ___ [vi], who is known to you and who is taking part in the work on ENORMOUS [ENORMOZ][vii].

2. [15 groups unrecovered]

- the well-known physicist - Gregory BREIT[viii], an emigrant from RUSSIA. According to available information BREIT is taking part in the work on ENORMOUS.

3. [4 groups unrecovered] 759[iii] of 8 February 1945 [2 groups unrecovered] with RAMSEY [RAMZAJ][ix].

4. By the next mail report on the carrying out of the instructions in our No. 416[iii] of 23 January 1945 concerning the collection through PETER[x] and the other agent network of information on the structure and activities of the Bureau of Standards.

No. 1745   VIKTOR[xi]

Footnotes: [i] ANTON: Leonid Romanovich KVASNIKOV, engineer in AMTORG.

[ii] Not available. Also referred to in NEW YORK's No. 1796 of 20 December 1944 (3/NBF/T489).

In March 1945 Moscow ordered an unidentified agent, code-named "Guron," to go to Chicago to reestablish contact with the head of Los Alamos, J. Robert Oppenheimer ("Veksel"). *(1 page)*

Appendix A

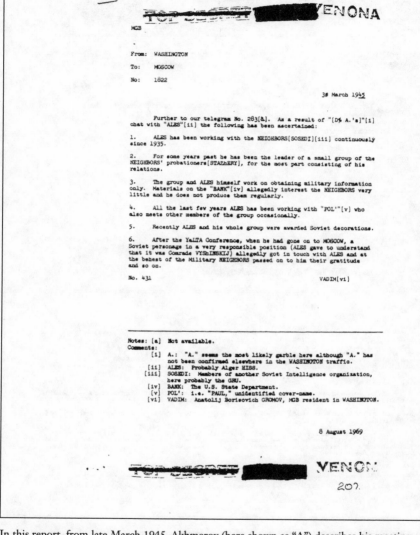

MGB

From: WASHINGTON

To: MOSCOW

No: 1822

3# March 1945

Further to our telegram No. 283[a]. As a result of "[D$ A.'s]"[i] chat with "ALES"[ii] the following has been ascertained:

1. ALES has been working with the NEIGHBORS[SOSEDI][iii] continuously since 1935.

2. For some years past he has been the leader of a small group of the NEIGHBORS' probationers[STAZhERY], for the most part consisting of his relations.

3. The group and ALES himself work on obtaining military information only. Materials on the "BANK"[iv] allegedly interest the NEIGHBORS very little and he does not produce them regularly.

4. All the last few years ALES has been working with "POL'"[v] who also meets other members of the group occasionally.

5. Recently ALES and his whole group were awarded Soviet decorations.

6. After the YALTA Conference, when he had gone on to MOSCOW, a Soviet personage in a very responsible position (ALES gave to understand that it was Comrade VYShINSKIJ) allegedly got in touch with ALES and at the behest of the Military NEIGHBORS passed on to him their gratitude and so on.

No. 431   VADIM[vi]

Notes: [a] Not available.
Comments:
   [i] A.: "A." seems the most likely garble here although "A." has not been confirmed elsewhere in the WASHINGTON traffic.
  [ii] ALES: Probably Alger HISS.
 [iii] SOSEDI: Members of another Soviet Intelligence organization, here probably the GRU.
  [iv] BANK: The U.S. State Department.
  [v] POL': i.e. "PAUL," unidentified cover-name.
 [vi] VADIM: Anatolij Borisovich GROMOV, MGB resident in WASHINGTON.

8 August 1969

In this report, from late March 1945, Akhmerov (here shown as "A") describes his meeting with Alger Hiss ("Ales"). The background information on "Ales" clearly describes Hiss, who visited Moscow after attending the Yalta Conference. *(1 page)*

Appendix A

BRIDE

~~TOP SECRET~~

USSR

Ref. No· 3/NBF/1914 (of 16/5/1957)

Issued : 27/5/1958

Copy No: 205.

<u>RE-ISSUE</u>

INSTRUCTIONS FOR "ALBERT" (1945)

From: MOSCOW

To: NEW YORK

No: 328   6 Apr. <u>45</u>

    Tell "ALBERT"[i] to make arrangements with "ROBERT"[ii] about maintaining contact with "RICHARD"[iii] and "PILOT"[iv] in BABYLON[VAVILON][v]

[9 groups unrecovered][a]

Note: [a] 4 of these should contain signature and serial numbers.

Comments: [i] ALBERT : Unidentified cover-name.

        [ii] ROBERT : Nathan Gregory SILVERMASTER.

       [iii] RICHARD : Harry Dexter WHITE.

      [iv] PILOT : William Ludwig ULLMAN.

       [v] BABYLON : SAN FRANCISCO.

<u>Distribution</u>

An April 1945 message from Moscow instructing Akhmerov ("Albert") to maintain contact with Silvermaster, White, and Ullman at the founding conference of the United Nations. *(1 page)*

Appendix A

Le 13 avril 1945.

1 8 AVR. 1945

29

Monsieur Max Horngacher,
F.E.S.E.
13 rue Calvin, Genève.

Cher Monsieur,

Je vous envoie ci-joint la lettre pour M. Dulles que je vous

ai promise ce matin.

Avec mes meilleures salutations.

Noel H. Field

An April 1945 letter, in French, from Noel Field to Soviet agent Max Horngacher regarding Allen Dulles of OSS. This letter would be used as evidence against Field in his trial in Hungary. *(1 page)*

Appendix A

~~TOP SECRET EIDER~~ BRIDE

~~TOP SECRET EIDER~~ BRIDE

(Re-issue)

1181.

From: WASHINGTON
To: MOSCOW
No: 3713-3715   29 June 1945

To the 8th Department. Material from "RAIDER [REJDER]".[i]

I am sending information extracted from the secret program of the "JOINT AIRCRAFT COMMITTEE" of the "DEPOT"[ii] of 25 May of this year concerning aircraft construction planned for 1945-1946.

In the first column is given the figure for the aircraft construction planned for April-December 1945; in the second column is the analogous figure for the whole of 1946.

1. Four engine heavy bomber long range for the USAAF [AVVS] type B-29:

[48 groups unrecoverable]

Ditto type B-24:	859;	none.
Ditto type B-32:	159;	none.

[53 groups unrecoverable]

USAAF type B-26:	2033;	1050.

No.	Type	Col 1	Col 2
1.	Single engine light bomber type (X) BTK:	20;	none
2.	Ditto, type BTM:	none;	766.
3.	Ditto, type BTD:	23;	none.
4.	Ditto, type BT2C:	6;	4.
5.	Ditto, type (X) BT2D:	15;	10.
6.	Ditto, type BT2D:	none;	579.
7.	Ditto, type SB2C:	1617;	2610.
8.	Ditto, type SBF:	22;	none.
9.	Ditto, type SBW:	353;	none.
10.	Ditto, type TBM:	3198;	4320.
11.	Ditto, type TBY:	799;	1800.
12.	Ditto, type TB3F:	none;	165.
	Total light bombers:	6053;	9804.

1. Twin engine fighters for the USAAF type P-38:   1011; none.

[51 groups unrecoverable]

No.		Col 1	Col 2
	F7F:	330;	1410.
2.	Ditto, type FD-1:	1;	99.
	Total twin engine fighters for the Navy:	331;	1509.

No.		Col 1	Col 2
1.	Single engine fighters for the USAAF types P-47D and P-47N:	3186;	3300.
2.	Ditto, types P-51, P-51D and P-51N:	5558;	4775.
3.	Ditto, type P-63:	1041;	150.
4.	Ditto, type P-80:	798;	2748.
5.	Ditto, type P-84:	13;	89.
	Total [6 groups unrecovered] :	10594;	11062.

[11 groups unrecoverable]

~~TOP SECRET EIDER~~ BRIDE

250.

Soviet agent Victor Perlo's June 1945 report to Moscow on U.S. aircraft construction. *(3 pages)*

Appendix A

```
                        G-1:  1133;   none.
2.          Ditto. type FG-4:   486;  2460.
3.          Ditto. type  FM :  1425;   208.
5.          Ditto. type F2M:     1;  1865.
6.          Ditto. type  FR:   275;  1400.
7.          Ditto. type F4V:  2679;  3600.
8.          Ditto. type F6F:  3625;
```

[68 groups unrecoverable]

```
                                ;     6.
Total single engine reconnaissance planes
            for the Navy:  446;  546.
```

Transport planes

[50 groups unrecoverable]

```
                  USAAF:  1080;  1132.

1.Ditto, for the Navy, type JRM:   14;    6.
2.          Ditto. type RY-3:   92;  none.
   Total four engine transport planes
            for the Navy:  106;    6.
```

[29 groups unrecoverable]

```
                          :   50;  913.
Total twin engine planes for
            the USAAF:  1273;  1963.

Medium twin engine transports
   for the USAAF, type C-47:  1293;  525.
        Ditto
```

[32 groups unrecoverable]

```
Light transports for the USAAF,
            type C-64:   20;  none.

  Ditto, for the Navy,
            type Y2F:   64;  none.
```

Training planes.

```
Single engine for the
      USAAF type AT6:  843;  none.
```

Liaison planes for the USAAF.

```
1.               Type L-4:  826;  none.
2.               Type L-14:  399;  1800.
3.               Type L-5:  1093;  1200.
     Total liaison planes:  2318;  3000.
```

```
Single engine helicopters(rotary)
         for the USAAF,

1.               Type R-5:  192;  285.
2.               Type R
```

[14 groups unrecoverable]

```
                        :  552;  605.
```

Special designation.

Appendix A

Single engine plane for the USAAF. type P.-14: 720; 960.

General total for the preceeding paragraphs:
1. Planes of all types for the USAAF : 28861; 25747.
2. Planes of all types for the Navy : 19901; 29159.
All planes: 48762; 54906.

"835   VADIM[iii]

Comment:
[i]   Victor PERLO
[ii] War Production Board
[iii] Anatolij Borisovich GROMOV

(page 3)

505

APPENDIX B

The Spies

THE SOVIET UNION RELIED on a far-reaching network of spies to conduct its aggressive espionage campaign. The United States was a particularly important target for the USSR's spying, and the Soviet intelligence services had great success recruiting Americans to help their cause. But the Soviets had agents all over the world working at the behest of the Moscow leadership—such as those who carried out Stalin's plans to assassinate rival Leon Trotsky.

What follows is a rogues' gallery of key Soviet intelligence officers and agents.

Max Bedacht, the leader of the Soviet underground in the United States, in 1935, the year he recruited Whittaker Chambers for espionage.

Pavel Fitin, head of the Foreign Department of the NKVD during World War II.

Iskhak Akhmerov, the NKVD "illegal" *Rezident* in the United States during World War II.

Jacob Golos, a senior NKVD agent in the United States during the 1930s and 1940s.

Appendix B

Vassiliy Zarubin, the NKVD *Rezident* in the United States during World War II.

Lisa Zarubina, the wife of Zarubin and an active NKVD officer in the United States in her own right.

Leonid Eitingon, the NKVD officer who organized the murder of Leon Trotsky.

Arthur Adams, a Soviet military intelligence (GRU) officer who worked in the United States from the 1920s through the 1940s. He was involved in the theft of America's atomic secrets.

KGB Archives

Anatoli Yatzkov (also known as Yakovlev), an NKVD officer who was active in the Soviets' atomic espionage.

National Security Agency

Gregory Kheifitz, the NKVD *Rezident* in San Francisco. This image is from an FBI surveillance camera.

Vicente Lombardo Toledano, a Mexican labor leader and an agent of the NKVD.

Appendix B

The Honored Chekist medal, which the NKVD issued to the most talented intelligence officers.

The Order of the Red Star, presented for bravery in combat or behind enemy lines. Several NKVD agents who served in the United States during the war received this honor, including Elizabeth Bentley, Harry Gold, Nathan Gregory Silvermaster, and Alger Hiss.

The Order of the Red Banner, issued for extreme bravery in combat or behind enemy lines. This medal was issued to a number of the NKVD officer who were in the United States in World War II as well as to Morris and Lona Cohen.

Appendix B

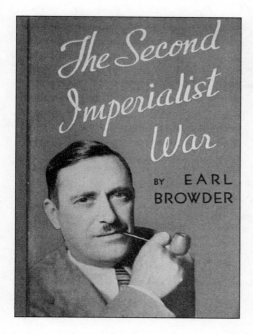

The cover of Earl Browder's book *The Second Imperialist War*, written during the period of the Soviet-Nazi alliance. Browder was the head of the American Communist Party from 1932 to 1945.

Soviet agents Morris and Lona Cohen, shown here in Moscow wearing their Order of the Red Banner medals.

Kitty Harris, the common-law wife of Earl Browder in the 1920s and 1930s, was an NKVD agent in Europe and Latin America before and during World War II.

Appendix B

State Department official and Soviet spy Alger Hiss (foreground) at a 1948 congressional hearing with his accuser, former Soviet agent Whittaker Chambers. Elizabeth Bentley, another former Soviet agent, is to Chambers's immediate right.

Julius and Ethel Rosenberg, both executed for passing atomic secrets to the Soviet Union.

Klaus Fuchs, who worked on the secret atomic bomb project and later confessed to passing classified information to the Soviets.

Appendix A

William Weisband of the U.S. Army Signal Security Agency, who alerted Moscow to the fact that the Americans had broken the Soviet code.

Judy Coplon, an NKVD spy in the Department of Justice.

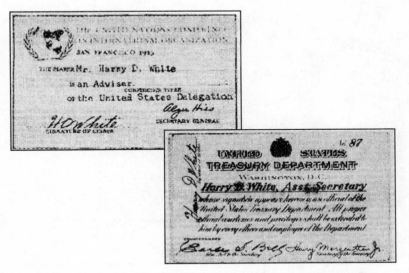

Assistant Secretary of the Treasury Harry Dexter White's credentials for the founding conference of the United Nations, signed by Alger Hiss. White, like Hiss, was a Soviet agent.

NOTES

PREFACE
1 *Sovetskaya Rossiya*, Moscow, April 22, 1993, p. 5.

CHAPTER 1
1 Memoirs of Professor S. Swianiewicz in *The Crime of Katyn: Facts and Documents*, with a foreword by General Wladyslaw Anders, pp. 31–32. Additional information about the murder of the Polish officers at Katyn may be found in J. P. Zawodny, *Death in the Forest: The Story of the Katyn Forest Massacre*, and Vladimir Abarinov, *The Murderers of Katyn*. Abarinov is a Russian journalist based in Moscow who utilized documents recently released from the Soviet archives.
2 Nataliya Lebedeva, "The Katyn Tragedy," *International Affairs*, Moscow, June 1990, pp. 106–7 and 114. Lebedeva is a Russian researcher who gained access to the Central State Archives of the USSR and of the Soviet army to see the records on the murder of the Polish officers. Many of these documents were later made available to the Polish government by Boris Yeltsin when he apologized for Soviet responsibility in the murder of the Polish officers.

3 Yevgeny Primakov, et al., editors, Foreign Intelligence Service of the Russian Federation, *Ocherki Istorii Rossiiskoi Vneshnei Razvedki* [*Essays on the History of Russian Foreign Intelligence*], vol. 3, pp. 391–93.
4 FBI Summary of Zarubin in case NY65-14702. Released under the Freedom of Information Act.
5 *Venona*, New York to Moscow, July 1, 1943.
6 Inez Cope Jeffery, *Inside Russia: The Life and Times of Zoya Zarubina, Former Soviet Intelligence Officer and Interpreter During the Stalin Years*, pp. 71–72. Although the book is extremely naive, it contains extensive direct quotes from former KGB officer Zoya Zarubina, the daughter of Vassiliy Zarubin with his first wife.
7 Robert Louis Benson and Michael Warner, *Venona: Soviet Espionage and the American Response, 1939–1957*, pp. 51–54.
8 German Propaganda Ministry, *Amtliches Material zum Massenmord von KATYN*, Gedruckt im Deutschen Verlag, Berlin, 1943.
9 *Venona*, New York to Moscow, August 23, 1944.
10 *Veteraniy Vneshnei Razvedki Rossii* [*Veterans of Foreign Intelligence of Russia*], pp. 14–16.

Notes

11 Walter Krivitsky, a high-ranking Soviet intelligence officer who defected to the West in 1937, revealed that Markin, who had once been his assistant, was probably murdered by the OGPU—as Krivitsky himself would be on February 10, 1941, by its successor, the NKVD. Krivitsky had been told by Abraham Slutsky, then chief of the foreign division of the OGPU, that Markin was a Trotskyite, which was considered a capital crime in Stalin's Russia and which indicated to Krivitsky the truth about Markin's death. W. G. Krivitsky, *In Stalin's Secret Service*, p. 171.

12 Primakov, et al., *Essays on the History of Russian Foreign Intelligence*, vol. 4, pp. 222–23; and Vitaliy Pavlov, *Operatziya "Sneg" [Operation "Snow"]*, pp. 24ff.

13 John Barron, *KGB: The Secret Work of Soviet Secret Agents*, p. 253.

14 See Chapter 5.

15 Romerstein discussion with retired KGB general Vadim Kirpichenko, October 1998.

16 Elizabeth Bentley, comprehensive statement to the FBI, November 1945, pp. 73–74. Released under the Freedom of Information Act.

17 *Venona*, Moscow to New York, March 29, 1945.

18 Barron, *KGB*, p. 253.

19 House of Representatives, Select Committee to Investigate the Federal Communications Commission, *Study and Investigation of the Federal Communications Commission*, p. 1934, and *New York Journal American*, October 18, 1943.

20 The difficulties and the opportunities that the American code breakers encountered were described by NSA cryptologist Cecil Phillips in a study prepared by the agency and published along with the declassified cables. Phillips described the Soviet error that initially proved critical to the decryption effort: "A Soviet code clerk preparing a message first reduced its text into numeric code groups drawn from a code book (a kind of dictionary in which the words and common phrases correspond to four-digit numbers). After encoding the plain text with numeric code groups, the clerk would obscure the code groups by adding them, digit by digit, to a string of random digits. The second series of digits—called the 'additive' or the 'key' was known to both the sender and receiver because it was printed on the pages of what was termed a 'one-time pad.' One-time pads were periodically pouched to Soviet consular missions in sealed packets. The pad pages—with sixty five-digit additive groups per page—were used in order, always starting with the group in the upper left-hand corner.... Code clerks in different Soviet missions used up these packets at varying rates, depending on the volume of messages to be enciphered or deciphered." Phillips went on to explain the security implications of this system, noting that "security... depends on both the randomness (that is unpredictability) of the 'key' on the one-time pad pages and the uniqueness of the pad sets held by the sender and the receiver." According to Phillips, "different Soviet organizations used their own codes, changing them every few years (probably more to improve vocabulary and convenience

Notes

than to enhance security)." And, in an effort to demonstrate the sophistication inherent in Moscow's transfer-of-information system, he emphasized that "the flaw in the Soviet messages resulted from the manufacturers' duplication of one-time pad pages, rather than from a malfunctioning random-number generator or extensive re-use of pages by code clerks." Phillips, in fact, has managed to pinpoint the precise moment at which the USSR's method failed: "for a few months in early 1942, a time of great strain on the Soviet regime, the KGB's crypto-graphic center in the Soviet Union, for some unknown reason, printed duplicate copies of the 'key' on more than 35,000 pages of additive and then assembled and bound them in one-time pads." Benson and Warner, *Venona*, xv.

21 From a pledge taken by two thousand new Communist Party members at a rally in 1935 where Earl Browder explained that the pledge was a condition for member-ship in the Communist Party. J. Peters, *The Communist Party: A Manual on Organization*, pp. 104–5.

22 *New York Times*, February 19, 1946.

23 *Fourth International*, New York, January 1942, p. 9.

24 *Venona*, Moscow to London, September 18, 1945.

25 *Venona*, Moscow to London, September 21, 1945.

26 *Venona*, Moscow to various posts, April 7, 1946.

27 Trotsky to Mexican attorney general, May 27, 1940, *Socialist Appeal*, June 15, 1940, p. 4.

28 Russian Center for the Storage and Study of Documents of Recent

History, Moscow [hereafter referred to as "Comintern Archives"], Fond 495, Opis 20, Delo 540.

29 *Izvestiya TsK KPSS*, April 1990, no. 4, p. 223.

30 Comintern Archives, Fond 495, Opis 18, Delo 1291, p. 47.

31 Comintern Archives, Fond 495, Opis 74, Delo 470, pp. 3–5 and Delo 473, pp. 1–26.

32 Adolf Hitler, *Speech Delivered in the Reichstag, January 30, 1939*, p. 42.

33 V. M. Molotov, *Molotov's Report to the Supreme Soviet*, pp. 4 and 6.

34 M. Ross, *A History of Soviet Foreign Policy*, pp. 44–45.

35 Comintern Archives, *Resolutionsentwurf zur amerikanischen Frage* [*Draft Resolution on the American Question*], June 20, 1941, Fond 495, Opis 20, Delo 513, pp. 37–38.

36 Comintern Archives, Dimitroff letter to Stalin, June 25, 1941, reporting on the instructions to the foreign Communist parties, Fond 495, Opis 73, Delo 112, p. 1.

37 Nigel West, *Venona*, pp. 61, 76–77.

38 *Venona*, London to Moscow, August 16, 1940.

39 *Venona*, London to Moscow, August 20, 1940.

40 *Venona*, London to Moscow, September 4, 1940.

41 *Venona*, London to Moscow, September 10, 1940.

42 *Venona*, London to Moscow, September 13, 1940.

43 *Venona*, London to Moscow, September 17, 1940.

44 *Venona*, London to Moscow, October 11, 1940.

45 *Venona*, London to Moscow, October 2, 1940.

46 *Venona*, London to Moscow, September 7, 1940.

Notes

47 *Venona*, London to Moscow,
October 16, 1940.

48 R. V. Jones, *The Wizard War: British
Scientific Intelligence, 1939–1945*,
p. 129.

49 *Venona*, London to Moscow,
October 30, 1940.

50 Bentley, FBI statement, p. 25.

51 Michael Warner and Robert Louis
Benson, "Venona and Beyond:
Thoughts on Work Undone,"
Intelligence and National Security,
Frank Cass, London, July 1997,
pp. 9–10. The story was based on
Robert Louis Benson's interview
with Frank Rowlett and Oliver
Kirby, who were involved in the
1944 conversation.

52 Benson and Warner, *Venona*,
xxvi–xxvii.

53 David A. Hatch and Robert Louis
Benson, *The Korean War: The Sigint
Background*, pp. 4–5.

CHAPTER 2

1 The KGB has been known under various names. From 1917 to 1922 it
was called the Cheka; from 1922 to
1934 it was called the GPU and
OGPU; from 1934 to 1946 it was
known as the NKVD and NKGB
(popularly referred to as NKVD); it
was the MGB from 1946 to 1953, the
MVD until 1954, and the KGB from
then until the collapse of the Soviet
Union in 1991. John J. Dziak,
Chekisty: A History of the KGB, pp.
184–85; and V. N. Chebrikov, et al.,
USSR, KGB, *Istoriya Sovetskikh
Organov Gosudarstvennoi Bezopasnosti
[History of Soviet State Security Organs]*
(marked Top Secret).

2 See Chapter 4.

3 Whittaker Chambers, extensive statement to the FBI, January 3–April 18,

1949, pp. 78, 86–87, 90, 94–95,
106–107, 109, 119. Released under
the Freedom of Information Act.

4 *Komsomolskaya Pravda*, December
21, 1990.

5 Ibid.

6 Vitaliy Pavlov, *Operatziya "Sneg"
[Operation "Snow"]*, pp. 13–14,
19–22, 30. Pavlov first told the story
of Operation Snow in the Moscow
magazine *Novosti Razvedki I
Kontrrazvedki [News of Intelligence
and Counterintelligence]*, 1995, no.
9–10, 11–12.

7 Primakov, et al., *Essays on the History
of Russian Foreign Intelligence*, vol. 3,
p. 175.

8 *Komsomolskaya Pravda*.

9 Memorandum from Pavel Fitin,
head of the Foreign Department of
NKVD, to George Dimitroff, head
of the Comintern, January 14, 1942,
Comintern Archives, Fond 495,
Opis 73, Delo 188, pp. 1, 3.

10 Julius Mader, *Dr. Sorge—Report*,
pp. 174–75.

11 Interrogation of Sorge, March 11,
1942, reprinted in *Far Eastern
Affairs*, Moscow, November 5, 1991,
p. 168.

12 William Z. Foster, *The War Crisis:
Questions and Answers*, pp. 5–7.

13 Comintern Archives, Fond 495,
Opis 20, Delo 513, *Resolutionsetwurf
zur amerikanischen Frage [Draft
Resolution on the American Question]*,
p. 34 (marked Secret).

14 Pavlov, p. 35.

15 Pavlov in *Novosti Razvedki I
Kontrrazvedki*, 1995, no. 11–12. The
Tanaka Memorial was a forgery
covertly released by the Soviet
Union in 1931. It was widely used to
create anti-Japanese sentiment in the
United States and Europe. The

Notes

document was supposedly written in 1927 by Baron Tanaka, prime minister of Japan from 1927 to 1929. In addition to its many internal contradictions, its tone was wrong and would not have been written that way by a Japanese official to the emperor. Leon Trotsky also inadvertently provided the evidence that it was a forgery. Trying to bolster its authenticity, Trotsky wrote in 1940 that he had seen the document in Moscow in 1925. It had been obtained by Soviet intelligence, he claimed. (*Fourth International*, New York, June 1941, "The 'Tanaka Memorial,'" by Leon Trotsky.) However, Tanaka was not prime minister until 1927, so he could not have written it in 1925. It is possible that some authentic document had been obtained from a Japanese source and was used as the exemplar to create the forgery.

The forgery first appeared in a Shanghai English-language newspaper, *The China Critic*, of September 24, 1931. The editor of the paper, in answer to an inquiry, wrote that "Whilst the source of the memorial is official, and the text was disclosed at the Kyoto Conference of the Institute of Pacific Relations, in 1929, by one of the delegates who was for a long time a student in Japan, we regret to say that we are not in a position to disclose to you the name of the delegate, which is kept confidential by his request." (Letter of May 7, 1932).

The introduction to a 1942 Communist Party USA version of the "document" says that it first came to light in 1929 after it was purchased by Chang Hsueh-liang, the young marshal of Manchuria (an erratic opportunist who sometimes cooperated with the Communists), from a Japanese. It was not until 1931 that it was released by the China Council of the Institute of Pacific Relations and published in the Shanghai newspaper. (*Japanese Imperialism Exposed: The Secret Tanaka Document.*)

In his article Trotsky revealed that the plan was first to release the "document" abroad and then publish it in the magazine *Communist International*. Shortly after the Shanghai newspaper published the forgery, it was republished in the December 30, 1931, issue of the *Communist International*, the official Comintern weekly.

In 1932, when the Comintern ordered the American branch of the front organization Pan-Pacific Trade Union Secretariat to publish the *Tanaka Memorial* in a Japanese-language edition to be smuggled to Japan, it had to be translated from English to Japanese. (Report of meeting, San Francisco Bureau of the Pan-Pacific Trade Union Secretariat, March 2, 1932, Comintern Archives, Fond 534, Opis 4, Delo 422.) As there was no Japanese-language version of the supposed document, it clearly was a forgery.

16 Pavlov, p. 39.

17 *Voyenno-Istoricheskiy Zhurnal* [*Military Historical Journal*], Moscow, June 1988.

18 Senate Internal Security Subcommittee, *Hearings on Institute of Pacific Relations*, Part I (U.S. Printing Office, Washington, D.C., 1951), p. 157.

19 Memorandum from Harry Dexter White to Secretary Henry

Notes

Morgenthau, Jr., May 1941 (written May 1941, sent to Secretary Morgenthau on June 6, 1941). *Morgenthau Diaries* (manuscript), vol. 405, pp. 471ff., Roosevelt Library, Hyde Park, NY, Morgenthau papers. Memorandum of Henry Morgenthau to President Roosevelt and Cordell Hull, November 18, 1942 (drafted by Harry Dexter White), in *Pearl Harbor Attack Hearings Before the Joint Committee on the Investigation of the Pearl Harbor Attack*, Part 19, pp. 3667ff. Hull Ultimatum, November 25, 1941, Ibid., pp. 3652ff.

20 Cordell Hull, *The Memoirs of Cordell Hull*, vol. 2, pp. 1072–73.

21 *Pearl Harbor Attack Hearings*, Testimony of General of the Army George C. Marshall, December 6, 1945, p. 1149.

22 Pavlov, p. 40.

23 Bentley, FBI statement, pp. 73–74.

24 House of Representatives Committee on Un-American Activities, *Hearing Regarding Communist Espionage in the United States Government*, Testimony of Elizabeth Bentley, July 31, 1948, p. 551.

25 Ibid., Testimony of Harry Dexter White, August 1, 1948, pp. 878, 893.

26 *Venona*, New York to Moscow, April 29, 1944.

27 Letter from Morgenthau to Admiral William B. Leahy, December 29, 1942, Senate Internal Security Subcommittee, *Interlocking Subversion in Government Department (The Harry Dexter White Papers)*, August 20, 1955, p. 2548.

28 *Venona*, New York to Moscow, August 4–5, 1944.

29 *Venona*, New York to Moscow, October 1, 1944.

30 *Venona*, Moscow to New York, March 19, 1945.

31 *Venona*, New York to Moscow, January 18, 1945.

32 *Venona*, New York to Moscow, August 4–5, 1944.

33 Senate Internal Security Subcommittee, *Interlocking Subversion*, Part 30, pp. 2639–640. Reprint of article from *United Nations World* by Fred Smith.

34 James Byrnes, director of war mobilization and later secretary of state, was in Paris in October 1944. A German-speaking G.I. who was monitoring the Nazi propaganda broadcasts to their own people told him about them. The broadcasts warned the Germans that the Morgenthau Plan "would destroy all industry and turn Germany into an agricultural state." The purpose of the Nazi propaganda was "to inspire the Germans to fight and die rather than surrender." James F. Byrnes, *Speaking Frankly*, p. 181.

35 Soviet surrender leaflet to the German troops, no. 1352, *Hitler ist nicht Deutschland* [*Hitler is not Germany*] (in the possession of the authors).

36 Senate Internal Security Subcommittee, *Interlocking Subversion*, p. 2527.

37 *Venona*, Moscow to New York, April 5, 1945. Code names for the agents were often changed.

38 *The United Nations Conference on International Organization, Provisional List of Members of the Delegations and Officers of the Secretariat*, San Francisco, April 1945, pp. 47, 59.

39 *Venona*, San Francisco to Moscow, May 5, 1945.

Notes

40 *Venona*, San Francisco to Moscow, June 8, 1945.

41 *Venona*, New York to Moscow, November 20, 1944.

42 FBI Summary Report on Nathan Gregory Silvermaster, June 9, 1952, p. 485.

43 FBI File on Harry Dexter White, #101-4053, Section 36, Memo January 13, 1965, from William Branigan to William Sullivan.

44 Senate Internal Security Subcommittee, *Interlocking Subversion*, Part 15, pp. 1115–116, letter from J. Edgar Hoover to Harry Vaughan, February 1, 1946.

45 J. W. Pickersgill and D. F. Forster (editors), *The Mackenzie King Record*, vol. 3, 1945–1946, p. 134.

46 Senate Internal Security Subcommittee, *Interlocking Subversion*, press statement of James F. Byrnes, November 9, 1953, p. 1086.

47 *Ottawa Citizen*, November 17, 1953.

48 Senate Internal Security Subcommittee, *Interlocking Subversion*, p. 1144.

49 Senate Internal Security Subcommittee, *Interlocking Subversion*, p. 2550.

50 House Committee on Un-American Activities, *Hearings Regarding Communist Espionage*, p. 881.

51 *New York Herald Tribune*, August 18, 1948, p. 1.

CHAPTER 3

1 *Komsomolskaya Pravda*, December 21, 1990, translated in FBIS-SOV 28 December 1990.

2 V. N. Chebrikov, et al., *History of Soviet State Security Organs*, p. 425.

3 *Venona*, New York to Moscow June 3, 1943, signed "Maksim," the code name for Zarubin.

4 The Comintern confirmed a decision of the CPUSA Politburo to appoint Browder to direct the day-to-day work of the Communist Party—"Organization Directives" Polit-Commission, Comintern, February 22, 1932, Comintern Archives, Fond 495, Opis 20, Delo 508, p. 172.

5 Frederick Vanderbilt Field, *From Right to Left: An Autobiography*, p. 173.

6 J. Peters, *The Communist Party: A Manual on Organization*, pp. 26, 104–5.

7 Special Committee on Un-American Activities (Dies Committee), 1939, vol. 7, pp. 4417–4418.

8 Peters, pp. 119–22.

9 *Communist International*, Organ of the Executive Committee of the Communist International, Petrograd, vol. 2, no. 13, pp. 2377–381 (1920). Few American Communists saw this rare magazine, but all read the Conditions of Admission when the United Communist Party of America reprinted the *Theses and Statutes of the Third (Communist) International*, adopted by the Second Congress, July 17–August 7, 1920, from the edition published in Moscow. As late as February 1934, the American Communist Party published the "conditions" as part of a pamphlet by the head of the Comintern's Organization Department, Osip Piatnitsky: *The Twenty-One Conditions of Admission into the Communist International*, Workers Library Publishers, New York, 1934.

10 *The Communist*, Official Organ, United Communist Party of America, vol. 1, no. 1, June 12, 1920, p. 3.

Notes

11 John Pepper, *Underground Radicalism*, p. 16.

12 Theodore Draper, *The Roots of American Communism*, p. 190.

13 *Theses and Resolutions Adopted at the III World Congress of the Communist International* (June 22–July 12, 1921), Press Bureau of the Communist International, Moscow, 1921, "Theses on Tactics," p. 20. A slightly different translation was released by the American Communist Party under the same title, published by Contemporary Publishing Association, New York City, 1921, pp. 40–41. Neither of these publications lists Lenin and the other authors of the theses. That is found in the draft "Theses on Tactics," Press Bureau of the Comintern, Moscow, 1921. The quotation appears on p. 6 and the list on p. 19.

14 *Program and Constitution: Workers Party of America, Adopted at the National Convention, New York City, December 24–25–26, 1921*. Benjamin Gitlow, *I Confess: The Truth About American Communism*, pp. 132–33.

15 Quoted in Pepper, 12.

16 Ibid., 17.

17 *The Communist*, vol. 1, no. 9, July 1922, p. 24. As this was an underground publication issued only to Party members, it showed no address of publication.

18 *The Communist*, vol. 1, no. 13, 1923, p. 2. Although this issue of the underground Communist Party organ did not show an exact date, it was probably about January 1923.

19 Translated from the German and quoted in Werner T. Angress, *Stillborn Revolution: The Communist Bid for Power in Germany, 1921–1923*, p. 428.

20 *Theses and Resolutions Adopted at the III World Congress of the Communist International (June 22–July 12, 1921)*, Resolution on "The Organizational Construction of the Communist Parties and the Methods and Scope of their Activity," Moscow edition, p. 54, New York edition, pp. 113–14.

21 *Protokoll des III Kongresses der Kommunistischen Internationale (Moskau, 22 Juni bis 12 Juli 1921)*, p. 1042.

22 Bernard Kaufmann, Eckhard Reisener, Dieter Schwips, and Henri Walther, *Der Nachrichtendienst der KPD, 1919–1937* [*The Intelligence Service of the Communist Party of Germany, 1919–1937*], document opposite p. 33, and pp. 35–36.

23 *An den Nachrichtenleiter, Berlin, den 27 Mai 1922* [*To Intelligence Leaders, Berlin, 27 May 1922*], *Stiftung Archiv der Parteien und Massenorganisationen der DDR im Bundesarchiv, Berlin* [hereafter referred to as "SAPMO"], Ry1/12/705/8, p. 33.

24 Lehen was once married to the daughter of Comintern official Otto Kuusinen. After World War II he went back to Finland, where he served in the leadership of the Finnish Communist Party. Lazitch, Branko, and Milorad M. Drachkovitch, *Biographical Dictionary of the Comintern*, pp. 251–52.

25 *Bericht über den Stand der N-Arbeit Ende Februar 1925* [*Report Concerning the State of the N (Intelligence)-Work End of February 1925*], in SAPMO, Ry1/12/705/2, pp. 208–11 (in German).

26 Kaufmann, et al., pp. 49–50.

27 *International Press Correspondence*, May 6, 1925, Vienna, English-

Notes

language edition. *Imprecorr*, as it was called, was a weekly publication of the Comintern for Party functionaries and writers in the member parties. The identification of Lovestone as "Powers" may be found in Theodore Draper, *American Communism and Soviet Russia*, p. 134.

28 "Membership Figures According to Dues Payments, By Language Sections, January to June 1925," in *The 4th National Convention, Workers (Communist) Party of America, held in Chicago, Illinois, August 21–30, 1925*, p. 37.

29 "Recruiting Drive," Resolution adopted at a meeting of the Organization Commission of the American Communist Party and reported to the Communist International, October 8, 1932, Comintern Archives, Fond 495, Opis 25, Delo 885, p. 26.

30 David J. Dallin, *Soviet Espionage*, pp. 52, 86.

31 *American Worker Correspondent*, Chicago, Illinois, April 1926, pp. 1, 4.

32 Ibid., July 1926, p. 4.

33 Dies Committee, vol. 7, pp. 4675–676.

34 Dies Committee, Executive Session, vol. 2, p. 568.

35 House Committee on Un-American Activities, *Hearings Regarding Communist Espionage*, 1948, p. 3556.

36 *The Red International of Labour Unions* [published by the Trade Union Education League as the English-language edition of the Moscow magazine], October 1929, pp. 369–74, "Letter to the National Convention of the Trade Union Education League."

37 *The Trade Union Unity League (American Section of the RILU): Its Program, Structure, Methods, and History*, Trade Union Unity League, New York (circa 1929), pp. 17, 21.

38 *Meeting of Bureau of Anglo-American Secretariat, January 13, 1934*, Comintern Archives, Fond 495, Opis 72, Delo 257, pp. 3, 6; *On the Work of Forming an Independent Federation of Labor in the USA*, Comintern Archives, Fond 495, Opis 5, Delo 408, pp. 161–63.

39 See Chapter 8.

40 Comintern Archives, Fond 495, Opis 20, Delo 515, p. 148.

41 "Statement of Earl Browder, General Secretary of Communist Party USA, to the McNaboe Committee, June 29, 1938" in *Report of the Joint Legislative Committee to Investigate the Administration and Enforcement of the Law, State of New York* [McNaboe Committee], vol. 2, pp. 551–2.

42 *Meeting of Bureau of Anglo-American Secretariat, May 11, 1933*, Comintern Archives, Fond 495, Opis 72, Delo 204, p. 30.

43 *Meeting of Bureau of Anglo-American Secretariat, April 27, 1933*, Ibid., p. 20.

44 The Comintern official Mehring was identified as the Estonian Communist Richard Mirring in Vilém Kahan, "A Contribution to the Identification of the Pseudonyms Used in the Minutes and Reports of the Communist International" in *International Review of Social History*, XXII (1978), p. 191.

45 *An Open Letter to All Members of the Communist Party*, Central Committee, Communist Party USA, New York, 1933.

46 Letter marked "Secret," Comintern Archives, Fond 495, Opis 72, Delo 274.

Notes

47 *The Way Out: A Program for American Labor. Manifesto and Principal Resolutions Adopted by the 8th Convention of the Communist Party of the USA*, p. 57.

48 *Meeting of Bureau of Anglo-American Secretariat, March 8, 1934*, Comintern Archives, Fond 495, Opis 72, Delo 257, p. 13.

49 All published by Workers Library Publishers in 1935.

50 William Z. Foster, *Toward Soviet America.*

51 William Z. Foster, and Benjamin Gitlow, *Acceptance Speeches, National Election Campaign Committee Workers (Communist) Party, 1928*, p. 12.

52 *List of Delegates of the Communist Party of America at the VII Congress of the Communist International*, Comintern Archives, Fond 494, Opis 1, Delo 467. The American Communist Party delegates were: Sam Don, under the name Sam Bryan; Earl Browder; John Williamson; Gilbert Green; Eisler; Jack Stachel; Sam Darcy; Margaret Cowl, also known as Krumbein and using the name Margaret Dean; Benjamin Carouthers; Claude Lightfoot, Eulolia Mondes, a Party leader in Connecticut, who used the name Anna Mart; Marcus Murphy; Paul Bochus, a CIO official using the name Robert Richards; John Steuben, a CIO official using the name John Stevenson; Martha Stein; Alexander Trachtenberg; Roy Hudson; James Ford; William Z. Foster; Ivan Elovich, an official of the CIO, using the name Ralph Shore; William Schneiderman, under the name Bill Sherman. Alternate delegates were: William Patterson and Lement Harris.

53 SAPMO IV 2/11/V749, p. 18 [in German]. In a later "Short biography" dated 1960, Eisler revealed that in 1923/24 he worked as a staff member of the German Communist Party Central Committee in the intelligence apparatus then called the "Information Department." In 1929, he went to Moscow to work in the Comintern. He said, "On their behalf I worked in China between 1929 and 1931. In 1931 I returned to Moscow and worked in the Anglo-American Secretariat of the Comintern. 1933–1935 I worked in the USA.... 1935 I was appointed a staff member of the Foreign Headquarters of the KPD and worked in that capacity in Prague, Paris and in Spain until 1939." Ibid. p. 48 [in German].

54 Letter, January 21, 1936, Comintern Archives, Fond 495, Opis 74, Delo 469, pp. 11–14, marked "Top Secret."

55 *Resolutions of the Ninth Convention of the Communist Party*, Workers Library Publishers, 1936, p. 17.

56 "Memorandum to Comrade Dimitroff," Comintern Archives, Fond 495, Opis 74, Delo 466, p. 29.

57 Comintern Archives, Fond 495, Opis 19, Delo 252, pp. 100–02.

58 "The Cadre Policy of the CP USA," Comintern Archives, Fond 495, Opis 20, Delo 515, p. 70.

59 Speech on National Groups by "Irene," Tenth Convention CPUSA, May 27, 1938, Comintern Archives, Fond 495, Opis 14, Delo 92, p. 74.

60 Memorandum on Raisa Borisovna Luganovskaia, 21 January 1938, Comintern Archives, Fond 495, Opis 74, Delo 459, pp. 22–23 (in Russian).

61 Dies Committee, vol. 7, p. 4440.

Notes

62 Dies Committee, Executive Hearings, October 27, 1944, pp. 3–8. (Although this hearing was printed in 1944, it was not released until 1951. At that time, printed copies were unavailable, and so they were never publicly distributed.)

63 Documents from the KGB Archives provided to us, September 17, 1993, by Oleg Tsarov and Yuri Kobaladze, officials of the Russian Foreign Intelligence Service, Moscow.

64 Dies Committee, vol. 7, pp. 4439–441.

65 "My Flight From Stalin" by W. G. Krivitsky, *Saturday Evening Post*, August 5, 1939, p. 76.

66 Krivitsky, p. 74.

67 FBI interview with an unidentified confidential informant (apparently Liston Oak) in early 1952 FBI file NY100-596645. Prosecutive Summary Report dated September 9, 1952, p. 20. Released under the Freedom of Information Act.

68 FBI File 100-20202, Report August 6, 1951, on Margaret Browder, pp. 1–2. Released under the Freedom of Information Act.

69 Ibid.

70 Morris Childs, a high-ranking Communist Party official and Soviet agent who began cooperating with the FBI in 1951, was Kweit's close friend in the 1920s and 1930s. While working for the FBI, Childs served as the liaison between the American Communist Party and the Soviet Communist Party. One of his functions was the transfer of Soviet funds to the American Communist Party through the KGB. We learned about Kweit from Childs and from a former Comintern radio specialist. Conversation between Morris Childs and Herb Romerstein, 1982; and conversation between a former Comintern radio specialist and Herb Romerstein, 1998. The radio specialist asked that his name not be used.

71 Romerstein discussion with former Comintern radio specialist, 1998.

72 Anthony Masters, *The Man Who Was M: The Life of Maxwell Knight*, pp. 30–34, 43–54.

73 MASK, Moscow to London, April 15, 1935.

74 MASK, London to Moscow, May 20, 1936 and Moscow to London May 25, 1936.

75 MASK, Moscow to Stockholm, November 13, 1935.

76 MASK, London to Moscow, November 7, 1934.

77 FBI File 100-287645, letter dated May 29, 1951. Released under the Freedom of Information Act.

78 Ibid., Interview Report, April 21, 1958.

79 FBI File NY65-14702. Released under the Freedom of Information Act.

80 FBI File 100-287645, Airtel from New York, April 24, 1958.

81 Ibid., Interview Report, April 21, 1958.

82 FBI File NY100-59645, Supplement, p. 10. (Booker's name is deleted by the FBI in some parts of the document, but included in others.)

83 Ibid., Prosecutive Summary Report, September 2, 1952, p. 29.

84 Ibid., Letter to the Director from New York, February 3, 1954.

85 Ibid., Letter to the Director, March 27, 1961.

86 An original used by the CPUSA is in the possession of the authors.

Notes

Another copy is in the Emory University Library, Atlanta, in the Philip Jaffe Collection.

87 Vassiliev wrote: "The first requisite: the letter must be in code ie., all aspects of illegal work are referred to by some special phrase or other. For example, the illegal printing press is called 'auntie'; 'type' is called 'sugar' and so on. A comrade writes: 'auntie asks you without fail to send her 20 lbs. of sugar,' that will mean that the press is in need of 20 lbs. of type or a comrade writes: 'we are experiencing great difficulty in finding a suitable flat for our aunt.' That means that it is question of finding a flat for the illegal printing press.

"Second requisite: besides a code, as above, ciphers are used, illegal parts of letters being put not only into code but also into cipher. There are many different systems of cipher. The simplest and at the same time most reliable system of cipher is the system of cipher by the help of a book. Some book or other is agreed upon beforehand and then the cipher is made in this way: simple fractions of decimals ciphered. The first figure of the first fraction shows the page of the book. Then further comes the actual cipher. For the numerator of the fraction we must take a line counting from above or below; for the denominator that counting from the left or from the right which it is necessary to put into cipher. For example, we need to put into cipher the letter 'A.' We look in the book and we see that this letter is in the third line from the top, the fourth letter from the left to the right. Then we cipher 3 over 4 (3/4), that is the third line from the top, fourth letter from left to right. You can agree also on this method; for example, counting the line not from above but from below, then the 3 will be not the third line from above but the third line from below. You can agree to count the letter in the line not from left to right but from right to left. Finally, for the greater complexity in order to keep the sense from the police, you can also add to the fraction some figure or other. Let us say the numerator is increased by 3 and the denominator by 4. In this case, in order to decipher, it will be necessary first to subtract in the numerator and denominator of every fraction. A whole number of similar complications can be thought out in order to complicate the cipher. The advantage of such a cipher is that it is not only very simple but also that each letter can be designated by a great number of different signs and in such a way that the cipher designation of letters are not repeated. The book cipher can be used without a book. In place of a book some poem or other can be chosen, learned by heart and the ciphering done according to it. When it is necessary to cipher or decipher, the poem must be written out in verses and then the ciphering or deciphering done and the poem destroyed.

"The third requisite which it is also recommended should be observed in correspondence, is writing in chemical inks, that is, with such inks that it is impossible to read them without special adaptations. If a secret Party letter falls into the hands of the police written in

Notes

invisible ink they must first of all guess that it is written in invisible ink; the open text of such letters must be made perfectly blameless, for example, a son is writing to his mother that he is alive and well and of the good things he wishes her. Not a word about revolution. The police must guess first of all that under this apparent innocent text there is a hidden text. Having discovered this secret the police tumble against a cipher, if they succeed in decipher-code. But all this takes time in the course of which the police can do nothing. If the police succeed in reading it in the course of two or three weeks, then by that time the Party organization has been able to cover up all the consequences of the question which was written about in the letter.

"What kind of invisible ink should be used? Invisible inks exist in a very great number. They can be bought in any chemist's shop. Finally, comrades must use the latest inventions of chemistry in this direction. The simplest invisible ink which can be recommended and which can be found everywhere, is, for example, onion juice and pure water." B. Vassiliev, "How the Communist International Formulates at Present the Problem of Organization," mimeographed, circa 1930, pp. 19–20.

88 Comintern Archives, Fond 495, Opis 74, Delo 470, marked Confidential.

89 John J. Abt, *Advocate and Activist, Memoirs of an American Communist Lawyer*, p. 117.

90 Comintern Archives, Fond 495, Opis 74, Delo 484, pp. 35–38 (marked Secret).

CHAPTER 4

1 "To the Communist Party of America from the Executive Committee of the Communist International" in *The Communist, Official Organ of the Communist Party of American (Section of the Communist International)*, vol. 1, no. 13, 1923, pp. 1–2. This was an internal publication to be given only to Communist Party members.

2 Ibid., vol. 1, no. 9, July 1922, pp. 2–3.

3 Workers (Communist) Party of America, *The 4th National Convention, Held in Chicago, Illinois, August 21–30, 1925*, p. 37.

4 In 1919 two Communist parties were formed, the Communist Party and the Communist Labor Party. They merged the next year on Moscow's orders.

5 Whittaker Chambers, *Witness*, p. 208.

6 Solon De Leon, *The American Labor Who's Who*, pp. 86, 141, 201.

7 Theodore Draper, *American Communism and Soviet Russia*, p. 244.

8 Ben Gitlow, *The "Red Ruby,"* Communist Labor Party, New York, circa 1920, front cover.

9 One of these pins is in the possession of the authors.

10 Earl Browder, "Socialism in America" in David Footman, editor, *International Communism*, p. 101.

11 Joseph Stalin, *Stalin's Speeches on the American Communist Party*, p. 28.

12 Ibid., p. 32.

13 Ibid., p. 38.

14 Ibid., p. 19, 31.

15 Chambers, *Witness*, p. 32, 271.

16 Chambers, FBI statement, p. 13.

17 Ibid., pp. 13–14.

18 Ibid., p. 20.

19 Grace Hutchins, *Labor and Silk*.

20 Chambers, FBI statement, pp. 20, 133.

Notes

21 *New York World Telegram*, December 15, 1948.

22 Dies Committee, vol. 11, and *Communist International*, New York, July 20, 1935, pp. 862–76.

23 Herbert Romerstein, *Heroic Victims: Stalin's Foreign Legion in the Spanish Civil War*, p. 52.

24 Chambers, FBI statement, p. 21.

25 Whittaker Chambers, *Can You Hear Their Voices? A Short Story*.

26 Comintern Archives, Fond 495, Opis 261, Delo 34, p. 14.

27 Comintern Archives, Fond 495, Opis 74, Delo 472, pp. 39–40, letter from head of the Cadre Department of the Executive Committee of the Comintern, Gulyaev, to George Dimitroff, December 21, 1939, and Fond 495, Opis 74, Delo 485, pp. 45–46, Reichman to Dimitroff, November 9, 1944, and Dimitroff to Reichman, November 17, 1944.

28 Max Bedacht, "Appeal to Party Members to Study the Documents Relating to the Expulsion of Comrade Max Bedacht" in *Toward Socialism*, New York, May 1, 1949 (mimeographed).

29 *New York Star*, January 6, 1949, p. 9.

30 Chambers, FBI statement, pp. 26–27.

31 Ibid., p. 29.

32 Ibid., p. 30.

33 Ibid., pp. 40–43.

34 Handwritten autobiography in Comintern Archives, Fond 495, Opis 261, Delo 1677, pp. 1–11.

35 *Daily Worker*, New York, December 28, 1928, and Mink's appeal for reinstatement, Comintern Archives, Fond 515, Opis 1, Delo 1570, pp. 105–6.

36 MASK, Moscow to Copenhagen, March 15, 1935, and March 18, 1935.

37 MASK, Moscow to Copenhagen, March 27, 1935, Moscow to Copenhagen, August 4, 1935.

38 Dies Committee, vol. 14, Testimony of Richard Krebs (also known as Jan Valtin), May 26, 1941, p. 8483.

39 MASK, Moscow to Copenhagen, April 25, 1935, and Copenhagen to Moscow, May 16, 1935.

40 MASK, Copenhagen to Moscow, May 18, 1935 and May 21, 1935.

41 MASK, Moscow to Copenhagen, July 9, 1936.

42 Nadezhda and Maya Ulanovsky, *Istoriya Odnoi Cemi* [*The History of One Family*], p. 120. The authors were the widow and daughter of Chambers's Soviet control officer, Ulrich.

43 Vittorio Vidali, *Diary of the Twentieth Congress of the Communist Party of the Soviet Union*, p. 44.

44 Primakov, et al., *Essays on the History of Russian Foreign Intelligence*, vol. 3, p. 11.

45 Memo from Pat Toohey to George Dimitroff, November 19, 1938, Comintern Archives, Fond 495, Opis 74, Delo 466.

46 Ted Morgan, *A Covert Life*.

47 Letter from Lovestone to Ella Wolf, October 19, 1926, in Comintern Archives, Fond 515, Opis 1, Delo 763, p. 7.

48 Dies Committee, Testimony of Jay Lovestone, vol. 11, p. 7147.

49 FBI reports read into transcript of case, *United States of America* v. *Judith Coplon*, June 10, 1949, vol. XXXI, pp. 5529, 5546–547, 5570–571.

50 *Daily Worker*, July 19, 1947, p. 3.

51 Chambers, FBI statement, p. 60.

52 H. Puro, "The Tasks of the Party in the Work Among the Farmers" in

Notes

The Communist Position on the Farmers Movement, pp. 32–33.

53 Ibid., p. 29.

54 *What is the United Farmers League, Program and By-Laws?*, p. 8.

55 Comintern Archives, Fond 515, Opis 1, Delo 3448, p. 342.

56 The report of the CIO on the expulsion of this union was presented to the Senate by Hubert Humphrey and may be found in the Report of the Subcommittee on Labor and Labor-Management Relations of the Committee on Labor and Public Welfare, *Communist Domination of Certain Unions*, pp. 19ff.

57 Chambers, FBI statement, p. 73.

58 Ibid., p. 74.

59 Ibid., pp. 72, 75.

60 Hearings before the Senate Special Committee Investigating the Munitions Industry, March 29, 1935, pp. 6349–358.

61 Chambers, FBI statement, pp. 78, 83, 84.

62 MASK, Moscow to Basel, September 13–14, 1934, and September 16, 1934, and Moscow to London, two messages of September 15, 1934.

63 Chambers, FBI statement, p. 86.

64 Ibid., p. 110.

65 Comintern Archives, Fond 495, Opis 20, Delo 115, p. 148, Report of T. Ryan (Eugene Dennis), August 9, 1937.

66 Chambers, FBI statement, pp. 91–92. Chambers's meeting with Krivitsky was described to a 1947 American Legion seminar by the man who brought the two defectors together, journalist Isaac Don Levine, one of the most knowledgeable Americans on Communist espionage. When Levine spoke at the meeting, Chambers had not yet gone public, so Levine didn't reveal his name. Instead, he talked about a meeting between Krivitsky and "an American citizen who had become an agent of the Soviet military intelligence in this country...." Levine described how "[i]t was interesting to watch these two men go on from dinner time until 1:00 o'clock in the morning, and when I retired then and got up at 7:00, they were still checking things.... I can see how these two men, who had never known each other, one an American with a Long Island background and the other who held a little rank in the Soviet intelligence, who originally came from Austrian Poland, how these two men knew so many things in common. One would mention somebody who under such and such passport had got to the United States in 1932 or '33, and immediately the other one would pick it up and give a description of the man...." Isaac Don Levine, "Communism in the Government, State Department Case" in *Addresses, Counter-Subversion Seminar*, Sponsored by Americanism Commission, the American Legion, Washington D.C., November 17–20, 1947 (mimeographed 1948), p. 139.

67 Chambers, FBI statement, p. 93.

68 Ibid., p. 94.

69 Ibid., pp. 96–98.

70 Ibid., pp. 99–100.

71 Ibid., p. 107.

72 Ibid., pp. 89–90.

73 *Foreign Relations of the United States, Diplomatic Papers, The Soviet Union 1933–39*, pp. 497–98, 708–9, 718, 908–9, 911.

74 Ikal KGB File, handwritten protocol of the interrogation, December 14, 1937.

Notes

75 For more information on Dozenberg, see: Herbert Romerstein and Stanislav Levchenko, *The KGB Against the "Main Enemy": How the Soviet Intelligence Service Operates Against the United States*, pp. 6–9.

76 Chambers, FBI statement, p. 60.

77 Ikal File, handwritten protocol, December 22, 1937.

78 Ibid., handwritten protocol, December 24, 1937.

79 Ibid., typewritten interrogation, January 8, 1939, and January 24, 1939.

80 Sam Tanenhaus, *Whittaker Chambers: A Biography*, p. 130.

81 "The Faking of Americans," Part I, "The Soviet Passport Racket" in Herbert Solow papers, Hoover Institution, Stanford, CA.

82 Ibid., pp. 3, 17, 18, 23.

83 Ibid., Part II, "Welcome, Soviet Spies!" p. 23.

84 Ibid., Solow Papers, Solow to Lovestone, April 16, 1939.

85 Ibid., Solow Memorandum, November 13, 1938, 10.

86 Ibid., p. 13.

87 Chambers to Robert Cantwell, no date, circa 1938, in Robert Cantwell Papers, Special Collections, Knight Library, University of Oregon.

88 Comintern Archives, Fond 495, Opis 14, Delo 73, p. 28.

89 Although a few of the books published by Modern Age Books were by non-Communists such as the well-known journalist H. V. Kaltenborn, most of them were by Communist Party members like Bruce Minton, the former husband of Soviet agent Louise Bransten, and pro-Soviet propagandists like Corliss Lamont, Hewlett Johnson, the dean of Canterbury, and Anna Louise Strong.

90 FBI Report, background information on Alfred K. Stern in File NY100-65568, May 18, 1955, p. 12.

91 The Berle notes and Chambers's comments were in Chambers, FBI statement, pp. 225–34.

92 Chambers, *Witness*, p. 470.

93 Department of State press release, February 19, 1945.

94 Department of State press release, December 10, 1946.

95 Testimony of Dean Acheson before the Senate Foreign Relations Committee, *Executive Sessions of the Senate Foreign Relations Committee (Historical Series)*, vol. 2, 1949–1950, pp. 11, 12.

96 Attachment to FBI Report 65-56402-2944, Letter from John F. Cronin to Mr. Patrick Coyne, Federal Bureau of Investigation, October 14, 1947. The FBI had contacted Father Cronin because two journalists had told the bureau that the priest had interviewed a former Communist operative who had information about Communist infiltration of the U.S. government.

97 House Committee on Un-American Activities, *Hearings Regarding Communist Espionage in the United States Government*, Testimony of Whittaker Chambers, August 3, 1948, p. 565.

98 Chambers, FBI statement, p. 230.

99 *New York Journal American*, December 21, 1948.

100 For example: *Venona*, New York to Moscow, June 30, 1943, and March 20, 1943.

101 *Venona*, New York to Moscow, July 22, 1944.

102 *American Mercury*, New York,

Notes

February 1949, pp. 153, 158–59.

103 FBI Report on Priscilla Fansler Hobson Hiss in File 100-376016, dated May 20, 1955, p. 1.

104 *Chicago Tribune*, December 9, 1949.

105 Chambers, FBI statement, pp. 87, 88.

106 Comintern Archives, Fond 515, Opis 1, Delo 3150.

107 Dies Committee, *Report on the C.I.O. Political Action Committee*, pp. 12, 54.

108 *Official Reports on the Expulsion of Communist Dominated Organizations from the CIO*, Congress of Industrial Organizations, Washington, D.C., 1954, pp. 34ff.

109 FBI, New York to Director, in File 65-1642-26.

110 Chambers, FBI statement, p. 147.

111 Czech National Archives, Ministry of National Security File #4523, March 30, 1955.

112 Maria Schmidt, *Behind the Scenes of the Showtrials of Central-Eastern Europe*, Budapest, 1993 (uncorrected manuscript), quoting from Archives of the Ministry of the Interior, Noel Field's file, transcript, September 23, 1954, and September 29, 1954.

113 Noel Field, "Hitching Our Wagon to a Star" in *Mainstream*, New York, January 1961.

114 Department of State telegram, September 14, 1970.

115 *New York Journal American*, July 1, 1949.

116 *Venona*, Washington to Moscow, March 30, 1945.

117 FBI Memo from Belmont to Ladd, May 15, 1950, released to Senator Daniel Patrick Moynihan in 1998.

118 State Department Security Archives in U.S. National Archives,

Memo, September 12, 1946, to Director of Intelligence from Colonel R. F. Ennis, OSC, Chief, Intelligence Group; memorandum for the files, Department of State, Samuel Klaus and memo from J. Anthony Panuch to Alger Hiss and John Ross, October 2, 1946.

119 Yevgenia Albats, *The State Within a State: The KGB and Its Hold on Russia—Past, Present, and Future*, p. 250. She originally published this document in June 1992 in an article in the Moscow newspaper *Izvestia*, which had by then become prodemocratic.

120 *Venona*, New York to Moscow, July 15, 1944.

121 *Fortune*, December 3, 1979.

122 *Washington Post*, April 5, 1962, p. A10.

123 *New York Times*, October 29, 1992, and *Washington Post*, October 31, 1992.

124 *Nezavisimaya Gazeta*, Moscow, November 24, 1992, p. 4.

125 *New York Times*, December 17, 1992.

126 *New York Times*, December 7, 1995.

127 *The New Republic*, December 30, 1996.

CHAPTER 5

1 A translation of the document appears in Harvey Klehr, et al., *The Secret World of American Communism*, pp. 87ff. The translation uses the term "Secret Apparatus," but the original Russian-language document in Comintern Archives, Fond 495, Opis 74, Delo 472, p. 12, shows the term as *"Konspirativnogo Apparata,"* which is more properly translated as "Conspiratorial Apparatus."

533

Notes

2 Leaflet addressed to all members in Detroit, signed R. Baker District Organizer, circa 1928; biography of Rudy Baker in Comintern Archives Fond 495, Opis 74, Delo 472, pp. 8, 9 (translated in Klehr, pp. 120–21); catalog, Workers' School New York, Spring Term, 1931.

3 Comintern Archives, Fond 495, Opis 24, Delo 484, p. 12.

4 Comintern Archives, Fond 495, Opis 184, Delo 3, p. 4. The text was typed in English and handwritten in Russian. The English was so poor grammatically that we had it translated from the Russian. This and the next document were found in the Comintern Archives by Fridrikh Firsov and made available to us by John Haynes.

5 Comintern Archives, Fond 495, Opis 184, Delo 19.

6 *House Investigation of Communist Activities in the Buffalo, NY, Area— Part 1*, October 2, 1957, where the job application was reproduced. Wolkenstein took the Fifth Amendment at the hearings.

7 See Chapter 7.

8 Comintern Archives, Fond 495, Opis 74, Delo 480, translated in Klehr, 208–12.

9 *Venona*, New York to Moscow, July 25, 1944, and September 8, 1944.

10 Primakov, et al., *Essays on the History of Russian Foreign Intelligence*, vol. 3, ch. 16.

11 Ibid., p. 185.

12 Bentley, FBI statement, pp. 2–4, 7–8.

13 Ibid., p. 18.

14 *Venona Historical Monograph #3: The 1944–45 New York and Washington–Moscow KGB Messages.*

15 FBI Summary Report on Silvermaster, p. 36.

16 Silberstein, reports and letters; American Legion California and Washington, letters regarding Silberstein, copies in private collection.

17 FBI Summary Report on Silvermaster, p. 35.

18 Ibid., pp. 42, 45.

19 Bentley, FBI statement, pp. 18–19.

20 *Venona*, New York to Moscow, May 25, 1942, and May 27, 1942.

21 Memo from Colonel J. T. Bissell, General Staff, Chief, Counter-Intelligence Group, to Major General G. V. Strong, G-2, June 3, 1942; Memorandum from N. Gregory Silvermaster to General Strong, June 9, 1942, and Robert P. Patterson, Undersecretary of War, to Milo Perkins, Board of Economic Warfare, July 3, 1942, Senate Internal Security Subcommittee, *Interlocking Subversion*, pp. 2562–567.

22 *Venona*, New York to Moscow, September 2, 1943.

23 FBI Summary Report on Silvermaster, p. 53.

24 Bentley, FBI statement, p. 25.

25 *Venona*, Moscow to New York, February 15, 1945.

26 *Venona*, New York to Moscow, July 1, 1944.

27 B. H. Liddell Hart, *History of the Second World War.*

28 *Venona*, New York to Moscow, December 13, 1944.

29 *Venona*, New York to Moscow, December 26, 1944.

30 *Venona*, New York to Moscow, January 15, 1945.

31 *Venona*, Moscow to New York, February 22, 1945.

32 *Venona*, New York to Moscow, November 21, 1944 and Moscow to New York, April 8, 1945.

Notes

33 *Venona*, New York to Moscow, October 17, 1944.

34 *Venona*, Moscow to New York, April 8, 1945 and March 11, 1945.

35 *Venona*, New York to Moscow, January 11, 1945 and Moscow to New York, March 25, 1945.

36 FBI Summary Report on Silvermaster, September 23, 1946, pp. 9, 45, 46.

37 *House Hearings on Communist Espionage in the United States Government*, August 9, 1948, pp. 704–13.

38 *New York Times*, October 1, 1948; *New York Times*, October 20, 1948; *New York Sun*, January 31, 1949; and *New York Times*, January 10, 1950.

39 *Venona*, New York to Moscow, January 4, 1945.

40 Vladimir Pozniakov, "A NKVD/ NKGB Report to Stalin: A Glimpse into Soviet Intelligence in the United States in the 1940s," in *Bulletin, Cold War International History Project*, Woodrow Wilson Center, Washington, D.C., March 1998, pp. 220–22.

41 *Venona*, New York to Moscow, November 21, 1944.

42 *Venona*, New York to Moscow, February 10, 1945.

43 Comintern Archives, Fond 495, Opis 72, Delo 201, p. 98.

44 *Venona*, New York to Moscow, May 27, 1943 and June 22, 1943.

45 Comintern Archives, Fond 495, Opis 74, Delo 486, pp. 2, 3.

46 Bentley, FBI statement, pp. 50–52.

47 *Venona*, New York to Moscow, July 21, 1943, and July 22, 1943.

48 See Chapter 9.

49 *Venona*, New York to Moscow, April 29, 1944.

50 *Venona*, New York to Moscow, May 13, 1944.

51 *Venona*, New York to Moscow, May 30, 1944.

52 Comintern Archives, Fond 495, Opis 74, Delo 485, p. 35.

53 *Venona*, New York to Moscow, February 23, 1944.

54 *Venona*, New York to Moscow, July 11, 1944.

55 See Chapter 11.

56 *Venona*, New York to Moscow, July 28, 1944.

57 Ibid.

58 *Venona*, New York to Moscow, November 30, 1944.

59 *Venona*, New York to Moscow, June 28, 1944.

60 *Venona*, New York to Moscow, January 18, 1945.

61 Senate Internal Security Subcommittee, *Interlocking Subversion*, May 6, 1953, Part 6, pp. 377–79.

62 FBI logs of the wiretap on Thomas Corcoran in Case Philip Jacob Jaffe, et al., File 100-2673601516, May 28, 1950.

63 *Venona*, New York to Moscow, June 16, 1943.

64 Testimony of T. A. Bisson, March 31, 1952, Senate, *Hearings on Institute of Pacific Relations*, vol. 12, p. 4188.

65 Testimony of T. A. Bisson, April 9, 1943, Dies Committee, Executive Hearings, vol. 7, pp. 3467ff.

66 *Venona*, New York to Moscow, June 16, 1943, and June 24, 1943. For additional information from Bisson through Bernstein see *Venona*, June 17, 1943.

67 IPR Report, p. 7, and Hearings, p. 4161.

68 FBI Report on Lauchlin Currie, November 8, 1945, in Silvermaster Case File 65-56401, vol. 2.

Notes

Released under the Freedom of
Information Act.

69 Report to German Communist
Party leadership, SAPMO, Berlin,
Ry1/12/3404, p. 1.

70 Karl Frank (Paul Hagen),
"Autobiographical Data" sent to
OSS 1942 in Paul Hagen papers,
Hoover Institution, Stanford, CA,
p. 9.

71 Germany Communist Party
Archives, SAPMO, Berlin,
Ry1/12/3404, p. 49.

72 Ibid., Ry1/12/3/405, pp. 45–6 and
50–2.

73 Ibid., pp. 13–15.

74 *Venona*, New York to Moscow,
August 31, 1943.

75 *Venona*, New York to Moscow,
May 26, 1943.

76 Joseph P. Lash, *Eleanor Roosevelt, A
Friends Memoir*, p. 30.

77 Associated Press, October 13, 1995.

78 Joseph P. Lash and James A.
Wechsler, *War—Our Heritage.*

79 Comintern Archives, Fond 495,
Opis 14, Delo 68, "Minutes of
Politburo Meeting—Thursday,
January 14, 1937," and report on
American Students, Union
Convention, January 14, 1937.

80 Dies Committee, December 1,
1939, vol. 11, pp. 706ff.

81 Daniel Bell, "Y.C.L. Puts Skids
Under Joe Lash as Student Union
Leader Deviates," *New Leader*, New
York, December 23, 1939.

82 Comintern Archive, Fond 495, Opis
73, Delo 82, pp. 63–74.

83 Dies Committee, Executive
Hearings, vol. 5, Hearing of January
21, 1942, Testimony of Joseph P.
Lash, pp. 2793–810.

84 Letters, Benjamin Mandel to
Mrs. Roosevelt, December 16,

1940; Eleanor Roosevelt to
Benjamin Mandel, December 21,
1940; and Benjamin Mandel to
Eleanor Roosevelt, December 26,
1940; Eleanor Roosevelt collection.
The original letter from Mrs.
Roosevelt to Mandel is in the
possession of the authors.

85 Comintern Archives, Fond 495,
Opis 14, Delo 26b, p. 233.

86 Letters, Benjamin Mandel to Mrs.
Roosevelt, March 18, 1941; Mrs.
Roosevelt to Mandel, March 24,
1941; Mandel to Mrs. Roosevelt,
March 31, 1941; and Mrs. Roosevelt
to Mandel, April 7, 1941. Roosevelt
Library, Eleanor Roosevelt collec-
tion. The original letters from Mrs.
Roosevelt to Mandel are in the
possessions of the authors.

87 *The Correspondent of the Descendants
of the American Revolution*, New
York, August 1940, p. 3; October
1940, p. 6; and November 1940, p.
1 (mimeographed).

88 Ibid., January 1941, 1, 3, 6.

89 *Venona*, New York to Moscow,
July 31, 1943.

90 Comintern Archives, Fond 495,
Opis 74, Delo 485, p. 21 (in
Russian).

91 Leaflet, "Free Browder Meeting,"
Cooper Union, New York,
December 8, 1941.

92 The letter of the Social Democratic
Federation read: "We Social-
Democrats are at all times loath to
criticize the president, whose
domestic and foreign policies as a
whole we heartily support. A sense
of duty to our country and to
democracy, however, forbids us to
keep silence in regard to his statement in commuting the prison sentence of Earl Browder.

Notes

"Had the commutation been granted solely as an act of mercy, criticism might have been out of place. But the president has seen fit to say that he hopes by this act to 'promote national unity' and to allay any feeling that Browder's sentence was a penalty imposed upon him because of his political views.

"No thoughtful person has ever believed that Browder was being punished for his political views. If his views and those of his party involve criminal acts, then unity with them will be a danger to the American people.

"For good and sufficient reasons the law says that an American who seeks to go abroad must truthfully inform the government as to his purposes. Earl Browder intentionally and persistently violated this law. Three times he obtained passports under a false name and by false statements, and twice thereafter he falsely denied ever having received those passports. His repeated perjuries were all pursuant to a single end. He was and is the representative of an organization which is devoted to the principle of minority dictatorship as against democracy, of rule by force and terror as against rule by discussion and consent, and which for twenty-three years has consistently paid allegiance to a foreign and dictatorial government. It was to report for his party to the Moscow dictatorship and to receive orders from it that Browder secretly went to Russia. This was the motive of the unlawful acts of which he was convicted.

"In 1939 Browder and his party applauded the Soviet Government for joining with Hitler in the invasion of Poland, in attempting the conquest of Finland, and in forcibly subjugating Estonia, Latvia and Lithuania.

"They collaborated with Nazis in this country and with native Fascists in condemning our own government for its anti-Nazist attitude and opposing all preparations for national defense. In the service of Moscow they continued their unpatriotic and anti-democratic activities until in June, 1941, Hitler broke the pact and invaded Russia. Only then, and because Moscow needed American help, did they feign devotion to American interests and institutions.

"In a democratic country there can be no sincere agreement between the advocates of dictatorship and the supporters of democracy. The cause of national unity is not served, but gravely injured, by words from the White House which tend to conceal this fact. The president's public statement cannot assure the loyalty of the Communists. It wrongs and offends all who are on principle opposed to dictatorship and who are working and fighting for democracy." Roosevelt Library, Franklin Roosevelt correspondence.

93 Comintern Archives, Fond 495, Opis 74, Delo 485, p. 21 (in Russian).

94 Ibid., Josephine Adams to Eleanor Roosevelt, July 4, 1944, and Secretary to Mrs Roosevelt to Earl G. Harrison, July 12, 1944, Eleanor Roosevelt Collection.

95 See Chapter 3.

96 Earl G. Harrison, *Americans of Foreign Birth in the War Program for*

537

Notes

Victory, American Committee for Protection of Foreign Born.

97 John J. Abt, *Advocate and Activist, Memoirs of an American Communist Lawyer*, p. 117. This book was published posthumously, and Abt might have had second thoughts about identifying Communists in Congress had he been alive when the book was published.

98 Comintern Archives, Fond 495, Opis 184, Delo 19, p. 28. Dimitroff to Browder Radio message received June 12, 1943.

99 Roosevelt Library, Franklin Roosevelt correspondence, Earl Browder to President Roosevelt, June 14, 1943; President Roosevelt to Browder, June 23, 1943; President Roosevelt to Browder, June 26, 1943; and Browder to President Roosevelt, July 12, 1943.

100 *Venona*, New York to Moscow, July 18, 1943, and Comintern Archives, Fond 495, Opis 74, Delo 484, pp. 32–34. The Comintern document also carried information from a report sent by NKVD officer Stepan Apresyan of June 21, 1943. Apresyan succeeded Klarin as *Rezident* in 1944. A translation of the Comintern file document appears in Harvey Klehr, and John Earl Haynes, *The Secret World of American Communism*, pp. 249–50.

101 Roosevelt Library, Josephine Truslow Adams to Mrs. Roosevelt, no date (filed October 6, 1944), Eleanor Roosevelt Collection.

102 *Venona*, New York to Moscow, June 1, 1944, and New York to Moscow, October 27, 1944.

103 *Venona*, New York to Moscow, August 2, 1944.

104 Chambers, FBI statement. The most complete version of this part of the statement appears in Edith Tigar, editor, *In Re Alger Hiss*, p. 205.

105 *Congressional Record*, Daily Report, December 19, 1950, p. H16928.

106 House Committee on Un-American Activities, *Hearings Regarding Communist Espionage*, 1948, pp. 552, 556.

107 *Venona*, New York to Moscow, August 10, 1943.

108 *Venona*, New York to Moscow, June 24, 1944.

109 *Venona*, Moscow to New York, February 15, 1945.

110 *Venona*, New York to Moscow, October 14, 1944.

111 *Venona*, Moscow to New York, March 20, 1945.

112 Associated Press, March 26 and March 28, 1956.

113 House Committee on Un-American Activities, *Interim Report on Hearing Regarding Communist Espionage in the United States Government*, 1948, p. 5.

114 Victor Perlo, *The Big Tax Swindle and How to Stop it*, and a letter to all members of Congress signed by Arnold Johnson, legislative director of the Communist Party USA, which was mailed with the pamphlet.

115 John Abt, *Advocate and Activist*, p. 42.

116 L. L. Sharkei, *An Outline History of the Australian Communist Party*, pp. 81–83.

117 *Venona*, Moscow to New York, San Francisco, Ottawa, Canberra, etc., September 12, 1943.

118 *Venona*, New York to Moscow, February 9 and February 24, 1944.

119 *Venona*, New York to Moscow, June 15, 1944.

Notes

120 English translation in *On the Struggle Against Revisionism*, Communist Party USA.

121 Earl Browder, *Modern Resurrections and Miracles*, p. 49.

122 Comintern Archives, Fond 495, Opis 74, Delo 482, pp. 63–65.

123 Pavlov, pp. 73–74.

124 Ibid., pp. 100–3.

125 See Chapter 2.

CHAPTER 6

1 Douglas J. MacEachin, *The Final Months of the War With Japan: Signals Intelligence, U.S. Invasion Planning, and the A-Bomb Decision*, pp. 1–11.

2 Harry S. Truman, *Year of Decisions*, p. 416, and Winston S. Churchill, *Triumph and Tragedy*, pp. 669–70.

3 The identification of Potapova comes from Vladimir Tschikow [Chikov] and Gary Kern, *Perseus: Espionage in Los Alamos*, p. 45. Written by a former KGB officer and the knowledgeable American researcher Gary Kern, this book provides some valuable data on atomic espionage. It is seriously flawed, however. Chikov, to hide the identities of some of the Soviet agents, added disinformation and confusion. The book originally appeared in French as *Comment Staline a volé la bombe atomique aux Américains*, Dossier KGB no. 13676, Robert Laffont, Paris, 1996, where the identification of Potapova appears on p. 42.

4 Pavel Sudoplatov, et al., *Special Tasks*, pp. 475, 437. Sudoplatov provided translations of documents originally published in Russian in *Voprossi Istorii Estestvoznania I Tekhniki* [*Questions of History of Natural Science and Technology*] in

1992. He incorrectly identified "List" as Donald Maclean. We know from *Venona* that Maclean was "Gomer."

5 John Cairncross, *The Enigma Spy: An Autobiography*, pp. 9, 10, 85. Sudoplatov gave the agent's code name as "Leaf." The Russian original shows it is "List." While the Russian word "list" translates as "leaf," according to Gary Kern, Cairncross's GRU handler, Vladimir Barkowsky, told Chikov that Cairncross was given the name "List" because of his interest in classical music and the Hungarian composer Liszt. Ibid., p. 49.

6 Sudoplatov, pp. 179, 439–41, 480. Sudoplatov's memoirs were published in 1994, coauthored by his son and the American journalists Jerrold and Leona Schecter. There is much valuable information in the book. However, writing fifty years after the incidents from memory, Sudoplatov sometimes got code names confused. *Venona* provides us with the correct identifications of most of these agents and confirms much of what Sudoplatov wrote.

7 Pavlov, p. 69.

8 *Venona*, New York to Moscow, August 12, 1943.

9 *The Report of the Royal Commission to Investigate the Facts Relating to and the Circumstances Surrounding the Communication, by Public Officials and Other Persons in Positions of Trust, of Secret and Confidential Information to Agents of a Foreign Power*, June 27, 1946, pp. 113–14.

10 Ibid., p. 375.

11 *Yearbook, 8th Convention, Young Communist League of Canada*, Toronto, 1938.

Notes

12 Proceedings, Canadian House of Commons, April 30, 1946, pp. 1040–41.

13 *Royal Commission*, pp. 97–98.

14 Handwritten form filled out by Carr, September 17, 1937, in Comintern Archives, Fond 495, Opis 261, Delo 26.

15 *Royal Commission*, pp. 714–15.

16 Childs discussion with Romerstein, April 14, 1982.

17 *Canadian Tribune*, May 22, 1989.

18 *Royal Commission*, pp. 57–58, 85–86, 447–55.

19 *Venona*, Moscow to London, September 18, 1945.

20 *Royal Commission*, pp. 455–57.

21 Napoli had worked with the senior Soviet agent Jacob Golos, who by then had died. Bentley, FBI statement, p. 44.

22 *Venona*, New York to Moscow, December 2, 1944.

23 *Soviet Russia Today*, September 1949, p. 20, and FBI Report in Case *U.S. v. Judith Coplon*, vol. XXX, p. 5344. Quoted in House Committee on Un-American Activities, *Testimony of Philip O. Keeney and Mary Jane Keeney and Statement Regarding their Background, May 24–25 and June 9, 1949*, p. 221.

24 *Venona*, New York to Moscow, June 17, 1943, two messages.

25 *Venona*, New York to Moscow, October 5, 1944.

26 *Daily Worker*, New York, July 19, 1949, p. 2, and *Soviet Russia Today*, September 1949, p. 20.

27 *Venona*, New York to Moscow, November 12, 1944.

28 *Venona*, New York to Moscow, January 23, 1945.

29 When Romerstein and *Reader's Digest* senior editor Ralph Bennett met with

Hall in Cambridge, England, in 1995, Hall remembered being horrified that he might actually have to go through basic training. But he was instead sent back to Los Alamos.

30 *Venona*, Moscow to New York, March 31, 1945.

31 *Venona*, New York to Moscow, May 26, 1945.

32 See Chapter 8.

33 *Venona*, Moscow to New York, July 5, 1945.

34 FBI Report CH65-3403, August 25, 1950. A mail cover was not a mail opening; the postman would record the return addresses on envelopes.

35 FBI Report CH65-59122-241, March 31, 1951.

36 Ralph Kinney Bennett and Herbert Romerstein, "Secrets of Venona" in *Reader's Digest*, September 1996.

37 Joseph Albright, and Marcia Kunstel, *Bombshell, The Secret Story of America's Unknown Atomic Spy Conspiracy*, pp. 288–89.

38 *Guardian*, London, February 27, 1996.

39 See note 4.

40 FBI Airtel from New York to Headquarters, February 11, 1958, in Case NY100-103389.

41 Comintern Archives, Fond 545, Opis 6, Delo 846, p. 100, Evaluation of Morris Cohen showing pseudonyms Israel Altman and Baruch Prichett.

42 Comintern Archives, Fond 545, Opis 6, Delo 846, List of American Communist Party members in the International Brigades, p. 1.

43 Alexandr Feklisov, *Za Okeanom I Na Ostrove [Across the Ocean and On the Island]*, Dem, Moscow, 1944, p. 22. Feklisov, under the name Fomin, returned to the United States as the KGB *Rezident* in the Khrushchev

Notes

period and served as President Kennedy's back channel to the Soviet dictator during the 1962 Cuban missile crisis.

44 Ibid., p. 24.

45 *Komsomolskaya Pravda*, Moscow, July 10, 1993, translated in FBIS August 30, 1993, pp. 11–14.

46 House Committee on Un-American Activities, *List of Communist Party Registrations in New York City 1936*, pp. 31–32.

47 Ibid., *List of Signers of New York Nominating Petitions*, pp. 142, 144.

48 FBI Report, Los Angeles to Headquarters, February 21, 1958, in Case LA100-4457, p. 2.

49 FBI Reports, New Haven to Headquarters, February 7, 1955, Case no. NH100-15936, and New York to Headquarters, August 1, 1957, Case no. NY100-103389.

50 Tschikow and Kern, p. 392.

51 *Venona*, New York to Moscow, August 30, 1944.

52 Feklisov, pp. 102–4. As with most KGB memoirs and officially sponsored "history," the code names of the agents and some identifying characteristics were changed to protect their identities. By separating out known information, one can sometimes identify the agents. In this case, Feklisov gave the agent the false code name "Rupert" and said that he had been stationed in the Pacific, while Weisband was actually in Europe. It was possible to identify Weisband based on the information he supplied the NKVD.

53 Benson and Warner, *Venona*, xxvii, xxviii, and pp. 167–70.

54 FBI Memo, Hennrich to Belmont, October 3, 1951, in File 65-59439-4.

55 Tschikow and Kern, p. 392.

56 FBI Report, Los Angeles to Headquarters, February 21, 1958 in Case LA100-55567, p. 4.

57 See Chapter 7.

58 FBI Report, New York to Headquarters, May 12, 1955, in Case NY100-103338, p. 2.

59 FBI Memo, August 1, 1957, in Case 100-406659.

60 FBI Airtel, New York to Headquarters, August 2, 1957, in Case NY100-103389.

61 FBI Memo, Legat, Bern to Headquarters, March 27, 1970, in Case 100-406659-2294.

62 *New York Times*, New York, July 5, 1995.

63 *Veterani Vneshnei Razvedki Rossii [Veterans of Russian Foreign Intelligence]*, Foreign Intelligence Service of the Russian Federation, Moscow, 1995, pp. 68–73.

64 House Committee on Un-American Activities, *Hearings Regarding Shipment of Atomic Material to the Soviet Union During World War II*, December 5, 1949; Testimony of Louis Russell, p. 903, and December 7, 1949; Testimony of Lieutenant General Leslie R. Groves, pp. 936, 940, 947.

65 Ibid., Testimony of George Racey Jordan, p. 927.

66 George Racey Jordan, *From Major Jordan's Diaries*.

67 Robert E. Sherwood, *Roosevelt and Hopkins: An Intimate History*, p. 1.

68 Christopher Andrew and Oleg Gordievsky, *KGB: The Inside Story*, pp. 287–88.

69 *Venona*, Washington to Moscow, March 3, 1943 and April 22, 1943.

70 *Venona*, New York to Moscow, May 29, 1943.

Notes

71 Eduard Mark, "Venona's Source 19 and the 'Trident' Conference of May 1943: Diplomacy or Espionage?" in *Intelligence and National Security*, London, Summer 1998, pp. 1–31.

72 Sudoplatov, pp. 226–27.

73 *Krasnaya Zvezda*, July 24, 1992, p. 3.

74 See Chapter 4.

75 George McJimsey, *Harry Hopkins: Ally of the Poor, Defender of Democracy*, p. 74. McJimsey described the group as "informal meetings" to discuss "various projects to help the poor...."

76 House Committee on Un-American Activities, *Hearings Regarding Communist Espionage in the United States Government*, August 20, 1948, pp. 1022–28.

77 House Committee on Un-American Activities, *Hearings Regarding Communism in the United States Government—Part 2*, Testimony of Lee Pressman, August 28, 1950, pp. 2850, 2853–885, 2879.

78 Ibid., pp. 246–49.

79 *Correspondence Between the Chairman of the Council of Ministers of the USSR [Stalin] and the Presidents of the USA and the Prime Ministers of Great Britain During the Great Patriotic War of 1941–1945*, Foreign Languages Publishing House, Moscow, 1957, vol. 2, pp. 156–57.

80 Memo of General F. L. Anderson on his meeting with Harry Hopkins, September 7, 1944, in Carl Spaatz papers, Library of Congress, Box 182.

81 *Foreign Relations of the United States, Diplomatic Papers, The Conference of Berlin [Potsdam Conference], 1945*, Government Printing Office, Washington, D.C., 1960, vol. 1, p. 28.

82 McJimsey, pp. 189, 228–29.

83 V. N. Chebrikov, et al., *History of Soviet State Security Organs*, Chapter 9 (marked Top Secret).

84 McJimsey, p. 360.

85 *Venona*, New York to Moscow, June 21, 1943 and June 22–23, 1943.

86 See Chapter 5.

87 Memo from J. Edgar Hoover, director of the FBI, to State Department, March 12, 1946, U.S. National Archives, no. 861.20211/3-1246 CS/A and House, *Report on Soviet Espionage Activities in Connection with the Atom Bomb, September 28, 1948*, Government Printing Office, Washington, D.C., 1948, pp. 176–77.

88 The NSA has tentatively identified "Ramsey" as possibly Norman Foster Ramsey. This appears to be incorrect. The circumstantial evidence indicates that "Ramsey" was Hiskey.

89 *Venona*, New York to Moscow, May 4, 1944.

90 House Committee on Un-American Activities, *Excerpts from Hearings Regarding Investigation of Communist Activities in Connection with the Atom Bomb*, September 9, 1948, p. 3.

91 Ibid., pp. 54–55.

92 *Venona*, New York to Moscow, July 20, 1944.

93 *Excerpts*, pp. 55–57.

94 *Venona*, New York to Moscow, September 18, 1944 and December 5, 1944.

95 *Venona*, Moscow to New York, March 30, 1945.

96 John Barron, *Operation Solo: The FBI's Man in the Kremlin*.

97 FBI Report to State Department, p. 9.

98 SAPMO, DY 301V2/11, p. 53.

99 Part of the confession is contained in Joint Committee on Atomic

Notes

Energy, *Soviet Atomic Espionage*, p. 16.

100 *Venona*, London to Moscow, August 10, 1941.

101 Joint Committee, p. 16.

102 Sudoplatov, 193, and Ruth Werner, *Sonjas Rapport*. Even after the fall of the Berlin Wall, she continued to live in Berlin under the name Werner. She died in 2000.

103 A picture of one of her Orders of the Red Banner appears in her memoirs, Ibid., p. 207.

104 Harry Gold, Supplemental Statement to FBI, July 10, 1950, while he was in prison. FBI File no. PH65-3407 and Senate Internal Security Subcommittee, *Scope of Soviet Activity in the United States*, Part 20, Testimony of Harry Gold, April 26, 1956.

105 *Venona*, New York to Moscow, February 9, 1944.

106 Gold Testimony, pp. 1026–27.

107 *Venona*, New York to Moscow, June 15, 1944.

108 FBI Report, September 26, 1949, reproduced in Benson and Warner, *Venona*, pp. 141–43.

109 Robert J. Lamphere, *The FBI-KGB War: A Special Agent's Story*, p. 151.

110 *Venona*, New York to Moscow, October 5, 1944.

111 *Venona*, New York to Moscow, August 29, 1944.

112 *Venona*, New York to Moscow, September 22, 1944.

113 Harry Gold, Scope, testimony, pp. 1031–32.

114 *Prisma* published in Berlin, East Germany, Issue no. 2 for 1984, p. 10.

115 *Chicago Sun-Times*, January 29, 1988.

116 Kim Philby, *My Silent War*, pp. 208–9.

CHAPTER 7

1 Senate Internal Security Subcommittee, *Scope*, Testimony of Harry Gold, pp. 1045–46.

2 Senate Internal Security Subcommittee, *Scope*, May 17, 1956, Testimony of Thomas L. Black, pp. 1114–121.

3 Ibid., pp. 1020–21.

4 *Venona*, Moscow to New York, March 21, 1945.

5 Vladimir Pozniakov, "A NKVD/NKGB Report to Stalin: A Glimpse into Soviet Intelligence in the United States in the 1940s" in *Cold War International History Project Bulletin*, March 1998, pp. 220–22.

6 *Venona*, New York to Moscow, December 13, 1944.

7 Senate Internal Security Subcommittee, *Scope*, Testimony of David Greenglass, April 27, 1956, pp. 1090–91, and Transcript of Record, *United States of America* v. *Julius Rosenberg et al.*, Case on Appeal, pp. 419–20.

8 *Venona*, New York to Moscow, September 21, 1944.

9 Ibid.

10 Walter and Miriam Schneir, *Invitation to an Inquest*.

11 Walter and Miriam Schneir, "Cryptic Answer" in *The Nation*, August 14/21, 1995.

12 *Venona*, New York to Moscow, November 27, 1944.

13 Transcript, Rosenberg Case, pp. 444–53.

14 *Venona*, New York to Moscow, December 16, 1944.

15 Transcript, Rosenberg Case, pp. 444–53.

16 Ibid., pp. 457–59.

17 Ibid., pp. 821–28.

18 *Venona*, New York to Moscow,

Notes

October 22, 1944.

19 *Venona*, New York to Moscow, December 20, 1944. NSA in releasing the document identified Sidorovich's wife as Ann Hanusiak Sidorovich.

20 *Venona*, New York to Moscow, September 14, 1944.

21 *Venona*, Moscow to New York, March 5, 1945.

22 *Venona*, Moscow to New York, April 5, 1945. At the time this message was sent, the Communist Party called itself the Communist Political Association. It returned to the name Communist Party in July 1945. Moscow made no distinctions between the Party's real name and its temporary pseudonym.

23 *Venona*, New York to Moscow, September 14, 1944.

24 Transcript, Rosenberg Case, pp. 207–11, 235–37.

25 Lamphere, p. 91.

26 This was one of the few cases in which the NSA deleted someone's name. It has not explained the reason.

27 *Venona*, New York to Moscow, June 24, 1944.

28 See Chapter 8.

29 Senate Permanent Subcommittee on Investigations of the Committee on Government Operations, *Army Signal Corps—Subversion and Espionage, December 8 and 9, 1953,* Part I, pp. 51–52, 57–62; Part II, pp. 70–72, 79–82, 87–90.

30 Transcript, Rosenberg Case, pp. 1099, 1284.

31 *Venona*, New York to Moscow, May 5, 1944.

32 *Venona*, New York to Moscow, November 14, 1944.

33 *Venona*, New York to Moscow, May 22, 1944. Rosenberg's code

name was changed from "Antenna" to "Liberal" according to a *Venona* message, New York to Moscow, September 2, 1944.

34 *Venona*, New York to Moscow, July 11, 1944.

35 *Venona*, Moscow to Mexico City, July 28, 1944.

36 *Venona*, New York to Moscow, November 17, 1944.

37 *Venona*, New York to Moscow, December 5, 1944.

38 FBI Teletype, New York to Headquarters, December 12, 1950; Memos, March 20, March 23, and March 26, 1951, in File NY65-15348.

39 FBI Report, New York to Headquarters, March 17, 1952, File NY65-15360.

40 FBI Report, Seattle to Headquarters, August 7, 1950, File SE65-3114.

41 FBI Teletype, Albany to Headquarters, July 26, 1950.

42 FBI Memo, Albany to Headquarters, September 10, 1951, and Headquarters to Albany, September 22, 1951.

43 FBI Teletype, Albany to New York, Cleveland, and Newark, July 23, 1950.

44 *New York Times*, September 19, 1983.

45 For more on the anti-Semitic Slansky case, see Chapter 6.

46 Documents from the files of the Czechoslovak Ministry of State Security were made available to the authors by the Czech journalist Karel Pacner.

47 *Los Angeles Times*, October 14, 1992.

48 *New York Times*, August 16, 1998.

49 Letter, Ann Rivington to William Patterson, July 13, 1949, copy

Notes

provided in 1960 to Romerstein by
John Lautner, head of the New York
State Control Commission of the
Communist Party until 1950 and
later a government witness.

50 Transcript, Rosenberg Case,
pp. 1615–616.

51 Ibid., pp. 1620, 1624.

52 Morton Sobell letter, "To Whom It
May Concern."

53 1952 leaflets and other material
from the Rosenberg Committee.

54 Memo, Lyman B. Kirkpatrick, assistant director of the CIA, to the
director of the FBI, July 30, 1952,
obtained from CIA web site.

55 Dr. S. Andhil Fineberg, *The
Rosenberg Case: Fact and Fiction*,
pp. 55–57.

56 Memorandum March 31, 1953 from
the Czech government to the Soviet
government, Files of the Ministry of
Internal Affairs, Prague,
Czechoslovakia, courtesy of Czech
journalist Karel Pacner.

57 *New York Times*, April 26 and 27,
1951, and May 17, 1953.

58 Ethel and Julius Rosenberg,
*The Testament of Ethel and Julius
Rosenberg*, Letter of June 16, 1953,
pp. 181ff. The publisher was not
quite openly Communist. Angus
Cameron and Albert Kahn were
both secret members of the
Communist Party—Kahn was
involved in a Soviet spy ring. The
book was printed by Prompt Press,
the Communist Party's print shop.
An earlier edition titled *Death House
Letters*, Jero Publishing Company,
Inc., New York, 1953, appeared to
be non-Communist. However, it
was also printed by Prompt Press.

59 D. N. Pritt, *The Rosenberg Case*,
National Committee to Secure

Justice in the Rosenberg Case; *The
Case of Morton Sobell*, National
Committee to Secure Justice for
Morton Sobell in the Rosenberg
Case, New York, no date; and *An
Appeal for Clemency*, published by the
National Guardian, New York, circa
1953 (a reprint of the first listed).

60 For more on Pritt and the Soviet
money supplied to him for
"honoraria," see Chapter 10.

61 FBI Summary of February 5, 1954,
interview with Jack Childs, in
Morris Childs Collection, Hoover
Institution, Stanford, California.

62 House Committee on Un-American
Activities, *Investigation of Communist
Activities (The Committee to Secure
Justice in the Rosenberg Case and
Affiliates—Part II)*, pp. 2222–224,
and brochure of the National
Committee to Secure Justice in the
Rosenberg Case, *Perjury in the
Rosenberg Case*, p. 2.

63 Nathan Glazer, *A New Look at the
Rosenberg-Sobell Case*. Published as a
supplement to the magazine's issue
of July 2, 1956, and reprinted for
free distribution by the Tamiment
Institute. The Tamiment Institute
Library is now part of the library of
New York University.

64 Document reproduced in *Cold War
International History Project Bulletin*,
"New Findings on the Korean War"
by Kathryn Weathersby, Fall 1993,
pp. 15–16.

CHAPTER 8

1 For more on Rudy Baker, see
Chapter 1.

2 In 1980 Branigan participated in a
conference of the Consortium for the
Study of Intelligence in Washington,
D.C. He commented on a paper

Notes

presented by Herbert Romerstein on "Soviet Intelligence in the United States." Branigan said, "Romerstein refers also to the early cases of atomic espionage. He specifically refers to a man named Joe, later identified as Joseph Woodrow Weinberg, who met Steve Nelson, then the Communist Party functionary in East Bay. The meeting occurred in March 1943. He also refers to a meeting between Vassiliy Zubilin and Steve Nelson a few days later. I was the fortunate FBI agent who intercepted both of those meetings. I mention this not because of the personal satisfaction derived and not because it was those meetings that really changed my career in counterintelligence but for a very simple purpose: following those meetings, the FBI first learned of the Manhattan Project, the experiment to develop an atomic bomb." Roy Godson, editor, *Intelligence Requirements for the 1980s: Counterintelligence*, p. 201.

3 CIA memorandum, February 6, 1948, in Benson and Warner, *Venona*, pp. 105ff.; and FBI Memo in Senate Internal Security Subcommittee *Interlocking Subversion*, part 15, pp. 1049–51. Some of the sources list St. Francis Hospital, but this is incorrect. The meeting took place at St. Joseph's Hospital.

4 House Committee on Un-American Activities, *Hearings Regarding Communist Infiltration of Radiation Laboratory and Atomic Bomb Project at the University of California*, vol. 1, April 26, 1949, p. 317.

5 House Committee on Un-American Activities, *Report on Atomic Espionage (Nelson-Weinberg and Hiskey-Adams Cases)*, September 29, 1949, pp. 7, 8.

6 House Committee, *Hearings Regarding Communist Infiltration of Radiation Laboratory and Atomic Bomb Project*, vol. 2, pp. 102–3.

7 Senate Internal Security Subcommittee, *Interlocking Subversion*.

8 *Venona*, San Francisco to Moscow, April 18, 1945.

9 *Venona*, San Francisco to Moscow, February 20, 1946.

10 Steve Nelson, James R. Barrett, Rob Ruck, *Steve Nelson: American Radical*, p. 294.

11 In addition to doing the same work as the agent with the code name "Butcher," Nelson entered the country in 1920 under the name Joseph Fleischinger, a German name related to meat. As we have seen in other cases, NKVD frequently played on words or related names for their code names.

12 *Venona*, San Francisco to Moscow, January 17, 1944.

13 Comintern Archives, Fond 545, Opis 3, Delo 436, pp. 78–80; Delo 452, pp. 76, 79.

14 For more on the execution of American volunteers by the Communist authorities in Spain, see Romerstein, *Heroic Victims*.

15 Francis King and George Matthews, editors, *About Turn, The British Communist Party and the Second World War, The Verbatim Record of the Central Committee Meetings of 25 September and 2–3 October 1939*, p. 305.

16 *Venona*, New York to Moscow, August 13, 1943.

17 Dies Committee, *Report on the CI.O. Political Action Committee*, p. 56.

18 *Venona*, New York to Moscow, September 21, 1944.

Notes

19 House Committee on Un-American Activities, *Hearing,* June 21, 1950, pp. 2649–651.

20 Comintern Archives, Moscow, Fond 515, Opis 1, Delo 3458, pp. 132–33.

21 Ibid., Fond 515, Opis 1, Delo 3761, p. 6.

22 Max M. Kampelman, *The Communist Party* vs. *The C.I.O.,* p. 45.

23 Senate Committee on Labor and Public Welfare, *Communist Domination of Certain Unions,* 1951, pp. 3ff. Reports on the CIO expulsion of Communist-dominated unions were published at the request of Senator Hubert Humphrey.

24 *Venona,* San Francisco to Moscow, February 8, 1944.

25 *Venona,* San Francisco to Moscow, November 1, 1943.

26 *Venona,* San Francisco to Moscow, November 9, 1943.

27 Comintern Archives, Fond 495, Opis 19, Delo 617, pp. 19, 20.

28 *Venona,* San Francisco to Moscow, December 7, 1943. The GRU, Soviet military intelligence, had both a navy and army unit functioning in the United States.

29 *Venona,* San Francisco to Moscow, December 31, 1943.

30 House Committee on Un-American Activities, *The Shameful Years—Thirty Years of Soviet Espionage in the United States,* December 31, 1951, p. 40.

31 Robert Louis Benson, *Venona Historical Monograph #4: The KGB in San Francisco and Mexico City,* National Security Agency, p. 4.

32 *Venona,* San Francisco to Moscow, April 3, 1945.

33 *Venona,* San Francisco to Moscow, April 2, 1945 and April 18, 1945.

34 *Venona,* San Francisco to Moscow, November 13, 1945.

35 FBI Summary Report on J. Robert Oppenheimer, File 100-17828, pp. 6–7.

36 United States Atomic Energy Commission, *In the Matter of J. Robert Oppenheimer, Transcript of Hearing before Personnel Security Board, Washington, D.C., April 12, 1954, through May 6, 1954,* Testimony of J. Robert Oppenheimer, pp. 183–85.

37 Comintern Archives, Moscow, Fond 515, Opis 1, Delo 3875.

38 *In the Matter of J. Robert Oppenheimer,* p. 191.

39 See Chapter 10. Minton subsequently married Ruth McKinney, the author of the book, later a major film, *My Sister Eileen.*

40 Sudoplatov, p. 79.

41 Ibid., p. 86.

42 FBI Summary Report on Oppenheimer, p.10. Pozner was the father of the Gorbachev-era Soviet propagandist with the American accent.

43 *Venona,* New York to Moscow, July 13, 1943.

44 *Venona,* New York to Moscow, November 21, 1943.

45 FBI Blind Memo, April 16, 1954, in Case 100-17828.

46 FBI Summary Report in Case 100-17828, p. 27.

47 FBI Summary on Oppenheimer in File 100-17828, pp. 23, 26.

48 FBI Memo on Unknown Subject, March 23, 1950, Case SF65-4154, p. 4.

49 *In the Matter of J. Robert Oppenheimer,* p. 130.

50 Ibid., 572, and FBI Summary Report on Oppenheimer, p. 26.

Notes

51 Comintern Archives, Fond 545, Opis 3, Delo 453, pp. 176–77; Joe Dallet, *Letters from Spain*, p. 53 (these were letters to Kitty and were published by the American Communist Party).

52 FBI Blind Memo on J. Robert Oppenheimer, March 18, 1946, in File 100-17828, p. 5.

53 Comintern Archives, Fond 545, Opis 3, Delo 453, p. 79.

54 FBI Report on J. Robert Oppenheimer, July 30, 1954, in File CG105-1688, pp. 2, 9–12.

55 *Venona*, San Francisco to Moscow, November 13, 1945.

56 Photostatic copies of the 1937 and 1938 membership books and 1938 stub are in a private collection made available to the authors. It is believed that the committee did not actually see copies of the membership books but only notations about them. The committee advised Frank Oppenheimer that he had been issued Communist Party book #56385 in 1937 under the name Frank Folsom. However, an examination of the membership book shows his name given as Frank Oppenheimer. In 1938 he was issued Communist Party book #60493, and that, too, was in the name Frank Oppenheimer, and the stub sent to the Party State headquarters also showed the name Frank Oppenheimer.

57 Ibid.

58 House Committee on Un-American Activities, *Hearings Regarding Communist Infiltration of Radiation Laboratory*, vol. 1, pp. 355–81.

59 *Los Angeles Times*, July 13, 1947.

60 *Venona*, New York to Moscow, December 16, 1944.

61 *Venona*, Moscow to New York, March 21, 1945.

62 Robert Louis Benson, *Introductory History of VENONA and Guide to the Translations*, p. 10.

63 Sudoplatov, pp.190, 194.

64 *New York Times*, May 1, 1994.

65 Sudoplatov, pp. 479–81.

66 Letter from Louis Freeh to Les Aspin, May 1, 1995.

67 *Izvestia*, April 30, 1994.

68 *Pravda*, Moscow, April 26, 1996.

69 *New York Times*, September 28, 1996.

70 FBI report on Albert Einstein, February 13, 1950, in File 61-7089-25.

71 *New York Times*, June 1, 1998.

72 Associated Press, Moscow, June 3, 1998.

73 FBI report on Albert Einstein, February 28, 1952, in File 100-32986, p. 3.

74 FBI report on Paul Jacob Pontecorvo (brother of Bruno), December 14, 1950, in File Boston 117-50, #7.

75 Comintern Archives, Fond 17, Opis 125, Delo 391, pp. 140, 141, in Vladislav Zubok and Constantine Pleshakov, *Inside the Kremlin's Cold War, From Stalin to Khrushchev*, p. 15.

76 *Moscow News*, October 15–22, 1989, p. 8 (English-language edition).

CHAPTER 9

1 Thomas F. Troy, *Donovan and the CIA: A History of the Establishment of the Central Intelligence Agency*, pp. 423, 427.

2 Harold Smith, *Attack for Victory*, Veterans of the Abraham Lincoln Brigade, and Earl Browder, *The People's Front*, p. 182.

3 *Party News*, Communist Party USA, New York, July 1940, pp. 8, 9 (issued only to members of the Communist Party).

4 Comintern Archives, Fond 515, Opis

Notes

1, Delo 4178, pp. 287–88, typescript sent to Moscow on microfilm.

5 Milton Wolff, typescript of keynote speech at VALB convention, May 1941, exhibit #98 in Subversive Activities Control Board Case, *Attorney General* v. *VALB*.

6 Comintern Archives, Fond 495, Opis 74, Delo 469, pp. 108–112, which contains the full text of an early September 1939 radio message from the Comintern to the American Communist Party setting out the line the CPUSA was to take regarding the war.

7 Comintern Archives, Fond 495, Opis 18, Delo 1293, pp. 2, 3, 6, 267–68.

8 Milton Wolff, *Western Front Now!*, Veterans of the Abraham Lincoln Brigade, November 1941.

9 Comintern Archives, Fond 495, Opis 74, Delo 484, pp. 27–31.

10 Comintern Archives, Fond 495, Opis 73, Delo 188, p. 10.

11 Comintern Archives, Fond 495, Opis 74, Delo 484, pp. 14–15.

12 Comintern Archives, Fond 545, Opis 6, Delo 1015. Wolff's hand-filled-out biographical form on the letterhead of the International Brigades, November 1, 1938.

13 National Archives, OSS Files, Directorate of Operations, 216 Box 1.

14 VALB letterhead April 14, 1941, Comintern Archives, Fond 495, Opis 14, Delo 25, p. 59.

15 Joseph Albright and Marcia Kunstel, *Bombshell*, Times Books, New York, 1997, p. 44.

16 See Chapter 6.

17 National Archives, transcript of Hearing in OSS files, pp. 125, 177, 180, 184, 190.

18 *Venona*, New York to Moscow, August 11, 1943.

19 House Committee on Un-American Activities, Hearings on Communist Party of Western Pennsylvania, February 21, 1950, p. 1220, and *The Slavic American*, New York, Fall 1947, p. 9.

20 Senate Internal Security Subcommittee, *Interlocking Subversion*, Part 12, pp. 765ff.

21 *Venona*, New York to Moscow, July 1, 1943.

22 National Archives, OSS files.

23 Report of Dimitri Manuilsky to the 18th Congress of the Communist Party of the Soviet Union in *The Land of Socialism Today and Tomorrow: Reports and Speeches at the Eighteenth Congress of the Communist Party of the Soviet Union (Bolsheviks), March 10–21, 1939*, p. 89.

24 Bentley, FBI statement, pp. 3–45, 52. See also Chapter 5.

25 House Committee on Un-American Activities, *Hearing Regarding Communist Espionage in the United States Government*, 1948, p. 723.

26 Senate Internal Security Subcommittee, *Subversive Influence in the Educational Process*, Part 6, March 26, 1953, pp. 668, 673–74.

27 House Committee on Un-American Activities, *Investigation of Communist Activities in the San Francisco Area—Part 1*, Hearing, December 1, 1953, pp. 3138ff.

28 *Venona*, New York to Moscow, May 26, 1943.

29 *Venona*, New York to Moscow, September 15, 1944.

30 *Venona*, Moscow to New York, September 20, 1944.

31 *Venona*, New York to Moscow, September 22, 1944.

32 *Venona*, New York to Moscow, September 23, 1944.

Notes

33 *Venona*, New York to Moscow, October 10, 1944.

34 *Venona*, New York to Moscow, June 9, 1944.

35 *Venona*, New York to Moscow, June 8, 1943.

36 Senate Internal Security Subcommittee, *Interlocking Subversion*, Part 10, pp. 605ff.

37 *Venona*, New York to Moscow, October 14, 1944.

38 *Venona*, New York to Moscow, June 8, 1943, and House Committee on Un-American Activities, *Communist Political Subversion*, pp. 6247–255 and *Daily Worker*, June 28, 1947.

39 Oleg Kalugin, *The First Directorate*, p. 45.

40 *Venona*, New York to Moscow, June 16, 1942.

41 FBI File 100-352385-2576, memo on Jane Foster Zlatovski and George Michael Zlatovski, January 17, 1957.

42 FBI Report published by Senate Internal Security Subcommittee, *Expose of Soviet Espionage*, May 1960, pp. 25–26.

43 Jane Foster, *An Un-American Lady*, p. 243.

44 Department of State Archives, cable to the secretary of state from Paris, January 29, 1951, and FBI Files 100-1469, memo to the director from Special Agent in Charge, New York, August 13, 1959, re: William Edwin Browder.

45 Dies Committee, Executive Hearings, vol. 7, pp. 3415–416, 3419, 3421.

46 Comintern Archives, Fond 515, Opis 1, Delo 3750, p. 34.

47 Comintern Archives, Fond 495, Opis 14, Delo 1, p. 28.

48 Workers' School, *Winter Term Announcement of Courses*, 1937, p. 11.

49 *Venona*, New York to Moscow, July 12, 1943, signed Moliere, the code name for Pavel Mikhailov, the GRU *Rezident*.

50 *Venona*, New York to Moscow, August 16, 1943.

51 *Venona*, New York to Moscow, September 8, 1943.

52 *Venona*, New York to Moscow, August 17, 1943, and Senate Internal Security Subcommittee, *Interlocking Subversion*, p. 701.

53 Senate Internal Security Subcommittee, *Interlocking Subversion*, Ibid., Part 11, pp. 679ff.

54 Bentley, FBI statement, pp. 38–41.

55 Comintern Archives, Fond 495, Opis 74, Delo 485, pp. 42–44.

56 Comintern Archives, Fond 495, Opis 74, Delo 481, and U.S. National Archives, OSS Files, INT27SP-208.

57 *Venona*, New York to Moscow, November 29, 1944.

58 *Venona*, New York to Moscow, July 20, 1944.

59 *Venona*, New York to Moscow, December 31, 1944.

60 House Committee on Un-American Activities, *Exposé*, pp. 17–18.

61 House Committee on Un-American Activities, *Hearing Regarding Communist Espionage in the United States Government*, p. 518.

62 Comintern Archives, Fond 495, Opis 74, Delo 485, p. 55.

63 *Venona*, New York to Moscow, November 20, 1945.

64 Bentley, FBI statement, p. 42.

65 *Venona*, New York to Moscow, April 29, 1943, and May 19, 1943.

66 *Venona*, New York to Moscow, May 29, 1943. Also, see Nigel West, editor, *British Security Coordination, the Secret History of British*

Notes

Intelligence in the Americas 1940–45.

67 Comintern Archives, Fond 495, Opis 74, Delo 478.

68 Pierre Cot, *Triumph of Treason.*

69 *Venona*, New York to Moscow, June 26, 1942, and Moscow to New York, July 1, 1942.

70 Thierry Wolton, *Le Grand Recrutement*, p. 248. This document was found in the Comintern Archives by French journalist Thierry Wolton.

71 *Venona*, New York to Moscow, June 3, 1943.

72 *Venona*, New York to Moscow, July 1, 1943.

73 *Venona*, New York to Moscow, July 22, 1943.

74 *Venona*, London to Moscow, July 17, 1940.

75 *Venona*, London to Moscow, August 10, 1940.

76 *Venona*, London to Moscow, September 23, 1940.

77 *Venona*, London to Moscow, September 6, 1940.

CHAPTER 10

1 Although the term "Rats" was used by NKVD both for Jews, generally, and for the Zionists, then a significant minority of the Jewish community who advocated a Jewish state in Palestine, the Soviets paid little mind to the distinction. They considered all Jews "Jewish nationalists," i.e., Zionists, and even distrusted the small group of Jewish Communists.

2 *W. I. Lenin und die Gesamtrussische Tscheka, Dokumentensammlung* (1917–1922) pp. 43–44 (in German). This is a translation of the Russian *V. I. Lenin I Vchka*, Publishing House of Political Literature, Moscow, 1975. The German edition was published by the East Germany Ministry of State Security (Stasi) Higher School, and marked for internal use only.

3 V. N. Chebrikov, et al., *History of Soviet State Security Organs.*

4 *Aus der Geschichte der Allrussischen Auflerordentlichen Kommission* (1917–1921), *Eine Sammlung von Dokumenten* [*From the History of the All Russian Extraordinary Commission (1917–1921), a collection of Documents*] p. 20. (This is a translation of the Russian *Iz Istorii Vserossiysskoi Chrezvichainoi Komissii*, published by the State Publishing House of Political Literature, Moscow, 1958. The German edition was published for the Stasi Higher School and marked for internal use only.)

5 V. N. Chebrikov, et al., *History of Soviet State Security Organs.*

6 Primakov, et al., *Essays on the History of Russian Foreign Intelligence*, p. 14.

7 Material on this case from the KGB Archives was made available to some Soviet scholars. It appears in a series of three articles by Soviet historian Leonid Mkhatylov, which were published in *Nedelya*, Moscow, November 27–December 3, 1989.

8 V. N. Chebrikov, et al., *History of Soviet State Security Organs.*

9 Ibid.

10 *The Trident*, published by the Organization for Rebirth of Ukraine, New York, April–May 1939, p. 31.

11 Sudoplatov, pp. 23–24, 26–27.

12 The Workers Party of America, *The White Terrorists Ask for Mercy*, pp. 4–5.

13 Statement of the City Executive Committee of Baltimore in Regards to Action Taken by Baltimore

Notes

Jewish Branch Abramovich Meeting, mimeographed, April 1925, in files of the American Communist Party maintained at the Communist International in Moscow, Fond 515, Opis 1, Delo 551, pp. 33, 34.

14 *The Menshevik Trial, the Text of the Indictment of the Counter-Revolutionary Menshevik Organization, the Trial of the All Union Bureau of the Central Committee of the Counter-Revolutionary Menshevik Party*, pp. 73–77.

15 Friedrich Adler, R. Abramovich, Leon Blum, and Emile Vandervelde, *The Moscow Trial and the Labour and Socialist International.*

16 Robert Conquest, *Stalin and the Kirov Murder*, pp. 45–47.

17 MASK, Moscow to Amsterdam, January 1, 1935.

18 SAPMO Archives, RY1 I 2/3/250, p. 225.

19 MASK, Moscow to London, January 28, 1935. A similar message was intercepted on the same date from Moscow to Basel.

20 Branko Lazitch, *Biographical Dictionary of the Comintern*, revised edition, pp. 290, 411.

21 M. Katz, *The Assassination of Kirov*, p. 22. Trotsky's name was often spelled with a z.

22 MASK, Moscow to Basel, January 3, 1935.

23 Lazitch, pp. 217–18.

24 *International Press Correspondence*, January 26, 1935, pp. 110–11.

25 Lazitch, 412.

26 *The Case of the Trotskyite-Zinovievite Terrorist Center, Report of Court Proceedings, August 19–24, 1936*, pp. 95–96. This abridged trial transcript was published in Moscow in many languages.

27 Max Shachtman, *Behind the Moscow Trial: The Greatest Frame-up in History*, p. 96.

28 *The Case of the Trotskyite-Zinovievite Terrorist Center*, pp. 88–90.

29 L. Sedov, *Livre Rouge sur le Procés de Moscou (Red Book on the Moscow Trial)*, pp. 40–41.

30 Comintern Archives Fond 495, Opis 14, Delo 20, pp. 24–25.

31 *The Case of Trotskyite-Zinovievite Terrorist Center*, p. 100.

32 Sedov, *Livre Rouge*, pp. 89–93.

33 D. N. Pritt, *The Moscow Trial*, preface.

34 D. N. Pritt, *At the Moscow Trial.*

35 MASK, Moscow to London, October 23, 1936.

36 MASK, Moscow to Stockholm, Copenhagen and Amsterdam, October 22, 1936.

37 D. N. Pritt, *Reports on Investigation in Korea and China, March–April 1952*, introduction.

38 Comintern Archives, Fond 495, Opis 14, Delo 81, p. 15. Confidential memo April 23, 1937, from Randolph (Sam Darcy) to Ercoli (Palmiro Togliatti).

39 Leaflet, "Solidarity Meeting," March 19, 1937 (in possession of the authors).

40 *Culture and the Crisis, An Open Letter to the Writers, Artists, Teachers, Physicians, Engineers, Scientists and other Professional Workers of America.*

41 Eugene Lyons, *The Red Decade, The Stalinist Penetration of America*, p. 369.

42 "Minutes of Polboro Meeting—February 11, 1937," and "Meeting of Sub-Committee in Campaign Against Trotskyism" [no date—1937] in Comintern Archives, Fond 495, Opis 14, Delo 68, pp. 115, 122–24, 160–61.

Notes

43 Call for the formation of the American Committee for the Defense of Leon Trotsky in *World Voices on the Moscow Trials from the Labor and Liberal Press*, published for The American Committee for the Defense of Leon Trotsky, p. 2.

44 MASK, Moscow to Stockholm, December 4, 1935.

45 *Bulletin of the Executive Committee of the Communist International*, Petrograd, July 7, 1922, no. 5, p. 126. (This rare publication was reprinted by photo offset by Feltrinelli, Milan, 1967.)

46 Isaac Deutscher, *The Prophet Outcast*, pp. 336–56.

47 Letter from Trotsky to Comrades in Norway, December 19, 1937, in *Writings of Leon Trotsky (1937–38)*.

48 Mauritz A. Hallgren, *Why I Resigned From the Trotsky Defense Committee*.

49 Pavel Sudaplatov, et al., *Special Tasks*, p. 74.

50 Comintern Archives, Fond 495, Opis 14, Delo 70, pp. 122–24.

51 Ibid.

52 Comintern Archives, Fond 495, Opis 14, Delo 75, p. 213.

53 *Direction*, Darien, Connecticut, May–June 1939, p. 1, and *Daily Worker*, New York, April 5, 1941.

54 *World Voices on the Moscow Trials from the Labor and Liberal Press*.

55 Friedrich Adler, *The Witchcraft Trial in Moscow*, p. 7.

56 Leon Trotsky, *I Stake My Life!*, pp. 2, 5.

57 Comintern Archives, Fond 495, Opis 14, Delo 69, pp. 20–22.

58 Sidney Hook, *Out of Step, An Unquiet Life in the 20th Century*, p. 227.

59 *Labor Condemns Trotskyism: Resolution Unanimously Adopted by First National Congress of the Mexican Confederation of Labour*.

60 *The Case of Leon Trotsky, Report of Hearings on the Charges Made Against Him in the Moscow Trials By the Preliminary Commission of Inquiry, John Dewey, Chairman*, pp. 32–34, 51–52, 273, 412–17.

61 Comintern Archives, Fond 495, Opis 20, Delo 536, pp. 7–8.

62 Joseph E. Davies, "How Russia Blasted Hitler's Spy Machine" in *The American Magazine*, December 1941, p. 80, 81, 110–12.

63 Frederick C. Giffin, "Improving the Image of Stalin's Russia: Joseph Davies's Mission to Moscow" in *Social Science*, Winter 1977.

64 This ad appeared in *The Nation*, New York, May 1, 1943, p. 641.

65 *New York Times*, May 21, 1943. The full text appeared in *The New Leader*, New York, May 29, 1943, p. 2.

66 *Daily Worker*, New York, May 20, 1943.

67 Veterans of Foreign Wars of the United States, Washington, D.C., press release May 28, 1943.

68 *Venona*, New York to Moscow, July 14, 1943.

69 Leon Trotsky, *Leon Sedoff—Son—Friend—Fighter*, pp. 23–24.

70 Ibid., p. 26.

71 Senate Internal Security Subcommittee, *Scope of Soviet Activity in the United States*, Part 4, Testimony of Mark Zborowski, February 29, 1956, pp. 88–89, 92.

72 Copies of exchange of telegrams were made available to Herbert Romerstein by the late Ruth Matthews, the widow of J. B. Matthews.

73 Leon Trotsky, *Writings of Leon Trotsky (1939–40)*, pp. 110–12.

Notes

74 Sanchez Salazar and Julian Gorkin, *Murder in Mexico, The Assassination of Leon Trotsky*, pp. 91–93.

75 Sudoplatov, p. 74.

76 Primakov, et al., *Essays on the History of Russian Foreign Intelligence*, vol. 3, 1933–41, p. 101.

77 Joseph Hansen, "The Attempted Assassination of Leon Trotsky" in *Fourth International*, New York, August 1940, pp. 85–91.

78 Letter addressed "Dear Friend" signed "J. P. Cannon, Farrell Dobbs and Rose Karsner," May 24, 1940, mailed from New York, 10 PM, on that date.

79 Joseph Hansen, "With Trotsky to the End" in *Fourth International*, New York, October 1940, p. 115.

80 *Fourth International*, New York, October 1940, p. 138.

81 *Fourth International*, New York, November 1940, pp. 148ff.

82 Sanchez Salazar, with the collaboration of Julian Gordin, *Murder in Mexico: The Assassination of Leon Trotsky*. Natalia Sedov's account appears on pp. 111–24.

83 Albert Goldman, *The Assassination of Leon Trotsky: The Proofs of Stalin's Guilt*. The text of the "confession" appears on pp. 5–8.

84 See Chapter 5.

85 House Committee on Un-American Activities, *American Aspects of the Assassination of Leon Trotsky*, pp. v–viii, 3401ff., 3409ff.

86 Primakov, et al., *Essays on the History of Russian Foreign Intelligence*, pp. 254–55.

87 Ibid., p. 258.

88 Ibid., p. 259.

89 *Venona*, Moscow to Mexico City, April 8, 1944, and May 27, 1944.

90 *Venona*, Moscow to Mexico City, April 29, 1944 and May 10, 1944; Mexico City to Moscow, May 3, 1944.

91 *Venona*, Mexico City to Moscow, December 6, 1943.

92 Primakov, et al., *Essays on the History of Russian Foreign Intelligence*, vol. 2, p. 259.

93 Ibid., vol. 3, p. 260.

94 Sudoplatov, pp. 70–72, 107–8.

95 Salazar, Appendix by Gorkin, pp. 231–35.

96 For more on the NKVD use of the passports of American volunteers in Spain, see Romerstein, *Heroic Victims*, pp. 21–25.

97 *Moscow News*, no. 12, 1989, p. 16.

98 Sudoplatov, pp. 80–81.

99 *Venona*, Mexico City to Moscow, March 14, 1944.

100 Primakov, et al., *Essays on the History of Russian Foreign Intelligence*, vol. 3, p. 106.

101 *Venona*, Mexico City to Moscow, December 23, 1943.

102 *Venona*, Mexico City to Moscow, December 29 and 30, 1943, and January 3, 1944.

103 *Venona*, Mexico City to Moscow, March 29, 1944.

104 Salazar, p. 222.

105 *Venona*, Mexico City to Moscow, June 6, 1944.

106 Salazar, p. 222.

107 *Venona*, San Francisco to Moscow, August 3, 1944, and August 19, 1944.

108 *Venona*, Moscow to Mexico City, February 27, 1944.

109 *Venona*, Moscow to Mexico City, August 24, 1944.

110 Senate Internal Security Subcommittee, *Scope*, Part 23A, p. 40.

111 Ruth's name and Party membership appears on a list of

Notes

Communist Party and Young Communist League members prepared by the International Brigades in 1937. Jacob was not on the list, as he had not yet arrived in Spain. Comintern Archives, Fond 545, Opis 6, Delo 846, p. 14.

112 *Venona*, Moscow to New York, March 21, 1945.

113 House Committee on Un-American Activities, *American Aspects of the Assassination of Leon Trotsky*, pp. 3345–354.

114 *Venona*, New York to Buenos Aires, February 1, 1943.

115 House Committee on Un-American Activities, *American Aspects*, p. 3376.

116 *Venona*, New York to Buenos Aires, September 29, 1943.

117 *Venona*, Buenos Aires to New York, July 5, 1942.

118 House Committee on Un-American Activities, *American Aspects*, pp. 3371–77.

119 *Venona*, Buenos Aires to New York, December 6, 1942.

120 House Committee on Un-American Activities, *American Aspects*, pp. 3354–360.

121 Comintern Archives, Fond 495, Opis 73, Delo 195, pp. 94–5.

122 *Venona*, Moscow to Mexico City, October 6, 1944.

123 *Venona*, Moscow to Montevideo, June 16, 1945.

124 *Venona*, Moscow to Mexico City, March 2, 1945, and March 9–10, 1945.

125 *Venona*, Moscow to Mexico City, May 31, 1945.

126 *Venona*, Moscow to Mexico City, August 1, 1945.

127 *Venona*, Moscow to Mexico City, August 26, 1945.

128 *Chicago Tribune*, May 24, 1954.

129 Sudoplatov, pp. 413, 120, 36.

CHAPTER 11

1 Cable, U.S. Embassy, London, to Department of State, September 14, 1962.

2 State Department Chronology regarding Robert Soblen, July 10, 1962, and cable, U.S. Embassy, London, to Department of State, July 1, 1962.

3 Cable, U.S. Embassy, London, to Department of State, August 2, 1962.

4 *International Bulletin of the Communist Left Opposition*, published for the International Secretariat by the Communist League of America (opposition), New York, Issue no. 3, May 1931, p. 6; no. 5, August 1931, pp. 15–18; no. 6, June 1931, p. 5ff; and no. 7, no date, entire issue.

5 FBI Summary Report on the Soble/Soblen Case, NY65-14702.

6 *Venona*, New York to Moscow, May 5, 1944.

7 Senate Internal Security Subcommittee, *Exposé of Soviet Espionage, May 1960*, FBI Report, Government Printing Office, 1960, p. 24.

8 Boris Morros, *My Ten Years as a Counterspy*, pp. 26–46.

9 Senate Internal Security Subcommittee, *Exposé of Soviet Espionage*, p. 24.

10 House Committee on Un-American Activities, *American Aspects*, pp. vii–ix.

11 *Venona*, New York to Moscow, June 16, 1943.

12 Transcript of Sylvia Doxsee's testimony before the grand jury was published by a Trotskyite splinter group in the 1980s as *Confession of a*

Notes

GPU Spy: Full transcript of the secret testimony of Sylvia Franklin before a New York Grand Jury, October 7, 1954 and June 18, 1958, New Park Publications, London.

13 *Venona*, New York to Moscow, June 6, 1943 and August 26, 1943.

14 *Venona*, New York to Moscow, May 26, 1944.

15 Senate Internal Security Subcommittee, *Strategy and Tactics of World Communism, Recruiting for Espionage—Part 15*, Hearing, June 30, 1955, Testimony of Charles Grutzner, p. 1403.

16 Ibid., *Communist Underground Printing Facilities and Illegal Propaganda*, Hearing, March 31, 1953, pp. 166, 187, 195.

17 Philip J. Jaffe, *The Rise and Fall of American Communism*, pp. 50–52.

18 *Venona*, New York to Moscow, July 21, 1943.

19 Richard McCarthy to Herbert Romerstein, January 1998.

20 *Venona*, New York to Moscow, May 1, 1944.

21 *Venona*, New York to Moscow, May 2, 1944.

22 *Venona*, New York to Moscow, May 3, 1944.

23 *Venona*, New York to Moscow, May 9, 1944.

24 *Venona*, New York to Moscow, May 19, 1944.

25 *Venona*, New York to Moscow, May 20, 1944.

26 *Venona*, New York to Moscow, May 19, 1944.

27 *Venona*, New York to Moscow, May 24, 1944.

28 *Venona*, New York to Moscow, June 26, 1944, and July 4, 1944.

29 *Venona*, New York to Moscow, August 10, 1944.

30 House Committee on Un-American Activities, Testimony of Victor A. Kravchenko, July 22, 1947; Victor Kravchenko, *I Chose Freedom: The Personal and Political Life of a Soviet Official*; and *I Chose Justice*.

31 *I Chose Justice*, Ibid., 8, 9, 13.

32 *Washington Post*, February 26, 1944.

33 *Venona*, New York to Moscow, August 10, 1944.

34 *Venona*, Moscow to New York, April 5, 1945.

35 Jean van Heijenoort, *With Trotsky in Exile: From Prinkipo to Coyoacan*.

36 *Venona*, New York to Moscow, September 2, 1944.

37 *Venona*, New York to Moscow, October 14, 1944.

38 *Venona*, New York to Moscow, December 22, 1944.

39 Zborowski had learned the whereabouts of Reiss through Trotsky's son Leon Sedov. He reported it to the NKVD.

40 *Venona*, New York to Moscow, November 3, 1944.

41 *Venona*, New York to Moscow, May 26, 1943, and June 10, 1943.

42 *Venona*, New York to Moscow, January 19, 1945.

43 For more on Hopkins's role as a Soviet agent, see Chapter 8.

44 McJimsey, 359–60. This extremely pro-Hopkins book provides valuable circumstantial evidence of Hopkins's work for the Soviets.

45 *Surveillance and Counter Espionage News*, a public web site expressing the views of the Russian Foreign Intelligence Service, 1998.

46 *Venona*, Mexico City to Moscow, June 29, 1944.

47 Senate Internal Security Subcommittee, *The Legacy of Alexander Orlov*, 1973, pp. 37–38.

Notes

48 Senate Internal Security Subcommittee, *Scope of Soviet Activity in the United States, Part 5,* Testimony of Lila Dallin, March 2, 1956, pp. 137–38.

49 Senate Internal Security Subcommittee, *Legacy of Alexander Orlov,* pp. 20–4.

50 Ibid.; and Senate Internal Security Subcommittee, *Scope, Parts 4 and 5.*

51 Senate Internal Security Subcommittee, *Exposé of Soviet Espionage, May 1960, Report by the FBI,* July 2, 1960, pp. 24, 27.

52 Mark Zborowski, *Life Is with People.*

53 Zborowski, *People in Pain.*

54 *San Francisco Chronicle,* May 12, 1960 (obituary), and May 15, 1990 (letter from former colleague).

55 Morros, pp. 45–50.

56 FBI report on Alfred K. Stern case, September 29, 1955, NY100-65568.

57 FBI report on Alfred K. Stern case, July 2, 1957, NY100-65568.

58 Ibid., letter Boris Vinogradov to Martha Dodd, July 11, 1934.

59 FBI report on the Alfred K. Stern case, June 24, 1958, NY100-65568.

60 Martha Dodd Stern papers, Manuscript Division, Library of Congress, Sigrid Schultz to Martha Dodd Stern, March 14, 1970.

61 Martha Dodd Stern papers, Stern to Ehrenberg, October 29, 1957.

62 Martha Dodd, *Through Embassy Eyes,* p. 261.

63 FBI Reports on Alfred K. Stern case, July 31, 1957, NH65-1169, and February 26, 1958, NY100-65568.

64 FBI Report on Alfred K. Stern case, June 30, 1949, NY100-65568.

65 *Venona,* New York to Moscow, January 4, 1945 (two messages sent on the same day).

66 FBI report on Alfred K. Stern case, June 27, 1960, NY100-65568.

67 *New York Herald Tribune,* April 11, 1957.

68 FBI report on Alfred K. Stern case, June 24, 1958, NY100-65568.

69 See Chapter 11.

70 *CTK Information Bulletin* (issued by Czechoslovak News Agency), Prague, September 6, 1957, "Press Release of Mrs. Martha Dodd Stern and Mr. Alfred K. Stern in Prague," Martha Dodd Stern papers.

71 Cable, Prague to State Department, September 7, 1957. Released under the Freedom of Information Act.

72 Martha Dodd, *The Searching Light.*

73 The inscribed copy is in the possession of the authors.

74 FBI Memo, New York to Headquarters, in Case NY100-65568, August 11, 1971.

75 FBI Teletype, New York to Headquarters, September 21, 1971.

76 Memo from FBI Director to Assistant Attorney General, Internal Security Division, March 13, 1972.

77 See Victor Rabinowitz, *Unrepentant Leftist, A Lawyer's Memoir,* where he admits Party membership while doing his best to conceal the dates or its significance.

78 Memo from FBI Director to Acting Assistant Attorney General, Internal Security Division, June 15, 1972.

79 FBI Memo, New York to Headquarters, January 30, 1974.

80 FBI Teletype, New York to Headquarters, April 23, 1975.

81 Letter Leonard Boudin to Kevin T. Maroney, Dept. of Justice, July 25, 1975.

82 Memo FBI Director to Assistant Attorney General Criminal Division, July 31, 1975.

Notes

83 Letter Congressman Don Edwards to Attorney General Griffin Bell, June 30, 1977 (all of the correspondence on this matter from Congressman Edwards was made available to the press by his office).

84 FBI report on Alfred Stern case, NY100-65568, May 7, 1957.

85 Ibid., June 27, 1960.

86 Letter, Assistant Attorney General Benjamin Civiletti by Robert Keuch to Congressman Don Edwards, July 18, 1977.

87 Letter, Congressman Don Edwards to Robert Lipshutz, December 20, 1977.

88 Letter, Congressman Don Edwards to Griffin Bell, March 3, 1978.

89 Letter, Benjamin Civiletti to Congressman Don Edwards, April 10, 1978.

90 Letter, Congressman Don Edwards to Anne Wexler, June 12, 1978.

91 FBI Director to Assistant Attorney General, Criminal Division, August 11, 1978.

92 FBI Cable, New York to Headquarters, November 29, 1978, and FBI Memo, undated, in Case NY100-655680.

93 *Washington Post*, March 23, 1979.

94 FBI Memo, undated, in Case NY100-65568.

95 Martha Dodd Stern papers, letter, Martha Dodd to George and Eleanor Wheeler, May 6, 1979.

96 Ibid., Congressman Don Edwards to Mr. and Mrs. Alfred Stern, November 30, 1979.

97 *Los Angeles Times*, June 24, 1986.

CHAPTER 12

1 *Venona*, Moscow to New York, Mexico City, Paris, etc., March 10, 1945.

2 *Venona*, Moscow to Mexico City, February 21, 1945.

3 *Venona*, Moscow to Mexico City, etc., March 6, 1946.

4 *Venona*, New York to Moscow, May 25, 1945. (The code word "Rats" was used by NKVD for both Jews generally and Zionists particularly. At the same time that NKVD used this term, the Nazis were distributing airborne leaflets to the Soviet troops with a picture of a rat and the caption "Jews are like rats.")

5 Report from Andreev of the Comintern Cadre Department to Dimitroff, head of the Comintern, on the members of the Politburo of the American Communist Party, Comintern Archives, Fond 495, Opis 74, Delo 457, p. 53.

6 Earl Browder, et al., *The Communist Position on the Negro Question*, Workers Library Publishers, circa 1931, "Resolution of Communist International October 26, 1928," pp. 56–64.

7 *"On this first day in October," Dr. W. E. B. DuBois's application to join the Communist Party and Gus Hall's reply*, Communist Party USA, New York, 1961.

8 *The Crisis*, September 1931, p. 315.

9 Tim Ryan (Eugene Dennis), Report on "The Organizational Position of the CPUSA," March 3, 1941, Comintern Archives, Fond 515, Opis 1, Delo 4091, pp. 3–4.

10 Comintern Archives, Fond 495, Opis 74, Delo 467, p. 39.

11 Herbert Hill, "The Communist Party—Enemy of Negro Equality," *The Crisis*, June–July 1951, p. 371.

12 Alfred J. Kutzik, *The Communist Party and the Jews*, p. 14.

13 Ibid., p. 70.

Notes

14 By 1929 all of the Communist parties had been cleansed of dissident elements. The Comintern referred to this as "Bolshevization." From then until Khrushchev's secret speech denouncing Stalin in 1956, Communists were not permitted to deviate from the Party line in any way.

15 *Report on Mass Agitation and Propaganda*, March 2, 1937, Comintern Archives, Fond 495, Opis 14, Delo 76, p. 30.

16 J. V. Stalin, *Works*, vol. 2, pp. 51–52.

17 "Report on Organizational Condition of the CPUSA" by a Comintern instructor who had studied the Party apparatus from September to November 1929, Comintern Archives, Fond 495, Opis 25, Delo 869, p. 96, and Marie Syrkin, *The Communists and the Arab Problem*, League for Labor Palestine, circa 1936, p. 4.

18 *Two Decades of the Communist Party USA*, New York State, p. 13, and Comintern Archives, Fond 495, Opis 14, Delo 92, p. 111.

19 Comintern Archives, Ibid., p. 97.

20 Sam Darcy, *An Eye-Witness at the Wreckers' Trial*.

21 The Soviet line on this trial may be found in H. R. George, *Eight Soviet Generals Plotted Against Peace*.

22 Comintern Archives, Fond 495, Opis 14, Delo 67, p. 338.

23 *Soviet Russia Today*, New York, January 1939, p. 24.

24 MASK, Moscow to Copenhagen, June 1, 1936, and Moscow to London, June 15, 1936.

25 *Speech by Comrade Wm. Z. Foster at Meeting of National Council of Jewish Communists*, March 2, 1940 (mimeographed).

26 Tim Ryan (Eugene Dennis), "The Organizational Position of the CPUSA."

27 *Nazi-Soviet Relations 1939–1941, Documents from the Archives of the German Foreign Office*, p. 163.

28 Leaflet of Jewish-American Council, Communist Party of Illinois, circa June 1940.

29 FBI Supplemental Correlation Summary, December 30, 1957, pp. 10, 11. Released under the Freedom of Information Act.

30 FBI Report on Alfred K. Stern, June 24, 1958, in NY100-65568, p. 75.

31 *Venona*, New York to Moscow, May 6, 1944.

32 FBI Report NY100-8150, August 2, 1957, pp. 10, 11. Released under the Freedom of Information Act.

33 Bentley, FBI statement, November 30, 1945, pp. 28, 29.

34 Tom O'Connor, *The Truth About Anti-Semitism in the Soviet Union*.

35 Letterhead American Birobidjan Committee, May 14, 1946.

36 Melech Epstein, *The Jew and Communism 1919–1941*, p. 311.

37 J. M. Wachman, *Why the Jewish Masses Must Rally to the Defense of the Soviet Union*, p. 12.

38 Yarmulke is the Russian word for the skull cap worn by religious Jews.

39 Comintern Archives, Fond 495, Opis 14, Delo 55, p. 129.

40 Comintern Archives, Fond 495, Opis 19, Delo 299, pp. 12–14, 19, 54.

41 Brochure of pictures published by Workers International Relief circa 1931, p. 1.

42 See Chapter 8.

43 *R. W. R. Reporter*, published by Russian War Relief, Inc., March 1942, p. 1.

44 *Response to Fellow Jews in the Soviet Union*, Committee of Jewish Writers

Notes

and Artists in the United States, New York, December 1941.

45 *The Case of Henryk Erlich and Victor Alter, compiled by the General Jewish Workers' Union "Bund" of Poland,* pp. 4, 5, 9, 10, 12, 13, 14, 17–19.

46 *Daily Worker,* March 25, 1943, p. 2.

47 Earl Browder, *A Conspiracy Against Our Soviet Ally, A Menace to America,* Illinois State Committee Communist Party, 1943.

48 *Polish-Soviet Relations 1918–1943,* Official Documents, pp. 180, 245–46.

49 See Chapter 4.

50 *Open Letter to the American People on American-Soviet Friendship,* p. 7.

51 *The Ghetto Speaks,* American Representation of the General Jewish Workers' Union of Poland (The Bund), July 1, 1943, p. 5.

52 Ibid., September 1, 1943, p. 8.

53 *Jews Have Always Fought for Freedom,* National Reception Committee to the Delegation from the USSR, New York, 1943; *Birobidjan and the Jews in the Post-War World: A series of addresses on the occasion of the visit to the USA of Prof. Mikhoels and Lt.-Col. Feffer of the USSR,* American Committee for the Settlement of Jews in Birodidjan (Ambijan), New York, 1943; *Admiration Is Not Enough! Calling All Jews to Action,* Jewish Fund for Soviet Russia, Affiliated to Mrs. Churchill's Red Cross Aid-to-Russia Fund, London, 1943.

54 *Venona,* New York to Moscow, May 31, 1944.

55 Arkady Vaksberg, *Stalin Against the Jews.*

56 *Revelations from the Russian Archives, Documents in English Translation,* Library of Congress, Washington, D.C., 1997, pp. 218–19 (translation corrected after comparison with Russian original).

57 B. Z. Goldberg, *The Jewish Problem in the Soviet Union,* pp. 100–4.

58 Shimon Redlich, *Propaganda and Nationalism in Wartime Russia, the Jewish Antifascist Committee in the USSR, 1941–1948,* pp. 158–59.

59 See Chapter 8.

60 Sudoplatov, pp. 214, 298.

61 Vaksberg, pp. 227–36.

62 Memo, "Charges Preferred Against Comrade Paul Novick" from National Organization Department to all members of the Communist Party USA, 1971.

63 *New York Times,* July 13, 1943 (ad).

64 *The (Jewish) Sentinel,* Chicago, August 5, 1943.

65 *Chicago Tribune,* January 23, 1944.

66 *Daily Worker,* New York, July 12, 1943, and July 28, 1943.

67 *The (Jewish) Sentinel,* Chicago, October 19, 1944.

68 *Chicago Tribune,* October 20, 1944.

69 *New York Post,* January 22, 1945 (ad).

70 FBI Report, January 22, 1946, on Jacob Landau in Silvermaster File 65-56402 Volume 22, Serial 491.

71 *Venona,* Mexico City to Moscow, January 15, 1944.

72 *Venona,* New York to Moscow, February 2, 1944.

73 *Venona,* New York to Moscow, May 6, 1944.

74 *Venona* Mexico City to Moscow, September 7, 1944.

75 See Chapter 11.

76 *New York World Telegram,* September 13, 1948; *Hearings on Communist Activities Among Aliens and National Groups,* Special Subcommittee to Investigate Immigration and Naturalization of the Committee on the Judiciary, September 15, 1949,

Notes

Testimony of Larry E. Kerley
Former Special Agent, Federal
Bureau of Investigation, pp. 803–4.

77 E. Yaroslavsky, *Religion in the USSR,*
pp. 36–37.

78 Earl Browder, *A Message to Catholics,*
p. 15.

79 Fond 495, Opis 14, Delo 95, Speech
by Louis Budenz, Central
Committee CPUSA Plenum,
December 1938, p. 63a.

80 Fond 495, pp. 1, 2, 3, 7.

81 Dies Committee, vol. 2, p. 1054.

82 *Five Years of International Workers
Order, 1930–1935,* National
Executive Committee, IWO, New
York, May 1935, pp. 9, 11.

83 S. Gusev, et al., *The Next Step in
Britain, America, and Ireland:
Speeches at the 12th Plenum of the
Executive Committee of the
Communist International,* p. 29.

84 *We Support the Communist Candidate
in This Year's Election, Every Member
of the International Workers Order
Must Rally Behind the Communist
Election Platform,* p. 14.

85 See Chapter 4.

86 Gusev, pp. 67ff., and "35 Lat W
USA" ["35 Years in the USA"] by
Boleslaw Gebert in *Z Pola Walki,*
Warsaw, 1959, no. 3, p. 174.

87 Arthur Bliss Lane, *I Saw Poland
Betrayed: An American Ambassador
Reports to the American People,*
pp. 131–32.

88 *Venona,* New York to Moscow,
August 8, 1944.

89 *Venona,* New York to Moscow,
May 17, 1944.

90 *Venona,* New York to Moscow,
May 27, 1944.

91 *Venona,* New York to Moscow,
June 7, 1944, and July 1, 1944.

92 *Venona,* New York to Moscow,
July 6, 1944.

93 *Venona,* New York to Moscow,
August 29, 1944.

94 *Venona* New York to Moscow,
October 6, 1944.

95 *Venona,* New York to Moscow,
July 3, 1943.

96 *Venona,* New York to Moscow,
June 20, 1944.

97 *Venona,* Moscow to New York,
February 9, 1945.

98 *Venona,* New York to Moscow,
February 10, 1945.

99 *Venona,* Moscow to New York,
February 15, 1945.

100 Bentley, FBI statement; p. 29.

101 Proceedings 6th National
Convention IWO, July 2–7, 1944,
New York City, p. 225.

102 FBI Report. Released under the
Freedom of Information Act.

103 OSS Files in National Archives,
INT 29UK146, 148.

104 See Chapter 11.

105 Albert Parry, *Russian Cavalcade: A
Military Record.*

106 Michael Sayers, and Albert E.
Kahn, *The Great Conspiracy: The
Secret War Against Soviet Russia.* A
magazine size paperback edition
was published in May 1946 by
Boni & Gaer, New York, a
Communist-controlled publishing
house. In June 1947 a pocket-sized
paperback edition was published by
Boni & Gaer.

107 Eugene Dennis to all state and district secretaries of the Communist
Party, on letterhead of the Communist Party USA, April 11, 1947.

108 Bentley, FBI statement, pp. 28–29.

109 *Venona,* New York to Moscow,
June 18, 1943.

110 *Venona,* New York to Moscow,
February 2, 1944.

Notes

111 *Venona*, New York to Moscow, June 7, 1944.

112 *Venona*, New York to Moscow, June 20, 1944.

113 *Venona*, San Francisco to Moscow and New York, June 14, 1946.

114 Memo, Shelepin to Central Committee CPSU, June 7, 1960, translated in *Cold War International History Project Bulletin*, Woodrow Wilson International Center for Scholars, Washington, D.C., Fall 1994, pp. 25–27, 32.

115 Bob Edward and Kenneth Dunne, *A Study of a Master Spy (Allen Dulles)*, and CIA report "The Soviet and Communist Bloc Defamation Campaign" placed in the *Congressional Record*, by Congressman Melvin Price of Illinois, September 28, 1965, p. 24477.

116 V. N. Chebrikov, et al., *History of Soviet State Security Organs*, ch. 10 (marked Top Secret).

117 Richard Squires, *Auf Dem Kreigspfad [On the War Path]*, pp. 209–10. Although the book never appeared in English, it said on the copyright page, "Title of the English original: *On the War Path*."

118 Albert E. Kahn, Introduction to *The Diary of General Grow as Exposed by Major Richard Squires*, p. 1.

119 An extensive discussion of the case may be found in George F. Hofmann, *Cold War Casualty; The Court-Martial of Major General Robert W. Grow*.

120 *Proceedings, Sixth National Convention International Workers Orders, July 2–7, 1944*, p. 135.

121 Sam Milgrom, *7th Convention Report*.

122 *Proceedings Seventh General Convention, International Worker Order, June 16 to 18, 1947*, pp. 215–17.

123 *Daily Worker*, New York, September 7, 1977, p. 7.

124 *New York* v. *International Workers Order*, transcript, Case on Appeal, New York State Supreme Court, Appellate Division—First Department, Index no. 21205-1950, p. 2550.

125 Comintern Archives, Fond 545, Opis 1, Delo 11, p. 68.

126 Alexander Polyukhov, "The Raoul Wallenberg Mystery," *New Times*, Moscow, December 18–24, 1990, pp. 32–35.

127 *For a Lasting Peace, for a People's Democracy!* Bucharest, November 21 and November 28, 1952. (This incredibly named newspaper was the organ of the Cominform).

128 *The Anti-Semitic Nature of the Czechoslovak Trial (November–December 1952)*, p. 1.

129 Henry Ford's *The International Jew [Mezhdunarodnoe Evreistvo]* was published in Moscow as late as 1993 by Moskvityanin. The book contained ads for such hard-line Communist journals as *Den* and *Ruskii Vestnik*.

130 A. A. Ivan, *Osobennosti Verbovochnoi Razrabotki Zarubezhnikh Evreev, Etnicheski Svyazannikh SSSR [The Peculiarity of Recruit Development of Foreign Jews Who Are Ethnically Tied to the USSR]*, Moscow, 1986, pp. 25, 30, 33, 36, 38, 53 (marked Secret).

CHAPTER 13

1 *Venona*, New York to Moscow, May 17, 1944.

2 Comintern Archives, Fond 495, Opis 74, Delo 485.

Notes

3 *Venona*, New York to Moscow, August 17, 1944.

4 *Venona*, New York to Moscow, September 9, 1944.

5 *Venona*, New York to Moscow, September 9, 1944, and September 14, 1944.

6 *Venona*, New York to Moscow, October 28, 1944.

7 *Venona*, New York to Moscow, September 13, 1944.

8 *Venona*, New York to Moscow, October 10, 1944.

9 Ibid.

10 Senate Internal Security Subcommittee, *Institute of Pacific Relations*, Part 2, p. 490.

11 *Venona*, New York to Moscow, October 23, 1944.

12 *Venona*, New York to Moscow, December 23, 1944.

13 I. F. Stone, *The Truman Era*, p. 196.

14 *The Independent*, London, March 12, 1992.

15 Kalugin, in two private conversations with Romerstein, revealed that the agent to whom he had referred was the late I. F. Stone. However, he said, the money he took was not for him personally but for his publication, *I. F. Stone's Weekly*, and he would write the same thing whether he was paid or not. While not identifying Kalugin as the source, both Romerstein and Breindel wrote articles about the I. F. Stone case.

Stone's relatives and friends created a firestorm, denying the allegations and claiming that Stone was the victim of a smear. *The New York Review of Books* carried extensive correspondence arguing both sides of the issue.

Brown later spoke to Kalugin again and reported that the retired KGB general had confirmed that he was referring to Stone during his Exeter speech. However, Kalugin later claimed that Stone was not an agent, nor had he taken KGB money, the opposite of what he said in his speech. (*The New York Review of Books*, October 8, 1992, p. 21).

16 *I. F. Stone's Weekly*, Washington, September 23, 1968, p. 4.

17 L. Beria, *The Great Inspirer and Organizer of the Victories of Communism*, p. 24.

18 *The Daily Compass*, New York, December 21, 1949, p. 5.

19 *The Daily Compass*, New York, December 23, 1949.

20 I. F. Stone, *The Hidden History of the Korean War*, p. 27.

21 *I. F. Stone's Weekly*, Washington, D.C., September 26, 1966, p. 3.

22 Committee on Armed Services, United States Senate, *Imprisonment and Escape of Lt. (JG) Dieter Dengler, USNR*, Hearing, September 16, 1966, p. 8.

23 *I. F. Stone's Weekly*, Washington, D.C., January 8, 1968, p. 3.

24 Bentley, FBI statement, December 3, 1945, p. 15.

25 *Venona*, New York to Moscow, June 8, 1943.

26 Bentley, FBI statement, p. 94.

27 *Venona*, New York to Moscow, August 28, 1944.

28 Letterhead, Southern Conference for Human Welfare, with typed address in Greensboro, NC, September 7, 1945.

29 Comintern Archives, Fond 495, Opis 18, Delo 1290, pp. 104–5.

30 Comintern Archives, Fond 495, Opis 14, Delo 131, p. 18.

31 Comintern Archives, Fond 495, Opis 73, Delo 84, pp. 20, 28.

Notes

32 Harry Hopkins memo, March 10, 1943, and Davies diary, March 12 and 14, 1943, both at Roosevelt Library, Hyde Park, New York. Cited in McJimsey, p. 291.

33 Comintern Archives, Fond 495, Opis 73, Delo 173, pp. 1–69.

34 Günter Bohnsack and Herbert Brehmer, *Auftrag: Irreführung, Wie die Stasi Politik im Western machte*, pp. 25–27.

CHAPTER 14

1 Regina and Philip Frankfeld, *A Discussion Article on Trumanism and McCarthyism*, pp. 6, 10.

2 J. Stalin, *Defects in Party Work and Measures for Liquidating Trotskyite and Other Double-Dealers, Report and Speech in Reply to Debate at the Plenum of the Central Committee of the C.P.S.U., March 3–5, 1937*, pp. 21, 29.

3 Leon Trotsky, *In Defense of the Soviet Union, A Compilation 1927–1937*, pp. 18, 20.

4 Rumanian Government, *Trial of the Group of Spies and Traitors in the Service of the Espionage of Tito's Fascist Clique*, and Hungarian Government, *Tito-Fascist Kidnappers before the Court*, 1952.

5 George Charney, *A Long Journey*, p. 233.

6 *American Mercury*, July 1953.

7 The ACLU resolution said: "The Board of Directors and the National Committee of the American Civil Liberties Union therefore hold it inappropriate for any person to serve on the governing committees of the Union or on its staff, who is a member of any political organization which supports totalitarian dictatorship in any country, or who by his public declarations indicates his support of such a principle.

"Within this category we include organizations in the United States supporting the totalitarian governments of the Soviet Union and of the Fascist and Nazi countries (such as the Communist Party, the German-American Bund and others); as well as native organizations with obvious anti-democratic objectives or practices."—Corliss Lamont, editor, *The Trial of Elizabeth Gurley Flynn by the American Civil Liberties Union, including The Transcript of the Extraordinary Meeting of the Board of Directors of the American Civil Liberties Union* (May 7, 1940), p. 43.

8 Committee on Post Office and Civil Service, United States Senate, *Administration of the Federal Employees' Security Program*, Part I, pp. 261, 263.

9 Committee on Government Operations, United States Senate, *Commission on Government Security*, p. 439.

10 Committee on Labor and Public Welfare United States Senate, *Communist Domination of Certain Unions*. See also Congress of Industrial Organizations, *Official Reports on the Expulsion of Communist Dominated Organizations from the CIO*.

11 *The Communist Party and the Labour Party*, p. 4.

12 Harold J. Laski, *The Secret Battalion, An Examination of the Communist Attitude to the Labour Party*, p. 12.

13 Barron, *Operation Solo*.

BIBLIOGRAPHY

Abarinov, Vladimir, *The Murderers of Katyn*, Hippocrene Books, New York, 1993.

Abt, John J., *Advocate and Activist: Memoirs of an American Communist Lawyer*, University of Illinois Press, Urbana and Chicago, 1993.

Adler, Friedrich, R. Abramovich, Leon Blum, and Emile Vandervelde, *The Moscow Trial and the Labour and Socialist International*, The Labour Party, London, 1931.

Adler, Friedrich, *The Witchcraft Trial in Moscow*, Pioneer Publishers, 1937.

Albright, Joseph, and Marcia Kunstel, *Bombshell: The Secret Story of America's Unknown Atomic Spy Conspiracy*, Times Books, New York, 1997.

American Committee for the Defense of Leon Trotsky, *World Voices on the Moscow Trials from the Labor and Liberal Press*, Pioneer Publishers, New York, 1936.

American Jewish Committee, *The Anti-Semitic Nature of the Czechoslovak Trial (Nov.–Dec. 1952)*, New York, 1952.

Anders, General Wladyslaw (Foreword), *The Crime of Katyn, Facts and Documents*, Polish Cultural Foundation, London, 1965.

Andrew, Christopher, and Oleg Gordievsky, *KGB: The Inside Story*, HarperCollins, New York, 1990.

Angress, Werner T., *Stillborn Revolution: The Communist Bid for Power in Germany, 1921–1923*, Princeton University Press, Princeton, 1963.

Aus der Geschichte der Allrussischen Auss erordentlichen Kommission (1917–1921), Eine Sammlung von Dokumenten [*From the History of the All Russian Extraordinary Commission (1917–1921), a Collection of Documents*] Ministerium für Staatssicherheit, Juristische Hochschule, Potsdam, 1974.

Barron, John, *KGB: The Secret Work of Soviet Secret Agents*, Reader's Digest Press, New York, 1974.

Barron, John, *Operation Solo: The FBI's Man in the Kremlin*, Regnery Publishing, Washington, D.C., 1996.

Benson, Robert Louis, and Michael Warner, *Venona: Soviet Espionage and the American Response 1939–1957*, United States National Security Agency and Central Intelligence Agency, Washington, D.C., 1996.

Benson, Robert Louis, six monographs issued by the National Security Agency with the release of the Venona documents. (1) *Introductory History of Venona and Guide to the Translations*, (2) *Venona Historical Monograph #2: The 1942–43 New*

565

Bibliography

York-Moscow KGB Messages, (3) *Venona Historical Monograph #3: The 1944–45 New York and Washington–Moscow KGB Messages,* (4) *Venona Historical Monograph #4: The KGB in San Francisco and Mexico. The GRU in New York and Washington,* (5) *Venona Historical Monograph #5: The KGB and GRU in Europe, South America, and Australia,* (6) *Venona Historical Monograph #6: Venona: New Released, Special Reports, and Project Shutdown,* National Security Agency, Fort Meade, Maryland.

Beria, L., *The Great Inspirer and Organizer of the Victories of Communism,* Foreign Languages Publishing House, Moscow, 1950.

Bohnsack, Günter, and Herbert Brehmer, *Auftrag: Irreführung, Wie die Stasi Politik im Western machte,* Carlsen, Germany.

Browder, Earl, *A Message to Catholics,* Workers Library Publishers, New York, 1938.

Browder, Earl, *Modern Resurrections and Miracles,* privately published, Yonkers, New York, 1950.

Browder, Earl, *The People's Front,* International Publishers, New York, 1938.

Byrnes, James F., *Speaking Frankly,* Harper & Brothers, New York, 1947.

Cairncross, John, *The Enigma Spy: An Autobiography,* Century, London, 1997.

Canada, Government of, *The Report of the Royal Commission to Investigate the Facts Relating to and the Circumstances Surrounding the Communication, by Public Officials and Other Persons in Positions of Trust, of Secret and Confidential Information to Agents of a Foreign Power, June 27, 1946,* Controller of Stationery, Ottawa, 1946.

Chambers, Whittaker, *Can You Hear Their Voices? A Short Story,* International Pamphlets, New York, 1932.

Chambers, Whittaker, *Witness,* Random House, New York, 1952.

Charney, George, *A Long Journey,* Quadrangle Books, Chicago, 1968.

Chikov, Vladimir, and Gary Kern, *Perseus: Espionage in Los Alamos,* Ferlag Volk & Welt, Berlin, 1996.

Churchill, Winston, *Triumph and Tragedy,* Houghton Mifflin Company, Boston, 1953.

Communist International, *Protokoll des III. Kongresses der Kommunistischen Internationale (Moskau, 22 Juni bis 12 Juli 1921),* Verlag der Kommunistischen Internationale, Auslieferungstelle für Deutschland, Carl Hoym Nachf., Hamburg, 1921.

Communist International, *Thesis and Resolutions Adopted at the III World Congress of the Communist International (June 22–July 12, 1921),* Press Bureau of the Communist International, Moscow, 1921.

Communist Party of Great Britain, *The Communist Party and the Labour Party,* London, 1943.

Communist Party New York State, *Two Decades of the Communist Party USA, New York State,* New York, September 1939.

Communist Party of the Soviet Union, *The Land of Socialism Today and Tomorrow, Reports and Speeches at the Eighteenth Congress of the Communist Party of the Soviet Union (Bolsheviks), March 10–21, 1939,* Foreign

Bibliography

Languages Publishing House, Moscow, 1939.

Communist Party USA, *On the Struggle Against Revisionism*, New York, January 1946.

Communist Party USA, *The Way Out: A Program for American Labor;— Manifesto and Principal Resolutions Adopted by the 8th Convention of the Communist Party of the USA*, Workers Library Publishers, New York, May 1934.

Conquest, Robert, *Stalin and the Kirov Murder*, Oxford University Press, New York, 1989.

Cot, Pierre, *Triumph of Treason*, Ziff Davis, Chicago, 1944.

Dallet, Joe, *Letters from Spain*, Workers Library Publishers, New York, 1938.

Dallin, David J., *Soviet Espionage*, Yale University Press, New Haven, 1955.

Darcy, Sam, *An Eye-Witness at the Wreckers' Trial*, Workers Library Publishers, 1937.

Davies, Joseph E., *Mission to Moscow*, Simon and Schuster, New York, 1941.

De Laon, Solon, *The American Labor Who's Who*, Hanford Press, New York, 1925.

Deutscher, Isaac, *The Prophet Outcast*, Oxford University Press, London, 1963.

Dewey, John (chairman), *The Case of Leon Trotsky, Report of Hearings on the Charges Made Against Him in the Moscow Trials By the Preliminary Commission of Inquiry*, Harper & Brothers, New York, 1937.

Dodd, Martha, *The Searching Light*, Citadel Press, New York, 1955.

Dodd, Martha, *Through Embassy Eyes*, Harcourt, Brace and Company, New York, 1939.

Draper, Theodore, *American Communism and Soviet Russia*, Viking Press, New York, 1960.

Draper, Theodore, *The Roots of American Communism*, Viking Press, New York, 1957.

Dziak, John J., *Chekisty: A History of the KGB*, Lexington Books, Lexington, Massachusetts, 1988.

Edwards, Bob, and Kenneth Dunne, *A Study of a Master Spy (Allen Dulles)*, Housmans Publishers and Book-sellers, London (circa 1961).

Epstein, Melech, *The Jew and Communism, 1919–1941*, Trade Union Sponsoring Committee, New York, 1959.

Feklisov, Alexandr, *Za Okeanom I Na Ostrove [Across the Ocean and on the Island]*, Dem, Moscow, 1994.

Field, Frederick Vanderbilt, *From Right to Left: An Autobiography*, Lawrence Hill & Company, Westport, Connecticut, 1983.

Fineberg, Dr. S. Andhil, *The Rosenberg Case: Fact and Fiction*, Oceana Publications, New York, 1953.

Ford, Henry, *Mezhdunarodnoe Evreisvo [The International Jew]*, Moskvityanin, Moscow, 1993.

Foreign Intelligence Service of the Russian Federation, *Ocherki Istorii Rossiiskoi Vneshnei Razvedki [Essays in the History of Russian Foreign Intelligence]*, Mezhdunarodnaya Otnosheniya, Moscow, vol. 2, 1996; vol. 3, 1997; and vol. 4, 1999.

Foreign Intelligence Service of the Russian Federation, *Veteraniy Vnechnei Razvedki Rossii [Veterans of Foreign Intelligence of Russia]*, Sluzhba Vneshnei Razvedki Rossiiskoi Federatsii, Moscow, 1995.

Foster, Jane, *An Un-American Lady*, Sidgwick & Jackson, London, 1980.

Bibliography

Foster, William Z., and Benjamin Gitlow, *Acceptance Speeches, National Election Campaign Committee, Workers (Communist) Party*, 1928.

Foster, William Z., *The War Crisis: Questions and Answers*, Workers Library Publishers, New York, January 1940.

Foster, William Z., *Toward Soviet America*, Coward-McCann and International Publishers, New York, 1932.

Fraina, Louis C., *Report of Louis C. Fraina, International Secretary of the Communist Party of America, to the Executive Committee of the Communist International*, Communist Party of America, Chicago (circa 1920).

Frankfeld, Regina and Philip, *A Discussion Article on Trumanism and McCarthyism*, privately printed, Baltimore, 1951.

General Jewish Workers' Union "Bund" of Poland, *The Case of Henryk Erlich and Victor Alter*, London, 1943.

George, H. R., *Eight Soviet Generals Plotted Against Peace*, Friends of the Soviet Union, London (circa 1937).

German Propaganda Ministry, *Amtliches Material zum Massenmord von KATYN*, Gedruckt im Deutschen Verlag, Berlin, 1943.

Gitlow, Benjamin, *I Confess: The Truth About American Communism*, E. P. Dutton & Company, New York, 1940.

Glazer, Nathan, *A New Look at the Rosenberg-Sobell Case*, The New Leader, New York, 1956.

Godson, Roy (editor), *Intelligence Requirements for the 1980s: Counterintelligence*, Transaction Books, New Brunswick, 1980.

Goldberg, B. Z., *The Jewish Problem in the Soviet Union*, Crown Publishers, New York, 1961.

Goldman, Albert, *The Assassination of Leon Trotsky: The Proofs of Stalin's Guilt*, Pioneer Publishers, New York, 1940.

Government of Poland, *Polish-Soviet Relations, 1918–1943*, Official Documents, Polish Embassy, Washington, D.C., 1943.

Gusev, S., et al., *The Next Step in Britain, America, and Ireland: Speeches at the 12th Plenum of the Executive Committee of the Communist International*, Workers Library Publishers, New York (circa 1932).

Hallgren, Mauritz A., *Why I Resigned from the Trotsky Defense Committee*, International Publishers, New York, 1937.

Harrison, Earl G., *Americans of Foreign Birth in the War Program for Victory*, American Committee for Protection of Foreign-Born, New York, 1942.

Hatch, David A., and Robert Louis Benson, *The Korean War: The Sigint Background*, National Security Agency, Maryland, 2000.

Hitler, Adolf, *Speech Delivered in the Reichstag, January 30, 1939*, M. Müller & Sohn K.G., Berlin, 1939.

Hook, Sidney, *Out of Step: An Unquiet Life in the 20th Century*, Harper & Row, New York, 1987.

Hull, Cordell, *The Memoirs of Cordell Hull*, MacMillan Company, New York, 1948.

Hungarian Government, *Tito-Fascist Kidnappers before the Court*, State Publishing House, Budapest, 1952.

Hutchins, Grace, *Labor and Silk*, International Publishers, New York, 1929.

Bibliography

International Workers Order, *Five Years of International Workers Order, 1930–1935*, New York, 1935.

International Workers Order, *Proceedings, 6th National Convention IWO, July 2–7, 1944, New York City*, New York, 1944.

International Workers Order, *We Support the Communist Candidate in This Year's Election, Every Member of the International Workers Order Must Rally Behind the Communist Election Platform*, New York, 1932.

Jaffe, Philip J., *The Rise and Fall of American Communism*, Horizon Press, New York, 1975.

Japanese Imperialism Exposed: The Secret Tanaka Document, International Publishers, New York, 1942.

Jeffery, Inez Cope, *Inside Russia: The Life and Times of Zoya Zarubina, Former Soviet Intelligence Officer and Interpreter During the Stalin Years*, Eakin Press, Austin, Texas, 1999.

Jones, R. V., *The Wizard War: British Scientific Intelligence 1939–1945*, Coward, McCann & Geoghegan, Inc., New York, 1978.

Jordan, George Racey, *From Major Jordan's Diaries*, Harcourt, Brace and Company, New York, 1952.

Kahn, Albert E. (introduction), *The Diary of General Grow as Exposed by Major Richard Squires*, Hour Publishers, New York, 1952.

Kalugin, Oleg, *The First Directorate*, St. Martin's Press, New York, 1994.

Kampelman, Max M., *The Communist Party vs. The CIO*, Frederick A. Praeger, New York, 1957.

Katz, M., *The Assassination of Kirov*, Workers Library Publishers, New York, February 1935.

Kaufmann, Bernard, Eckhard Reisener, Dieter Schwips, and Henri Walther,

Der Nachrichtendienst der KPD, 1919–1937 [The Intelligence Service of the Communist Party of Germany, 1919–1937], Dietz Verlag, Berlin, 1993.

King, Francis, and George Matthews (editors), *About Turn: The British Communist Party and the Second World War—The Verbatim Record of the Central Committee Meetings of 25 September and 2–3 October 1939*, Lawrence & Wishart, London, 1990.

Klehr, Harvey, and John Earl Haynes, *The Secret World of American Communism*, Yale University Press, New Haven, 1995.

Krivitsky, W. G., *In Stalin's Secret Service*, Harper & Brothers, New York, 1939.

Kutzik, Alfred J., *The Communist Party & The Jews*, Red Balloon Collective, Brooklyn, New York, 1994.

Lamont, Corliss (editor), *The Trial of Elizabeth Gurly Flynn by the American Civil Liberties Union, including The Transcript of the Extraordinary Meeting of the Board of Directors of the American Civil Liberties Union (May 7, 1940)*, Horizon Press, New York, 1968.

Lamphere, Robert J., *The FBI-KGB War: A Special Agent's Story*, Random House, New York, 1986.

Lane, Arthur Bliss, *I Saw Poland Betrayed: An Americn Ambassador Reports to the American People*, Bobbs-Merrill Company, New York, 1948.

Lash, Joseph P., and James A. Wechsler, *War—Our Heritage*, International Publishers, New York, 1936.

Lash, Joseph P., *Eleanor Roosevelt: A Friend's Memoir*, Doubleday & Company, Garden City, New York, 1964.

569

Bibliography

Laski, Harold J., *The Secret Battalion: An Examination of the Communist Attitude to the Labour Party*, Labour Publications Department, London, 1946.

Lazitch, Branko, and Milorad M. Drachkovitch, *Biographical Dictionary of the Comintern*, Hoover Institution Press, Stanford, 1986.

League of Professional Groups for Foster and Ford, *Culture and the Crisis: An Open Letter to the Writers, Artists, Teachers, Physicians, Engineers, Scientists, and Other Professional Workers of America*, New York, 1932.

Lyons, Eugene, *The Red Decade: The Stalinist Penetration of America*, Bobbs-Merrill Company, Indianapolis, 1941.

MacEachin, Douglas J., *The Final Months of the War with Japan: Signals Intelligence, U.S. Invasion Planning and the A-Bomb Decision*, Center for the Study of Intelligence, Washington, D.C., 1999.

Mader, Julius, *Dr. Sorge—Report*, Militarverlag der DDR, Berlin, 1985.

Masters, Anthony, *The Man Who Was M: The Life of Maxwell Knight*, Basil Blackwell, Oxford, England, 1984.

McJimsey, George, *Harry Hopkins: Ally of the Poor, Defender of Democracy*, Harvard University Press, Cambridge, 1987.

The Menshevik Trial: The Text of the Indictment of the Counter-Revolutionary Menshevik Organisation, The Trial of the All-Union Bureau of the Central Committee of the Counter-Revolutionary Menshevik Party, Workers Library Publishers, New York, 1931.

Mexican Confederation of Labour, *Labor Condemns Trotskyism: Resolution Unanimously Adopted by First National Congress of the Mexican Confederation of Labour*, International Publishers, New York, 1938.

Milgrom, Sam, *7th Convention Report*, International Workers Order, New York, 1947.

Molotov, V. M., *Molotov's Report to the Supreme Soviet*, Workers Library Publishers, New York, 1939.

Morgan, Ted, *A Covert Life: Jay Lovestone—Communist, Anti-Communist, and Spy Master*, Random House, New York, 1999.

Morros, Boris, *My Ten Years as a Counterspy*, Viking Press, New York, 1959.

National Council of American Soviet Friendship, *Open Letter to the American People on American-Soviet Friendship*, New York, 1943.

Nelson, Steve, et al., *Steve Nelson: American Radical*, University of Pittsburgh Press, Pittsburgh, 1981.

New York State Joint Legislative Committee to Investigate the Administration and Enforcement of the Law (McNaboe Committee), J. B. Lyon Company, Printer, Albany, New York, 1939.

New York State Supreme Court, *New York International Workers Order*, transcript, Case on Appeal, New York State Supreme Court, Appellate Division—First Department, Index no. 21205-1950.

O'Connor, Tom, *The Truth About Anti-Semitism in the Soviet Union*, American Committee of Jewish Writers, Artists, and Scientists, New York (circa 1949).

Bibliography

Parry, Albert, *Russian Cavalcade: A Military Record*, Ives Washburn, Inc., New York, 1944.

Pavlov, Vitaliy, *Operatziya "Sneg" (Operation "Snow")*, Geya, Moscow, 1996.

Pepper, John, *"Underground Radicalism": An Open Letter to Eugene V. Debs and to All Honest Workers within the Socialist Party*, Workers Party of America, New York City (1923).

Perlo, Victor, *The Big Tax Swindle and How to Stop It*, New Outlook Publishers, New York, May 1969.

Peters, J., *The Communist Party: A Manual on Organization*, Workers Library Publishers, New York, July 1935.

Philby, Kim, *My Silent War*, Grove Press, Inc., New York, 1968.

Pickersgill, J. W. and D. F. Forster (editors), *The Mackenzie King Record*, University of Toronto Press, Toronto.

Pritt, D. N. (preface), *The Moscow Trial (1936)*, Anglo-Russian Parliamentary Committee, London, 1936.

Pritt, D. N., *At the Moscow Trial*, International Publishers, New York, 1937.

Pritt, D. N. (introduction), *Reports on Investigation in Korea and China March–April 1952*, International Association of Democratic Lawyers, Brussels, 1952.

Pritt, D. N., *The Rosenberg Case*, National Committee to Secure Justice in the Rosenberg Case, New York (circa 1953).

Rabinowitz, Victor, *Unrepentant Leftist: A Lawyer's Memoir*, University of Illinois Press, Urbana, 1996.

Redlich, Shimon, *Propaganda and Nationalism in Wartime Russia: The Jewish Antifascist Committee in the USSR, 1941–1948*, East European Quarterly, 1982.

Romerstein, Herbert, and Stanislav Levchenko, *The KGB Against the Main Enemy: How the Soviet Intelligence Service Operates Against the United States*, Lexington Books, Lexington, Massachusetts, 1989.

Romerstein, Herbert, *Heroic Victims*, The Council for the Defense of Freedom, Washington, D.C., 1994.

Rosenberg, Ethel and Julius, *The Testament of Ethel and Julius Rosenberg*, Cameron & Kahn, New York, 1954.

Ross, M., *A History of Soviet Foreign Policy*, Workers Library Publishers, New York, 1940.

Rumanian Government, *Trial of the Group of Spies and Traitors in the Service of the Espionage of Tito's Fascist Clique*, Bucharest, 1950.

Salazar, Sanchez, and Julian Gorkin, *Murder in Mexico: The Assassination of Leon Trotsky*, Secker & Warburg, London, 1950.

Sayers, Michael, and Albert E. Kahn, *The Great Conspiracy: The Secret War Against Soviet Russia*, Little Brown and Company, Boston, 1946.

Schneir, Walter and Miriam, *Invitation to an Inquest*, Doubleday & Company, Garden City, New York, 1965.

Sedov, L., *Livre Rouge sur le Procés de Moscou [Red Book on the Moscow Trial]*, Éditions Populaires, Paris, 1936.

Shachtman, Max, *Behind the Moscow Trial: The Greatest Frame-up in History*, Pioneer Publishers, New York, 1936.

Sharkei, L. L., *An Outline History of the Australian Communist Party*, Australian Communist Party, Sydney, Australia, December 1944.

Bibliography

Sherwood, Robert E., *Roosevelt and Hopkins: An Intimate History*, Harper & Brothers, New York, 1948.

Smith, Harold, *Attack for Victory*, Veterans of the Abraham Lincoln Brigade, New York, 1942.

Squires, Richard, *Auf Dem Kreigspfad [On the War Path]*, Rutten & Loening, Berlin, 1951.

Stalin, J., *Defects in Party Work and Measures for Liquidating Trotskyite and Other Double-Dealers: Report and Speech in Reply to Debate at the Plenum of the Central Committee on the C.P.S.U., March 3–5, 1937*, Operative Publishing Society of Foreign Workers in the USSR, Moscow, 1937.

Stalin, Joseph, *Stalin's Speeches on the American Communist Party*, Central Committee Communist Party USA, New York (circa 1930).

Stalin, J. V., *Works*, Foreign Languages Publishing House, Moscow, 1953.

Stone, I. F., *The Hidden History of the Korean War*, Monthly Review Press, New York, 1952.

Stone, I. F., *The Truman Era*, Vintage Books, New York, 1973.

Sudoplatov, Pavel, et al., *Special Tasks*, Little Brown & Company, Boston, 1994.

Tanenhaus, Sam, *Whittaker Chamber: A Biography*, Random House, New York, 1997.

Trotsky, Leon, *In Defense of the Soviet Union: A Compilation, 1927–1937*, Pioneer Publishers, New York, 1937.

Trotsky, Leon, *Leon Sedoff:—Son—Friend—Fighter*, Young People's Socialist League (Fourth Internationalists), New York, March 1938.

Trotsky, Leon, *Writings of Leon Trotsky*, Pathfinder Press, New York, various dates.

Troy, Thomas F., *Donovan and the CIA: A History of the Establishment of the Central Intelligence Agency*, Central Intelligence Agency Center for the Study of Intelligence, 1981.

Truman, Harry S., *Year of Decisions*, Doubleday & Company, Garden City, New York, 1955.

Ulanovsky, Nadezhda and Maya, *Istoriya Odnoi Cemi [The History of One Family]*, Chalidze Publications, New York, 1982.

United Farmers League, *What Is the United Farmers League, Program and By-Laws?*, United Farmers League, Chicago, Illinois, 1934.

United States Atomic Energy Commission, *In the Matter of J. Robert Oppenheimer: Transcript of Hearings Before Personnel Security Board, Washington, D.C., April 12, 1954–May 6, 1954*, Government Printing Office, Washington, D.C., 1954.

United States Department of State, *Foreign Relations of the United States, Diplomatic Papers, the Soviet Union, 1933–1939*, Government Printing Office, Washington, D.C., 1952.

United States Department of State, *Nazi-Soviet Relations, 1939–1941, Documents from the Archives of the German Foreign Office*, Washington, D.C., 1948.

United States House of Representatives Committee on Un-American Activities, Government Printing Office, Washington, D.C., 1945–1968.

United States House of Representatives Special Committee on Un-American Activities (Dies Committee), Government Printing Office, Washington, D.C., 1938–1944.

Bibliography

United States House of Representatives, Select Committee to Investigate the Federal Communications Commission, Government Printing Office, Washington, D.C., 1943.

United States Joint Committee on Atomic Energy, *Soviet Atomic Espionage*, Government Printing Office, Washington, D.C., 1951.

United States Joint Committee on the Investigation of the Pearl Harbor Attack, Government Printing Office, Washington, D.C., 1946.

United States Library of Congress, *Revelations from the Russian Archives, Documents in English Translation*, Washington, D.C., 1997.

United States Senate Committee on Armed Services, *Imprisonment and Escape of Lt. (JG) Dieter Dengler, USNR*, Government Printing Office, Washington, D.C., 1966.

United States Senate Committee on Government Operations, *Commission on Government Security*, Government Printing Office, Washington, D.C., 1955.

United States Senate Committee on Labor and Public Welfare, *Communist Domination of Certain Unions*, Government Printing Office, Washington, D.C., 1951.

United States Senate Committee on Post Office and Civil Service, *Administration of the Federal Employees' Security Program*, Government Printing Office, Washington, D.C., 1956.

United States Senate Foreign Relations Committee, *Executive Sessions of the Senate Foreign Relations Committee (Historical Series)*, Government Printing Office, Washington, D.C., various dates.

United States Senate Internal Security Subcommittee, Government Printing Office, Washington, D.C., 1951–1978.

United States Senate Permanent Subcommittee on Investigations of the Committee on Government Operations, *Army Signal Corps—Subversion and Espionage*, Government Printing Office, Washington, D.C., 1953 and 1954.

United States Senate Special Committee Investigating the Munitions Industry, Government Printing Office, Washington, D.C., 1936.

United States Senate Special Subcommittee to Investigate Immigration and Naturalization, 1949.

USSR KGB, *Istoriya Sovetskikh Organov Gosudarstevvoiy Bezoposnosti* [*History of Soviet State Security Organs*], F. E. Dzerzhinskiy Red Banner Higher School of the Committee of State Security, Moscow, 1977 (marked Top Secret).

USSR People's Commissariat of Justice, *The Case of the Trotskyite-Zinovievite Terrorist Center, Report of Court Proceedings, August 19–24, 1936*, Moscow, 1936.

Vaksberg, Arkady, *Stalin Against the Jews*, Alfred A. Knopf, New York, 1994.

Van Heijenoort, Jean, *With Trotsky in Exile: From Prinkipo to Coyoacan*, Harvard University Press, Cambridge, 1978.

Vidali, Vittorio, *Diary of the Twentieth Congress of the Communist Party of the Soviet Union*, Lawrence Hill & Company, Westport, Connecticut, 1974.

W. I. Lenin und die Gesamtrussische Tscheka, Dokumentensammlung (1917–1922), Ministerium für

Bibliography

Staatssicherheit, Juristische Hochschule, Potsdam, 1977.

Wachman, J. M., *Why the Jewish Masses Must Rally to the Defense of the Soviet Union*, ICOR, New York, 1932.

Werner, Ruth, *Sonjas Rapport*, Verlag Neues Leben, Berlin, 1977.

West, Nigel (editor), *British Security Coordination: The Secret History of British Intelligence in the Americas, 1940–1945*, St. Ermine's Press, London, 1998.

West, Nigel, *Venona*, HarperCollins, London, 1999.

Wolff, Milton, *Western Front Now!*, Veterans of the Abraham Lincoln Brigade, New York, 1941.

Wolton, Thierry, *Le Grand Recrutement*, Bernard Grasset, Paris, 1993.

Workers (Communist) Party of America, *The 4th National Convention, Workers Communist Party of America, Held in Chicago, Illinois, August 21–30, 1925*, Daily Worker Publishing Co., Chicago, 1925.

Workers Party of America, *Program and Constitution, Workers Party of America, Adopted at National Convention, New York City December 24, 25, 26, 1921*, Lyceum and Literature Department Workers Party, New York City (circa 1921).

Workers Party of America, *The White Terrorists Ask for Mercy*, Daily Worker Publishing Co., Chicago, February 1925.

Yaroslavsky, E., *Religion in the USSR*, International Publishers, New York, 1934.

Zawodny, J. P., *Death in the Forest: The Story of the Katyn Forest Massacre*, University of Notre Dame Press, Notre Dame, Indiana, 1952.

Zborowski, Mark, and Elizabeth Herzog, *Life Is with People*, International Universities Press, New York, 1952.

Zborowski, Mark, *People in Pain*, Jossey-Bass, San Francisco, 1969.

Zubok, Vladislav, and Constantine Pleshakov, *Inside the Kremlin's Cold War: From Stalin to Khrushchev*, Harvard University Press, Cambridge, Massachusetts, 1996.

ACKNOWLEDGMENTS

MANY PEOPLE HELPED to put this book together. They include those who provided good advice as well as those who provided documents.

We thank: Sam Tanenhaus, Allan Cullison, James Ryan, Harvey Klehr, John Haynes, and others who shared documents from the Comintern archives in Moscow; Olga Novikova, who assisted us in the Moscow archives and translated many of the documents; Francoise Thom, who provided KGB documents; Oleg Tsarev and Yuri Kobaladze of the Russian Foreign Intelligence Service, who provided documents from the KGB archives; Karel Skrabek and Karel Pacner, who helped in the Czech archives and also provided documents that they found; Andreas Weisse, who helped us in the German Communist Party archives in Berlin; and the most helpful archivists we have ever met, Volker Lange, Annemarie Müller, and Carola Aehlich of the German federal archives, which now contain the German Communist Party archives.

We also thank those who translated foreign language documents for us. We received invaluable help from Dick Markel, who not only translated from German but also provided valuable insights into German history; Mahir Ibrahimov and Jeff Moore, who translated from Russian; George Sever, who translated from Czech; and Henry Plater-Zybeck, who translated from Polish.

We received advice and help from Ruth Matthews, Stan Evans, Allan Ryskind, John Barron, Ralph Bennett, Peter Marwitz, Michael

Acknowledgments

Chapman, Larry Cott, Eric Fettman, Jack Dziak, and Jim Srodes, and the leading NSA experts on *Venona*, Cecil Phillips and Lou Benson.

We thank the Olin Foundation and the Earhart Foundation for their generous support, and our agent, Mort Janklow, who was of great help. Our excellent and knowledgeable editors, Trish Bozell and Jed Donahue, and our publisher, Al Regnery, were indispensable. But most of all we thank Pat Romerstein, who helped in the archives, typed the manuscript, and kept Herb organized.

INDEX

Index

Index

Index

Index

Bittleman, Alexander, 97, 101
Bjoze, Jack, 289
Black, Thomas, 231–32
"Blin." *See* Stone, I. F.
Bloch, Emanuel, 253; Rosenberg defense and, 247–48
Bloomfield, Sidney, 331
Blum, Leon, 315
Board of Economic Warfare, 152
"Boets." *See* Kahn, Albert
Bohlen, Charles, 218
Bohr, Niels, 275
Bolshakov, 176
Bolshevik Revolution, 38
Bolsheviks, 177, 313, 316, 391–92
Booker, Lucy Jane, 90, 362
"Boris." *See* Saprykin, Aleksandr
Borodin, Mikhail, 330
Boudin, Leonard, 383, 384–85
Boyer, Raymond, 197
Bradley, Omar, 441
Branigan, William, 255, 257
Brantsen, Louise, 257, 263, 266
Brantsen, Richard, 266
"Braun." *See* Horngacher, Max
Breindel, Eric, vii–ix, 436
"Breme." *See* Babin, Toma
Britain: Comintern work in, 144; Communist Party in, 23–25, 86; as enemy, 38; Gouzenko's defection and, 12; intelligence activities in, 14, 23, 86, 225; intelligence of, 301–2; Nazi-Soviet alliance and, 20; Soviet agents in, 14
British Campaign for Nuclear Disarmament, 205
British Labour Party, 457–58
British Military Finance Department, 24
British Security Coordination (BSC), 301–2
British Uranium Committee, 192
Bronstein, Lev Davidovich. *See* Trotsky, Leon
Brooklyn Eagle, 363
"Brooks," 134

"Brother." *See* Toohey, Pat
Browder, Earl, 8, 71, *513*; American Communist Party and, 72–74, 97–99, 102, 188–89, 433, 463; Bedacht and, 104; burglary of Lovestone's files and, 111; Catholics and, 412–13; Congressional testimony of, 78–80; Dies Committee and, 20, 58, 80–82; expulsion of, 187; Hall's contact with, 200–201; murders of Erlich and Alter and, 401–2; names used by, 57, 76, 145; NKVD and, 84; Perlo ring and, 160, 162–63; power of, 166; recruitment of Party members by, x, 57; release of, 177; Roosevelt and, 178–80; Silvermaster ring and, 150, 165
Browder, Margaret: death of, 91; FBI testimony of, 89–91; names used by, 81; underground activities of, 80–83, 84–85, 88–89
Browder, Raisa, 84; deportation of, 77–78, 177–78; immigration visa of, 79; intelligence activities of, 77–79; names used by, 77
Browder, Rose, 89, 379
Browder, William, 88, 89, 188, 380, 383
Brown, Andrew, 435
Brown, F. *See* Alpi, Mario
Bruce, David K. E., 283
BSC. *See* British Security Coordination
Budenz, Louis, 342–44, 360–61, 413, 424
Bukharin, 62
Bukovsky, Vladimir, 438
"Bund." *See* Jewish Workers' Union
Burd, Michael W., 180
Burgess, Guy, 14, 26
Burnham, James, 337
Bursler, Norman, 184, 301
Burstein, Isidor. *See* Peters, J.
Burtan, William, 70
"Butcher," 259
Butkevich, 37
Bykov, Boris, 31, 32, 116–18
Byrnes, James F., 51–55, 126

Index

Cachin, Marcel, 305
Cahan, Abraham, 402
Cahiers du Communisme, 188
Caldwell, Sylvia. *See* Franklin, Sylvia
California: atom bomb development in,
    255; Communist leaders in, 151;
    Communist Party in, 145, 255
California State Emergency Relief
    Administration (SERA), 152
Callahan, Jerome Michael, 264
Camp Ritchie, 370
Camp X, 284, 287
Canada: atomic espionage in, 193–99;
    Comintern work in, 144; Communist
    Party in, 13, 194; Gouzenko's defec-
    tion and, 12; Soviet espionage in,
    12–13
Canadian Department of National
    Defense, 418
Canadian Information Services, 196
Canadian Royal Commission, 12
Cannon, James, 97, 100, 120, 360, 362
Cantor, Eddie, 409–10
Cantwell, Robert, 124
Can You Hear Their Voices? (Chambers),
    104
Carnegie Endowment for International
    Peace, 125, 126
Carr, Sam: atomic espionage and,
    194–95; as Canadian agent, 13; con-
    viction of, 195; intelligence work of,
    195–96; Lesovian parliament and,
    476; names used by, 195, 196
Carter, Jimmy, 139, 383
Castro, Fidel, 348
"Catherine." *See* Lowry, Helen
Catholic Church, 411–15
"Cavalryman." *See* Kournakoff, Sergei
Celler, Emanuel, 136
Central Intelligence Agency (CIA), viii,
    26, 250–51, 379
Cerf, Bennett, 378
Chambers, Esther, 102, 103
Chambers, Whittaker, *514*; Apparatus A
    and, 114–15; Bedacht and, 416;

break with Communism of, 121–23;
    as Communist, 95–97; defection of,
    32, 44, 102–3, 143; exchange of doc-
    uments and, 116–18; fear for life of,
    123–24; Hiss and, 95, 141; House
    Committee on Un-American
    Activities and, 53, 126–30; identifica-
    tion of spies by, 127–28, 167; literary
    career of, 102, 104, 125; *Meet the
    Press* and, 129–30; Niles and, 181;
    recruiting of, 433–34; reinstatement
    to Communist Party of, 104–5; reve-
    lations of, 124–25; Robinson/Rubens
    case and, 118–21; Silvermaster ring
    and, 44; as source of information, 95;
    Soviet espionage and, 64; Soviet
    Union as "focus of evil" and, xi;
    underground activities of, 64, 105–7,
    113; White and, 31–32
Chanin, Nathan, 402
Chapa, Esther, 349, 350
Chapin, John, 223
Chapman, Abraham, 409
"Charles." *See* Fuchs, Klaus
Cheka. *See* Council of People's
    Commissars to Fight Against
    Counterrevolution and Sabotage
Chemator, Inc., 210, 211
"Chen." *See* Franklin, Irving
Cheptsov, General, 407–8
Chester, Bernie, 188, 222, 239, 343;
    Franklin and, 362–63; Hall and Sax
    and, 202–3; Jack Childs and, 223–24;
    names used by, 223; OSS structure
    and, 299–300; Rosenberg and, 233;
    Scherer and, 260; Stone's recruit-
    ment and, 432; Zborowski and, 370
Chevalier, Haakon, 268–70
Chicago Post, 285
Chicago Tribune, 376
Chikov, Vladimir, 208–9
Childs, Eva, 224, 460
Childs, Jack, 222, 223–24, 459–60
Childs, Morris, 196, 222, 224, 274,
    459–60

582

Index

Index

Index

Index

Index

Index

Glazer, David, 86, 253
Goddard, Henry W., 130
Gold, Bela, 157–58, 184
Gold, Harry: arrest of, 231; atomic espionage and, 477; confession of, 231, 233; Fuchs and, 226–28; Greenglass and, 236; industrial espionage and, 231–32; names used by, 226, 228; as NKVD agent, 226; Red Star medal of, 158, 232; *Venona* identification of, 26
Gold, Sonia: names used by, 167; Silvermaster ring and, 157–58, 167, 185
Gold, William. *See* Gold, Bela
Goldberg, B. Z., 405–7
Goldberger, Sandor. *See* Peters, J.
Goldman, Albert, 365
Gold Star, 210
Gollanz, 322
Golos, Jacob, 333, *509*; agent network of, 146–47; American Communist Party and, 146; Bentley and, 9, 88, 148–50; career of, 146; Communist penetration of OSS and, 298–99; cover business of, 146; Dies Committee and, 148; FBI arrest of, 147; funeral of, 103; importance of work of, 147–48; Klarin and, 150; names used by, 146, 147; NKVD work of, 146; Perlo ring and, 158–60, 164; Peters and, 464; reactivation of, 145; Silvermaster ring and, 150, 162
Golovin, Igor, 280–81
Gomez, Elena Vazquez, 410, 411
Gomez, Rosendo, 349
Gompertz, Hedda. *See* Massing, Hede
Gordievsky, Oleg, 212, 213
Gorkin, Julian, 337, 347, 349, 350
Gottwald, Klement, 286
Gouzenko, Igor: atomic espionage and, 193–94; Carr and, 196; defection of, 12–18, 198; knowledge of Soviet intelligence operations and, 13–14; Soviet response to defection of, 14–16; White's espionage and, 51

GPU. *See* Council of People's Commissars to Fight Against Counterrevolution and Sabotage
Granich, Grace. *See* Maul, Grace
Gray, Gordon, 268
Gray, Olga, 86–87
The Great Conspiracy (Kahn and Sayers), 420
Great Depression, 91
Great Terror, 33
Green, William, 400
Greenglass, David: arrest of, 208; atomic espionage and, 235–36; Gold and, 232, 236; names used by, 235; Rosenbergs and, 232–33, 235, 252–53; sentence of, 248; *Venona* identification of, 26; YCL and, 232
Greenglass, Ruth, 233–35, 273
"Greg." *See* Silvermaster, Nathan Gregory
Grigulevich, Joseph, 338
Gromyko, Andrei, 213, 219
"Group X," 23–25
Groves, Leslie, 211
Grow, Robert, 422–23
GRU. *See* Soviet military intelligence
Grutzner, Charles, 363
Guardian, 205
Gubitchev, Valentine, 300–301
"Guidelines for Intelligence Leaders," 65–66
"Guron," 273
"Gus." *See* Gold, Harry
Gusev, S., 415–16
Gutzeit, Pavel, 34, 146

Hagen, Paul, 169–71, 172
Haldane, J. B. S., 23–25
Hall, Theodore: atomic espionage and, 192, 200, 202–5, 273; description of, 202; FBI interview of, 204; Kournakoff and, 202; names used by, 192; recruitment of, 493; *Venona* identification of, 26

Index

Index

Index

Index

Index

Index

Index

Index

Index

Index

Index

Index

Index

Index

Solow, Herbert, 121, 123–24
Somary, Felix, 301
Somervell, Brehan, 226
"Son." *See* Baker, Rudy
"Sonia." *See* Kuczynski, Ruth
Sons of the American Revolution, 176
Sorge, Richard, 44; as Soviet spy in
    Japan, 36–37
Southern Conference for Human
    Welfare, 440
South Korea, viii, 253
Soviet Communist Party, 64; Central
    Committee of, 61; Cheka and, 310;
    intelligence gathering of, 67–68
Soviet Counter-Intelligence Service, 255
Soviet-Finnish War, 93
Soviet foreign intelligence service: activi-
    ties of, viii; agents of, 509–11,
    513–15; *Amerasia* espionage opera-
    tions and, 168–69; American
    Communist Party and, 11–12, 95,
    109–10, 238; American journalists
    and, 429–45; atomic espionage and,
    192–93, 220, 280–81; attitude toward
    Jews of, 110; Bentley and, 189;
    British Communists and, 23–25;
    Browder and, 84; in Canada, 12–13;
    disinformation and, viii, 108–9,
    419–23; former Communist Party
    members and, 103; Gouzenko's
    defection and, 13–14; handling of
    Polish prisoners by, 4–7; internal
    repression and, 4, 16–17, 33; in
    Japan, 35–37; Jewish organizations
    and, x; Jews and, 309; Justice
    Department and, 300–301; local
    Communists' role in, 12–13, 15–16;
    Moscow headquarters of, 7; OSS
    and, 291–92, 299–300, 303, 307;
    Pavlov and, 33–35; Perlo ring and,
    160; planning for, 59; postwar rivals
    and, 387; purges and, 33; radio com-
    munications and, 86–88, 144;
    recruiting of American Communists
    for, x, xii, 11–12, 91–93; security

problems in, 9–10; Silvermaster and,
    157; Silvermaster ring and, 44,
    161–62; Stalin's purges and, 143; sta-
    tions of, 3–4; Stone's relationship
    with, 434–36; trade union movement
    and, 70; Trotsky's revelations about,
    17–18; Trotskyites and, 309, 315,
    356–57, 388. *See also* atomic espi-
    onage; Soviet military intelligence
Soviet Gold Star, 210
Soviet military intelligence: atomic espi-
    onage and, 194, 220; British
    Communists and, 24; intelligence
    collection of, 3; Mins in, 297–98;
    Stalin's purges and, 143; training
    school of, 84–85; U.S. operations of,
    3; usefulness of, 66–67. *See also*
    Soviet foreign intelligence service
Soviet Purchasing Commission, 365
Soviet Russia Today, 393, 403
Soviet Union: American Communist loy-
    alty to, 37–38; American loyalty to,
    xvi, 11, 20–22; anti-Semitism in, 231,
    387–89; archives of, viii–ix; atom
    bomb development of, x–xi, 253;
    atomic espionage and, 13; in Cold
    War, xi; demise of, xiii; discrediting
    of, xi; espionage advantage of, xvi; as
    "focus of evil," xi–xii; German inva-
    sion of, 19, 22–23; Japan and, 35;
    loyalty to, 55–56; mass immigration
    and, 393–94; military might of, xiv;
    nationalist movements and, 311–15;
    nature of, xi; Nazi Germany and,
    231; non-Communist resistance
    movements and, 303–7; struggle
    between United States and, xvi;
    Venona and, 27
Spain, 298
Spanish Civil War, 270, 364
SPD. *See* Social Democratic Party
Special Committee on Un-American
    Activates. *See* Dies Committee
Special House of Representatives
    Committee on Military Affairs, 289

Index

Index

Tenney, Helen, 298–99, 301, 492
"Tenor." *See* Burd, Michael W.
Thailand, 42
Third American Writers Congress, 327
Thomas, Norman, 328
Through Embassy Eyes (Dodd), 378
Tiempo, 349
Tilton, Alfred, 120
Time magazine, xi
Tito, Marshal, 436, 453
Tkach, Michael, 418
Today, 406
Todd, Lawrence, 431
"Tom." *See* Eitingon, Leonid
Toohey, Pat, 75, 92; burglary of
    Lovestone's files and, 110–11; clan-
    destine radio communications and,
    144–45; Comintern orders and, 287;
    Gitlow's testimony and, 21; names
    used by, 144
Toronto Star, 406
To Secure Justice, 249
Toward Soviet America (Foster), 75
Trade Union Education League, 70
trade union movement: American
    Communist Party and, 39, 70–72;
    atomic espionage and, 260–64; Buro
    and, 71; Soviet foreign intelligence
    service and, 70
Trade Union Unity League (TUUL), 70
Transport Workers Union, 414
Treasury Department, 8, 152, 167
Trilling, Lionel, 332
Trillisser, Moishe, 196
Trotsky, Leon, 13; American Communist
    Party's aboveground presence and,
    62; assassination attempt on, 17,
    337–42; assassination of, 341–45;
    Communist campaign against,
    319–29; deportation to Mexico of,
    325, 330; Dies Committee and,
    335–37; Kirov murder and, 316–18;
    murderer of, 57; Socialists and, 328;
    Soviet espionage revelations of,
    17–18; Stalin and, 17, 316, 325–26,

328, 337; Stalinists and, 334; trial of,
    319–25, 332–33; Zborowski and, 373
Trotsky, Seva, 339
Trotskyites: Franklin and, 363; Gestapo
    and, 320; Justice Department and,
    363; NKVD and, 309, 342–54, 388;
    recruiting for, 360; Smith Act and,
    363; Soble/Soblen spy ring and,
    359–61, 364; Socialist Party and,
    361; Soviet persecution of, 315–19;
    Stalin and, 315, 452; Stalinist dis-
    crediting of, 323; Swiss Communist
    Party and, 318–19; as threat to
    Soviet Union, 388; YPSL and, 361;
    Zborowski and, 368–70
Truman, Harry, 30, 249; atomic bomb
    development and, 191–92; atomic
    espionage and, 192; Communist
    movement and, 451–52; espionage
    role of local Communists and, 17;
    investigation of Hiss and, 455;
    Stone's writing about, 437; UN
    founding conference and, 50; White
    and, xv, 50, 51–53
Trumanism, 452, 453
Tukhachevsky, Mikhail, 393
"Tulip." *See* Zborowski, Mark
"Tur," 154
TUUL. *See* Trade Union Unity League

"U." *See* Bentley, Elizabeth
U.S. Army, 3
U.S. Army Signal Corps, 238, 240
Udet, Ernst, 376, 378
Ukrainian Daily News, 418
Ukrainian independence movement,
    311–12
Ulanovsky, Alexander: false passports of,
    113, 123; names used by, 106, 107,
    123; underground activities of, 106–7
Ullman, William Ludwig: names used by,
    49; Operation Anvil and, 485;
    Silvermaster ring and, 152–55, 157,
    185; UN founding conference and,

604

Index

49; White's financial problems and, 50; White's information and, 45
"Ulrich." *See* Ulanovsky, Alexander
Ultra, vii
"Umnitsa." *See* Bentley, Elizabeth
UN. *See* United Nations
Un-American Activities Committee. *See* House Committee on Un-American Activities
"Uncle." *See* Folkoff, Isaac
Unitarian Service Committee, 134
United Electrical Workers, 261
The United Farmer, 114
United Farmers League, 114
United Federal Workers of America, 131
United Front, 91
United Jewish Appeal, 397
United Nations (UN), 48–50, 95, 324
United Nations Relief and Rehabilitation Administration, 357
United Nations World, 47
United Office and Professional Workers (UOPWA), 261
United Palestine Appeal, 396
United Press International, 139
United Public Workers. *See* United Federal Workers of America
United States: agriculture in, 114–15; air strength of, 466, 469; anti-Semitism in, 249–52; atomic bomb program in, 193; British intelligence in, 302; Communist movement in, 39; economic policies of, 29; Gouzenko's defection and, 12; intelligence gathering and, xiv; invasion of Japan and, 191–92; Japanese relations with, 41–44; manipulation of policy of, 40; Nazi-Soviet alliance and, 20; policy of, 35; postwar military and, 155; rearming of, 38; "Soviet colony" in, 7; Soviet intelligence and, ix, 3–4, 12–13, 35–37; struggle between Soviet Union and, xvi; World War II and, 44, 125. *See also* United States government

United States government: American Communist Party and, 61; Communist penetration of, 11, 52–53, 92–93; domestic security and, xiii; prewar spy ring in, 30; view of American Communists of, ix–x
United States Information Agency, viii
United States Public Health Service, 375
University of California at Berkeley, 255
University of Montreal, 197
UOPWA. *See* United Office and Professional Workers
USSR. *See* Soviet Union
Utah, 264

Vaksberg, Arkady, 408
VALB. *See* Veterans of the Abraham Lincoln Brigade
Vandenberg, Arthur H., 50
Vandervelde, Emil, 315
van Heijenoort, Jean, 364, 368, 369
"Vardo." *See* Zarubin, Elizabeth
Vassiliev, B., 91
Vaughan, Harry, 51
"Veksel." *See* Oppenheimer, J. Robert
Veksler, Sara. *See* Judey, Sara
Venona: Akhmerov in, 34–35; *Amerasia* espionage operations and, 168–69; Apresyan and Akhmerov and, 7–8; atomic espionage and, 194, 204, 205; Bentley and, 25, 182; British Communists and, 23–24, 25; Browder and, 84; Childs family and, 224; code breaking and, 26–28, 207–8, 233–34; confirmation of Chambers's revelations by, 128; declassification of, xii; documents of, 463–505; evidence of, 448–49; financial help given to agents and, 31; Gouzenko's defection and, 14, 15; Hiss and, 136–37; Hopkins and, 214; identification of spies and, 26–27; Karr's political connections and, 139; Kravchenko affair and, 366, 367;

Index

Index

tion and, 48–49; Silvermaster ring
and, 44–45, 153, 154; Soviet appreci-
ation of, 31; Soviet espionage and,
xv; Soviet influence on, 30–31;
Venona identification of, 26
"White Guards," 316
"The White Terrorists Ask for Mercy,"
313
Wholesale Radio Service Company, 221
Wiita, John. *See* Puro, Henry
Willert, Paul, 123–24
Willkie, Wendell, 179, 442
Wilson, Edmund, 332
Wilson, Ruth. *See* Epstein, Ruth Wilson
Winter Help Work, xiv
Wisdom, 414, 415
Wise, James Waterman, 323
Wise, Stephen S., 323
Wishnak, George, 19
The Witchcraft Trial in Moscow (Adler),
328
*With Trotsky in Exile: From Prinkipo to
Coyoacan* (van Heijenoort), 369
Witness (Chambers), 97
Witt, Nathan, 114, 127, 216
Witte, Peter, 152
WJC. *See* World Jewish Congress
Wolfe, Bertram, 332, 409
Wolff, Erwin, 340
Wolff, Manny, 227
Wolff, Milt, 284, 285, 287, 289, 290
Wolston, Arnold, 357
Wolston, Ilya, 370
Woolwich Arsenal Case, 87
Workers Ex-Servicemen's League, 151
Workers International Relief, 98, 399
Workers Party of America, 62–63, 96,
342
Workman's Circle, 415
Works Progress Administration, 216
World Bank, 29
World Jewish Congress (WJC), 394
World Party. *See* Communist
International
World Socialist Revolution, 33

World Tourists, Inc., 146, 147, 166–67
World War I, 61
World War II: American involvement in,
125; influence operations of, 33;
Nazi-Soviet alliance and, 18; United
States and, 44
Wright, Richard, 177
The Writer, 381
Wuchinich, George, 290

Yakir, Ion, 393
"Yakov." *See* Perl, William
Yakovlev, Anatoli, 202, *511*; atomic espi-
onage and, 242; Gold and, 228, 236;
Sax and, 203
Yalta Conference, 136–37
Yatzkov, Anatoli. *See* Yakovlev, Anatoli
"Yaz." *See* Krafsur, Samuel
YCL. *See* Young Communist League
Yeltsin, Boris, ix, 139, 210
Yezhov, Nikolai, 80, 372
York, James Orin, 208
Young, C. W. "Bill," viii
Young, Martin. *See* Platt, Leon
Young Communist International, 194
Young Communist League (YCL):
American Communist Party and,
172; Greenglass and, 232; Rose and,
194; Wolff and, 289
Young People's Socialist League (YPSL),
131, 361
"Yunga," 56
"Yurij." *See* Tarasov, Lev

Zabotin, 195, 197–98
Zaitsev, 37
Zarubin, Elizabeth, 89, 379, *510*; names
used by, 172; recruiting of Eleanor
Roosevelt and, 172; as secret agent, 6
Zarubin, Vassiliy, *510*; Akhmerov and, 7;
atomic espionage and, 257–58; clandestine radio communications and, 145;
duties of, 56–57; early work of, 4–7;

Index